IF FOUND, please notify and arrange return to owner. This text is an important study guide for the owner's career and/or exam preparation.

Name: _____

Address: _____

City, State, ZIP: _____

Telephone: (_____) _____ Email: _____

Gleim Publications, Inc., offers five university-level study systems:

Auditing & Systems Exam Questions and Explanations with Test Prep CD-Rom
Business Law/Legal Studies Exam Questions and Explanations with Test Prep CD-Rom
Federal Tax Exam Questions and Explanations with Test Prep CD-Rom
Financial Accounting Exam Questions and Explanations with Test Prep CD-Rom
Cost/Managerial Accounting Exam Questions and Explanations with Test Prep CD-Rom

The following is a list of Gleim examination review systems:

CIA Review: Part I, Internal Audit Role in Governance, Risk, and Control
CIA Review: Part II, Conducting the Internal Audit Engagement
CIA Review: Part III, Business Analysis and Information Technology
CIA Review: Part IV, Business Management Skills

CMA Review: Part 1, Business Analysis
CMA Review: Part 2, Management Accounting and Reporting
CMA Review: Part 3, Strategic Management
CMA Review: Part 4, Business Applications

CPA Review: Financial
CPA Review: Auditing
CPA Review: Business
CPA Review: Regulation

EA Review: Part 1, Individuals
EA Review: Part 2, Businesses
EA Review: Part 3, Representation, Practice, and Procedures

An order form is provided at the back of this book or contact us at www.gleim.com or (800) 87-GLEIM.

Groundwood Paper and Highlighters — All Gleim books are printed on high quality groundwood paper. We recommend you use a non-bleed-through (dry) highlighter (e.g., the Avery *Glidestick*™ -- ask for it at your local office supply store) when highlighting page items within these books.

REVIEWERS AND CONTRIBUTORS

Garrett Gleim, B.S., CPA (not in public practice), University of Pennsylvania, is one of our vice presidents. Mr. Gleim coordinated the production staff, reviewed the manuscript, and provided production assistance throughout the project.

Grady M. Irwin, J.D., is a graduate of the University of Florida College of Law, and he has taught in the University of Florida College of Business. Mr. Irwin provided substantial editorial assistance throughout the project.

John F. Rebstock, B.S.A., is a graduate of the Fisher School of Accounting at the University of Florida. He has passed the CIA and CPA exams. Mr. Rebstock reviewed portions of the manuscript.

Stewart B. White, B.M., *Cum Laude*, University of Richmond, B.S., Virginia Commonwealth University, has passed the CPA and CISA exams and has worked in the fields of retail management, financial audit, IT audit, COBOL programming, and data warehouse management. He extensively revised portions of this manuscript.

A PERSONAL THANKS

This manual would not have been possible without the extraordinary effort and dedication of Jacob Brunny, Kyle Cadwallader, Julie Cutlip, Mumbi Ngugi, Eileen Nickl, Teresa Soard, and Joanne Strong, who typed the entire manuscript and all revisions and drafted and laid out the diagrams and illustrations in this book.

The authors appreciate the proofreading and production assistance of Christine Bertrand, Ellen Buhl, Katherine Goodrich, James Harvin, Jean Marzullo, Shane Rapp, Victoria Rodriguez, and Martha Willis.

The authors also appreciate the critical reading assistance of Christy Carlson, Will Clamons, Corinne Contento, Margaret Curtis, Ellie Gonzalez, Holly Johnson, and Jeremy Wright.

Finally, we appreciate the encouragement, support, and tolerance of our families throughout this project.

NONDISCLOSED EXAM

The CMA is a nondisclosed exam, and you will encounter questions that may be totally unfamiliar to you. That is the nature of nondisclosed exams. Please follow the study suggestions on pages 12 through 17. We have the best and most efficient CMA exam prep system for success.

FOURTEENTH EDITION

GLEIM's

CMA Review

Part 3
Strategic Management

by

Irvin N. Gleim, Ph.D., CPA, CIA, CMA, CFM

and

Dale L. Flesher, Ph.D., CPA, CIA, CMA, CFM

ABOUT THE AUTHORS

Irvin N. Gleim is Professor Emeritus in the Fisher School of Accounting at the University of Florida and is a member of the American Accounting Association, Academy of Legal Studies in Business, American Institute of Certified Public Accountants, Association of Government Accountants, Florida Institute of Certified Public Accountants, The Institute of Internal Auditors, and the Institute of Management Accountants. He has had articles published in the *Journal of Accountancy, The Accounting Review,* and *The American Business Law Journal* and is author/coauthor of numerous accounting and aviation books and CPE courses.

Dale L. Flesher is the Arthur Andersen Alumni Professor in the School of Accountancy at the University of Mississippi and has written over 300 articles for business and professional journals, including *Management Accounting, Journal of Accountancy,* and *The Accounting Review,* as well as numerous books. He is a member of the Institute of Management Accountants, American Institute of Certified Public Accountants, The Institute of Internal Auditors, American Accounting Association, and American Taxation Association. He is a past editor of *The Accounting Historians' Journal* and is a trustee and past president of the Academy of Accounting Historians.

iv

Gleim Publications, Inc.
P.O. Box 12848
University Station
Gainesville, Florida 32604
(800) 87-GLEIM or (800) 874-5346
(352) 375-0772
FAX: (352) 375-6940
Internet: www.gleim.com
Email: admin@gleim.com

This is the first printing of the fourteenth edition of *CMA Review: Part 3*. Please email update@gleim.com with **CMA 3 14-1** included in the subject or text. You will receive our current update as a reply. Updates are available until the next edition is published.

EXAMPLE:

To:	update@gleim.com
From:	*your email address*
Subject:	**CMA 3 14-1**

ISSN: 1093-2569

ISBN: 978-1-58194-663-5

First Printing: June 2008

ACKNOWLEDGMENTS

The authors are indebted to the Institute of Certified Management Accountants for permission to use problem materials from past CMA examinations. Questions and unofficial answers from the Certified Management Accountant Examinations, copyright © 1982 through 1997 by the Institute of Management Accountants, are reprinted and/or adapted with permission.

The authors are also indebted to The Institute of Internal Auditors, Inc. for permission to use Certified Internal Auditor Examination Questions and Suggested Solutions, copyright © 1985 through 1996 by The Institute of Internal Auditors, Inc.

The authors also appreciate and thank the American Institute of Certified Public Accountants, Inc. Material from Uniform Certified Public Accountant Examination questions and unofficial answers, Copyright © 1981-2006 by the American Institute of Certified Public Accountants, Inc., is reprinted and/or adapted with permission.

This publication was printed and bound by Corley Printing Company, St. Louis, MO, a registered ISO-9002 company. More information about Corley Printing Company is available at www.corleyprinting.com or by calling (314) 739-3777.

Visit our website (www.gleim.com) for the latest updates and information on all of our products.

This publication is designed to provide accurate and authoritative information with regard to the subject matter covered. It is sold with the understanding that the publisher is not engaged in rendering legal, accounting, or other professional service.

If legal advice or other expert assistance is required, the services of a competent professional person should be sought.

(From a declaration of principles jointly adopted by a Committee of the American Bar Association and a Committee of Publishers.)

TABLE OF CONTENTS

PREFACE FOR CMA PART 3 CANDIDATES

The purpose of this book is to help **you** prepare **yourself** to pass Part 3 of the CMA examination. The overriding consideration is to provide an inexpensive, effective, and easy-to-use study program. This manual

1. Defines topics tested on Part 3 of the CMA exam.

2. Explains how to optimize your exam score by analyzing how the CMA exam is constructed, administered, and graded.

3. Outlines the new subject matter tested on Part 3 of the CMA exam in 20 easy-to-use study units.

4. Presents questions to prepare you to answer questions on Part 3 of the CMA exam. The answer explanations are presented to the immediate right of the questions for your convenience. You MUST cover these answers until you commit to the correct answer. Use the bookmark provided at the back of this book.

5. Illustrates individual question-answering techniques to minimize selecting incorrect answers and to maximize your exam score.

6. Suggests exam-taking techniques to help you maintain control and achieve success.

This is the Fourteenth Edition of *CMA Review* for Part 3, which covers only Part 3 of the CMA exam. This new edition includes the following features and benefits:

1. Gleim's content and structure are organized to closely follow the IMA's Learning Outcome Statements, thus ensuring your study time is spent preparing to Pass the Exam!

2. Core Concepts at the end of each Knowledge Transfer Outline allow CMA candidates to obtain an overview of each study unit, as well as ensure that they understand the basic concepts.

3. Many examples throughout the Knowledge Transfer Outlines clarify harder-to-understand concepts.

4. Comprehensive coverage of all topics, including economics, quantitative methods, and ratios.

To maximize the efficiency of your review program, begin by **studying** (not reading) the introduction in this book. "Preparing for and Taking the CMA Exam" is very short but very important. It has been carefully organized and written to provide you with important information to assist you in successfully completing Part 3 of the CMA examination.

Thank you for your interest in our review materials. We very much appreciate the thousands of letters and suggestions we have received from CIA, CMA, and CPA candidates since 1974. Please give us feedback concerning this book. Do NOT disclose information about individual questions beyond subject matter not covered in our books. Tell us which part and which topics were NOT covered or were inadequately covered. The last page has been designed to help you note corrections and suggestions throughout your study process. Please tear it out and mail or fax it to us with your comments.

Finally, THANK YOU for recommending our products to others.

Good Luck on the Exam,

Irvin N. Gleim
Dale L. Flesher
June 2008

PREPARING FOR AND TAKING THE CMA EXAM

ABOUT THE CMA EXAM

Introduction

CMA is the acronym for Certified Management Accountant.

The CMA examination has been and will continue to be developed and offered by the Institute of Certified Management Accountants (ICMA) in approximately 200 locations in the U.S. and an additional 200 international locations.

The CMA exam consists of four parts: Business Analysis, Management Accounting and Reporting, Strategic Management, and Business Applications. Parts 1, 2, and 3 must be successfully completed before the candidate can register for Part 4. Holders of certain professional certifications may be granted a waiver for Part 1 (Business Analysis).

CMA Review: Part 3 contains this 20-page Introduction and 20 study units of outlines and multiple-choice questions that cover all of the material tested on Part 3 of the CMA exam. This Introduction discusses exam content, pass rates, administration, organization, background information, preparing for the CMA exam, and taking the CMA exam. We urge you to read the next 19 pages carefully because they will help you dramatically improve your study and test-taking procedures.

Corporate Management Accounting

1. Objective: Maximize the value of the firm by optimizing

    a. Long-term investment strategies
    b. The capital structure, i.e., how these long-term investments are funded
    c. Short-term cash flow management

2. Corporate financial management involves a financial manager, usually a vice-president/chief financial officer, who is assisted by the

    a. Treasurer -- cash, credit, capital outlay management
    b. Controller -- financial, cost, tax accounting

3. All accounting and finance personnel are beneficiaries of CMA participation.

4. The body of knowledge necessary for proficiency in management accounting is set forth in the ICMA's Content Specification Outlines and Learning Outcome Statements for the CMA exam.

5. The diagram below illustrates an entity combining the factors of production into finished goods (arrows to the right) with money flowing to the left.

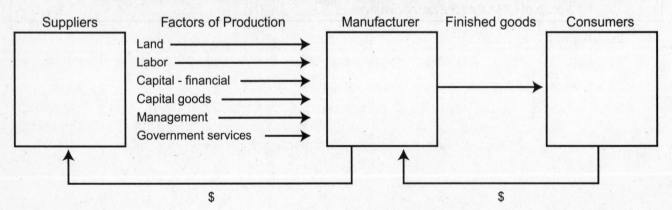

6. Put CMA in perspective when considering the production of goods or services in our capitalistic society. An entity combines the factors of production into finished goods.

   a. Note that the CMA program focuses on financial capital and the other factors of production as well as the finished goods market, while the CEO (chief executive officer) has overall responsibility for the entity's operations.

Objectives of the CMA Examination

The CMA certification program has four objectives:

- *To establish management accounting as a recognized profession by identifying the role of the management accountant and financial manager, the underlying body of knowledge, and a course of study by which such knowledge is acquired;*
- *To encourage higher educational standards in the management accounting field;*
- *To establish an objective measure of an individual's knowledge and competence in the field of management accounting; and*
- *To encourage continued professional development by management accountants.*

The exam tests the candidates' knowledge and ability with respect to the current state of the field of management accounting.

We have arranged the subject matter tested on the CMA examination into 20 study units for each part. Each part is presented in a separate book. All of these books contain review outlines and prior CMA exam questions and answers.

Requirements to Attain the CMA Designation

The CMA designation is granted only by the ICMA. Candidates must complete the following steps to become a CMA:

1. Become a member of the Institute of Management Accountants. You can submit an application for IMA membership with your application for certification.

2. Complete the certification information section on the IMA application and register for the CMA examination.

3. Pass all four parts of the CMA examination. "Continuous candidacy" is required to retain credit after successful completion of one or more parts. "Continuous candidacy" includes IMA membership, and candidates must pass all four parts of the exam within 4 years. The 4-year period begins with the first part passed.

4. Fulfill or expect to fulfill the education requirements (see the next page).

5. Be employed or expect to be employed in a position that meets the experience requirement (see the next page).

6. Provide two character references proving you are of good moral character, if requested.

7. Comply with the IMA's Statement of Ethical Professional Practice.

Credit can be retained indefinitely as long as these requirements are fulfilled. Once a designation is earned, the CMA is a member of the Institute of Certified Management Accountants and must comply with the program's CPE requirement and maintain IMA membership in good standing.

Education and Experience Requirements

Candidates seeking admission to the CMA program must meet one of the following **educational credentials**:

1. Hold a bachelor's degree, in any area, from an accredited college or university. Degrees from foreign institutions must be evaluated by an independent agency approved by the ICMA (visit www.imanet.org/certification_started_education_partial_Int.asp for a list of foreign universities that are acceptable without an evaluation); or

2. Pass the U.S. CPA examination or hold another professional qualification issued in a foreign country that is comparable to the CPA, CMA, etc.; or

3. Achieve a score in the 50th percentile or higher on either the Graduate Management Admission Test (GMAT) or the Graduate Record Examination (GRE).

NOTE: Educational credentials must be submitted when applying or within 7 years of passing the examination. The educational credentials must qualify in order to be certified.

Two continuous years of **professional experience** in financial management and/or management accounting are required any time prior to or within 7 years of passing the examination.

1. Professional experience shall be defined as full-time continuous experience at a level where judgments are regularly made that employ the principles of financial management and/or management accounting, e.g.,
   a. Financial analysis
   b. Budget preparation
   c. Management information systems analysis
   d. Financial management
   e. Management accounting
   f. Auditing in government, finance, or industry
   g. Management consulting
   h. Auditing in public accounting
   i. Research, teaching, or consulting related to management accounting (for teaching, a significant portion required to be above the principles level)

2. Employment in functions that require the occasional application of financial management or management accounting principles, but are not essentially management accounting oriented, will not satisfy the requirement, e.g.,
   a. Computer operations
   b. Sales and marketing
   c. Manufacturing
   d. Engineering
   e. Personnel
   f. Employment in internships, trainee, clerical, or nontechnical positions

3. Continuous part-time positions of 20 hours per week meeting the definition of qualified experience will count toward the experience requirement at a rate of one year of experience for every two years of part-time employment.

If you have any questions about the acceptability of your work experience or bachelor's degree, please write or call the ICMA. Include a complete description of your situation. You will receive a response from the ICMA as soon as your request is evaluated.

Institute of Certified Management Accountants
10 Paragon Drive
Montvale, NJ 07645-1759
(201) 573-9000
(800) 638-4427

NOTE: The ICMA Board of Regents has compiled a list of U.S. and international certifications for which they will grant a waiver of Part 1. To be granted the waiver, acceptable proof must be supplied to the ICMA along with the appropriate waiver fee of $190. For example, you can waive Part 1 of the CMA exam if you have passed the U.S. CPA exam. To receive the waiver, you must request that a letter from your state board be sent directly to the ICMA confirming your licensure or passing of the U.S. CPA exam; copies are not acceptable. Visit www.imanet.org/certification_started_waivers.asp for the complete listing of accepted certifications.

Content Specification Outlines

The ICMA has developed content specification outlines and has committed to follow them on each examination. A complete CSO for Part 3 is presented in Appendix B beginning on page 471. Thus, each examination will cover the major topics specified below; e.g., Strategic Planning will constitute 15% of the Part 3 examination.

Candidates for the CMA designation are expected to have a minimum level of business knowledge that transcends all examination parts. This minimum level includes knowledge of basic financial statements, time value of money concepts, and elementary statistics. Specific discussion of the ICMA's Levels of Performance (A, B, and C) is provided below.

ICMA'S CMA CONTENT SPECIFICATION OVERVIEW

Part 1: Business Analysis
(3 hours – 110 questions)

Business Economics	25%	Level B
Global Business	20%	Level B
Internal Controls	15%	Level A
Quantitative Methods	15%	Level B
Financial Statement Analysis	25%	Level B

Part 2: Management Accounting and Reporting
(4 hours – 140 questions)

Budget Preparation	15%	Level C
Cost Management	25%	Level C
Information Management	15%	Level A
Performance Measurement	20%	Level C
External Financial Reporting	25%	Level B

Part 3: Strategic Management
(3 hours – 110 questions)

Strategic Planning	15%	Level B
Strategic Marketing	15%	Level A
Corporate Finance	25%	Level B
Decision Analysis	25%	Level C
Investment Decisions	20%	Level C

Part 4: Business Applications (Level C)
(3 hours – 3-7 essays)

All topics from Parts 1, 2, and 3 plus:

Organization Management
Organization Communication
Behavioral Issues
Ethical Considerations

Level of Performance Required

All parts of the exam appear to be tested at the skill level of a final examination for the appropriate course at a good school of business. The ICMA has specified three levels of coverage as reproduced on the next page and indicated in its content specification outlines. You will evaluate and compare the difficulty of each part of the CMA exam as you work the questions in this book.

Authors' Note: Rely on the questions at the end of each study unit in each *CMA Review* book and in *CMA Test Prep* CD-Rom and *CMA Gleim Online*.

Level A: Requiring the skill levels of knowledge and comprehension.

Level B: Requiring the skill levels of knowledge, comprehension, application, and analysis.

Level C: Requiring all six skill levels: knowledge, comprehension, application, analysis, synthesis, and evaluation.

See Appendix D for a reprint of the ICMA's discussion of "Types and Levels of Exam Questions."

Gleim Study Unit Listing

LISTING OF GLEIM STUDY UNITS*

Part 1: Business Analysis

1. Factors Affecting the Firm
2. Consumption and Production
3. Market Structures and the Market for Inputs
4. Macroeconomic Issues, Measures, and Cycles
5. Government Participation in the Economy
6. Comparative Advantage and Free Trade
7. Trade Barriers and Agreements
8. Foreign Exchange
9. Other Global Business Topics
10. Risk Assessment and Controls
11. Internal Auditing
12. Systems Controls and Security Measures
13. Forecasting Analysis
14. Linear Programming and Network Analysis
15. Probability, Decision Trees, and Other Techniques
16. The Development of Accounting Standards
17. Financial Statement Assurance
18. Liquidity, Capital Structure, and Solvency
19. Return on Investment, Profitability, and Earnings
20. Other Analytical Issues

Part 2: Management Accounting and Reporting

1. Budgeting Concepts and Budget Systems
2. Annual Profit Plan and Supporting Schedules
3. Cost Management Terminology and Concepts
4. Cost Accumulation Systems
5. Cost Allocation Techniques
6. Overview of Information Systems
7. Technology of Information Systems
8. Electronic Commerce and Other Topics
9. Cost and Variance Measures
10. Responsibility Accounting and Financial Measures
11. The Balanced Scorecard and Quality Considerations
12. Overview of External Financial Reporting
13. Cash and Receivables
14. Inventories and Investments
15. Long-Lived Assets
16. Liabilities
17. Equity and Revenue Recognition
18. Other Income Statement Items
19. Business Combinations and Derivatives
20. SEC Requirements and the Annual Report

Part 3: Strategic Management

1. Strategic and Tactical Planning
2. Manufacturing Paradigms
3. Business Process Performance
4. Marketing's Strategic Role within the Firm
5. Marketing Information and Market Segmentation
6. Other Marketing Topics
7. Risk and Return
8. Financial Instruments
9. Cost of Capital
10. Managing Current Assets
11. Financing Current Assets
12. The Decision Process
13. Data Concepts Relevant to Decision Making
14. Cost-Volume-Profit Analysis
15. Marginal Analysis
16. Cost-Based Pricing
17. The Capital Budgeting Process
18. Discounted Cash Flow and Payback
19. Ranking Investment Projects
20. Risk Analysis and Real Options

Part 4: Business Applications

1. Organization Structures
2. Jobs and Teams
3. Leadership Styles and Sources of Power
4. Motivational Theories and Diversity Issues
5. Organization Communication
6. Behavior – Alignment of Organizational Goals
7. Behavior – Budgeting and Standard Setting
8. Behavior – Reporting and Performance Evaluation
9. Ethics as Tested on the CMA Exam
10. Part 1 Review – Business Economics and Global Business
11. Part 1 Review – Internal Controls and Quantitative Methods
12. Part 1 Review – Financial Statement Analysis
13. Part 2 Review – Budget Preparation and Cost Management
14. Part 2 Review – Information Management and Performance Measurement
15. Part 2 Review – External Financial Reporting I
16. Part 2 Review – External Financial Reporting II
17. Part 3 Review – Strategic Planning and Strategic Marketing
18. Part 3 Review – Corporate Finance
19. Part 3 Review – Decision Analysis
20. Part 3 Review – Investment Decisions

---

*WARNING!!!

About 30% of CMA test questions will require mathematical calculations.
Practice computational questions to prepare for exam success!

Each study unit begins with the Learning Outcome Statements from the Institute of Management Accountants, followed by our Knowledge Transfer Outline, then our Core Concepts, and finally multiple-choice questions.

The *CMA Review* study unit titles and organization differ somewhat from the subtopic titles used by the ICMA in its content specification outlines (see the previous page) for the CMA exam. The selection of study units for *CMA Review: Part 3* is based on the types and number of questions that have appeared on past CMA exams, as well as the extensiveness of past and expected future exam coverage as defined in both the ICMA Content Specification Outlines and Learning Outcome Statements.

Learning Outcome Statements

In addition to the Content Specification Outlines, the ICMA has published Learning Outcome Statements (LOSs) that specify in detail what skills a candidate should possess. Before you study our knowledge transfer outline, read the LOS at the beginning of each study unit. This will alert you to what is expected and required of you.

Conceptual vs. Calculation Questions

About 30% of CMA Part 3 test questions will be calculations in contrast to conceptual questions. When you take the test, it may appear that more than 40% of the questions are calculation-type because they take longer and are "more difficult." The ICMA has approved the use of two new calculators (see page 19) to assist in this area. As an additional benefit, beginning in Spring of 2009, the exam will include a new spreadsheet function to assist with calculations, including net present value.

How Ethics Are Tested

Ethical issues and considerations will be tested on Part 4, Business Applications. At least one (essay) question in this part will be devoted to an ethical situation presented in a business-oriented context. Candidates will be expected to evaluate the issues involved and make recommendations for the resolution of the situation.

The Institute of Management Accountants (IMA)

Conceived as an educational organization to develop the individual management accountant professionally and to provide business management with the most advanced techniques and procedures, the IMA was founded as the National Association of Cost Accountants in 1919 with 37 charter members. It grew rapidly, with 2,000 applications for membership in the first year, and today it is the largest management accounting association in the world, with approximately 67,000 members and more than 230 chapters in the U.S. and 10 abroad.

The IMA has made major contributions to business management through its continuing education program, with courses and seminars conducted in numerous locations across the country; its two magazines, *Strategic Finance*, which is a monthly publication, and *Management Accounting Quarterly*, which is a new online journal; other literature, including research reports, monographs, and books; a technical inquiry service; a library; the annual international conference; and frequent meetings at chapter levels.

Membership in the IMA is open to all persons interested in advancing their knowledge of accounting or financial management. It is required for CMA candidates and CMAs.

IMA Dues in the USA, Canada, and Mexico (as of January 1, 2008)*

1. **Regular:** 1 year, $195
2. **Associate:** 1st year, $65
3. **Associate:** 2nd year, $130
4. **Educator:** $98; must be a full-time faculty member and reside in the U.S., Canada, or Mexico
5. **Student:** $39; must have 6 or more equivalent hours per semester and reside in the U.S., Canada, or Mexico

* All new members (except Students and Associates) also pay a one-time registration fee of $15.

Membership application forms may be obtained by writing the Institute of Management Accountants, 10 Paragon Drive, Montvale, NJ 07645-1759, or calling (201) 573-9000 or (800) 638-4427. A sample of the two-page form appears in Appendix A on pages 466 and 467. Or, visit the IMA's website and complete the form online.

The Institute of Certified Management Accountants (ICMA)

The ICMA is located at the IMA headquarters in Montvale, New Jersey. The only function of the ICMA is to offer and administer the CMA designation. The staff consists of the managing director, the director of examinations, and support staff. The ICMA occupies about 2,000 square feet of office space in the IMA headquarters. This office is where new examination questions are prepared and where all records are kept.

ICMA Board of Regents Staff

The ICMA Board of Regents is a special committee of the IMA established to direct the CMA program for management accountants through the ICMA.

The Board of Regents consists of 16 regents, one of whom is designated as chair by the president of the IMA. The regents are appointed by the president of the IMA to serve 3-year terms. Membership on the Board of Regents rotates, with one-third of the regents being appointed each year. The regents usually meet twice a year for 1 or 2 days.

The managing director of the ICMA, the director of examinations, and the ICMA staff are located at the ICMA office in Montvale, NJ. They undertake all of the day-to-day work with respect to the CMA program.

How to (1) Apply and (2) Register for the CMA Exam

First, you are required to **apply both for membership** in the IMA **and for admission** into the Certification Program (see sample application form in Appendix A on pages 468 and 469).

Apply to join the IMA and the Certification Program **today** -- it takes only a few minutes. Application to the certification program requires education, employment, and reference data. The educational and experience requirements are discussed on page 4. You must provide two references if requested: one from your employer and the second from someone other than a family member or fellow employee. An official transcript providing proof of graduation is also required after you have completed the exams. There is a $200 Certification Entrance Fee ($75 for students), and everyone who enters the certification program by paying the fee receives 4 electronic books in .pdf format that contain sample questions and exam content information and a knowledge assessment exam. Once a person has become a candidate, there is no participant's fee other than IMA membership dues, unless a candidate does not complete the exam within 4 years, in which case the entrance fee must be paid again to take the exam.

Second, it is necessary to **register** each time you wish to sit for the exams. The exam registration form (see pages 466 and 467) is very simple (it takes about 2 minutes to complete). The registration fee for each part of the exam is $190. Graduating seniors, full-time graduate students, and full-time faculty are charged special rates as discussed below.

Order a registration booklet and IMA membership application form from the ICMA at (800) 638-4427, extension 510. The IMA encourages candidates to view information and complete an IMA application and exam registration forms online. Visit the IMA's website at www.imanet.org for more information.

Special Student Examination Fee

U.S., Canadian, and Mexican college students may take up to four examinations at $95 per part (versus the normal $190). These discounts must be used within the year following application or they will be forfeited. To be eligible for this discount, students must

1. Provide the name of someone who can verify student status.
2. Apply to the ICMA while enrolled in school.
3. Upon graduation, arrange for an official copy of your transcript to be sent to the ICMA.

Fees for Full-Time Professors

Full-time faculty members are permitted to take up to four examination parts once at no charge. The fee for any parts that must be retaken is 50% of the normal fee. To qualify, a faculty member must submit a letter on school stationery affirming his/her full-time status. Faculty should sit for the CMA examinations because a professor's status as a CMA encourages students to enter the program. Full-time doctoral students who plan to pursue a teaching career are treated as faculty members for purposes of qualifying for the free examination.

CMA Test Administration

After registering for an exam part, the ICMA will send you authorization to take the exam. Until December 31, 2008, candidates have 120 days from receipt of authorization to sit for the exam and the exam is offered year-round (except for Part 4, which is only offered in the second month of every calendar quarter). Beginning January 1, 2009, however, the authorization period will shorten so that candidates will have a 60-day window for Parts 1, 2, and 3 and a 30-day window for Part 4. The periods during which the exam parts are available will also change (see table below for testing windows as of January 1, 2009). The authorization will instruct you to call the Prometric registration office at (800) 479-6370 and register for your test at a local Prometric testing center. You may also register online at www.prometric.com. Call your testing center a day or two before your test to confirm your time and obtain directions to the testing center or visit www.prometric.com.

January and February:	Parts 1, 2, and 3
March:	No exam parts
April:	Part 4 only
May and June:	Parts 1, 2, and 3
July:	No exam parts
August:	Part 4 only
September and October:	Parts 1, 2, and 3
November:	No exam parts
December:	Part 4 only

DOMESTIC INSTRUCTIONS TO CANDIDATES

The letter accompanying these instructions is your authorization to schedule the taking of your examination part(s) with Prometric. Please note that you have a separate authorization number for each part that you registered to take. Questions regarding your registration with ICMA should be directed to 800-638-4427, ext. 1521.

You should contact Prometric for your appointment(s) **at your earliest convenience**, as ICMA is not responsible if you delay scheduling and there are no longer appointments available within your authorization period.

Scheduling with Prometric

The interval dates shown on your authorization letter represent the time/authorization period during which you are authorized to take CMA examination part(s).

- Before contacting Prometric, select two or three dates during your authorization period that are convenient for you to take the examination in case your first choice is not available. Please be aware that Saturdays fill quickly and you may not be able to get a Saturday appointment.
- Choose a Prometric Center by checking the list of sites at www.prometric.com or ask the Prometric Call Center representative to suggest a center close to your home or office.
- Be sure you have your authorization number(s) from the accompanying letter handy, as you will be required to provide this information.
- To schedule your examination, you can log onto the Internet 24 hours, 7 days a week by visiting www.prometric.com. You can also call Prometric's Candidate Service Call Center at 800-479-6370 or the local Prometric Testing Center of your choice. Online is the recommended choice to schedule your test.
- Once you have scheduled your appointment, it is strongly suggested that you confirm the date and time of your appointment by visiting www.prometric.com and selecting the View/Print Appointment option.

Reschedule or Cancellation of a Scheduled Appointment

If you find that you are unable to keep a scheduled appointment at Prometric or wish to move your appointment to another date, **you must do so three business days** before the appointment. To cancel or reschedule your appointment, please have your confirmation number ready and visit www.prometric.com or call 800-479-6370 and select option 1 to be directed to the automated system. Both options are available 24 hours, 7 days a week. If you cancel an appointment, you must wait 72 hours before calling to make a new appointment. If you do not comply with this **reschedule/cancellation policy**, you will be considered a "no-show" and you will need to reregister with ICMA and REPAY the examination fee.

Cancellation Examples

- If your exam date is on Friday at 3 pm, you must cancel by noon on the Tuesday before your scheduled appointment date.
- If your exam date is on Thursday at 8 am, you must cancel by 8 am on the Monday before your scheduled appointment date.
- If your exam date is on Saturday at 10 am, you must cancel by 10 am on the Wednesday before your scheduled appointment date.
- Upon written request, ICMA will consider limited time period extensions of the authorization period. For a processing fee of $60, ICMA can grant a one-time 60-day extension for parts 1, 2, and 3. For a processing fee of $50, ICMA can grant a one-time extension to the following monthly testing window for part 4.

ICMA Credit Policy

If you do not take an examination within the authorized time period, you will not receive any credit for your exam fees. However, students and faculty who registered at a discounted fee will have their discounts restored for future use.

General Instructions

- You should arrive at the Prometric Testing Center **30 minutes** before the time of your appointment. If you are more than 15 minutes late for your scheduled appointment, you may lose your scheduled sitting and be required to reschedule at a later date at an additional cost.
- You will be required to sign the Prometric Log Book when you enter the center.
- For admission to the examination, you will be required to present **two** forms of identification, one with a photograph, both with your signature. Approved IDs are a passport, driver's license, military ID, credit card with photo, or company ID. Student IDs are **not** acceptable. You **will not be** permitted into the examination without proper identification.
- Small lockers are available at the test centers for personal belongings. Items such as purses, briefcases, and jackets will not be allowed in the testing room.
- Small battery or solar powered electronic calculators restricted to a maximum of six functions - addition, subtraction, multiplication, division, square root, and percent - are allowed. The calculator must be non-programmable and must not use any type of tape. Candidates may alternatively choose to bring either a Texas Instruments BAII Plus or a Hewlett Packard 10bII calculator. Candidates **will not** be allowed to use calculators that do not comply with these restrictions.
- Candidates will receive ONE scratch paper booklet initially during their examination. However, if you require more sheets during the exam in order to complete calculations, you should raise your hand and ask the test center personnel for ONE additional booklet. Candidates are able to keep one used booklet in case they need to refer back to previous calculations. Candidates will be permitted to trade in ONE or TWO used booklets for ONE or TWO new booklets. Candidates are only permitted to have TWO booklets at any given time. The test center personnel will then collect and destroy ALL booklets from each candidate at the end of their testing session.
- The test center will provide pencils for use in making calculations, etc., on the provided scratch paper booklet(s).
- The staff at the Prometric Testing Center is not involved in the development of the examination or the procedures governing the evaluation of your performance. Questions or comments on the examination content or performance evaluation should be directed only to the ICMA, as this is a nondisclosed examination.
- At the beginning of your test administration, you will be given the opportunity to take a tutorial that introduces the testing screens; the tutorial is not part of your testing time and may be repeated if the candidate wishes; however, total tutorial time is limited.
- Upon completion of each examination part, your performance results will be displayed on the screen, and you will also receive a printed and embossed copy of your results before leaving the testing center. (Part 4 "Revised" - Business Applications is graded offline and there is no immediate performance feedback. Grades are mailed to candidates approximately 30 days after each testing period.)

Computer Testing Procedures

When you arrive at the computer testing center, you will be required to check in. Be sure to bring your authorization letter and two forms of identification, one with a photograph, both with your signature. If you have any questions, please call the IMA at (800) 638-4427.

Next, you will be taken into the testing room and seated at a computer terminal. You will be provided with pencils and scrap paper. You are permitted to use a 6-function, non-programmable calculator; a Texas Instruments BAII Plus calculator; or a Hewlett Packard 10bII calculator. A person from the testing center will assist you in logging on the system, and you will be asked to confirm your personal data. Then you will be prompted and given an online introduction to the computer testing system and you will view a tutorial.

If you have used our *CMA Test Prep* CD-Rom, you will be conversant with the computer testing methodology and environment, and you will probably want to skip the tutorial and begin the actual test immediately. Once you begin your test, you will be allowed 3 hours to complete the actual test. This is just over 1.6 minutes per question. You may take a break during the exam, BUT the clock continues to run during your break. Before you leave the testing center, you will be required to check out of the testing center.

ICMA Refund Policy

If you do not take an examination within the authorized time period, you will not receive any credit for your exam fees. However, students and faculty who registered at a discounted fee will have their discounts restored for future use.

Pass/Fail and Grade Reports

"Candidates are given different 'forms' of the exam and it is therefore necessary to establish a passing score for each form, taking into consideration the relative difficulty of the items contained in each form. In order to equate all scores for all forms of the exam, the scores for each part are placed along a scale from 200 to 700. On this scale, a score of 500 represents the minimum passing scaled score. One form of the exam might require a passing percentage of 70% and another a passing percentage of 65%; both of these passing percentages would represent a scaled score of 500. The scaled score allows candidates to know how they performed in relation to the passing standard of 500." If you fail the exam, you may register to take it again as soon as you like. However, you may not sit for any part more than three times in a one-year period.

Maintaining Your CMA Designation

Membership in the IMA is required to maintain your CMA certificates. The general membership fee is $195. There is no additional participant fee.

Continuing professional education is required of CMAs to maintain their proficiency in the field of management accounting. Beginning the calendar year after successful completion of the CMA exams, 30 hours of CPE must be completed, which is about 4 days per year. Qualifying topics include management accounting, corporate taxation, statistics, computer science, systems analysis, management skills, marketing, business law, and insurance. All CMAs are required to complete 2 hours of CPE on the subject of ethics as part of their 30-hour annual requirement.

Credit for hours of study will be given for participation in programs sponsored by businesses, educational institutions, or professional and trade associations at either the national or local level.

Programs conducted by an individual's employer must provide for an instructor or course leader. There must be formal instructional training material. On-the-job training does not qualify. An affidavit from the employer is required to attest to the hours of instruction. The programs may be seminars, workshops, technical meetings, or college courses under the direction of an instructor. The method of instruction may include lecture, discussion, case studies, and teaching aids such as training films and cassettes.

Credit for hours of study may be given for technical articles published in business, professional, or trade journals, and for major technical talks given for the first time before business, professional, or trade organizations. The specific hours of credit in each case will be determined by the Institute.

PREPARING FOR THE CMA EXAM

How Many Parts to Take

We suggest that you take one part at a time. For a list of the Gleim/Flesher study units in each part, see page 6. See page 5 for the ICMA Content Specification Overview for all parts.

CMA Part 1:   Business Analysis
CMA Part 2:   Management Accounting and Reporting
CMA Part 3:   Strategic Management
CMA Part 4:   Business Applications

Candidates can maintain credit for passed parts as long as they maintain continuous candidacy. "Continuous candidacy" includes IMA membership, and candidates must pass all four parts of the exam within 4 years. Note that a candidate receives 12 hours of continuing professional education for each exam part passed.

How to Study a Study Unit Using Gleim's Complete System

To ensure that you are using your time effectively, we recommend that you follow the steps listed below when using all of the materials together (books, CD-Rom, audios, and Gleim Online):

1.   (25-30 minutes) In Gleim Online, complete Multiple-Choice Quiz #1 in 20-25 minutes (excluding the review session). It is expected that your scores will be low on the first quiz.

   a.   Immediately following the quiz, you will be prompted to review the questions you marked and/or answered incorrectly. For each question, analyze and understand why you answered it incorrectly. This step is an essential learning activity.

2.   (15-30 minutes) Use the audiovisual presentation for an overview of the study unit. The Gleim *CMA Review Audios* can be substituted for audiovisual presentations and can be used while driving to work, exercising, etc.

3.   (30-45 minutes) Complete the 30-question True/False quiz. It is interactive and most effective if used prior to studying the Knowledge Transfer Outline.

4.   (60 minutes) Study the Knowledge Transfer Outline, specifically the troublesome areas identified from the multiple-choice questions in Gleim Online. The Knowledge Transfer Outlines can be studied either online or from the books.

5.   (25-30 minutes) Complete Multiple-Choice Quiz #2 in Gleim Online.

   a.   Immediately following the quiz, you will be prompted to review the questions you marked and/or answered incorrectly. For each question, analyze and understand why you answered it incorrectly. This step is an essential learning activity.

6. (40-50 minutes) Complete two 20-question quizzes while in Test Mode from the *CMA Test Prep* CD-Rom.

7. (30-90 minutes) Complete all of the essay questions in at least two scenarios in Gleim Online. (This only applies to Part 4 since there are no essays in Parts 1, 2, and 3.)

When following these steps, you will complete all 20 units in about 70-80 hours. Then spend about 10-20 hours using the *CMA Test Prep* CD-Rom to create customized tests for the problem areas that you identified. To review the entire part before the exam, use the *CMA Test Prep* CD-Rom to create 20-question quizzes that draw questions from all twenty study units. Continue taking 20-question quizzes until you approach a 75%+ proficiency level.

Avoid studying Gleim questions to learn the correct answers. Use questions to help you <u>learn</u> how to answer CMA questions <u>under exam conditions</u>. Expect the unexpected and be prepared to deal with the unexpected. Always take one 20-question test in test mode *before* studying the material in each study unit. These test sessions will allow you to practice answering questions you have not seen before. Become an educated guesser when you encounter questions in doubt; you will outperform the inexperienced exam taker.

After you complete each 20-question test, ALWAYS do a study session of questions you missed. FOCUS on why you selected the incorrect answer, NOT the correct answer. You want to learn from your mistakes during study so you avoid mistakes on the exam.

CMA Gleim Online

CMA Gleim Online is a versatile, interactive, self-study review program delivered via the Internet. With *CMA Gleim Online*, Gleim guarantees that you will pass the CMA exam on your first sitting. It is divided into four courses (one for each part of the CMA exam).

Each course is broken down into 20 individual, manageable study units. Completion time per study unit will vary from 1-5 hours. Each study unit in the course contains an audiovisual presentation, 30 true/false study questions, 10-20 pages of Knowledge Transfer Outlines, and two 20-question multiple-choice quizzes. Essay questions are also included with each study unit in Part 4.

CMA Gleim Online provides you with a Personal Counselor, who will provide support to ensure your competitive edge. *CMA Gleim Online* is a great way to get confidence as you prepare with Gleim. This confidence will continue during and after the exam.

Gleim/Flesher Audio Reviews

Gleim/Flesher *CMA Review* audios provide a 15- to 40-minute introductory review for each study unit. Each review provides a comprehensive overview of the outline or (for the review study units in Part 4) the LOSs and Core Concepts in the *CMA Review* book. The purpose is to get candidates "started" so they can relate to the questions they will answer before reading the study outlines and/or Core Concepts in each study unit.

The audios are short and to the point, as is the entire Gleim System for Success. We are working to get you through the CMA exam with the minimum time, cost, and frustration. You can listen to an informative discussion about the CMA exam and hear a sample of two audio reviews (Cost Volume Profit Analysis and CVP Applications) on our website at www.gleim.com/accounting/demos/.

How to Study a Study Unit (Books and CD-Rom)

Twenty-question tests in the *CMA Test Prep* CD-Rom will help you to focus on your weaker areas. Make it a game: How much can you improve?

Our *CMA Test Prep* forces you to commit to your answer choice before looking at answer explanations; thus, you are preparing under true exam conditions. It also keeps track of your time and performance history for each study unit, which is available in either a table or graphical format.

Simplify the exam preparation process by following our suggested steps listed below. DO NOT omit the step in which you diagnose the reasons for answering questions incorrectly; i.e., learn from your mistakes while studying so you avoid making similar mistakes on the CMA exam.

1. In test mode, answer a 20-question diagnostic test from each study unit before studying any other information.

2. Study the Knowledge Transfer Outline for the corresponding study unit in your Gleim/Flesher book. Place special emphasis on the weaker areas that you identified with the initial diagnostic quiz in Step 1.

3. Take two or three 20-question tests in test mode after you have studied the Knowledge Transfer Outline.

4. Immediately following the quiz, you will be prompted to review the questions you marked and/or answered incorrectly. For each question, analyze and understand why you answered it incorrectly. This step is an essential learning activity.

5. Continue this process until you approach a predetermined proficiency level, e.g., 75%+.

6. Modify this process to suit your individual learning process.

    a. Learning from questions you answer incorrectly is very important. Each question you answer incorrectly is an **opportunity** to avoid missing actual test questions on your CMA exam. Thus, you should carefully study the answer explanations provided until you understand why the original answer you chose is wrong, as well as why the correct answer indicated is correct. This study technique is clearly the difference between passing and failing for many CMA candidates.

    b. Also, you **must** determine why you answered questions incorrectly and learn how to avoid the same error in the future. Reasons for missing questions include:

        1) Misreading the requirement (stem)
        2) Not understanding what is required
        3) Making a math error
        4) Applying the wrong rule or concept
        5) Being distracted by one or more of the answers
        6) Incorrectly eliminating answers from consideration
        7) Not having any knowledge of the topic tested
        8) Employing bad intuition (WHY?) when guessing

    c. It is also important to verify that you answered correctly for the right reasons. Otherwise, if the material is tested on the CMA exam in a different manner, you may not answer it correctly.

    d. It is imperative that you complete your predetermined number of study units per week so you can review your progress and realize how attainable a comprehensive CMA review program is when using Gleim/Flesher books and CD-Rom. Remember to meet or beat your schedule to give yourself confidence.

Study Plan and Time Budget

Complete one study unit at a time. Initially, budget 3 to 4 hours per study unit (1 to 2 hours studying the outline and 1 to 2 minutes each on all the multiple-choice questions). Depending on your background, you may need more or less time to prepare.

This Introduction	2
20 study units at 4 hours each	80
General review	8
Total Hours	90

Each week, you should evaluate your progress and review your preparation plans for the time remaining prior to the exam. Use a calendar to note the exam dates and the weeks to go before the exam. Marking a calendar will facilitate your planning. Review your commitments, e.g., out-of-town assignments, personal responsibilities, etc., and note them on your calendar to assist you in keeping to your schedule.

Control: How To Be in

You have to be in control to be successful during exam preparation and execution. Control is a process that we use in all of our activities, implicitly or explicitly. The objective is to improve performance as well as to be confident that the best possible performance is being generated. Control is a process whereby you

1. Develop expectations, standards, budgets, and plans.
2. Undertake activity, production, study, and learning.
3. Measure the activity, production, output, and knowledge.
4. Compare actual activity with expected and budgeted activity.
5. Modify the activity, behavior, or study to better achieve the desired outcome.
6. Revise expectations and standards in light of actual experience.
7. Continue the process or restart the process in the future.

Most accountants study this control process in relation to standard costs, i.e., establish cost standards and compute cost variances. Just as it helps them in their jobs, the control process will help you pass the CMA exam.

Every day, you rely on control systems implicitly. For example, when you groom your hair, you have expectations about the desired appearance of your hair and the time required to style it. You monitor your progress and make adjustments as appropriate. The control process, however, is applicable to all of your endeavors, both professional and personal. You should refine your personal control processes specifically toward passing the CMA exam.

Unless you are a natural at something, most endeavors will improve with explicit control. This is particularly true with the CMA exam.

1. Develop an explicit control system over your study process.
2. Practice your question-answering techniques (and develop control) as you prepare solutions to practice questions/problems during your study program.
3. Plan to use the Gleim Time Management System at the exam.

Multiple-Choice Question-Answering Technique

The following suggestions are to assist you in maximizing your score on each part of the CMA exam. Remember, knowing how to take the exam and how to answer individual questions is as important as studying/reviewing the subject matter tested on the exam.

1. **Budget your time.**

   a. We make this point with emphasis. Just as you would fill up your gas tank prior to reaching empty, so too should you finish your exam before time expires.

   b. You have 180 minutes to answer 110 questions, i.e., 1.6 minutes per question. We suggest you attempt to answer eight questions every 10 minutes, which is 1.25 minutes per question. This would result in completing 110 questions in 137 minutes to give you almost 45 minutes to review questions that you have marked. See 3.c.2) on the next page for a brief discussion on marking questions at Prometric. On Part 2, you have 4 hours to answer 140 questions, or roughly 1.7 minutes per question. Stick with averaging 1.25 minutes per question so that you still allow yourself ample review time.

   c. On your Prometric computer screen, the time remaining (starting with 3:00:00 or 4:00:00) appears at the lower left corner of your screen for Parts 1, 2, and 3.

2. **Answer the questions in consecutive order.**

   a. Do **not** agonize over any one item. Stay within your time budget.

   b. Mark any questions you are unsure of and return to them later.

   c. Never leave a multiple-choice item unanswered. Make your best guess in the time allowed. Remember that your score is based on the number of correct responses. You will not be penalized for guessing incorrectly.

3. **For each multiple-choice question,**

   a. **Read the question stem** carefully (the part of the question that precedes the answer choices) to determine the precise requirement.

      1) Focusing on what is required enables you to ignore extraneous information and to proceed directly to determining the correct answer.

         a) Be especially careful to note when the requirement is an **exception**; e.g., "All of the following statements regarding a company's internal rate of return are true except:"

   b. **Determine the correct answer** before reading the answer choices. The objective is to avoid allowing the answer choices to affect your reading of the question.

      1) When four answer choices are presented, three of them are incorrect. They are called distractors for a very good reason.

      2) Read each answer choice with close attention.

         a) Even if answer (A) appears to be the correct choice, do not skip the remaining answer choices. Answer (B), (C), or (D) may be better.

         b) Treat each answer choice as a true/false question.

c. **Select the best answer.** The answer is selected by either pressing the answer letter on your keyboard or by using your mouse. Select the most likely or best answer choice. If you are uncertain, make an educated guess.

1) The CMA does not penalize guessing because your score is determined by the number of correct responses. Thus, you should answer every question.

2) As you answer a question, you can mark it by pressing the "Mark" button or unmark a marked question by pressing the "Marked" button. After you have answered, marked, or looked at and not answered all 110 or 140 questions, you will be presented with a review screen that shows how many questions you did not answer and how many you marked. You then have the option of revisiting all of the unanswered questions and "marked" questions.

4. **Prometric Computer Screen Layout**

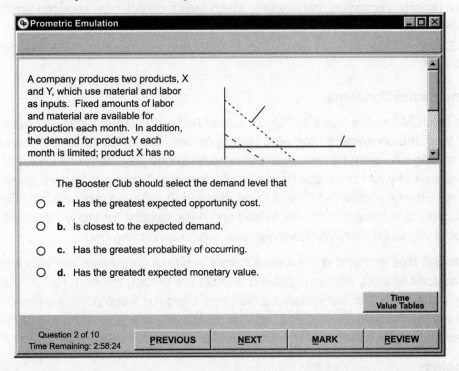

NOTE: A menu offering a number of options is displayed at the bottom of the question screen. The options enable you to view the previous question or the next question, mark a question to be revisited, or request help. You may select an option by pressing the appropriate symbol key or highlighted letter on your keyboard or by clicking on the symbol or letter with your mouse.

a) View the previous question by indicating the letter **P** or the left arrow key.
b) View the next question by indicating the letter **N** or the right arrow key.
c) Mark a question by indicating the letter **M**.
d) Request help by indicating the question mark.

USE GLEIM/FLESHER *CMA TEST PREP* CD-Rom. It emulates the Prometric testing procedures and environment including computer screen layout, software operation, etc.

TAKING THE CMA EXAM

CMA Examination Checklist

1. Acquire your study materials. Rely on this book, *CMA Test Prep* CD-Rom, and *CMA Gleim Online*. Consider our audios as a supplement, which can be used while you commute, exercise, etc.

2. **Apply** for membership in the IMA (see pages 466 and 467). **Register** to take the desired part of the exam using the examination registration form (pages 468 and 469) and send it with your application to the ICMA. Take one part at a time. When you register and pay $190 for a part, you have 60 days to take Parts 1, 2, and 3 and 30 days to take Part 4.* Upon receipt of authorization to take the exam, contact Prometric to schedule your test.

3. Plan your preparation process. It's easy. You have 20 study units to complete.

4. Utilize orderly, controlled preparation, which builds confidence, reduces anxiety, and produces success!

5. PASS THE EXAMINATION (study this Introduction and Gleim's *CMA Review: A System for Success*)!

Logistical and Health Concerns

As soon as the ICMA sends you a computer-based test authorization, call and schedule your test at a convenient time and convenient Prometric testing center. In almost all cases, you should be able to drive to your testing site, take the test, and return home in one day. If the exam is not being given within driving distance of your home, call Prometric Technology Centers to inquire about accommodations. Stay by yourself at a hotel to be assured of avoiding distractions. The hotel room should be soundproof and have a comfortable bed and desk suitable for study. If possible, stay at a hotel with the recreational facilities you normally use, e.g., a swimming pool.

Proper exercise, diet, and rest in the weeks before you take your exam are very important. High energy levels, reduced tension, and an improved attitude are among the benefits. A good aerobic fitness program, a nutritious and well-balanced diet, and a regular sleep pattern will promote your long-term emotional and physical well-being, as well as contribute significantly to a favorable exam result. Of course, the use of health-undermining substances should be avoided.

Exam Psychology

Plan ahead and systematically prepare. Then go to the exam and give it your best: neither you nor anyone else can expect more. Having undertaken a systematic preparation program, you will do fine.

Maintain a positive attitude and do not become depressed if you encounter difficulties before or during the exam. An optimist will usually do better than an equally well-prepared pessimist. Remember, you have reason to be optimistic because you will be competing with many less-qualified persons who have not prepared as well as you have.

---

* Authorization periods effective January 1, 2009. Through December 31, 2008, the authorization period is 120 days for all 4 parts.

Calculators

Simple six-function calculators are permitted (i.e., addition, subtraction, multiplication, division, square root, percent). Alternatively, candidates may choose to bring either a Texas Instruments BAII Plus or a Hewlett Packard 10bII calculator. Candidates are responsible for providing their own calculators. You should be thoroughly experienced in the operations of your calculator. Make sure it has fresh batteries just prior to the examination.

1. Consider bringing a backup calculator with you.
2. The calculator must be small, quiet, and battery- or solar-powered so it will not be distracting to other candidates.
3. The calculator may have a memory. However, the memory must be temporary and erase when the memory is cleared or the calculator is turned off.
4. The calculator must not use any type of tape.
5. The calculator must be nonprogrammable.
6. Nonconforming calculators and calculator instruction books are not permitted.
7. We suggest that you study using the calculator that you will be bringing to the exam so that you are completely comfortable using it.

Examination Tactics

1. Remember to bring your authorization and appropriate identification to the exam site. The photo ID requirement is strictly enforced.
2. Arrive at the test center at least 30 minutes prior to the scheduled exam time to allow for orientation and check-in procedures. Your appointment may be canceled if you are more than 15 minutes late.
3. Dressing for exam success means emphasizing comfort, not appearance. Be prepared to adjust for changes in temperature, e.g., to remove or put on a sweater.
4. Do not bring notes, this text, other books, etc., into the Prometric testing center. You will only make yourself nervous and confused by trying to cram the last 5 minutes before the exam. Books are not allowed in the testing room, anyway. You should, however, bring an appropriate calculator.
5. Adequate scratch paper and pencils are provided. You must turn in your scratch paper as you leave the exam site. Any breath mints, gum, etc., should be in your pocket as they may distract other persons taking the test.
6. As soon as you complete the exam, we would like you to email, fax, or write to us with your comments on our books, CD-Rom, audios, and Gleim Online. We are particularly interested in which topics need to be added or expanded in our materials. We are NOT asking about specific CMA questions; rather we are asking for feedback on our materials.

Recap of CMA Part 3 Exam Coverage

ICMA Major Topics and Percent Coverage	Gleim/Flesher Study Units
A. Strategic Planning--15% (Level B)	1. Strategic and Tactical Planning 2. Manufacturing Paradigms 3. Business Process Performance
B. Strategic Marketing--15% (Level A)	4. Marketing's Strategic Role Within the Firm 5. Marketing Information and Market Segmentation 6. Other Marketing Topics
C. Corporate Finance--25% (Level B)	7. Risk and Return 8. Financial Instruments 9. Cost of Capital 10. Managing Current Assets 11. Financing Current Assets
D. Decision Analysis--25% (Level C)	12. The Decision Process 13. Data Concepts Relevant to Decision Making 14. Cost-Volume-Profit Analysis 15. Marginal Analysis 16. Cost-Based Pricing
E. Investment Decisions--20% (Level C)	17. The Capital Budgeting Process 18. Discounted Cash Flow and Payback 19. Ranking Investment Projects 20. Risk Analysis and Real Options

WARNING!!!

About 30% of CMA test questions will require mathematical calculations. Practice computational questions to prepare for exam success!

GO FOR IT!
IT'S YOURS TO PASS!

STUDY UNIT ONE
STRATEGIC AND TACTICAL PLANNING

(20 pages of outline)

Strategic and tactical planning are a big part of a management accountant's job and thus are emphasized on the CMA examination. Exam coverage in this area includes manufacturing paradigms, such as JIT, MRP, and the theory of constraints. Value chain analysis and benchmarking are also a part of the strategic planning process, as are activity-based management (ABM) and the philosophy of continuous improvement.

This study unit is the **first of three** on **strategic planning**. The relative weight assigned to this major topic in Part 3 of the exam is **15%** at **skill level B** (four skill types required). The three study units are

Study Unit 1: Strategic and Tactical Planning
Study Unit 2: Manufacturing Paradigms
Study Unit 3: Business Process Performance

After studying the outline and answering the multiple-choice questions, you will have the skills necessary to address the following topics listed in the IMA's Learning Outcome Statements:

Part 3 – Section A.1. Strategic and tactical planning

The candidate should be able to:

a.　discuss how strategic planning determines the path an organization chooses for attaining its long-term goals and missions

b.　identify the time frame appropriate for a strategic plan

c.　identify the external factors that should be analyzed during the strategic planning process and explain how this analysis leads to recognition of organizational opportunities, limitations, and threats

d.　identify the internal factors that should be analyzed during the strategic planning process and understand how this analysis leads to recognition of organizational strengths, weaknesses, and competitive advantages

e.　demonstrate an understanding of how the analysis of external and internal factors leads to the development of the overall organizational mission and that this mission leads to the formulation of long-term business objectives such as business diversification, the addition or deletion of product lines, or the penetration of new markets

f.　identify the role of capital budgeting and capacity planning in the strategic planning process

g.　explain why short-term objectives, tactics for achieving these objectives, and operational planning (master budget) must be congruent with the strategic plan and contribute to the achievement of long-term strategic goals

h.　explain why performance measurement and other reporting systems must be congruent with and support measurement of progress on strategic and operational measures

i.　identify the characteristics of successful strategic/tactical planning

j.　define contingency planning and discuss its importance, particularly where changes in external factors might adversely impact strategic plans

1.1 NATURE OF THE STRATEGIC PLANNING PROCESS

1. **Planning** is the determination of **what** is to be done and of **how, when, where,** and **by whom** it is to be done. Plans serve to direct the activities that all organizational members must undertake and successfully perform to move the organization from where it is to where it wants to be (accomplishment of its objectives).

    a. Planning must be completed before undertaking any other managerial function.

        1) **Forecasting** is the basis of planning because it projects the outcomes of events, their timing, and their future values.

    b. Planning establishes the means to reach organizational ends (objectives).

        1) This **means-end relationship** extends throughout the organizational hierarchy and ties together the parts of the organization so that the various means all focus on the same end.

        2) One organizational level's ends provide the next higher level's means and so on.

            a) EXAMPLE: One purpose of **management by objectives (MBO)** is to establish relationships between an employee's job objectives (ends) and the immediate supervisor's objectives (ends). Thus, the employee can understand how his/her job is the means by which the supervisor's job is accomplished.

    c. Planning and the setting of objectives are **necessarily, but not entirely, top-down processes**. At higher levels in the firm's hierarchy, plans are longer-term and objectives are broader than at lower levels.

    d. Plans may be described as strategic, intermediate, or operational.

2. **Strategic management** is the continuing process of pursuing a favorable competitive fit between the firm and its dynamic environment.

    a. **Strategy** may be defined simply as an integrated, environment-centered approach to accomplishing the firm's mission.

    b. Business strategy theorist **Michael E. Porter** in *Harvard Business Review*, November-December 1996, defined strategy as "the creation of a unique and valuable position, involving a different set of activities." It involves "making tradeoffs in competing," that is, "deciding what not to do." Moreover, strategy also involves "creating fit among a company's activities."

    c. The following is a common approach to classifying strategy:

        1) The firm's **corporate strategy** reflects its values and ultimate objectives. This strategy applies across the range of the firm's businesses. It addresses choice of businesses, how they will be controlled, and what resources should be allocated to them.

        2) The firm's **competitive strategy** addresses how to establish a successful position in a given industry, preferably one providing sustained, superior returns. Thus, it is a strategy adopted for a strategic business unit (SBU).

            a) The competitive strategy must identify customers, how to provide value to them, and the means for creating that value. Accordingly, in Porter's terms, a fit must be created among the firm's activities to ensure that they function synergistically. They should cooperate to exploit the firm's competitive advantages and create customer value.

        3) The firm's **functional strategies** (e.g., R&D, finance, and marketing) complement the competitive strategy. Formulating strategies for specific activities and processes in a business determines how well they fit.

d.   Strategic management has a **long-term planning horizon**. Thus, a strategic orientation is traditionally associated with senior management. However, this orientation should pervade the organization because it encourages farsightedness by all employees. Strategic thinking also helps employees understand and implement managerial decisions. Moreover, it is consistent with the modern trend toward cooperation and teamwork and away from authoritarian managerial styles.

3.   **Strategic planning** follows a formal five-step process.

a.   **Formulate the mission statement.**

1)   A mission statement formally conveys the definition of the firm for the stakeholders, the firm's vision, a broad description of how to realize that vision, firm **priorities**, and common **objectives**.

2)   Moreover, it should state a **philosophy** that informs all firm activities and inspires all members of the firm to believe they are important to its success.

3)   Accordingly, a mission statement should address reasonably limited **objectives**, define the firm's major **policies and values** (e.g., service, quality, social responsibility, and financial performance), and state the firm's primary **competitive scopes** (e.g., industries, products and services, applications, core competencies, market segments, degree of vertical integration, and geographic markets).

b.   **Analyze the firm's internal environment.**

1)   A **situational analysis** considers organizational **strengths and weaknesses** (a capability profile) and their interactions with environmental **opportunities and threats**. Such an evaluation is also called a **SWOT analysis**.

2)   Strengths and weaknesses (the internal environment) are usually identified by considering the firm's **capabilities, resources, and limitations**.

a)   Strengths and weaknesses are internal resources or a lack thereof.

i)   For example, technologically advanced products, a broad product mix, capable management, leadership in R&D, modern production facilities, and a strong marketing organization.

b)   What the firm does particularly well or has in greater abundance are known as **core competencies**. Core competencies are the source of **competitive advantages**.

i)   For example, speed in reacting to environmental changes or in introducing new products.

ii)   To exploit a competitive advantage to the fullest, the organization may have to reengineer its processes.

c)   Cost and quality are other basic factors highlighted in the SWOT analysis.

c.   **Analyze the firm's external environment.**

1)   Opportunities and threats (the external environment) are identified by considering **macroenvironment factors** (economic, demographic, political, legal, social, cultural, and technical) and **microenvironment factors** (suppliers, customers, distributors, competitors, and other competitive factors in the industry).

2)   Opportunities and threats arise from such **externalities** as government regulation, advances in technology, and demographic changes. They may be reflected in such competitive conditions as

a)   Raising or lowering of barriers to entry into the firm's industry by competitors

b)   Changes in the intensity of rivalry within the industry, for example, because of overcapacity or high exit barriers

    c)   The relative availability of substitutes for the firm's products or services

    d)   Bargaining power of customers, which tends to be greater when switching costs are low and products are not highly differentiated

    e)   Bargaining power of suppliers, which tends to be higher when suppliers are few

    3)   Risks should be assessed based on forecasts of the effects of factors relevant to the organization, such as market trends, technology development, international competition, governmental changes, and social evolution.

    d.   **Select appropriate strategies and create strategic business units.**

    1)   Businesses should be defined in market terms, that is, in terms of needs and customer groups. Moreover, a distinction should be made between a **target market definition** and a **strategic market definition**. For example, a target market for a railroad might be freight hauling, but a strategic market might be transportation of any goods and people.

    2)   A business also may be defined with respect to **customer groups**, their needs, and the technology required to satisfy those needs.

    3)   A large firm has multiple businesses. Thus, the concept of the **strategic business unit (SBU)** is useful for strategic planning by large firms. An SBU is a business (or a group) for which separate planning is possible. An SBU also has its own competitors and a manager who engages in strategic planning and is responsible for the major determinants of profit.

        a)   Determining the strength of each SBU with respect to its potential markets and the position of businesses in those markets is called **business portfolio management** (see Subunit 4.3).

    e.   **Implement the chosen strategies.**

    1)   Strategic plans must be **filtered down** the organizational structure through development of plans at each lower level that are congruent with higher level plans.

    2)   This process is most likely to succeed if the structure is compatible with strategic planning, personnel have the necessary abilities, the organizational culture is favorable or can be changed, and controls exist to facilitate implementation.

4.   **Strategic controls** should be established to monitor progress, isolate problems, identify invalid assumptions, and take prompt corrective action.

    a.   As plans are executed at each organizational level, control measurements are made to determine whether objectives have been achieved. Thus, objectives flow down the organizational hierarchy, and control measures flow up.

    1)   One category of strategic control measures relates to **external effectiveness**.

        a)   At the **business-unit level**, these measures concern performance in the marketplace (market share, etc.).

        b)   At the **business-operating-system level**, these measures concern customer satisfaction and flexibility.

        c)   At the **departmental or work-center level**, these measures concern quality and delivery.

    2)   A second category of strategic control measures relates to **internal efficiency**.

        a)   At the **business-unit level**, these measures concern financial results.

        b)   At the **business-operating-system level**, these measures concern flexibility (both an external effectiveness and internal efficiency issue).

        c)   At the **departmental or work-center level**, these measures concern cycle time (time to change raw materials into a finished product) and waste.

b.   The trend in performance evaluation is the **balanced scorecard** approach to managing the implementation of the firm's strategy. The balanced scorecard is an accounting report that connects the firm's critical success factors to measurements of its performance.

   1)   **Critical success factors (CSFs)** are specific, measurable, financial and nonfinancial elements of a firm's performance that are vital to its competitive advantage. They are formulated during the SWOT analysis.

   2)   Once the firm has identified its CSFs, it establishes **specific measures for each CSF** that are relevant to the firm's success and reliably stated. By providing measures that are financial and nonfinancial, long-term and short-term, and internal and external, the balanced scorecard de-emphasizes short-term financial results and focuses attention on CSFs.

5.   **Capital budgeting** is a part of the strategic planning process that addresses expenditures for assets (including such intangible assets as a customer base or brand name) with long-range returns. Once made, capital outlays tend to be relatively inflexible because the commitments extend well into the future.

   a.   However, without proper timing, **additional capacity** generated by the acquisition of capital assets may not coincide with changes in demand for output, resulting in capacity excess or shortage. Thus, **accurate forecasting** is needed to anticipate changes in demand so that full economic benefits flow to the firm when the capital asset is available for use.

   b.   Moreover, a capital budget usually involves substantial expenditures, and the sources and costs of these funds are critical.

   c.   Planning is also important because of possible rapid changes in capital markets, inflation, interest rates, and the money supply. Firms constantly need to budget and plan for capital expenditures to hold a relative position in a dynamic economic environment.

   d.   Capital budgeting requires **choosing among investment proposals**, for example, to add a product or product line, a business segment, or a customer. Thus, a ranking procedure is needed for such decisions.

   1)   The **first step in the ranking procedure** is to determine the asset cost or net investment. The **net investment** is the net outlay, or gross cash requirement, minus cash recovered from the trade or sale of existing assets, plus or minus adjustments for tax effects. Cash outflows in subsequent periods must also be considered.

   a)   The investment required also includes funds to provide for increases in **working capital**, for example, the additional receivables and inventories resulting from the acquisition of a new manufacturing plant. This investment in working capital is treated as an initial cost of the investment (a cash outflow) that will be recovered (as an inflow) at the end of the project. If the project is expected to reduce working capital during its life, the analysis should include an initial inflow and an outflow at the end of the project.

   2)   The **second step in the ranking procedure** is to calculate the estimated cash flows, period by period, using the acquired assets. **Net cash flow** is the economic benefit, period by period, resulting from the investment. Hence, reliable estimates of cost savings or revenues are necessary, and the economic life of the asset should be distinguished from its depreciable life.

   a)   The **economic life** is the time period over which the benefits of the investment proposal are expected to be obtained as distinguished from the physical or technical life of the asset involved.

    b)   The **depreciable life** is the period used for accounting and tax purposes over which the asset's cost is to be systematically and rationally allocated. It is based upon permissible or standard guidelines and may have no particular relevance to economic life.

    c)   The **disposal** of the acquired assets usually increases cash inflows at the end of the project.

    3)   The **third step in the ranking procedure** is to relate the cash-flow benefits to their cost by using quantitative methods to evaluate the investment proposals.

    a)   The best evaluation methods (e.g., net present value and internal rate of return) use present value and future value calculations. These calculations are essential to capital budgeting. They are based on the **compound interest** concept that a quantity of money sometime in the future is worth less than the same amount of money today. The difference is measured in terms of interest calculated according to the appropriate discount rate.

    b)   Capital-budgeting (long-term funding) decisions require knowledge of the **firm's cost of capital**. Investments with a return in excess of the cost of capital increase the value of the firm. The cost of capital is the weighted-average cost of debt (net of tax) and the implicit cost of equity capital to be invested in long-term assets.

    c)   Capital-budgeting decisions also require knowledge of the firm's **optimal capital structure**. This structure minimizes the firm's weighted-average cost of capital and maximizes the value of the firm.

    e.   See also Study Unit 17.

6.   **Capacity planning** is an element of strategic planning that is closely related to capital budgeting. Statement on Management Accounting (SMA) 4Y, *Measuring the Cost of Capacity* (issued by the IMA in March 1996), states that maximizing the value created within an organization starts with understanding the nature and capabilities of all of the company's resources. Thus, capacity should be defined from several different perspectives. Managing the cost of that capacity starts when a product or process is first envisioned. It continues through the subsequent disposal of resources downstream. Effective capacity cost management requires the following:

    a.   In the short run, **optimizing capital decisions** and the effective and flexible use of investments that have already been made

    b.   Maximizing the value delivered to **customers**

    c.   Helping **minimize requirements** for future investment

    d.   Supporting effective matching of a firm's **resources** with current and future market **opportunities**

    e.   Closing any gap between **market demands** and a firm's capabilities

    1)   At times, the firm may have excess capabilities; at others, shortages may exist. These capabilities may be physical, human, technological, or financial.

    f.   **Eliminating waste** in the short, intermediate, and long run

    g.   Providing useful **costing information** on current process costs versus those proposed in current or future investment proposals

    h.   Supporting the establishment of capacity **usage measurements** that identify the cost of capacity and its impact on business cycles and overall company performance

    i.   Identifying the capacity required to meet **strategic and operational objectives** and to estimate current available capacity

    j.   Detailing the **opportunity cost** of unused capacity and suggesting ways to account for that cost

k.   Supporting **change efforts** by providing predecision information and analysis on the potential resource and cost implications of a planned change

l.   Creating a **common language** for, and understanding of, capacity cost management

7.   **Capacity expansion.** According to Michael E. Porter, whether to expand capacity is a major **strategic decision** because of the capital required, the difficulty of forming accurate expectations, and the long timeframe of the lead times and the commitment. The key forecasting problems are **long-term demand** and **behavior of competitors**. The key strategic issue is **avoidance of industry overcapacity**. Capacity expansion is also referred to as market penetration because it involves increasing the amount of an existing product in an existing market.

a.   **Undercapacity** in a profitable industry tends to be a short-term issue. Profits ordinarily lure additional investors. Overcapacity tends to be a long-term problem because firms are more likely to compete intensely rather than reverse their expansion.

b.   The formal **capital budgeting** process entails predicting future cash flows related to the expansion project, discounting them at an appropriate interest rate, and determining whether the **net present value** is positive. This process permits comparison with other uses of the firm's resources.

1)   The apparent simplicity of this process is deceptive because it depends upon, among many other things, which expansion method is chosen, developments in technology, and profitability. The latter factor in turn depends on such uncertainties as total long-term demand and the expansion plans of rival firms.

c.   **Porter's model** of the decision process for **capacity expansion** has the following interrelated steps:

1)   The firm must **identify the options** in relation to their size, type, degree of vertical integration (if any), and possible response by competitors.

2)   The second step is to **forecast demand, input costs, and technology developments**. The firm must be aware that its technology may become obsolete or that future design changes to allow expansion may or may not be possible. Moreover, the expansion itself may put upward pressure on input prices.

3)   The next step is **analysis of competitors** to determine when each will expand. The difficulty is that forecasting their behavior depends on knowing their expectations. Another difficulty is that each competitor's actions potentially affect all other competitors' actions, with the industry leader being most influential.

4)   Using the foregoing information, the firm predicts **total industry capacity and firms' market shares**. These estimates, together with the expected demand, permit the firm to predict **prices and cash flows**.

5)   The final step is **testing for inconsistencies**.

d.   The extent of **uncertainty about future demand** is a crucial variable in determining the nature of industry expansion. For example, if uncertainty is great, firms willing to take greater risks because of their large cash resources or strategic stake in the industry will act first. Other firms will await events.

1)   When demand uncertainty is low, firms will tend to adopt a strategy of **preemption**, usually with strong market signals, to forestall competitors' expansion plans. Excess preemption leads to excess industry capacity because firms overestimate their competitive strengths, misunderstand market signals, or fail to accurately assess competitors' intentions.

e. **Preemptive strategies** require investments in plant facilities and the ability to accept short-term unfavorable results. The strategy is risky because it anticipates demand and often sets prices in the expectation of future cost efficiencies. Moreover, a failed preemption strategy may provoke intense, industry-damaging conflict. The following conditions must be met for the strategy to succeed:

   1) The expansion must be **large relative to the market**, and competitors must believe that the move is preemptive. Hence, the firm should know competitors' expectations about the market or be able to influence them favorably. A move that is too small is by definition not preemptive.

   2) **Economies of scale** should be large in relation to demand, or the **learning-curve effect** will give an initial large investor a permanent cost advantage. For example, the preemptive firm may be able to secure too much of the market to allow a subsequent firm to invest at the efficient scale. That is, the residual demand available to be met by the later firm is less than the efficient scale of production. The later firm therefore must choose between intense competition at the efficient scale or a cost disadvantage.

   3) The preempting firm must have **credibility** to support its statements and moves, such as resources, technology, and a history of credibility.

   4) The firm must provide **credible signals before action by competitors**.

   5) The **competitors** of the firm should be willing not to act. This condition may not be met if competitors have noneconomic objectives, the business is strategically vital to them, or they have greater ability or willingness to compete.

8. Strategic management is facilitated when managers think synergistically. **Synergy** occurs when the combination of formerly separate elements has a greater effect than the sum of their individual effects. The following are types of synergy observed in business:

   a. **Market synergy** arises when products or services have positive complementary effects. Shopping malls reflect this type of synergy.

   b. **Cost synergy** results in cost reduction. It manifests itself in many ways, for example, in recycling of by-products or in the design, production, marketing, and sales of a line of products by the same enterprise.

   c. **Technological synergy** is the transfer of technology among applications. For example, technology developed for military purposes often has civilian uses.

   d. **Management synergy** also entails knowledge transfer. For example, a firm may hire a manager with skills that it lacks.

9. An **operations strategy** formulates a long-term plan for using enterprise resources to reach strategic objectives. The following are five operations strategies:

   a. A **cost** strategy is successful when the enterprise is the low-cost producer. However, the product (e.g., a commodity) tends to be undifferentiated in these cases, the market is often very large, and the competition tends to be intense because of the possibility of high-volume sales.

   b. A **quality** strategy involves competition based on product quality or process quality. Product quality relates to design, for example, the difference between a luxury car and a subcompact car. Process quality concerns the degree of freedom from defects.

   c. A **delivery** strategy may permit an enterprise to charge a higher price when the product is consistently delivered rapidly and on time. An example firm is UPS.

d.   A **flexibility** strategy entails offering many different products. This strategy also may reflect an ability to shift rapidly from one product line to another. An example firm is a publisher that can write, edit, print, and distribute a book within days to exploit the public's short-term interest in a sensational event.

e.   A **service** strategy seeks to gain a competitive advantage and maximize customer value by providing services, especially post-purchase services such as warranties on automobiles and home appliances.

10. Stop and review! You have completed the outline for this subunit. Study multiple-choice questions 1 through 10 beginning on page 41.

1.2 STRUCTURAL ANALYSIS OF INDUSTRIES

1.   The characteristics of the industries in which the firm wants to compete and of potential competitors are crucial **external factors (opportunities and threats)** analyzed during strategic planning. A useful tool for understanding these external factors is Michael E. Porter's comprehensive model of the structure of industries and competition. One feature of the model is an analysis of the five competitive forces that determine long-term profitability measured by long-term return on investment. This analysis determines the attractiveness of the industry. The **five competitive forces** are

a.   Rivalry among existing firms
b.   Threats of, and barriers to, entry
c.   Threat of substitute goods and services
d.   Threat of buyers' bargaining power
e.   Threat of suppliers' bargaining power

2.   **Rivalry** among existing firms will be intense when an industry contains many strong competitors. Price-cutting, large advertising budgets, and frequent introduction of new products are typical of intense competitive rivalry. The intensity of rivalry and the threat of entry vary with the following factors:

a.   The stage of the **industry life cycle**, e.g., introduction, rapid growth, growth, maturity, decline, or rapid decline. Thus, growth is preferable to decline. In a declining or even a stable industry, a firm's growth must come from winning other firms' customers, thereby requiring intensified competition.

b.   The **degree of product differentiation** and the **costs of switching** from one competitor's product to another. Less differentiation tends to heighten competition based on price, with price cutting leading to lower profits. On the other hand, high costs of switching suppliers weakens competition.

c.   Whether **fixed costs** are high in relation to variable costs. High fixed costs indicate that rivalry will be intense. The greater the cost to generate a given amount of sales revenues, the greater the **investment intensity** and the greater the need to operate at or near capacity. Hence, price cutting to sustain demand is typical of such firms.

d.   **Capacity expansion.** If it must be made in **large increments**, competition will be more intense. The need for large-scale expansion to achieve production efficiency may result in an excess of industry capacity over demand.

e.   **Concentration and balance**, e.g., when no firm is dominant. If an industry has a few equal competitors, the situation tends to be unstable and the rivalry intense.

f.   The extent of **exit barriers**. Low exit costs make an industry more attractive.

g.   **Competitors' incentives** to remain in the industry. When incentives are low, competitors are less likely to incur the costs and risks of intense rivalry.

3.   **Threats of, and barriers to, entry.** The prospects of long-term profitability are contingent upon the industry's exit and entry barriers.

    a.   Factors that **increase the threat of entry** are the following:

        1)   **Economies of scale** (and learning curve effects) are not significant.

        2)   **Brand identity** of existing products is weak.

        3)   **Costs of switching suppliers** are low.

        4)   Existing firms do not enjoy the cost advantages of **vertical integration.**

        5)   Proprietary **product differences** are few.

        6)   **Access to existing suppliers** is not blocked, and distribution channels are willing to accept new products.

        7)   **Capital requirements** are low.

        8)   **Retaliation against a new firm** by existing firms that follow the industry leader is unlikely.

        9)   The **government's policy** is to encourage new entrants.

    b.   The most favorable industry condition is one in which entry barriers are high and exit barriers are low. The following grid reflects Porter's view of the **relationship of returns to entry barriers and exit barriers**:

		Exit Barriers	
		Low	High
Entry Barriers:	Low	Low, stable returns	Low, risky returns
	High	High, stable returns	High, risky returns

        1)   When the threat of new entrants is minimal and exit is not difficult, returns are high, and risk is reduced in the event of poor performance.

        2)   Low entry barriers keep long-term profitability low because new firms can enter the industry, increasing competition and lowering prices and the market shares of existing firms.

        3)   **Exit barriers** are reasons for a firm to remain in an industry despite poor (or negative) profits. They include

            a)   Assets with a low residual value because of obsolescence or specialization

            b)   Legal or ethical duties to stakeholders, such as employees, creditors, suppliers, or customers

            c)   Governmental regulations

            d)   Lack of favorable alternative investments

            e)   Substantial vertical integration

            f)   Emotional factors, such as history and tradition

4.   The **threat of substitutes** limits price increases and profit margins. The greater the threat, the less the attractiveness of the industry to potential entrants. **Substitutes** are types (not brands) of goods and services that have the same purposes, for example, plastic and metal or minivans and SUVs. Hence, a change in the price of one such product or service causes a change in the demand for its substitutes.

    a.   The **price elasticity of demand** is a measure of the threat posed by substitutes. It is the ratio of the percentage change in the quantity of a product or service demanded to the percentage change in the price causing the change in the quantity.

      1)   Demand is **elastic** when the ratio exceeds 1.0 (ignoring the minus sign that results because the price and demand changes are in opposite directions). If demand is elastic, the effect of a price change on a firm's **total revenue** will be in the opposite direction of the change.

            a)   If demand is **inelastic** (the ratio is less than 1.0), the price effect on total revenue is greater than the quantity effect. Thus, a firm could increase total revenue by raising its prices.

      2)   The better the substitutes for a product or service, the more likely that demand is elastic and the greater the threat of substitutes.

    b.   **Structural considerations** affecting the threat of substitutes are

      1)   Relative prices,
      2)   Costs of switching to a substitute, and
      3)   Customers' inclination to substitute.

5.   As the **threat of buyers' bargaining power** increases, the appeal of an industry to potential entrants decreases. Buyers seek lower prices, better quality, and more services. Moreover, they use their purchasing power to obtain better terms, possibly through a bidding process. Thus, buyers affect competition.

    a.   **Buyers' bargaining power** varies with the following factors:

      1)   When purchasing power is **concentrated** in a few buyers or when buyers are well organized, their bargaining power is greater. This effect is reinforced when sellers are in a capital-intensive industry.

      2)   High (low) **switching costs** decrease (increase) buyers' bargaining power.

      3)   The threat of **backward (upstream) vertical integration**, that is, the acquisition of a supply capacity, increases buyers' bargaining power.

      4)   Buyers are most likely to bargain aggressively when their profit margins are low and a supplier's product accounts for a substantial amount of their costs.

      5)   Buyers are in a stronger position when the supplier's product is **undifferentiated**.

      6)   The more important the supplier's product is to buyers, the less bargaining power they have.

    b.   The foregoing analysis applies whether buyers are end users or intermediaries (e.g., distributors).

    c.   A supplier may seek to limit buyers' power by choosing those with the least ability to bargain or switch to other suppliers. However, a preferable response is to make offers that are difficult to reject.

6.   As the **threat of suppliers' bargaining power** increases, the appeal of an industry to potential entrants decreases. Accordingly, suppliers affect competition through pricing and the manipulation of the quantity supplied.

    a.   **Suppliers' bargaining power** is greater when

      1)   Switching costs are substantial.
      2)   Prices of substitutes are high.
      3)   They can threaten forward (downstream) vertical integration.
      4)   They provide something that is a significant input to the value added by the buyer.
      5)   Their industry is concentrated, or they are organized.

    b.   Buyers' best responses are to develop favorable, mutually beneficial relationships with suppliers or to diversify their sources of supply.

7.   Stop and review! You have completed the outline for this subunit. Study multiple-choice questions 11 through 17 beginning on page 43.

1.3 PLANNING PREMISES AND OBJECTIVES

1. **Premises** are the **underlying assumptions** about the expected environment in which plans will operate. Thus, the next step in planning is premising, or the generation of planning assumptions.

   a. Premises should be limited to those crucial to the success of the plans.

   b. Managers should ask, "What internal and external factors would influence the actions planned for this organization (division, department, program)?" Premises must be considered at all levels of the organization.

      1) Thus, capital budgeting plans should be premised on assumptions (forecasts) about economic cycles, price movements, etc.

      2) The parts department's plans might be premised on stability of parts prices or on forecasts that prices will rise.

   c. EXAMPLES:

      1) The general economy will suffer an 11% decline next year.

      2) Our closest competitor's new model will provide greater competition for potential sales.

      3) Union negotiations will result in a general wage increase of 8%.

      4) Over the next 5 years, the cost of our raw materials will increase by 30%.

      5) The elasticity of demand for the company's products is 1.2.

2. **Objectives and goals.** These terms are often used synonymously. Some writers distinguish between overall organizational objectives and individual, departmental, or subunit goals. Other writers adopt the opposite approach. In this text, the term "objectives" is used regardless of the organizational level or time frame involved.

   a. The determination of organizational objectives is the first step in planning.

      1) A **mission statement** is a formal, written document that defines the organization's purpose in society.

   b. Organizations usually have multiple objectives, which are often contradictory.

      1) The objective of maximizing profit and the objective of growth could be mutually exclusive within a given year. Maximizing short-term profit might hamper or preclude future growth.

      2) Conflict among an organization's objectives is common.

   c. Objectives vary with the organization's type and stage of development.

3. **Management Objectives**

   a. Management's primary task is to reach organizational objectives effectively and efficiently.

      1) **Effectiveness** is the degree to which the objective is accomplished.

      2) **Efficiency** is maximizing the output for a given quantity of input.

      3) In practice, effectiveness is of prime importance, and efficiency may be secondary because trade-offs are frequently made between effectiveness and efficiency.

         a) EXAMPLE: In a hospital, efficiency is much less important than effectiveness. Reducing the night nursing staff to the theoretical minimum might increase efficiency by reducing payroll, but if even one patient dies because of inadequate care, the hospital has failed to carry out its mission effectively.

      4) Effectiveness is doing the right things. Efficiency is doing things right.

      b.   Subordinate objectives of management may include

          1)   Survival
          2)   Growth of market influence
          3)   Employee development
          4)   Social responsibility
          5)   Creativity
          6)   Personal need satisfaction

4.   Each **subunit** of an organization may have **its own objectives**.

      a.   Subunit objectives may conflict with overall organizational objectives.

      b.   Subunit objectives unite the efforts of the people in the subunit. Consequently,

          1)   The people in each subunit are bound by their collective wisdom, training, and experiences. Thus, they may have tunnel vision regarding the organization's purpose.

              a)   EXAMPLE: "Why doesn't anybody take the time to see our problems in production? After all, if it weren't for us, they wouldn't have anything to sell!"

          2)   Subunits tend to be designed to make decisions that optimize the results of each subunit to the possible detriment of the overall organization.

              a)   Decentralized profit centers are the classic illustration.

                  i)   EXAMPLE: A profit center that buys raw materials from another profit center in the same organization will seek to maximize its own welfare regardless of the consequences for corporate objectives.

      c.   **Congruence.** Subunit objectives must be established to translate broad corporate objectives into meaningful and measurable terms for the subunit members. Accordingly, the short-term objectives reflected in tactical and operational plans should be congruent with the long-term objectives reflected in strategic plans.

5.   Objectives should be

      a.   **Clearly stated in specific terms.** General or poorly defined objectives are not useful for guiding the actions of managers or measuring their performance.

      b.   **Easily communicated to all concerned.** The executives who determine objectives cannot have the desired impact on the organization until they successfully communicate the objectives to all from whom action is required.

      c.   **Accepted by the individuals concerned**. An objective is unlikely to be attained if it is thought to be unachievable by those affected.

6.   Broad objectives should be established at the top and retranslated in more specific terms as they are communicated downward in a **means-end hierarchy**.

      a.   EXAMPLE:

          1)   The **purpose** of any corporation is to provide investors with an adequate return on their investment.

          2)   The firm's **socioeconomic purpose**, such as providing food, is a means to that end.

          3)   The firm's **mission** is the accomplishment of its socioeconomic purpose through the production of breakfast cereal.

          4)   The firm develops long-range or **strategic objectives** with regard to profitability, growth, or survival.

          5)   **Divisional objectives** are developed, e.g., to increase the sales of a certain kind of cereal.

       6) **Departmental objectives** are developed, e.g., to reduce waste in the packaging department.

       7) Lower-level managers and supervisors develop **personal performance and development objectives**.

7. A divergence of opinions exists regarding the determination of organizational objectives.

    a. One view is that **service** (need satisfaction for the consumer) is primary and that profit results from service.

    b. Another view is that **profit** or **return on investment (ROI)** is primary and that service results from profit.

    c. The most relevant view for a given organization is contingent upon its particular situation or environment.

       1) EXAMPLE: A fast-food company has customer service as its primary objective and expects profits to result from the successful satisfaction of consumer needs. On the other hand, a private utility can provide service only if a reasonable return on investment attracts the capital needed for system maintenance and expansion. For a utility, service results from profit.

8. Objectives change over time.

    a. EXAMPLE: The 19th-century industrialist's main objectives were to make money and increase personal power. In the latter part of the 20th Century, **social responsibility** became a significant force to be accommodated. This change is evidenced by, for example, the expanding pressures for information disclosures to outside parties, for environmental-impact studies, and for training the unemployed.

9. After objectives and premises are formulated, the next step in the planning process is the development of policies, procedures, and rules. These elements are necessary at all levels of the organization and overlap both in definition and in practice.

10. Policies, procedures, and rules are standing plans for repetitive situations.

    a. Policies and procedures provide **feedforward control** because they anticipate and prevent problems and provide guidance on how an activity should be performed to best ensure that an objective is achieved.

11. **Policies** are general statements that guide thinking and action in decision making.

    a. Policies may be explicitly published by, or implied by the actions of, management.

       1) Managers should be certain that their subordinates do not misinterpret minor or unrelated decisions as precedents for policy.

    b. Policies indicate a preferred method for achieving objectives.

    c. Policies define a general area within which a manager may exercise discretion.

    d. Policies should

       1) Involve known principles

       2) Be consistent with higher-level policies and with those of parallel units in the organization

       3) Be clear and comprehensive

       4) Be workable

       5) Be published

  e. Difficulties arise in the administration of policies that are not properly

    1) Formulated
    2) Understood
    3) Flexible
    4) Communicated
    5) Updated
    6) Accepted

  f. A strong organizational culture means that the organization's key values are intensely held and widely shared. Thus, the need for formal written policies is minimized.

12. **Procedures** are specific directives that define how work is to be done.

  a. Procedures may be described as follows:

    1) Usually consist of a set of specific steps in chronological order
    2) Are found at every level of the organization
    3) Reduce the need for managerial direction of subordinates in the accomplishment of routine matters
    4) Improve efficiency through standardization of actions
    5) Facilitate the training of personnel
    6) Provide coordination among different departments of the organization

  b. Procedures should be

    1) Balanced
    2) Efficient in use of resources
    3) Subject to organized control
    4) Flexible enough to handle most normal situations
    5) Clearly defined and easily accessible, as in procedures manuals

13. **Rules** are specific, detailed guides that restrict behavior.

  a. Rules are the simplest plans.
  b. A rule requires a specific action to be taken with regard to a given situation.
  c. Rules allow no discretion or flexibility.
  d. A procedure may contain a sequence of rules, or a rule may stand alone.
  e. For example, "No smoking in the paint shop. Violators will be dismissed without exception."

14. Stop and review! You have completed the outline for this subunit. Study multiple-choice questions 18 through 22 beginning on page 45.

1.4 PROGRAMS AND BUDGETS

1. A **program** is an organized set of objectives, policies, procedures, and rules designed to carry out a given course of action.

  a. A major program may call for many derivative programs (subprograms).
  b. Most significant programs depend upon or affect other programs within an enterprise.

2. A **budget** is a plan that contains a quantitative statement of expected results. A budget may be defined as a quantified program.

  a. Budgets are useful **control** devices, but their formulation is a **planning function**.
  b. The following are typical budgets:

    1) The **master budget** encompasses the organization's operating and financial plans for a specified period (ordinarily a year).

2) The **operating budget** is the part of the master budget that consists of the pro forma income statement and related budgets. Its emphasis is on obtaining and using resources.

    a) The **sales budget** (revenues budget) presents sales in units at their projected selling prices and is usually the first budget prepared. Accordingly, accurate sales forecasts are crucial.

    b) The **production budget** (for a manufacturing firm) is based on the sales forecast in units, plus or minus the desired inventory change. It is prepared for each department and used to plan when items will be produced.

        i) When the production budget has been completed, it is used in conjunction with the **ending inventory budget** to prepare budgets for direct labor, direct materials, and overhead.

    c) The **cost of goods sold budget** reflects direct materials usage, direct labor, factory overhead, and the change in finished goods inventory.

    d) **Other budgets** prepared during the operating budget process are for other stages in the value chain: R&D, marketing, distribution, customer service, and administrative costs.

3) The **financial budget** is the part of the master budget that includes the cash budget, capital budget, pro forma balance sheet, and pro forma statement of cash flows. Its emphasis is on obtaining the funds needed to purchase operating assets.

    a) The **capital budget** is not part of the operating budget because it is not part of normal operations. The capital budget may be prepared more than a year in advance.

    b) The **cash budget** is vital because an organization must have adequate cash at all times. Thus, cash budgets are prepared not only for annual and quarterly periods but also for monthly and weekly periods.

        i) A cash budget projects cash receipts and disbursements for planning and control purposes. Hence, it helps prevent not only cash emergencies but also excessive idle cash.

    c) Once the individual budgets are complete, budgeted financial statements can be prepared. They are often called **pro forma** statements because they are prepared before actual activities commence.

        i) The **pro forma income statement** is the culmination of the operating budget process. It is the pro forma operating income statement adjusted for interest and taxes.

        ii) The **pro forma balance sheet** is prepared using the cash and capital budgets and the pro forma income statement. Thus, it and the pro forma statement of cash flows culminate the financial budget process. The pro forma balance sheet is a beginning-of-the-period balance sheet that has been updated for projected changes in cash, receivables, payables, inventory, etc.

        iii) The **pro forma statement of cash flows** classifies cash receipts and disbursements depending on whether they are from operating, investing, or financing activities.

c. **Flexible budgets** are prepared based on many levels of activity.

d. **Zero-based budgeting** is an effective means of bringing objective thinking to the budgeting process and avoiding a tendency to add to the preceding year's budget.

    1) The programs of the organization are divided into **packages** that include goals, activities, and resources.

2) The cost of each package for the coming period is calculated, starting from zero.

3) The principal advantage of this approach is that managers are forced to review each program in its entirety (justify all expenditures) at the beginning of every budget period, rather than merely extrapolate the historical figures (costs).

e. A **life-cycle budget** involves estimates of a product's revenues and expenses over its expected life cycle (i.e., from research and development through introduction to maturity, and subsequently to the decline or harvest stage).

3. **Purposes.** Budgets serve to

a. Present organizational plans in a formal, logical, integrated manner.

b. Quantify objectives and the means selected for achieving them by relating expected occurrences to the resources available.

c. Force consideration of all the events needed to meet the objectives of each organizational function and thus serve as a motivational tool.

d. Provide a basis for coordinating the plans of all the subunits of the organization into an integrated whole, thereby promoting congruence.

e. Provide a means for communicating detailed plans to all concerned.

f. Provide a basis for control of performance through comparisons of actual with budgeted data. They permit analysis of variations from plans and signal the need for corrective managerial action.

4. **Program budgets** are formulated by objective rather than function and can cut across functional lines.

5. The budget for an operating unit should include as much specific information from that unit's management as possible, but

a. Budgets must be congruent with the strategic plans of corporate management.

1) Top management provides a context within which operational managers can prepare their budgets.

2) Corporate support might include economic forecasts, overall market sales forecasts, capital budgets, etc.

b. Input from the lowest relevant unit must be included because managers at this level have knowledge of actual production needs, etc., without which overall planning may be ineffective or inaccurate.

c. Successful budgets represent a compromise between top-level and operating management.

6. A fundamentally different use of the word budget is common in **governmental organizations**.

a. Because governmental endeavor is difficult to measure (often no revenue function exists), the use of budgets in the **appropriation process** is extremely important.

b. Also, the **stewardship function** is emphasized; thus, spending limits are important. Governmental units are encouraged to expend all of their appropriated funds.

7. Budgets have a significant **behavioral impact**. The setting of realistic and attainable objectives has been shown to have a positive effect on performance.

a. Unrealistically high or low targets have a negative effect on performance.

b. **Participation** in the budgeting process by the individuals affected usually improves performance by fostering a sense of involvement. Also, participants better understand what is expected of them.

8. Stop and review! You have completed the outline for this subunit. Study multiple-choice questions 23 through 27 beginning on page 47.

1.5 TYPES OF PLANS AND GENERAL PRINCIPLES

1.   Planning can be either formal or informal.

    a.   **Formal plans** are written in a stylized format for distribution to those concerned with carrying them out. Examples are

        1)   Budgets
        2)   Schedules
        3)   Business plans in the form of pro forma income statements
        4)   Statements of specific objectives

    b.   **Informal plans** are made by an individual to guide his/her activities. They may consist of lists or notes on what (s)he plans to accomplish during a day, or they may cover a longer period of time.

2.   Plans have different **planning horizons** (periods of time).

    a.   **Short-range, tactical, or operational planning** is usually considered to be for 1 year or less. All organizations create short-range, relatively specific plans concerning such matters as

        1)   Production
        2)   Materials procurement
        3)   Expenses and revenues
        4)   Cash flows

    b.   **Strategic (long-range) planning** is for periods from 1 to as many as 20 years (although 10 is more common). These plans are sometimes divided into **intermediate** (6 months to 2 years) and strategic (1 to 10 years or more).

        1)   Strategic plans are difficult to make because of uncertainty about future conditions. Thus, strategic plans are more general and exclude operational detail.

        2)   Strategic plans concern such matters as

            a)   New product development
            b)   Capital budgeting
            c)   Major financing
            d)   Mergers, acquisitions, or divestitures

    c.   The expansion of computer capabilities and the decrease in cost of computer acquisition and operation have increased the use of quantitative models for strategic as well as tactical planning purposes.

        1)   This effect is particularly evident in large organizations in which quantitative models may be used with greater statistical reliability.

3.   Plans may be single-purpose or standing-purpose.

    a.   **Single-purpose plans** are for objectives of known duration. Examples are

        1)   Construction of a plant
        2)   Installation of a new accounting system
        3)   Introduction of a marketing program

    b.   **Standing-purpose plans** are for objectives that will continue to exist for the foreseeable future. Examples are

        1)   Maintenance of market share
        2)   Operation of an existing production facility
        3)   Administration of a pension plan

4. **Contingency planning** is based on different sets of premises. It stipulates different sets of actions for management based on these premises.

    a. Contingency planning allows for forecasting error.

    b. Contingency planning is more expensive than formulating a single plan, so this additional cost must be more than balanced by improved performance.

5. **Participation.** Although planning and objective-setting are necessarily top-down processes, the lowest possible relevant units of management should be involved in the planning process. This form of upward communication is important for several reasons.

    a. Lower-level managers are aware of operational details and limitations. Thus, they can contribute to the feasibility and precision of the plan with regard to their individual areas of responsibility.

    b. Plans prepared at higher levels, without the participation of the managers who will be involved in their execution, appear to be dictated to the lower-level managers, with a consequent reduction in performance.

6. **Additional general planning principles**

    a. Plans should not allocate more than the known available resources.

    b. Planning must precede action.

    c. Plans must be coordinated among related functions.

    d. Plans must be flexible and recognized as subject to change.

    e. Plans should be limited to only highly probable future events; it is impossible to include every possible action and consequence.

7. Stop and review! You have completed the outline for this subunit. Study multiple-choice questions 28 and 29 on page 48.

1.6 CORE CONCEPTS

Nature of the Strategic Planning Process

- **Strategic planning** is a function of **strategic management**, which is the continuing process of pursuing a favorable competitive fit between the firm and its dynamic environment.

- A common **classification of strategies** is: corporate strategies, competitive strategies, and functional strategies.

- **Strategic planning** follows a formal five-step process: (1) formulate the mission statement, (2) analyze the firm's internal environment, (3) analyze the firm's external environment, (4) select appropriate strategies and create strategic business units, and (5) implement the chosen strategies.

- A **situational analysis** (also called a SWOT analysis) considers organizational **strengths and weaknesses** and their interactions with **opportunities and threats**.

- Strengths and weaknesses are inherent in the organization's **internal environment**; opportunities and threats are aspects of the **external environment**.

- A firm's **core competencies** are the source of its competitive advantages.

- **Strategic controls** should be established to monitor progress, isolate problems, identify invalid assumptions, and take prompt corrective action.

Structural Analysis of Industries

- **Michael E. Porter's comprehensive model** of the structure of industries and competition provides a tool for understanding the **external factors** analyzed during strategic planning.

- The **five competitive forces** named by Porter are (1) rivalry among existing firms; (2) threats of, and barriers to, entry; (3) threat of substitute goods and services; (4) threat of buyers' bargaining power; and (5) threat of suppliers' bargaining power.

<u>Planning Premises and Objectives</u>

- **Premises** are the underlying **assumptions** about the expected environment in which plans will operate.
- Managers should ask, "What internal and external factors would influence the actions planned for this organization (division, department, program)?" Premises must be considered at all levels of the organization.
- A **mission statement** is a formal, written document that defines the organization's purpose in society.
- Management's primary task is to **reach organizational objectives** effectively and efficiently.
- **Effectiveness** is the degree to which the objective is accomplished. **Efficiency** is maximizing the output for a given quantity of input.
- Each **subunit** of an organization may have its own objectives. Broad objectives should be established at the top and retranslated in more specific terms as they are communicated downward in a **means-end hierarchy**.
- **Policies** are general statements that guide thinking and action in decision making. **Procedures** are specific directives that define how work is to be done. **Rules** are specific, detailed guides that restrict behavior.

<u>Programs and Budgets</u>

- A **program** is an organized set of objectives, policies, procedures, and rules designed to carry out a given course of action.
- A **budget** is a plan that contains a quantitative statement of expected results. A budget may be defined as a quantified program.
- The **master budget** encompasses the organization's **operating** and **financial plans** for a specified period.
- Budgets serve **multiple functions**, e.g., they quantify objectives and the means for achieving them and provide a means for communicating the organization's objectives to all levels of personnel.

<u>Types of Plans and General Principles</u>

- **Short-range, tactical, or operational planning** is usually considered to be for **one year or less** concerning such matters as production, materials procurement, expenses and revenues, and cash flows.
- **Strategic, or long-range, planning** is for periods from one to **as many as 20 years** (although 10 is more common) concerning such matters as new product development, capital budgeting, major financing, and mergers and acquisitions.
- **Contingency planning** is based on different sets of premises. It stipulates different sets of actions for management based on these premises.
- Although planning and objective-setting are necessarily top-down processes, the **lowest possible** relevant units of management should be **involved in the planning process**.

QUESTIONS

1.1 **Nature of the Strategic Planning Process**

1. A distinction between forecasting and planning

A. Is not valid because they are synonyms.

B. Arises because forecasting covers the short term and planning does not.

C. Is that forecasts are used in planning.

D. Is that forecasting is a management activity, whereas planning is a technical activity.

Answer (C) is correct. *(CMA, adapted)*
REQUIRED: The distinction between forecasting and planning.
DISCUSSION: Planning is the determination of what is to be done, and of how, when, where, and by whom it is to be done. Plans serve to direct the activities that all organizational members must undertake to move the organization from where it is to where it wants to be. Forecasting is the basis of planning because it projects the future. A variety of quantitative methods are used in forecasting.
Answer (A) is incorrect because forecasting is a basis for planning. Answer (B) is incorrect because forecasting and planning may be short or long term. Answer (D) is incorrect because forecasting is often more technical than planning. It can involve a variety of mathematical models.

2. Strategy is a broad term that usually means the selection of overall objectives. Strategic analysis ordinarily excludes the

A. Trends that will affect the entity's markets.

B. Target product mix and production schedule to be maintained during the year.

C. Forms of organizational structure that would best serve the entity.

D. Best ways to invest in research, design, production, distribution, marketing, and administrative activities.

Answer (B) is correct. *(CMA, adapted)*
REQUIRED: The item ordinarily excluded from the process of strategic analysis.
DISCUSSION: Strategic analysis is the process of long-range planning. It includes identifying organizational objectives, evaluating the strengths and weaknesses of the organization, assessing risk levels, and forecasting the future direction and influences of factors relevant to the organization, such as market trends, changes in technology, international competition, and social change. The final step is to derive the best strategy for reaching the objectives. Setting the target product mix and production schedule for the current year is not a concern of strategic analysis because it is a short-term activity.
Answer (A) is incorrect because strategic analysis includes examining marketing trends. Answer (C) is incorrect because strategic analysis evaluates organizational structure. Answer (D) is incorrect because strategic analysis includes evaluation of the best ways to invest in research, design, etc.

3. Strategic planning, as practiced by most modern organizations, includes all of the following except

A. Top-level management participation.

B. A long-term focus.

C. Strategies that will help in achieving long-range goals.

D. Analysis of the current month's actual variances from budget.

Answer (D) is correct. *(CMA, adapted)*
REQUIRED: The item not an element of strategic planning.
DISCUSSION: Strategic planning is the process of setting overall organizational objectives and goals. It is a long-term process aimed at charting the future course of the organization. Strategic planning is based on assessing risk levels, evaluating the strengths and weaknesses of the organization, and forecasting the future direction and influences of factors relevant to the organization such as market trends, changes in technology, international competition, and social change. Analysis of the current month's budget variances is not an aspect of strategic planning.

4. Which one of the following reasons is not a significant reason for planning in an organization?

A. Promoting coordination among operating units.

B. Forcing managers to consider expected future trends and conditions.

C. Developing a basis for controlling operations.

D. Monitoring profitable operations.

Answer (D) is correct. *(CMA, adapted)*
REQUIRED: The item not a significant reason for planning.
DISCUSSION: Monitoring profitable operations is not a significant reason for planning. Monitoring is a control function, whereas planning has a control purpose that precedes control in the planning-control cycle. Planning establishes standards against which the control function compares preliminary or final results.
Answer (A) is incorrect because planning helps to ensure goal congruence. Answer (B) is incorrect because, by definition, planning is forward looking. It compels managers to determine their objectives, the methods of achieving those objectives, and the resources required. Answer (C) is incorrect because plans are the criteria with which results are compared during the planning-control cycle to determine whether objectives are being achieved.

5. Certain phases of the planning process should be formalized for all of the following reasons except that

    A. Informal plans and goals lack the necessary precision, understanding, and consistency.

    B. Formal plans can act as a constraint on the decision-making freedom of managers and supervisors.

    C. Formalization requires the establishment and observance of deadlines for decision making and planning.

    D. Formalization provides a logical basis for rational flexibility in planning.

Answer (B) is correct. *(CMA, adapted)*
    REQUIRED: The statement not a reason for formalizing certain phases of the planning process.
    DISCUSSION: A formal plan is a prescription for organizational behavior and a set of goals. Management decision making is therefore necessarily constrained by the limitations established in the plan.
    Answer (A) is incorrect because formal planning compels managers to establish specific goals and avoid pursuit of contradictory objectives. It also requires managers to think carefully about what the organization should accomplish and how goals are to be met. Answer (C) is incorrect because plans entail commitment to achieving specified results within a given future time frame. Hence, deadlines are an essential part of formal planning. Answer (D) is incorrect because formal plans should be the product of a disciplined, objective process of gathering evidence and reasoning. It recognizes that assumptions must be made about future conditions and that plans must be flexible enough to allow for changes in those assumptions.

6. All of the following are characteristics of the strategic planning process except the

    A. Emphasis on the long run.

    B. Analysis of external economic factors.

    C. Review of the attributes and behavior of the organization's competition.

    D. Analysis and review of departmental budgets.

Answer (D) is correct. *(CMA, adapted)*
    REQUIRED: The item that is not a characteristic of the strategic planning process.
    DISCUSSION: Strategic planning is the process of setting the overall organizational objectives and goals, and involves the drafting of strategic plans. Long-range (strategic) planning is based on identifying and specifying organizational goals and objectives, evaluating the strengths and weaknesses of the organization, assessing risk levels, forecasting the future direction and influences of factors relevant to the organization (such as market trends, changes in technology, international competition, and social change), and deriving the best strategy for reaching the objectives given the organization's strengths and weaknesses and the relevant future trends. Analyzing and reviewing departmental budgets is an aspect of operational management and not a part of strategic planning.

7. The first step in the sales planning process is to

    A. Assemble all the data that are relevant in developing a comprehensive sales plan.

    B. Develop management guidelines specific to sales planning, including the sales planning process and planning responsibilities.

    C. Prepare a sales forecast consistent with specified forecasting guidelines, including assumptions.

    D. Secure managerial commitment to attain the goals specified in the comprehensive sales plan.

Answer (B) is correct. *(CMA, adapted)*
    REQUIRED: The first step in the sales planning process.
    DISCUSSION: Sales planning is a starting point for many other plans. The resources required, revenues to be earned, and costs to be incurred depend on sales. The sales plan of an operating unit should include as much specific information from that unit's management as possible, but it must conform to the strategic plans of corporate management. Thus, top management must provide a context within which operational managers can prepare their plans. Corporate support might include economic forecasts, overall market sales forecasts, and capital budgets.
    Answer (A) is incorrect because top management must develop guidelines and outline planning responsibilities before assembling data. Answer (C) is incorrect because top management must develop guidelines and outline planning responsibilities before preparing a forecast. Answer (D) is incorrect because top management must develop guidelines and outline planning responsibilities before securing managerial commitment.

8. The capital budget is a(n)

A. Plan to ensure that sufficient funds are available for the operating needs of the company.

B. Exercise that sets the long-range goals of the company including the consideration of external influences.

C. Plan that coordinates and communicates a company's plan for the coming year to all departments and divisions.

D. Plan that assesses the long-term needs of the company for plant and equipment purchases.

Answer (D) is correct.   *(CMA, adapted)*
REQUIRED: The true statement about the capital budget.
DISCUSSION: Capital budgeting is the process of planning expenditures for long-lived assets. It involves choosing among investment proposals using a ranking procedure. Evaluations are based on various measures involving rate of return on investment.
Answer (A) is incorrect because capital budgeting involves long-term investment needs, not immediate operating needs. Answer (B) is incorrect because strategic planning establishes long-term goals in the context of relevant factors in the firm's environment. Answer (C) is incorrect because an operating budget communicates a company's plan for the coming year to all departments.

9. Capital budgeting techniques are least likely to be used in evaluating the

A. Acquisition of new aircraft by a cargo company.

B. Design and implementation of a major advertising program.

C. Adoption of a new method of allocating nontraceable costs to product lines.

D. Sale by a conglomerate of an unprofitable division.

Answer (C) is correct.   *(CMA, adapted)*
REQUIRED: The decision least likely to be evaluated using capital budgeting techniques.
DISCUSSION: Capital budgeting is the process of planning expenditures for investments that are expected to generate returns over a period of more than one year. Thus, capital budgeting concerns the acquisition or disposal of long-term assets and the financing ramifications of such decisions. The adoption of a new method of allocating nontraceable costs to product lines has no effect on a company's cash flows, does not relate to the acquisition of long-term assets, and is not concerned with financing. Hence, capital budgeting is irrelevant to such a decision.
Answer (A) is incorrect because new aircraft represent a long-term investment in capital goods. Answer (B) is incorrect because a major advertising program is a high-cost investment with long-term effects. Answer (D) is incorrect because disinvestment decisions should be approached with long-term planning methods applicable to investments.

10. The capital budgeting model that is ordinarily considered the best model for long-range decision making is the

A. Payback model.

B. Accounting rate of return model.

C. Unadjusted rate of return model.

D. Discounted cash flow model.

Answer (D) is correct.   *(CMA, adapted)*
REQUIRED: The best capital budgeting model for long-range decision making.
DISCUSSION: The capital budgeting methods that are generally considered the best for long-range decision making are the internal rate of return and net present value methods. These are both discounted cash flow methods.
Answer (A) is incorrect because the payback method gives no consideration to the time value of money or to returns after the payback period. Answer (B) is incorrect because the accounting rate of return does not consider the time value of money. Answer (C) is incorrect because the unadjusted rate of return does not consider the time value of money.

1.2 Structural Analysis of Industries

11. Which of the following factors is not typical of an industry that faces intense competitive rivalry?

A. Price-cutting.

B. Large advertising budgets.

C. Frequent introduction of new products.

D. Inelastic demand.

Answer (D) is correct.   *(Publisher, adapted)*
REQUIRED: The situation not typical in an industry facing intense rivalry.
DISCUSSION: Rivalry among existing firms will be intense when an industry has many strong competitors. Inelastic demand exists when quantity purchased is not greatly affected by price changes. Thus, price cutting does not increase sales for the industry and is therefore atypical of an intensely competitive industry.
Answer (A) is incorrect because price-cutting is typical for a firm in an industry with intense competitive rivalry. Answer (B) is incorrect because a large advertising budget is typical for a firm in an industry with intense competitive rivalry. Answer (C) is incorrect because frequent introduction of new products is typical for a firm in an industry with intense competitive rivalry.

12. Intense rivalry among firms in an industry increases when there is

I.   A low degree of product differentiation
II.   Low consumer switching costs

    A. I only.

    B. II only.

    C. Both I and II.

    D. Neither I nor II.

Answer (C) is correct. *(Publisher, adapted)*
    REQUIRED: The situation(s), if any, that increase the intensity of rivalry in an industry.
    DISCUSSION: The degree of product differentiation and the costs of switching from one competitor's product to another increase the intensity of rivalry and competition in an industry. Less differentiation tends to heighten competition based on price, with price cutting leading to lower profits. Low costs of switching products also increase competition.
    Answer (A) is incorrect because low consumer switching costs also increase rivalry. Answer (B) is incorrect because a low degree of product differentiation also increases rivalry. Answer (D) is incorrect because both low consumer switching costs and a low degree of product differentiation increase rivalry.

13. The prospect for the long-term profitability of an existing firm is greater when

    A. The firm operates in an industry with a steep learning curve in its production process.

    B. The costs of switching suppliers is low.

    C. New entrants are encouraged by government policy.

    D. Distribution channels are willing to accept new products.

Answer (A) is correct. *(Publisher, adapted)*
    REQUIRED: The circumstance improving the prospect of long-term profitability.
    DISCUSSION: The prospects of long-term profitability are contingent upon the industry's exit and entry barriers. The entry of new firms in a market decreases the prospect for long-term profitability. When a firm operates in an industry that has a steep learning curve, it is more difficult for new firms to enter the market. Thus, the prospects of long-term profitability are greater for an existing firm.
    Answer (B) is incorrect because, when the costs of switching suppliers is low, the threat of entry by new firms is increased. Answer (C) is incorrect because, when new entrants are encouraged by government policy, the threat of entry by new firms is increased. Answer (D) is incorrect because, when distribution channels are willing to accept new products, the threat of entry by new firms is increased.

14. Structural considerations affecting the threat of substitutes include all of the following except

    A. Relative prices.

    B. Brand identity.

    C. Cost of switching to substitutes.

    D. Customers' inclination to use a substitute.

Answer (B) is correct. *(Publisher, adapted)*
    REQUIRED: The structural consideration that does not affect the threat of substitutes.
    DISCUSSION: Substitutes are types of goods and services that serve the same purpose. All products that can replace a good or service should be considered substitutes. For example, bicycles and cars are substitutes for public transportation. Structural considerations determine the effect substitutes have on one another. However, because substitutes are types (not brands) of goods and services that have the same purposes, brand identity is not a structural consideration affecting the threat of substitutes.
    Answer (A) is incorrect because relative price is a structural consideration affecting the threat of substitutes. Answer (C) is incorrect because the cost of switching is a structural consideration affecting the threat of substitutes. Answer (D) is incorrect because a customers' inclination to use a substitute is a structural consideration affecting the threat of substitutes.

15. Logistics Corp. is performing research to determine the feasibility of entering the truck rental industry. The decision to enter the market is most likely to be deterred if

    A. Buyer switching costs are high.

    B. Buyers view the product as differentiated.

    C. The market is dominated by a small consortium of buyers.

    D. Buyers enjoy large profit margins.

Answer (C) is correct. *(Publisher, adapted)*
    REQUIRED: The deterrent to market entry.
    DISCUSSION: When purchasing power is concentrated in a few buyers or when buyers are well organized, their bargaining power is greater. This effect is reinforced when sellers are in a capital-intensive industry such as trucking.
    Answer (A) is incorrect because high switching costs decrease buyers' bargaining power. Answer (B) is incorrect because buyers are in a weaker position when the supplier's product is differentiated. Answer (D) is incorrect because buyers are most likely to bargain aggressively when their profit margins are low, especially if the supplier's product accounts for a substantial amount of their costs.

16. Which industry factor does not contribute to competitive rivalry?

  A. Price-cutting, large advertising budgets, and frequent introduction of new products.

  B. A firm's growth must come from winning other firms' customers.

  C. High costs of switching suppliers.

  D. High fixed costs.

Answer (C) is correct. *(Publisher, adapted)*
  REQUIRED: The industry factor that does not contribute to competitive rivalry.
  DISCUSSION: If it is expensive to switch suppliers, customers will be less motivated to respond to competitor advances.
  Answer (A) is incorrect because price-cutting, large advertising budgets, and frequent introduction of new products are characteristic of intense competitive rivalry. Answer (B) is incorrect because winning other firms' customers is essential to a firm's growth and strengthens competition. Answer (D) is incorrect because, the greater the fixed cost to generate a given amount of sales revenues, the greater the incentive to compete on price, service, etc., to maintain and increase sales levels.

17. Which condition does not increase the threat of new competitor entry into the industry?

  A. Strong brand identity.

  B. Existing firms do not enjoy the cost advantages of vertical integration.

  C. Few proprietary product differences.

  D. Low capital requirements.

Answer (A) is correct. *(Publisher, adapted)*
  REQUIRED: The condition that decreases the threat of new competition.
  DISCUSSION: Strong brand identity decreases the threat that new competitors will enter an industry. New competitors have difficulty because potential customers are loyal to established firms in the industry.
  Answer (B) is incorrect because cost advantages of existing firms make entry difficult for new competitors. Answer (C) is incorrect because proprietary product differences make entry more difficult. Answer (D) is incorrect because high capital requirements make entry more difficult.

1.3 Planning Premises and Objectives

18. Which one of the following management considerations is usually addressed first in strategic planning?

  A. Outsourcing.

  B. Overall objectives of the firm.

  C. Organizational structure.

  D. Recent annual budgets.

Answer (B) is correct. *(CMA, adapted)*
  REQUIRED: The management consideration usually addressed first in strategic planning.
  DISCUSSION: Strategic planning is the process of setting overall organizational objectives and drafting strategic plans. It is a process of long-term planning. Setting ultimate objectives for the firm is a necessary prelude to developing strategies for achieving those objectives. Plans and budgets are then needed to implement those strategies.
  Answer (A) is incorrect because outsourcing is an operating decision of a more short-term nature. Answer (C) is incorrect because organizational structure, although important in strategic planning, is based upon the firm's overall objectives. Answer (D) is incorrect because recent annual budgets are a basis for short-term planning.

19. A firm's statement of broad objectives or mission statement should accomplish all of the following except

  A. Outlining strategies for technological development, market expansion, and product differentiation.

  B. Defining the purpose of the company.

  C. Providing an overall guide to those in high-level, decision-making positions.

  D. Stating the moral and ethical principles that guide the actions of the firm.

Answer (A) is correct. *(CMA, adapted)*
  REQUIRED: The purpose not achieved by a mission statement.
  DISCUSSION: The determination of organizational objectives is the first step in the planning process. A mission statement is a formal, written document that defines the organization's purpose in society, for example, to produce and distribute certain goods of high quality in a manner beneficial to the public, employees, shareholders, and other constituencies. Thus, a mission statement does not announce specific operating plans. It does not describe strategies for technological development, market expansion, or product differentiation because these are tasks for operating management.
  Answer (B) is incorrect because a mission statement defines the purpose of the company (some writers differentiate between purpose and mission). Answer (C) is incorrect because broad objectives provide guidance to those in high-level positions who are responsible for long-range planning. Answer (D) is incorrect because mission statements increasingly are concerned with ethical principles.

20. Policies and procedures provide guidance to management and employees. Would policies and procedures normally be found for the senior management of a multinational organization?

- A. Yes, all policies and procedures are developed by senior management.
- B. No, senior management develops policies and procedures for lower levels only.
- C. Yes, policies and procedures are used throughout an organization's ranks.
- D. No, only middle managers and below develop and use policies and procedures.

Answer (C) is correct. *(CIA, adapted)*
REQUIRED: Whether the senior management of a multinational corporation would be subjected to policies and procedures.
DISCUSSION: Research has shown that policies and procedures are referred to by all levels of management on an as-needed basis.
Answer (A) is incorrect because senior management develops and refers to some, but not all, policies and procedures. Answer (B) is incorrect because senior management does develop policies and procedures for their own use. Answer (D) is incorrect because senior management also develops and uses policies and procedures.

21. The management of an organization has stated that two members of the same family may not be employed in the same department. Identify the component of organizational planning that is being demonstrated by management's action.

- A. A strategy.
- B. A policy.
- C. An objective.
- D. A mission statement.

Answer (B) is correct. *(CIA, adapted)*
REQUIRED: The component of organizational planning that prohibits employment of family members in the same department.
DISCUSSION: Top management establishes policies as guides to middle- and lower-management decision making. Policies are relatively broad guidelines for making routine decisions consistent with overall objectives or goals. They channel thinking in a certain direction but allow for some managerial discretion.
Answer (A) is incorrect because a strategy is a broad, overall concept of operation. Objectives are implemented by strategies. Answer (C) is incorrect because objectives are long-range and general in nature. They guide the organization toward its mission. Answer (D) is incorrect because an organization's mission is its basic task or function.

22. In an organization with empowered work teams, organizational policies

- A. Should define the limits or constraints within which the work teams must act if they are to remain self-directing.
- B. Become more important than ever. Without clear rules to follow, empowered work teams are almost certain to make mistakes.
- C. Should be few or none. The work teams should have the freedom to make their own decisions.
- D. Should be set by the teams themselves in periodic joint meetings.

Answer (A) is correct. *(CIA, adapted)*
REQUIRED: The impact of organizational policies on empowered work teams.
DISCUSSION: Work teams are not "empowered" to do anything they please. The organization has certain expectations for what is to be accomplished and how the teams are to go about accomplishing these expectations. Once the organization defines its objectives and sets appropriate policies, the work teams are able to make and implement decisions within those boundaries. Policies in this context are usually quite broad (e.g., relating to ethical business conduct) but nevertheless important.
Answer (B) is incorrect because policies are not more important than ever. Policies are usually important guides for decision making. They enable empowered work teams to make decisions within boundaries. Answer (C) is incorrect because policies are necessary to define boundaries within which the empowered work teams can make decisions. Such boundaries promote achievement of the organization's objectives. Answer (D) is incorrect because empowered work teams are not free to do as they please.

1.4 Programs and Budgets

23. After the goals of the company have been established and communicated, the next step in the planning process is development of the

    A. Production budget.

    B. Direct materials budget.

    C. Selling and administrative budget.

    D. Sales budget.

Answer (D) is correct. *(CMA, adapted)*

REQUIRED: The first budget to be prepared.

DISCUSSION: The sales budget is the first step in the operating budget process because it is needed to prepare all of the other budgets. For example, the production budget cannot be prepared until the sales department has determined how many units are needed.

Answer (A) is incorrect because the production budget depends on the sales budget, and the direct materials, direct labor, factory overhead, and cost of goods sold budgets depend on the production budget. Answer (B) is incorrect because the production budget depends on the sales budget, and the direct materials, direct labor, factory overhead, and cost of goods sold budgets depend on the production budget. Answer (C) is incorrect because selling and administrative costs are dependent on projected sales.

24. In planning and controlling capital expenditures, the most logical sequence is to begin with

    A. Analyzing capital addition proposals.

    B. Making capital expenditure decisions.

    C. Analyzing and evaluating all promising alternatives.

    D. Identifying capital addition projects and other capital needs.

Answer (D) is correct. *(CMA, adapted)*

REQUIRED: The most logical first step in planning and controlling capital expenditures.

DISCUSSION: Capital budgeting is a long-term planning process for investments. This process begins with the identification of capital needs, that is, of projects required to achieve organizational goals. The next step is to search for specific investments. The third step is to acquire and analyze information about the potential choices. The fourth step is to select specific investments after considering both qualitative and quantitative factors. The fifth step is to finance the undertakings. The final step is implementation and monitoring.

Answer (A) is incorrect because analyzing capital addition proposals is a step subsequent to identifying capital addition projects and other capital needs. Answer (B) is incorrect because making capital expenditure decisions is a step subsequent to identifying capital addition projects and other capital needs. Answer (C) is incorrect because analyzing and evaluating all promising alternatives is a step subsequent to identifying capital addition projects and other capital needs.

25. The process of developing plans for a company's expected operations and controlling the operations to help carry out those plans is

    A. Preparing a period budget.

    B. Preparing a master budget.

    C. Budgetary control.

    D. Participative budgeting.

Answer (C) is correct. *(CMA, adapted)*

REQUIRED: The process of developing plans for expected operations and controlling the operations to help carry out those plans.

DISCUSSION: The budget has the same structure as the organization itself. The complete budget is made up of a hierarchy of smaller budgets, each representing the plan of a division, department, or other unit in the organizational structure. Successful budgeting requires completion of a plan that states organizational goals before the budgeting process. Prevention and detection of deviations from the budget are the control purposes of budgets.

Answer (A) is incorrect because the simple preparation of a budget does not address the control aspect of the process. Answer (B) is incorrect because the simple preparation of a budget does not address the control aspect of the process. Answer (D) is incorrect because participative budgeting implies a budget that is prepared jointly by management and lower-level employees; it is only one of many processes of budget development.

26. Zero-based budgeting forces managers to

A. Estimate a product's revenues and expenses over its expected life cycle.

B. Prepare a budget based on historical costs.

C. Formulate a budget by objective rather than function.

D. Justify all expenditures at the beginning of every budget period.

Answer (D) is correct.   *(Publisher, adapted)*
    REQUIRED: The characteristic of zero-based budgeting.
    DISCUSSION: Zero-based budgeting is a planning process in which each manager must justify his/her department's full budget for each period. The purpose is to encourage periodic reexamination of all costs in the hope that some can be reduced or eliminated.
    Answer (A) is incorrect because a life-cycle budget involves estimates of a product's revenues and expenses over its expected life cycle. Answer (B) is incorrect because a main objective of zero-based budgeting is to avoid budgeting based on historical costs. Answer (C) is incorrect because a program budget is formulated by objective rather than function.

27. Which of the following statements regarding budgets is false?

A. Budgets present organizational plans in a formal, logical, and integrated manner.

B. Budgets are used only as a planning function.

C. Budgets may be developed for cash flows or labor usage.

D. A budget is a plan that contains a quantitative statement of expected results.

Answer (B) is correct.   *(Publisher, adapted)*
    REQUIRED: The false statement about budgeting.
    DISCUSSION: Budget formulation is a planning function; however, budgets are also useful control devices. Budgets provide a basis for control of performance through comparisons of actual with budgeted data. They permit analysis of variations from plans and signal the need for corrective managerial action.

1.5 Types of Plans and General Principles

28. Strategic planning is

A. Short term.

B. Operational.

C. Long term.

D. Informal.

Answer (C) is correct.   *(Publisher, adapted)*
    REQUIRED: The term synonymous with strategic planning.
    DISCUSSION: Strategic planning, also called long-term planning, covers periods from 1 to 20 years. Strategic planning is somewhat difficult because of uncertainty about future conditions. Thus, long-range plans are more general and exclude operational detail.
    Answer (A) is incorrect because short-term planning covers a period of 1 year or less. Answer (B) is incorrect because operational planning is another name for short-term planning. Answer (D) is incorrect because informal planning can be either long term or short term.

29. Which of the following activities would likely not be a consideration in strategic planning?

A. New product development.

B. Capital budgeting.

C. Mergers.

D. Materials procurement.

Answer (D) is correct.   *(Publisher, adapted)*
    REQUIRED: The activities not included in the strategic planning process.
    DISCUSSION: Strategic, or long-term, planning covers long periods of time and is concerned with matters such as new product development; capital budgeting; major financing; and mergers, acquisitions, and divestitures. Operational matters, such as materials procurement, are not a part of strategic planning, but they are a consideration in short-term, or operational, planning.

Use Gleim's **CMA Test Prep** for interactive testing with **over 2,000 additional multiple-choice questions**!

STUDY UNIT TWO
MANUFACTURING PARADIGMS

(11 pages of outline)

This study unit is the **second of three** on **strategic planning**. The relative weight assigned to this major topic in Part 3 of the exam is **15%** at **skill level B** (four skill types required). The three study units are:

Study Unit 1: Strategic and Tactical Planning
Study Unit 2: Manufacturing Paradigms
Study Unit 3: Business Process Performance

After studying the outline and answering the multiple-choice questions, you will have the skills necessary to address the following topics listed in the IMA's Learning Outcome Statements:

Part 3 – Section A.2. Manufacturing paradigms

The candidate should be able to:

a. define a just-in-time system and describe its central purpose

b. identify the operational benefits of implementing a just-in-time system

c. define the term kanban and describe how kanban is used in a just-in-time system

d. demonstrate an understanding of work cells and how they relate to just-in-time processes

e. define material resource planning (MRP) and identify its benefits

f. calculate subunits needed to complete an order for a finished product using MRP

g. demonstrate an understanding of the concept of outsourcing and identify the benefits and limitations of choosing this option

h. demonstrate an understanding of the theory of constraints and the steps involved in theory of constraints analysis

i. define and calculate throughput contribution and demonstrate an understanding of its relationship to the theory of constraints

j. demonstrate an understanding of a drum-buffer-rope system as a tool for managing product flow

k. discuss how the theory of constraints and activity-based costing are complementary analytical tools

l. identify other contemporary productivity concepts such as automation and the use of robots, computer-aided design, computer-integrated manufacturing, and flexible manufacturing systems

2.1 JUST-IN-TIME SYSTEMS

1.   Modern inventory planning favors the **just-in-time (JIT)** model. Many companies have traditionally built parts and components for subsequent operations on a preset schedule. Such a schedule provides a cushion of inventory so that the next operation will always have parts to work with – a just-in-case method.

    a.   In contrast, JIT limits output to the demand of the subsequent operation. Reductions in inventory levels result in **less money invested in idle assets**; reduction of storage space requirements; and lower inventory taxes, pilferage, and obsolescence risks.

        1)   High inventory levels often mask production problems because defective parts can be overlooked when plenty of good parts are available. If only enough parts are made for the subsequent operation, however, any defects will immediately halt production.

        2)   The **focus of quality control** under JIT shifts from the discovery of defective parts to the prevention of quality problems, so zero machine breakdowns (achieved through preventive maintenance) and zero defects are ultimate goals. Higher quality and lower inventory go together.

    b.   **Objectives.** JIT is a reaction to the trends of global competition and rapid technological progress that have resulted in shorter product life-cycles and greater consumer demand for product diversity.

        1)   Higher productivity, reduced order costs as well as carrying costs, faster and cheaper setups, shorter manufacturing cycle times, better due date performance, improved quality, and more flexible processes are objectives of JIT methods.

        2)   The ultimate objectives are increased competitiveness and higher profits.

    c.   JIT systems are based on a **manufacturing philosophy** popularized by the Japanese that combines purchasing, production, and inventory control.

        1)   **Minimization of inventory** is a goal because many inventory-related activities are viewed as nonvalue-added. Indeed, carrying inventory is regarded as a symptom of correctable problems, such as poor quality, long cycle times, and lack of coordination with suppliers.

    d.   However, JIT also encompasses changes in the **production process** itself.

        1)   JIT is a **pull system**; items are pulled through production by current demand, not pushed through by anticipated demand.

        2)   Thus, one operation produces only what is needed by the next operation, and components and raw materials arrive just in time to be used.

    e.   One feature of the lower inventory levels in a JIT system is **elimination of the need for certain internal controls**.

        1)   Frequent receipt of deliveries from suppliers often means less need for a sophisticated inventory control system and for control personnel.

        2)   JIT also may eliminate central receiving areas, hard copy receiving reports, and storage areas. A central warehouse is not needed because deliveries are made by suppliers directly to the area of production.

        3)   The quality of parts provided by suppliers is verified by use of statistical controls rather than inspection of incoming goods. Storage, counting, and inspecting are eliminated in an effort to perform only value-adding work.

    f.   In a JIT system, the **suppliers' dependability** is crucial. Organizations that adopt JIT systems therefore develop close relationships with a few carefully chosen suppliers who are extensively involved in the buyer's processes.

        1)   Long-term contracts are typically negotiated to reduce order costs. Indeed, some major retailers have agreed to **continuous replenishment** arrangements whereby a supplier with superior demand forecasting ability essentially tells the buyer when and how much to reorder.

        2)   Buyer-supplier relationships are further facilitated by **electronic data interchange (EDI)**, a technology that allows the supplier access to the buyer's online inventory management system. Thus, electronic messages replace paper documents (purchase orders and sales invoices), and the production schedules and deliveries of the parties can be more readily coordinated.

2.   The Japanese term **kanban** and JIT have often been confused. JIT is the total system of purchasing, production, and inventory control. Kanban is one of the many elements in the JIT system as it was developed by the Toyota Motor Corporation (kanban is not characteristic of Japanese industry as a whole).

    a.   Kanban means **ticket**. Tickets (also described as cards or markers) control the flow of production or parts so that they are produced or obtained in the needed amounts at the needed times.

    b.   A basic kanban system includes a **withdrawal kanban** that states the quantity that a later process should withdraw from its predecessor, a **production kanban** that states the output of the preceding process, and a **vendor kanban** that tells a vendor what, how much, where, and when to deliver.

    c.   U.S. companies have not been comfortable with controlling production using tickets on the production floor. **Computerized information systems** have been used for many years, and U.S. companies have been reluctant to give up their computers in favor of the essentially manual kanban system. Instead, U.S. companies have integrated their existing systems, which are complex computerized planning systems, with the JIT system.

3.   To implement a JIT approach to inventory management and to eliminate waste of materials, labor, factory space, and machine usage, the **factory is reorganized** to permit what is often called **lean production**.

    a.   **Plant layout** in a JIT-lean production environment is not arranged by functional department or process but by **manufacturing cells (work cells)**. Cells are sets of machines, often grouped in semicircles, that produce a given product or product type.

    b.   Each worker in a cell must be able to operate all machines and, possibly, to perform support tasks, such as setup activities, preventive maintenance, movement of work-in-process within the cell, and quality inspection.

        1)   In such a pull system, workers might often be idle if they are not multi-skilled.

    c.   Central support departments are reduced or eliminated, space is saved, fewer and smaller factories may be required, and materials and tools are brought close to the point of use.

        1)   **Manufacturing cycle time** and **setup time** are also reduced. As a result, **on-time delivery performance** and response to changes in markets are enhanced, and production of customized goods in small lots becomes feasible.

    d.   A cellular organization requires workers to operate as effective teams, so **employee empowerment** is crucial in a JIT-lean production system.

        1)   Greater participation by employees is needed to achieve the objectives of **continuous improvement** and **zero defects**, so they may, for example, have the power to stop production to correct a problem, be consulted about changes in processes, or become involved in hiring co-workers. Thus, managers in such a system usually play more of a facilitating than a support role.

4.   Stop and review! You have completed the outline for this subunit. Study multiple-choice questions 1 through 13 beginning on page 60.

2.2 MATERIALS REQUIREMENTS PLANNING AND OUTSOURCING

1.   The short-range (tactical or operational) plans described in Subunit 1.5 must be converted into **specific production targets** for finished goods. The **raw materials** going into the creation of these end products must be carefully scheduled for delivery.

    a.   The yearly/quarterly/monthly numbers and styles of finished goods called for in the demand forecasts included in the operational plans must be turned into specific dates for completion and availability for shipment to the customer. This is the task of the **master production schedule (MPS)**.

    b.   A **materials requirements planning (MRP)** system enables a company to efficiently fulfill the requirements of the MPS by coordinating both the manufacture of component parts for finished goods and the arrival of the raw materials necessary to create the intermediate components.

        1)   As computers were introduced into manufacturing, it was common for firms to have a production scheduling system and an inventory control system. MRP joins the two into a single application.

        2)   The three overriding goals of MRP are the arrival of the **right part** in the **right quantity** at the **right time**.

2.   MRP is a **push system**, that is, the demand for raw materials is driven by the forecasted demand for the final product, which can be programmed into the computer.

    a.   For example, an automobile manufacturer need only tell the computer how many autos of each type are to be manufactured.

    b.   The MRP system consults the **bill of materials (BOM)**, a record of which (and how many) subassemblies go into the finished product. The system then generates a complete list of every part and component needed.

    c.   MRP, in effect, creates schedules of when items of inventory will be needed in the production departments.

        1)   If parts are not in stock, the system automatically generates a purchase order on the proper date (considering lead times) so that deliveries will arrive on time.

        2)   The **timing of deliveries** is vital to avoid both production delays AND a pileup of raw materials inventory that must be stored.

    d.   Some **benefits** of MRP are

        1)   Reduced idle time.
        2)   Lower setup costs.
        3)   Lower inventory carrying costs.
        4)   Increased flexibility in responding to market changes.

3. **Manufacturing resource planning (MRP II)** is a closed-loop manufacturing system that integrates all facets of a manufacturing business, including production, sales, inventories, schedules, and cash flows. The same system is used for both the financial reporting and managing operations (both use the same transactions and numbers).

   a. Because manufacturing resource planning encompasses materials requirements planning, MRP is a component of an MRP II system.

4. **Outsourcing** is the management or day-to-day execution of an entire business function by a third-party service provider. Outsourced services may be provided on or off premises, in the same country, or in a separate country.

   a. Outsourcing enables a company to focus on its core business rather than having to be concerned with marginal activities. For example, payroll preparation is often outsourced because a company does not want to maintain a full-time staff to perform what is only a weekly or monthly activity.

   b. **Business process outsourcing** is the outsourcing of back office and front office functions typically performed by white collar and clerical workers. Examples of these functions include data processing, accounting, human resources, and medical coding and transcription.

      1) **Insourcing** is the transfer of an outsourced function to an internal department of a company to be managed entirely by company employees. The term has also been used to describe a foreign company's locating of facilities in a host country where it employs local workers.

      2) **Cosourcing** is performance of a business function by both internal staff and external resources, such as consultants or outsourcing vendors, who have specialized knowledge of the business function.

   c. **Benefits** of outsourcing include reliable service, reduced costs, avoidance of the risk of obsolescence, and access to technology. **Disadvantages** include dependence on an outside party and loss of control over a necessary function.

5. Stop and review! You have completed the outline for this subunit. Study multiple-choice questions 14 through 18 beginning on page 63.

2.3 THEORY OF CONSTRAINTS AND THROUGHPUT COSTING

1. The **theory of constraints (TOC),** devised by Israeli physicist and business consultant Eliyahu Goldratt (b. 1948), is a system to improve human thinking about problems. It has been greatly extended to include manufacturing operations.

   a. The basic premise of TOC as applied to business is that improving any process is best done not by trying to maximize efficiency in every part of the process, but by focusing on the **slowest part of the process**, called the **constraint**.

      1) EXAMPLE: During the early days of the American Civil War, several units calling themselves legions were formed, consisting of combined infantry, artillery, and cavalry. This arrangement did not last because the entire unit could only maneuver as fast as the slowest part. The artillery was the constraint.

      2) Increasing the efficiency of processes that are not constraints merely creates backup in the system.

2. The **steps in a TOC analysis** are as follows (they are described in more detail under item 3.):

   a. **Identify** the constraint.
   b. **Determine** the most profitable product mix given the constraint.
   c. **Maximize** the flow through the constraint.
   d. **Increase** capacity at the constraint.
   e. **Redesign** the manufacturing process for greater flexibility and speed.

3.   The detailed steps in performing a TOC analysis are described below and on the next page:

    a.   **Identify the constraint.**

        1)   The **bottleneck operation** can usually be identified as the one where work-in-process backs up the most.

        2)   A more sophisticated approach is to analyze available resources (number and skill level of employees, inventory levels, time spent in other phases of the process) and determine which phase has negative slack time, i.e., the phase **without enough resources** to keep up with input.

    b.   **Determine the most profitable product mix** given the constraint.

        1)   A basic principle of TOC analysis is that short-term profit maximization requires maximizing the contribution margin **through the constraint**, called the **throughput margin** or throughput contribution.

            a)   TOC thus helps managers to recognize that the product they should produce the most of is not necessarily the one with the highest contribution margin per unit, but the one with the **highest throughput margin per unit**, i.e., managers must make the most profitable use of the bottleneck operation.

        2)   **Throughput costing**, sometimes called **supervariable costing**, recognizes **only direct materials costs** as being truly variable and thus relevant to the calculation of throughput margin. All other manufacturing costs are ignored because they are considered fixed in the short run.

$$\textit{Throughput margin = Sales - Direct materials}$$

        3)   EXAMPLE: (Authors' Note: This is the same example as that used in item 3. in Subunit 5.1 of Gleim's *CMA Review, Part 2,* with a subtotal for supervariable costing added.)

            a)   During its first month in business, a firm produced 100 units and sold 80 while incurring the following costs:

Direct materials	$1,000
Manufacturing costs used in supervariable costing	**$1,000**
Direct labor	2,000
Variable overhead	1,500
Manufacturing costs used in variable costing	**$4,500**
Fixed overhead	3,000
Manufacturing costs used in absorption costing	**$7,500**

            b)   The impact on the financial statements of using one method over another can be seen in the following calculations. Note that, because throughput costing capitalizes so few costs as product costs, **ending inventory and cost of goods sold are much lower** than under variable costing.

Cost per unit:

Absorption ($7,500 ÷ 100 units)	$75
Variable ($4,500 ÷ 100 units)	45
Supervariable ($1,000 ÷ 100 units)	10

Ending inventory:

Absorption ($75 × 20 units)	$1,500
Variable ($45 × 20 units)	900
Supervariable ($10 × 20 units)	200

c) Below is a comparison of the calculation of operating income under two of the methods.

    i) The units were sold at a price of $100 each.

    ii) The company incurred $200 of variable selling and administrative expenses and $600 of fixed selling and administrative expenses.

    iii) Note the drastic reduction in operating income resulting from the treatment of so many costs as period costs under throughput costing.

Variable Costing			Supervariable Costing		
Sales		$ 8,000	Sales		$ 8,000
Beginning inventory	$ 0		Beginning inventory	$ 0	
Variable manufacturing costs	4,500		Direct materials costs	1,000	
Goods available for sale	$ 4,500		Goods available for sale	$1,000	
Less: ending inventory	(900)		Less: ending inventory	(200)	
Variable cost of goods sold		(3,600)	Supervariable cost of goods sold		(800)
Variable S&A expenses		(200)			
Contribution margin		$ 4,200	Throughput margin		$7,200
			Direct labor		(2,000)
			Variable overhead		(1,500)
			Variable S&A expenses		(200)
Fixed overhead		(3,000)	Fixed overhead		(3,000)
Fixed S&A expenses		(600)	Fixed S&A expenses		(600)
Operating income		$ 600	Operating loss		$ (100)

4) To determine the most profitable use of the bottleneck operation, a manager next calculates the throughput margin **per unit of time spent in the constraint**.

    a) **Profitability is maximized** by keeping the bottleneck operation busy with the product with the highest throughput margin per unit of time.

c. **Maximize the flow** through the constraint.

    1) **Production flow** through a constraint is managed using the **drum-buffer-rope (DBR)** system.

        a) The **drum** (i.e., the beat to which a production process marches) is the bottleneck operation. The constraint sets the pace for the entire process.

        b) The **buffer** is a minimal amount of work-in-process input to the drum that is maintained to ensure that it is always in operation.

        c) The **rope** is the sequence of activities preceding and including the bottleneck operation that must be coordinated to avoid inventory buildup.

d. **Increase capacity** at the constraint.

    1) In the short-run, TOC encourages a manager to make the best use of the bottleneck operation. The medium-term step for improving the process is to increase the **bottleneck operation's capacity**.

e. **Redesign** the manufacturing process for greater flexibility and speed.

    1) The **long-term solution** is to reengineer the entire process. The firm should take advantage of new technology, product lines requiring too much effort should be dropped, and remaining products should be redesigned to ease the manufacturing process.

        a) **Value engineering** is useful for this purpose because it explicitly balances product cost and the needs of potential customers (product functions).

4.   **Extended Example:**

a.   **Identify the constraint.**

1)   A company makes three products: an airborne radar unit, a seagoing sonar unit, and a ground sonar unit. Under the current setup, the hours spent by each product in the two phases of the manufacturing process are as follows:

Product	Assembly	Testing
Airborne Radar	3	4
Seagoing Sonar	8	10
Ground Sonar	5	5

2)   The company has 150 hours available every month for testing. Under the current setup, therefore, the testing phase is the constraint.

b.   **Determine the most profitable product mix** given the constraint.

1)   The company calculates the throughput margin on each product and divides by the hours spent in testing:

	Radar	Seagoing Sonar	Ground Sonar
Price	$200,000	$600,000	$300,000
Less: Materials costs	(100,000)	(400,000)	(250,000)
Throughput margin	$100,000	$200,000	$ 50,000
Divided by: Constraint time	÷ 4	÷ 10	÷ 5
Throughput margin per hour	**$ 25,000**	**$ 20,000**	**$ 10,000**

2)   The crucial factor in determining the optimal product mix is not which product is the most profitable product in terms of absolute throughput margin (the seagoing sonar), but which one generates the **highest margin per time spent** in the bottleneck operation (the radar).

3)   To derive the most profitable product mix given finite resources, **customer demand** must be taken into account. The company has determined that it can sell 12 units of radar, 6 units of seagoing sonar, and 22 units of ground sonar per month.

4)   The **available time in the bottleneck operation** is first devoted to the product with the highest throughput margin (TM), then in descending order until the company is unable to meet demand.

a)   In the calculation below, the hours remaining after assignment to each product are the hours which can be devoted to the next product.

Product	Highest TM: Radar	2nd Highest TM: Seagoing Sonar	Lowest TM: Ground Sonar
Demand in unit	12	6	22
Hours per unit in bottleneck	× 4	× 10	× 5
Hours needed to fulfill demand	48	60	110
Hours available	150	102	42
Hours remaining	102	42	(68)

5)   Applying the principles of TOC, the company will forgo some sales of the ground sonar in favor of products that are more profitable given the current constraint.

c.   **Maximize the flow** through the bottleneck operation.

1)   The company will apply a drum-buffer-rope system to ensure that the bottleneck operation stays busy on high-TM products while keeping work-in-process inventory to a minimum.

    d.   **Increase capacity** at the bottleneck operation.

        1)   The company will hire and train more employees for the testing department.

    e.   **Redesign the manufacturing process** for greater flexibility and speed.

        1)   The company will examine its markets and new manufacturing technology to determine which products it wants to continue selling, whether to add new ones, and whether to retool the production line.

5.   **TOC analysis complements activity-based costing (ABC)** (see Subunit 4.3 in Gleim's *CMA Review, Part 2*) because they focus on different aspects of process improvement.

    a.   **TOC** has a **short-term focus** based on costs of materials and product mix; **ABC** has a **long-term focus** which considers all product costs and is concerned with strategic pricing and profit planning.

    b.   TOC analysis, unlike ABC, addresses the issues of resource constraints and operational capacity.

    c.   TOC ignores cost drivers, focusing mainly on process time; ABC requires defining cost drivers in every part of the organization.

6.   Stop and review! You have completed the outline for this subunit. Study multiple-choice questions 19 through 28 beginning on page 64.

2.4 OTHER PRODUCTION MANAGEMENT TECHNIQUES

1.   Modern manufacturing environments impose control and improve quality through **automation**, or the substitution of machines for humans. An automated environment may consist of one piece of equipment, a cell, or an integrated plant.

    a.   An example of the use of automation and advanced technologies is **flexible manufacturing**, which is the capacity of computer-controlled machinery to perform many different programmed functions.

        1)   By eliminating machine setup time, strengthening control, and automating handling processes, flexible manufacturing permits the efficient production of small numbers of different products by the same machines. A company can therefore more accurately match output with consumer tastes and avoid long production runs of identical goods.

        2)   A flexible manufacturing system consists of two or more computer-controlled machines linked by automated handling devices such as robots and transport systems. A **robot** is a machine that is programmed and computer controlled to perform repetitive functions.

2.   A **computer-integrated manufacturing (CIM)** system involves designing products using **computer-aided design (CAD)**, testing the design using computer-aided engineering (CAE), manufacturing products using computer-aided manufacturing (CAM), and integrating all components with a computerized information system.

    a.   Accordingly, CIM entails a **holistic approach** to manufacturing in which design is translated into product by **centralized processing and robotics**. The concept also includes materials handling. The advantages of CIM include flexibility, integration, and synergism.

        1)   **Flexibility** is a key advantage. A traditional manufacturing system might become disrupted from an emergency change, but CIM will reschedule everything in the plant when a priority requirement is inserted into the system.

2) The areas of flexibility include varying production volumes during a period, handling new parts added to a product, changing the proportion of parts being produced, adjusting to engineering changes of a product, adapting the sequence in which parts come to the machinery, adapting to changes in materials, rerouting parts as needed because of machine breakdowns or other production delays, and allowing for defects in materials.

b. **Benefits of CIM** include improved product quality (less rework), better customer service, faster response to market changes, greater product variety, lower production costs, and shorter product development times.

c. A **JIT system** is sometimes **adopted prior to CIM** because it simplifies production processes and provides a better understanding of actual production flow, which are essential factors for CIM success.

1) The flexibility offered by CIM is almost a necessity for suppliers in a JIT environment. For example, a company that provides JIT deliveries to automobile plants cannot adapt to changing customer production schedules with a manual system unless a high inventory level is maintained. The emphasis is on materials control rather than the direct labor control that is dominant in most cost systems.

2) CIM is an addition to, not a substitute for, other types of manufacturing concepts such as a JIT system. In other words, a JIT system should already be in place for CIM to work most effectively.

3. Stop and review! You have completed the outline for this subunit. Study multiple-choice questions 29 through 32 beginning on page 67.

2.5 CORE CONCEPTS

Just-in-Time Systems

- A just-in-time inventory management system **limits the output** of each function to the immediate demand of the next function. The accompanying **reductions in inventory levels** result in less money invested in idle assets.

- High inventory levels often **mask production problems** because defective parts can be overlooked when plenty of good parts are available.

- Higher productivity, reduced order costs as well as carrying costs, faster and cheaper setups, shorter manufacturing cycle times, better due date performance, improved quality, and more flexible processes are **objectives of JIT methods**.

- **Minimization of inventory** is a goal because many inventory-related activities are viewed as nonvalue-added. JIT is a **pull system**; items are pulled through production by current demand, not pushed through by anticipated demand.

- **Frequent receipt of deliveries** from suppliers often means less need for a sophisticated inventory control system and for control personnel. JIT also may **eliminate central receiving areas**, hard copy receiving reports, and storage areas. A central warehouse is not needed because deliveries are made by suppliers directly to the area of production.

- **Kanban**, a Japanese term meaning ticket, is one of the many elements in the JIT system as it was developed by the Toyota Motor Corporation. Tickets (also described as cards or markers) control the flow of production or parts so that they are **produced or obtained in the needed amounts** at the needed times.

- JIT also encompasses changes in the **production process** itself. To implement this approach and to eliminate waste of materials, labor, factory space, and machine usage, the **factory is reorganized** to permit what is often called **lean production**.

Materials Requirements Planning and Outsourcing

- A **materials requirements planning (MRP)** system enables a company to efficiently fulfill the requirements of the master production schedule by coordinating both the manufacture of component parts for finished goods and the arrival of the raw materials necessary to create the intermediate components.
- MRP is a **push system**, that is, the demand for raw materials is driven by the forecasted demand for the final product, which can be programmed into the computer.
- **Manufacturing resource planning (MRP II)** is a closed-loop manufacturing system that integrates all facets of a manufacturing business, including production, sales, inventories, schedules, and cash flows. The **same system** is used for both the **financial reporting and managing operations** (both use the same transactions and numbers).
- **Outsourcing** is the management or day-to-day execution of an entire business function by a third-party service provider. Outsourced services may be provided on or off premises, in the same country, or in a separate country.

Theory of Constraints and Throughput Costing

- The basic premise of the **theory of constraints (TOC)** as applied to business is that improving any process is best done not by trying to maximize efficiency in every part of the process, but by focusing on the **handful of factors** that are crucial, called **constraints**. Increasing the efficiency of processes that are not constraints merely creates backup in the system.
- The **steps in a TOC analysis** are: identify the bottleneck operation (the constraint); determine the most profitable profit mix given the constraint; maximize product flow through the bottleneck; increase capacity at the bottleneck; and redesign the manufacturing process.
- A basic principle of TOC analysis is that short-term profit maximization requires maximizing the **contribution margin through the constraint**, called the **throughput contribution** or throughput margin.
- **Throughput costing**, sometimes called **supervariable costing**, recognizes **only direct materials costs** as being truly variable and thus relevant to the calculation of throughput contribution. All other manufacturing costs are ignored because they are considered fixed in the short run.
- Production flow is managed using the **drum-buffer-rope** (DBR) system. The drum is the bottleneck operation, the buffer is the minimal amount of work-in-process input to the drum, and the rope is the sequence of activities preceding and including the bottleneck that must be coordinated.

Other Production Management Techniques

- Modern manufacturing environments impose control and improve quality through **automation**, or the substitution of machines for humans. An example of the use of automation and advanced technologies is **flexible manufacturing**, which is the capacity of computer-controlled machinery to perform many different programmed functions.
- A **computer-integrated manufacturing (CIM)** system involves designing products using **computer-aided design (CAD)**, testing the design using computer-aided engineering (CAE), manufacturing products using computer-aided manufacturing (CAM), and integrating all components with a computerized information system.
- CIM entails a **holistic approach** to manufacturing in which design is translated into product by **centralized processing and robotics**.

QUESTIONS

2.1 Just-in-Time Systems

1. Companies that adopt just-in-time purchasing systems often experience

A. A reduction in the number of suppliers.

B. Fewer deliveries from suppliers.

C. A greater need for inspection of goods as the goods arrive.

D. Less need for linkage with a vendor's computerized order entry system.

Answer (A) is correct. *(CMA, adapted)*
REQUIRED: The true statement about companies that adopt just-in-time (JIT) purchasing systems.
DISCUSSION: The objective of JIT is to reduce carrying costs by eliminating inventories and increasing the deliveries made by suppliers. Ideally, shipments of raw materials are received just in time to be incorporated into the manufacturing process. The focus of quality control under JIT is the prevention of quality problems. Quality control is shifted to the supplier. JIT companies typically do not inspect incoming goods; the assumption is that receipts are of perfect quality. Suppliers are limited to those who guarantee perfect quality and prompt delivery.
Answer (B) is incorrect because more deliveries are needed. Each shipment is smaller. Answer (C) is incorrect because, in a JIT system, materials are delivered directly to the production line ready for insertion in the finished product. Answer (D) is incorrect because the need for communication with the vendor is greater. Orders and deliveries must be made on short notice, sometimes several times a day.

2. The benefits of a just-in-time system for raw materials usually include

A. Elimination of nonvalue-adding operations.

B. Increase in the number of suppliers, thereby ensuring competitive bidding.

C. Maximization of the standard delivery quantity, thereby lessening the paperwork for each delivery.

D. Decrease in the number of deliveries required to maintain production.

Answer (A) is correct. *(CPA, adapted)*
REQUIRED: The benefit of a just-in-time system for raw materials.
DISCUSSION: Nonvalue-adding activities are those that do not add to customer value or satisfy an organizational need. Inventory activities are inherently nonvalue-adding. Thus, a system, such as JIT, that promotes lean production and reduces inventory and its attendant procedures (storage, handling, etc.) also reduces nonvalue-adding activities.
Answer (B) is incorrect because the dependability, not number, of suppliers is increased. Answer (C) is incorrect because standard delivery quality, not quantity, is increased. Answer (D) is incorrect because the number of deliveries is increased. Fewer goods are delivered at a time.

3. Bell Co. changed from a traditional manufacturing philosophy to a just-in-time philosophy. What are the expected effects of this change on Bell's inventory turnover and inventory as a percentage of total assets reported on Bell's balance sheet?

	Inventory Turnover	Inventory Percentage
A.	Decrease	Decrease
B.	Decrease	Increase
C.	Increase	Decrease
D.	Increase	Increase

Answer (C) is correct. *(CPA, adapted)*
REQUIRED: The expected effects of changing to JIT.
DISCUSSION: A JIT system is intended to minimize inventory. Inventory should be delivered or produced just in time to be used. Thus, JIT increases inventory turnover (cost of sales ÷ average inventory) and decreases inventory as a percentage of total assets.

4. Which changes in costs are most conducive to switching from a traditional inventory ordering system to a just-in-time ordering system?

	Cost per Purchase Order	Inventory Unit Carrying Costs
A.	Increasing	Increasing
B.	Decreasing	Increasing
C.	Decreasing	Decreasing
D.	Increasing	Decreasing

Answer (B) is correct. *(CPA, adapted)*
REQUIRED: The changes in costs most conducive to switching to a just-in-time ordering system.
DISCUSSION: A JIT system is intended to minimize inventory. Thus, if inventory carrying costs are increasing, a JIT system becomes more cost effective. Moreover, purchases are more frequent in a JIT system. Accordingly, a decreasing cost per purchase order is conducive to switching to a JIT system.

5. A manufacturing company is attempting to implement a just-in-time (JIT) purchase policy system by negotiating with its primary suppliers to accept long-term purchase orders which result in more frequent deliveries of smaller quantities of raw materials. If the JIT purchase policy is successful in reducing the total inventory costs of the manufacturing company, which of the following combinations of cost changes would be most likely to occur?

	Cost Category to Increase	Cost Category to Decrease
A.	Purchasing costs	Stockout costs
B.	Purchasing costs	Quality costs
C.	Quality costs	Ordering costs
D.	Stockout costs	Carrying costs

Answer (D) is correct. *(CIA, adapted)*
REQUIRED: The combination of cost changes.
DISCUSSION: The objective of a JIT system is to reduce carrying costs by eliminating inventories and increasing the deliveries made by suppliers. Ideally, shipments are received just in time to be incorporated into the manufacturing process. This system increases the risk of stockout costs because the inventory buffer is reduced or eliminated.
Answer (A) is incorrect because the supplier may seek a concession on the selling price that will raise purchasing costs, but the manufacturing company's stockout costs will increase. Answer (B) is incorrect because the cost of quality is not necessarily affected by a JIT system. Answer (C) is incorrect because fewer purchase orders are processed by the manufacturer, so the ordering costs are likely to decrease. However, the cost of quality is not necessarily affected by a JIT system.

6. In Belk Co.'s just-in-time production system, costs per setup were reduced from $28 to $2. In the process of reducing inventory levels, Belk found that there were fixed facility and administrative costs that previously had not been included in the carrying cost calculation. The result was an increase from $8 to $32 per unit per year. What were the effects of these changes on Belk's economic lot size and relevant costs?

	Lot Size	Relevant Costs
A.	Decrease	Increase
B.	Increase	Decrease
C.	Increase	Increase
D.	Decrease	Decrease

Answer (D) is correct. *(CPA, adapted)*
REQUIRED: The effect of a JIT production system on economic lot size and relevant costs.
DISCUSSION: The economic lot size for a production system is similar to the EOQ. For example, the cost per set-up is equivalent to the cost per order (a numerator value in the EOQ model). Hence, a reduction in the setup costs reduces the economic lot size as well as the relevant costs. The fixed facility and administrative costs, however, are not relevant. The basic EOQ model includes variable costs only.

7. The effectiveness of a JIT system is often facilitated by the elimination of some common forms of internal control. The elimination of which internal control is usually acceptable with a JIT system?

A. Preparation of hard copy receiving reports.

B. Voucher approval prior to paying accounts payable.

C. Two signatures required on large checks.

D. Locked doors on production areas.

Answer (A) is correct. *(Publisher, adapted)*
REQUIRED: The internal control that is not necessary with a JIT system.
DISCUSSION: Receiving departments are often eliminated with a JIT system so receiving reports are not needed. Also, the quantity received should be exactly equal to immediate production needs.

8. Just-in-time manufacturing practices are based in part on the belief that

A. High inventory levels provide greater flexibility in production scheduling.

B. Attempting to reduce inventory to a consistently low level can lead to "panic" situations.

C. Goods should be "pulled" through the production process, not "pushed."

D. Beefed-up internal control in the central warehouse can greatly enhance productivity in the production areas.

Answer (C) is correct. *(Publisher, adapted)*
REQUIRED: The concept that is part of the philosophy of just-in-time manufacturing.
DISCUSSION: Just-in-time (JIT) manufacturing is a pull system; items are pulled through production by current demand, not pushed through by anticipated demand as in traditional manufacturing setups.
Answer (A) is incorrect because, under the JIT philosophy, high inventory levels often mask production problems. Answer (B) is incorrect because attempting to reduce inventory to a consistently low level is a core objective of JIT. Answer (D) is incorrect because, under JIT, central warehouses are often eliminated.

9. Key Co. changed from a traditional manufacturing operation with a job-order costing system to a just-in-time operation with a backflush costing system. What is(are) the expected effect(s) of these changes on Key's inspection costs and recording detail of costs tracked to jobs in process?

	Inspection Costs	Detail of Costs Tracked to Jobs
A.	Decrease	Decrease
B.	Decrease	Increase
C.	Increase	Decrease
D.	Increase	Increase

Answer (A) is correct. *(CPA, adapted)*
REQUIRED: The expected effects of changing to JIT.
DISCUSSION: In a JIT system, materials go directly into production without being inspected. The assumption is that the vendor has already performed all necessary inspections. The minimization of inventory reduces the number of suppliers, storage costs, transaction costs, etc. Backflush costing eliminates the traditional sequential tracking of costs. Instead, entries to inventory may be delayed until as late as the end of the period. For example, all product costs may be charged initially to cost of sales, and costs may be flushed back to the inventory accounts only at the end of the period. Thus, the detail of cost accounting is decreased.
Answer (B) is incorrect because both inspection costs and the detail of costs tracked to jobs decrease. Answer (C) is incorrect because a JIT system is intended to minimize inventory. Inventory should be delivered or produced just in time to be used. Thus, JIT increases inventory turnover (cost of sales ÷ average inventory) and decreases inventory as a percentage of total assets. Answer (D) is incorrect because both inspection costs and the detail of costs tracked to jobs decrease.

10. If a worker encounters a production kanban at his/her workstation, the worker should

A. Release the requested item to the next stage in the process.

B. Begin manufacturing the requested item.

C. Initiate a purchase order with the supplier of the requested item.

D. Confirm the amount of the item requested and present the kanban to the production supervisor.

Answer (B) is correct. *(Publisher, adapted)*
REQUIRED: The action a worker should take upon being presented with a production kanban.
DISCUSSION: In a kanban inventory control system, a production kanban is an indication to a worker to begin producing the item referred to on the kanban.
Answer (A) is incorrect because release of an item to a subsequent stage in production is initiated with a withdrawal kanban. Answer (C) is incorrect because a purchase from a supplier is indicated by a vendor kanban. Answer (D) is incorrect because, under a kanban system, a worker is authorized to take action upon being presented with a kanban; involving the production supervisor only slows down the process.

11. A firm that is deploying just-in-time manufacturing for the first time will

A. Establish contracts with many suppliers since an interruption in supply is extremely disruptive of the production process.

B. Establish contracts with a few carefully chosen suppliers since an interruption in supply is extremely disruptive of the production process.

C. Maintain a carefully calibrated safety stock since interruptions in supply are inevitable.

D. Acquire considerable computer processing capability to manage the demands of the data-dependent kanban inventory management system.

Answer (B) is correct. *(Publisher, adapted)*
REQUIRED: The aspect of employing just-in-time (JIT) inventory management.
DISCUSSION: In a JIT system, the suppliers' dependability is crucial. Organizations that adopt JIT systems develop close relationships with a few carefully chosen suppliers who are extensively involved in the buyer's processes.
Answer (A) is incorrect because, in a JIT system, the suppliers' dependability is crucial. Organizations that adopt JIT systems develop close relationships with a few carefully chosen suppliers who are extensively involved in the buyer's processes. Answer (C) is incorrect because the use of safety stock is considered a nonvalue-adding activity under a JIT system, and interruptions in supply are not considered inevitable. Answer (D) is incorrect because a JIT system does not necessarily require the employment of kanban inventory management. Also, kanban is essentially a manual system.

12. Which of the following is not a benefit of lean production?

A. Reduced setup time.

B. Lower central support costs.

C. Lower training costs.

D. Improved on-time delivery.

Answer (C) is correct. *(Publisher, adapted)*
REQUIRED: The choice that is not a benefit of lean production.
DISCUSSION: Since every worker in a manufacturing cell must be able to operate every piece of machinery in the cell, reduced training costs do not necessarily accompany the deployment of lean production.
Answer (A) is incorrect because reduced setup time is a benefit of lean production. Answer (B) is incorrect because central support departments are reduced or eliminated under lean production. Answer (D) is incorrect because on-time delivery mostly improves under lean production.

13. Which of the following internal controls is not one typically eliminated when a just-in-time inventory system is introduced?

    A. Sophisticated inventory tracking system.

    B. Central receiving dock.

    C. Statistical methods for quality assurance.

    D. Hard copy receiving report.

Answer (C) is correct. *(Publisher, adapted)*
    REQUIRED: The internal control that is not one typically eliminated when a just-in-time (JIT) inventory system is introduced.
    DISCUSSION: Under a JIT system, the quality of parts provided by suppliers is verified by use of statistical controls rather than inspection of incoming goods. Storage, counting, and inspection are eliminated in an effort to perform only value-adding work.
    Answer (A) is incorrect because frequent receipt of deliveries from suppliers often means less need for a sophisticated inventory control system and for control personnel. Answer (B) is incorrect because, under JIT, a central receiving area and central warehouse are not needed because deliveries are made by suppliers directly to the area of production. Answer (D) is incorrect because, with the elimination of central receiving areas and central warehouses that typically accompanies the institution of a JIT system, hard copy receiving reports are unnecessary.

2.2 Materials Requirements Planning and Outsourcing

14. A company uses a planning system that focuses first on the amount and timing of finished goods demanded and then determines the derived demand for raw materials, components, and subassemblies at each of the prior stages of production. This system is

    A. An economic order quantity model.

    B. Materials requirements planning.

    C. Linear programming.

    D. Just-in-time purchasing.

Answer (B) is correct. *(CIA, adapted)*
    REQUIRED: The planning system that calculates derived demand for inventories.
    DISCUSSION: Materials requirements planning (MRP) is a system that translates a production schedule into requirements for each component needed to meet the schedule. It is usually implemented in the form of a computer-based information system designed to plan and control raw materials used in production. It assumes that forecasted demand is reasonably accurate and that suppliers can deliver based upon this accurate schedule. MRP is a centralized push-through system; output based on forecasted demand is pushed through to the next department or to inventory.
    Answer (A) is incorrect because the EOQ model focuses on the trade-off between carrying and ordering costs. Answer (C) is incorrect because linear programming is a decision model concerned with allocating scarce resources to maximize profit or minimize costs. Answer (D) is incorrect because JIT is a decentralized demand-pull system. It is driven by actual demand.

15. In contrast to just-in-time manufacturing, materials requirements planning is a

    A. Push system.

    B. Pull system.

    C. Automated system.

    D. Manual system.

Answer (A) is correct. *(Publisher, adapted)*
    REQUIRED: The description of materials requirements planning (MRP) that stands in contrast to just-in-time manufacturing.
    DISCUSSION: MRP is a push system, that is, the demand for raw materials is driven by the forecasted demand for the final product, which can be programmed into the computer. This is in contrast with just-in-time manufacturing, which is a pull system, meaning items are pulled through production by current demand, not pushed through by anticipated demand.
    Answer (B) is incorrect because just-in-time manufacturing is a pull system. Answer (C) is incorrect because both systems may be automated. Answer (D) is incorrect because neither system need be manual.

16. Materials requirements planning (MRP) sometimes results in

    A. Longer idle periods.

    B. Less flexibility in responding to customers.

    C. Increased inventory carrying costs.

    D. Decreased setup costs.

Answer (D) is correct. *(Publisher, adapted)*
    REQUIRED: The result of implementing a materials requirements planning (MRP) system.
    DISCUSSION: Among the benefits of MRP are reduced idle time, lower setup costs, lower inventory carrying costs, and increased flexibility in responding to market changes.
    Answer (A) is incorrect because MRP often results in reduced idle time. Answer (B) is incorrect because MRP often results in increased flexibility in responding to market changes. Answer (C) is incorrect because MRP often results in lower inventory carrying costs.

17. The manufacturing concept that relates demand forecasts to specific dates for completion is

- A. Master production schedule.
- B. Materials requirements planning.
- C. Manufacturing resource planning.
- D. Bill of materials.

Answer (A) is correct. *(Publisher, adapted)*
   REQUIRED: The concept that relates demand forecasts to specific dates for completion.
   DISCUSSION: The yearly/quarterly/monthly numbers and styles of finished goods called for in the demand forecasts included in the operational plans must be turned into specific dates for completion and availability for shipment to the customer. This is the task of the master production schedule (MPS).
   Answer (B) is incorrect because materials requirements planning is a system that enables a company to efficiently fulfill the goals of the master production schedule. Answer (C) is incorrect because manufacturing resource planning is a closed-loop manufacturing system that integrates all facets of a manufacturing business, including production, sales, inventories, schedules, and cash flows. Answer (D) is incorrect because a bill of materials is a record of which (and how many) subassemblies go into the finished product. The system then generates a complete list of every part and component needed.

18. Which of the following is not a typical benefit of an outsourcing arrangement?

- A. Reduced costs.
- B. Access to technology.
- C. Avoidance of risk of obsolescence.
- D. Increased control over a necessary function.

Answer (D) is correct. *(Publisher, adapted)*
   REQUIRED: The item that is not a typical benefit of outsourcing.
   DISCUSSION: Outsourcing results in a loss of control over the outsourced function.

2.3 Theory of Constraints and Throughput Costing

19. Under throughput costing, the only cost considered to be truly variable in the short run is

- A. Direct materials.
- B. Direct labor.
- C. Manufacturing overhead.
- D. All manufacturing costs are considered variable.

Answer (A) is correct. *(Publisher, adapted)*
   REQUIRED: The variable cost under throughput costing.
   DISCUSSION: Throughput costing, also called supervariable costing, recognizes only direct materials costs as being truly variable and thus relevant to the calculation of throughput margin.
   Answer (B) is incorrect because, under throughput costing, direct labor is considered fixed because of labor contracts and employment levels. Answer (C) is incorrect because, under throughput costing, overhead is considered fixed in the short run. Answer (D) is incorrect because, under throughput costing, only direct materials costs are considered variable in the short run.

20. The immediate goal of a theory of constraints (TOC) analysis is to

- A. Maximize the efficiency of the entire production process.
- B. Minimize direct materials cost.
- C. Maximize contribution margin through the constraint.
- D. Smooth production flow to eliminate backup in the system.

Answer (C) is correct. *(Publisher, adapted)*
   REQUIRED: The immediate goal of a theory of constraints analysis.
   DISCUSSION: A basic principle of TOC analysis is that short-term profit maximization requires maximizing the contribution margin through the constraint, called the throughput margin or throughput contribution.
   Answer (A) is incorrect because, under the principles of TOC, maximizing the efficiency of processes that have excess capacity merely creates backup in the system. Answer (B) is incorrect because holding down direct materials costs, while an important part of improving contribution margin, is not part of a TOC analysis. Answer (D) is incorrect because, while eliminating backup is a goal of a TOC analysis, it is not done by simply "smoothing" production flow, since this could mean slowing down the entire process to match the bottleneck.

21. A manufacturer can sell its single product for $660. Below are the cost data for the product:

Direct Materials	$170
Direct Labor	225
Manufacturing Overhead	90

The relevant margin amount when beginning a theory of constraints (TOC) analysis is

A. $490

B. $345

C. $265

D. $175

Answer (A) is correct. *(Publisher, adapted)*
REQUIRED: The relevant margin amount when beginning a theory of constraints (TOC) analysis.
DISCUSSION: A theory of constraints (TOC) analysis proceeds from the assumption that only direct materials costs are truly variable in the short run. This is called throughput, or supervariable, costing. The relevant margin amount is throughput margin, which equals price minus direct materials. Thus, the relevant margin amount for this manufacturer is $490 ($660 – $170).
Answer (B) is incorrect because $345 results from subtracting conversion cost, rather than throughput cost, from selling price. Answer (C) is incorrect because $265 results from subtracting prime cost, rather than throughput cost, from selling price. Answer (D) is incorrect because $175 results from subtracting all manufacturing costs, rather than just throughput cost, from selling price.

22. Below are data concerning the hours spent by a manufacturer's two products in its two processes.

	Assembly	Painting
Product A	21	14
Product B	32	8

The constraint is

A. Product A.

B. Product B in Assembly.

C. The assembly activity.

D. Cannot be determined from the information given.

Answer (C) is correct. *(Publisher, adapted)*
REQUIRED: The constraint (bottleneck).
DISCUSSION: In theory of constraints (TOC) analysis, the constraint (bottleneck) operation is the slowest part of the process. It can usually be identified as the one where work-in-process backs up the most. Of this manufacturer's two operations, the one that requires the most total time is assembly.
Answer (A) is incorrect because an operation, not a product, is a constraint. Answer (B) is incorrect because an operation as a whole is a constraint, not a particular product in an operation. Answer (D) is incorrect because the operation that requires the most total time is determinable from the information given.

23. Tocon Company produces two components: A-1 and A-2. The unit throughput contribution margins for A-1 and A-2 are $150 and $300, respectively. Each component must proceed through two processes: Operation 1 and Operation 2. The capacity of Operation 1 is 180 machine hours, with A-1 and A-2 requiring 1 hour and 3 hours, respectively. Furthermore, Tocon can sell only 45 units of A-1 and 100 units of A-2. However, Tocon is considering expanding Operation 1's capacity by 90 machine hours at a cost of $80 per hour. Assuming that Operation 2 has sufficient capacity to handle any additional output from Operation 1, Tocon should produce

	Units of A-1	Units of A-2
A.	180	0
B.	45	100
C.	45	75
D.	0	60

Answer (C) is correct. *(Publisher, adapted)*
REQUIRED: The optimal product mix given expanded capacity.
DISCUSSION: A-1's throughput contribution margin per unit of the scarce resource (the internal binding constraint) is $150 ($150 UCM ÷ 1 machining hour). A-2's throughput contribution margin per unit of the scarce resource is $100 ($300 UCM ÷ 3 machine hours). Consequently, Tocon should produce as much A-1 as it can sell (45 units). If Tocon adds 90 machine hours to increase the capacity of Operation 1 to 270 hours (180 + 90), it cannot produce additional units of A-1 because the external binding constraint has not been relaxed. However, it can produce additional units of A-2. Given that the UCM per machine hour of A-2 is $100 and that the cost is $80 per hour, adding capacity to Operation 1 is profitable. Thus, Tocon should use 45 machine hours to produce 45 units of A-1. The remaining 225 machine hours (270 – 45) should be used to produce 75 units (225 ÷ 3 hours) of A-2. The latter amount is within the external binding constraint.
Answer (A) is incorrect because Tocon can sell only 45 units of A-1. Answer (B) is incorrect because Tocon can produce only 75 units of A-2 if it produces 45 units of the more profitable A-1. Answer (D) is incorrect because Tocon should produce as much of A-1 as it can sell.

Questions 24 through 26 are based on the following information. Rosecrans Manufacturing produces kerosene lanterns.
The company can sell all of its output. Each unit sells for $120, and direct materials costing $48 per unit are added at the
start of the first operation. Other variable costs are immaterial. Production data for one of its products is presented below:

	Operation 1	Operation 2	Operation 3
Total capacity per year	200,000 units	150,000 units	180,000 units
Total output per year	150,000 units	150,000 units	150,000 units
Fixed cost of operations	$1,200,000	$1,800,000	$2,250,000

24. Rosecrans hires additional workers at a cost of
$50,000 per year to expedite setups and materials
handling in the bottleneck operation. As a result, the
annual output of the bottleneck operation increases
by 500 units. The change in operating income
attributable to the increase in workers is

A. $50,000

B. $36,000

C. $(14,000)

D. $(20,000)

Answer (C) is correct. *(Publisher, adapted)*
REQUIRED: The change in operating income.
DISCUSSION: Operation 2 is the bottleneck because it is
functioning at its capacity. The incremental annual throughput
contribution (revenues – direct materials costs) from adding
workers to Operation 2 is $36,000 [500 units × ($120 unit price –
$48 DM per unit)]. Because the cost of the additional workers is
$50,000, the change in operating income is $(14,000).
Answer (A) is incorrect because $50,000 is the incremental
cost. Answer (B) is incorrect because $36,000 is the incremental
throughput contribution. Answer (D) is incorrect because
$(20,000) is based on the assumption that an additional $12 per
unit of fixed costs will be applied.

25. Tullahoma Company has offered to perform the
Operation 2 function on 1,000 units at a unit price of
$40, excluding direct materials cost. Chattanooga
Company has offered to perform the Operation 1
function on 1,000 units at a price of $7, excluding
direct materials cost. Chickamauga Company has
made an offer to perform the Operation 1 function on
5,000 units at a unit cost of $5 (excluding direct
materials cost). Which of these mutually exclusive
offers is acceptable to Rosecrans?

A. Tullahoma's offer.

B. Chattanooga's offer.

C. Chickamauga's offer.

D. None of the offers should be accepted.

Answer (A) is correct. *(Publisher, adapted)*
REQUIRED: The acceptable offer(s), if any.
DISCUSSION: Tullahoma's offer should be accepted
because its cost is $40,000 (1,000 units × $40), and the increase
in throughput contribution is $72,000 [1,000 units × ($120 unit
price – $48 DM per unit)]. Hence, the relevant cost of
Tullahoma's offer is less than the incremental throughput
contributed. Tullahoma's offer effectively increases the capacity
of the bottleneck operation. Chattanooga's and Chickamauga's
offers should both be rejected because, even though their $7 and
$5 unit costs are less than the $8 unit operating cost (excluding
direct materials) for Operation 1 ($1,200,000 fixed costs ÷
150,000 units), they will result in the incurrence of additional
costs with no increase in throughput contribution, given that
Operation 2 is already producing at its 150,000-unit capacity.
Answer (B) is incorrect because Chattanooga's offer will
result in the incurrence of additional costs that merely add
capacity to a non-bottleneck operation. Answer (C) is incorrect
because Chickamauga's offer does nothing to address the
bottleneck operation. Answer (D) is incorrect because
Tullahoma's offer will result in improved throughput contribution.

26. Operation 1 produces 500 unsalable units and
Operation 2 also produces 500 unsalable units. The
relevant cost of the unsalable units to Rosecrans is

A. $24,000

B. $60,000

C. $84,000

D. $120,000

Answer (C) is correct. *(Publisher, adapted)*
REQUIRED: The relevant cost of the unsalable units.
DISCUSSION: The cost of the unsalable units in Operation
1 consists solely of the wasted direct materials because idle
capacity is available to replace the defective units. As a
consequence, Operation 1 can still transfer the maximum
150,000 units that Operation 2 can process, and no throughput
contribution is lost. The cost of the unsalable units in Operation 1
is thus $24,000 (500 units × $48 DM). In Operation 2, however,
the lost throughput contribution is an opportunity cost because no
idle capacity exists to replace the defective units. The cost of the
unsalable units in Operation 2 is $60,000 {(500 units × $48 DM) +
[500 units × ($120 unit price – $48 DM cost)]}. Hence, the total
relevant cost of the unsalable units is $84,000 ($24,000 +
$60,000).
Answer (A) is incorrect because $24,000 equals the direct
materials cost of 500 units. Answer (B) is incorrect because
$60,000 equals the lost throughput contribution and wasted direct
materials cost of 500 units. Answer (D) is incorrect because
$120,000 equals the lost throughput contribution and wasted
direct materials cost of 1,000 units.

27. In a theory of constraints (TOC) analysis, the bottleneck operation (the constraint) corresponds to which part of the drum-buffer-rope model?

A. Drum.

B. Buffer.

C. Rope.

D. No part of TOC analysis corresponds to the drum-buffer-rope model.

Answer (A) is correct. *(Publisher, adapted)*
REQUIRED: The component of a TOC analysis that corresponds to the drum-buffer-rope model.
DISCUSSION: Production flow through a constraint is managed using the drum-buffer-rope (DBR) system. The drum (i.e., the beat to which a production process marches) is the bottleneck operation. The constraint sets the pace for the entire process. The buffer is a minimal amount of work-in-process input to the drum that is maintained to ensure that it is always in operation. The rope is the sequence of activities preceding and including the bottleneck operation that must be coordinated to avoid inventory buildup.

28. Which pairs of systems are considered complementary because they inherently focus on different time frames?

	Short-term	Long-term
A.	Operation costing	Theory of constraints
B.	Activity-based costing	Theory of constraints
C.	Theory of constraints	Operation costing
D.	Theory of constraints	Activity-based costing

Answer (D) is correct. *(Publisher, adapted)*
REQUIRED: The pair of systems often considered to be complementary.
DISCUSSION: Theory of constraints (TOC) has a short-term focus based on costs of materials and product mix; activity-based costing has a long-term focus which considers all product costs and is concerned with strategic pricing and profit planning.
Answer (A) is incorrect because theory of constraints has a short-term focus. Answer (B) is incorrect because theory of constraints has a short-term focus. Answer (C) is incorrect because operation costing is a hybrid of job-order and process costing that is employed when a manufacturer's products uses some similar processes and some custom processes. It cannot be classified as having a short- or long-term focus.

2.4 Other Production Management Techniques

29. A major justification for investments in computer-integrated manufacturing (CIM) projects is

A. Reduction in the costs of spoilage, reworked units, and scrap.

B. Lower book value and depreciation expense for factory equipment.

C. Increased working capital.

D. Stabilization of market share.

Answer (A) is correct. *(CIA, adapted)*
REQUIRED: The major justification for investments in CIM.
DISCUSSION: Automating and computerizing production processes requires a substantial investment in fixed assets and an increase in risk because of greater fixed costs. CIM also necessitates an increase in software costs and extensive worker retraining. However, the costs of spoilage, rework, and scrap are reduced along with labor costs. The qualitative advantages of CIM are increased flexibility, shorter manufacturing lead time, quicker development of new products, better product delivery and service, faster response to market changes, and improved competitiveness.
Answer (B) is incorrect because an increase in fixed assets results in higher book value and depreciation expense. Answer (C) is incorrect because working capital normally is reduced as investments shift from current to fixed assets. Answer (D) is incorrect because actual or potential market share changes may trigger investments in CIM.

30. Increased competition, technological innovation, and a shift from mass production of standardized products to custom-produced products in many industries have increased the need for productivity improvement and flexibility of production systems. In response to these demands, organizations have increased their reliance on automation and the use of advanced technologies in their operations. Which of the following is an example of the use of automation and advanced technologies?

A. Flexible manufacturing system (FMS).

B. Just-in-time (JIT) system.

C. Master budgeting system (MBS).

D. Economic order quantity (EOQ).

Answer (A) is correct. *(CIA, adapted)*
REQUIRED: The example of the use of automation and advanced technologies.
DISCUSSION: Flexible manufacturing is the capacity of computer-controlled machinery to perform many different programmed functions. By eliminating machine setup time, strengthening control, and automating handling processes, flexible manufacturing permits the efficient production of small numbers of different products by the same machines. A company can therefore more accurately match output with consumer tastes and avoid long production runs of identical goods. A flexible manufacturing system consists of two or more computer-controlled machines linked by automated handling devices such as robots and transport systems.
Answer (B) is incorrect because a JIT system involves the purchase of materials and production of components immediately preceding their use. Answer (C) is incorrect because a master budget is the detailed financial plan for the next period. Answer (D) is incorrect because the EOQ is the quantity that minimizes total costs.

31. A manufacturing arrangement characterized by low or no setup times and the ability to switch quickly from producing one product to another is called a

    A. Just-in-time manufacturing system.

    B. Computer-integrated manufacturing system.

    C. Flexible manufacturing system.

    D. Robot.

Answer (C) is correct. *(Publisher, adapted)*
    REQUIRED: The manufacturing system with low setup costs and the ability to change products quickly.
    DISCUSSION: An example of the use of automation and advanced technologies in the manufacturing field is flexible manufacturing, which is the capacity of computer-controlled machinery to perform many different programmed functions. By eliminating machine setup time, strengthening control, and automating handling processes, flexible manufacturing permits the efficient production of small numbers of different products by the same machines. A company can therefore more accurately match output with consumer tastes and avoid long production runs of identical goods.
    Answer (A) is incorrect because just-in-time is more properly treated as an inventory management system rather than a manufacturing paradigm. Answer (B) is incorrect because a computer-integrated manufacturing (CIM) system involves designing products using computer-aided design (CAD), testing the design using computer-aided engineering (CAE), manufacturing products using computer-aided manufacturing (CAM), and integrating all components with a computerized information system. Answer (D) is incorrect because a manufacturing arrangement characterized by low or no setup times and the ability to switch quickly from producing one product to another can be facilitated by the use of robots, but a robot cannot constitute the entire system.

32. Benefits of computer-integrated manufacturing (CIM) include all of the following except:

    A. Faster response to market changes.

    B. Lower production costs.

    C. Greater oversight by upper management.

    D. Improved product quality.

Answer (C) is correct. *(Publisher, adapted)*
    REQUIRED: The feature that is not a benefit of computer-integrated manufacturing (CIM).
    DISCUSSION: An computer-integrated manufacturing (CIM) provides many benefits, among them improved product quality (less rework), better customer service, faster response to market changes, greater product variety, lower production costs, and shorter product development times. Greater oversight by upper management is debatable as a positive good and is does not inhere in CIM in any case.

Use Gleim's ***CMA Test Prep*** for interactive testing with **over 2,000 additional multiple-choice questions**!

STUDY UNIT THREE
BUSINESS PROCESS PERFORMANCE

(10 pages of outline)

This study unit is the **last of three** on **strategic planning**. The relative weight assigned to this major topic in Part 3 of the exam is **15%** at **skill level B** (four skill types required). The three study units are

Study Unit 1: Strategic and Tactical Planning

Study Unit 2: Manufacturing Paradigms

Study Unit 3: Business Process Performance

After studying the outline and answering the multiple-choice questions, you will have the skills necessary to address the following topics listed in the IMA's Learning Outcome Statements:

Part 3 – Section A.3. Business process performance

The candidate should be able to:

a. define value chain analysis

b. identify the steps in value chain analysis

c. demonstrate an understanding of how value chain analysis is used to better understand a firm's competitive advantage

d. define a value-added activity and explain how the value-added concept is related to improving performance

e. demonstrate an understanding of process analysis and how to improve business process performance through business process reengineering

f. analyze a sequence of tasks, activities, and processes

g. define the Pareto principle

h. demonstrate an understanding of benchmarking process performance

i. identify the benefits of benchmarking in creating a competitive advantage

j. apply activity-based management principles to recommend process performance improvements

k. demonstrate an understanding of the relationship among continuous improvement techniques, activity-based management, and quality performance

l. demonstrate an understanding of the concept of continuous improvement (kaizen) and how it relates to implementing ideal standards and quality improvements

m. define best practice analysis and discuss how it can be used by an organization to improve performance

3.1 VALUE CHAIN ANALYSIS

1. To remain on the market, a product must provide **value to the customer** and a **profit to the seller**.

   a. Customers assign value to a product. The producer can affect the customer's perception of value by **differentiating the product** and **lowering its price**.

   b. The producer's profit is the difference between its costs and the price it charges for the product. Thus, by keeping costs low, the producer has more flexibility in pricing.

   c. The relationship of these three aspects of value creation can be graphically depicted as follows:

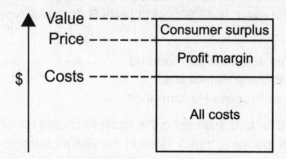

2. The **value chain** is a model for depicting the way in which every function in a company adds value to the final product. "The value chain approach for assessing competitive advantage is an integral part of the strategic planning process." (SMA 4X, *Value Chain Analysis for Assessing Competitive Advantage*, March 1996)

   a. A value chain depicts how costs and customer value accumulate along a chain of activities that lead to an end product or service. A value chain consists of the internal processes or activities a company performs: R&D, design, production, marketing, distribution, and customer service.

   b. Another view is that the value chain consists of all of the value-creating activities leading to the ultimate end-use product delivered into the final consumers' hands. In other words, a value chain is a firm's overall chain of value-creating (value-added) processes.

   c. **Primary activities** deal with the product directly. **Support activities** lend aid to the primary activity functions. The value chain can be graphically depicted as follows:

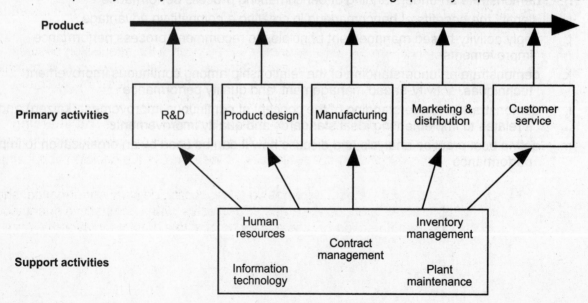

    d.   **Value-chain analysis** is a strategic analysis tool that allows a firm to focus on those activities that are consistent with its overall strategy.

        1)   Value-chain analysis allows a firm to decide **which parts of the value chain** it wants to occupy and how each activity then contributes to the firm's competitive advantage by adding customer value or by reducing costs.

        2)   Because the value chain identifies and connects the organization's strategic activities, value chain analysis improves the firm's knowledge of its relations with customers, suppliers, and competitors.

            a)   It also facilitates the strategic determination of the phase(s) of the industry's value chain in which the firm should operate.

        3)   The first step in a value-chain analysis is to **identify** the firm's **value-creating activities**.

        4)   The second step is to determine how each value-creating activity can **produce a competitive advantage** for the firm. This step has multiple substeps.

            a)   Identify the firm's competitive advantage (e.g., cost reduction, product differentiation) so that the firm's position in the industry's value chain can be clarified.

            b)   Identify the ways in which the firm's value-creating activities can generate additional customer value.

            c)   Identify activities that are candidates for cost reduction or, in the case of non-core competencies, outsourcing.

            d)   Identify value-adding ways in which the firm's remaining activities can be linked.

        5)   Value-chain analysis is a team effort. Management accountants need to collaborate with engineering, production, marketing, distribution, and customer service professionals to focus on the strengths, weaknesses, opportunities, and threats identified in the value-chain analysis results.

        6)   Value-chain analysis offers an excellent opportunity to integrate strategic planning and management accounting to guide the firm to survival and growth.

3.   The **supply chain** is the flow of materials and services from their original sources to final consumers. Moreover, it usually encompasses more than one firm. Firms seeking to improve performance and reduce costs must analyze all phases of the supply chain as well as the value chain. Thus, a firm must reduce the cost of, and increase the value added by, its purchasing function.

    a.   **Purchasing** is the management function that concerns the acquisition process. It includes choice of vendors, contract negotiation, the decision whether to purchase centrally or locally, and **value analysis**. The process is initiated by purchase requisitions issued by the production control function.

        1)   Purchase requisitions ultimately result from **insourcing vs. outsourcing (make vs. buy)** decisions made when production processes were designed.

        2)   For a retailer, the purchase decision is the same as the decision about what to sell.

        3)   The choice of vendors depends on price, quality, delivery performance, shipping costs, credit terms, and service. Purchasers with a competitive orientation and considerable economic power may be able to extract very favorable terms from vendors.

4) Purchasers with a cooperative orientation adopt a longer-term approach: **supply chain coordination**. The purchaser and the vendor are viewed as committed to a partnership involving joint efforts to improve quality.

    a) For example, in the case of a major manufacturer and one of its suppliers, this orientation may include the purchaser's willingness to help develop the vendor's managerial, technical, and productive capacities. Thus, it tends to result in minimizing the number of vendors.

    b) Supply chain analysis and coordination should extend to all parties in the chain, from initial sources of materials to retailers.

    c) Coordination has special relevance to **inventory management**. By sharing information among all parties, demand uncertainty is reduced at each level, with consequent decreases of inventory at each level, minimization of stockouts, and avoidance of overproduction and rush orders.

        i) For example, such cooperation counteracts what has been called the **bullwhip or backlash effect**. This phenomenon occurs when demand variability increases at each level of the supply chain. Thus, retailers face only customer demand variability, but the manufacturer must cope with retailer demand variability that is greater than customer demand variability because retailers' purchases vary with additional factors, such as batching of orders and trade promotions. Similarly, the variability of manufacturer demands on suppliers may be greater than the variability of retailer demands on manufacturers.

    b. **Critical success factors**. Value-chain and supply-chain analysis should be used to meet customer requirements for better performance regarding

        1) Cost reduction,
        2) Efficiency,
        3) Continuous improvement of quality to meet customer needs and wants,
        4) Minimization or elimination of defects,
        5) Faster product development and customer response times, and
        6) Constant innovation.

4. **Value engineering** is a means of reaching targeted cost levels. It is a systematic approach to assessing all aspects of the value chain cost buildup for a product. The purpose is to minimize costs without sacrificing customer satisfaction. Value engineering requires distinguishing between cost incurrence and **locked-in costs**.

    a. **Cost incurrence** is the actual use of resources, but **locked-in (designed-in)** costs will result in use of resources in the future as a result of past decisions. Thus, value engineering emphasizes controlling costs at the design stage, that is, before they are locked in.

    b. **Life-cycle costing** is sometimes used as a basis for cost planning and product pricing. Life-cycle costing estimates a product's revenues and expenses over its expected life cycle. The result is to highlight upstream and downstream costs in the cost planning process that often receive insufficient attention. Emphasis is on the need to price products to cover all costs, not just production costs.

5.   **Process analysis** is a means of linking a firm's internal processes to its overall strategy.

   a.   **Types of process**

   1)   **Continuous**, such as candy bars squirted out by machinery.
   2)   **Batch**, such as beer brewing.
   3)   **Hybrid**, in which both continuous and batch processes are used.
   4)   **Make-to-stock**, such as automobile assembly.
   5)   **Make-to-order**, such as deli sandwich making.

   b.   **Process interdependence.** The degree of interdependence among the stages in a process is referred to as "tightness."

   1)   A **tight process** is one in which breakdown in one stage brings the succeeding stages to a halt. This is characteristic of continuous processes that do not have buffer work-in-process inventories.
   2)   A **loose process** is one in which subsequent stages can continue working after a breakdown in a previous stage. This is characteristic of batch processes and any others with extensive work-in-process inventories.

   c.   **Bottlenecks.** Very few processes run at the precise same speed in every stage.

   1)   One part of the process is almost always the slowest, referred to as the "bottleneck." If capacity is added at that point, the bottleneck simply shifts to the next slowest operation.

   a)   The theory of constraints was developed to deal with this challenge (see Subunit 2.3)

   2)   The bottleneck issue only arises when demand for the firm's product is sufficient to absorb all of the output. When a production line is running at less than full capacity, bottlenecks can be avoided.

6.   **Process value analysis** is a comprehensive understanding of how an organization generates its output. It involves a determination of which activities that use resources are **value-adding** or **nonvalue-adding** and how the latter may be reduced or eliminated.

   a.   This linkage of **product costing** and **continuous improvement** of processes is **activity-based management (ABM)**. ABM redirects and improves the use of resources to increase the value created for customers and other stakeholders. It encompasses activity analysis, cost driver analysis, and quality performance measurement.

   b.   An **activity analysis** determines what is done, by whom, at what cost in time and other resources, and the value added by each activity.

   1)   A **value-added activity** is necessary to remain in business. It may be mandated (e.g., a regulatory requirement) or discretionary. The latter produces some changes not otherwise achievable that enables other activities to occur.
   2)   A **value-added cost** is incurred to perform a value-added activity without waste.
   3)   A **nonvalue-added activity** is unnecessary and should be eliminated.
   4)   A **nonvalue-added cost** is caused by a nonvalue-added activity or inefficient performance of a value-added activity. Thus, **managing the causes of cost** results in elimination of unnecessary activities as well as greater efficiency of activities.

5) Financial and nonfinancial **measures of activity performance** address efficiency, quality, and time. The purpose is to assess how well activities meet customer demands. To satisfy customer needs and wants, activities should be **efficient** (a favorable input-to-output ratio) so that customers are willing to pay the prices charged. Activities should produce defect-free output (high **quality**), and that output should be produced in a **timely** manner (with less resource usage and in response to customer requirements).

6) The **selection of value-added activities** in each place of the value chain reflects the firm's determination of its **competitive advantage** and its choice of **competitive strategy**. For example, different design strategies require different activities and costs. A firm might choose to be the low-cost producer of an undifferentiated product rather than compete on the basis of superior product quality.

7. One aspect of process analysis is the management of **time**.

a. **Product development time** is a crucial factor in the competitive equation. A company that is first in the market with a new product has obvious advantages.

1) Reducing development time is also important because product life cycles are becoming shorter.

2) Companies need to respond quickly and flexibly to new technology, changes in consumer tastes, and competitive challenges.

b. One financial measure of product development is **breakeven time**, which is the time from management approval of the project to the time when the cumulative present value of its cash inflows equals the cumulative present value of the investment cash outflows.

1) The most popular method of determining breakeven time calculates the time required for the present value of the cumulative cash flows to equal zero.

a) An alternative that results in a longer breakeven time is to consider the time required for the present value of the cumulative cash inflows to equal the present value of all the expected future cash outflows.

c. **Customer-response time** is the delay from placement of an order to delivery of the good or service. Response time is a function of time drivers, e.g., uncertainty about arrivals of customers in the queue and bottlenecks (points at which capacity is reached or exceeded). Response time consists of order receipt time (delay between the placement of an order and its readiness for setup), manufacturing cycle time (delay from the moment the order is ready for setup to its completion), and order delivery time.

1) Manufacturing cycle (throughput) time equals order waiting time plus manufacturing time.

2) Queuing (waiting-line) theory is a group of mathematical models for systems involving waiting lines. The objective of queuing theory is to minimize the total cost of the system, including both service and waiting costs, for a given rate of arrivals. Mathematical solutions are available for simple systems having unscheduled random arrivals. For other systems, simulation must be used to find a solution.

8. Stop and review! You have completed the outline for this subunit. Study multiple-choice questions 1 through 9 on page 78.

3.2 OTHER PERFORMANCE MEASUREMENT TOOLS

1. Technological advances have increased the popularity of **total quality management (TQM)** techniques and **business process reengineering**.

    a. A **process** is how something is accomplished in a firm. It is a set of activities directed toward the same objective. Reengineering is process innovation and core process redesign. Instead of improving existing procedures, it finds new ways of doing things. Thus, reengineering should be contrasted with **process improvement**, which consists of incremental but constant changes that improve efficiency.

        1) Accordingly, reengineering and TQM techniques eliminate many traditional controls. They exploit modern technology to improve productivity and decrease the number of clerical workers. Thus, the emphasis is on developing controls that are automated and self-correcting and require minimal human intervention.

    b. The emphasis therefore shifts to monitoring internal control so management can determine when an operation may be out of control and corrective action is needed.

        1) Most reengineering and TQM techniques also assume that humans will be motivated to work actively in improving operations when they are full participants in the process.

    c. **Monitoring** assesses the quality of internal control over time. Management considers whether internal control is properly designed and operating as intended and modifies it to reflect changing conditions. Monitoring may be in the form of separate, periodic evaluations or of ongoing monitoring.

        1) Ongoing monitoring occurs as part of routine operations. It includes management and supervisory review, comparisons, reconciliations, and other actions by personnel as part of their regular activities.

2. **Pareto analysis** is based on the concept that about 80% of results or effects are caused by about 20% of people or events. Thus, managers should concentrate on the relatively few people or events that have the most significant effects. **Pareto diagrams** are bar charts in which the frequencies of the various types of adverse conditions that may occur in a given process are depicted.

    a. For example, an auditor might construct a Pareto diagram of the types and numbers of control deviations found in the receiving department. The tallest (or longest) bar signifies the most common type of problem.

3. SMA 4V, *Practices and Techniques: Effective Benchmarking* (July 1995), describes techniques for improving the effectiveness of benchmarking, which is a means of helping companies with productivity management and business process reengineering.

    a. "**Benchmarking** involves continuously evaluating the practices of best-in-class organizations and adapting company processes to incorporate the best of these practices." It "analyzes and measures the key outputs of a business process or function against the best and also identifies the underlying key actions and root causes that contribute to the performance difference."

        1) Benchmarking is an ongoing process that entails quantitative and qualitative measurement of the difference between the company's performance of an activity and the performance by the best in the world. The benchmark organization need not be a competitor.

b.   The first phase in the benchmarking process is to **select and prioritize benchmarking projects**.

1)   An organization must understand its critical success factors and business environment to identify key business processes and drivers and to develop parameters defining what processes to benchmark. The criteria for selecting what to benchmark relate to the reasons for the existence of a process and its importance to the entity's mission, values, and strategy. These reasons relate in large part to satisfaction of end users or customer needs.

c.   The next phase is to organize **benchmarking teams**. A team organization is appropriate because it permits an equitable division of labor, participation by those responsible for implementing changes, and inclusion of a variety of functional expertise and work experience. Team members should have knowledge of the function to be benchmarked, respected positions in the company, good communication skills, teaming skills, motivation to innovate and to support cross-functional problem solving, and project management skills.

d.   The benchmarking team must thoroughly **investigate and document internal processes**. The organization should be seen as a series of processes, not as a fixed structure. A process is "a network of related and independent activities linked by the outputs they exchange." One way to determine the primary characteristics of a process is to trace the path a request for a product or service takes through the organization.

1)   The benchmarking team must also develop a **family of measures** that are true indicators of process performance and a process taxonomy, that is, a set of process elements, measures, and phrases that describes the process to be benchmarked.

e.   **Researching and identifying best-in-class performance** is often the most difficult phase. The critical steps are setting up databases, choosing information-gathering methods (internal sources, external public domain sources, and original research are the possible approaches), formatting questionnaires (lists of questions prepared in advance), and selecting benchmarking partners.

f.   The **data analysis phase** entails identifying performance gaps, understanding the reasons they exist, and prioritizing the key activities that will facilitate the behavioral and process changes needed to implement the benchmarking study's recommendations. Sophisticated statistical and other methods may be needed when the study involves many variables, testing of assumptions, or presentation of quantified results.

g.   Leadership is most important in the **implementation phase** of the benchmarking process because the team must be able to justify its recommendations. Moreover, the process improvement teams must manage the implementation of approved changes.

4.   **Kaizen** is the Japanese word for the continuous pursuit of improvement in every aspect of organizational operations.

a.   For example, a budget prepared on the kaizen principle projects costs based on future improvements. The possibility of such improvements must be determined, and the cost of implementation and the savings therefrom must be estimated.

5.   The trend in managerial performance evaluation is the **balanced scorecard** approach. Multiple measures of performance permit a determination as to whether a manager is achieving certain objectives at the expense of others that may be equally or more important. For example, an improvement in operating results at the expense of new product development would be apparent using this approach.

   a.   The scorecard is a **goal congruence tool** that informs managers about the nonfinancial factors that top management believes to be important.

   b.   As mentioned previously, measures may be financial or nonfinancial, internal or external, and short term or long term.

   c.   The balanced scorecard facilitates best practice analysis. **Best practice analysis** is a method of accomplishing a business function or process that is considered to be superior to all other known methods. A lesson learned from one area of a business can be passed on to another area of the business or between businesses. Thus, the whole concept of **benchmarking** is aimed at identifying best practices.

   d.   A typical scorecard includes measures in four categories:

      1)   Financial
      2)   Customer
      3)   Learning, growth, and innovation
      4)   Internal business processes

6.   Stop and review! You have completed the outline for this subunit. Study multiple-choice questions 10 through 15 beginning on page 81.

3.3 CORE CONCEPTS

Value Chain Analysis

- The **value chain** is a model for depicting the way in which every function in a company adds value to the final product. **Primary activities** (R&D, manufacturing, etc.) deal with the product directly. **Support activities** (human resources, inventory management, etc.) lend aid to the primary activity functions.

- The **supply chain** is the flow of materials and services from their original sources to final consumers. Moreover, it usually encompasses more than one firm.

- **Value engineering** is a means of reaching targeted cost levels. It is a systematic approach to assessing all aspects of the value chain cost buildup for a product. The purpose is to minimize costs without sacrificing customer satisfaction. Value engineering requires distinguishing between **cost incurrence** and **locked-in costs**.

- **Cost incurrence** is the actual use of resources, but **locked-in (designed-in)** costs will result in the use of resources in the future as a result of past decisions. Thus, value engineering emphasizes **controlling costs at the design stage**, that is, before they are locked in.

- **Life-cycle costing** is sometimes used as a basis for cost planning and product pricing. Life-cycle costing estimates a product's revenues and expenses over its expected life cycle. The result is to **highlight upstream and downstream costs** that often receive insufficient attention in the cost planning process.

- **Process value analysis** is a comprehensive understanding of how an organization generates its output. It involves a determination of which activities that use resources are **value-adding** or **nonvalue-adding** and how the latter may be reduced or eliminated.

Other Performance Measurement Tools

- Technological advances have increased the popularity of **total quality management (TQM)** techniques and **business process reengineering**. Reengineering should be contrasted with **process improvement**, which consists of incremental but constant changes that improve efficiency.

- **Pareto analysis** is based on the concept that about 80% of results or effects are caused by about 20% of people or events. Thus, managers should concentrate on the relatively few people or events that have the **most significant effects**.

- **Benchmarking** is an ongoing process that entails quantitative and qualitative measurement of the difference between the company's performance of an activity and the performance by the best in the world.

- **Kaizen** is the Japanese word for the continuous pursuit of improvement in every aspect of organizational operations.

- The trend in managerial performance evaluation is the **balanced scorecard** approach. Multiple measures of performance permit a determination as to whether a manager is achieving certain objectives at the expense of others that may be equally or more important. The scorecard is a **goal congruence tool** that informs managers about the nonfinancial factors that top management believes to be important.

QUESTIONS

3.1 Value Chain Analysis

1. Process value analysis is a key component of activity-based management that links product costing and

- A. Reduction of the number of cost pools.
- B. Continuous improvement.
- C. Accumulation of heterogeneous cost pools.
- D. Overhead rates based on broad averages.

Answer (B) is correct. *(Publisher, adapted)*
REQUIRED: The element of process value analysis.
DISCUSSION: Design of an ABC system starts with process value analysis, a comprehensive understanding of how an organization generates its output. It involves a determination of which activities that use resources are value-adding or nonvalue-adding and how the latter may be reduced or eliminated. This linkage of product costing and continuous improvement of processes is activity-based management (ABM). It encompasses driver analysis, activity analysis, and performance measurement.
Answer (A) is incorrect because ABC tends to increase the number of cost pools and drivers used. Answer (C) is incorrect because ABC's philosophy is to accumulate homogeneous cost pools. Thus, the cost elements in a pool should be consumed by cost objects in proportion to the same driver. Homogenizing cost pools minimizes broad averaging of costs that have different drivers. Answer (D) is incorrect because ABC's philosophy is to accumulate homogeneous cost pools. Thus, the cost elements in a pool should be consumed by cost objects in proportion to the same driver. Homogenizing cost pools minimizes broad averaging of costs that have different drivers.

2. A systematic approach to reaching targeted cost levels during value chain analysis is known as

- A. Value engineering.
- B. Life-cycle costing.
- C. Process value analysis.
- D. Activity analysis.

Answer (A) is correct. *(Publisher, adapted)*
REQUIRED: The term referring to a systematic approach to reaching targeted cost levels during value chain analysis.
DISCUSSION: Value engineering is a means of reaching targeted cost levels. It is a systematic approach to assessing all aspects of the value chain cost buildup for a product.
Answer (B) is incorrect because life-cycle costing is a basis for cost planning and product pricing. Answer (C) is incorrect because process value analysis is a way of understanding how a company generates its output. Answer (D) is incorrect because activity analysis determines what is done, by whom, at what cost in time and other resources, and the value added by each activity.

3. Gram Co. develops computer programs to meet customers' special requirements. How should Gram categorize payments to employees who develop these programs?

	Direct Costs	Value-Adding Costs
A.	Yes	Yes
B.	Yes	No
C.	No	No
D.	No	Yes

Answer (A) is correct. *(CPA, adapted)*
REQUIRED: The proper categorization of employee costs.
DISCUSSION: Direct costs may be defined as those that can be specifically associated with a single cost object and can be assigned to it in an economically feasible manner. Wages paid to labor that can be identified with a specific finished good are direct costs. Value-adding costs may be defined as the costs of activities that cannot be eliminated without reducing the quality, responsiveness, or quantity of the output required by a customer or by an organization. Clearly, the amounts paid to programmers add value to computer programs.
Answer (B) is incorrect because the activities performed by programmers add value to computer programs. Therefore, the payments to employees who develop these programs is considered a value-adding cost. Answer (C) is incorrect because payments to programmers are both direct costs and value-adding costs of computer programs. Answer (D) is incorrect because wages paid to labor that can be identified with a specific finished good are direct costs. Therefore, payments to employees who develop computer programs is a direct cost.

4. The term referring to the excess of the price of a good over its cost is

- A. Consumer surplus.
- B. Profit margin.
- C. Contribution margin.
- D. Value-added transfer.

Answer (B) is correct. *(Publisher, adapted)*
REQUIRED: The term referring to the excess of the price of a good over its cost.
DISCUSSION: To remain in the market, a product must provide value to the customer and a profit to the seller. The producer's profit (profit margin) is the difference between its costs and the price it charges for the product.
Answer (A) is incorrect because consumer surplus is the excess of the value a consumer places on a good over the price (s)he pays for it. Answer (C) is incorrect because contribution margin is the excess of the sales price over variable costs. Answer (D) is incorrect because value-added transfer is not a meaningful term in this context.

5. Which of the following is not a component of the value chain?

- A. Primary activities.
- B. Secondary activities.
- C. Support activities.
- D. The product.

Answer (B) is correct. *(Publisher, adapted)*
REQUIRED: The items not a component of the value chain.
DISCUSSION: The value chain is a model for depicting the way in which every function in a company adds value to the final product. Primary activities deal with the product directly. Support activities lend aid to the primary activity functions.
Answer (A) is incorrect because, in value-chain analysis, primary activities are those that deal with the product directly. Answer (C) is incorrect because, in value-chain analysis, support activities lend aid to the primary activity functions. Answer (D) is incorrect because the product is the ultimate reason for having a value chain.

6. The flow of materials and services from their original sources to final consumers is the

- A. Value chain.
- B. Product chain.
- C. Supply chain.
- D. Value process.

Answer (C) is correct. *(Publisher, adapted)*
REQUIRED: The term referring to the flow of materials and services from their original sources to final consumers.
DISCUSSION: The supply chain usually encompasses more than one firm. Firms seeking to improve performance and reduce costs must analyze all phases of the supply chain as well as the value chain.
Answer (A) is incorrect because the value chain is a model for depicting the way in which every function in a company adds value to the final product. Answer (B) is incorrect because product chain is not a meaningful term in this context. Answer (D) is incorrect because value process is not a meaningful term in this context.

7. Which of the following is not a phase in a value-chain analysis?

    A. Identify activities that are candidates for cost reduction.

    B. Identify ways to generate additional customer value.

    C. Identify means for improving product cost efficiency.

    D. Identify the firm's competitive advantage.

Answer (C) is correct. *(Publisher, adapted)*
    REQUIRED: The item not a phase in a value-chain analysis.
    DISCUSSION: The second step in a value-chain analysis is to determine how each value-creating activity can produce a competitive advantage for the firm. This step has multiple substeps: (1) Identify the firm's competitive advantage (e.g., cost reduction, product differentiation) so that the firm's position in the industry's value chain can be clarified. (2) Identify the ways in which the firm's value-creating activities can generate additional customer value. (3) Identify activities that are candidates for cost reduction or, in the case of non-core competencies, outsourcing. (4) Identify value-adding ways in which the firm's remaining activities can be linked.
    Answer (A) is incorrect because identifying activities that are candidates for cost reduction or, in the case of non-core competencies, outsourcing, is one of the phases of a value-chain analysis. Answer (B) is incorrect because identifying ways in which the firm's value-creating activities can generate additional customer value is one of the phases of a value-chain analysis. Answer (D) is incorrect because identifying the firm's competitive advantage (e.g., cost reduction, product differentiation) so that the firm's position in the industry's value chain can be clarified is one of the phases of a value-chain analysis.

8. Which of the following is not a type of process?

    A. Make-to-stock.

    B. Make-to-order.

    C. Buffer.

    D. Hybrid.

Answer (C) is correct. *(Publisher, adapted)*
    REQUIRED: The term not referring to a type of process.
    DISCUSSION: A buffer in the context of process analysis is a quantity of work-in-process inventory that allows some stage(s) of the overall process to continue operating when an earlier stage breaks down.
    Answer (A) is incorrect because the value chain is a model for depicting the way in which every function in a company adds value to the final product. Answer (B) is incorrect because product chain is not a meaningful term in this context. Answer (D) is incorrect because value process is not a meaningful term in this context.

9. Which of the following is not an appropriate time measure for use in process analysis?

    A. Product development time.

    B. Breakeven time.

    C. Customer-response time.

    D. Process value time.

Answer (D) is correct. *(Publisher, adapted)*
    REQUIRED: The term not referring to an appropriate time measure for use in process analysis.
    DISCUSSION: The three common time measures for process analysis are product development time, breakeven time, and customer-response time. Process value time is not a meaningful term in this context.
    Answer (A) is incorrect because product development time is a crucial factor in the competitive equation Answer (B) is incorrect because breakeven time is a financial measure of product development, and thus is an appropriate time measure for process analysis. Answer (C) is incorrect because customer-response time is one of the common time measures for process analysis.

3.2 Other Performance Measurement Tools

Questions 10 and 11 are based on the following information. An organization has collected data on the complaints made by personal computer users and has categorized the complaints.

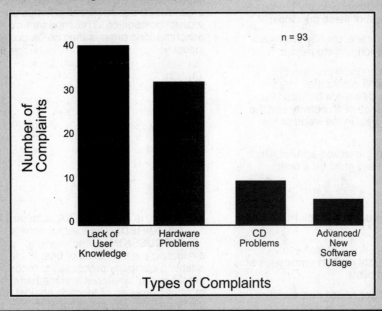

10. Using the information collected, the organization should focus on the

A. Total number of personal computer complaints that occurred.

B. Number of computer complaints associated with CD problems and new software usage.

C. Number of computer complaints associated with the lack of user knowledge and hardware problems.

D. Cost to alleviate all computer complaints.

Answer (C) is correct. *(CIA, adapted)*
REQUIRED: The organization's focus based on the data.
DISCUSSION: Complaints based on lack of user knowledge and hardware problems are by far the most frequent according to this chart. Consequently, the company should devote its resources primarily to these issues.
Answer (A) is incorrect because more detailed information is not available. The Pareto diagram does not focus on the total quantity of computer complaints. Answer (B) is incorrect because complaints about CD and software are infrequent. Answer (D) is incorrect because cost information is not provided.

11. The chart displays the

A. Arithmetic mean of each computer complaint.

B. Relative frequency of each computer complaint.

C. Median of each computer complaint.

D. Absolute frequency of each computer complaint.

Answer (D) is correct. *(CIA, adapted)*
REQUIRED: The information provided by the chart.
DISCUSSION: This Pareto diagram depicts the frequencies of complaints in absolute terms. It displays the actual number of each type of complaint.
Answer (A) is incorrect because the chart does not display arithmetic means of each type of complaint. Answer (B) is incorrect because the chart does not display relative frequencies of each type of complaint. Answer (C) is incorrect because the chart does not display medians of each type of complaint.

12. A statement that "80% of our profits come from 20% of our products" is an example of the application of

A. Pareto analysis.

B. Benchmarking.

C. Value chain analysis.

D. Life-cycle costing.

Answer (A) is correct. *(Publisher, adapted)*
REQUIRED: The concept that assumes that 80% of results are caused by 20% of people or events.
DISCUSSION: Pareto analysis assumes that 80% of results are caused by 20% of people or events.
Answer (B) is incorrect because benchmarking is essentially a nonsense alternative as used here. Answer (C) is incorrect because value chain analysis is essentially a nonsense alternative as used here. Answer (D) is incorrect because life-cycle costing is essentially a nonsense alternative as used here.

13. Which of the following statements regarding benchmarking is false?

A. Benchmarking involves continuously evaluating the practices of best-in-class organization and adapting company processes to incorporate the best of these practices.

B. Benchmarking, in practice, usually involves a company forming benchmarking teams.

C. Benchmarking is an ongoing process that entails quantitative and qualitative measurement of the difference between the company's performance of an activity and the performance by the best in the world or the best in the industry.

D. The benchmarking organization against which a firm is comparing itself must be a direct competitor.

Answer (D) is correct. *(Publisher, adapted)*
REQUIRED: The false statement about benchmarking.
DISCUSSION: Benchmarking is an ongoing process that entails quantitative and qualitative measurement of the difference between the company's performance of an activity and the performance by a best-in-class organization. The benchmarking organization against which a firm is comparing itself need not be a direct competitor. The important consideration is that the benchmarking organization be an outstanding performer in its industry.

14. An example of an internal nonfinancial benchmark is the

A. Labor rate of comparably skilled employees at a major competitor's plant.

B. Average actual cost per pound of a specific product at the company's most efficient plant becoming the benchmark for the company's other plants.

C. Company setting a benchmark of $50,000 for employee training programs at each of the company's plants.

D. Percentage of customer orders delivered on time at the company's most efficient plant becoming the benchmark for the company's other plants.

Answer (D) is correct. *(CIA, adapted)*
REQUIRED: The internal nonfinancial benchmark.
DISCUSSION: Benchmarking "involves continuously evaluating the principles of best-in-class organizations and adapting company processes to incorporate the best of these practices." It "analyzes and measures the key outputs of a business process or function against the best and also identifies the underlying key actions and root causes that contribute to the performance difference" (SMA 4V). The percentage of orders delivered on time at the company's most efficient plant is an example of an internal nonfinancial benchmark.
Answer (A) is incorrect because the labor rate of a competitor is a financial benchmark. Answer (B) is incorrect because the cost per pound of a product at the company's most efficient plant is a financial benchmark. Answer (C) is incorrect because the cost of a training program is a financial benchmark.

15. Which of the following statements is false with respect to best practices analysis?

A. The balanced scorecard facilitates best practice analysis.

B. Best practice analysis is a way or method of accomplishing a business function or process that is considered to be superior to all other known methods.

C. Best practices analysis assumes that a lesson learned from one area of a business can be passed on to another area of the business or between businesses.

D. The concept of benchmarking is incompatible with best practices analysis.

Answer (D) is correct. *(Publisher, adapted)*
REQUIRED: The false statement about best practices analysis.
DISCUSSION: Best practice analysis is a method of accomplishing a business function or process that is considered to be superior to all other known methods. The balanced scorecard facilitates best practice analysis. A lesson learned from one area of a business can be passed on to another area of the business or between businesses. The whole concept of benchmarking is aimed at identifying best practices.
Answer (A) is incorrect because the balanced scorecard facilitates best practice analysis. Answer (B) is incorrect because the best practice analysis is a method of accomplishing a business function or process that is considered to be superior to all other known methods. Answer (C) is incorrect because a lesson learned in one area of a business can be passed on to another area of the business or between businesses.

Use Gleim's **CMA Test Prep** for interactive testing with **over 2,000 additional multiple-choice questions!**

STUDY UNIT FOUR
MARKETING'S STRATEGIC ROLE WITHIN THE FIRM

(30 pages of outline)

Management accountants often work with the area of marketing to provide information needed for effective marketing management. Thus, the CMA exam covers the strategic role of marketing, market segmentation, managing products and services, pricing strategies, the promotional mix, and distribution strategy.

This study unit is the **first of three** on **strategic marketing**. The relative weight assigned to this major topic in Part 3 of the exam is **15%** at **skill level A** (two skill types required). The three study units are

Study Unit 4: Marketing's Strategic Role within the Firm
Study Unit 5: Marketing Information and Market Segmentation
Study Unit 6: Other Marketing Topics

After studying the outline and answering the multiple-choice questions, you will have the skills necessary to address the following topics listed in the IMA's Learning Outcome Statements:

Part 3 – Section B.1. Strategic role within the firm

The candidate should be able to:

a. identify the interrelationships between a firm's overall strategy and its marketing process
b. demonstrate an understanding of the process of setting company marketing strategies, as well as the objectives and tactics to reach those strategic marketing goals
c. demonstrate an understanding of Strengths/Weaknesses/Opportunities/Threats (SWOT) analysis
d. explain the critical importance of identifying customer needs and providing value to satisfy those customer needs
e. define and demonstrate an understanding of business portfolio concepts
f. demonstrate an understanding of the marketing process, including analyzing marketing opportunities, selecting target markets, developing the marketing mix, and managing the marketing effort
g. demonstrate an understanding of the interrelationships among marketing analysis, planning, implementation, and control
h. define strategic groups within industries and discuss why they require unique marketing strategies
i. identify Porter's three generic strategies
j. demonstrate an understanding of competitive changes during an industry's evolution
k. differentiate among embryonic industries, growth industries, industry shakeout, mature industries, and declining industries
l. demonstrate an understanding of the effect of globalization on industry structure
m. identify internal competitive advantage and its components, including efficiency, quality, innovation, and customer satisfaction
n. demonstrate an understanding of the value creation chain

o.   identify distinctive competencies, resources, and capabilities

p.   identify reasons that marketing strategies fail and identify ways to sustain competitive advantage, including continuous improvement and benchmarking

4.1 THE MARKETING PROCESS

1.   The marketing process involves

a.   Analyzing marketing opportunities

b.   Choosing target markets

c.   Formulating marketing strategies

d.   Planning the marketing program and mix

e.   Managing the marketing effort

2.   Businesses should be defined in market terms, that is, in terms of needs and customer groups. Moreover, a distinction should be made between a **target market definition** and a **strategic market definition**. For example, a target market for a railroad might be freight hauling, but a strategic market might be transportation of any goods and people. A business also may be defined with respect to **customer groups and their needs** and the technology required to satisfy those needs.

3.   The categories of controllable elements in a **marketing program** reflect the decisions to be made about the **marketing mix** (the combination of marketing tools). From the seller's perspective, the categories of marketing tools are **product, price, place,** and **promotion** (sometimes called the "4 Ps" of marketing). The seller chooses tools from these categories to develop a marketing mix for achieving its objectives in the target market. From the buyer's perspective, each class of marketing tools corresponds to a customer benefit: **customer solution** (product), **customer cost** (price), **convenience** (place), and **communication** (promotion). Thus, a firm will succeed by using the 4 Ps to deliver the **4 Cs** of marketing.

a.   The **product** category of marketing tools includes offering different varieties, sizes, and features. Quality, design, and packaging also may vary. Different brands may be marketed, and a product may be sold subject to a multitude of warranty and service agreements and return policies.

b.   **Pricing tools** include offerings of various discounts, allowances, credit arrangements, and payment periods.

c.   Marketing tools related to **place** include choices among distribution (marketing) channels, delivery (transportation) options, inventory policies, locations, and coverage.

d.   The mix of **promotion** tools includes the types of sales promotions, advertising methods, direct marketing media (e.g., the Internet, telemarketing, and regular mail), public relations efforts, and in-person selling.

4.   The **scope of marketing** may be broadly defined as demand management. It extends to marketing not only goods and services but also experiences, people, events, entities, places, information, properties, and ideas. Thus, marketers engage in

a.   Selling products to those who demand them.

b.   Creating demand for a known product where none exists by linking the product's benefits with people's needs.

c.   Reversing negative or declining demand.

d.   Changing the pattern (e.g., seasonal) of demand **(synchromarketing)**.

e.   **Demarketing** in the overall market or selectively to reduce demand, e.g., because segments are unprofitable.

f.   Maintaining full demand.

g.   Discouraging unhealthful demand, such as that for tobacco and illegal drugs.

h. Discovering demands that are not currently being met **(latent demand)** and developing products that can fill those unmet needs.

i. Distributing products in the most effective and efficient manner.

5. A firm should provide customer value profitably. The **traditional approach** is to treat value delivery as having **two stages**: making and then selling (marketing) the product. However, this approach is ineffective in a highly competitive economy in which customers have many options, and the mass market has divided into many micromarkets.

6. The **business-process approach** to value creation and delivery is to involve marketing in all phases, including strategic planning.

    a. The firm chooses the value to be delivered in the **strategic marketing** stage. This stage consists of

        1) **Market (customer) segmentation.** Segments are defined by analysis of buyer differences (income, age, location, attitudes, etc.).

        2) Choosing **target markets**. These segments provide the best **marketing opportunities**. A "marketing opportunity is an area of buyer need or potential interest in which a company can perform profitably" (Philip Kotler, *Marketing Management*).

            a) An opportunity arises, for example, when

                i) The buying process can be improved.
                ii) A product or service can be customized.
                iii) Informational needs are unmet.
                iv) More rapid or cheaper delivery is possible.
                v) The firm can offer a capability not matched by any rival.

            b) **Market opportunity analysis** determines whether

                i) Benefits (value) can be communicated effectively to the target markets.
                ii) The communication can be done with a cost effective promotional mix and distribution strategy.
                iii) The firm has the necessary resources.
                iv) The firm can provide the chosen value better than its possible competitors.
                v) Profits will at least equal the firm's targeted return on investment.

            c) **Developing and positioning the offering.** Positioning is the process of designing the offering so that it will have a distinct and favorable place **in the minds of customers**. Thus, the firm's value proposition (the combination of benefits offered) should give customers in the target market good reasons to purchase the offering.

    b. The firm delivers and communicates value in the **tactical marketing** stage.

        1) **Delivery of value** entails product or service development (choice of features), setting prices, production or outsourcing, and distribution.

        2) **Communication of value** is done through an integrated marketing communication process. Instead of an emphasis on one method (e.g., advertising or the sales force), modern marketers combine promotional methods so that a consistent and favorable **image** will be communicated to customers whenever they have contact with the brand.

            a) A **brand** is "an offering from a known source" (Kotler). A brand image is the aggregate of associations that customers have with the brand.

c.   Japanese writers suggest that the objectives of the marketing process should include:

1)   Continuous receipt of feedback as a basis for better products and marketing efforts.
2)   Implementing improvements as quickly as feasible.
3)   Using just-in-time inventory systems.
4)   Minimizing production set-up time and cost.
5)   Minimizing product defects.

7.   **Planning the marketing program and mix** is the process of determining how marketing strategies formulated in accordance with a SWOT (strengths, weaknesses, opportunities, and threats) analysis (see item 3. in Study Unit 1, Subunit 1) may be implemented.

a.   The firm must decide what resources should be devoted to the marketing effort, for example, budgeting outlays as a percentage of sales. Total expenditures may be increased to secure a larger market share.

b.   The next step is to allocate the budgeted resources to the elements of the marketing mix (the 4 Ps or 4 Cs of marketing).

8.   **Managing the marketing effort** involves organizing the resources provided for achieving the objectives of the marketing strategy, implementing the marketing plan, and controlling the process.

a.   The **marketing organization** should be able to implement the marketing plan. The following are types of marketing organizations.

1)   Sales department only
2)   Sales department with some marketing functions, such as advertising and research
3)   Marketing department separate from sales
4)   Marketing and sales departments reporting to a vice-president of marketing and sales
5)   Process and outcome organizations, with departments replaced by cross-disciplinary teams managed by process leaders

b.   The **marketing department** itself may be organized by

1)   Functional specializations
2)   Geographic areas
3)   Products
4)   Brands
5)   Market segments
6)   Product and market matrix
7)   Corporate-divisional structure, with varying emphasis on marketing at different levels

c.   **Marketing implementation** determines how marketing **strategies and plans** will be executed, when, where, and by whom.

1)   The skills needed for efficient and effective implementation are

a)   Recognition of problems and diagnosis of causes.
b)   Determining where in the firm the problem exists (marketing policy, program, or function).
c)   The abilities to assign resources, organize activities, and motivate others.
d)   The ability to track and assess performance.

d. Marketing Control

1) **Annual-plan control** should be overseen by senior and middle management. It is applied at all levels of the firm using **management-by-objectives (MBO)** methods. Annual plan control is directed toward reaching sales, profitability, and other objectives defined in the annual plan. Interim-period objectives are set, performance is monitored, the causes of variances are identified, and corrective action is taken. The following are frequently used **marketing metrics**:

    a) **Sales-variance analysis** determines the effects of specific variables, such as price and volume (see Gleim's *CMA Review, Part 2*, Subunit 9.7).

        i) The components of the sales quantity variance are the market size and the market share variances. The **market size variance** equals the budgeted market share percentage, times the difference between the actual market size in units and the budgeted market size in units, times the budgeted weighted-average UCM. The **market share variance** equals the difference between the actual market share percentage and the budgeted market share percentage, times the actual market size in units, times the budgeted weighted-average UCM.

    b) **Microsales analysis** addresses particular products, geographic areas, customers, etc.

    c) **Market-share analysis** may determine

        i) Overall market share (sales ÷ total market sales)

        ii) Served market share (sales ÷ the served market, i.e., all buyers willing and able to buy the firm's product)

        iii) Relative market share (sales ÷ sales of largest competitor, so a share exceeding 1.0 signifies market leadership)

    d) The **overall market share in dollar terms** is the product of the following:

        i) Customer penetration (firm customers ÷ all customers)

        ii) Customer selectivity (average purchase from the firm ÷ average purchase from the average firm)

        iii) Customer loyalty (purchases from the firm ÷ total purchases from sellers of the same products)

        iv) Price selectivity (firm's average price ÷ average price of all firms)

    e) **Marketing expense-to-sales ratio.** Fluctuations may be tracked on a control chart with upper and lower limits. These ratios may include

        i) Advertising ÷ sales

        ii) Sales promotion ÷ sales

        iii) Sales force ÷ sales

        iv) Sales administration ÷ sales

        v) Marketing research ÷ sales

    f) **Rate of return on net worth** results from multiplying ROI (return on investment, or profit margin × asset turnover) by financial leverage.

$$\text{Profit Margin} \times \text{Asset Turnover} \times \text{Financial Leverage} = \text{RRNW}$$

$$\frac{Net\ profits}{Net\ sales} \times \frac{Net\ sales}{Total\ assets} \times \frac{Total\ assets}{Net\ worth} = \frac{Net\ profits}{Net\ worth}$$

g) **Return on Marketing Investment**

$$\frac{Net\ marketing\ contribution\ (revenues\ -\ total\ variable\ costs)}{Marketing\ expenditures}$$

    i)   The numerator omits overhead and operating expenses.

h) **Market-Based Scorecard**

    i)   A **customer-performance scorecard** contains measures of new customers, lost customers, customer satisfaction, brand awareness, customer loyalty, identification of intended positioning and differentiation, perception of product or service quality compared with a chief rival, and others.

    ii)   A **stakeholder-performance scorecard** provides measures of the satisfaction of shareholders, creditors, employees, suppliers, and distributors.

2) **Profitability control** is the responsibility of the marketing controller.

a) Actual profits should be calculated for each

    i)   Product
    ii)   Customer group
    iii) Territory
    iv) Market segment
    v)   Trade channel
    vi) Order size

b) A problem is that the accounting system needs to be organized to provide the necessary data.

c) Marketing profitability control applies to each marketing activity. Functional expenses need to be identified and assigned and an income statement prepared for each marketing entity.

3) **Efficiency control** is the responsibility of line and staff managers and the marketing controller. It monitors and improves the efficiency of marketing expenditures. Measures should be developed to determine the efficiency of

a) The sales force
b) Promotions
c) Advertising
d) Distribution

4) **Strategic control** is the responsibility of senior management and the marketing auditor. It determines whether marketing strategy is appropriate for market conditions and the optimal marketing opportunities are being addressed. The firm should perform

a) A **marketing effectiveness review**. Marketing effectiveness is a function of

    i)   Strategic awareness
    ii)   Operational efficiency
    iii) Integration of the firm's marketing efforts
    iv) Customer centeredness
    v)   Gathering of sufficient information

b) A **marketing audit**. This audit should address all marketing activities, be done in a systematic order, be done by an independent group (e.g., outside consultants), and be done periodically.

c) A firm also may perform reviews for excellence and ethical and social responsibility.

9. Stop and review! You have completed the outline for this subunit. Study multiple-choice questions 1 through 13 beginning on page 112.

4.2 MARKETING STRATEGIES

1. The analysis of **marketing opportunities** begins with market-oriented strategic planning (see Study Unit 1). It addresses the structural analysis of industries and competition, including the **five competitive forces**, the nature of a firm's **competitive advantages** (its competencies, resources, and capabilities), and the **generic strategies** based on those advantages.

   a. For outlines covering the **value creation chain** and such ways of perpetuating competitive advantage as **continuous improvement** of quality and **benchmarking**, see Study Unit 2.

   b. For an outline of strategic planning **portfolio techniques** used to devise strategies for the firm's businesses, see Subunit 4.3.

2. **Industry approach to competition.** An **industry** consists of firms selling products or services that are substitutes.

   a. One way to describe an industry considers the **number of sellers** and the **extent of differentiation** of products and services, an approach used in microeconomics.

      1) A **monopoly** consists of a single seller of a product or service in an area, such as a utility. A monopoly may be regulated so as to compel better service and a lower price.

      2) An **oligopoly** consists of a few large firms. If products are standardized, competition may be based solely on price. If products are partially differentiated, each firm may attempt to lead the industry regarding a given attribute, e.g., price, quality, service, or features.

      3) In **monopolistic competition**, an industry has numerous sellers who offer differentiated products and services.

      4) In **pure competition**, differentiation is absent, and the same prices are charged by all sellers.

   b. Another way to characterize an industry is by reference to its **entry, exit,** or **mobility barriers**.

      1) **Entry barriers** may be high or low. Industries vary as to the necessary capital investment, economies of scale, intellectual property, materials, locations, distribution channels, and other factors.

      2) **Exit barriers** may consist of legal and moral obligations, regulatory requirements, lack of alternative investments, vertical integration, low residual value of assets, and tradition.

      3) **Mobility barriers** restrict movement within an industry's segments. They are similar to industry entry barriers.

      4) In general, high entry and mobility barriers and low exit barriers promote profitability.

   c. The **cost structure** of an industry affects the competitive strategies available to firms in the industry. For example, the physical plant and distribution costs of oil refineries are much greater than those of restaurants. Other industries may have especially high R&D costs (pharmaceutical industry) or marketing costs (the brewery industry).

d.   The degree of backward or forward **vertical integration** along the value chain varies with the industry. For example, a manufacturer that has acquired suppliers is **backward integrated**, and a movie producer that has acquired a chain of theaters is **forward integrated**.

1)   Integration may reduce costs, and a firm may be able to choose where in the value chain to earn profits and pay the lowest taxes.

2)   However, an integrated firm may be inflexible and face high exit barriers.

e.   The extent of **globalization** varies with the industry. For example, restaurants are in a local industry, and manufacturers of large passenger aircraft are in a global industry, one that requires large R&D outlays and economies of scale.

3.   **Strategic groups.** To analyze competition within an industry, its **strategic groups** should be evaluated. Hence, a potential entrant into an industry must consider which strategic group to target. The choice of strategic group and a firm's ability to implement its competitive strategy will determine profitability.

a.   A strategic group consists of firms in an industry that have adopted **similar competitive strategies**. The analysis of strategic groups addresses such issues as

1)   Their composition, number, and size.

2)   **Mobility barriers**, i.e., barriers to movement among groups. The ability to move depends on the firm's current strategic group and its targeted group.

3)   The bargaining power of a group.

4)   The degree of the threat of substitutes.

5)   Intergroup competition. The level of competition primarily depends on

a)   **Market interdependence**, i.e., the extent to which different groups pursue the same customers. The greater the interdependence, the stronger the competition.

b)   **Product differentiation** or substitutability. Lower substitutability means less competition.

c)   **Number and size of groups.** The greater the number and the more equal their size, the greater the competition.

b.   The **dimensions of the competitive strategies** adopted by the firms in a strategic group include specialization, brand identification (e.g., within the distribution channels or with ultimate consumers), selection of channels, product or service quality, technical leadership, cost, service, price, degree of integration, degree of leverage, relationship with regulators, and relationship with the parent firm.

c.   An **overall industry analysis** considers

1)   The characteristics of the industry (growth, demand, technology, strength of suppliers and buyers, and other factors)

2)   The industry's strategic groups in relation to the five competitive forces

3)   How the firm compares with the competitors within the chosen strategic group, e.g., on the basis of its scale of operations, the intensity of group rivalry, and the differences in the ability of the group members to implement their strategies

d.   A **strategic group analysis**

1)   Determines what mobility barriers exist.

2)   Determines which groups are weak.

3)   Forecasts future group actions and trends.

4)   Predicts reaction patterns to events such as competitive attacks.

      5) Addresses the risks confronting the firms in the group. These risks include those that lower mobility barriers, those that arise from the investments needed to raise protective mobility barriers, and those resulting from entering a new strategic group.

      6) Helps the firm to make competitive choices, such as whether to move to another strategic group, improve the strategic group's structural position or the firm's relative position within the group, or to establish its own strategic group.

4. **Analysis of competitors** begins with determining the firm's actual and potential competitors. Accordingly, a firm must consider which other firms attempt to satisfy the **same customer needs** (a market approach to competitive analysis). Moreover, a firm may be more threatened by new entrants or the evolution of technology (notably, the Internet) than by existing competition.

    a. Each **competitor's characteristics** should be considered, e.g., revenues, profits, market share, financial position, and relations with its parent firm. Moreover, the strategic business unit (SBU) and product-market entry sales and market share are especially interesting. They are measures of the effectiveness of a competitor's strategy.

    b. Each **competitor's objectives** also should be considered.

      1) The organizational structure suggests the significance of given functions, where decisions are made, and the status of the competitor within a larger entity.

      2) Tradeoffs may be made among financial and market position goals, in particular in the short run. For example, some firms emphasize short-run profits, but others may concentrate on market-share growth and long-run profits.

      3) The competitor may believe itself to be the overall market leader or a leader in price or technology. An issue is what the competitor will do to remain in that position. The competitor's assumptions about its products, its position, and other firms in its strategic group may reveal probable objectives and possible blindspots.

      4) The incentive and control systems of the competitor affect its ability to react to competitive pressures.

      5) The experience, background, and attitudes of senior managers and directors may be clues to the competitor's objectives. Such factors may also be indicative of the nature of the corporate culture.

      6) Various commitments (e.g., debt or joint ventures) may limit a competitor's flexibility.

      7) Regulatory restraints, e.g., on price, may also limit a competitor's options.

      8) Recent setbacks or successes are often predictors of future behavior.

      9) The analysis of the parent of a competitor may provide many insights, for example, the reasons for the parent's entry into the competitor firm's business, its significance to the parent, the parent's use of generic strategies with other businesses it controls, the parent's corporate strategies, and the parent's results.

      10) The competitor's portfolio of businesses should be assessed to determine which are successful.

      11) A crucial question about a competitor's objectives is whether it plans to expand.

    c. The **competitor's history** may be revealing. Its current and past performance, record in relevant markets, successful and unsuccessful actions, and past reactions to strategic moves by rivals are factors identifying past and current **competitor strategies**.

d.   A competitor's **strengths and weaknesses** indicate whether and how it may be attacked.

   1)   Areas to be addressed are **innovation** (ability to develop new products and technologies), **manufacturing** (capacity, efficiency, workforce, access to materials, degree of integration), access to **financing** at low cost, **product** quality and availability, **marketing and selling** (brands, distribution, advertising, customer orientation, diversity of products, relations with retailers), **service**, **management** skills at all levels (quality of decisions, loyalty), the firm's **portfolio** (investments, degree of diversification), and the **organizational structure**.

   2)   A firm should identify a competitor's **core competencies** and assess its growth potential, ability to respond quickly to threats and opportunities, and staying power in the industry.

   3)   Evaluating a competitor's market position is necessary to judge how and whether to challenge it. According to Arthur D. Little, an organization of consultants, a competitor firm may hold one of the following **competitive positions**:

      a)   A **dominant firm** has a choice of strategies. It controls other firms' actions.

      b)   A **strong firm** can act independently and sustain its long-term status irrespective of the behavior of others.

      c)   A firm in a **favorable position** has strengths to use that give it a better-than-average chance to improve its status.

      d)   The performance of a firm in a **tenable position** justifies continuation of the business, but its chance for improvement is below average.

      e)   The performance of a firm in a **weak position** must change, or it must withdraw from the business.

      f)   A **nonviable firm** is a poor performer with no chance of improvement.

   4)   Arthur D. Little also suggests a three-factor model for assessing a competitor's current and future market share.

      a)   **Market share** is the share of the target market.

      b)   **Mind share** is the percentage of customers who name the firm as the first "that comes to mind" in the industry.

      c)   **Heart share** is the percentage of customers who name the firm as the one from which they "would prefer to buy."

      d)   A competitor that improves its mind share and heart share will ultimately increase its market share and profits.

   5)   Bruce Henderson has analyzed firms' **reaction patterns** when confronted with competitive attacks. A key to the analysis is **competitive equilibrium**.

      a)   Almost **identical competitors** have an unstable equilibrium because differentiation cannot be sustained. Price wars are common.

      b)   When one major factor is the **critical factor**, the equilibrium is unstable. A cost advantage obtained through economies of scale, technology gains, or experience allows a firm to gain market share.

      c)   Given **multiple critical factors** (quality, service, price, convenience, etc.), differentiation is more likely. More competitors can secure an advantage with respect to a critical factor in a market segment or niche.

      d)   The **number of competitors** is directly related to the number of critical factors.

      e)   When one competitor has approximately twice the **market share** of a second competitor, equilibrium exists. The costs of gaining market share outweigh the benefits to either party.

e. A competitor analysis may be used to assess a firm's best strategy for **countering a competitive move**.

1) The **offensive ability** of a firm to make a competitive move depends on

   a) Its satisfaction with the status quo.
   b) Its probable competitive moves.
   c) The strength and seriousness of its competitive moves.

2) A firm's **defensive ability** to respond to a competitive move depends on

   a) Its vulnerability to environmental threats.
   b) The extent of the provocation, that is, the moves that cause a reaction.
   c) The effectiveness of retaliation.

      i) A competitor may be unable to respond quickly to some events.

5. **Porter's Generic Strategies**

   a. Although profitability is substantially determined by the industry in which the firm functions, its relative position in the industry is also important. The firm's understanding of that position is determined by the analysis of its strengths, weaknesses, opportunities, and threats. This SWOT analysis (see item 3. in Study Unit 1, Subunit 1) identifies the firm's competitive advantages as a basis for choosing its **competitive strategy**.

   b. Michael E. Porter's **generic strategies model** is well known. It is based on the concept that each of a firm's **competitive advantages** ultimately may be categorized as either a **cost** advantage or a **differentiation** advantage.

   1) The firm's advantages should be used within the firm's **competitive (target) scope** to achieve its objectives. This scope may be **broad** (e.g., industry wide) or **narrow** (e.g., a market segment).

   c. Using the variables of **competitive advantage** (cost and differentiation) and **competitive scope** (broad and narrow), Porter described four generic strategies to be applied by business units.

   1) **Cost leadership** is the generic strategy favored by firms that seek competitive advantage through **lower costs** and that have a **broad competitive scope**. Such a firm can earn higher profits than its competitors at the industry average price or charge a lower price to increase market share.

      a) A firm may **acquire a cost advantage** over its competitors by

         i) Vertical integration
         ii) Exclusive access to low-cost materials
         iii) Economies of scale or other production efficiencies resulting in low unit cost
         iv) Outsourcing

      b) **Strengths of cost leaders.** The typical firm that follows a cost leadership strategy has low profit margins, a high volume of sales, and a substantial market share. Such a firm

         i) Has efficient supply and distribution channels
         ii) Is capable of large capital investment
         iii) If it is a manufacturer, has strengths in product design and process engineering
         iv) Closely supervises its labor force

    c) The **risks** of this strategy include the possibility that advances in technology or successful imitation may allow other firms to erase the cost leader's advantage.

        i) Furthermore, multiple firms following a strategy with a **narrow focus on cost** may achieve advantages in their market segments.

        ii) Still another risk is that the emphasis on cost may cause managers to overlook product and marketing changes. For example, the cost advantage must suffice to outweigh the differentiation advantages held by others.

    d) **Organization.** A cost leader is ordinarily highly structured to achieve close control of costs. Detailed reports are provided with great frequency, and benefits are tied to numerical goals.

2) **Differentiation** is the generic strategy favored by firms that seek competitive advantage through providing a **unique product or service**. This strategy has a **broad competitive scope**. Such a firm may earn higher profits because consumers are willing to pay a price increment above the amount charged by competitors. However, that increment must exceed the additional cost of the differentiated product or service.

    a) A successful differentiation strategy creates a buyer perception that few, if any, **substitutes** are available. Thus, the firm that adopts this strategy may have the additional advantage of being able to pass supplier **cost increases** to consumers.

        i) Uniqueness may be based on, for example, massive promotion, excellence of design, superior service, technical leadership, or brand identification.

        ii) A differentiation strategy does not signify a disregard for cost control, but simply a greater emphasis on creating a perception of the uniqueness of the product or service.

    b) Typical **strengths** of successful broad-scope differentiators are

        i) An effective R&D function

        ii) Creative product development

        iii) A strong marketing function that communicates (or helps to create) the uniqueness of the product or service that is perceived by the mass audience

        iv) A reputation for quality or technical leadership

        v) A tradition reaching back for decades

        vi) Effective coordination with suppliers and distributors

        vii) An ability to apply the expertise of other enterprises

    c) The **risks** of a differentiation strategy include the following:

        i) The maturing of the industry produces successful imitation by competitors.

        ii) Consumer tastes evolve as they become more sophisticated buyers or as they have less need for the differentiating factor.

        iii) Multiple firms following a strategy with a narrow focus on differentiation can achieve advantages in their market segments.

        iv) The differentiating factor may no longer justify its premium price. Brand loyalty may erode as lower-cost competitors may improve the quality and image of their products or services.

       d)   An **organization** adopting a differentiation strategy usually has close cooperation among its R&D and marketing functions. Incentive compensation is often based on relatively subjective performance measures, and the firm must succeed in attracting highly skilled or creative individuals.

   3)   **Cost focus** is the generic strategy favored by firms that seek competitive advantage through **lower costs** and that have a **narrow competitive scope** (e.g., a regional market or a specialized product line). The rationale for a focus strategy is that the narrower market can be better served because the firm knows it well.

       a)   Firms that successfully adopt a focus strategy achieve very strong **customer loyalty**, a disincentive to potential competitors.

       b)   The **strengths** of successful firms employing a focus strategy are similar to those of broad-target firms.

       c)   The **risks** of a focus strategy include the following:

          i)   A narrow focus means lower purchasing volume and therefore a weaker position relative to suppliers.

          ii)   The cost (or differentiation) advantage of servicing a narrow target may be more than offset by the cost advantage achieved by broad-target competitors through economies of scale and other factors.

          iii)   Even more narrowly focused competitors may serve their niches better.

          iv)   A firm following a broad-target strategy may, by imitation or otherwise, change its product or service to compete more effectively in the narrower market.

          v)   The narrower market itself may change.

       d)   The **organizational attributes** of firms employing a focus strategy are similar to those of broad-target firms.

   4)   **Focused differentiation** is the generic strategy favored by firms that seek competitive advantage through providing a **unique product or service** but with a **narrow competitive scope**, e.g., a regional market or a specialized product line.

       a)   The analysis of these firms is similar to that for cost-focus firms.

  d.   Porter's generic strategies can be graphically depicted as follows:

		Competitive Advantage	
		Low Cost	**Product Uniqueness**
Competitive Scope	**Broad (industry)**	Cost Leadership	Differentiation
	Narrow (niche)	Focus Strategy (cost)	Focus Strategy (differentiation)

   1)   According to Porter, using a **combination of generic strategies** may leave the firm "**stuck in the middle**," i.e., unable to create or sustain a competitive advantage. The danger is that attempting to follow more than one generic strategy will prevent the firm from achieving a competitive advantage. Thus, pursuit of both cost leadership and differentiation, for example, may interfere with reaching either objective. Furthermore, even if the firm could succeed by following multiple generic strategies, the result might be an ambiguous public image.

2)   In Porter's view, a firm that pursues multiple generic strategies may be more likely to succeed if it creates a separate **strategic business unit** to implement each strategy.

   a)   However, some writers disagree with Porter's advice not to pursue a combination of strategies. They argue that following a single strategy may not serve the needs of customers who want the best combination of product attributes, e.g., price, service, and quality.

3)   A firm also may become stuck in the middle as a result of the changes that occur as the firm, its products or services, and the industry proceed through their **life cycles**.

   a)   For example, an appropriate and successful focus strategy may need to be changed to a cost leadership strategy as the firm matures.

e.   **Porter's generic strategies** are responses to the **five competitive forces**.

   1)   **Rivalry among Existing Firms**

      a)   **Cost leadership** permits a firm to compete by charging lower prices.

      b)   **Differentiation** strengthens brand loyalty.

      c)   **Focus strategies** provide superior attention to customer needs, whether for quality, price, or other product attributes.

   2)   **Threats of, and Barriers to, Entry**

      a)   **Cost leadership** permits a firm to reduce prices as a deterrent to potential entrants.

      b)   **Differentiation** creates brand loyalty that a new entrant may not be able to overcome.

      c)   **Focus strategies** develop core competencies in a narrow market that potential entrants may not be able to match.

   3)   **Threat of Substitutes**

      a)   **Cost leadership** may result in low prices that substitutes cannot match.

      b)   **Differentiation** may create unique product (service) attributes not found in substitutes.

      c)   **Focus strategies** are efforts to develop core competencies or unique product attributes that may protect against substitutes as well as potential entrants.

   4)   **Buyers' Bargaining Power**

      a)   **Cost leadership** may enable a firm to remain profitable while charging the lower prices required by strong buyers.

      b)   **Differentiation** may reduce the leverage enjoyed by strong buyers because of the uniqueness of the product and the resulting lack of close substitutes.

      c)   **Focus strategies** also may reduce buyers' ability to negotiate in a narrow market. Substitutes may not be able to compete on price, quality, etc.

   5)   **Threat of Suppliers' Bargaining Power**

      a)   **Cost leadership** provides protection from strong suppliers.

      b)   **Differentiation** may permit a firm to increase its price in response to suppliers' price increases.

      c)   **Focus strategies** must allow for the superior bargaining power of suppliers when sellers operate in a narrow, low-volume market. For example, focused differentiation may permit the firm to pass along suppliers' price increases.

6. **Target Market Approach to Competitive Strategies**

   a. The dominant firm in a market pursues a **market-leader strategy**.

      1) The leader should attempt to **increase total demand** in the market because the market leader will gain the most. Demand will increase if the firm

         a) Attracts **new users**.

            i) A **market-penetration strategy** focuses on customers who might use the product or service.

            ii) A **new-market segment strategy** pursues customers who have never used the product or service.

            iii) A **geographical expansion strategy** targets users in previously unserved localities.

         b) Encourages **new uses** of the product or service.

         c) Promotes **increased use**, for example, by planned obsolescence.

      2) The leader must **defend market share** through offensive and defensive actions.

         a) Constant innovation to improve products and services, control costs, and increase distribution effectiveness is the basis for a good **offensive strategy**. The leader must continuously improve the value offered to customers.

         b) Kotler and Singh have identified **six defense strategies**.

            i) A **position defense** strengthens the firm's **brand power**.

            ii) A **flank defense** creates outposts that protect the leader's position. For example, a firm might respond to a competitor's price attack on one of its major products by introducing new brands. One of these might be sold at the same price as the attacker's brand and a second at a lower price, in effect outflanking the attacker.

            iii) A **preemptive defense** anticipates an attack, such as by targeting particular competitors before they can launch assaults, flooding the market with products for every segment and niche, or by sending **market signals** indicating ways in which the leader intends to anticipate attacks.

            iv) A **counteroffensive defense** is a counterattack. For example, the leader may meet an attacker's price cuts in one market by slashing prices in another market that is more important to the attacker.

            v) A **mobile defense** may involve **market broadening**, a reorientation from a specific product to the underlying need. An example is the repositioning of oil companies as energy companies. An alternative is **market diversification**, an effect of conglomerate mergers of firms in wholly different industries.

            vi) A **contraction defense** is planned contraction or strategic withdrawal. This defense involves concentrating resources in the areas of greatest strength rather than defending all of the firm's positions.

      3) The leader may attempt to obtain a **greater market share**. In general, a firm that increases its market share in its **served (target) market**, as opposed to the total market, will increase profits if it adopts an appropriate strategy.

         a) This strategy must avoid the risk of **antitrust** suits.

         b) The **economic cost** of the strategy must be acceptable. Beyond a certain **optimal market share**, profits may decline. The incremental market share may not provide economies of scale and experience, costs borne by the market leader (e.g., legal and lobbying costs) may increase, and customers may want more than one supplier.

  c) The leader must adopt the right **marketing mix** (the marketing methods used). For example, market share should be earned, not bought by lower profit margins.

    i) Most firms that gain market share ordinarily are leaders in introducing new products, product quality, and marketing outlays.

 b. Trailing (runner-up) firms may choose a **market challenger strategy**.

  1) A challenger must determine its strategic objective (such as leadership or a larger market share) and specific targets

    a) The challenger may attack the leader, for example, by across-the-board innovation or by better serving the market.

    b) The attack may be directed at firms of similar size that are not serving the market, e.g., by failing to introduce new products or by overpricing.

    c) The challenger may seek to grow by absorbing small firms.

  2) Philip Kotler suggests five general **attack strategies** by a challenger.

    a) A **frontal attack** directly pits the firm's products, prices, promotions, and methods of distribution against the target's.

      i) An example of a modified frontal attack is price cutting, a strategy that may succeed if there is no retaliation and the perception is that the product's quality equals that of the target.

    b) A **flank attack** may be directed at a geographic or segmental weakness of the target (an underserved market) or an unmet need (such as the desire for more healthful fast food).

      i) A flank attack succeeds when market segments shift. The result is a gap in need fulfillment that the attacker can convert into a strong position in a profitable segment.

    c) An **encirclement attack** is used by a challenger with an advantage in resources. It is an assault on multiple marketing fronts.

    d) The **bypass attack** directs the assault against markets other than those where the competitive target is strong. It may involve diversification of products or geographic markets. It may also entail developing next-generation technology so as to move the competition to an arena where the challenger is in a stronger position.

    e) **Guerilla warfare** consists of numerous small attacks designed to reduce the strength of the target, e.g., by ad campaigns, carefully chosen price decreases, and lawsuits. Such warfare ordinarily must be followed by a different (and stronger) type of attack if the challenge is to succeed.

  3) The market challenger also must devise combinations of strategies that are more specific than the general strategies.

    a) **Price discounting** tends to succeed if buyers are price sensitive, the product and service are similar to the market leaders, and the discounts are not matched.

    b) **Lower-price goods** of average quality may substantially outsell higher quality goods if the price is much lower.

    c) **Prestige goods** are high-quality items sold at a high price.

    d) **Product proliferation** is a strategy based on better product variety.

    e) Other specific strategies emphasize improved service, development of a new distribution channel, increased marketing expenditures, or manufacturing efficiencies.

    c. **Market-follower strategies** are adopted by firms that do not wish to challenge the leader.

        1) These firms may adhere to the view that **product imitation** may be preferable to **product innovation**. Because the innovator has already incurred the expenses of bringing the new product to market, the imitator that introduces a similar product may be profitable without being the leader.

        2) Some industries are characterized by **conscious parallelism**. These industries (e.g., fertilizers and chemicals) tend to have high fixed costs and little product and image differentiation. Market followers tend to imitate the leader because competing for a greater market share provokes painful retaliation.

        3) A market follower requires a strategy to maintain its share of current and new customers, fend off challengers, protect its advantages (e.g., service or location), lower its costs, and improve the quality of its products and services.

            a) A **counterfeiter** operates illegally by selling copies on the underground market.

            b) A **cloner** sells cheap variations of a product with sufficient differentiation to avoid liability for counterfeiting.

            c) An **imitator** sells a product that is significantly differentiated, e.g., with respect to price, promotion, location, and packaging.

            d) An **adapter** improves products and may operate in different markets or evolve into a market challenger.

        4) Market followers ordinarily have lower percentage returns than market leaders.

    d. **Market-nicher** strategies are followed by small or mid-size firms that compete in small (niche) markets that may be overlooked by large firms.

        1) Successful niche marketers often have higher rates of return than firms in large markets. They often sell high quality products at premium prices and have low manufacturing costs.

            a) These firms excel in need satisfaction because they know their markets well.

        2) Successful niche marketers have high profit margins. By contrast, mass marketers sell in high volume.

        3) Niche marketers must create, expand, and protect their niches. The risk is that a niche may evaporate or be entered by a large firm.

        4) The essence of niche marketing is **specialization**. However, success often depends on **multiple niching**. Creating new niches diversifies risk and increases the firm's probability of survival.

    e. Choosing and implementing an effective target-market-based competitive strategy should never be at the expense of maintaining a customer orientation. Firms with this orientation are more likely to be alert to customer-related needs, threats, and opportunities than firms that are competitor oriented.

7. **Industry evolution.** The **five competitive forces** within an industry or market identified by Porter are a basis for analyzing its structure. However, that structure and the firm's competitive strategies appropriate to it will evolve. Early recognition of change and prompt adjustment of strategies are essential to maintaining a competitive advantage. The costs of adjustments will be lower and their benefits greater the sooner they are made.

    a. The analysis of industry evolution should begin with how it affects each competitive force (see Study Unit 1).

b.   Another concept useful in forecasting industry evolution is the **product life cycle (PLC)**. It has the following stages:

1)   **Precommercialization** (product development). The **strategy** in this stage is to innovate by conducting R&D, marketing research, and production tests. During product development, the firm has no sales, but it has high investment costs.

2)   The **introduction (embryonic) stage** is characterized by slow sales growth and lack of profits because of the high expenses of promotion and selective distribution to generate awareness of the product and encourage customers to try it. Thus, the per-customer cost is high. Competitors are few, basic versions of the product are produced, and higher-income customers (innovators) are usually targeted. Cost-plus prices are charged. They may initially be high to permit cost recovery when unit sales are low.

   a)   The **strategy** is to infiltrate the market, plan for financing to cope with losses, build supplier relations, increase production and marketing efforts, and plan for competition.

3)   In the **growth stage**, sales and profits increase rapidly, cost per customer decreases, customers are early adopters, new competitors enter an expanding market, new product models and features are introduced, and promotion spending declines or remains stable.

   a)   The **strategy** is to enter new market segments and distribution channels and attempt to build brand loyalty and achieve the maximum share of the market. Thus, prices are set to penetrate the market, distribution channels are extended, and the mass market is targeted through advertising. The firm advances by these means and by achieving economies of productive scale.

4)   Some writers identify a separate stage between growth and maturity. During the **shakeout period**, the overall growth rate falls, price cutting occurs, industry profits decrease, and weaker firms leave the market. The growth phase tends to result in too many competitive entrants, brands, and models; greater intensity of competition; and too much capacity. Furthermore, as technology evolves, industry standards develop and product differentiation is more difficult to sustain. Still another aspect of the shakeout stage is that other firms in the distribution channel may act in ways that have a negative effect on low-share competitors. For example, wholesalers and retailers may lower their costs by carrying fewer brands. Consequently, a firm's costs increase and its profits decrease during the shakeout stage. R&D, marketing, customer service, and trade incentives costs may increase as price cutting occurs because of overcapacity. As weaker competitors leave the market, the objective of a surviving firm is to further strengthen its position and gain market share.

   a)   The **strategy** is to eliminate weak products and product lines, strength R&D and engineering efforts, reduce prices through effective promotions, and improve relationships with other firms in the distribution channel (e.g., by reducing inventory carrying costs).

   b)   To implement its strategy, the firm must recognize the **beginning of the shakeout period**. The firm thereby avoids over-estimation of sales and too rapid expansion of capacity with its increase in per-unit costs.

   c)   The firm also must ensure that it has a **sustainable competitive advantage** as growth declines and competition increases. For example, the firm must recognize that an early quality advantage may disappear as competing products improve and customers focus more on price and service.

d) Finally, the firm should not emphasize short-term profits at the expense of long-term market share. Reducing marketing, R&D, and other costs to maintain profit levels may in the long-term reduce market share and increase per-unit costs.

5) In the **maturity stage**, sales peak but growth declines, competitors are most numerous but may begin to decline in number, and per-customer cost is low. Profits are high for large market-share firms. For others, profits may fall because of competitive price-cutting and increased R&D spending to develop improved versions of the product.

 a) The **strategy** is to defend market share and maximize profits through diversification of brands and models to enter new market segments, still more intensive distribution, cost cutting, advertising and promotions to encourage brand switching, and emphasizing customer service.

6) During the **decline stage**, sales and profits drop as prices are cut, and some firms leave the market. Customers include late adopters (laggards), and per-customer cost is low. Weak products and unprofitable distribution media are eliminated, and advertising budgets are pared to the level needed to retain the most loyal customers.

 a) The **strategy** is to withdraw by reducing production, promotion, and inventory.

7) **Criticisms** of the PLC concept are that some stages may be hard to distinguish, and their length may vary substantially among industries. Moreover, sales growth may not follow the pattern described on the previous page and above, partly because the firm's strategies affect growth. Still another consideration is that industry characteristics (degree of concentration, R&D costs, advertising costs, price competition, etc.) differ among industries.

c. According to Porter, the focus of the analysis of industry evolution should be on the **evolutionary processes** that cause structural change in an industry. They operate to move an industry from its **initial structure** (technology, entry and exit barriers, power of suppliers and buyers, product traits, beginning size constraints, etc.) to its **potential structure**. The nature of that structure and the speed at which it will be achieved are unlikely to be known. They depend on numerous factors that are hard to predict, such as innovations in technology and marketing, resources and skills of firms, favorable or unfavorable random events, and judgments about investments (e.g., which marketing or technology approaches to follow).

1) **Long-run changes in the industry growth rate** occur because of changes in external factors: demographic traits (such as consumer ages and income levels), trends in needs of buyers (caused by changes in regulation, tastes, lifestyles), relative positions of substitute products, relative positions of complementary products, and sales to new customers (market penetration). Product innovation, an internal factor, alters the industry's position regarding the external factors.

2) **Changes in buyer (customer) segments served** occur when new segments are created (e.g., sale of computers to scientists, then to business, and finally to consumers), existing segments are subdivided, and old segments are no longer served.

3) **Learning by buyers** who become more sophisticated and better informed causes a decrease in product differentiation. These buyers tend increasingly to demand similar product characteristics (quality, service, etc.). Thus, products may become more akin to commodities. This effect may be offset by changes in the product or its marketing and by attracting new, inexperienced customers.

4) **Reduction of uncertainty** about such factors as the potential market size, resolution of technical problems, possible buyers, and marketing methods occurs as a result of experimentation. Successful strategies will be imitated and unsuccessful strategies will be discarded. Moreover, the reduction in risk will attract new and often larger competitors, especially if the potential market is large.

5) **Proprietary knowledge** may become more available to potential competitors as the industry evolves. This diffusion may result from reverse engineering (a form of imitation) or another form of competitive intelligence (e.g., that obtained from suppliers, distributors, or customers), expiration of patents, purchase, migration of personnel to new firms, and spinoffs of operating segments. The problem of diffusion may be met by creation of a substantial capacity to develop new proprietary knowledge.

6) **Accumulation of experience** (the learning-curve effect) permits unit costs of manufacturers to decrease. This lead may not be sustainable because of diffusion of proprietary knowledge. A one-time leader may then be at a disadvantage because it has incurred costs not borne by its competitor-imitators.

7) **Expansion** of industry scale and firm scale permits a broader group of strategies to be implemented, with potentially greater economies of scale, capital needs, and desirability and feasibility of vertical integration. Also, suppliers and customers in an expanding industry will gain bargaining power. All these factors raise entry barriers.

   a) An increase in the scale of the industry may attract new, large firms once the scale has reached a level that provides sufficient opportunity to justify the necessary investment.

   b) Contraction of an industry has effects opposite to those of expansion.

8) **Changes in input costs** most directly affect the cost and price of the product and the demand for it. These changes also affect the existence of economies of scale and may promote substitution of inputs, reorganization of production, and use of different marketing media. Distribution channels and geographic market boundaries also may be altered.

9) **Product innovation** may broaden markets or increase product differentiation. Furthermore, barriers are affected because innovation may involve high costs to market new products. It may also change marketing, distribution, and manufacturing methods and the related economies of scale.

   a) Innovation cancels buyer experience and therefore changes purchasing behavior.

   b) Product innovation may come from external sources and from suppliers and buyers.

10) **Marketing innovation** (e.g., in media, channels, or themes) may increase demand by differentiating the product, appealing to new buyers, or lowering costs. Indirect effects may include changes in economies of scale, e.g., as a result of changing to a wider-scope but more expensive medium.

11) **Process innovation** in manufacturing may affect the degree to which it is more or less capital intensive, economies of scale, vertical integration, the proportions of fixed and variable costs, and the gaining of experience, among other things.

12) **Structural changes in suppliers' and customers' industries** affect their bargaining power. For example, as concentration of customers' industries increases, the tendency is for sellers' industries to become more concentrated so as to counter their greater power.

13) **Government policies** affect industry evolution by explicit regulation of entry, competitive practices, licensing, and pricing. Moreover, strong government regulation has profound effects on foreign trade and global competition.

14) **Entry** changes industry structure, especially when strong outsiders with special skills and large resources are the entrants. Entry occurs when outside firms believe that potential growth and profits justify the costs of entry.

15) **Exit** is motivated by diminished returns on investment. It is impeded by exit barriers. Exit improves the position of the remaining firms, but exit barriers weaken those firms.

16) Firms should consider how each evolutionary process may affect industry structure, their strategic position, and the ways of coping with the resulting change. Thus, firms must monitor the environment for the **strategic signals** relative to each evolutionary process. Moreover, firms must be aware that some processes (e.g., learning) may be operating without the occurrence of obvious external events.

d. **Key Relationships**

1) An industry is a **system**. Hence, a change in one subsystem (e.g., marketing) tends to trigger cascading changes elsewhere (e.g., in manufacturing methods leading to greater economies of scale and backward vertical integration that reduces suppliers' power).

2) **Industry concentration and mobility barriers** are directly correlated. Thus, increasing barriers normally predict increasing concentration.

3) **Low or decreasing barriers** generally signify an absence of concentration because unsuccessful exiting firms will likely be replaced.

4) **Exit barriers** keep unsuccessful firms in the industry and therefore limit concentration to the detriment of successful firms.

5) **Potential for above-average long-term profits** for the remaining firms depends on an industry's structure in its maturity stage, i.e., the presence of high mobility barriers.

6) **Industry boundaries** change, for example, when refrigeration and genetic engineering allowed perishables to be transported long distances.

7) Firms may **influence industry structure** by initiating changes (e.g., product, marketing, or process innovation) or responding to changes (e.g., by influencing regulation or licensing externally developed technology to control its diffusion).

8. Stop and review! You have completed the outline for this subunit. Study multiple-choice questions 14 through 26 beginning on page 116.

4.3 BUSINESS PORTFOLIO CONCEPTS

1. A large firm has multiple businesses. Thus, the concept of the **strategic business unit** is useful for strategic planning by large firms. An SBU is a business (or a group) for which separate planning is possible. An SBU also has its own competitors and a manager who engages in strategic planning and is responsible for the major determinants of profit. Accordingly, a large firm may be viewed as a portfolio of investments in the form of SBUs.

2. **Techniques of portfolio analysis** have been developed to aid management in making decisions about resource allocation, new business startups and acquisitions, downsizing, and divestitures.

    a. One of the two portfolio models most frequently used for competitive analysis was created by the **Boston Consulting Group (BCG)**. This model, the **growth-share matrix**, has two variables. The **market growth rate (MGR)** is on the vertical axis, and each SBU's **relative market share (RMS)** is on the horizontal axis. The size of each circle indicates the size of the SBU.

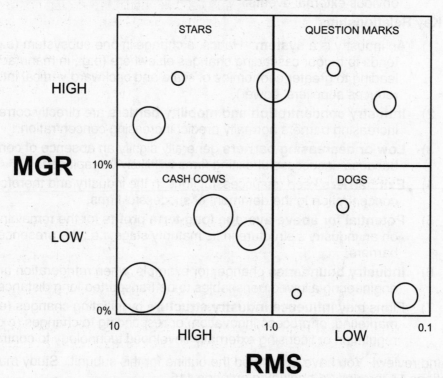

1) The annual MGR is stated in constant units of the currency used in the measurement. It reflects the maturity and attractiveness of the market and the relative need for cash to finance expansion.

    a) An MGR of **10% or more** is generally regarded as high.

2) The RMS reflects the SBU's competitive position in the market segment. It equals the SBU's absolute market share divided by that of its leading competitor.

    a) An RMS of **1.0 or more** signifies that the SBU has a strong competitive position.

3) The growth-share matrix has four quadrants. The firm's SBUs are commonly represented in their appropriate quadrants by circles. The size of a circle is directly proportional to the SBU's sales volume.

   a) **Dogs** (low RMS, low MGR) are weak competitors in low-growth markets. Their net cash flow (plus/minus) is modest.

   b) **Question marks** (low RMS, high MGR) are weak competitors in high-growth markets. They need large amounts of cash not only to finance growth and keep pace with the market but also to increase RMS, but do poorly in cash generation. If RMS increases significantly, a question mark may become a star. If not, it becomes a dog.

   c) **Cash cows** (high RMS, low MGR) are strong competitors and cash generators. An SBU that is a cash cow ordinarily enjoys high profit margins and economies of scale. Financing for expansion is not needed, so the SBU's excess cash can be used for investments in other SBUs. However, marketing and R&D expenditures should not necessarily be slashed excessively. Maximizing net cash inflow might precipitate a premature decline from cash cow to dog.

   d) **Stars** (high RMS, high MGR) are strong competitors in high growth markets. Such an SBU is profitable, but needs large amounts of cash for expansion, R&D, and to meet competitors' attacks. Net cash flow (plus/minus) is modest.

   e) A portfolio of SBUs should not have too many dogs and question marks or too few cash cows and stars.

4) Each SBU should have objectives, a strategy should be formulated to achieve those objectives, and a budget should be allocated.

   a) A **hold strategy** is used for strong cash cows.

   b) A **build strategy** is necessary for a question mark with the potential to be a star.

   c) A **harvest strategy** maximizes short-term net cash inflow. Harvesting means zero-budgeting R&D, reducing marketing costs, not replacing facilities, etc. This strategy is used for weak cash cows and possibly question marks and dogs.

   d) A **divest strategy** is normally used for question marks and dogs that reduce the firm's profitability. The proceeds of sale or liquidation are then invested more favorably.

      i) A harvest strategy may undermine a future divestiture by decreasing the fair value of the SBU.

5) The **life cycle of a successful SBU** is reflected by its movement within the growth-share matrix. The progression is from question mark to star, cash cow, and dog. Accordingly, a firm should consider an SBU's current status and its probable progression when formulating a strategy.

6) A serious **mistake** is not to tailor objectives (e.g., rates of return or growth) to the circumstances of each SBU.

   a) Cash cows should not be underfunded. The risk is premature decline. However, overfunding cash cows means less investment in SBUs with greater growth prospects.

   b) A large investment in a dog with little likelihood of a turnaround is also a typical mistake.

   c) A firm also should not have too many question marks. Results are excess risk and underfunded SBUs.

b.   The other most frequently used (and more detailed) portfolio model for competitive analysis was developed by **General Electric**. Shell, McKinsey and Company, and Arthur D. Little also have developed portfolio models. The GE model is a multifactor portfolio matrix with two variables. **Business strength or competitive position (BUS)** is on one axis, and **market attractiveness (MAT)** is on the other.

1)   BUS is classified as strong, medium, or weak, and MAT is classified as high, medium, or low. Thus, the matrix in this model is 3 × 3 and has **nine cells**.

2)   SBUs are shown in the matrix as **circles**. **Circle size** is directly proportional to the **size of the related market**, with a shaded portion in the circle that represents the SBU's **market share**.

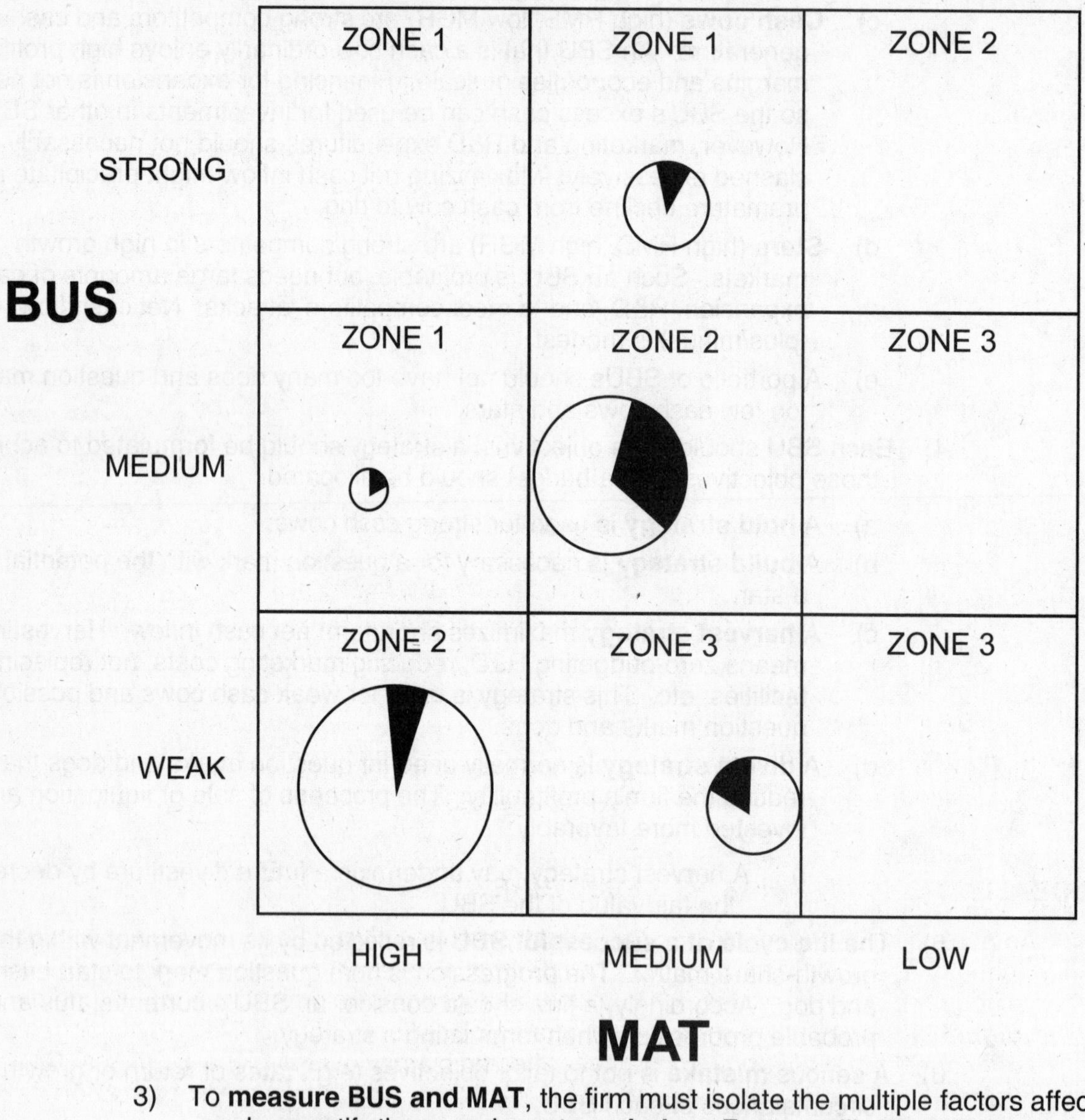

	HIGH	MEDIUM	LOW
STRONG	ZONE 1	ZONE 1	ZONE 2
MEDIUM	ZONE 1	ZONE 2	ZONE 3
WEAK	ZONE 2	ZONE 3	ZONE 3

BUS

MAT

3)   To **measure BUS and MAT**, the firm must isolate the multiple factors affecting each, quantify them, and create an **index**. Factors will vary with each business. The measurements will provide the values on the axes of the matrix.

a)   Typical **BUS factors** are the SBU's size, market share, growth rate, customer loyalty, profit margins, distribution network, technology position, and marketing skills.

b)   Typical **MAT factors** are market size, growth rate, competitive intensity, price levels, profit margins, technology requirements, and degree of regulation.

        c)   One approach to the computation of BUS or MAT is to rate each factor on a scale from 1 to 5 (the highest ranking), weight each ranking by the factor's relative significance (0 to 1.0 each for a total of 1.0), and add the results.

    4)   The nine cells in the matrix may be classified into **three zones**.

        a)   **Zone 1 (strong BUS and high MAT, medium BUS and high MAT, strong BUS and medium MAT).** The SBUs in the three cells in the upper left corner have strong overall attractiveness. Investment and growth are indicated.

        b)   **Zone 2 (strong BUS and low MAT, medium BUS and MAT, weak BUS and high MAT).** The SBUs in the three cells on the diagonal from the lower left to the upper right of the matrix have medium overall attractiveness. Selective investment and management for earnings are indicated.

        c)   **Zone 3 (medium BUS and low MAT, weak BUS and medium MAT, weak BUS and low MAT).** The SBUs in the three cells in the lower right corner have low overall attractiveness. A harvest or divest strategy is indicated.

    5)   Forecasts for the next 3-5 years should be made to estimate each SBU's position given the current strategy, the stage of the product life cycle, competitor actions, and other events. These forecasts may be indicated by arrows drawn on the matrix.

  c.   Portfolio models should be used with care. They may over-emphasize entry into high growth markets and increasing market share and may lead to inadequate attention to current SBUs.

    1)   Moreover, because averages and weights are used in many models, they are subject to manipulation. Also, businesses in the same cell may have very different ratings for the multiple analytical factors.

    2)   Strategies for SBUs in the middle positions may be hard to determine.

    3)   Synergies among SBUs are ignored. Thus, divesting a low-rated SBU may be a mistake because of benefits it offers to other SBUs, such as a vital core competency.

3.   Stop and review! You have completed the outline for this subunit. Study multiple-choice questions 27 through 29 beginning on page 120.

4.4 GLOBALIZATION AND INDUSTRY STRUCTURE

1.   An analysis of the competition in an industry requires consideration of the economics of the industry and the characteristics of competitors. However, in a global industry, the analysis extends not to one market, but to all markets (geographic or national) taken together. A **global industry** is "one in which the strategic positions of competitors in major geographic or national markets are fundamentally affected by their overall global positions" (Michael E. Porter). The rapid proliferation of global industries, also known as **globalization**, is an extremely significant development.

  a.   A true global industry is one that requires a firm to compete internationally. Accordingly, an **industry is not global** simply because some or all competitors are multinational. When nonmultinationals can compete in a geographic or national market, the industry is not global.

b.   Global competition obviously differs in important ways from national competition. For example, costs, market characteristics, and the roles of governments vary among countries. Available resources, competitive monitoring, and objectives also vary. Nevertheless, the **five competitive forces** and the basic, underlying **structural factors** are the same as in national competition. Of course, the structural analysis of the forces and factors must still address foreign competitors, a larger group of possible entrants, a wider range of substitute products, and an even higher probability that firms will vary in their strategic objectives and corporate cultures.

c.   The primary issues are whether a firm should compete and the extent of the threat to the firm from global competition.

2.   **Sources of Global Competitive Advantage**

a.   Participation in foreign markets is usually by **licensing; export**; or, after the firm has obtained experience, **direct investment**. A genuinely global industry will have significant export activity or direct investment. Nevertheless, direct investment does not necessarily signal the existence of global competition. Direct investment also may occur when purely national factors determine a subsidiary's competitive position.

b.   An industry becomes global because it perceives a **net strategic advantage** to competing. Thus, the sources of competitive advantage must have greater weight than the impediments. A firm should consider the materiality of the source of advantage to total cost. Moreover, it also should consider the element of the business where the firm has a global competitive advantage. Still another consideration is that the sources of advantage reflect the implied presence of **mobility barriers**.

c.   The **competitive advantage** of a nation regarding the cost or quality of a product means that it will produce and export the product. Consequently, a global firm's position in that nation is vital.

d.   **Economies of scale in centralized production** may yield a cost advantage achievable only when output exceeds the demand in one country and exports are feasible. Vertical integration may provide the necessary scale.

e.   **Global experience** may result in more rapid movement along the learning curve when similar products are sold in multiple national markets. Thus, the global firm may be first to achieve the maximum cost advantage from experience. Its cumulative production volume grows more rapidly than that of a purely national firm.

f.   **Logistical economies of scale** may be attained by a global firm that spreads its fixed costs by supplying multiple national markets. A logistical cost advantage also may result because a global firm uses specialized logistical systems.

g.   **Marketing economies of scale** may exceed the volume achievable in a national market even though much marketing is necessarily local. For example, one sales force may be employed globally when buyers are few and technical considerations are complex. Furthermore, some brands require no incremental investment to have international strength. Also, some advertising campaigns may be effective across national borders.

h.   **Purchasing economies of scale** may confer a cost advantage. A global firm will make larger purchases than a purely national firm. One result may be longer and therefore more economical production runs. Another result may be greater bargaining power versus suppliers.

i.   **Product differentiation** through enhanced image and reputation may be achieved in national markets by operating globally.

j.   **Proprietary technology** may be applicable in multiple national markets, thereby creating a global competitive advantage. Furthermore, achieving such an advantage may only be feasible in a global industry. Economies of scale for R&D may only be attainable when the market is global. Also, global operation may help a firm to stay in touch with new developments.

k.   **Mobility of production** allows a global firm to more readily achieve economies of scale and share proprietary technology among operating activities in multiple national markets. For example, a construction firm may have a larger organization than would be feasible in a national market. The fixed costs of that organization and of developing its technology will be lower relative to revenues because the global market is greater. Global operation is more likely to be profitable when construction crews and equipment are mobile.

3.   **Impediments to Global Competition**

a.   Impediments may increase direct costs, make management more difficult, be imposed by governments or institutions, or consist of perceptual or resource limitations. Impediments that do not block global competition may still create niches for national firms.

b.   **High transportation and storage costs** may require construction of plants in each market.

c.   **Product needs may differ** from country to country because of culture, climate, degree of economic development, income, legal requirements, technical standards, and other factors. This barrier limits global procurement and achievement of economies of scale and experience. The height of the barrier depends on the costs of product modifications. **Complex segmentation within geographic markets** has similar effects.

d.   Access to **established distribution channels** may be **difficult**, especially when large volumes of low-cost items are sold. Concessions required to persuade a channel to substitute the product for a domestic producer's may be too great.

e.   The **need for a direct sales force** creates a barrier based on a diseconomy of scale, especially if local competitors' sales agents market wide product lines. The need for **local repair** is similar.

f.   Sensitivity to lead times means that global firms may not respond with the necessary rapidity to **changes in fashion, technology, etc.**, in a national market. Centralized functions may be at too great a distance from that market to meet quickly evolving customer needs, especially when local needs vary. The relevant lead times include those for physical transportation at an economically acceptable cost.

g.   **Lack of world demand** may derive from the product's lack of appeal except in a few markets or its early position in the **product life cycle of world trade**. Initial introduction of the product is in a few markets where the product has the greatest appeal. Demand then builds elsewhere by product imitation and technology diffusion, resulting in exports and foreign investment by the pioneer firms. Greater demand and diffusion may also result in production in other markets by foreign firms. During the maturity stage, the product is standardized, price competition increases, and local firms enter the market. Thus, global competition may require some industry maturity, but the level of maturity is lower when experienced global competitors can rapidly spread the product to new markets.

h.   **Differing marketing tasks** are required in different national markets. Hence, local firms with superior marketing experience in their countries may have the advantage. A possible solution is to have a local marketing function.

i.   Local firms tend to be more responsive than global firms when **intensive local services** or other customer contacts are necessary. Hence, the local firm's advantages in marketing and other services could outweigh the global firm's advantages.

j.   **Governmental impediments** to global competition are generally imposed for the announced purpose of protecting local firms and jobs and developing new industries. They also may have the effect of raising revenue. Examples of impediments are tariffs; duties; quotas; domestic content rules; preferences for local firms regarding procurement, taxes, R&D, labor regulations, and other operating rules; and laws (e.g., anti-bribery or tax) enacted by a national government that impede national firms from competing globally. These impediments are most likely when industries are viewed as crucial.

k.   **Perceptual impediments** arise because the complexities of global competition may impair the firm's ability to identify (visualize) global opportunities.

l.   **Resource impediments** consist of information and search costs, the costs of large-scale facilities construction, and the investments needed to penetrate new markets.

4.   **Evolution of Global Markets**

a.   The **triggers** of this evolution establish or exploit the **sources** of global competitive advantage. In the alternative, if resources are adequate, they negate the **impediments** to global competition. Moreover, a **strategic innovation** is always necessary for the industry to become global.

1)   **Access to the largest markets** also may be critical to the successful globalization of an industry.

b.   **Environmental triggers** include an increase in any of the types of economies of scale, lower transportation or storage costs, changes in distribution channels that facilitate access by foreign firms, changes in the costs of the factors of production, increased similarity of economic and social conditions in other nations, and reduction of governmental limitations.

c.   **Strategic innovations** may begin globalization even if environmental triggers are not present.

1)   **Product redefinition** may take the form of a reduction in national product differences resulting from industry maturity and product standardization. However, a marketing innovation that redefines the product's concept or image may make it more acceptable in global markets.

2)   **Identification of common market segments** among countries that are badly served by national firms is possible even if national product differences persist.

3)   Despite national product differences, **reducing the costs of adapting the product**, for example, by modularization or increasing the product's range of compatibility, may permit global competition. **Design changes** may have the same impact when they result in standardization of components.

4)   Combining centralized production with local assembly (deintegration of production) may satisfy governmental requirements while creating sufficient economies of scale to trigger global competition.

5)   **Elimination of resource or perceptual constraints** may result from entry of new firms with greater resources or with a fresher perspective that is helpful in developing new strategies and identifying new opportunities.

5.   **Strategic Alternatives in Global Industries**

a.   **Broad line global competition** is competition over the full product line of the firm based on differentiation or low cost. The firm needs large resources for this long-term strategy. Governmental relations should emphasize impediment reduction.

b.   A **global focus strategy** is limited to an industry segment with low impediments where the firm can defend its position against broad line firms. The focus of competition is low cost or product differentiation.

    c.   A **national focus strategy** is limited to a national market or the segments with the greatest impediments to global competitors. Low cost or product differentiation is the focus of competition.

    d.   A **protected niche strategy** is applied in nations where global competitors are discouraged by governmental impediments. The strategy is designed to be effective in markets with governmental constraints and requires close attention to the national government.

    e.   **Transnational coalitions** may be created to help the firms overcome impediments to executing the broader strategies, for example, market access or technology barriers.

6.   **Trends in Global Competition**

    a.   **Economic differences** among developed and newly developed countries have narrowed.

    b.   Some countries are pursuing more **aggressive industrial policies** by providing resources to stimulate industries to achieve global status.

    c.   **Governmental protection of distinctive national assets**, such as natural assets, is reflected in direct ownership or joint ventures with private firms. A large labor pool is another asset increasingly recognized by some governments.

7.   Stop and review! You have completed the outline for this subunit. Study multiple-choice questions 30 through 33 beginning on page 121.

4.5 CORE CONCEPTS

The Marketing Process

- The **marketing process** involves: analyzing marketing opportunities, choosing target markets, formulating marketing strategies, planning the marketing program and mix, and managing the marketing effort.
- Businesses should be **defined in market terms**, that is, in terms of needs and customer groups.
- The **scope of marketing** may be broadly defined as demand management.
- The **business-process approach** to value creation and delivery is to involve marketing in all phases, including strategic planning.

Marketing Strategies

- The analysis of **marketing opportunities** begins with market-oriented strategic planning. It addresses the structural analysis of industries and competition, including the five **competitive forces**, the nature of a firm's **competitive advantages** (its competencies, resources, and capabilities), and the **generic strategies** based on those advantages.
- One way to describe an industry considers the **number of sellers** and the **extent of differentiation** of products and services, an approach used in microeconomics.
- Another way to characterize an industry is by reference to its **entry, exit, or mobility barriers**.
- A **strategic group** consists of firms in an industry that have adopted **similar competitive strategies**. Hence, a potential entrant into an industry must consider which strategic group to target.
- Michael E. Porter describes **four generic strategies** to be applied to business units: cost leadership, differentiation, cost focus, and focused differentiation.
- Porter's generic strategies are responses to the **five competitive forces**: rivalry among existing firms; threats of, and barriers to, entry; the threat of substitutes; buyers' bargaining power; and the threat of suppliers' bargaining power.

Business Portfolio Concepts

- The **growth-share matrix**, created by the Boston Consulting Group, plots a firm's SBUs relative to two variables, market growth rate (high or low) and relative market share (high or low). The interaction of these two factors allows the firm to classify its SBUs into four categories: dogs, question marks, cash cows, and stars.
- The other most frequently used portfolio model was developed by **General Electric**. The two variables are business strength (strong, medium, or weak) and market attractiveness (high, medium, or low). A firm can determine the proper strategy for an SBU after plotting into which of three zones the SBU is classified.

Globalization and Industry Structure

- The **five competitive forces** and the basic, underlying structural factors **are the same** in global competition as in national competition.
- **Global competitive advantage** may be gained by, for example, economies of scale in centralized production, product differentiation, and mobility of production.
- **Impediments** to global competition include high transportation and storage costs; the need for a direct sales force; difficulty of responding to changes in fashion, technology, etc.; and governmental impediments.
- **Strategic alternatives in global industries** include broad line global competition, a global focus strategy, a national focus strategy, a protected niche strategy, and transnational coalitions.

QUESTIONS

4.1   The Marketing Process

1. Which of the following is an example of the market-oriented definition of a business?

A. We make air conditioners and furnaces.

B. We supply energy.

C. We produce movies.

D. We sell men's shirts and pants.

Answer (B) is correct. *(CIA, adapted)*
REQUIRED: The market-oriented business definition.
DISCUSSION: Businesses should be defined in market terms, that is, in terms of needs and customer groups. Moreover, a distinction should be made between a target market definition and a strategic market definition. For example, a target market for a railroad might be freight hauling, but a strategic market might be transportation of any goods and people. Accordingly, stating that a business supplies energy is a market-oriented definition as opposed to the product-oriented definition.
Answer (A) is incorrect because air conditioners and furnaces are products, not customer needs. Answer (C) is incorrect because movies are products, (i.e., entertainment), not a customer need. Answer (D) is incorrect because shirts and pants are products, not an underlying need.

2. The scope of marketing extends to

A. Synchromarketing to reverse declining demand.

B. Demarketing to reverse negative demand.

C. Management of demand.

D. Making consumers aware of existing products that satisfy latent demand.

Answer (C) is correct. *(Publisher, adapted)*
REQUIRED: The scope of marketing.
DISCUSSION: The scope of marketing may be broadly defined as demand management. It extends to marketing not only goods and services but also experiences, people, events, entities, places, information, properties, and ideas. These tasks vary with the nature, volume, components, and timing of demand for what is marketed.
Answer (A) is incorrect because synchromarketing changes the demand pattern (e.g., from seasonal to year round). Answer (B) is incorrect because intentional demand reduction is demarketing. Answer (D) is incorrect because latent demand is not currently being met by existing products.

3. The elements of the marketing mix from the seller's perspective are known as the 4 Ps. Each class of marketing tools corresponds to one of the 4 Cs, the classes of customer benefits. Which of the following is a correspondence between a customer's 4 Cs and a seller's 4 Ps?

    A. Customer solution - Price.

    B. Convenience - Place.

    C. Customer cost - Perception.

    D. Communication - Process.

Answer (B) is correct. *(Publisher, adapted)*
    REQUIRED: The correspondence between the 4 Ps and the 4 Cs.
    DISCUSSION: The categories of controllable elements in a marketing program reflect the decisions to be made about the marketing mix (the combination of marketing tools). From the seller's perspective, the categories of marketing tools are product, price, place, and promotion (sometimes called the "4 Ps" of marketing). The seller chooses tools from these categories to develop a marketing mix for achieving its objectives in the target market. From the buyer's perspective, each class of marketing tools corresponds to a customer benefit: customer solution (product), customer cost (price), convenience (place), and communication (promotion). Thus, a firm will succeed by using the 4 Ps to deliver the 4 Cs of marketing. For example, decisions about place (distribution channels, delivery options, locations, etc.) should provide the optimal feasible convenience for customers.
    Answer (A) is incorrect because product corresponds to the customer solution benefit. Answer (C) is incorrect because price is customer cost. Answer (D) is incorrect because promotion corresponds to communication with customers.

4. Marketing is involved in all phases of the business-process approach to value creation and delivery. In the tactical marketing phase, the firm

    A. Defines market segments.

    B. Selects target markets.

    C. Develops the offering.

    D. Uses an integrated marketing process to communicate value.

Answer (D) is correct. *(Publisher, adapted)*
    REQUIRED: The tactical marketing activity.
    DISCUSSION: The firm delivers and communicates value in the tactical marketing stage. Communication of value is done through an integrated marketing communication process. Instead of an emphasis on one method (e.g., advertising or the sales force), modern marketers combine promotional methods so that a consistent and favorable image will be communicated to customers whenever they have contact with the brand.
    Answer (A) is incorrect because the firm defines market segments in the strategic marketing phase. Answer (B) is incorrect because the firm selects target markets in the strategic marketing phase. Answer (C) is incorrect because the firm develops the offering in the strategic marketing phase.

5. Positioning the market offering most likely requires

    A. Establishing the offering in the minds of customers.

    B. Entering a target market.

    C. Anticipating or countering a competitor's move in a market.

    D. Providing value to customers.

Answer (A) is correct. *(Publisher, adapted)*
    REQUIRED: The nature of market positioning.
    DISCUSSION: Positioning is the process of designing the offering so that it will have a distinct and favorable place in the minds of customers. Thus, the firm's value proposition (the combination of benefits offered) should give customers in the target market good reasons to purchase the offering.
    Answer (B) is incorrect because segmenting, targeting, and positioning involve choosing value. Market entry begins the process of delivering value. Answer (C) is incorrect because many competitive moves do not involve positioning. Answer (D) is incorrect because delivery of value entails product or service development (choice of features), setting prices, production or outsourcing, and distribution.

6. Strategic marketing involves

    A. Market opportunity analysis.

    B. Developing a brand.

    C. Developing a brand image.

    D. Delivering value.

Answer (A) is correct. *(Publisher, adapted)*
    REQUIRED: The element of strategic marketing.
    DISCUSSION: The strategic marketing stage includes choosing target markets. These segments provide the best marketing opportunities. A "marketing opportunity is an area of buyer need or potential interest in which a company can perform profitably" (Kotler, *Marketing Management*). Market opportunity analysis determines whether benefits (value) can be communicated effectively to the target markets, the communication can be done with a cost effective promotional mix and distribution strategy, the firm has the necessary resources, and the firm can provide the chosen value better than its possible competitors.
    Answer (B) is incorrect because developing a brand is done in the tactical marketing stage. It involves communication of value. Answer (C) is incorrect because developing a brand image is done in the tactical marketing stage. It involves communication of value. Answer (D) is incorrect because the firm delivers and communicates value in the tactical marketing stage.

7. According to Japanese researchers, an objective of the marketing program should include

    A. Determining the optimal level of inventory.

    B. Intermittent receipt of feedback.

    C. The earliest possible implementation of improvements.

    D. Treating product defects as a function of the production process.

Answer (C) is correct. *(Publisher, adapted)*
REQUIRED: The objective of the marketing program.
DISCUSSION: Japanese writers suggest that the objectives of the marketing process should include continuous receipt of feedback as a basis for better products and marketing efforts, implementing improvements as quickly as feasible, using just-in-time inventory systems, minimizing production set-up time and cost, and minimizing product defects.
    Answer (A) is incorrect because the Japanese stress JIT principles. Answer (B) is incorrect because feedback should be continuous. Answer (D) is incorrect because product defects are everyone's concern.

8. Which of the following is accomplished during the process of planning the marketing program and mix?

    A. Organizing resources.

    B. A SWOT analysis.

    C. Determining when, where, how, and by whom plans will be executed.

    D. Conducting sales variance analysis.

Answer (B) is correct. *(Publisher, adapted)*
REQUIRED: The element of the process of planning the marketing program and mix.
DISCUSSION: Planning the marketing program and mix is the process of determining how marketing strategies formulated in accordance with a SWOT (strengths, weaknesses, opportunities, and threats) analysis may be implemented. The firm must decide what resources should be devoted to the marketing effort, for example, budgeting outlays as a percentage of sales. Total expenditures may be increased to secure a larger market share. The next step is to allocate the budgeted resources to the elements of the marketing mix (the 4 Ps or 4 Cs of marketing).
    Answer (A) is incorrect because organizing resources is part of managing the marketing effort. Answer (C) is incorrect because marketing implementation determines how marketing strategies and plans will be executed, when, where, and by whom. Answer (D) is incorrect because conducting sales variance analysis is a marketing control procedure.

9. The marketing organization may take which forms?

  I.   A cross-disciplinary team
  II. A sales department team
  III. Separate sales and marketing departments
  IV. Sales and marketing reporting to a vice-president

    A. I and IV only.

    B. I and II only.

    C. II, III, and IV only.

    D. I, II, III, and IV.

Answer (D) is correct. *(Publisher, adapted)*
REQUIRED: The forms of the marketing organization.
DISCUSSION: The marketing organization should be able to implement the marketing plan. The following are types of marketing organizations: sales department only; sales department with some marketing functions, such as advertising and research; marketing department separate from sales; marketing and sales departments reporting to a vice-president of marketing and sales; the same, except that everyone is customer- and market-centered; and process and outcome organizations, with departments replaced by cross-disciplinary teams managed by process leaders.
    Answer (A) is incorrect because a sales department performing a purely selling function is the simplest form of marketing organization. Another possible form of marketing organization is a marketing department separate from sales. Answer (B) is incorrect because separate sales and marketing departments reporting to a vice-president of marketing and sales and a marketing department separate from sales with no specialized vice-president responsible for both are possible organizational forms. Answer (C) is incorrect because a cross-disciplinary team is the latest stage in the evolution of marketing organizations.

10. Which necessary approach to marketing control is the responsibility of senior and middle management and is directed toward achievement of planned objectives?

    A. Annual-plan control.

    B. Profitability control.

    C. Efficiency control.

    D. Strategic control.

Answer (A) is correct. *(Publisher, adapted)*
    REQUIRED: The approach to marketing control directed toward achievement of planned objectives.
    DISCUSSION: Annual-plan control should be overseen by senior and middle management. It is applied at all levels of the firm using management-by-objectives (MBO) methods. Annual plan control is directed toward reaching sales, profitability, and other objectives defined in the annual plan. Interim-period objectives are set, performance is monitored, the causes of variances are identified, and corrective action is taken.
    Answer (B) is incorrect because profitability control is the responsibility of the marketing controller. It is limited to profitability analysis. Answer (C) is incorrect because efficiency control is the responsibility of line and staff managers and the marketing controller. It monitors and improves the efficiency of marketing expenditures. Answer (D) is incorrect because strategic control is the responsibility of senior management and the marketing auditor. It determines whether marketing strategy is appropriate for market conditions and the optimal marketing opportunities are being addressed.

11. In a market-share analysis, the relative market share equals

    A. Sales divided by total market sales.

    B. Sales divided by sales of largest competitor.

    C. Sales divided by the served market.

    D. Firm customers divided by all customers.

Answer (B) is correct. *(Publisher, adapted)*
    REQUIRED: The relative market share.
    DISCUSSION: The relative market share measures a firm's competitive position. If it exceeds 1.0, the firm is the market leader. A rising measurement signifies that the firm is gaining.
    Answer (A) is incorrect because sales divided by total market sales is overall market share. Answer (C) is incorrect because sales divided by the served market is served market share. Answer (D) is incorrect because firm customers divided by all customers is customer penetration.

12. The served market share

    A. Decreases when profits decrease.

    B. Measures customer loyalty.

    C. Always exceeds overall market share.

    D. Must be less than overall market share.

Answer (C) is correct. *(Publisher, adapted)*
    REQUIRED: The true statement about the served market share.
    DISCUSSION: Served market share (sales ÷ the served market, i.e., all buyers willing and able to buy the firm's product) must exceed the overall market share. The served market is smaller than the total market.
    Answer (A) is incorrect because a market-share decrease may result in higher profits if unprofitable products have been dropped. Answer (B) is incorrect because customer loyalty equals purchases from the firm divided by total purchases of the same products. Answer (D) is incorrect because the served market is smaller than the total market.

13. Assuming other factors are held constant, the dollar value of the firm's overall market share will increase when

    A. Customer penetration decreases.

    B. The average purchase from the average firm increases.

    C. Total purchases from sellers of the same products increases.

    D. Price selectivity increases.

Answer (D) is correct. *(Publisher, adapted)*
    REQUIRED: The reason the dollar value of the firm's overall market share will increase.
    DISCUSSION: An increase in price selectivity (firm's average price ÷ average price of all firms) results in an increase in the dollar value of the overall market share. Thus, the firm's average price may have risen, or the average price of its competitors may have fallen.
    Answer (A) is incorrect because, when customer penetration decreases, overall market share decreases if other factors are held constant. Answer (B) is incorrect because, when customer selectivity (average purchase from the firm ÷ average purchase from the average firm) decreases, overall market share decreases. Answer (C) is incorrect because, when customer loyalty (purchases from the firm ÷ total purchases from sellers of the same products) decreases, overall market share decreases.

4.2 Marketing Strategies

14. In which industry structure is differentiation absent, and all sellers charge the same price?

    A. Monopoly.

    B. Monopolistic competition.

    C. Oligopoly.

    D. Pure competition.

Answer (D) is correct. *(Publisher, adapted)*
    REQUIRED: The industry structure in which differentiation is absent and the same prices are charged by all sellers.
    DISCUSSION: An industry consists of firms selling products or services that are substitutes. One way to describe an industry considers the number of sellers and the extent of differentiation of products and services. In pure competition, differentiation is absent and the same prices are charged by all sellers.
    Answer (A) is incorrect because a monopoly consists of a single seller of a product or service. Answer (B) is incorrect because, in monopolistic competition, an industry has numerous sellers who offer differentiated products and services. Answer (C) is incorrect because an oligopoly consists of a few large firms whose products may be standardized. In that case, competition may be based solely on price.

15. The retail petroleum industry consists of a few large firms that sell a standardized product. Which of the following best describes this industry?

    A. Monopoly.

    B. Oligopoly.

    C. Monopolistic competition.

    D. Pure competition.

Answer (B) is correct. *(Publisher, adapted)*
    REQUIRED: The type of industry that describes the retail petroleum industry.
    DISCUSSION: An oligopoly consists of a few large firms. If products are standardized, competition may be based solely on price. If products are partially differentiated, each firm may attempt to lead the industry regarding a given attribute, e.g., price, quality, service, or features. The retail petroleum industry is dominated by a small number of firms that control a vast majority of the market. Furthermore, it is an example of an industry that sells a standardized product with competition based primarily on price.
    Answer (A) is incorrect because a monopoly consists of a single seller of a product or service, such as a utility. Answer (C) is incorrect because monopolistic competition has numerous sellers that offer differentiated products and services. Answer (D) is incorrect because pure competition has numerous sellers that offer undifferentiated products.

16. Which of the following statements is true with regard to a vertically integrated acquisition?

    A. A grocery store chain that purchases a dairy and begins to make milk-based products under its own brand is forward integrated.

    B. A movie producer that acquires a chain of theaters is backward integrated.

    C. A clothing manufacturer that acquires a chain of clothing stores is forward integrated.

    D. A soda maker that purchases its leading competitor is backward integrated.

Answer (C) is correct. *(Publisher, adapted)*
    REQUIRED: The true statement regarding a vertically integrated acquisition.
    DISCUSSION: Vertical integration occurs upstream (backward) by acquiring suppliers or downstream (forward) by acquiring wholesalers and retailers. An example of forward integration is a clothing manufacturer's acquisition of a chain of clothing stores in which to sell its products.
    Answer (A) is incorrect because a grocery store chain that begins to make its own brand of dairy products is backward integrated. It acquired a supplier. Answer (B) is incorrect because a movie producer that acquires a chain of theaters is forward integrated. Answer (D) is incorrect because the acquisition of a leading competitor is horizontal integration.

17. A strategic group analysis does all but which of the following?

    A. Determines what mobility barriers exist.

    B. Forecasts future group actions and trends.

    C. Considers how the firm compares with the competitors within the chosen strategic group.

    D. Predicts reaction patterns to events such as competitive attacks.

Answer (C) is correct. *(Publisher, adapted)*
    REQUIRED: The false statement regarding a strategic group analysis.
    DISCUSSION: An overall industry analysis, not a strategic group analysis, considers how the firm compares with the competitors within the chosen strategic group, e.g., on the basis of its scale of operations, the intensity of group rivalry, and the differences in the ability of the group members to implement their strategies.
    Answer (A) is incorrect because a strategic group analysis determines what mobility barriers exist. Answer (B) is incorrect because a strategic group analysis forecasts future group actions and trends. Answer (D) is incorrect because a strategic group analysis predicts reaction patterns to events such as competitive attacks.

18. According to Arthur D. Little, a competitor firm that can act independently and sustain its long-term status irrespective of the behavior of others holds which of the following competitive positions?

    A. A dominant position.

    B. A strong position.

    C. A favorable position.

    D. A tenable position.

Answer (B) is correct. *(Publisher, adapted)*
    REQUIRED: The competitive position held by a competitor firm that can act independently and sustain its long-term status irrespective of the behavior of others.
    DISCUSSION: Evaluating a competitor's market position is necessary to judge how and whether to challenge it. A firm that is in a strong competitive position can act independently and sustain its long-term status irrespective of the behavior of others.
    Answer (A) is incorrect because a competitor firm in a dominant position has a choice of strategies, and it controls other firm's actions. Answer (C) is incorrect because a firm in a favorable position has strengths to use that give it a better-than-average chance to improve its status. Answer (D) is incorrect because the performance of a firm in a tenable position justifies continuation of the business, but its chance for improvement is below average.

19. A runner-up firm in a market may choose a market-challenger strategy. Which general attack strategy adopted by a market challenger is directed at a gap in customer need fulfillment?

    A. Guerilla warfare.

    B. Bypass attack.

    C. Frontal attack.

    D. Flank attack.

Answer (D) is correct. *(Publisher, adapted)*
    REQUIRED: The general attack strategy adopted by a market challenger to exploit a need-fulfillment gap.
    DISCUSSION: A flank attack may be directed at a geographic or segmental weakness of the target (an underserved market) or an unmet need (such as the desire for more healthful fast food). A flank attack succeeds when market segments shift. The result is a gap in need fulfillment that the attacker can convert into a strong position in a profitable segment.
    Answer (A) is incorrect because guerilla warfare consists of numerous small attacks designed to reduce the strength of the target, e.g., by ad campaigns, carefully chosen price decreases, and lawsuits. Such warfare ordinarily must be followed by a different (and stronger) type of attack if the challenge is to succeed. Answer (B) is incorrect because the bypass attack directs the assault against markets other than those where the competitive target is strong. It may involve diversification of products or geographic markets. It may also entail developing next-generation technology so as to move the competition to an arena where the challenger is in a stronger position. Answer (C) is incorrect because a frontal attack directly pits the firm's products, prices, promotions, and methods of distribution against the target's.

20. The dominant firm in a market pursues a market-leader strategy. This strategy may involve

    A. Holding the market stable to avoid attracting new competitors.

    B. A flank defense to strengthen the firm's brand.

    C. Sending market signals as a mobile defense.

    D. Innovations as an offensive strategy.

Answer (D) is correct. *(Publisher, adapted)*
    REQUIRED: The action taken by a market leader.
    DISCUSSION: Constant innovation to improve products and services, control costs, and increase distribution effectiveness is the basis for a good offensive strategy. The leader must continuously improve the value offered to customers.
    Answer (A) is incorrect because, as the firm most likely to gain, the leader should attempt to increase total demand, for example, by attracting new users, encouraging new uses, and promoting increased use. Answer (B) is incorrect because a position defense strengthens the firm's brand power. Answer (C) is incorrect because a preemptive defense anticipates an attack, such as by targeting particular competitors before they can launch assaults, flooding the market with products for every segment and niche, or by sending market signals indicating ways in which the leader intends to anticipate attacks.

21. Of the major processes affecting the evolution of an industry, which one affects rivalry, entry, expansion, and supply?

    A. Long-run changes in the industry growth rate.

    B. Changes in input costs.

    C. Structural changes in suppliers' and customers' industries.

    D. Government policies.

Answer (A) is correct. *(Publisher, adapted)*
    REQUIRED: The evolutionary process that affects rivalry, entry, expansion, and supply.
    DISCUSSION: Long-run changes in the industry growth rate affect rivalry, entry, expansion, and supply. These changes occur because of changes in five external factors: demographic traits (such as consumer ages and income levels), trends in needs of buyers (caused by changes in regulation, tastes, lifestyles), relative positions of substitute and complementary products, sales to new customers (market penetration), and product innovation–an internal factor–alters the industry's position regarding the external factors.
    Answer (B) is incorrect because changes in input costs most directly affect the cost and price of the product and the demand for it. Answer (C) is incorrect because structural changes in suppliers' and customers' industries affect their bargaining power. Answer (D) is incorrect because government policies affect industry evolution by explicit regulation of entry, competitive practices, licensing, and pricing.

22. In a product's life cycle, the first symptom of the decline stage is a decline in the

    A. Firm's inventory levels.

    B. Product's sales.

    C. Product's production cost.

    D. Product's prices.

Answer (B) is correct. *(CIA, adapted)*
    REQUIRED: The initial symptom of the decline stage in a product's life cycle.
    DISCUSSION: The sales of most product types and brands eventually decrease permanently. This decline may be slow or rapid. This first symptom of the decline stage of a product's life cycle triggers such other effects as price cutting, narrowing of the product line, and reduction in promotion budgets.
    Answer (A) is incorrect because a decline in the firm's purchases–resulting in a decline in the firm's inventory levels–is not the first symptom. It will occur only when production declines as a result of a drop in sales. Answer (C) is incorrect because a decline in production costs may be due to many factors, e.g., new plant technology or the increased availability of raw materials. Moreover, production costs may decrease in any stage of a product's life cycle and not specifically in the decline stage. Answer (D) is incorrect because a change in prices is a marketing decision. It is an action that may be taken in the maturity stage to compete in the market. Moreover, a decrease in the product's prices is a response to a permanent decline in sales.

23. At the introduction stage of an innovative product, the profit growth is normally slow due to

    A. Expensive sales promotion.

    B. High competition.

    C. A mass market.

    D. Available alternatives.

Answer (A) is correct. *(CIA, adapted)*
    REQUIRED: The reason for slow profit growth during the introduction stage of an innovative product.
    DISCUSSION: The introduction stage is characterized by slow sales growth and lack of profits because of the high expenses of promotion and selective distribution to generate awareness of the product and encourage customers to try it. Thus, the per-customer cost is high. Competitors are few, basic versions of the product are produced, and higher-income customers (innovators) are usually targeted. Cost-plus prices are charged. They may initially be high to permit cost recovery when unit sales are low. The strategy is to infiltrate the market, plan for financing to cope with losses, build supplier relations, increase production and marketing efforts, and plan for competition.
    Answer (B) is incorrect because, during the introduction stage, little competition exists. Competitors tend not to enter the market until they have greater assurance of profits. Answer (C) is incorrect because no mass market is available during the introduction stage. Answer (D) is incorrect because, by definition, not many alternatives are available during the introduction stage of an innovative product.

24. An emerging industry is new or newly formed and is small in size initially. It results from innovation, changes in cost structures, new customer needs, or another factor that creates an attractive opportunity for selling a product or service. Which of the following is a structural characteristic of an emerging industry?

A. A long time horizon for product development.

B. Low initial costs and a shallow learning curve.

C. Mobility barriers include economies of scale and brand identification.

D. The presence of embryonic companies and spinoffs.

Answer (D) is correct. *(Publisher, adapted)*
REQUIRED: The characteristics of an emerging industry.
DISCUSSION: Embryonic companies (firms newly formed and not new units of established entities) are numerous in the emerging phase of industry evolution. Entry is not discouraged by the presence of economies of scale or strategic certainty. Spin-offs from existing firms also are common. Given the strategic uncertainties and the lure of equity interests, employees of these firms may have the incentive, and be well-placed, to create new firms. Their motive is to exploit ideas that may not have received a favorable reception by their former employers.
Answer (A) is incorrect because the time horizon for product and customer development is short. Thus, policies may evolve for reasons other than well-researched decision making. Answer (B) is incorrect because initial costs are high, but the learning curve is steep. When the efficiency gains from experience combine with economies of scale achieved by growth, cost decreases are dramatic. Answer (C) is incorrect because early mobility barriers tend to consist of willingness to accept risk, proprietary technology, access to resource supplies, and the lower costs of experienced firms. Branding, economies of scale, and the need for capital tend not to be barriers.

25. A firm in a declining industry ordinarily adopts one of four strategies. A firm that follows a

A. Quick divestment strategy should have divested during the maturity phase.

B. Leadership strategy may assume that success will enable it to subsequently pursue a harvest strategy.

C. Harvest strategy seeks a pocket of stable demand.

D. Niche strategy is engaged in a gradual liquidation.

Answer (B) is correct. *(Publisher, adapted)*
REQUIRED: The true statement about a strategy followed by a firm in a declining industry.
DISCUSSION: A leadership strategy is pursued by a firm that believes it can achieve market share gains to become the dominant firm. An assumption is that additional investment can be recovered. A second assumption is that success will put the firm in a better position to hold its ground or subsequently to follow a harvest strategy. This strategy may entail aggressive pricing, marketing, or other investments that raise the stakes for competitors; reducing competitors' exit barriers by acquisitions of their capacity or products, assuming their contracts, and producing spare parts and generic versions of goods for them; demonstrations of strength and resolve to remain in the industry; and publicizing accurate data about the reality of future decline so as to dispel competitors' uncertainty.
Answer (A) is incorrect because a quick divestment strategy assumes that the highest net recovery is obtained by sale early in the decline phase. It is then that uncertainty about the industry's future is greatest and other markets for the assets are most favorable. Indeed, divestiture may be indicated. Answer (C) is incorrect because a niche strategy seeks a market segment (pocket of demand) with stable or slowly decreasing demand with the potential for above-average returns. Some of the moves undertaken when following a leadership strategy may be appropriate. The firm may eventually change to a harvest or divest strategy. Answer (D) is incorrect because a harvest strategy is in effect a controlled, gradual liquidation. It maximizes cash flow by minimizing new investment, R&D, advertising, service, maintenance, etc., and by exploiting the firm's remaining strengths (e.g., goodwill) to increase prices or maintain sales volume.

26. Strategic choices in an emerging industry are inherently subject to great uncertainty and risk with regard to competitors, industry structure, and competitive rules. Accordingly, a firm considering entry into an emerging industry

    A. Has little need to be concerned with industry cooperation.

    B. Is least likely to be able to shape the industry structure at this stage.

    C. May enjoy such benefits of pioneering as experience advantages and early commitment to suppliers.

    D. Must be prepared for responding vigorously to competitors' moves.

Answer (C) is correct. *(Publisher, adapted)*
    REQUIRED: The true statement about strategic considerations by a potential entrant into an emerging industry.
    DISCUSSION: Timing of entry is a critical choice. Pioneering firms face high risk but low barriers and may earn high returns. The following are factors favoring early entry: pioneering improves the firm's reputation, the learning curve (experience) advantage is important and will persist, customer loyalty will be high, and cost advantages (through early commitment to suppliers or distributors) can be secured.
    Answer (A) is incorrect because a firm in an emerging industry needs to consider externalities in industry development. It should balance its self interest with the need to promote the image and credibility of the industry. Thus, to appeal to first-time buyers and encourage substitution, the firm's enlightened self-interest ordinarily resides in industry cooperation, improved quality, and standardization. However, as the industry matures, the firm should be less industry-oriented. Answer (B) is incorrect because the firm is best able to shape the industry structure when the industry is emerging. It is best able to influence to its advantage industry approaches on such matters as pricing, marketing, and product policy. Answer (D) is incorrect because responding to competitors during the emerging phase of industry development is often a poor strategic choice. A firm is frequently best served by reinforcing its strengths and by developing the industry, perhaps through encouraging new entrants (e.g., by licensing) who will sell the industry's product and expedite its technological evolution.

4.3 Business Portfolio Concepts

27. A strategic business unit (SBU) has a relative market share (RMS) of 2.0 and a market growth rate (MGR) of 9.5%. According to the portfolio model for competitive analysis created by the Boston Consulting Group, such an SBU is considered a

    A. Star.

    B. Question mark.

    C. Cash cow.

    D. Dog.

Answer (C) is correct. *(Publisher, adapted)*
    REQUIRED: The appropriate quadrant of the growth-share matrix for an SBU that is a strong competitor in a low-growth market.
    DISCUSSION: The annual MGR reflects the maturity and attractiveness of the market and the relative need for cash to finance expansion. An MGR of 10% or more is generally regarded as high. The RMS reflects an SBU's competitive position in the market segment. An RMS of 1.0 or more signifies that the SBU has a strong competitive position. Cash cows have high RMS and low MGR. They are strong competitors and cash generators in low-growth markets.
    Answer (A) is incorrect because stars have both high RMS and high MGR because they are strong competitors in high growth markets. Answer (B) is incorrect because question marks are weak competitors in high-growth markets, meaning they have a low RMS and a high MGR. Answer (D) is incorrect because dogs have both low RMS and low MGR, meaning they are weak competitors in low-growth markets.

28. General Electric has popularized a model for competitive analysis. In this portfolio matrix,

    A. Each of the firm's businesses is represented by a circle proportional to its size.

    B. Business strength and market attractiveness are measured using a multifactor index.

    C. The number of cells varies with the number of factors used by the firm in its analysis.

    D. The four quadrants represent combinations of high or low market growth rates and business profitability.

Answer (B) is correct. *(Publisher, adapted)*
    REQUIRED: The nature of the GE portfolio model for competitive analysis.
    DISCUSSION: The GE model is a multifactor portfolio matrix with two variables. Business strength or competitive position (BUS) is on one axis, and market attractiveness (MAT) is on the other. To measure BUS and MAT, the firm must isolate the multiple factors affecting each, quantify them, and create an index. Factors will vary with each business. The measurements will provide the values on the axes of the matrix.
    Answer (A) is incorrect because each circle is proportional to the size of the related market. Answer (C) is incorrect because the GE model has two variables. Business strength is classified as strong, medium, or weak, and market attractiveness is classified as high, medium, or low. Answer (D) is incorrect because the matrix is 3 × 3 and has nine cells.

29. A weak competitor in a high-growth market is sometimes called a

A. Dog.

B. Question mark.

C. Cash cow.

D. Star.

Answer (B) is correct. *(Publisher, adapted)*
REQUIRED: The term applied to a weak competitor in a high-growth market.
DISCUSSION: A weak competitor in a high-growth market is called a question mark. They need large amounts of cash to finance growth. However, if market share increases substantially, the question mark can become a star.
Answer (A) is incorrect because a dog is in a low-growth market. Answer (C) is incorrect because cash cows are strong competitors. Answer (D) is incorrect because stars are strong competitors.

4.4 Globalization and Industry Structure

30. Which of the following is a source of global competitive advantage?

A. Low fixed costs.

B. Production economies of scale.

C. Weak copyright protection.

D. Intensive local service requirements.

Answer (B) is correct. *(CIA, adapted)*
REQUIRED: The source of global competitive advantage.
DISCUSSION: Production economies of scale exist when a firm can produce and sell the output at which the average total cost of production is minimized. (The archetypal example is oil refining.) In other words, economies of scale in centralized production may yield a cost advantage achievable only when output exceeds the demand in one country and exports are feasible.
Answer (A) is incorrect because low fixed costs generally imply weak barriers to entry, and the consequent ability of local competitors to compete effectively against a larger global firm. Answer (C) is incorrect because weak intellectual property rights enforcement enables small local competitors to produce efficiently, if illicitly, in the short term. Answer (D) is incorrect because intensive local service requirements dilute the advantage of a large and efficient global competitor.

31. A global industry is one that

A. Contains competitors that are multinationals.

B. Has secured a competitive advantage based on economies of scale in centralized production.

C. Has a strategic advantage by establishing coordinated competition in many national markets.

D. Has made large direct investments abroad.

Answer (C) is correct. *(Publisher, adapted)*
REQUIRED: The nature of a global industry.
DISCUSSION: The analysis of a competition in an industry requires consideration of the economics of the industry and the characteristics of competitors. However, in a global industry, the analysis is not limited to one market, but extends to all markets (geographic or national) taken together. Michael E. Porter defines a global industry as "one in which the strategic positions of competitors in major geographic or national markets are fundamentally affected by their overall global positions." Thus, an industry becomes global because it perceives a net strategic advantage to competing, as Porter says, "in a coordinated way in many national markets."
Answer (A) is incorrect because a true global industry is one that requires a firm to compete internationally. Accordingly, an industry is not global simply because some or all competitors are multinational. When nonmultinationals can compete in a geographic or national market, the industry is not global. Answer (B) is incorrect because economies of scale in centralized production may yield a cost advantage achievable only when output exceeds the demand in one country and exports are feasible. Vertical integration may provide the necessary scale. However, a global competitive advantage may be based on other factors, such as other economies of scale (purchasing, marketing, or logistical), proprietary technology, product differentiation, or mobility of production. Answer (D) is incorrect because participation in foreign markets is usually by licensing; export; or, after the firm has obtained experience, direct investment. A genuinely global industry will have significant export activity or direct investment, but the presence of the latter does not necessarily signal the existence of global competition. Direct investment also may occur when national factors only determine a subsidiary's competitive position.

32. Governments restrict trade to

I. Help foster new industries.
II. Protect declining industries.
III. Increase tax revenues.

   A. I only.

   B. I and II only.

   C. II and III only.

   D. I, II, and III.

Answer (D) is correct. *(CIA, adapted)*
   REQUIRED: The reason(s) governments restrict trade.
   DISCUSSION: Governmental impediments to global competition are generally imposed for the announced purpose of protecting local firms and jobs and developing new industries. They also may have the effect of raising revenue. Examples of impediments are tariffs; duties; quotas; domestic content rules; preferences for local firms regarding procurement, taxes, R&D, labor regulations, and other operating rules; and laws (e.g., anti-bribery or tax) enacted by a national government that impede national firms from competing globally. These impediments are most likely when industries are viewed as crucial.
   Answer (A) is incorrect because developing new industries is only one reason governments restrict trade. Answer (B) is incorrect because governments also restrict trade to increase tax revenues. Answer (C) is incorrect because governments also restrict trade to protect declining industries.

33. Which strategy in a global industry is most likely to be facilitated by a transnational coalition?

   A. A protected niche strategy.

   B. A national focus strategy.

   C. A national segment strategy.

   D. Broad line global competition.

Answer (D) is correct. *(Publisher, adapted)*
   REQUIRED: The strategy in a global industry most likely to be facilitated by a transnational coalition.
   DISCUSSION: Broad line global competition is competition over the full product line of the firm based on differentiation or low cost. The firm needs large resources for this long-term strategy. Governmental relations should emphasize impediment reduction. Transnational coalitions may be created to help the firms overcome impediments to executing the broader strategies, for example, market access or technology barriers.
   Answer (A) is incorrect because a protected niche strategy is applied in nations where global competitors are discouraged by governmental impediments. The strategy is designed to be effective in markets with governmental constraints and requires close attention to the national government. Answer (B) is incorrect because a national focus strategy is limited to a national market or the segments with the greatest impediments to global competitors. Low cost or differentiation is sought. Answer (C) is incorrect because a national focus strategy is limited to a national market or the segments with the greatest impediments to global competitors. Low cost or differentiation is sought.

Use Gleim's ***CMA Test Prep*** for interactive testing with **over 2,000 additional multiple-choice questions**!

STUDY UNIT FIVE
MARKETING INFORMATION AND
MARKET SEGMENTATION

(24 pages of outline)

This study unit is the **second of three** on **strategic marketing**. The relative weight assigned this major topic in Part 3 of the exam is **15%** at **skill level A** (two skill types required). The three study units are

Study Unit 4: Marketing's Strategic Role within the Firm
Study Unit 5: Marketing Information and Market Segmentation
Study Unit 6: Other Marketing Topics

After studying the outline and answering the multiple-choice questions, you will have the skills necessary to address the following topics listed in the IMA's Learning Outcome Statements:

Part 3 – Section B.2. Managing marketing information

The candidate should be able to:

   a.   identify marketing information needs
   b.   demonstrate an understanding of the marketing information development process, including internal data collection, marketing intelligence, and marketing research
   c.   define customer relationship management
   d.   identify efficient methods of compiling, distributing, and using marketing information

Part 3 – Section B.3. Market segmentation, targeting, and positioning

The candidate should be able to:

   a.   identify target marketing steps, including market segmentation, targeting, and positioning
   b.   identify and define mass marketing, segment marketing, niche marketing, and micromarketing
   c.   demonstrate an understanding of segmenting consumer markets, business markets, and international markets
   d.   identify requirements for effective segmentation
   e.   demonstrate an understanding of market targeting, including evaluating and selecting market segments
   f.   define positioning strategy

5.1 MANAGING MARKETING INFORMATION

1. **Marketing information needs.** Each firm has unique requirements for information about customer needs and wants, preferences, and behavior in all of its markets, including those abroad.

2. **Internal data collection** begins with the firm's accounting transaction processing system for the order-to-payment cycle. This cycle generates information about the results of transactions involving cash and credit, sales, billing and receivables, production, inventories, shipping, purchasing, receiving, payables, and payroll.

   a. **Sales information systems** using the Internet, extranets, and EDI allow the generation and sharing of up-to-date information about prices, per-item sales, per-store sales, inventories at any level, and more.

   b. **Databases**, such as those for customers and products, may be analyzed and combined. Hence, promotions may be customized based on customer characteristics to reduce costs and improve response rates.

      1) A firm with a decision-support system (DSS) may exploit advanced database technology to analyze vast amounts of data. One approach is **online analytical processing**, or **multidimensional data analysis**. It allows a user to have multiple perspectives of the same data. Another approach is **data mining**. It allows a user to discover hidden relationships in the data, such as associations (links to a given event), sequences of events, classifications (descriptions of the group to which an item belongs), or clusters (new groupings not previously known). Consequently, a firm might detect trends or underserved customer market segments. Data mining requires advanced statistical and mathematical methods, for example, predictive modeling, neural networking, and automatic interaction detection.

      2) A **data warehouse** contains not only current operating data but also historical information from throughout the organization. Thus, data from all operational systems are integrated, consolidated, and standardized into an organization-wide database into which data are copied periodically. These data are maintained on one platform and can be read but not changed. Graphics and query software and analytical tools assist users. Accordingly, data mining is facilitated by a data warehouse.

3. Philip Kotler in *Marketing Management* defines a **marketing intelligence system** as "a set of procedures and sources used by managers to obtain everyday information about developments in the marketing environments."

   a. The members of the firm's **sales force** should be a primary source of intelligence because of their close contact with customers. Sales agents should be trained to gather relevant information and communicate it to appropriate people in the firm.

   b. **Intermediaries** are another source of intelligence. They include not only the firm's own suppliers, distributors, and retailers, but also outside specialists, for example, ghost shoppers who report on how sales people treat customers.

   c. **Competitive intelligence** is a subset of marketing intelligence. It is discussed in item 5. on page 127.

   d. Information may be purchased from **external researchers**. Moreover, massive amounts of information, much of it free, may be obtained over the Internet.

   e. A firm may consult its **customers**, especially the largest, most sophisticated, or most representative.

4. **Marketing research** is defined by Kotler *(Marketing Management)* as "the systematic design, collection, analysis, and reporting of data and findings relevant to a specific marketing situation." For example, the research may be in the form of a customer survey in a target market, a demand forecast, or an assessment of a promotional program.

   a. The **first phase** in the marketing research process is to **define the task**. This definition should have enough specificity to avoid gathering unnecessary data but enough breadth to obtain sufficient data to achieve the objectives of the project. Thus, specific objectives must be established and decision variables defined.

   b. The **second phase** of the marketing research process is **developing a research plan**.

      1) **Suppliers of information.** Large firms usually have their own market researchers. Small firms usually purchase market research from specialists, who may gather information and sell it to any buyer (syndicated research), execute a specific commission to conduct a study (customized research), or perform a specific type of research service (e.g., survey taking or shopping).

      2) **Sources of information** may be secondary (already existing in materials available from, for example, government publications, books, periodicals, commercial services, and the Internet). If the less expensive secondary information is not adequate, the researchers must gather **primary information**. The following are the types of **research approaches** used to gather primary information:

         a) **Observations** may be made of competitors, customers, employees, or others.

         b) **Focus group** discussions are guided by a moderator and recorded for later analysis. This approach collects information about participants' attitudes toward a product, company, service, etc. Consumer goods research has popularized the use of focus groups.

         c) **Surveys** are conducted about attitudes, awareness, customer satisfaction levels, and other matters that provide descriptive information.

         d) Evidence of **customer purchasing behavior** is recorded in many ways, e.g., in scanning data or catalog purchases.

         e) **Experimentation** determines the cause of some observed result by isolating the effects of a variable. This technique requires that people with similar traits be divided into groups that receive different treatment. The difference is the factor that is being researched.

      3) The following are the most common **research instruments**:

         a) **Questionnaires.** These must be expertly drafted and sequenced to minimize bias and achieve the research objectives.

            i) **Closed-end questions** yield results that are relatively simple to analyze because the range of answers is finite. Examples are yes/no, multiple choice, agree/disagree on a given scale, intention-to-buy scale, semantic differential scale (big to little, competent to incompetent, etc.), importance scale, or rating scale.

            ii) **Open-end questions** ask for personalized responses and are most useful when researchers are exploring thought processes. Examples are picture interpretation, word association, sentence or story completion, and thematic apperception testing (creating a story about a given picture).

      b)   **Psychological Methods**

          i)   **Laddering** entails posing an initial question to a subject and then a series of follow-up questions to determine the individual's ultimate motivation.

          ii)   **Depth interviewing** elicits latent feelings about products or services.

          iii)   **Use of metaphors.** An example is showing pictures to test subjects that represent a range of reaction to a product.

      c)   **Mechanical methods.** An example is a lie detector.

      d)   **Qualitative methods.** For example, researchers may videotape consumers or conduct field interviews in informal locations, such as restaurants.

      e)   **Customer prototyping.** This procedure attempts to delineate a target customer type using qualitative variables.

      f)   **Articulative interviewing.** The objective is to use wide-ranging, general discussions to extract information about values and other factors affecting purchasing choices.

    4)   The **sampling plan** is based on determination of the **sampling unit** (such as types of people to be interviewed), the **size of the sample** needed to achieve reliable results at reasonable cost, and the **sampling method** (e.g., simple random sampling, stratified sampling, or judgment sampling).

    5)   **Contacts** may be via arranged interview, intercept interview (e.g., requesting an interview from a person on the street), telephone, the postal service, or online.

      a)   **Mail questionnaires** avoid interviewer bias and reach people who would not allow a personal interview.

      b)   **Telephone** contact is quick and has a better response rate than mail questionnaires but encounters general hostility to telemarketers and use of answering machines to screen calls. Prepaid phone cards are a common incentive to participate in phone surveys.

      c)   **Personal interviewing** provides depth and observational advantages (such as viewing of body language and attire) but is costly and administratively complex.

      d)   **Online contacts** may be on a popular website, in chat rooms, in the firm's own chat room, or on the firm's website. For example, observation of a visitor's **clickstream** (movement through the website and the progression to other sites) may be captured by **cookies**.

  c.   The **third phase** of the marketing research process is **data collection**. It is the most expensive because subjects may be unavailable, uncooperative, biased, or dishonest. Interviewers also may be biased or dishonest.

  d.   The **fourth phase** of the marketing research process is **analysis** using statistical methods, e.g., to calculate means and standard deviation for the variables.

  e.   The **fifth phase** of the marketing research process is to **report the relevant findings**.

  f.   The **sixth and final phase** of the marketing research process is to consider the findings and **make a decision**. This decision may be to begin or cancel the project or to seek more data.

5.   A **competitive intelligence system** should be established to identify competitor strategies, monitor their new product introductions, analyze markets for the firm's own new product introductions and acquisitions, obtain information about nonpublic firms, evaluate competitor R&D activity, learn about competitors' senior executives, and perform other necessary information-gathering tasks.

   a.   **Setting up the system** involves determining the kinds of information to be collected, sources, and persons responsible.

   b.   **Data collection** should be a continuous process. Field sources include the firm's own sales agents, distributors, and suppliers. Trade associations and market researchers are also useful sources.

   1)   Other information may come from competitors' customers, suppliers, retailers, and distributors; purchases of their products and services; attending meetings of shareholders; open houses; trade shows; observation of competitors' advertising and other promotions; and competitors' other market signals, that is, actions providing indications of intentions, motives, objectives, or internal situations.

      a)   **Market signals** (such as prior announcements of actions, after-the-fact announcements, choice of conciliatory or aggressive tactics, or entry into a competitor's key market) may be true signals or bluffs. The types of signals vary with the nature of the competitor's signaling behavior and the media used.

   2)   An enormous amount of published information is publicly available from various services (Dun & Bradstreet, Moody's, Standard & Poor's, and others), newspapers, general business periodicals, special business publications, government data, reports submitted to government regulators (e.g., SEC filings of public companies), and more.

   3)   The Internet, e.g., websites of competitors, trade associations, and governments, is a fertile source of business intelligence. Patent applications, help wanted ads, licensing agreements, and many other activities may be revealing.

   c.   **Data analysis** entails validating and processing the intelligence gathered.

   d.   **Information dissemination** to decision makers is the final step in the establishment of an intelligence system. The system should be able to transmit timely information and to respond to queries.

6.   Competitive intelligence permits a firm to create effective competitive strategies that target the appropriate competitors.

   a.   A starting point is **customer value analysis (CVA)**. The premise of CVA is that customers choose from competitors' products or services the brands that provide the greatest customer value. Customer value equals **customer benefits** (product, service, personnel, and image benefits) minus **customer costs** (price and the costs of acquisition, use, maintenance, ownership, and disposal). The **steps in a CVA** are to

   1)   Determine what customers value.

   2)   Assign quantitative amounts to the elements of customer value and have customers rank their relative significance.

   3)   Evaluate how well the firm and its competitors perform relative to each element.

   4)   Focus on performance with respect to each element compared with an important competitor in a given market segment. For example, if the firm outperforms the competitor in every way, it may be able to raise its price.

   5)   Repeat the foregoing steps as circumstances change.

7.   Using the results of the CVA, the firm may then target a given **class of competitors**.

   a.   Targeting **weak competitors** may be the cheapest way to gain market share. However, targeting **strong competitors** also may be appropriate because this strategy forces the firm to improve. Moreover, a strong competitor may have an exploitable weakness.

   b.   **Close competitors**, that is, firms that are similar, are the usual targets. Nevertheless, **distant competitors** are also threats. For example, any beverage may be a competitor of soft drink makers.

   c.   **Bad competitors** should be targeted rather than **good competitors**. The former disturb the competitive equilibrium, e.g., by excessive expansion of capacity or overly risky behavior. The latter make sound business decisions that promote the long-term health of the industry, e.g., about prices, entry into new segments, and pursuit of market share.

8.   Stop and review! You have completed the outline for this subunit. Study multiple-choice questions 1 through 7 beginning on page 147.

5.2 CUSTOMER VALUE AND RELATIONSHIP MANAGEMENT

1.   **Customer Value and Satisfaction**

   a.   A marketer responds to **customer needs** by stating a **value proposition**, that is, the benefits offered to satisfy those needs. The value proposition is an attempt to affect customer **wants** (needs focused on particular satisfiers). It becomes tangible in an **offering**, which may consist of products, services, and other things that are intended to satisfy the needs of target buyers.

      1)   **Value** is an aggregate of the elements of the **customer value triad**: quality, service, and price. Value increases as quality and service increase and price decreases.

      2)   Value also may be defined as a **benefits-to-costs ratio**: the sum of functional and emotional benefits divided by the sum of monetary, time, energy, and psychic costs. The value of the offering is increased by any means that increases the ratio, such as lowering benefits by less than a decrease in costs.

         a)   A customer will be indifferent between two offerings with equal ratios.

         b)   **Customer perceived value** is an estimate of a given offering and the alternative. Total customer value is what a customer believes to be the financial value of the benefits of an offering. Total customer cost is the sum of all costs to the customer related to the offering.

   b.   **Customer satisfaction** is the relation between the offering's perceived performance and the customer's expectations. High customer satisfaction tends to create high customer loyalty that results in repurchases. However, at lower satisfaction levels, customers are more likely to switch when a superior alternative becomes available.

      1)   **Expectations** are a function of a customer's experience, marketing information, and other factors. Marketers should not raise expectations above the level at which they can be satisfied. However, some superior firms have had great success by adopting a **total customer satisfaction** approach, that is, by elevating expectations and then satisfying them.

      2)   **High customer loyalty** is an emotional as well as rational bond that develops when a firm provides high customer value. To obtain such loyalty, the firm needs to develop a value proposition that has superior competitiveness in the target market segment. Crucially, it must be supported by an effective **value delivery system**, the accumulation of all the experiences the customer has with the offering. Thus, brand value must be supported by **core business processes** that actually deliver the promised customer value.

3) **Customer satisfaction information** is gathered by

    a)   Complaint and suggestion systems, such as websites and hotlines

    b)   Customer surveys

    c)   Lost customer analysis (e.g., exit interviews and determination of the customer loss rate)

    d)   Testing of the treatment customers receive when purchasing the firm's (or competitors') products (ghost shopping)

4) Customer satisfaction must be balanced against the satisfaction level of the firm's **other stakeholders** (e.g., shareholders, employees, suppliers, and retailers). Thus, raising customer satisfaction at the expense of profit or other stakeholders may not be appropriate.

    a)   **High-performance business model.** According to Arthur D. Little (a consulting firm), a business should establish satisfaction objectives for **stakeholder groups**. To achieve the objectives, it must devise strategies, reengineer and coordinate its **core processes**, and appropriately allocate resources in accordance with organizational arrangements (structure, culture, etc.).

        i)   The firm may retain its **core resources** and outsource the rest.

        ii)   Core processes and resources are tied to **core competencies**. The competencies provide substantial customer value and therefore are sources of competitive advantage. Moreover, they have many applications and are hard for rivals to emulate.

        iii)   **Distinctive capabilities** provide superiority in certain overall business functions. According to George Day, an organization should have effective market sensing, customer linking, and channel bonding capabilities.

5) High **customer satisfaction rankings** may be an effective marketing tool. See, for example, the J.D. Powers rankings of automotive industry performance or the American Customer Satisfaction Index measurements applicable to national economies, industries, and sectors as well as firms.

c.   The **value creation chain** consists of the activities of a firm that create customer value and incur costs. They consist of five **primary activities** and four support activities. The following is Michael E. Porter's model:

    1)   **Inbound logistics** activities involve the firms' capture of materials to be processed.

    2)   **Operations** activities are conversion processes.

    3)   **Outbound logistics** activities include shipment of products.

    4)   **Marketing and sales** activities are the promotion and sale of final products.

    5)   **Service** activities provide customer service.

    6)   The four **support activities** are infrastructure (e.g., administration, finance, and planning), procurement, human resources, and technology development.

d.   To sustain customer value, the firm must seek **continuous improvement** of value-creating activities. Benchmarking the best performance attributes of top firms and emulating their best practices is a key continuous improvement technique.

e.   **Effective coordination** of the following core business processes is crucial:

1)   **Market sensing** consists of obtaining, distributing, and acting upon market intelligence.

2)   **New offering realization** should be timely and efficient. It involves R&D and the launch of products, services, and other elements of offerings.

3)   **Customer acquisition** defines target markets and researches for customers.

4)   **Customer relationship management** seeks to increase the value of the customer base by developing long-term relationships with individual customers by such methods as customer service, customized (if not personalized) offerings, and choice of marketing messages and media.

5)   **Fulfillment management** relates to order processing, on-time delivery, and collection.

f.   The **value-delivery network** is another source of competitive advantage. **Partner relationship management** involves coordinating with suppliers and distributors in this network (the supply chain) to provide better customer value.

2.   Kotler *(Marketing Management)* defines **customer relationship management** as "the process of managing detailed information about individual customers and carefully managing all the customer 'touchpoints' with the aim of maximizing customer loyalty." Its purpose is to create optimal customer equity. Thus, the process involves more than merely attracting customers (through media advertising, direct mail, etc.) and satisfying them (something competitors also may do).

a.   The firm should seek to minimize customer churn (customer loss) because **customer retention** through customer satisfaction is a key to profitability.

1)   **High customer satisfaction** means a longer relationship with the firm, repeat purchases of new offerings and upgrades, favorable word-of-mouth, and less concern about price and competitors' offerings. Moreover, the highly satisfied repeat customer is less costly than a new customer and is more likely to provide helpful feedback.

2)   **The listening process.** Accordingly, the firm should measure customer satisfaction frequently, facilitate complaints and suggestions, and act rapidly on the results.

3)   A less effective method of customer retention is to create high **switching costs**, such as loss of discounts.

b.   The firm should emphasize customer retention because the **customer base** is an important intangible asset.

1)   Loss of some customers is unavoidable. For example, a customer may cease operations.

2)   Customer retention is far less costly than customer attraction.

3)   Increasing the retention rate increases profits exponentially.

4)   The longer the customer relationship, the more profitable it is.

c.   **Analysis of customer loss** entails the following steps:

1)   Determining the retention rate

2)   Identifying causes that can be managed, such as bad products, lack of service, or uncompetitive prices

3)   Approximating the lost profit

4)   Calculating the cost of increasing the retention rate

d.   A firm should estimate **customer lifetime value**, the net present value of the cash flows (purchases – costs of acquiring, selling to, and serving the customer) related to a particular customer. This amount indicates whether a given investment in a customer is justified.

e. **Customer equity** is the sum of the customer lifetime values for all firm customers. According to Rust, Zeithaml, and Lemon, it has certain drivers (value, brand, and relationship equity) and subdrivers. A firm must determine the subdrivers that should be improved to increase customer equity and profits.

   1) **Value equity** is an estimate of the benefits-to-cost ratio. It is based on the following subdrivers: quality, price, and convenience. Value equity is most important when products are differentiated or require a formal assessment by the buyer.

   2) **Brand equity** is a subjective evaluation. Subdrivers are the customer's awareness of, and attitude toward, the brand and the customer's belief about brand ethics. Brand equity is most significant when the product is not differentiated but has emotional appeal.

   3) **Relationship equity** is the likelihood that customer loyalty is not based on any appraisal of the brand's value. Subdrivers are **programs to build customer loyalty, recognition, community, and knowledge**. This driver is most significant when the supplier-customer relationship is vital or when a customer may simply be habit-bound.

f. Jill Griffin has described the process of attracting and retaining customers as follows:

   1) Identifying **suspects** (all potential customers)
   2) Separating **prospects** from the suspects
   3) Persuading prospects to be **first-time customers**
   4) Giving preferred treatment to **repeat customers** to make them clients
   5) Creating a membership program to transform clients into **members**
   6) Converting members into **advocates** for the firm, its products, and its services
   7) Making advocates into **partners**

g. A firm may be able to **regain lost customers** more inexpensively than it could attract new ones using existing information and the results of surveys and exit interviews. A firm must determine the appropriate **investment in building customer relationships**. The levels of investment depend on unit profit margins and the numbers of customers. According to Kotler, the following are the corresponding levels of relationship marketing:

   1) **Basic marketing** is merely selling (low-margin, many customers).

   2) **Reactive marketing** includes encouragement of customer communication (low-to-medium margin and many customers or low margin and medium number of customers).

   3) **Accountable marketing** involves seller-initiated communication to ask about problems or suggestions (low margin and few customers, medium margin and medium number of customers, or high margin and many customers).

   4) **Proactive marketing** involves seller-initiated communication about new products or uses of old ones (high margin and medium number of customers or medium margin and few customers).

   5) **Partnership marketing** entails continuous assistance to big customers (high margin and few customers).

h. **Strengthening ties with customers** to improve customer satisfaction and retention may be accomplished in the following ways:

1) Firm-wide coordination of planning and management of the process
2) Making every business decision from customer as well as a firm perspective
3) Marketing superior offerings
4) Developing a comprehensive and accessible customer database
5) Facilitating customer communications with appropriated firm employees
6) Giving awards for employee achievement
7) Providing financial benefits, such as club memberships and frequent-buyer programs
8) Turning customers into clients through socially sensitive, personalized relationships
9) Creating structural relationships, e.g., by providing equipment, software, or EDI linkages; entering into long-term contracts; or offering bulk discounts

i. **Customer profitability analysis** determines all revenues and all costs assignable to specific customers. Kotler provides the following classification of customers:

1) **Platinum** – most profitable (highest investment)
2) **Gold** – profitable (high investment, with objective of converting to platinum)
3) **Iron** – low profit but desirable (lower investment with objective of converting to gold)
4) **Lead** – not profitable or desirable (drop or provide low investment while raising prices or lowering costs of serving)

3. Stop and review! You have completed the outline for this subunit. Study multiple-choice questions 8 through 15 beginning on page 149.

5.3 MARKETING COMMUNICATION

1. The **marketing communications mix** consists of **five promotional tools** or media chosen as the means of reaching current stakeholders (customers, employees, shareholders, suppliers, etc.), possible future stakeholders, and the public.

a. **Advertising** is defined by Kotler *(Marketing Management)* as "any paid form of nonpersonal presentation and promotion of ideas, goods, or services by an identified sponsor." It may occur on many platforms. Examples are television, radio, films, the Internet, packaging, billboards, point-of-purchase and other displays, brochures, videos, and trademarks. Advertising may have long-term (e.g., image building) or short-term (e.g., a one-day-only sale) effects and may or may not require outlays (national television versus leaflets). Advertising is

1) **Impersonal.** Advertising may be effective in part because people do not feel that they are required to give it attention.
2) **Expressive.** The communication may be enhanced through creative means, such as storytelling, music, and color.
3) **Pervasive and repetitive.** These qualities permit customer comparison. They also suggest that the firm is large and successful and that it offers substantial customer value.
4) **Public.** This quality combined with pervasiveness legitimizes the advertiser's offering and also implies standardization.

b. **Sales promotion** offers customers short-term incentives to try or purchase the offering. Some possible platforms are coupons, samples, premiums, gifts, contests (e.g., lotteries), trade-ins, no-interest financing, and rebates. Sales promotion

1) Provides some additional customer value in exchange for inviting immediate action
2) Draws attention to the offering

c. **Public relations** consists of methods of protecting the image of the firm or a product. Typical platforms are lobbying, sponsorships (e.g., the U.S. Postal Service's sponsorship of a cycling team), community outreach, gifts to charity, and the firm's annual report. Public relations campaigns may

1) Be more credible than advertising.
2) Reach those who avoid advertising.

d. **Personal selling** involves human interaction and mutual observation. It is the best method of inducing action in the end stages of the purchasing process. Among the platforms are meetings, presentations, fairs, and trade shows. Personal selling

1) Allows the development of relationships
2) May generate a sense of obligation by the potential customer

e. **Direct marketing** involves sending a promotional message directly to consumers rather than through a mass medium. Some examples are email, voice mail, fax, mail, telemarketing, and home shopping by television.

1) Direct marketing is customized, updated, interactive, and nonpublic.
2) The greatest benefit of direct marketing programs is that results are easily measurable. It is the most quantifiable method of marketing communication, and more information can be learned about customers' wants and needs because the communication is interactive.
3) Ethical questions sometimes arise with respect to direct marketing because sellers know so much about their customers that they can target the same customers for other types of products.

2. **Variables in selecting a mix.** A firm should choose and assign resources to the interchangeable promotional tools in a coordinated manner. The actual mix varies among and within industries because of such factors as

a. The **product market** (e.g., consumer versus business markets)
b. **Readiness of buyers** (e.g., awareness, comprehension, conviction, ordering, or reordering)
c. Stage of the **product life cycle** (e.g., advertising may be most effective in the introduction stage and sales promotion in the decline stage)

3. A firm should follow an **integrated marketing communications process** (IMCP), an approach that emphasizes comprehensive and coordinated planning and management of the marketing effort. Thus, each promotional tool should be integrated into a single process so that marketing communications (messages) are clear, consistent, and mutually reinforcing.

a. Central to the IMCP is the basic communications process. A **sender** transmits a **message** to a **receiver**. The message is **encoded** by the sender and may be sent in various **media**. The receiver **decodes** the message and makes a **response**. The sender creates **feedback channels** to monitor responses. **Noise** is anything (e.g., a competing message) that interferes with the communication process.

1) The sender must identify receivers (target audiences) and the desired responses. It must then encode messages (marketing communications) in a manner that facilitates decoding by the target audiences. Moreover, media (promotional tools) must be selected that are most likely to reach those audiences.

2) The goal is for every **brand contact** made through the process described on the previous page and above to provide an impression that enhances the receiver's (customer's) perception of the sender (marketer firm).

   b.   Marketing communications will be efficient and effective if

1) **Target audiences** are properly identified. **Image analysis** of the firm, its offerings, and its competitors is important for this purpose.

2) **Objectives** are clearly defined. The firm may want to gain attention, alter attitudes, or induce action. Thus, customers go through cognitive, affective, and behavioral stages (but not necessarily in that order). Understanding this model (and the sequence for a given audience) aids planning.

3) **Messages** are well **designed**. The design issues are content (e.g., rational, emotional, or moral appeals), structure (e.g., one-sided or two-sided arguments), format (variable with the medium), and source (e.g., choice of celebrity endorsers).

4) **Communication channels** are appropriate for the messages (e.g., personal or nonpersonal).

5) The **total budget** is adequate but not excessive. The budget may be based on affordability; percentage of sales; competitive parity; or an analysis of objectives, the tasks to be accomplished to reach them, and the costs of those tasks.

6) The right **marketing communications mix** is chosen.

   c.   **Results are measured** in terms of the effects on the target audiences and eventually behavioral changes.

4.   **Advertising**

   a.   The advertising process may be defined in terms of the 5 Ms:

1) The **mission** consists of sales and advertising objectives.
2) The **money** to be spent is stated in the budget.
3) The **message** to be communicated is crafted using a creative strategy.
4) The **media** are chosen to communicate the message.
5) The **measurement** of communication and sales effects determines the effectiveness of the process.

   b.   The **objectives** of advertising are determined by choices of target markets (audiences), positioning, and the marketing communications mix. Objectives may be to

1) **Inform** (raise awareness and knowledge)
2) **Persuade** (generate liking, preference, and conviction)
3) **Remind** (encourage repeat customers)
4) **Reinforce** (avoid dissatisfaction by existing customers)

   c.   The spending described in the **advertising budget** is a current expense for most accounting purposes, but it also represents a long-term investment in brand equity. Budgeted amounts depend on

1) A **product's life-cycle stage.** New products are usually more heavily advertised than old.

2) **Market share.** Advertising costs to maintain share decline as a percentage of sales when that share is large. Increasing market share is more costly.

       3) **Competition.** When a market has many competitors or is cluttered by noncompetitive messages, costs are higher.

       4) **Frequency** needed to communicate the message to customers.

       5) A high degree of potential **product substitution**. A high degree of substitutability increases the need for advertising.

  d. The **advertising message** is the result of a **creative strategy** that reflects four developmental stages:

       1) **Generating an effective message.** This creative step includes deciding how many benefits to stress and researching the target audiences. It also may involve testing alternative advertisements. A **deductive framework** also may be used. For example, a message may reflect a combination of rewards (ego, rational, social, or sensory) and experiences (result-of-use, in-use, or incidental-to-use).

       2) **Message evaluation**, for example, as to whether it is desirable (interesting), exclusive (distinct), and believable.

       3) **Message execution.** Some messages may reflect emotional positioning and others rational positioning. **Styles** (technical, testimonial, scientific, fantasy, realism, etc.) and **tone** should be suitable. Wording should be distinctive, and the format (size, color, graphics, etc.) should attract attention.

       4) The message must be within the bounds of the law, taste, and **social responsibility**.

  e. **Advertising media** are chosen to maximize, subject to cost constraints, the total exposures of each desired type experienced by members of the targeted audiences.

       1) Reach, frequency, and impact are key variables in determining the relationship of exposures to audience awareness.

          a) **Reach** (R) is the total number of individuals (or households) exposed during a defined interval of time.

          b) **Frequency** (F) is the average number of exposures per individual (household) during an interval of time.

          c) **Impact** (I) is the qualitative effect of an exposure.

          d) Total exposures **(gross rating points)** equals R times F.

          e) The weighted number of exposures equals R times F times I.

       2) **Choice of media.** Media (and vehicles within each medium) vary in their reach, frequency, impact, and cost. Choices are based on many variables, for example,

          a) Media exposure of the targeted audiences

          b) Nature of the product

          c) Attributes of the message (e.g., content and timeliness)

          d) Size of the audience for the vehicle chosen within the medium. The audience may be defined as follows:

             i) Circulation (physical units of the medium)
             ii) Individuals in the audience
             iii) The individuals exposed having the targeted traits
             iv) Actual ad-exposed individuals with the desired traits

3) **Media timing** involves considering seasonal and business cycle factors (macrotiming). Variables are **carryover effects** of advertising and **habitual behavior** (i.e., repeat purchasing independent of advertising).

   a) The microtiming issue is how to schedule advertising outlays for best effect during a short period. Variables considered in choosing the pattern are **buyer turnover** (entry of new buyers), **purchase frequency**, and the **forgetting rate**. The higher these rates, the greater the continuity of advertising should be. For a new product launch, advertising may follow one of the following approaches:

      i) Continuity means distributing expenditures evenly over the period, especially in a growing market, with frequently purchased goods, or when buyer categories are narrowly defined.

      ii) Concentration in one period is typical for a seasonal product.

      iii) Pulsing maintains low level continuity with bursts of more intense activity. It is a compromise approach that promotes buyer learning while reducing costs.

      iv) Flighting is intermittent advertising with periods of no activity. Flighting is useful when funding is low, purchases are infrequent, or when goods are seasonal.

4) **Geographical advertising** choices also must be made, e.g., national buys, spot buys (in areas of dominant influence or designated marketing areas), and local buys.

  f. **Advertising Evaluation**

   1) One approach is to test a campaign in one or a few local markets before a nationwide effort is made.

   2) **Communication-effect research** (copy testing) pretests and sometimes post-tests the effectiveness of an advertisement using

     a) Customer feedback to key questions
     b) Portfolio tests of multiple advertisements for customer recall levels
     c) Laboratory testing of physical responses

   3) **Sales-Effect Research**

     a) The measurement of these advertising effects and benefits is difficult because of the existence of both immediate and lagged responses. Also, the measurement problem is complicated by the difficulty of isolating the advertising effects from those of other elements of the marketing mix, competitors' actions, economic conditions, and other factors.

     b) When a firm uses more than one form of advertising (such as TV and magazines), the benefits derived from each medium is nearly impossible to derive (at least in the short run).

     c) One view is that the share of expenditures for advertising a product results in a **share of voice** (firm advertising ÷ all advertising of the product). This in turn results in a **share of customers' minds and hearts**. The final result is share of market. One researcher found that the voice-market share ratio was one-to-one for established products but was high for new products.

     d) Other approaches are to use statistical methods to analyze historical or experimental information to estimate the effect of advertising sales.

5. While advertising provides **reasons** to buy, sales promotion provides **incentives**.

    a. **Targets.** Promotions may be directed toward consumers, distributors and retailers (trade promotion), the firm's sales force, and other businesses.

    b. **Promotion costs** have increased as a percentage of marketing budgets because consumers are more price conscious, brands have proliferated and are less differentiated, distributors and retailers have greater bargaining power, advertising has become less efficient, firms are under greater pressure to increase sales in the near term, and managers are more accepting of promotional methods.

    c. **Sales promotion objectives with respect to consumers** include

        1) Attraction of new users of the product
        2) Strengthening ties with current users
        3) Providing incentives for switching from other brands
        4) Motivating users to buy bigger sizes of the product

    d. **Sales promotion objectives with respect to retailers** include giving them incentives to

        1) Stock the firm's new products.
        2) Stock larger amounts.
        3) Purchase during off-peak periods.
        4) Not respond to the promotions of the firm's competitors.
        5) Buy other items in the firm's product line.
        6) Develop loyalty to the firm's brand.
        7) Carry the firm's products for the first time.

    e. **Sales promotion objectives with respect to the sales force** include motivating them to

        1) Make more sales in off-peak periods.
        2) Do more prospecting for new customers.
        3) Express genuine support for new products.

    f. **Sales promotion tools** vary depending on whether the targets are consumers, the trade (distributors and retailers), businesses, or the sales force.

        1) **Consumer tools** include gifts, coupons, rebates, reduced price packs of the same product or related products, contest prizes, frequent-purchaser programs, trial offers, warranties, point-of-purchase marketing, tie-ins, and cross promotion (marketing a noncompetitor brand).

        2) **Trade tools** include offering free units of the product in exchange for buying in bulk or displaying the product favorably, allowances paid for advertising and display of the firm's product(s), and discounts.

        3) **Business and sales force tools** include contests, use of specialty items (e.g., pens, calendars, or key chains), conventions, and trade shows.

    g. Developing the **strategy** for a sales promotion requires determining

        1) The amount and extent of the offers needed to be effective
        2) Conditions for participants
        3) Length of the program and its frequency
        4) The vehicle used
        5) The timing of the activity
        6) The budget
        7) The extent and nature of pretesting
        8) Implementation and control plans that address both **lead-time** (preparation time) and **sell-in time** (time to distribute most incentives) activities

h.   **Evaluation of sales promotion** is done using

1)   Scanner sales data (e.g., Nielsen television ratings). This information indicates the kinds of customers reached, their pre-promotion purchases, and their post-promotion behavior.
2)   Customer surveys.
3)   Experimental results.

6.   **Public relations** is defined by Kotler *(Marketing Management)* to encompass "programs designed to promote or protect a company's image or its individual products."

a.   A public relations organization

1)   Manages **media relations** so that the firm is seen in the best possible light
2)   Publicizes the firm's products
3)   Manages internal and external **corporate communications**
4)   Lobbies governmental entities
5)   Provides advice to management

b.   **Marketing public relations** (publicity) supports the marketing department, especially by increasing audience awareness and brand knowledge. Its traditional role was to obtain free media coverage. This function may be less expensive than advertising and sales promotions. Furthermore, publicity is often perceived to be more trustworthy because it appears in news stories and features. Thus, it may affect people who avoid other elements of the promotional mix. Moreover, publicity may dramatize the firm and its products. Other purposes of marketing public relations are

1)   Publicizing new products
2)   Developing a different position for an existing product
3)   Creating (or restoring) interest in a classification of products, such as a type of commodity
4)   Building goodwill in a targeted group
5)   Restoring a tarnished product image after some negative public event
6)   Improving the corporate image so that its products are indirectly benefited

c.   Public relations **tools** include

1)   Publishing newsletters, reports, magazines, and other materials
2)   Holding special events
3)   Inducing news media to cover the firm, its products, and its employees
4)   Sponsoring sports teams, cultural activities, charities, etc.
5)   Performing community service activities
6)   Providing speakers
7)   Using identity media, such as logos, forms, stationery, business cards, and uniforms

7.   **Personal selling** is the most basic (and the oldest) form of direct marketing. The great majority of industrial firms use a professional sales force or hire manufacturers' representatives or other agents to perform the in-person task of selling. Also, consumer firms may engage in direct sales (e.g., Avon and Tupperware).

a.   **The sales process.** The sales force engages in prospecting (searching for new customers), qualifying customers (determining interest and financial status), learning about prospects (the preapproach phase of the selling process), approaching customers, presenting and demonstrating products, overcoming psychological and rational resistance, closing sales, following up, and maintaining and growing accounts.

b. The sales force should be trained in solving customer problems. This **customer-oriented approach** relies on listening and inquiry (questioning) skills to determine needs and find solutions. Thus, the members of the sales force should not be mere **order takers**. Moreover, high-pressure selling is inconsistent with modern concepts of **sales professionalism**.

c. **Negotiation** is another skill that members of the sales force should possess when the terms of exchange are not **routinized**. It is the process of reaching terms of exchange agreeable to the parties.

d. **Relationship marketing** involves building a strong, long-term, mutually beneficial customer relationship by finding out who the firm's customers are and what they want, then tailoring products and services to meet those specific needs. Successful relationship marketers seek opportunities for personalized treatment of customers. Also, customers are shown how much they are appreciated. Accordingly, the emphasis in relationship marketing is equally on managing customers and managing products and services.

8. **Direct marketing** employs potential customers that bypass marketing intermediaries. **Direct-order marketing** is intended to elicit an immediate and measurable result (e.g., orders), and **customer-relationship marketing** may use direct-marketing methods to develop long-term relationships.

a. Direct marketing has grown as a result of **market demassification** (the fragmentation of markets into many niches), the popularity of home shopping, the availability of next-day delivery, and telecommunications advances (toll-free numbers, the Internet, email, cell phones, and fax machines).

b. **Ethical issues.** Some direct marketers overstep ethical boundaries to create problems that may result in customer distaste for direct marketing, decreased response rates, and increased regulation (e.g., the national do-not-call list created by federal legislation).

   1) Consumers may be irritated by hard-sell tactics, calls at inappropriate times, callers who are not well trained, and leaving prerecorded voice-mail messages.

   2) Some direct marketers may unfairly target unsophisticated, elderly, or impulsive buyers.

   3) Direct marketers may in some cases indulge in outright **fraud**. Representations about price, performance, or products may be intentionally false and misleading.

   4) Direct marketing raises **invasion of privacy issues**. The reasons are the proliferation of computerized databases and the sale or misuse of the names, addresses, personal histories, and purchasing information they contain.

c. **Benefits**

   1) **Customers** benefit by the increased convenience and decreased complexity of the buying experience. Comparative shopping is facilitated by catalogs and online access. Selection is expanded, and ordering is simplified.

   2) **Sellers** benefit because of the availability of customized mailing lists, the ability to personalize messages, and the opportunity to build customer relationships. The effect is a higher response rate. Moreover, direct marketing allows a firm to manage the timing of messages to prospects, test a variety of marketing media and messages, measure responses, and reduce the visibility of its effects to competitors.

d.   The **forms of direct marketing** include

1) In-person selling
2) Direct mail
3) Email
4) Voice mail
5) Fax mail
6) Catalogs
7) Telemarketing (use of telephones and call centers)

a) Customer service and support
b) Teleprospecting
c) Telecoverage (maintenance of customer relationships)
d) Telesales (taking orders and making outbound calls)

8) Kiosk marketing
9) E-marketing

e.   **Integrated direct marketing**, also known as integrated marketing communications or maximarketing, combines and coordinates tools in planning and executing a campaign. Thus, a multiple-vehicle, multiple-stage campaign might integrate news releases about a new product, advertising combined with a customer response option, direct mail, telemarketing calls, in-person sales efforts, and some form of repeated communication.

1) One key is to determine the appropriate amount and allocation of the budget.

9.   Stop and review! You have completed the outline for this subunit. Study multiple-choice questions 16 through 24 beginning on page 151.

5.4 SEGMENTATION, TARGETING, AND POSITIONING

1.   **Levels of Market Segmentation**

a.   **Mass marketing** groups people into large categories based solely on their demographic traits, e.g., age, income, gender, or education level. It assumes most people in the same category will react similarly to one marketing message. Mass marketers primarily use mass media (television and print) to reach their targets in large numbers.

1) Mass marketing is directed toward an average, anonymous customer, not one with whom the firm has a relationship. Thus, it should be contrasted with **customer relationship marketing**.

2) A standard product is offered that is mass produced, distributed, advertised, and otherwise promoted. This approach differs from modern trends toward customized output and individualized distribution and promotion.

3) Mass marketing relies on **economies of scale** and a large share of the largest possible market to reduce costs and thereby lower prices or raise profit margins. The current trend is toward **economies of scope** and **share of the customer**, that is, identifying potential customers, maximizing net customer lifetime value, and not pursuing unprofitable customers. Accordingly, firms that avoid mass marketing emphasize customer retention, not attraction.

4) A **disadvantage** of mass marketing is that promotional media (over-the-air television, cable television, radio, the Internet, niche magazines, telemarketing, and others) and distribution channels (mail-order-catalogs, home shopping, the Internet, warehouse stores, malls, and others) have increased. The effect is to fragment markets.

        a) Another disadvantage of mass marketing is that all people in a group do not share the same interests, desires, and needs simply because they have the same broad demographic traits.

   b. The alternative to mass marketing is **micromarketing**.

     1) **Segment marketing** focuses on people who share particular wants, such as married, first-time homeowners buying kitchen appliances on limited budgets.

        a) A **sector** differs from a segment. The customers in a sector may vary considerably in their wants. For example, first-time homeowners buying kitchen appliances constitute a sector.

        b) Identifying and targeting a segment permits **customization** of products, services, prices, distribution channels, and marketing media. Competitive analysis also is facilitated.

        c) Within a segment, a **flexible market offering** may be made. The **naked solution** has characteristics desired by all segment customers. **Discretionary options** are available, usually at added cost.

     2) **Niche marketing** is a specialized strategy based on devoting all marketing efforts toward a subsegment of a market segment.

        a) Niche marketing typically appeals to smaller firms with limited resources, but larger firms also engage in niche marketing. It is attractive to these firms due to its cost effectiveness, the result of focusing marketing funds on a targeted group.

        b) Diverse types of niche marketing include **end-user strategy**, which is based on serving only one type of end-user customer; **vertical-level strategy**, which calls for specialization in one level of the production and distribution cycle and offering a unique product or service that is not available from another firm; and **geographic strategy**, which involves selling in one specific geographic area.

        c) Niche customers have unique wants and will pay higher prices for their satisfaction. Moreover, an ideal niche attracts little if any competition, has growth and profit potential, and confers production and marketing advantages that derive from **specialization** (e.g., knowledge of customers). The Internet is especially conducive to niche (and **microniche**) marketing because websites may be established inexpensively.

     3) **Local marketing** addresses the wants of neighborhood and other local groups. The disadvantages of local marketing are that it decreases economies of scale, dilutes brand image, and creates logistical problems.

     4) **Individual customer marketing** involves mass customization of products and services for each individual's wants. For example, an Internet firm may offer an interactive **choiceboard** that allows a customer to designate product and service features, prices, and means of delivery. This approach facilitates customized marketing because of the real-time research information gained about an individual's preferences.

2. **Patterns of segmentation** may be defined in terms of customer preferences.

   a. **Homogeneous preferences** indicate that a market lacks natural segments.

   b. **Diffuse preferences** signify great variety of preferences. The first firm in the market will position itself to satisfy average preference and thus the most customers.

   c. If **preferences are clustered**, natural market segments exist.

3.   Because segments evolve, they should be identified periodically.

   a.   **Needs-based segmentation** has the following steps:

   1)   Group customers by similarity of needs and wants relative to a given type of consumption.

   2)   Isolate demographic traits and behaviors that make segments identifiable.

   3)   Assess the attractiveness of segments based on accessibility, growth, etc.

   4)   Estimate profitability.

   5)   Establish a value proposition and a positioning strategy suitable to each segment.

   6)   Test the positioning strategy.

   7)   Determine the full marketing mix (the 4 Ps) for each segment.

   b.   **Market positioning** identifies segments by considering the **hierarchy of attributes** that customers use to make purchasing decisions. For example, customers may be primarily influenced by price, product type, brand, service, or quality.

   c.   **Effective segmentation** has the following requirements:

   1)   Segment characteristics should be measurable.

   2)   A segment should be large enough to be profitable when served with a customized marketing program.

   3)   A segment should be accessible.

   4)   Segments should be differentiable. Each must require a distinct marketing mix.

   5)   The firm must be able to take action to serve a segment well.

4.   **Segmenting Consumer Markets**

   a.   **Geographic segmentation** is by region, size of metropolitan area, population density (e.g., suburban versus rural), or climate. Knowing where the firm's customers live is an aid in targeting communications.

   b.   **Demographic segmentation** is by age group, generation (e.g., baby boomers, Generation X, Generation Y, etc., were shaped by different events and cultural factors), stage in the family life cycle, size of the family, sex, level of income, job, level of education, social class, religion, race, or ethnicity. Demographic traits are the most common bases for segmentation because they correlate with customer behavior and are readily measurable.

   c.   **Psychographic segmentation** is by personality traits, lifestyle (attitudes, activities, interests), or core values. Thus, marketers may attempt to build a brand personality, design offerings targeted to time-constrained or money-constrained individuals, or appeal to beliefs at a deeper level than attitudes and behaviors.

   d.   **Behavioral segmentation** is by regular or special **occasions** (e.g., holidays, critical life events, transitions, business activities, or holidays), **benefits** wanted (e.g., price, speed of delivery, quality, or service), **status of users** (e.g., nonusers and former, potential, or regular users), **rate of usage**, degree of loyalty (e.g., hard-core to switchers), **readiness** to buy (e.g., from unaware of the product to intending to purchase), or **attitude** (e.g., from hostile toward the product to enthusiastic).

   e.   **Multiattribute segmentation (geoclustering)** uses two or more characteristics to specify more precise targets. For example, Claritas, Inc. has developed **PRIZM**, or Potential Rating Index by Zip Markets. It categorizes U.S. residential areas as belonging to 62 lifestyles (clusters) based on 39 variables. The five types of variables are education and affluence, urbanization, family life cycle, race and ethnicity, and mobility.

5. **Segmenting Business Markets**

    a.   Certain variables (e.g., geographic areas or benefits wanted) that are used in segmenting consumer markets also apply to business markets.

    b.   **Demographic segmentation** is by industry, customer firm size, or geographic area.

    c.   **Operational segmentation** is by customer technology, degree of customer usage, or customer service needs.

    d.   **Purchasing segmentation** is by extent of centralization of the customer purchasing activity, current relationship with the customer, power structure (e.g., engineering or finance oriented), purchasing policies (e.g., leasing, service contracts, or sealed competitive bidding), or purchase criteria (e.g., quality or price).

    e.   **Situational segmentation** is by degree of urgency of delivery or service, applications of the product by customer firms, or order size.

    f.   **Personal segmentation** is by similarity of the buyer-seller firms' values and personnel, risk attitudes (e.g., risk averse or risk seeking), or loyalty to suppliers.

    g.   A business usually defines segments by applying **sequential segmentation**, beginning with macrosegmentation and ending with microsegmentation using the factors described above.

    h.   Businesses want different benefits from a supplier depending on whether they are novices in the purchasing process, first-time buyers from a seller, or sophisticated customers. They also vary in their preferences for marketing channels. For example, EDI may be preferred by a sophisticated buyer.

6. **Market Targeting**

    a.   Once market segments have been identified, the firm selects its target(s). The process of **evaluating and selecting market segments** requires consideration of

        1)   Segment attractiveness in terms of potential growth and profits, risk, available economies of scale, and size

        2)   The firm's resources, competencies, and objectives

    b.   **Single-segment concentration** provides the advantages of more focused marketing, savings from specialized production and distribution, and strong customer relationships. However, the risks are that demand will shrink or competitors will enter the segment.

    c.   **Selective specialization** is a risk-diversification approach. The segments selected are attractive and consistent with the firm's resources, competencies, and objectives, but they may not provide synergy.

    d.   **Product specialization** is the sale of different versions of one product to multiple segments. The risk is technological obsolescence.

    e.   **Market specialization** entails selling multiple products to one customer group. Hence, the risk is that the group will suffer a loss of purchasing power.

    f.   **Full market coverage** provides all the products wanted by all customer groups. This approach is possible only for a very large firm.

        1)   **Undifferentiated marketing** covers the market by mass distribution and advertising of one offering. Costs of R&D, production, transportation, inventory, marketing research, and product management are minimized, and a lower price can be charged to attract price sensitive buyers.

        2)   **Differentiated marketing** covers the market by offering different products in different segments. Sales are higher than under undifferentiated marketing, but costs (product modification, inventory, manufacturing, administration, and promotion) are higher.

g.   Market targeting should have a **social responsibility** element. For example, targeting children with certain product appeals has drawn much adverse reaction. Thus, socially responsible marketing considers the welfare of targeted groups as well as that of the marketers.

h.   **Economies of scope** arise when a firm targets multiple segments that are interrelated regarding cost, performance, and technology.

1)   A **supersegment** consists of multiple segments with some commonality that the firm can leverage.

i.   When a firm expects to enter multiple segments, it should formulate a **long-term invasion plan**. Ordinarily, the firm should conceal the plan from competitors and enter one segment at a time to avoid retaliation.

1)   **Megamarketing** is necessary when a market is blocked. This approach supplements the 4 Ps with political, public relations, and other techniques.

j.   Segment managers should be substantially autonomous but also cooperate with other entities in the firm.

7.   **Market Positioning**

a.   Positioning establishes a distinct and favorable place for the firm's offering and image **in the minds of customers**. Thus, the firm's **value proposition** (the combination of benefits offered) should give customers in the target markets good reasons to purchase. Moreover, positioning is the basis for the **marketing mix**.

b.   A firm should strive to position itself as the **leader** regarding its value position, for example, as the largest or best in a category. A competitor's **positioning strategy** may be to

1)   Improve its position in the minds of customers

2)   Occupy a position where it has no competition for its value proposition, for example, a food touted as the low-calorie alternative

3)   De-position or re-position a competitor, for example, by launching an attack

4)   Claim that it belongs to an exclusive group that includes the market leader

c.   According to Michael Treacy and Fred Wiersema, positioning strategy is based on choosing one of three **value disciplines**, becoming the leader in that discipline, performing satisfactorily in the other two, and continuously improving performance in all three. The value disciplines are

1)   Production (technological) leadership
2)   Operational excellence (reliability)
3)   Customer intimacy (responsiveness)

d.   Some marketing researchers advocate a strategy based on **single-benefit positioning** to avoid confusion in the minds of customers about the firm's value proposition. Hence, a firm might relentlessly market itself as offering the best value, lowest cost, greatest reliability, fastest service, etc. However, other researchers argue that **double-benefit positioning** (or even triple-benefit positioning) is preferable, especially if customers perceive that competitors also provide a particular benefit.

e.   The following are typical **positioning mistakes**:

1)   The brand image is vague (**underpositioning**).

2)   The brand image is too narrow (**overpositioning**). For example, customers may not believe that a low-cost retailer offers higher-quality products.

3)   The brand image may be confused in customers' perceptions because the value proposition has too many benefits or the positioning has been changed too often (**confused positioning**).

4)   Customers may not believe the firm's claims (**doubtful positioning**).

        f.   The following are some **positioning options**:

            1)   Leadership in some attribute, such as longevity
            2)   Leadership regarding a benefit
            3)   Leadership in a use or application of the product
            4)   Superiority to a competitor
            5)   Providing a product that is the best for a defined group of customers
            6)   Leadership in a product category
            7)   Best-value positioning

        g.   A firm's choice of which **positioning to promote** depends on the possible benefit(s) to be included in the value proposition and its standing and the standing of competitors in each area.

            1)   Other variables are the beliefs of customers about the importance of particular benefits and of any improvements that the firm might need to make to raise its standing. Still other considerations are the investment needed, the rapidity with which improvements can be made, and the ability of competitors to match the firm's moves.

        h.   **Communication of positioning** begins with a **positioning statement** that identifies a target group and its needs, the brand, the concept, and point(s) of difference from competitors.

            1)   Positioning then should be communicated using all aspects of the marketing mix.

   8.   Stop and review! You have completed the outline for this subunit. Study multiple-choice questions 25 through 29 beginning on page 154.

5.5 CORE CONCEPTS

<u>Managing Marketing Information</u>

- Each firm has unique requirements for **information about customer needs and wants**, preferences, and behavior in all of its markets, including those abroad.

- **Sales information systems** and **databases** of customers and products may be analyzed and combined.

- **Marketing research** is defined by Philip Kotler as "the systematic design, collection, analysis, and reporting of data and findings relevant to a specific marketing situation."

- The **six steps** in the marketing research process are: (1) define the task, (2) develop a research plan, (3) collect the data, (4) analyze the data, (5) report the findings, and (6) make a decision.

- A **competitive intelligence system** should be established to, among other things, identify competitor strategies and monitor their new product introductions.

- A starting point for competitive intelligence is **customer value analysis (CVA)**, the premise being that customers choose from competitors' products or services the brands that provide the greatest customer value.

Customer Value and Relationship Management

- A marketer responds to **customer needs** by stating a **value proposition**, that is, the benefits offered to satisfy those needs. The value proposition is an attempt to affect customer **wants** (needs focused on particular satisfiers).
- **Value** is an aggregate of the elements of the **customer value triad**: quality, service, and price.
- **Customer satisfaction** is the relation between the offering's perceived performance and the customer's expectations. High customer satisfaction tends to create high customer loyalty that results in repurchases.
- Kotler defines **customer relationship management** as "the process of managing detailed information about individual customers and carefully managing all the customer 'touchpoints' with the aim of maximizing customer loyalty."
- The firm should seek to minimize customer churn (customer loss) because **customer retention** through customer satisfaction is a key to profitability.
- **Customer equity** is the sum of the customer lifetime values for all firm customers. According to Rust, Zeithaml, and Lemon, it has certain drivers (value, brand, and relationship equity) and subdrivers.

Marketing Communication

- The **marketing communications mix** consists of **five promotional tools** or media chosen as the means of reaching current stakeholders (customers, employees, shareholders, suppliers, etc.), possible future stakeholders, and the public. The **five tools** are advertising, sales promotion, public relations, personal selling, and direct marketing.
- **Marketing communications** will be **efficient and effective** if target audiences are properly identified, objectives are clearly defined, messages are well designed, communication channels are appropriate, the total budget is adequate but not excessive, and the right marketing communications mix is chosen.
- The **advertising process** may be defined in terms of the **5 Ms**: mission, money, message, media, and measurement.
- **Sales promotion tools** vary: Consumer tools include gifts, coupons, rebates, etc.; trade tools include, e.g., bulk discounts; and business and sales force tools include contests, specialty items, conventions, and trade shows.
- **Public relations tools** include publishing newsletters, reports, etc.; holding special events; inducing news media to cover the firm; sponsoring sports teams, etc.; performing community service activities; providing speakers; and using identity media, such as logos, stationery, etc.
- **Personal selling** is the most basic (and the oldest) form of direct marketing. The great majority of industrial firms use a professional sales force or hire manufacturers' representatives or other agents to perform the in-person task of selling.
- **Direct marketing** employs means of access to potential customers that bypass marketing intermediaries.

Segmentation, Targeting, and Positioning

- **Mass marketing** groups people into large categories based solely on their demographic traits, e.g., age, income, gender, or education level. **Segment marketing** focuses on people who share particular wants, such as married, first-time homeowners buying kitchen appliances on limited budgets.
- **Segmenting** can be done on the basis of geography, demographics, psychographics, behavior, or on a multiattribute basis. Once market segments have been identified, the firm selects its **target(s)**.
- **Positioning** establishes a distinct and favorable place for the firm's offering and image in the minds of customers. Positioning is the basis for the marketing mix.

QUESTIONS

5.1 Managing Marketing Information

1. A firm may seek marketing information using its internally collected data. An approach that uses advanced statistical and mathematical methods to find hidden relationships in the data is

A. Data mining.

B. Data warehousing.

C. Multidimensional data analysis.

D. Electronic data interchange (EDI).

Answer (A) is correct. *(Publisher, adapted)*
REQUIRED: The approach that uses advanced statistical and mathematical methods to find hidden relationships in data.
DISCUSSION: A firm with a decision-support system (DSS) may exploit advanced database technology to analyze vast amounts of data. One approach is online analytical processing, or multidimensional data analysis. It allows a user to have multiple perspectives of the same data. Another approach is data mining. It allows a user to discover hidden relationships in the data, such as associations (links to a given event), sequences of events, classifications (descriptions of the group to which an item belongs, or clusters (new groupings not previously known). Consequently, a firm might detect trends or under-served customer market segments. Data mining requires advanced statistical and mathematical methods, for example, predictive modeling, neural networking, and automatic interaction detection.
Answer (B) is incorrect because a data warehouse contains not only current operating data but also historical information from throughout the organization. Thus, data from all operational systems are integrated, consolidated, and standardized into an organization-wide database into which data are copied periodically. These data are maintained on one platform and can be read but not changed. Graphics and query software and analytical tools assist users. Accordingly, data mining is facilitated by a data warehouse. Answer (C) is incorrect because multidimensional data analysis allows a user to have multiple perspectives of the same data. Answer (D) is incorrect because EDI is a means of transmitting electronic documents online.

2. Which element of the internal data collection process is most likely to yield up-to-date information about prices?

A. Marketing intelligence system.

B. Competitive intelligence system.

C. Sales information system.

D. Transaction processing system for the order-to-payment cycle.

Answer (C) is correct. *(Publisher, adapted)*
REQUIRED: The element of the internal data collection process most likely to yield up-to-date information about prices.
DISCUSSION: Sales information systems using the Internet, extranets, and EDI allow the generation and sharing of very up-to-date information about prices, per-item sales, per-store sales, inventories at any level, and much more.
Answer (A) is incorrect because Philip Kotler *(Marketing Management)* defines a marketing intelligence system as "a set of procedures and sources used by managers to obtain everyday information about developments in the marketing environment." Answer (B) is incorrect because a competitive intelligence system should be established to identify competitor strategies, monitor their new product introductions, analyze markets for the firm's own new product introductions and acquisitions, obtain information about nonpublic firms, evaluate competitor R&D activity, learn about competitors' senior executives, and perform other necessary information gathering tasks. Answer (D) is incorrect because internal data collection begins with the firm's accounting transaction processing system for the order-to-payment cycle. This cycle generates information about the results of transactions involving cash and credit, sales, billing and receivables, production, inventories, shipping, purchasing, receiving, payables, and payroll.

3. Marketing research may rely on primary or secondary sources of information. Which research approach gathers primary information through moderated discussions?

A. Surveys.

B. Focus groups.

C. Experimentation.

D. Evidence of purchasing behavior.

Answer (B) is correct. *(Publisher, adapted)*
REQUIRED: The research approach that gathers primary information through moderated discussions.
DISCUSSION: Focus group discussions are guided by a moderator and recorded for later analysis. This approach collects information about participant's attitudes toward a product, company, service, etc. Consumer goods research has popularized the use of focus groups.
Answer (A) is incorrect because surveys are conducted about attitudes, awareness, customer satisfaction levels, and other matters that provide descriptive information. Answer (C) is incorrect because experimentation determines the cause of some observed result by isolating the effects of a variable. This technique requires that people with similar traits be divided into groups that receive different treatment. The difference is the factor that is being researched. Answer (D) is incorrect because evidence of customer purchasing behavior is recorded in many ways, e.g., in scanning data or catalog purchases.

4. Which of the following is not a step in the establishment of a competitive intelligence system?

A. Data analysis.

B. Data collection.

C. Information dissemination.

D. Classification of competitors.

Answer (D) is correct. *(Publisher, adapted)*
REQUIRED: The choice that is not a step in the setup of a competitive intelligence system.
DISCUSSION: A competitive intelligence system is established to identify competitor strategies, monitor their new product introductions, analyze markets for the firm's own new product introductions and acquisitions, obtain information about nonpublic firms, evaluate competitor R&D activity, learn about competitors' senior executives, and perform other necessary information gathering tasks. Its establishment consists of setting up the system, collecting data, analyzing the data, and disseminating the information. Classification of competitors, however, is not a step in this process. Competitors are classified, and targeted by a firm based on that classification, following the results of a customer value analysis (CVA).
Answer (A) is incorrect because the data analysis phase of the establishment of a competitive intelligence system follows the data collection phase. Answer (B) is incorrect because the data collection phase of the establishment of a competitive intelligence system follows the system setup phase. Answer (C) is incorrect because the information dissemination phase of the establishment of a competitive intelligence system follows the data analysis phase.

5. Which of the following are steps in a customer value analysis (CVA)?

I. Determining what customers value.

II. Having customers rank the relative significance of the elements of customer value.

III. Evaluating how well the firm and its competitors perform relative to the elements of customer value.

IV. Focusing on performance with respect to each element of customer value.

A. I, III, and IV only.

B. I, II, and III only.

C. I, II, and IV only.

D. I, II, III, and IV.

Answer (D) is correct. *(Publisher, adapted)*
REQUIRED: The steps that are part of a customer value analysis (CVA).
DISCUSSION: The steps in a CVA are to

● Determine what customers value.

● Assign quantitative amounts to the elements of customer value and have customers rank their relative significance.

● Evaluate how well the firm and its competitors perform relative to each element.

● Focus on performance with respect to each element in relation to competitors in a given market segment.

● Repeat the foregoing steps as circumstances change.

6. The cheapest way to gain market share ordinarily is by targeting

    A. Close competitors.

    B. Distant competitors.

    C. Weak competitors.

    D. Bad competitors.

Answer (C) is correct. *(Publisher, adapted)*
    REQUIRED: The class of competitors to target to gain market share the most cheaply.
    DISCUSSION: Using the results of a customer value analysis, a firm may target a given class of competitors to gain market share. Targeting weak competitors is usually the cheapest way to gain market share because weak competitors generally do not offer much resistance.
    Answer (A) is incorrect because close competitors are firms that are similar and are the usual targets, but it is not necessarily easy or cheap to take market share from them. Answer (B) is incorrect because distant competitors are not direct competitors. They are indirect competitors that pose a remote threat. Thus, taking market share from them may not necessarily guarantee the firm the entire share taken. Moreover, such a move may be costly. Answer (D) is incorrect because bad competitors are ones that disturb the competitive equilibrium by engaging in such activities as excessive expansion of capacity or overly risky behavior. Although targeting a bad competitor often is a good move because it would improve the health of the industry, it may not necessarily be cheap.

7. Which marketing research instrument is based on follow-up questioning?

    A. Articulative interviewing.

    B. Customer prototyping.

    C. Closed-end questions.

    D. Laddering.

Answer (D) is correct. *(Publisher, adapted)*
    REQUIRED: The marketing research instrument based on follow-up questioning.
    DISCUSSION: Laddering entails posing an initial question to a subject and then a series of follow-up questions to determine the individual's ultimate motivation. It is a common psychological research instrument.
    Answer (A) is incorrect because articulative interviewing uses wide-ranging, general discussions to extract information about values and other factors affecting purchasing choices. Answer (B) is incorrect because customer prototyping attempts to delineate a target customer type using qualitative variables. Answer (C) is incorrect because closed-end questions have finite ranges of answers with no follow-up.

5.2 Customer Value and Relationship Management

8. A marketer states a value proposition to

    A. Create customer needs.

    B. Influence customer wants.

    C. Make the offering tangible.

    D. Define customer value and customer cost.

Answer (B) is correct. *(Publisher, adapted)*
    REQUIRED: The purpose of a marketer's value proposition.
    DISCUSSION: A marketer responds to customer needs by stating a value proposition, that is, the benefits offered to satisfy those needs. The value proposition is an attempt to affect customer wants (needs focused on particular satisfiers). It becomes tangible in an offering, which may consist of products, services, and other things that are intended to satisfy the needs of target buyers.
    Answer (A) is incorrect because a marketer influences wants but does not create needs. Needs are inherent in the human condition. Answer (C) is incorrect because the offering makes the value proposition tangible. Answer (D) is incorrect because the value proposition defines customer benefits, not costs.

9. Customer lifetime value for a particular customer is the

    A. Net present value of the cash flows related to a particular customer.

    B. Sum of the customer's purchases from the firm.

    C. Undiscounted amount of the net cash flows related to a particular customer.

    D. Customer equity.

Answer (A) is correct. *(Publisher, adapted)*
    REQUIRED: The measure of customer lifetime value.
    DISCUSSION: A firm should estimate customer lifetime value, the net present value of the cash flows (purchases – costs of acquiring, selling to, and serving the customer) related to a particular customer. This amount indicates whether a given investment in a customer is justified.
    Answer (B) is incorrect because the measurement of customer lifetime value also considers costs. Answer (C) is incorrect because customer lifetime value is a discounted amount. Answer (D) is incorrect because customer equity is the sum of the customer lifetime values for all of the firm's customers.

10. Customer satisfaction is related to the degree of customer loyalty. High customer loyalty

A. Requires a high degree of satisfaction of other stakeholders.

B. Results when quality, service, and price increase.

C. Depends on the effectiveness of the firm's core business processes.

D. Is directly proportional to customer expectations.

Answer (C) is correct. *(Publisher, adapted)*
REQUIRED: The true statement about high customer loyalty.
DISCUSSION: High customer loyalty is an emotional as well as rational bond that develops when a firm provides high customer value. To obtain such loyalty, the firm needs to develop a value proposition that has superior competitiveness in the target market segment. Crucially, it must be supported by an effective value delivery system, the accumulation of all the experiences the customer has with the offering. Thus, brand value must be supported by core business processes that actually deliver the promised customer value.
Answer (A) is incorrect because customer satisfaction must be balanced against the satisfaction level of the firm's other stakeholders (e.g., shareholders, employees, suppliers, and retailers). Thus, raising customer satisfaction at the expense of profit or other stakeholders may not be appropriate. Answer (B) is incorrect because customer value decreases when price increases. Answer (D) is incorrect because high customer loyalty is created by high customer satisfaction. Satisfaction is less likely when expectations are high.

11. In Michael E. Porter's model of the value creation chain, the primary activities include

A. Logistics, operations, marketing and sales, and service.

B. Procurement, infrastructure, operations, and service.

C. Procurement, infrastructure, operations, and technology development.

D. Procurement, infrastructure, human resources, and technology development.

Answer (A) is correct. *(Publisher, adapted)*
REQUIRED: The primary activities in the value creation chain.
DISCUSSION: The model consists of primary and supporting activities. The primary activities are inbound logistics, operations, outbound logistics, marketing and sales, and service. Inbound logistics activities involve the firms' capture of materials to be processed. Operations activities are conversion processes. Outbound logistics activities include shipment of products. Marketing and sales activities are the promotion and sale of final products. Service activities provide customer service. The four support activities are infrastructure (e.g., administration, finance, and planning), procurement, human resources, and technology development.
Answer (B) is incorrect because procurement and infrastructure are secondary activities. Answer (C) is incorrect because procurement, infrastructure, and technology development are secondary activities. Answer (D) is incorrect because procurement, infrastructure, human resources, and technology development are secondary activities.

12. Customer relationship management is best defined as

A. Coordination with members of the firm's supply chain.

B. Attracting and satisfying customers.

C. Market sensing.

D. Maximizing customer loyalty by managing customer "touchpoints."

Answer (D) is correct. *(Publisher, adapted)*
REQUIRED: The best definition of customer relationship management.
DISCUSSION: Philip Kotler *(Marketing Management)* defines customer relationship management as "the process of managing detailed information about individual customers and carefully managing all the customer 'touchpoints' with the aim of maximizing customer loyalty." Its purpose is to create optimal customer equity. Thus, the process involves more than merely attracting customers (through media advertising, direct mail, etc.) and satisfying them (something competitors also may do).
Answer (A) is incorrect because coordination with members of the firm's supply chain is partner relationship management. Answer (B) is incorrect because customer relationship management seeks to increase the value of the customer base by developing long-term relationships with individual customers by such methods as customer service, customized (if not personalized) offerings, and choice of marketing messages and media. Answer (C) is incorrect because market sensing consists of obtaining, distributing, and acting upon market intelligence.

13. The firm should emphasize customer retention

A. By creating low switching costs.

B. By maximizing customer churn.

C. Although new customers are less costly than old customers.

D. Because the customer base is an intangible asset.

Answer (D) is correct. *(Publisher, adapted)*
REQUIRED: The true statement about customer retention.
DISCUSSION: The firm should seek to minimize customer churn (customer loss) because customer retention through customer satisfaction is a key to profitability. The firm should emphasize customer retention because the customer base is an important intangible asset. The firm benefits from customer retention because it is far less costly than customer attraction. Indeed, increasing the retention rate increases profits exponentially. Moreover, the longer the customer relationship, the more profitable it is.
Answer (A) is incorrect because high switching costs tend to increase customer retention. Answer (B) is incorrect because the firm should minimize customer churn (customer loss). Answer (C) is incorrect because customer retention is less costly than customer attraction.

14. The drivers of customer equity are value equity, brand equity, and relationship equity. The subdriver most closely related to brand equity is

A. Quality.

B. Price.

C. Customer awareness.

D. Loyalty programs.

Answer (C) is correct. *(Publisher, adapted)*
REQUIRED: The subdriver most closely related to brand equity.
DISCUSSION: Brand equity is a subjective evaluation. Subdrivers are the customer's awareness of, and attitude toward, the brand and the customer's belief about brand ethics. Brand equity is most significant when the product is not differentiated but has emotional appeal.
Answer (A) is incorrect because quality is a subdriver of value equity. Answer (B) is incorrect because price is a subdriver of value equity. Answer (D) is incorrect because loyalty programs are subdrivers of relationship equity.

15. Which relationship marketing level is appropriate for a low unit profit margin and many customers?

A. Reactive marketing.

B. Basic marketing.

C. Partnership marketing.

D. Proactive marketing.

Answer (B) is correct. *(Publisher, adapted)*
REQUIRED: The relationship marketing level appropriate for a low unit profit margin and many customers.
DISCUSSION: A firm must determine the appropriate investment in building customer relationships. The levels of investment depend on unit profit margins and the numbers of customers. Basic marketing consists only of selling (low-margin, many customers).
Answer (A) is incorrect because reactive marketing includes encouragement of customer communication (low-to-medium margin and many customers or low margin and medium number of customers). Answer (C) is incorrect because partnership marketing entails continuous assistance to big customers (high margin and few customers). Answer (D) is incorrect because proactive marketing involves seller-initiated communication about new products or uses of old ones (high margin and medium number of customers or medium margin and few customers).

5.3 Marketing Communication

16. The 5 Ms of the advertising process include

I. Mission
II. Money
III. Market sensing
IV. Mass marketing
V. Media

A. I and III only.

B. I, II, and V only.

C. II, IV, and V only.

D. I, II, III, IV, and V.

Answer (B) is correct. *(Publisher, adapted)*
REQUIRED: The items included among the 5 Ms of the advertising process.
DISCUSSION: The advertising process may be defined in terms of the 5 Ms: (1) The mission consists of sales and advertising objectives, (2) the money to be spent is stated in the budget, (3) the message to be communicated is crafted using a creative strategy, (4) the media are chosen to communicate the message, and (5) the measurement of communication and sales determines the effectiveness of the process.
Answer (A) is incorrect because market sensing consists of gathering, disseminating, and acting on marketing intelligence. It is not part of the advertising process. Answer (C) is incorrect because the advertising process does not always involve mass marketing, a technique that is also not limited to advertising. Answer (D) is incorrect because market sensing and mass marketing are not among the 5 Ms.

17. Advertising budgets tend to decrease as a percentage of sales when

    A. Market share is already high.

    B. Clutter from noncompetitive messages exists.

    C. Products are new.

    D. Substitutability is high.

Answer (A) is correct. *(Publisher, adapted)*
    REQUIRED: The situation in which advertising budgets tend to decrease.
    DISCUSSION: Advertising costs to maintain share decline as a percentage of sales when that share is large. Increasing market share is more costly.
    Answer (B) is incorrect because, when a market has many competitors or is cluttered by noncompetitive messages, costs are higher. Answer (C) is incorrect because new products are usually more heavily advertised than old. Answer (D) is incorrect because, when substitutability is high, increased spending may be needed to differentiate the product, e.g., a commodity.

18. The marketing communication mix consists of five types of promotional tools or media. Electronic mail belongs to which class of promotional tools or media?

    A. Direct marketing.

    B. Advertising.

    C. Public relations.

    D. Personal selling.

Answer (A) is correct. *(Publisher, adapted)*
    REQUIRED: The class of promotional tools or media to which electronic mail belongs.
    DISCUSSION: Direct marketing involves sending a promotional message directly to consumers rather than through a mass medium. Some examples are email, voice mail, fax, mail, telemarketing, and home shopping by television.
    Answer (B) is incorrect because advertising is defined by Kotler *(Marketing Management)* as "any paid form of nonpersonal presentation and promotion of ideas, goods, or services by an identified sponsor." It may occur on many platforms: television, radio, films, the Internet, packaging, billboards, point-of-purchase and other displays, brochures, videos, and trademarks. Answer (C) is incorrect because public relations consists of methods of protecting the image of the firm or a product. Typical platforms are lobbying, sponsorships (e.g., the U.S. Postal Service's sponsorship of a cycling team), community outreach, gifts to charity, and the firm's annual report. Answer (D) is incorrect because personal selling involves human interaction and mutual observation. It is the best method of inducing action in the end stages of the purchasing process.

19. The weighted number of exposures to an advertising message equals

    A. Reach times frequency.

    B. Gross rating points times impact.

    C. Gross rating points.

    D. Frequency times impact.

Answer (B) is correct. *(Publisher, adapted)*
    REQUIRED: The weighted number of exposures to an advertising message in a given medium.
    DISCUSSION: Reach, frequency, and impact are key variables in determining the relationship of exposures to audience awareness. Reach (R) is the total number of individuals (or households) exposed during a defined interval of time. Frequency (F) is the average number of exposures per interval of time. Impact (I) is the qualitative effect of an exposure. Total exposures (gross rating points) equals R times F. Thus, the weighted number of exposures to an advertising message in a given medium equals gross rating points times impact, that is, R times F times I.
    Answer (A) is incorrect because reach times frequency equals gross rating points. Answer (C) is incorrect because gross rating points equals reach times frequency. Answer (D) is incorrect because frequency times impact must be multiplied by reach.

20. The element of the marketing communications mix that provides incentives to buy is

    A. Advertising.

    B. Public relations.

    C. Personal selling.

    D. Sales promotion.

Answer (D) is correct. *(Publisher, adapted)*
    REQUIRED: The element of the marketing communications mix that provides incentives to buy.
    DISCUSSION: Sales promotion offers customers short-term incentives to try or purchase the offering. Some possible platforms are coupons, samples, premiums, gifts, contests (e.g., lotteries), trade-ins, no-interest financing, and rebates. Sales promotion provides some additional customer value in exchange for inviting immediate action and draws attention to the offering.
    Answer (A) is incorrect because advertising provides reasons to buy. Answer (B) is incorrect because public relations consists of methods of protecting the image of the firm or a product. Answer (C) is incorrect because personal selling involves human interaction and mutual observation.

21. A firm is introducing a new product. Given a limited advertising budget and a low purchase frequency, the firm should adopt which microtiming approach for its advertising expenditures?

A. Pulsing.

B. Continuity.

C. Flighting.

D. Concentration.

Answer (C) is correct. *(Publisher, adapted)*
REQUIRED: The microtiming approach given a limited budget and a low purchase frequency.
DISCUSSION: The microtiming issue is how to schedule advertising outlays for best effect during a short time period. Variables considered in choosing the pattern are buyer turnover (entry of new buyers), purchase frequency, and the forgetting rate. The higher these rates, the greater the continuity of advertising should be. Flighting is intermittent advertising with periods of no activity. Flighting is useful when funding is low, purchases are infrequent, or when goods are seasonal.
Answer (A) is incorrect because pulsing, or low level continuity with bursts of more intense activity, is a compromise approach that promotes buyer learning while reducing costs. Answer (B) is incorrect because continuity means distributing expenditures evenly over the period, especially in a growing market with frequently purchased goods, or when buyer categories are narrowly defined. Answer (D) is incorrect because concentration in one period is typical for a seasonal project.

22. Personal selling is the promotion tool that is

A. The cheapest.

B. The most effective in the end stage of marketing.

C. Effective because it is impersonal.

D. Least effective when customers feel some obligation.

Answer (B) is correct. *(Publisher, adapted)*
REQUIRED: The characteristic of personal selling.
DISCUSSION: Personal selling involves human interaction and mutual observation. It is the best method of inducing action in the end stages of the purchasing process. Among the platforms are meetings, presentations, fairs, and trade shows. Personal selling allows the development of relationships and may generate a sense of obligation by the potential customer.
Answer (A) is incorrect because personal selling is labor intensive and relatively expensive. Answer (C) is incorrect because personal selling involves interaction with customers. Advertising may be effective because it is impersonal. Answer (D) is incorrect because one of personal selling's advantages is that personal interaction may generate a sense of obligation by the potential customer.

23. Direct marketing is a promotional tool that

A. Is more frequently used because of market demassification.

B. Avoids the invasion of privacy issues raised by other marketing methods.

C. Is more effective at eliciting direct orders than building customer relationships.

D. Makes greater use of marketing intermediaries than other promotional tools.

Answer (A) is correct. *(Publisher, adapted)*
REQUIRED: The characteristic of direct marketing.
DISCUSSION: Direct marketing has grown as a result of demassification (fragmenting of markets into many niches). It employs means of access to potential customers that bypass marketing intermediaries. Direct-order marketing is intended to elicit an immediate and measurable result (e.g., orders), and customer-relationship marketing may use direct-marketing methods to develop long-term relationships.
Answer (B) is incorrect because direct marketing raises invasion of privacy issues. The reasons are the proliferation of computerized databases and the sale or misuse of the names, addresses, personal histories, and purchasing information they contain. Answer (C) is incorrect because direct-order marketing is intended to elicit an immediate and measurable result (e.g., orders), and customer-relationship marketing may use direct-marketing methods to develop long-term relationships. Answer (D) is incorrect because direct marketing employs means of access to potential customers that bypass marketing intermediaries.

24. The most likely effect of a marketing public relations (publicity) campaign is to

A. Increase overall promotion costs.

B. Reach only people exposed to other promotional tools.

C. Provide greater credibility than other promotional tools.

D. Have little effect on the corporate image.

Answer (C) is correct. *(Publisher, adapted)*
REQUIRED: The most likely effect of a marketing public relations (publicity) campaign.
DISCUSSION: Marketing public relations (publicity) supports the marketing department, especially by increasing audience awareness and brand knowledge. Its traditional role was to obtain free media coverage. This function may be less expensive than advertising and sales promotions. Furthermore, publicity is often perceived to be more trustworthy because it appears in news stories and features. Thus, it may affect people who avoid other elements of the promotional mix. Moreover, publicity may dramatize the firm and its products.
Answer (A) is incorrect because public relations may be much cheaper than other promotional tools. Answer (B) is incorrect because public relations may reach people who avoid advertising, in-person selling, etc. Answer (D) is incorrect because public relations may be used to benefit product sales indirectly by improving the corporate image.

5.4 Segmentation, Targeting, and Positioning

25. Mass marketing relies on

A. Economies of scope.

B. Economies of scale.

C. Share of the customer.

D. Customer retention.

Answer (B) is correct. *(Publisher, adapted)*
REQUIRED: The basis of mass marketing.
DISCUSSION: Mass marketing groups people into large categories based solely on their demographic traits, e.g., age, income, gender, or education level. It assumes most people in the same category will react similarly to one marketing message. Mass marketers primarily use mass media (television and print) to reach their targets in large numbers. Moreover, mass marketing relies on economies of scale and a large share of the largest possible market to reduce costs and thereby to lower prices or raise unit profit margins.
Answer (A) is incorrect because economies of scope arise when a firm targets multiple segments that are interrelated regarding cost, performance, and technology. Answer (C) is incorrect because a share-of-the-customer approach identifies potential customers, maximizes net customer lifetime value, and avoids pursuit of unprofitable customers. Answer (D) is incorrect because mass marketing emphasizes customer attraction.

26. Which form of micromarketing is based on a specialized strategy directed toward a subsegment of a market segment?

A. Sector marketing.

B. Local marketing.

C. Flexible marketing offerings.

D. Niche marketing.

Answer (D) is correct. *(Publisher, adapted)*
REQUIRED: The form of micromarketing based on a specialized strategy directed toward a market subsegment.
DISCUSSION: Niche marketing is a specialized strategy based on devoting all marketing efforts toward a subsegment of a market segment. Niche marketing typically appeals to smaller firms with limited resources, but larger firms also engage in niche marketing. It is attractive to these firms due to its cost effectiveness, the result of focusing marketing funds on a targeted group. Diverse types of niche marketing include end-user strategy, which is based on serving only one type of end-user customer; vertical-level strategy, which calls for specialization in one level of the production and distribution cycle and offering a unique product or service that is not available from another firm; and geographic strategy, which involves selling in one specific geographic area.
Answer (A) is incorrect because segment marketing focuses on people who share particular wants, such as married, first-time homeowners buying kitchen appliances on limited budgets. A sector differs from a segment. The customers in a sector may vary considerably in their wants. For example, first-time homeowners buying kitchen appliances constitute a sector. Answer (B) is incorrect because local marketing addresses the wants of neighborhood and other local groups. Answer (C) is incorrect because flexible marketing offerings may be made within a segment or subsegment.

27. The type of consumer segmentation based on lifestyle or core values is

   A. Geographic.

   B. Demographic.

   C. Psychographic.

   D. Behavioral.

Answer (C) is correct. *(Publisher, adapted)*
   REQUIRED: The type of consumer segmentation based on lifestyle or core values.
   DISCUSSION: Psychographic segmentation is by personality traits, lifestyle (attitudes, activities, and interests), or core values. Thus, marketers may attempt to build a brand personality, design offerings targeted to time-constrained or money-constrained individuals, or appeal to beliefs at a deeper level than attitudes and behaviors.
   Answer (A) is incorrect because geographic segmentation is by region, size of metropolitan area, population density (e.g., suburban versus rural), or climate. Knowing where the firm's customers live is an aid in targeting communications. Answer (B) is incorrect because demographic segmentation is by age group, generation, stage in the family life cycle, size of the family, sex, level of income, job, level of education, social class, religion, race, or ethnicity. Answer (D) is incorrect because behavioral segmentation is by regular or special occasions, benefits wanted, status of users, rate of usage, degree of loyalty, readiness to buy, or attitude.

28. Market targeting is the process of evaluating and selecting market segments. A firm that elects full market coverage

   A. Reduces its costs by differentiated marketing.

   B. Ordinarily bases its approach on product specialization.

   C. Targets a supersegment.

   D. May adopt an undifferentiated marketing approach based on a single offering.

Answer (D) is correct. *(Publisher, adapted)*
   REQUIRED: The true statement about full market coverage.
   DISCUSSION: Full market coverage provides all the products wanted by all customer groups. This approach is possible only for a very large firm. Undifferentiated marketing covers the market by mass distribution and advertising of one offering. Costs of R&D, production, transportation, inventory, marketing research, and product management are minimized, and a lower price can be charged to attract price sensitive buyers.
   Answer (A) is incorrect because differentiated marketing covers the market by offering different products in different segments. Sales are higher than under undifferentiated marketing, but costs (product modification, inventory, manufacturing, administration, and promotion) are higher. Answer (B) is incorrect because product specialization is the sale of different versions of one product to multiple segments. The risk is technological obsolescence. Answer (C) is incorrect because a supersegment consists of multiple segments with some commonality that the firm can leverage. Hence, a supersegment does not cover the full market.

29. If a firm's value proposition has too many benefits, the result is most likely to be

   A. Confused positioning.

   B. Overpositioning.

   C. Underpositioning.

   D. Doubtful positioning.

Answer (A) is correct. *(Publisher, adapted)*
   REQUIRED: The effect when a firm's value proposition has too many benefits.
   DISCUSSION: The brand image may be confused in customers' perceptions because the value proposition has too many benefits or the positioning has been changed.
   Answer (B) is incorrect because overpositioning means that the brand image is too narrow. For example, customers may not believe that a low-cost retailer offers high-quality products. Answer (C) is incorrect because an underpositioned offering has a vague brand image. Answer (D) is incorrect because doubtful positioning results when customers do not believe the firm's claims.

Use Gleim's *CMA Test Prep* for interactive testing with **over 2,000 additional multiple-choice questions**!

STUDY UNIT SIX
OTHER MARKETING TOPICS

(22 pages of outline)

This study unit is the **last of three** on **strategic marketing**. The relative weight assigned to this major topic in Part 3 of the exam is **15%** at **skill level A** (two skill types required). The three study units are

Study Unit 4: Marketing's Strategic Role within the Firm

Study Unit 5: Marketing Information and Market Segmentation

Study Unit 6: Other Marketing Topics

After studying the outline and answering the multiple-choice questions, you will have the skills necessary to address the following topics listed in the IMA's Learning Outcome Statements:

Part 3 – Section B.4. Managing products and services

The candidate should be able to:

   a.   distinguish between products and services

   b.   classify products and services, including consumer products, industrial products, and other marketable entities

   c.   demonstrate an understanding of product attributes, branding, packaging, labeling, and product support services

   d.   demonstrate an understanding of product line decisions and product mix decisions

   e.   demonstrate an understanding of services marketing, including the nature and characteristics of service marketing strategies

   f.   demonstrate an understanding of new product development strategy and product life-cycle strategies

Part 3 – Section B.5. Pricing strategy

The candidate should be able to:

   a.   identify internal and external factors affecting pricing decisions

   b.   demonstrate an understanding of general pricing approaches, including cost-based pricing, value-based pricing, and competition-based pricing

   c.   discuss the role of the management accountant in pricing decisions.

   d.   demonstrate an understanding of new product pricing strategies, including market skimming pricing and market penetration pricing

   e.   demonstrate an understanding of product mix pricing strategies, including product line pricing, optional product pricing, captive product pricing, by-product pricing, and product bundle pricing

   f.   demonstrate an understanding of price adjustment strategies including discount and allowance pricing, segmented pricing, psychological pricing, promotional pricing, geographical pricing, and international pricing

   g.   demonstrate an understanding of how elasticity and the bargaining power of either the buyer or seller can impact the price

<u>Part 3 – Section B.6. Promotional mix and distribution strategy</u>

The candidate should be able to:

a.   define marketing communication mix

b.   demonstrate an understanding of the integrated marketing communication process, including the need for integrated marketing communications

c.   identify and define the components of the overall communication mix, including advertising, sales promotion, public relations, and personal selling

d.   demonstrate an understanding of the advertising process, including setting advertising objectives, setting the advertising budget, developing advertising strategy, and advertising evaluation

e.   demonstrate an understanding of the sales promotion process, including sales promotion objectives, tools, strategy, and evaluation

f.   demonstrate an understanding of public relations and identify related tools

g.   demonstrate an understanding of the role of the personal selling process as an element of promotional mix

h.   identify the most effective component of the marketing mix (advertising, sales promotion, public relations, or personal selling) to use in a given situation

i.   define relationship marketing

j.   demonstrate an understanding of the direct marketing model, its benefits, forms of direct marketing, integrated campaign process, and ethical issues

k.   define the nature and functions of distribution channels

l.   demonstrate an understanding of distribution channel behavior and organization, including vertical, horizontal, and hybrid marketing systems and channel disintegration trends

m.   demonstrate an understanding of distribution channel design decisions, including analysis of consumer service needs, defining channel objectives and constraints, identifying and evaluating major alternatives, and global implementation

6.1 PRODUCTS AND SERVICES

1.   A **product strategy** should align the approaches taken to choosing the product mix and product lines, branding, packaging, and labeling.

   a.   Kotler *(Marketing Management)* broadly defines a **product** as "anything that can be offered to a market to satisfy a want or need." This definition includes not only physical things such as goods, but also services, ideas, information, experiences, places, and people.

   b.   A **service** is "an act or performance" offered to another party. No transfer of ownership of anything is involved in the performance of a service.

2.   The attractiveness of the **offering** depends on the features and quality of the product, the mix and quality of the services, and price.

3.   A product may be analyzed in terms of the **customer value hierarchy**:

   a.   Core benefit (e.g., transportation)

   b.   Basic product (a car that simply provides the core benefit)

   c.   Expected product (a car with standard features and quality)

   d.   Augmented product (a car that exceeds expectations)

   e.   Potential product (a car that reflects every possible future augmentation and ways to differentiate the product)

4.   In industrialized nations, **product augmentation** through customer service, delivery options, packaging, financing, etc., is the basis for competition. Hence, the customer's **consumption system** must be understood, that is, how the customer acquires, uses, pays for, and maintains the product.

5. The relationships among products are described in the **product hierarchy**:

   a. Need family

   b. Product family (all product classes that satisfy the need reasonably well)

   c. Product class (products that are functionally related)

   d. Product line (products that are closely related)

   e. Product type (products in a line that share one of the forms of the product)

   f. Product variant, item, or storekeeping unit (a product distinguished by an attribute such as size or price)

6. **Product Classifications**

   a. **Durability and Tangibility**

      1) Nondurable goods (tangibles that are quickly consumed)

      2) Durable goods (tangibles that are multi-use)

      3) Services (intangibles that are indivisible, variable, and perishable)

   b. **Consumer Goods**

      1) Convenience goods (frequent purchase, low effort)

      2) Shopping goods (comparison before purchase)

         a) Homogeneous (price differentiated)

         b) Heterogeneous (feature or service differentiated)

      3) Specialty goods (special purchasing effort)

      4) Unsought goods (customers tend not to think of purchasing)

   c. **Industrial Goods**

      1) Materials and parts

         a) Raw materials (farm products and such natural products as crude oil or lumber)

         b) Manufactured materials and parts (component materials such as cement, tires)

      2) Capital items

         a) Installation (buildings and certain equipment, such as an elevator)

         b) Equipment (portable equipment and tools)

      3) Supplies

         a) Maintenance and repair products

         b) Operating supplies

      4) Business services

         a) Maintenance and repair

         b) Business advisory (e.g., accounting, legal, or IT)

7. **Branding** is the development, maintenance, and protection of a unique identity for the selling firm. Branding results from a large long-term investment in advertising, other forms of promotion, and packaging.

   a. A **brand name** is legally protected under U.S. **trademark** law for an indefinite period.

   b. A brand differentiates the seller's product in the minds of customers because it conveys any or a combination of the following meanings:

      1) The nature of the user

      2) A personality

      3) Core values

      4) A culture

      5) Product benefits

      6) Product attributes

c. Brand attributes (price, safety, quality, performance, etc.) are at the lowest level of the **brand pyramid**, benefits are in the middle, and beliefs and values are at the top. Thus, a brand name should be related in customer perceptions with a key benefit or, preferably, multiple benefits to protect against competitors' moves and changes in customers' preferences.

1) A strong brand usually has a strong emotional or nonrational appeal (the top of the pyramid).

d. **Brand identity** results not only from choices of the name, logo, colors, tagline, and symbol, but also from fulfilling the implicit promises to deliver specified benefits to customers. **Brand bonding** occurs when the total customer experience is consistent with the firm's promises. **Internal branding** is necessary to ensure that everyone in the firm acts consistently with those promises.

e. According to Kotler *(Marketing Management)*, **brand equity** is "the positive differential effect that knowing the brand name has on customer response to the product or service." It may be measured by the incremental price a customer will pay for the product. An effect of brand equity is customer preferences for the brand when another product is essentially identical.

1) **Brand valuation** is financial value. Some brands have valuations in the tens of billions of dollars.

2) Brand equity is a firm asset that correlates with the degree of customer loyalty. Thus, a brand may progress from being unknown to brand awareness, brand acceptability, brand preference, and brand loyalty. Brand equity is a component of **customer equity**, so management of brand equity is an important means of enhancing **customer lifetime value**.

f. The firm must make the following **decisions about branding**:

1) Whether to brand (see, for example, proliferation of generics in supermarkets)
2) Sponsorship

    a) Manufacturer (national) brand
    b) Distributor (private or reseller) brand
    c) Licensed brand name
    d) Private brands developed by wholesalers and resellers

3) Brand names

    a) Names for individual products (avoidance of risk to the firm's brand equity if the product fails)
    b) Blanket family names (advantages are lower development cost and immediate name recognition)
    c) Family names for different product lines
    d) Corporate name added to names for individual products

g. Brands may be **functional** brands (e.g., detergents), **image** brands (e.g., status symbols), or **experiential** brands (e.g., theme parks or coffee shops). Development of a brand may be in one of the firm's existing product categories or in a new product category.

1) **Line extension** (new items in the same product category, e.g., new ice cream flavors)
2) **Brand extension** (new product categories)
3) **Multibrands** (new brands, i.e., flanker brands, in a category)
4) **New brands** (new names and new categories)
5) **Co-branding** (dual branding, or an offering using different brand names, e.g., using one brand as an ingredient of another)

h. One effective means of developing and marketing new products is the use of **line extensions** and **brand extensions**. The concept behind extension is that consumers are already familiar with the firm's major brand names. Thus, if a new product carries the same brand name, it will be more likely to succeed. Carrying an established brand name enables a new product to more easily fill a niche in the marketplace. Furthermore, extensions make efficient use of promotional costs because customers are already familiar with the quality of the products created and manufactured under the brand. Most new products are line extensions.

8. **Packaging** is an element of the product strategy. It consists of designing and producing the container.

   a. An effective package makes a good general impression, attracts attention, is descriptive, and instills confidence.

   b. A customer may pay more for a better (more convenient, dependable, or prestigious) package.

   c. The package advertises the firm's and the brand's image.

   d. An invention of a new type of package may provide greater customer value, e.g., a better way of dispensing the product.

   e. **Package design** begins with deciding what it should do. Other decisions include size, shape, color, materials, text, environmental and safety features, and other matters. These decisions must be consistent with pricing and promotional strategies.

      1) Package testing includes not only engineering tests but also visual, retailer, and customer tests.

9. **Labeling** identifies the product and brand; describes the nature and grade of the product (if applicable), the producer, and the content; provides usage instructions; and serves as a promotional tool.

   a. Labels vary greatly in the amount of information conveyed, not least because legal disclosure requirements differ.

   b. Under the **Federal Trade Commission Act of 1914**, labels must not be false, misleading, or deceptive.

   c. The **Fair Packaging and Labeling Act of 1967** established required labeling standards.

10. A product mix contains **product lines**. A product line is often created by adding modular elements to a basic platform so as to satisfy different customer wants.

    a. Analysis of a product line should provide a basis for decisions about **product-line strategies**, such as building, maintaining, harvesting, or divesting a product line.

       1) A financial analysis should determine the **sales and profits** for each item in a product line. This process measures profit margins and the possibilities for increasing sales or profits through price increases or additional promotion.

       2) The **market profile** depicts how items in the product line are situated in relation to the competition. **Product mapping** is useful in comparing the locations of the firms' and competitors' products and customer wants. Mapping may reveal underserved market segments.

    b. The **length** should be profit-maximizing but also reflects other objectives.

       1) A line may be structured to take advantage of **upselling** of a more expensive product or **cross-selling** of a related product. It may also be **diversified** to hedge against changes in economic cycles.

       2) Longer lines reflect a desire for greater market share and market growth. Shorter lines may indicate an emphasis on profits.

       3) Longer lines reflect pressures to use excess capacity and to satisfy customers but also increase costs.

        4)   **Line stretching** may be **downmarket** to provide lower-priced products. The purpose may be to exploit a growth opportunity to move against a low-price competitor that has invaded the firm's markets, or to shift out of a declining market.

           a)   **Upmarket stretching** may reflect a search for growth, greater profit margins, or positioning as a full-product-line seller.

           b)   **Two-way stretching** is a middle market firm's move into the upmarket and the downmarket.

        5)   **Line filling** adds products within the firm's current range. This strategy may be counterproductive if it results in customer confusion and does not meet a customer need. A line-filling product should be differentiated in the minds of customers so that it has a **just-noticeable difference**.

    c.   **Line modernization** is essential to competitiveness. The issue is whether it should be incremental (less costly but also less competitively effective) or a complete makeover (more costly but giving competitors less time to respond). If markets are evolving quickly, the process should be continuous.

        1)   Timing is crucial. Premature modernization may harm sales of existing products, but delayed modernization may allow a competitor to establish an unassailable position.

    d.   If the firm considers **featuring** certain products in the line, it must decide whether to support underperforming products or to promote the most successful products.

    e.   **Pruning** is necessary when financial analysis reveals that a product is hurting profits or when the firm has capacity constraints.

11.   The **product mix** is the product assortment (everything the firm sells). Analysis of the attributes of the mix helps the firm to determine its marketing strategy and make decisions about its product lines.

    a.   The following are the attributes:

        1)   **Width** is the number of product lines.
        2)   **Length** equals the total items in the mix.
        3)   **Depth** equals the variants of each product.
        4)   **Consistency** is the degree of the relationship of the product lines, for example, as to uses by ultimate consumers or choices of distribution channels.

    b.   The firm may grow by adding to any attribute of the product mix.

12.   **Services Marketing**

    a.   Services are **intangible**, so customers need tangible evidence of their quality. Hence, **customer experience engineering** determines the desired perception of that experience and then develops **performance and context clues** that are consistent with it. An **experience blueprint** is a visual representation of those clues.

        1)   Services usually are rendered and consumed at the same time. Thus, the service provider-customer relationship is vital, and preferred providers charge a higher price.

        2)   Services vary greatly in quality. Accordingly, quality control must be managed effectively by selective hiring, strong training programs, standardizing the firm's services, and researching customer satisfaction.

        3)   Services are perishable. Because they cannot be inventoried, demand variability results in excess supply at nonpeak periods.

b. **Service Marketing Strategies**

1) Three more Ps apply:

a) **People.** The right employees, if well trained and motivated, enhance customer satisfaction because many services require substantial customer-employee interaction.

b) **Physical evidence and presentation** are what the customer perceives, such as the decorative features of a restaurant.

c) **Process.** A process is how the service is performed, for example, delivery of health care in a doctor's office, outpatient clinic, or hospital.

2) Service marketing involves external, internal, and interactive marketing.

a) **External marketing** (firm to customer) essentially reflects the 4 Ps.

b) **Internal marketing** (firm to employees) is the effort expended to induce employees to interact effectively with customers.

c) **Interactive marketing** (employees to customers) should have high functional as well as technical quality. The customer not only should be well served but also perceive that (s)he has been well served.

3) **Evaluation of services** is difficult for customers. Services tend to lack **search qualities**, or factors that can be evaluated beforehand. Services usually have **experience qualities** (factors that can be evaluated during and after performance) and **credence qualities** (factors that may be difficult to evaluate at any time).

a) Consequently, service customers may be less reliant on advertising than on testimonials by friends and users of the service. Moreover, they may rely heavily on physical clues, individual service providers, and prices to assess quality. Finally, customer satisfaction may lead to strong customer loyalty.

4) **Nonprice competitive differentiation** is a major issue for service firms. It may be achieved by

a) **Varying the offering** by including secondary service features with the primary service features. Innovation should be continuous because these features are readily imitated.

b) **Improving delivery** through greater reliability, resilience (e.g., coping with customer inquiries and emergencies), and innovation.

c) A **superior image**.

5) **Service quality** should be managed so that perceived service is better than expected service. Consequently, a firm must accurately determine customer expectations and service standards, communicate the nature and quality of the service to avoid distortion of expectations, and ensure that employees perform at least at the level of a consistent set of standards.

a) Service quality is a function of

i) Reliability of the service

ii) Responsiveness (motivation of providers to give good service)

iii) Assurance (capacity of providers to inspire confidence)

iv) Empathy (a caring attitude exhibited by providers)

v) Tangible factors (appearance of facilities, communications, employees, etc.)

    b)   Profitable service firms tend to be customer driven and therefore have a strategy for satisfying customer needs. They also set high standards. Moreover, senior management is committed to service quality. Still other characteristics of these firms are use of self-service technologies (e.g., ATMs), monitoring their own and competitors' performance, encouraging customers to register their complaints, effectively resolving those complaints, and attending to employee satisfaction.

    6)   Service firms may improve **productivity** by

        a)   Hiring and training better employees

        b)   Changing the quantity-quality tradeoff ratio

        c)   Treating the performance of the service as a manufacturing process

        d)   Creating a product that reduces the need for a service

        e)   Performing more substitute services (e.g., allowing a nurse practitioner to do some physician's work)

        f)   Giving customers reasons to provide labor (e.g., ATMs)

        g)   Using technology effectively and efficiently

    c.   Nonservice firms, such as equipment makers, may still need to provide **product support services**.

    1)   Customers are concerned about reliability, the rate of failure, length of time the product will be out of service, service dependability, and costs of maintenance and repair.

        a)   Thus, a buyer calculates the product's **life-cycle cost**, not just the purchase cost.

    2)   The firm should determine the services that are most important (and their rank order) and consider all elements of the **value chain** in developing new products. Proper design may reduce customer support costs.

    3)   Firms may offer different product-service packages. For example, different service contracts may have different effective periods and deductibles.

    4)   Services may

        a)   Be offered **presale**. They facilitate purchase and use (e.g., finance, installation, or training) or augment value (e.g., warranties).

        b)   Be offered **postsale**, for example, by parts-and-service departments, customer service departments, or authorized distributors and dealers. However, a customer that does its own servicing may negotiate for lower prices on the products it buys.

    5)   The following are trends in support services:

        a)   Customers are more sophisticated. Such customers may not desire bundled services.

        b)   Equipment is more reliable and easier to repair.

        c)   Service firms may now handle many different types of equipment.

        d)   Extended warranties have become less appealing as reliability improves.

        e)   Customer service competition is restraining price increases.

        f)   Firms have improved their call handling.

13.   Stop and review! You have completed the outline for this subunit. Study multiple-choice questions 1 through 6 beginning on page 179.

6.2 GLOBAL MARKETING ISSUES

1. **Methods of Expanding into International Markets**

   a. **Licensing** gives firms in foreign countries the right to produce or market products or services within a geographical area for a fee.

      1) Licensing a process, patent, trade secret, etc., is a way to gain a foothold in a foreign market with little immediate risk. However, the licensor may have insufficiency control over the licensee's operations, profits are lost if the arrangement succeeds, and the licensee ultimately may become a competitor.

   b. **Exporting** is the sale of goods manufactured in one country and then sold in other countries.

   c. In a **local storage and sale arrangement**, products manufactured in one country are then shipped to a marketing facility located in another country.

   d. **Local component assembly** involves shipping individual parts from one country to an assembly facility in a second country. They are then turned into a salable product and sold in the second country or exported to other countries.

   e. In **multiple or joint ventures**, several firms, even competitors, work together to create products that are sold under one or more brand names in different countries. They share responsibility, ownership, costs, and profits.

   f. An **indirect export strategy** operates through intermediaries, such as home-country merchants who buy and resell the product, home-country agents who negotiate transactions with foreign buyers for a commission, cooperatives that represent groups of sellers, and export-management firms that receive fees for administering the firm's export efforts. **Indirect export** requires lower investment than direct export and is less risky because of the intermediaries' expertise.

   g. **Direct investment** has many advantages: (1) cheaper materials or labor, (2) receipt of investment incentives from the host government, (3) a strong relationship with interested parties in the host country, (4) control of the investment, (5) a better image in the host country, and (6) market access when domestic contest rules are in effect. However, direct investment is risky because of exposure to currency fluctuations, expropriation, potentially high exit barriers, and restraints on sending profits out of the country.

   h. The **internationalization process** is of crucial interest to nations that wish to encourage local firms to grow and to operate globally. According to Swedish researchers, it involves the following steps:

      1) Lack of regular exports;
      2) Export via independent agents to a few markets, with later expansion to more countries;
      3) Creation of sales subsidiaries in larger markets; and
      4) Establishment of plants in foreign countries.

   i. **Attractiveness** of a foreign market is a function of such factors as geography, income, climate, population, and the product. Another major factor is the unmet needs of a developing nation, for example, China or India.

      1) Entry into a market abroad may be based on many factors, for example, **psychic proximity**. Thus, a first-time venture abroad might be in a market with a related culture, language, or laws.

2.   **Limited entry.** It has been suggested that firms emphasize the **triad markets** (the U.S., Western Europe, and the Far East). However, such an approach would have very adverse long-term effects on the world economy. Nevertheless, a firm may decide to enter only a few national markets.

    a.   According to Ayal and Zif, the following are factors indicating that few national markets should be entered:

        1)   Entry costs are high;

        2)   Market control costs are high;

        3)   Product adaptation costs are high;

        4)   Communication adaptation costs are high;

        5)   The first countries selected have large populations, high income, and a high rate of growth; and

        6)   A dominant firm can erect high entry barriers.

3.   **Organizational Progression of Marketing in the International Environment**

    a.   **Export division.** This is the first step for an organization when it begins selling products beyond its own borders. Generally, a firm's initial entry is in other markets that share a common language or similar cultural norms.

    b.   **International division.** Large corporations make this step before becoming true global organizations. They generally focus their efforts in certain geographical regions that are led either from a central structure or are locally run and managed. Moreover, operating units report to the head of the division, not to a CEO or executive committee. Operating units may be geographical units, world product groups, or subsidiaries.

    c.   **Global organization.** All elements of the organization are geared toward creating and selling products to a worldwide market. Thus, all elements of the firm can be made to be more efficient in the global arena. These elements include management, production facilities, and the procurement of raw materials and components.

        1)   **Glocalization** of a global organization localizes some of its elements but standardizes other elements.

4.   **Strategies for Global Marketing Organization**

    a.   A **multinational strategy** adopts a portfolio approach. Its emphasis is on national markets because the need for global integration is not strong.

        1)   The product is customized for each market and therefore incurs higher production costs.

        2)   Decision making is primarily local with a minimum of central control.

        3)   This strategy is most effective given large differences between countries.

        4)   Also, exchange rate risk is reduced when conducting business in this manner.

    b.   A **global strategy** regards the world as one market.

        1)   The product is essentially the same in all countries.

        2)   Central control of the production process is relatively strong.

        3)   Faster product development and lower production cost are typical.

    c.   A **glocal strategy** combines some elements of local responsiveness or adaptation with some elements of global integration.

        1)   Successful telecommunications firms are examples of balancing these elements.

        2)   **Local responsiveness** is indicated when local product tastes and preferences, regulations, and barriers are significant.

        3)   **Global integration** is indicated when demand is homogeneous and economies of productive scale are large.

5. **Global vs. Transnational Firms**

   a. **Global firms** are primarily managed from one central country. Even though their products may be sold throughout the globe, their headquarters and most of their policy decisions are set from a central base of operations.

   b. **Transnational firms** lack a national identity. These organizations rely on a decentralized structure for management and decision-making. They tend to be more attuned to local customs and market forces because they take much more of their input from a local or regional management team.

6. **International Trade Practices**

   a. **Regional Free Trade Zones**

      1) The **European Union (EU)** is a collection of 25 European nations that have lowered trade barriers among member states and share a common currency and trade policy.

      2) The **North American Free Trade Agreement (NAFTA)** was created among the U.S., Mexico, and Canada. NAFTA will likely be expanded into South American countries.

      3) **MERCOSUL** is a free-trade agreement among South American nations. They include Argentina, Brazil, Uruguay, and Paraguay. Chile and Bolivia are associate members.

      4) **APEC** (the Asian Pacific Economic Cooperation forum) is a collection of 21 Pacific-rim nations, including the NAFTA countries, China, and Japan, dedicated to fostering increased trade with each other and the rest of the world.

   b. **Cartels.** A cartel is an organization of sellers (e.g., the oil cartel OPEC) who undertake joint action to maximize members' profits by controlling the supply, and therefore the price, of their product. Under the laws of many nations, such collusive conduct is illegal when engaged in by firms subject to those laws. The reason is that, as a result of the monopolistic and anticompetitive practices of cartels, supply is lower, prices are high, competition is restrained, and the relevant industry is less efficient.

   c. **Dumping.** Dumping is an unfair trade practice that violates international agreements. It occurs when a firm charges a price (1) lower than that in its home market or (2) less than the cost to make the product. Dumping may be done to penetrate a market or as a result of export subsidies.

7. **International marketing programs.** Firms that operate globally must choose a marketing program after considering the need for **adaptation** to local circumstances. The possibilities lie on a continuum from a purely standardized marketing mix to a purely adapted marketing mix. The former chooses to standardize products, promotion, and distribution. The latter adapts the elements of the mix to each local market. Worldwide standardization of all elements should be the **lowest cost marketing strategy**. However, even well established global brands ordinarily undergo some adaptation to local markets.

   a. **Product and Promotion**

      1) Using a **straight extension** strategy, a higher profit potential exists because virtually no changes are made in the product or its promotion. There is a downside potential if foreign consumers are not familiar with this type of product or do not readily accept it.

      2) Using a **product adaptation** strategy, a firm makes changes in the product for each market but not in its promotion. This strategy can reduce profit potential but may also provide a marketing advantage by considering local wants and needs.

3) Using a **product invention** strategy, a new product is created specifically for a certain country or regional market. A product may either include advancements for developed countries or have certain elements removed in places where a lower cost is a key selling point. **Backward invention** is the reintroduction of an earlier version of the product to meet local needs. This variant of the invention strategy reflects the possibility that different countries may be in different stages of the international product life cycle. **Forward invention** requires developing a new product for the unique needs of a foreign market.

4) **Communication adaptation** is a strategy that does not change the products, but advertising and marketing campaigns are changed to reflect the local culture and beliefs.

5) A **dual adaptation** strategy changes both the product and the promotion to provide the best chance of acceptance in a foreign market.

b. **Price**

1) The gray market poses difficulties for a firm that sells products at different prices in different countries. In a **gray market**, products imported from one country to another are sold in a third country, or even in the original exporters country, by persons trying to make a profit from differences in retail prices.

2) The **price escalation** problem requires setting different prices in different countries. Price escalation is caused by an accumulation of additional costs, e.g., currency fluctuations; transportation expenses; profits earned by importers, wholesalers, and retailers; and import duties. Three strategies address this issue:

   a) A firm may set a **standard price** globally. However, this strategy may result in prices being unprofitable in some markets and too high in others.

   b) A firm may set a **market-based price** in each market. The drawback of this strategy is that it ignores cost differences. It also may create a gray market situation between certain regions.

   c) A firm may set a **cost-based price** in each market with a standard markup. In a region or country where costs are high, this strategy may result in prices that are too high to be competitive within the local market.

3) A **transfer price** is the price charged by one subunit of a firm to another. When the subsidiary-buyer is in a foreign country, the higher the transfer price, the higher the potential tariffs. However, the tax levied on a subsequent sale by the subsidiary will be lower because of its higher acquisition cost.

c. **Distribution channels** are a necessity to ensure goods are successfully transferred from the production facility to end users. These channels include three distinct links that must work smoothly together.

1) The **international marketing headquarters** (export department or international division) is where decisions are made with regard to the subsequent channels and other aspects of the marketing mix.

2) **Channels between nations** carry goods to foreign borders. They include air, land, sea, or rail transportation channels. At this stage, in addition to transportation methods, intermediaries are selected (e.g., agents or trading companies), and financing and risk management decisions are reached.

3) **Channels within nations** take the goods from the border or entry point to the ultimate users of the products. Among nations, the number of the levels of distribution, the types of channels, and the size of retailers vary substantially.

8. **Steps to brand globally.** The following steps should be taken to minimize the risks of expanding into foreign markets and to maximize growth potential:

   a. A firm must understand how diverse markets tie together to form a **global branding landscape**. Individual countries vary in their historical acceptance of products and services. However, firms may also capitalize on similarities that are found in certain areas and regions.

   b. Branding and brand-building must be a process. New markets must be developed from a zero base. Global firms must build awareness of the product and then create sources of **brand equity**.

   c. Establishing a **marketing infrastructure** is crucial. To create a successful marketing structure, the firm either must merge with the local marketing channels or create a completely new method of distribution.

   d. **Integrated marketing communications** should be developed. Markets must be approached with a broad range of messages. Sole reliance on advertising should be avoided. Other marketing communications include merchandising, promotions, and sponsorship.

   e. The firm may create **branding partnerships**. Global firms often form alliances with local distribution channels to increase their profitability while decreasing their marketing costs.

   f. The firm should determine the **ratio of standardization and customization**. Products that can be sold virtually unchanged throughout several markets provide a greater profit opportunity for a global firm. However, cultural differences may require extensive customization to appeal to markets in different countries.

   g. The firm should determine the **ratio of local to global control**. Local managers may understand the wants and needs of their market, but the global firm must still retain control of certain elements of the marketing process and strategy.

   h. The firm should establish **local guidelines** so the local sales and profit goals are met.

   i. The firm should create a **global brand equity tracking system**. This equity system is a set of research processes that provide the marketers with pertinent information. The marketers can use this tracking system to create both long- and short-term strategies for expanding product sales and reach.

   j. The firm should maximize **brand elements**. Large global firms can achieve much greater expansion rates when the brand elements are successfully employed at the launch of a product or service.

9. Stop and review! You have completed the outline for this subunit. Study multiple-choice questions 7 through 22 beginning on page 180.

6.3 PRICING DECISIONS

1. **Pricing** is the element of the 4 Ps of marketing that generates revenues, not costs. It is an important part of the marketing mix, and pricing alternatives should be test marketed in the same way as new products, packages, and advertising campaigns.

   a. The firm must determine its pricing objectives; estimate demand at each price; estimate learning curves and costs for different outputs; estimate costs of different marketing offers; consider competitors' actions (costs, prices, and offers); choose a pricing strategy; and establish a price.

   b. **Pricing objectives** include profit maximization. Classical economic theory assumes all firms always select the price that results in the highest profit.

      1) An alternative objective is **target margin maximization**. This objective is stated as a percentage ratio of profits to sales.

      2) **Volume-oriented objectives** set prices to meet target sales volumes or market shares.

        3) **Image-oriented objectives** set prices to enhance the consumer's perception of the firm's product mix.

        4) **Stabilization objectives** set prices to maintain a stable relationship between the firm's prices and the industry leader's prices.

  c. **External factors** to be considered include customer **price sensitivity**. For example, price sensitivity tends to be lower when the price is a relatively low proportion of the total cost of ownership, the product is low-cost, or it is rarely purchased.

     1) A thorough test marketing of pricing alternatives enables management to estimate the demand curve and the **price elasticity of demand** for a particular product. Without a knowledge of price elasticity, a firm may not charge the price that will maximize profits.

        a) **Price elasticity of demand.** If demand is price elastic (inelastic), the ratio of the percentage change in quantity demanded to the percentage change in price is greater (less) than 1.0. For example, if customer demand is price elastic, a price increase will result in the reduction of the seller's total revenue.

     2) **Other external factors** affect price. Competitors' products, costs, prices, and amounts supplied must be considered when setting the price of an item. Furthermore, supply of and demand for products and services are determined by customer demand, the actions of competitors, and costs.

  d. **Internal factors** that influence the prices charged include marketing objectives that may include survival, current profit maximization, market-share leadership, or product-quality leadership.

     1) The **marketing-mix strategy** influences the price charged. For instance, a firm may incur high advertising costs which must be covered by higher prices, but a competitor may do little advertising and try to compete solely on the basis of low prices.

     2) All **relevant costs** (variable, fixed, and total costs) in the value chain from R&D to customer service affect the amount of a product that the firm is willing to supply.

  e. The **organizational location** of pricing decisions may mean different prices depending on who makes the pricing decisions.

  f. **Capacity** also may be a pricing determinant. For example, under **peak-load pricing**, prices vary directly with capacity usage. Thus, when idle capacity is available, that is, when demand falls, the price of a product or service tends to be lower.

2. A product's position in its life cycle should be considered when establishing a price. The **product life cycle** is a history of a product's sales over the life of the product.

  a. As a product progresses through the various stages of its life cycle, the price elasticity of demand will usually change.

     1) During the **introductory stage**, prices can be kept high because competitors are few, and demand is weak. The firm essentially skims off the highest-priced segment of the market.

        a) **Market skimming pricing** is the practice of setting an introductory price relatively high to attract buyers who are not concerned about price and to recover value chain cost.

        b) **Penetration pricing** is the practice of setting an introductory price relatively low to gain deep market penetration quickly. Penetration pricing is the opposite of market skimming. The price is set low enough for the product to penetrate the market and reach a large number of consumers quickly.

           i)   Some firms begin with market skimming and then switch to a penetration strategy once those willing to pay a high price have been depleted.

           ii)   Penetration pricing is usually most effective when the firm's barriers to entry into a market are low, the market is price sensitive, the low price causes market growth, competitors are discouraged, and learning-curve effects are significant.

   2)   During the **growth stage**, prices are reduced but still kept high enough that profits increase.

   3)   During the **maturity stage**, many competitors have entered the market, and prices must be reduced to the lowest possible level.

   4)   During the **decline stage**, prices must be raised because per-unit costs rise as production decreases. Also, with few competitors left in the market, raising prices is more likely to be feasible.

3.   **Public policy** can sometimes influence pricing decisions. Certain pricing tactics are illegal. For example, pricing products below cost to destroy competitors **(predatory pricing)** is illegal. The U.S. Supreme Court has held that a price is predatory if it is below an appropriate measure of costs, and the seller has a reasonable prospect of recovering its losses in the future through higher prices or greater market share.

   a.   Another improper form of pricing is **collusive pricing**. Firms may not conspire to restrict output and set artificially high prices. Such behavior violates antitrust laws.

   b.   Another inappropriate pricing tactic is selling below cost in other countries **(dumping)**, which may trigger retaliatory tariffs and other sanctions.

   c.   The **Robinson-Patman Act of 1936** prohibits quoting different prices to competing customers unless the difference can be justified by differences in delivery or manufacturing costs. Both the buyer and the seller are liable for treble damages if a competitor can prove price discrimination. Thus, marketers should be aware of the requirements of the act because a violation may be costly.

   d.   However, much **discriminatory pricing** is legal. First-degree discrimination is based on customer demand intensity. Second-degree discrimination charges bulk purchasers lower per-unit prices. Third-degree discrimination prices products differently depending on the class of user.

      1)   The following variables are some bases for **third-degree price discrimination**:

         a)   Customer segments
         b)   The product's form
         c)   The product's image
         d)   Distribution channels
         e)   Locations
         f)   Times (seasons, days, or hours)

      2)   **Price discrimination is effective** when

         a)   Segmentation based on different demand intensities is feasible.
         b)   Resale from a lower- to a higher-price segment is not possible.
         c)   Competitors cannot offer a lower price in the higher-price segment.
         d)   The costs of segmenting the market are less than the incremental revenue.
         e)   The practice is legal.
         f)   Customer badwill does not develop.

4. **Cost-based pricing** begins with a cost determination followed by setting a price that will recover the value chain costs and provide the desired return on investment **(target-return pricing)**. When an industry is characterized by significant product differentiation, e.g., automobiles, cost-based and market-based pricing approaches are combined.

   a. A **cost-plus price** equals the cost plus a markup **(markup pricing)**. Cost may be defined in many ways. Most firms use either absorption manufacturing cost or total cost when calculating the price. Variable costs may be used as the basis for cost, but then fixed costs must be covered by the markup.

5. **Product-mix pricing** is a system that bases prices on the mix of products being offered.

   a. **Product-line pricing** sets price steps among the products in the line based on costs, consumer perceptions, and competitors' prices.

   b. **Optional-product pricing** requires the firm to choose which products to offer as accessories and which as standard features of a main product.

   c. **Captive-product pricing** applies to products that must be used with a main product, such as razor blades with a razor. Often the main product is relatively cheap, but the captive products have high markups.

   d. **Byproduct pricing** usually sets prices at any amount in excess of storing and delivering byproducts. Such prices allow the seller to reduce the costs and therefore the prices of the main products.

   e. **Product-bundle pricing** entails selling combinations of products at a price lower than the combined prices of the individual items. This strategy promotes sales of items consumers might not otherwise buy. An example is season tickets for sports events.

6. **Market-based pricing** determines prices according to the product's **perceived value** and competitors' actions rather than the seller's cost. Nonprice variables in the marketing mix (image, seller's reputation, warranties, customer service, and channel attributes) augment the perceived value. For example, a cup of coffee may have a higher price at an expensive restaurant than at a fast-food outlet. Market-based pricing is typical when competition is strong, and the product is undifferentiated. Examples are such commodities markets as agricultural products and natural gas.

   a. **Competition-based pricing** uses competitors' prices as benchmarks for setting prices. **Going-rate pricing** bases price largely on competitors' prices, and **sealed-bid pricing** bases price on a firm's perception of its competitors' prices.

   b. **Competitors' reactions** to the firm's price changes are most likely given few firms, relatively undifferentiated products, and informed buyers.

      1) To predict the response, the firm's competitive intelligence system should provide information about each competitor's financial position, sales volumes, objectives, degree of customer loyalty, and possible interpretations of the firm's price moves. For example, if a competitor wants to retain market share, it may match any price cut.

   c. **Competitors' Price Changes**

      1) If the product is relatively undifferentiated, the firm may augment its product or lower price. However, an increase might be matched only if it benefits the industry.

      2) If the product is relatively differentiated, a complex analysis is needed that determines the reason for the change, whether it is permanent, the effect on market share and profits of each possible response, and other firms' reaction to the response chosen.

    3)   A **market leader** may respond to price cuts by

        a) **Price maintenance.** This response is indicated when market share will not decline materially or can be recaptured, and the firm wishes not to lose profits. However, this response may embolden the attacker, demoralize the sales force, and result in greater than estimated loss of marketshare.

        b) **Price maintenance and augmented value.** The cost of lower profit margins may exceed the cost of improving the value offered.

        c) **Matching the decrease.** This response may be best when lower sales will mean loss of economies of scale; the product is price sensitive, and market share will be lost if the cut is not matched; and market share will be difficult to recapture.

        d) **Raising price and quality.** The leader also might introduce new brands. These flanker brands might be in higher-price and lower-price segments.

        e) **Introducing a fighter line.** This response involves offering lower-price items or brand.

7.   **Value-based pricing** charges relatively low prices relative to the quality delivered. This approach requires business-process reengineering to lower costs while maintaining quality.

    a. **Everyday low pricing** is a retail pricing strategy that employs few price promotions. It reduces promotional costs and caters to customers who do not want to shop for sales and use coupons.

    b. **High-low pricing** charges everyday higher prices but with frequent sales at prices below the everyday low price.

8.   **Geographical pricing** is a means of differentiating prices by geographic region.

    a. **FOB-origin pricing** charges each customer its actual freight costs.

    b. A seller that uses **uniform delivered pricing** charges the same price, inclusive of shipping, to all customers regardless of their location. All geographic customers are charged the same amount. This policy is easy to administer, permits the firm to advertise one price nationwide, and facilitates marketing to faraway customers.

    c. **Zone pricing** sets differential freight charges for customers on the basis of their location. Customers are not charged actual average freight costs.

    d. **Basing-point pricing** charges each customer the freight costs incurred from a specified city to the destination regardless of the actual point of origin of the shipment. A seller that uses freight-absorption pricing absorbs all or part of the actual freight charges. Customers are not charged actual delivery costs.

9.   **Discounts and allowances** can be used to change prices quickly or to differentiate between different classes of customers.

    a. **Cash discounts** promote prompt payment, improve cash flows, and avoid bad debts.

    b. **Quantity discounts** encourage large volume purchases.

    c. **Trade (functional) discounts** are offered to other members of the marketing channel for performing certain services, such as selling.

    d. **Seasonal discounts** smooth production by creating sales out of the busy season.

    e. **Psychological pricing** is based on consumer psychology. For example, consumers who cannot judge quality may assume higher prices correlate with higher quality. Moreover, pricing may exploit perceptual errors. For example, $9.99 may seem to be a much lower price than $10.

    f. **Promotional pricing** includes use of loss leaders to increase customer traffic at the seller's site, special-event pricing (e.g., holiday sales), rebates, reduced financial rates, offers of fringe benefits at low cost (e.g., warranties), and longer payment terms.

10. **Modification of a pricing strategy** may be necessary.

    a. **Price reductions** have certain risks. They may have a negative effect on perceived product quality, cause retaliation by stronger competitors, and result in increased market share but decreased customer loyalty. They may be indicated because of

        1) Overcapacity
        2) Loss of, or a desire to increase, market share
        3) A change to an overall cost leadership or a cost focus competitive strategy
        4) Macroeconomic factors

    b. **Prices may rise** because of

        1) Stronger demand
        2) Inflation (anticipatory demand)

    c. A firm that raises prices must determine whether the increase should be gradual or sharp and immediate. Furthermore, it must avoid the appearance of price gouging, e.g., by making low visibility moves first (such as ending discounts), giving notice, explaining the change, or including escalator clauses in contracts. A firm may **avoid higher prices** by, for example,

        1) Using less expensive product or packaging materials
        2) Reengineering processes to reduce costs
        3) Selling a smaller quantity for the same price
        4) Altering or eliminating services or features
        5) Offering generic brands
        6) Offering fewer sizes or models

11. Stop and review! You have completed the outline for this subunit. Study multiple-choice questions 23 through 31 beginning on page 185.

6.4 DISTRIBUTION CHANNELS

1. Distribution is one of the major facets of a firm's marketing mix. The distribution decision or **distribution strategy** involves determining the most profitable ways to reach the firm's markets.

    a. A **distribution channel** (marketing channel or trade channel) is an organized network of agencies and institutions (intermediaries) that in combination perform all the functions required to link producers of goods or services with end customers to accomplish the marketing task. It may be a sales, delivery, or service channel.

        1) **Selecting distribution channels** is an important decision because it affects the basic way a firm does business. It influences product development, marketing communication strategy, sales force size, and pricing. Essentially, the choice of distribution channels represents the foundation for a firm's other marketing policies.

        2) **Intermediaries** are used when they are more efficient in making products widely available. A one-level channel has one intermediary (e.g., a retailer), a two-level channel has two intermediaries (e.g., a wholesaler and a retailer), etc. The **functions** performed by channel intermediaries require backward or forward activity flows.

            a) Gathering and managing information flows about customers, competitors, and other relevant parties

            b) Providing promotional services

            c) Negotiation of contract terms allowing flows of goods and services

            d) Order placing

            e) Financing of inventories in the channel

        f)   Risk assumption related to channel activity

        g)   Storage and transportation of goods

        h)   Payment collection

        i)   Oversight of transfer of title

3) Many channels of distribution are available. Examples include mail order, door-to-door sales, grocery stores, discount stores, use of independent sales representatives, company-owned stores, wholesalers, retailers, dealers, value-added resellers, and the Internet.

4) A firm should know its **costs for each channel**. Adequate cost records may reveal that some channels are unprofitable even though they are generating significant sales.

5) One aspect of the distribution strategy is the determination of **distribution location**, which concerns the determination of the number and location of outlets that the seller uses.

6) **Distribution logistics** involve determining the best method to supply products to the intermediary sellers or the final market. High-quality service to customers should be provided to the extent benefits exceed costs.

b. Distribution channels are subject to constant change as management discovers better ways of serving customers or cutting costs.

1) Considerable **competition** may exist within some channels. Thus, a firm should not arbitrarily choose a particular channel. For example, food producers may find it difficult to obtain shelf space in grocery stores, and manufacturers may have to offer some retailers exclusive contracts before they will carry the manufacturer's products.

c. A **conventional marketing system** consists of separate, independent members that do not control the others.

d. A **vertical marketing system (VMS)** differs because it is a coordinated system with a **channel captain** that has substantial ability to control other members' behavior. The effect is to eliminate members' pursuit of conflicting objectives. Use of VMSs is the norm in the U.S. consumer market.

1) A **corporate channel** is a centrally owned and operated VMS that is designed for quick action and the achievement of certain economies of scale.

2) An **administered channel** is a VMS in which one firm is able to exercise administrative control over a vertical network because of its economic power.

3) A **contractual channel** is a VMS in which independent firms have combined on a contractual basis to achieve buying and selling power. Examples include wholesaler sponsored chains, retail cooperatives, and franchise operations.

e. A **horizontal marketing system** is a group of unrelated firms that share resources to exploit a marketing opportunity. An example is a fast-food company setting up stores in a Wal-Mart.

f. A **multichannel marketing system** is a hybrid in which a firm uses multiple channels to reach market segments. Advantages are better coverage of markets, lower costs, and specialized selling.

1) Thus, a firm should design the most efficient and effective **channel architecture** and understand its role in the system. The following are typical role patterns:

        a)   An **insider** in a dominant distribution channel has preferred sources of supply and benefits from the existing structure. It is a respected firm that enforces behavioral norms.

        b)   A **striver** wants to be an insider to gain access to preferred sources of supply. Hence, it follows behavioral norms.

     c)   A **complementer** may serve small segments, engage in functions not otherwise provided in the channel, or deal in smaller amounts of goods than other members. Because it gains from the existing arrangement, it follows the code of conduct.

     d)   A **transient** enters the dominant channel only when it perceives an opportunity. It is not a member and has only short-term objectives. Thus, it is less likely than other participants to abide by the industry code of conduct.

     e)   An **outside innovator** disrupts the existing structure by successfully creating different ways to do the work.

  g. **Channel disintegration** may result from conflict and competition. Firms may have irreconcilable objectives, badly defined roles and rights, perceptual disagreements (e.g., optimistic versus pessimistic demand forecasts), and resentment about dependency (e.g., when exclusive dealers sell a manufacturer's goods).

    1)   Conflict in the channel may be **vertical** (between different levels), **horizontal** (between firms on the same level), or **multichannel** (between different channels).

    2)   Conflict may be managed by

      a)   An appeal to superordinate goals (joint, overriding goals)
      b)   Co-optation, e.g., service of a manager of one firm on another's board
      c)   Joint membership in trade groups
      d)   Exchange of executives

  h. **Channel design** may involve the degree of emphasis on a **push strategy** (inducing intermediaries to promote and sell the firm's products) versus a **pull strategy** (motivating customers to pressure intermediaries to sell the firm's products).

    1)   **Analysis of customer service needs** is the first step in channel design. More service outputs mean greater cost. Service outputs include

      a)   Lot size (units per typical purchase)
      b)   Waiting time for delivery
      c)   Spatial convenience (e.g., more retailers, more consumer convenience)
      d)   Product variety (assortment available)
      e)   Service backup (e.g., financing, delivery, or repair)

    2)   **Channel objectives and constraints** should be defined.

      a)   Objectives are targeted service outputs and vary among products (e.g., perishable, bulky, or nonstandard). The firm minimize channel costs for a given level of service outputs.

      b)   Constraints include strengths and weaknesses of intermediaries, the channels available to competitors, economic conditions, and regulation.

    3)   **Channel alternatives** should be assessed.

      a)   Channels are very diversified, and each has specific strengths and weaknesses that must be evaluated in deciding on the channel mix. Preferably, each channel in the mix should reach different segments with appropriate products at minimum cost. An objective is to avoid channel conflict, loss of control, and excess cost.

      b)   Thus, the firm must choose the types of intermediaries. Innovative or unconventional channels may be selected when the dominant channels are not appropriate.

      c) Choice of the **number of intermediaries** is among

        i) Exclusive distribution

        ii) Selective distribution (more than a few but not all of the willing intermediaries)

        iii) Intensive distribution (as many outlets as possible)

      d) **Choice of the terms and responsibilities** of channel participants. The **trade-relations mix** consists of

        i) Pricing policies

        ii) Conditions of sale

        iii) Territorial rights

      e) **Evaluation of Channels**

        i) A **channel advantage** results when a firm can move customers to low-cost (often low-touch) channels without loss of revenues or service quality.

        ii) **Control** by the firm may be weaker when, for example, sales agents are used.

        iii) **Adaptability** of the firm to market changes may be reduced when it makes commitments to channel members. Hence, adaptability of channels and policies is a virtue.

2. Stop and review! You have completed the outline for this subunit. Study multiple-choice questions 32 through 36 beginning on page 187.

6.5 CORE CONCEPTS

Products and Services

- A **product strategy** should align the approaches taken in choosing the product mix and product lines, branding, packaging, and labeling.
- Products are commonly **classified** in three categories: durability and tangibility, consumer goods, and industrial goods.
- **Branding** is the development, maintenance, and protection of a unique identity for the selling firm.
- According to Philip Kotler, **brand equity** is "the positive differential effect that knowing the brand name has on customer response to the product or service."
- A product mix contains **product lines**. Analysis of a product line should provide a basis for decisions about **product-line strategies**, such as building, maintaining, harvesting, or divesting a product line.
- Services are **intangible**, so customers need tangible evidence of their quality. The three Ps are people, physical evidence and presentation, and process.

Global Marketing Issues

- Companies can expand into **international markets** through several means, including licensing, exporting, local component assembly, joint venture, and direct investment.
- **Strategies** for a global marketing organization include a multinational strategy (portfolio approach), a global strategy (regarding the world as one market), and a glocal strategy (combining elements of local responsiveness with global integration).
- **Global firms** are primarily managed from one central country. **Transnational firms** lack a national identity.

Pricing Decisions

- **Pricing** is the element of the 4 Ps of marketing that generates revenues, not costs.
- A firm's **steps** in the pricing process are to determine its pricing objectives, estimate demand at each price, estimate learning curves and costs for different outputs, estimate costs of different marketing offers, consider competitors' actions (costs, prices, and offers), choose a pricing strategy, and establish a price.
- A thorough test marketing of pricing alternatives enables management to estimate the demand curve and the **price elasticity of demand** for a particular product. Without a knowledge of price elasticity, a firm may not charge the price that will maximize profits.
- A product's position in its **life cycle** should be considered when establishing a price (introduction, growth, maturity, decline).
- **Cost-based pricing** begins with a cost determination followed by setting a price that will recover the value chain costs and provide the desired return on investment (also called target-return pricing).
- **Product-mix pricing** systems include product-line pricing, optional-product pricing, captive-product pricing, byproduct pricing, and product-bundle pricing.
- **Market-based pricing** determines prices according to the product's perceived value and competitors' actions rather than the seller's cost.
- **Value-based pricing** charges relatively low prices relative to the quality delivered.
- **Geographical pricing** is a means of differentiating prices by geographic region.

Distribution Channels

- Selecting distribution channels is an important decision because it affects the basic way a firm does business. It influences product development, marketing communication strategy, sales force size, and pricing. Essentially, the choice of distribution channels represents the **foundation for a firm's other marketing policies**.
- A **conventional marketing system** consists of separate, independent members that do not control the others.
- A **vertical marketing system** differs because it is a coordinated system with a channel captain that has substantial ability to control other members' behavior. The effect is to eliminate members' pursuit of conflicting objectives. Use of VMSs is the norm in the U.S. consumer market.
- A **horizontal marketing system** is a group of unrelated firms that share resources to exploit a marketing opportunity. An example is a fast-food company setting up stores in a Wal-Mart.
- A **multichannel marketing system** is a hybrid in which a firm uses multiple channels to reach market segments. Advantages are better coverage of markets, lower costs, and specialized selling.
- **Channel design** may involve the degree of emphasis on a **push strategy** (inducing intermediaries to promote and sell the firm's products) versus a **pull strategy** (motivating customers to pressure intermediaries to sell the firm's products).

QUESTIONS

6.1 Products and Services

1. Which attribute of the product mix corresponds to the number of product lines?

- A. Depth.
- B. Consistency.
- C. Width.
- D. Length.

Answer (C) is correct. *(Publisher, adapted)*
REQUIRED: The attribute of the product mix that corresponds to the number of product lines.
DISCUSSION: The product mix is the product assortment (everything the firm sells). A firm may grow by adding to any attribute of its product mix. The width attribute is the number of product lines.
Answer (A) is incorrect because depth equals the variants of each product. Answer (B) is incorrect because consistency is the degree of the relationship of the product lines, for example, as to uses by ultimate consumers or choices of distribution channels. Answer (D) is incorrect because length equals the total items in the mix.

2. Products may be classified in a hierarchy according to ascending levels of customer value. At which level of this customer value hierarchy does most competition occur in developed countries?

- A. Potential product.
- B. Augmented product.
- C. Expected product.
- D. Basic product.

Answer (B) is correct. *(Publisher, adapted)*
REQUIRED: The level of the customer value hierarchy where most competition occurs in developed countries.
DISCUSSION: An augmented product exceeds expectations. In industrialized nations, product augmentation through customer service, delivery options, packaging, financing, etc., is the basis for competition. Hence, the customer's consumption system must be understood, that is, how the customer acquires, uses, pays for, and maintains the product.
Answer (A) is incorrect because a potential product reflects every possible future augmentation and way to differentiate the product. Answer (C) is incorrect because the expected product has the standard features that buyers anticipate receiving. Answer (D) is incorrect because the basic product is the simplest expression of the core benefit provided.

3. The length of a product line should be structured to maximize profits and meet other objectives of the firm. Accordingly, the line may be structured to allow

- A. Upselling of a related product.
- B. Cross-selling of a more expensive product.
- C. Filling to reach an upmarket.
- D. Stretching to reach the downmarket.

Answer (D) is correct. *(Publisher, adapted)*
REQUIRED: The purpose of lengthening a product line.
DISCUSSION: Line stretching may be downmarket to provide lower-priced products. The purpose may be to exploit a growth opportunity, to move against a low-price competitor that has invaded the firm's markets, or to shift out of a declining market. Upmarket stretching may reflect a search for growth, greater profit margins, or positioning as a full-product-line seller. Two-way stretching is a middle market firm's move into the upmarket and the downmarket.
Answer (A) is incorrect because upselling is the sale of a more expensive product. Answer (B) is incorrect because cross-selling is the sale of a related product. Answer (C) is incorrect because line filling adds products within the firm's current range. This strategy may be counterproductive if it results in customer confusion and does not meet a customer need. A line-filling product should be differentiated in the minds of customers so that it has a just-noticeable difference.

4. The positive incremental effect that the brand name has on customer purchasing behavior is brand

- A. Valuation.
- B. Equity.
- C. Bonding.
- D. Identity.

Answer (B) is correct. *(Publisher, adapted)*
REQUIRED: The positive incremental effect that the brand name has on customer purchasing behavior.
DISCUSSION: According to Kotler *(Marketing Management)*, brand equity is "the positive differential effect that knowing the brand name has on customer response to the product or service." It may be measured by the incremental price a customer will pay for the product. An effect of brand equity is customer preference for the brand when another product is essentially identical.
Answer (A) is incorrect because brand valuation is financial value. Some brands have valuations in the tens of billions of dollars. Answer (C) is incorrect because brand bonding occurs when the total customer experience is consistent with the firm's promises. Answer (D) is incorrect because brand identity results not only from choices of the name, logo, colors, tagline, and symbol but also from fulfilling the implicit promises to deliver specified benefits to customers.

5. A brand may be developed in many ways. Which brand development strategy introduces new products in the same category under the same brand?

    A. Brand extension.

    B. Line extension.

    C. Flanker branding.

    D. Co-branding.

Answer (B) is correct. *(Publisher, adapted)*
    REQUIRED: The brand strategy that introduces new products in the same category under the same brand.
    DISCUSSION: One effective means of developing and marketing new products is the use of line extensions (new products in an already served category) and brand extensions. The concept behind extension is that consumers are already familiar with the firm's major brand names. Thus, if a new product carries the same brand name, it will be more likely to succeed. Carrying an established brand name enables a new product to more easily fill a niche in the marketplace. Furthermore, extensions make efficient use of promotional costs because customers are already familiar with the quality of the products created and manufactured under the brand. Most new products are line extensions.
    Answer (A) is incorrect because brand extension introduces products in new categories. Answer (C) is incorrect because multibranding introduces new brands (flanker brands) in the same product category. Answer (D) is incorrect because co-branding, or dual branding, is an offering using different brand names, e.g., using one brand as an ingredient of another.

6. Service marketing uses the traditional categories of marketing tools (the 4 Ps) as well as which additional methods?

    A. Price, place, and promotion.

    B. Price, place, and physical evidence.

    C. Process, promotion, and people.

    D. People, physical evidence, and process.

Answer (D) is correct. *(Publisher, adapted)*
    REQUIRED: The additional tools used by service marketers.
    DISCUSSION: The traditional 4 Ps are product, price, promotion, and place. The three additional Ps used in service marketing are people, physical evidence and presentation, and process. The right employees, if well trained and motivated, enhance customer satisfaction because many services require substantial customer-employee interaction. Physical evidence and presentation are what the customer perceives, such as the decorative features of a restaurant. A process is how the service is performed, for example, delivery of health care in a doctor's office, outpatient clinic, or hospital.
    Answer (A) is incorrect because price, place, and promotion are among the traditional 4 Ps. Answer (B) is incorrect because price and place are among the traditional 4 Ps. Answer (C) is incorrect because promotion is one of the traditional 4 Ps.

6.2 Global Marketing Issues

7. The least risky method of entering a market in a foreign country is by

    A. Indirect exports.

    B. Licensing.

    C. Direct exports.

    D. Direct investments.

Answer (A) is correct. *(Publisher, adapted)*
    REQUIRED: The least risky method of entering a market in a foreign country.
    DISCUSSION: An indirect export strategy operates through intermediaries, such as home-country merchants who buy and resell the product, home-country agents who negotiate transactions with foreign buyers for a commission, cooperatives that represent groups of sellers, and export-management firms that receive fees for administering the firm's export efforts. Indirect export requires lower investment than direct export and is less risky because of the intermediaries' expertise.
    Answer (B) is incorrect because licensing a process, patent, trade secret, etc., is a way to gain a foothold in a foreign market with little immediate risk. However, the licensor may have insufficient control over the licensee's operations, profits are lost if the arrangement succeeds, and the licensee ultimately may become a competitor. Answer (C) is incorrect because direct export involves higher risk and investment but may yield higher returns. Answer (D) is incorrect because direct investment has many advantages: (1) cheaper materials or labor, (2) receipt of investment incentives from the host government, (3) a strong relationship with interested parties in the host country, (4) control of the investment, (5) a better image in the host country, and (6) market access when domestic contest rules are in effect. However, direct investment is risky because of exposure to currency fluctuations, expropriation, potentially high exit barriers, and restraints on sending profits out of the country.

8. A global firm

A. Has achieved economies of scale in its domestic market.

B. Plans, operates, and coordinates business globally.

C. Relies on indirect export.

D. Tends to rely more on one product market.

Answer (B) is correct. *(Publisher, adapted)*
REQUIRED: The nature of a global firm.
DISCUSSION: According to Kotler, "Global firms plan, operate, and coordinate their activities on a worldwide basis." Thus, a global firm secures cost or product differentiation advantages not available to domestic firms.
Answer (A) is incorrect because one reason to go abroad is that economies of scale are so great that they cannot be achieved in a domestic market. Answer (C) is incorrect because global firms do not rely only on indirect export. They also rely on direct export, which is potentially more profitable. Answer (D) is incorrect because a global firm may be a small firm that sells one product or class of products, or it may be a large firm with a multiproduct line.

9. A firm expands into international markets to

A. Be in foreign markets.

B. Eliminate foreign competition.

C. Pursue new, higher-profit opportunities.

D. Preclude piracy of its products.

Answer (C) is correct. *(Publisher, adapted)*
REQUIRED: The reason to expand globally.
DISCUSSION: A firm may decide to go abroad for many reasons, for example, to respond to a competitive challenge in its home country by another global firm, to pursue opportunities yielding greater profits, to achieve economies of scale, to diversify, or to follow customers who need international service.
Answer (A) is incorrect because a firm should enter international markets for well-defined purposes, not for some vague reason such as establishing a presence. Answer (B) is incorrect because a firm's counterattack in a foreign market is not likely to eliminate the competitor. However, it may serve as a market signal that will influence the foreign competitor's behavior in a way favorable to the firm. Answer (D) is incorrect because expansion does not prevent piracy.

10. A firm wishing to become global must consider how many national markets to enter. A firm should enter fewer national markets when

A. Communication adaptation costs are low.

B. The product need not be adapted.

C. Entry costs are low.

D. The first countries chosen are heavily populated and have high incomes.

Answer (D) is correct. *(Publisher, adapted)*
REQUIRED: The reason for a global firm to enter fewer national markets.
DISCUSSION: According to Ayal and Zif, the following are factors indicating that few national markets should be entered: (1) entry costs are high; (2) market control costs are high; (3) product adaptation costs are high; (4) communication adaptation costs are high; (5) the first countries selected have large populations, high incomes, and high income growth; and (6) a dominant firm can erect high entry barriers.
Answer (A) is incorrect because low communication adaptation costs argue operations in many countries. Answer (B) is incorrect because low product adaptation costs argue for operations in many countries. Answer (C) is incorrect because low entry costs argue for operations in many countries.

11. An advantage of a direct investment strategy when entering a foreign market is

A. Reduction in the capital at risk.

B. Shared control and responsibility.

C. Assurance of access when the foreign country imposes domestic content rules.

D. Avoidance of interaction with the local bureaucracy.

Answer (C) is correct. *(Publisher, adapted)*
REQUIRED: The advantage of direct investment.
DISCUSSION: Direct investment has many advantages: (1) cheaper materials or labor, (2) receipt of investment incentives from the host government, (3) a strong relationship with interested parties in the host country, (4) control of the investment, (5) a better image in the host country, and (6) market access when domestic contest rules are in effect. However, direct investment is risky because of exposure to currency fluctuations, expropriation, potentially high exit barriers, and restraints on sending profits out of the country.
Answer (A) is incorrect because direct investment maximizes capital at risk. Answer (B) is incorrect because direct investment avoids shared control and responsibility. Answer (D) is incorrect because direct investment means a closer relationship with governmental entities in the host country.

12. A firm that moves from not exporting on a regular basis to establishing plants in foreign countries has

    A. Globalized.

    B. Nationalized.

    C. Glocalized.

    D. Internationalized.

Answer (D) is correct. *(Publisher, adapted)*

    REQUIRED: The process of moving from not exporting on a regular basis to establishing plants in foreign countries.

    DISCUSSION: The internationalization process is of crucial interest to nations that wish to encourage local firms to grow and to operate globally. According to Swedish researchers, it involves the following steps: (1) Lack of regular exports; (2) export via independent agents with a few markets, with later expansion to more countries; (3) creation of sales subsidiaries in larger markets; and (4) establishment of plants in foreign countries.

    Answer (A) is incorrect because all elements of a global organization are geared toward selling in a worldwide market. Answer (B) is incorrect because nationalization is the takeover of an industry by a national government. Answer (C) is incorrect because glocalization of a global organization localizes some of its elements but standardizes other elements.

13. Which strategy for a global marketing organization is based on a portfolio of national markets?

    A. Creation of a division to manage international marketing.

    B. A multinational strategy.

    C. A glocal strategy.

    D. Creation of an export department.

Answer (B) is correct. *(Publisher, adapted)*

    REQUIRED: The global organization strategy based on a portfolio of national markets.

    DISCUSSION: International marketing efforts take three basic forms: creation of an export department, creation of a division to manage international marketing, or global organization. The latter encompasses genuinely worldwide functions, e.g., manufacturing, marketing, finance, and logistics. Thus, worldwide operations are the organization's focus, not merely that of a department or division of a national firm. A global organization may follow a multinational, global, or glocal strategy. A multinational strategy adopts a portfolio approach. Its emphasis is on national markets because the need for global integration is not strong. The product is customized for each market and therefore incurs higher production costs. Decision making is primarily local with a minimum of central control. This strategy is most effective given large differences between countries. Also, exchange rate risk is reduced when conducting business in this manner.

    Answer (A) is incorrect because export departments and international divisions are organizational arrangements that precede the firm's evolution into a global organization. Answer (C) is incorrect because glocal strategy balances local responsiveness and global integration. Answer (D) is incorrect because export departments and international divisions are organizational arrangements that precede the firm's evolution into a global organization.

14. Which strategy for a global marketing organization balances local responsiveness and global integration?

    A. Global.

    B. Multinational.

    C. Glocal.

    D. Transnational.

Answer (C) is correct. *(Publisher, adapted)*

    REQUIRED: The strategy for a global marketing organization that balances local responsiveness and global integration.

    DISCUSSION: A glocal strategy combines some elements of local responsiveness or adaptation with some elements of global integration. Successful telecommunications firms are examples of balancing these elements. Local responsiveness is indicated when local product tastes and preferences, regulations, and barriers are significant. Global integration is indicated when demand is homogeneous and economies of productive scale are large.

    Answer (A) is incorrect because a global strategy is weighted toward global integration. Answer (B) is incorrect because a multinational strategy is weighted toward local responsiveness. Answer (D) is incorrect because the term "transnational" is sometimes applied to firms that operate internationally but with a decentralized overall structure.

15. Which of the following is the most significant reason that domestic governments and international organizations seek to eliminate cartels?

A. The increased sales price reduces the amount of corporate tax revenues payable to the government.

B. True competition keeps prices as low as possible, thus increasing efficiency in the marketplace.

C. Small businesses cannot survive or grow without government protection.

D. The economic stability of developing countries depends on a global free market.

Answer (B) is correct. *(CIA, adapted)*
REQUIRED: The best reason to eliminate cartels.
DISCUSSION: A cartel is an organization of sellers (e.g., the oil cartel OPEC) who undertake joint action to maximize members' profits by controlling the supply and therefore the price of their product. Under the laws of many nations, such collusive conduct is illegal when engaged in by firms subject to those laws. The reason is that, as a result of the monopolistic and anticompetitive practices of cartels, supply is lower, prices are high, competition is restrained, and the relevant industry is less efficient. Accordingly, governmental and international organizations seek to protect consumers and the health of the domestic and global economy through anti-cartel efforts.
Answer (A) is incorrect because an increased sales price would raise corporate profits. Thus, the tax revenue lost through eliminating cartel activity would serve as a disincentive to government anti-cartel efforts. Answer (C) is incorrect because, although the effect of cartel activities may be harmful to small businesses, the greatest impact is on the overall economy. Macroeconomic effects are the primary reasons for anti-cartel efforts by governments and international organizations. Answer (D) is incorrect because the contribution of a free market to the stability of developing countries' economies does not provide a compelling reason for domestic anti-cartel efforts in industrialized countries.

16. When a multinational firm decides to sell its products abroad, one of the risks it faces is that the government of the foreign market charges the firm with dumping. Dumping occurs when

A. The same product sells at different prices in different countries.

B. A firm charges less than it costs to make the product to enter or win a market.

C. Lower quality versions of the product are sold abroad so as to be affordable.

D. Transfer prices are set artificially high so as to minimize tax payments.

Answer (B) is correct. *(CIA, adapted)*
REQUIRED: The nature of dumping.
DISCUSSION: Dumping is an unfair trade practice that violates international agreements. It occurs when a firm charges a price (1) lower than that in its home market or (2) less than the cost to make the product. Dumping may be done to penetrate a market or as a result of export subsidies.
Answer (A) is incorrect because, in a gray market, the same product sells at different prices in different countries. The effect differs from that of dumping. A seller in a low-price market tries to sell the goods in a higher-price market. Products are not dumped to penetrate a market. Instead, a dealer seeks to resell at a favorable price. Answer (C) is incorrect because selling a lower quality product at a fair price is a perfectly acceptable strategy. Answer (D) is incorrect because a transfer price is a price charged to a subunit of an enterprise. Setting a high price to avoid an unfavorable tax rate has the opposite effect of dumping, assuming the subunit passes the cost on to its customers.

17. Firms that sell products worldwide are most likely to have the lowest costs with a marketing mix that is

A. Adapted to each market.

B. Standardized for all markets.

C. A combination of new and adapted products in each market.

D. A combination of standardized products and adapted promotions.

Answer (B) is correct. *(Publisher, adapted)*
REQUIRED: The marketing mix most likely to have the lowest costs.
DISCUSSION: Firms that operate globally must choose a marketing program after considering the need for adaptation to local circumstances. The possibilities lie on a continuum from a purely standardized marketing mix to a purely adapted marketing mix. The former chooses to standardize products, promotion, and distribution. The latter adapts the elements of the mix to each local market. Worldwide standardization of all elements should be the lowest cost marketing strategy. However, even well-established global brands ordinarily undergo some adaptation to local markets.
Answer (A) is incorrect because adaptation to each market incurs greater costs. Some economies of scale are lost. Answer (C) is incorrect because pure standardization of products, promotion, and distribution is likely to be the lowest-cost, but not necessarily highest-revenue, strategy. Answer (D) is incorrect because pure standardization of products, promotion, and distribution is likely to be the lowest-cost, but not necessarily highest-revenue, strategy.

18. A firm that manufactures refrigerators sold ice boxes in urban areas of less developed countries. Many residents lacked electricity to power refrigerators but could purchase blocks of ice from local vendors for use in ice boxes. According to Keegan's model of adaptation strategies, this firm adopted a strategy of

    A. Product adaptation.

    B. Dual adaptation.

    C. Backward invention.

    D. Forward invention.

Answer (C) is correct. *(Publisher, adapted)*
    REQUIRED: The adaptation strategy followed.
    DISCUSSION: Using a product invention strategy, a new product is created specifically for a certain country or regional market. A product may either include advancements for developed countries or have certain elements removed in places where a lower cost is a key selling point. Thus, an ice box, a precursor of the modern refrigerator, is a backward invention.
    Answer (A) is incorrect because the refrigerator was not adapted. An older precursor product was reintroduced. Answer (B) is incorrect because dual adaptation involves product adaptation, not invention. Answer (D) is incorrect because forward invention is the development of a new product.

19. A firm buys like-new computer equipment from bankrupt companies and resells it in foreign markets at prices significantly below those charged by competitors. The firm is

    A. Engaged in dumping.

    B. Engaged in price discrimination.

    C. Operating in a gray market.

    D. Operating in a black market.

Answer (C) is correct. *(Publisher, adapted)*
    REQUIRED: The term for sale in a higher-price market of goods acquired cheaply in another market.
    DISCUSSION: In a gray market, products imported from one country to another are sold by persons trying to make a profit from the difference in retail prices between the two countries. In essence, the seller firm in this case was exploiting a price difference between markets.
    Answer (A) is incorrect because dumping is sale below cost or at less than the price charged in the home market. Answer (B) is incorrect because price discrimination involves illegally selling the same products at different prices to different customers. Answer (D) is incorrect because black market operations are illegal.

20. A firm ships its product to a foreign subsidiary and charges a price that may increase import duties but lower the income taxes paid by the subsidiary. The most likely reason for these effects is that the

    A. Price is an arm's-length price.

    B. Price is a cost-plus price.

    C. Transfer price is too low.

    D. Transfer price is too high.

Answer (D) is correct. *(Publisher, adapted)*
    REQUIRED: The reason that sale to a subsidiary results in high import duties.
    DISCUSSION: A transfer price is the price charged by one subunit of a firm to another. When the subsidiary-buyer is in a foreign country, the higher the transfer, the higher the potential tariffs. However, the tax levied on a subsequent sale by the subsidiary will be lower because of its higher acquisition cost.
    Answer (A) is incorrect because an arm's-length price is what a competitor would charge in that market. Answer (B) is incorrect because a cost-plus price does not necessarily trigger higher import duties. Answer (C) is incorrect because, if the transfer price is too low, import duties would be lower and taxes would be higher.

21. Developing brand equity in a foreign market may be desirable but is subject to considerable risk. A global firm launching a new product in a new market most likely should

    A. Initially place most of its emphasis on advertising geared to the local culture.

    B. Fully decentralize control of the marketing process.

    C. Avoid creating partnerships with local distribution channels to avoid dilution of the brand.

    D. Balance standardization and customization of the product.

Answer (D) is correct. *(Publisher, adapted)*
    REQUIRED: The most likely step taken by a global firm launching a new product in a new market.
    DISCUSSION: The firm should determine the ratio of standardization and customization. Products that can be sold virtually unchanged throughout several markets provide a greater profit opportunity for a global firm. However, cultural differences may require extensive customization to appeal to markets in different countries.
    Answer (A) is incorrect because integrated marketing communications should be developed. Markets must be approached with a broad range of messages. Sole reliance on advertising should be avoided. Other marketing communications include merchandising, promotions, and sponsorship. Answer (B) is incorrect because the firm should determine the ratio of local to global control. Local managers may understand the wants and needs of their market, but the global firm must still retain control of certain elements of the marketing process and strategy. Answer (C) is incorrect because the firm may create branding partnerships. Global firms often form alliances with local distribution channels to increase their profitability while decreasing their marketing costs.

22. A global firm establishes a cost-based price for its product in each country. The most likely negative outcome is that this pricing strategy will

    A. Set too high a price in countries where the firm's costs are high.

    B. Overprice the product in some markets and underprice it in others.

    C. Create a gray market.

    D. Result in dumping.

Answer (A) is correct. *(Publisher, adapted)*
    REQUIRED: The most likely negative result of a cost-based pricing strategy.
    DISCUSSION: A firm may set a cost-based price in each market with a standard markup. In a region or country where costs are high, this strategy may result in prices that are too high to be competitive within the local market.
    Answer (B) is incorrect because a uniform pricing policy may overprice the product in some markets and underprice it in others. Answer (C) is incorrect because charging what consumers can afford in each country may create a gray market. Answer (D) is incorrect because dumping often entails charging a below-cost price.

6.3 Pricing Decisions

23. Which pricing objective is stated as a percentage ratio of profits to sales?

    A. Image enhancement.

    B. Stabilization.

    C. Target margin maximization.

    D. Achievement of market share.

Answer (C) is correct. *(Publisher, adapted)*
    REQUIRED: The pricing objective that is stated as a percentage ratio of profits to sales.
    DISCUSSION: Pricing objectives include profit maximization. Classical economic theory assumes all firms always select the price that results in the highest profit. An alternative objective is target margin maximization. This objective is stated as a percentage ratio of profits to sales.
    Answer (A) is incorrect because image-oriented objectives set prices to enhance the consumer's perception of the firm's product mix. Answer (B) is incorrect because stabilization objectives set prices to maintain a stable relationship between the firm's prices and the industry leader's prices. Answer (D) is incorrect because volume-oriented objectives set prices to meet target sales volumes or market shares.

24. Internal factors that influence the prices charged include

    A. Price sensitivity.

    B. Desire for market-share leadership.

    C. Price elasticity.

    D. Competitors' capacity.

Answer (B) is correct. *(Publisher, adapted)*
    REQUIRED: The internal factor that influences the prices charged.
    DISCUSSION: Internal factors that influence the prices charged include such marketing objectives as survival, current-profit maximization, market-share leadership, and product-quality leadership.
    Answer (A) is incorrect because price sensitivity is an external factor. Answer (C) is incorrect because price elasticity tests the change in demand when the price is changed. It is an external factor. Answer (D) is incorrect because competitors' capacity is an external factor.

25. During which stage of the product life cycle will prices most likely be reduced to the lowest possible level?

    A. Introductory stage.

    B. Growth stage.

    C. Maturity stage.

    D. Decline stage.

Answer (C) is correct. *(Publisher, adapted)*
    REQUIRED: The product life cycle stage during which prices will most likely be reduced to the lowest possible level.
    DISCUSSION: During the maturity stage, many competitors are in market. Given a decline in absence of growth or negative growth, the industry also may have excess capacity. For these and other reasons, competitive rivalry will be strong. Firms may attempt to modify the market, the product, or the marketing mix. Thus, price competition (an element of the marketing mix) will be most intense during the maturity stage
    Answer (A) is incorrect because, during the introductory stage, prices can be kept high. There are few or no competitors and few products to sell. The firm essentially skims off the highest priced segment of the market. Answer (B) is incorrect because, during the growth stage, prices can be reduced, but they are still kept high enough that profits are high. Answer (D) is incorrect because, during the decline stage, prices must be raised. Per-unit costs rise as production decreases. Also, with few competitors left in the market, raising prices will encounter less opposition.

26. Which form of product-mix pricing applies to products that must be used with a main product?

- A. Captive-product pricing.
- B. By-product pricing.
- C. Product-bundle pricing.
- D. Optional-product pricing.

Answer (A) is correct. *(Publisher, adapted)*
REQUIRED: The form of product-mix pricing that applies to products that must be used with a main product.
DISCUSSION: Captive-product pricing applies to products that must be used with a main product, such as razor blades with a razor. Often, the main product is relatively cheap, but the captive products have high markups.
Answer (B) is incorrect because by-product pricing usually sets prices at any amount in excess of the costs of storing and delivering by-products. Answer (C) is incorrect because product-bundle pricing entails selling combinations of products at a price lower than the combined price of the individual items. Answer (D) is incorrect because optional-product pricing requires the firm to choose which products to offer as accessories and which as standard features of a main product.

27. Several surveys show that most managers use full product costs, including unit fixed costs and unit variable costs, in developing cost-based pricing. Which one of the following is least associated with cost-based pricing?

- A. Price stability.
- B. Price justification.
- C. Target pricing.
- D. Fixed-cost recovery.

Answer (C) is correct. *(CMA, adapted)*
REQUIRED: The concept least associated with cost-based pricing.
DISCUSSION: A target price is the expected market price of a product, given the firm's knowledge of its customers and competitors. Hence, under target pricing, the sales price is known before the product is developed. Subtracting the unit target profit margin determines the long-term unit target cost. If cost-cutting measures do not permit the product to be made at or below the target cost, it will be abandoned.
Answer (A) is incorrect because full-cost pricing promotes price stability. It limits the ability to cut prices. Answer (B) is incorrect because full-cost pricing provides evidence that the firm is not violating antitrust laws against predatory pricing. Answer (D) is incorrect because full-cost pricing has the advantage of recovering the full long-term costs of the product. In the long term, all costs are relevant.

28. Market-skimming pricing strategies are appropriate when

- A. No buyers want the product at a high price.
- B. The costs of producing a small volume are low.
- C. Competitors can easily enter the market.
- D. The product is of poor quality.

Answer (B) is correct. *(CIA, adapted)*
REQUIRED: The circumstances in which market-skimming pricing strategies are appropriate.
DISCUSSION: Market-skimming pricing is used when a new product is introduced at the highest price possible given the benefits of the product. For market skimming to work, the product must appear to be worth its price, the costs of producing a small volume cannot be so high that they eliminate the advantage of charging more, and competitors cannot enter the market and undercut the price.
Answer (A) is incorrect because, if no buyers want the product at a high price, this marketing strategy is inappropriate. Answer (C) is incorrect because, if competitors can easily enter the market, they can undercut the price. Answer (D) is incorrect because the product quality and image must support a high price.

29. Which of the following price adjustment strategies is designed to stabilize production for the selling firm?

- A. Cash discounts.
- B. Quantity discounts.
- C. Functional discounts.
- D. Seasonal discounts.

Answer (D) is correct. *(CIA, adapted)*
REQUIRED: The price adjustment strategy intended to stabilize production.
DISCUSSION: Seasonal discounts are designed to smooth production by the selling firm. For example, a ski manufacturer offers seasonal discounts to retailers in the spring and summer to encourage early ordering.
Answer (A) is incorrect because cash discounts encourage prompt payment. Answer (B) is incorrect because quantity discounts encourage large volume purchases. Answer (C) is incorrect because functional or trade discounts are provided to channel members in return for the performance of certain functions, such as selling, storing, and record keeping.

30. In which product-mix pricing strategy is it appropriate for the seller to accept any price that exceeds the storage and delivery costs for the product?

    A. By-product pricing.

    B. Optional-product pricing.

    C. Captive-product pricing.

    D. Product-bundle pricing.

Answer (A) is correct. *(CIA, adapted)*
    REQUIRED: The pricing strategy that accepts any price greater than storage and delivery costs.
    DISCUSSION: A by-product is a product of relatively minor importance generated during the production of one or more other products. Its production entails no additional costs. Any amount received above the storage and delivery costs for a by-product allows the seller to reduce the main product's price to make it more competitive.
    Answer (B) is incorrect because optional products are offered for sale along with the main product. They are unlikely to have a zero production cost, so the seller must receive a price above their storage and delivery costs. Answer (C) is incorrect because captive products must be used along with the main product, such as film for use with a camera. Sellers often make their profits on the captive products rather than on the main product, which is sold at a low price. The captive products therefore will be priced well above the storage and delivery costs. Answer (D) is incorrect because product bundles are combinations of products sold together at a reduced price, such as season tickets for a theater. Products are bundled to promote the sale of certain items that consumers might not otherwise purchase. The combined price of the bundle must be low enough to encourage consumers to buy the bundle but must recover production costs and provide some profit for the seller, so the price must exceed storage and delivery costs.

31. If a U.S. manufacturer's price in the U.S. market is below an appropriate measure of costs, and the seller has a reasonable prospect of recovering the resulting loss in the future through higher prices or a greater market share, the seller has engaged in

    A. Collusive pricing.

    B. Dumping.

    C. Predatory pricing.

    D. Price discrimination.

Answer (C) is correct. *(Publisher, adapted)*
    REQUIRED: The pricing strategy characterized by charging a price that is below an appropriate measure of costs when the seller reasonably expects to recover the loss through higher prices or a greater market share.
    DISCUSSION: Predatory pricing is intentionally pricing below cost to eliminate competition and reduce supply. Federal statutes and many state laws prohibit the practice. The U.S. Supreme Court has held that pricing is predatory when two conditions are met: (1) the seller's price is below "an appropriate measure of its costs," and (2) it has a reasonable prospect of recovering the resulting loss through higher prices or greater market share.
    Answer (A) is incorrect because collusive pricing involves a conspiracy to set higher prices. Answer (B) is incorrect because dumping is defined under U.S. law as sale by a non-U.S. company in the U.S. market of a product below its market value in the country where it was produced. Such sale is illegal if it threatens material injury to a U.S. industry. Answer (D) is incorrect because price discrimination entails charging different prices to different customers for essentially the same product if the effect is to lessen competition substantially; to tend to create a monopoly; or to injure, destroy, or prevent competition.

6.4 Distribution Channels

32. A distribution channel

    A. May consist only of a producer and an ultimate customer.

    B. Performs sales and goods delivery functions only.

    C. Is chosen after other marketing policies are determined.

    D. Performs functions that involve only forward flows of activities.

Answer (A) is correct. *(Publisher, adapted)*
    REQUIRED: The true statement about a distribution channel.
    DISCUSSION: Direct marketing (a zero-level channel) is the simplest distribution channel. Because direct marketing eliminates all intermediaries, it consists only of a producer and an ultimate customer.
    Answer (B) is incorrect because a channel also may provide services. Answer (C) is incorrect because channel selection affects the basic way a firm does business. It influences product development, marketing communications strategy, sales force size, and pricing. Essentially, the choice of distribution channels represents the foundation for a firm's other marketing policies. Answer (D) is incorrect because activity flows also may be backward, e.g., order receiving and payment collection.

33. The form of distribution channel organization characterized by substantial overall control by one channel member is a

A. Conventional marketing system (CMS).

B. Horizontal marketing system (HMS).

C. Vertical marketing system (VMS).

D. Multichannel marketing system (MMS).

Answer (C) is correct.　*(Publisher, adapted)*
　　REQUIRED: The distribution channel organization with overall control by one channel member.
　　DISCUSSION: A CMS consists of separate, independent members that do not control the others. A VMS differs because it is a coordinated system with a channel captain that has the substantial ability to control other members' behavior. The effect is to eliminate members' pursuit of conflicting objectives. Use of VMSs is the norm in the U.S. consumer market.
　　Answer (A) is incorrect because the members of a CMS are independent. Answer (B) is incorrect because an HMS is a group of unrelated firms that share resources to exploit a marketing opportunity. An example is a fast-food company that sets up stores in a Wal-Mart. Answer (D) is incorrect because an MMS is a hybrid in which a firm uses multiple channels to reach market segments. Advantages are better coverage of markets, lower costs, and specialized selling.

34. Different firms in a distribution channel system play different roles. The firms least likely to respect the industry code of conduct are

A. Transients.

B. Strivers.

C. Complementers.

D. Insiders.

Answer (A) is correct.　*(Publisher, adapted)*
　　REQUIRED: The firms least likely to respect the industry code of conduct.
　　DISCUSSION: A transient enters the dominant channel only when it perceives an opportunity. It is not a member and has only short-term objectives. Thus, it is less likely than other participants to abide by the industry code of conduct.
　　Answer (B) is incorrect because a striver wants to be an insider to gain access to preferred sources of supply. Hence, it follows behavioral norms. Answer (C) is incorrect because a complementer may serve small segments, engage in functions not otherwise provided in the channel, or deal in smaller amounts of goods than other members. Because it gains from the existing arrangement, it follows the code of conduct. Answer (D) is incorrect because an insider in a dominant distribution channel has preferred sources of supply and benefits from the existing structure. It is a respected firm that enforces behavioral norms.

35. Multichannel marketing

A. Is ownership of channels by multiple cooperating firms.

B. Introduces conflict when channels compete for customers.

C. Tends to increase coverage and cost.

D. Improves control by customizing the selling process.

Answer (B) is correct.　*(Publisher, adapted)*
　　REQUIRED: The nature of multichannel marketing.
　　DISCUSSION: Conflict in the channel may be vertical (between different levels), horizontal (between firms on the same level), or multichannel (between different channels). Channels may compete for the same customers and be unwilling to cooperate, especially when they have been added recently.
　　Answer (A) is incorrect because multichannel marketing is use of two or more channels by one firm. Answer (C) is incorrect because cost decreases when lower-cost channels are adopted successfully. Answer (D) is incorrect because controlling multiple channels is more difficult than controlling one channel. Customizing the selling process for different customers is an advantage, but it may create control problems.

36. Effective design of distribution channels involves balancing many factors. Accordingly, the firm should

A. Emphasize a push strategy by motivating customers to pressure intermediaries to sell the firm's products.

B. Adopt a pull strategy by pressuring intermediaries to sell the firm's products.

C. Decrease costs by increasing service outputs.

D. Select channels that reach different segments.

Answer (D) is correct.　*(Publisher, adapted)*
　　REQUIRED: The appropriate channel design choice.
　　DISCUSSION: Channels are very diversified, and each has specific strengths and weaknesses that must be evaluated in deciding on the channel mix. Preferably, each channel in the mix should reach different segments with appropriate products at minimum cost. An objective is to avoid channel conflict, loss of control, and excess cost.
　　Answer (A) is incorrect because a push strategy involves a firm's pressure on intermediaries. Answer (B) is incorrect because a pull strategy involves a firm's pressure on customers. Answer (C) is incorrect because more service outputs, such as convenience, variety, and service, mean greater cost.

Use Gleim's *CMA Test Prep* for interactive testing with **over 2,000 additional multiple-choice questions!**

STUDY UNIT SEVEN
RISK AND RETURN

(17 pages of outline)

The area of corporate finance is a heavily tested area on the CMA exam. Candidates must know the types of risk, measures of risk, elements of portfolio management, the use of options and futures contracts, and the types of capital instruments available for long-term financing. Dividend policy is also covered, as are factors influencing the optimum capital structure, the cost of capital, and the effective and efficient management and financing of working capital.

This study unit is the **first of five** on **corporate finance**. The relative weight assigned to this major topic in Part 3 of the exam is **25%** at **skill level B** (four skill types required). The five study units are

Study Unit 7: Risk and Return
Study Unit 8: Financial Instruments
Study Unit 9: Cost of Capital
Study Unit 10: Managing Current Assets
Study Unit 11: Financing Current Assets

After studying the outline and answering the multiple-choice questions, you will have the skills necessary to address the following topics listed in the IMA's Learning Outcome Statements:

Part 3 – Section C.1. Risk and return

The candidate should be able to:

    a.   calculate rates of return

    b.   identify and demonstrate an understanding of the different types of risk [systematic (market), unsystematic (company), industry, country, etc.]

    c.   demonstrate an understanding of the relationship between risk and return

    d.   calculate expected return, standard deviation of return, and coefficient of variation

    e.   identify the different types of attitudes toward risk and infer how attitude might affect the management of risk

    f.   define a portfolio and distinguish between individual security risk and portfolio risk

    g.   define value at risk (VAR)

    h.   demonstrate an understanding of diversification

    i.   differentiate between systematic and unsystematic risk

    j.   demonstrate an understanding of how individual securities affect portfolio risk

    k.   define beta and identify the meaning of a security's beta

    l.   calculate the expected risk-adjusted returns using the capital asset pricing model (CAPM) and arbitrage pricing theory (APT)

    m.   define hedging and demonstrate how hedging can be used to manage financial risk

7.1 CALCULATING RETURN

1.   A **return** is the amount received by an investor as compensation for taking on the risk of the investment. The **rate of return** is the return stated as a percentage of the amount invested.

> *Rate of return = (Amount received - Amount invested) ÷ Amount invested*

2.   The **expected rate of return** on an investment is determined using an **expected value** calculation. It is an average of the outcomes weighted according to their probabilities. Consequently, the expected rate of return is the mean of the probability distribution of the possible outcomes. If k_i is the return from the ith possible outcome and p_i is its probability, the expected return ($\hat{k}$) may be expressed as

$$\hat{k} = \sum_{i=1}^{n} k_i \, p_i$$

a.   The **greater the standard deviation** of the expected return, the **riskier the investment**. A large standard deviation implies that the range of possible returns is wide; i.e., the probability distribution is broadly dispersed. Conversely, the smaller the standard deviation, the tighter the probability distribution and the lower the risk.

b.   The **standard deviation** gives an exact value for the tightness of the distribution and the riskiness of the investment. The standard deviation (σ) is the square root of the variance. If k_i is the return from the ith outcome, p_i is its probability, and $\hat{k}$ is the expected (mean) return, the variance (σ^2) is

$$\sigma^2 = \sum_{i=1}^{n} (k_i - \hat{k})^2 p_i$$

1)   EXAMPLE:

Stock X

Return (k_i)	Probability (p_i)	$k_i \times p_i$	$(k_i - \hat{k})^2 p_i$
4.5	0.25	1.125	4.6764063
−5.2	0.25	−1.30	7.2226563
6.3	0.25	1.575	9.3789063
−4.9	0.25	−1.225	6.4389063
		0.175	27.716875

$$\hat{k} = 0.175$$
$$\sigma^2 = 27.716875$$
$$\sigma = 5.264681852$$

Stock Y

Return (k_i)	Probability (p_i)	$k_i \times p_i$	$(k_i - \hat{k})^2 p_i$
10.2	0.25	2.55	7.317025
−8.07	0.25	−2.0175	41.3449
9.63	0.25	2.4075	5.8564
7.4	0.25	1.85	1.703025
		4.79	56.22135

$$\hat{k} = 4.79$$
$$\sigma^2 = 56.22135$$
$$\sigma = 7.498089757$$

Stock Y, having the greater standard deviation, is the riskier investment.

c. The **coefficient of variation** is useful when the rates of return and standard deviations of two investments differ. It measures the risk per unit of return because it divides the standard deviation (σ) by the expected return (k̂).

$$Coefficient\ of\ variation\ =\ \frac{\sigma}{\hat{k}}$$

1) EXAMPLE:

Stock X		Stock Y	
σ ÷ k̂	= 5.264681852 ÷ 0.175	σ ÷ k̂	= 7.498089757 ÷ 4.79
	= 30.0839		= 1.5654

Thus, when compared on a per-unit-of-return basis, Stock X is far riskier.

3. Stop and review! You have completed the outline for this subunit. Study multiple-choice question 1 on page 205.

7.2 TYPES OF RISK

1. **Investment risk** is analyzed in terms of the probability that the **actual return** on an investment will be lower than the **expected return**. Accordingly, the concepts of probability distributions and expected value are basic to risk measurement.

   a. The risk of an investment may be considered in isolation. It may also be viewed from the perspective of its inclusion in a portfolio of investments chosen to minimize the riskiness of the whole. **Diversification** is a basic risk minimization technique that seeks to spread the risk from a single task or asset to multiple tasks or assets with returns that are not perfectly positively correlated.

2. **Specific Types of Investment Risks**

   a. **Interest-rate risk** is the risk of fluctuations in the value of an asset due to changes in interest rates. In general, it is greater the longer the maturity of the asset.

      1) One component of interest-rate risk is **price risk**. Thus, the value of bonds declines when interest rates increase.

      2) A second component of interest-rate risk is **reinvestment-rate risk**. If interest rates decline, lower returns will be available for reinvestment of interest and principal payments received.

      3) **Immunization** is protection against interest-rate risk by holding assets and liabilities such that the product of the value of the assets times their duration equals the product of the value of the liabilities times their duration.

   b. **Purchasing-power risk** is the risk that a general rise in the price level will reduce what can be purchased with a fixed sum of money. Accordingly, required returns include an inflation premium.

   c. **Default risk** is the risk that a borrower will be unable to repay debt. Hence, the higher the default risk, the higher the return required by an investor.

   d. **Systematic risk** is the risk that changes in price will result from changes that affect all firms. Prices of all securities, even the values of portfolios, are correlated to some degree with broad swings in the economy caused by recession, inflation, high interest rates, etc. For this reason, systematic risk is also known as **market** or **nondiversifiable risk**.

   e. **Unsystematic risk** or **specific risk** is the risk that is influenced by an individual firm's policies and decisions. Unsystematic risk is diversifiable because it is specific to each firm. Thus, it is also known as **diversifiable** or **nonmarket risk**. Diversification reduces risk.

f. **Portfolio risk** is the risk remaining after allowing for the risk-reducing effects of combining securities into a portfolio. Portfolio risk is attributable to the poor balance of risks within the portfolio.

g. **Total risk** is the risk of a single asset, whereas market risk is the asset's risk if it is held in a large portfolio of diversified securities.

h. **Liquidity risk** is the possibility that an asset cannot be sold on short notice for its market value. If an asset must be sold at a deep discount, it is said to have a substantial amount of liquidity risk.

i. **Business risk** is the risk of fluctuations in earnings before interest and taxes or in operating income when the firm uses no debt. It is the risk inherent in its operations that excludes **financial risk**, which is the risk to the shareholders from the use of financial leverage. Business risk depends on factors such as

    1) Demand variability
    2) Sales price variability
    3) Input price variability
    4) Amount of operating leverage

j. **Exchange-rate risk** is the risk that a foreign currency transaction will be negatively exposed to fluctuations in exchange rates.

k. A thorough knowledge of the market is necessary to be able to manage **commodities risk**. Commodities risk includes many possibilities, for example, that

    1) An entire investment may be lost,
    2) It may be impossible to liquidate a position under certain market conditions,
    3) Spread positions may not be less risky than simple long or short positions,
    4) The use of leverage can lead to large losses, and
    5) Managed commodity accounts are subject to substantial management fees.

l. **Political risk** is the probability of loss from actions of governments, such as from changes in tax laws or environmental regulations or from expropriation of assets.

3. **Financing Risk**

    a. The **financial structure** of a firm encompasses the right-hand side of the balance sheet, which describes how the firm's assets are financed. Capital structure is the permanent financing of the firm and is represented primarily by

        1) Long-term debt

            a) Most firms renew (roll over) their long-term obligations. Thus, long-term debt is often effectively permanent.

        2) Preferred stock
        3) Common equity

            a) Common stock
            b) Additional paid-in capital
            c) Retained earnings

    b. The following factors influence financial structure:

        1) Growth rate and stability of future sales
        2) Competitive structures in the industry
        3) Asset makeup of the individual firm
        4) Attitude toward risk of owners and management
        5) Control position of owners and management
        6) Rating agencies' and lenders' attitudes toward the industry and a particular firm
        7) Tax considerations

4. **Leverage** is the relative amount of the fixed cost of capital, principally debt, in a firm's capital structure. Leverage, by definition, creates financial risk, which relates directly to the question of the cost of capital. The more leverage, the higher the financial risk, and the higher the cost of debt capital.

    a. **Earnings per share (EPS)** will ordinarily be higher if debt is used to raise capital instead of equity, provided that the firm is not over-leveraged. The reason is that the cost of debt is lower than the cost of equity because interest is tax deductible. However, the prospect of higher EPS is accompanied by greater risk to the firm resulting from required interest costs, creditors' liens on the firm's assets, and the possibility of a proportionately lower EPS if sales volume fails to meet projections.

    b. **The degree of financial leverage (DFL)** for a period is expressed by the following ratio:

$$\frac{Operating\ income}{Net\ income}$$

        Financial leverage is the degree of risk assumed by a firm from the use of fixed costs in its financing structure (analogous to operating leverage measuring the use of fixed costs in its production environment). Thus, the greater the financial leverage, the riskier the firm.

        1) EXAMPLE: A company has the following data:

	Year 4	Year 3
Operating Income	$150,000	$70,000
Net income	$42,000	$21,000
DFL	3.57	3.33

        2) The company is more leveraged in the most recent year and is thus riskier.

    c. The DFL at a particular level of EBIT can be calculated as follows:

$$DFL\ at\ one\ level\ of\ EBIT = \frac{EBIT}{EBIT - Interest}$$

        1) If the firm has **preferred stock**, the formula is further modified as follows (if P = preferred dividends and T is the tax rate):

$$\frac{EBIT}{EBIT - Interest - \left[P \div (1 - T)\right]}$$

        2) If the return on assets exceeds the cost of debt, additional leverage is favorable.

    d. The **degree of operating leverage (DOL)** for a period is expressed by the following ratio.

$$\frac{Contribution\ margin}{Operating\ income}$$

        It measures the extent to which a firm incurs fixed rather than variable costs in operations. A firm with a high percentage of fixed costs is more risky than a firm in the same industry that relies more heavily on variable production costs. Thus, the greater the DOL, the greater the risk of loss when revenues decline and the greater the reward when revenues increase.

        1) EXAMPLE: The company's contribution margin was $900,000 and $600,000 for Years 4 and 3, respectively. It's DOL figures were thus 6.00 and 8.57.

        2) The company was less leveraged in the most recent year.

3) The assumption is that firms with larger investments (and greater fixed costs) will have higher contribution margins and more operating leverage. Thus, as they invest in better and more expensive equipment, their variable production costs should decrease.

4) If Q equals the number of units sold, P is unit price, V is unit variable cost, and F is fixed cost, the DOL also can be calculated by dividing **total contribution margin** by net operating income (total contribution margin − fixed cost). This formula is derived from the formula on the previous page, but the derivation is not given.

$$\frac{Q(P - V)}{Q(P - V) - F} = \frac{Total\ contribution\ margin\ (TCM)}{Net\ operating\ income}$$

5) The DOL is calculated with respect to a given **base level of revenues**. The significance of the DOL is that a given percentage increase in revenues yields a percentage increase in net operating income equal to the DOL for the base revenues level times the percentage increase in revenues.

6) Furthermore, the DOL is related to the **margin of safety percentage (MSP)**. The DOL equals 1 divided by the MSP, and the MSP equals 1 divided by the DOL. The reason for this relationship is that the margin of safety (net operating income) is the excess of the TCM over fixed costs (the amount by which the TCM may be reduced without incurring a loss). Thus, the MSP equals net operating income divided by the TCM, which is the inverse of the DOL (TCM ÷ net operating income).

e. **The degree of total leverage (DTL)** combines the DFL and the DOL. It equals the degree of financial leverage times the degree of operating leverage. Thus, it also equals the percentage change in EPS that is associated with a given percentage change in revenues:

$$DTL = DFL \times DOL = \frac{Contribution\ margin}{\%\ \Delta\ Net\ income}$$

1) EXAMPLE: The company's degree of total leverage can be calculated as follows:

Year 4: 3.57 × 6.00 = 21.43

Year 3: 3.33 × 8.57 = 28.57

2) Firms with a high degree of operating leverage do not usually employ a high degree of financial leverage and vice versa. One of the most important considerations in the use of financial leverage is operating leverage.

a) EXAMPLE: A manufacturer has a highly automated production process. Because of automation, the degree of operating leverage is 5. If the firm wants a degree of total leverage not exceeding 6, it must restrict its use of debt so that the degree of financial leverage is not more than 1.2. If the firm had committed to a production process that was less automated and had a lower DOL, more debt could be employed, and the firm could have a higher degree of financial leverage.

5. Stop and review! You have completed the outline for this subunit. Study multiple-choice questions 2 through 15 beginning on page 206.

7.3 RELATIONSHIP BETWEEN RISK AND RETURN

1. Whether the expected return on an investment is sufficient to entice an investor depends on its risk, the risks and returns of alternative investments, and the **investor's attitude toward risk**.

   a. Most serious investors are **risk averse**. They have a diminishing marginal utility for wealth. In other words, the utility of additional increments of wealth decreases. The utility of a gain for serious investors is less than the disutility of a loss of the same amount. Due to this risk aversion, risky securities must have higher expected returns.

   b. A **risk neutral** investor adopts an expected value approach because (s)he regards the utility of a gain as equal to the disutility of a loss of the same amount. Thus, a risk-neutral investor has a purely rational attitude toward risk.

   c. A **risk-seeking** investor has an optimistic attitude toward risk. (S)he regards the utility of a gain as exceeding the disutility of a loss of the same amount.

2. **Financial instruments**. Financial managers may select from a wide range of financial instruments in which to invest and with which to raise money.

   a. Ranked from the lowest **rate of return** to the highest (and thus the lowest **risk** to the highest), the following is a short list of widely available long-term financial instruments:

      1) U.S. Treasury bonds
      2) First mortgage bonds
      3) Second mortgage bonds
      4) Subordinated debentures
      5) Income bonds
      6) Preferred stock
      7) Convertible preferred stock
      8) Common stock

   b. These instruments also are ranked according to the level of security backing them. An unsecured financial instrument is much riskier than an instrument that is secured. Thus, the riskier asset earns a higher rate of return. Mortgage bonds are secured by assets, but common stock is completely unsecured. Accordingly, common stock will earn a higher rate of return than mortgage bonds. For more on long-term financing, see Subunit 8.1.

   c. Short-term financial instruments increase the liquidity of an entity. For a discussion of the asset management aspects of short-term instruments, see Subunit 10.3.

3. Stop and review! You have completed the outline for this subunit. Study multiple-choice questions 16 through 18 beginning on page 210.

7.4 RISK AND RETURN IN A PORTFOLIO CONTEXT

1. The calculations in Subunit 7.1 apply to investments in individual securities. When a portfolio is held, however, additional considerations apply. **Risk and return** should be evaluated for the **entire portfolio**, not for individual assets.

   a. The expected return on a portfolio is the **weighted average** of the returns on the individual securities.

   b. However, the risk of the portfolio is usually not an average of the standard deviations of the particular securities. Thanks to the diversification effect, **combining securities** results in a **portfolio risk that is less** than the average of the standard deviations because the returns are imperfectly correlated.

1) The **correlation coefficient (r)** has a range from 1.0 to −1.0. It measures the degree to which any two variables, e.g., two stocks in a portfolio, are related. Perfect positive correlation (1.0) means that the two variables always move together, and perfect negative correlation (−1.0) means that the two variables always move in the opposite direction.

    a) Given perfect positive correlation, risk for a two-stock portfolio with equal investments in each stock would be the same as that for the individual assets.

    b) Given perfect negative correlation, risk would in theory be eliminated.

2) In practice, securities are usually positively but imperfectly correlated. The normal range for the correlation of two randomly selected stocks is .50 to .70. The result is a reduction in, but not elimination of, risk.

c. The measurement of the standard deviation of a portfolio's returns is based on the same formula as that for a single security.

1) An important measurement used in portfolio analysis is the **covariance**. It measures the **volatility** of returns together with their correlation with the returns of other securities. For two stocks X and Y, if $\hat{k}$ is the expected return, k_i is a given outcome, and p_i is its probability, the covariance of X and Y is

$$COV_{xy} = \sum_{i=1}^{n}(k_{xi} - \hat{k}_x)(k_{yi} - \hat{k}_y)p_i$$

    a) EXAMPLE: The following is based on the data for Stock X and Stock Y in the example of the calculation of the variance and standard deviation in Subunit 7.1.

| Monthly Returns | | $(k_i - \hat{k})$ | | |
Stock X	Stock Y	Stock X	Stock Y	$(k_{xi} - \hat{k}_x)(k_{yi} - \hat{k}_y)$
4.5	10.2	4.325	5.41	23.39825
−5.2	−8.07	−5.375	−12.86	69.1225
6.3	9.63	6.125	4.84	29.645
−4.9	7.4	−5.075	2.61	−13.24575
$\hat{k}_x =$ 0.175	$\hat{k}_y =$ 4.79			108.92

$$COV_{xy} = 108.92 \times .25^*$$
$$= 27.23$$

*The probability assumed for each return for computational simplicity. See tables on page 190.

2) The correlation coefficient (r) mentioned earlier is calculated to facilitate comparisons of covariances. It standardizes the covariance by dividing by the product of the standard deviations of the two assets. Moreover, if r_{xy}, σ_x, and σ_y are known, the covariance can be determined.

$$r_{xy} = \frac{COV_{xy}}{\sigma_X \sigma_Y}$$

    a) EXAMPLE: The following is based on the data from the previous Stock X and Stock Y examples:

$$COV_{xy} = 27.23$$
$$\sigma_x = 5.264681852$$
$$\sigma_y = 7.498089757$$
$$r_{xy} = 27.23 \div (5.26 \times 7.5)$$
$$= 0.69$$

3)   The standard deviation of a two-asset portfolio may be calculated from the following formula if p is the portion invested in x and (1 – p) is the portion invested in y:

$$\sqrt{p^2\sigma_x^2 + (1 - p)^2\sigma_y^2 + 2p(1 - p)r_{xy}\sigma_x\sigma_y}$$

a)   EXAMPLE: This computation is based on the data from the previous Stock X and Stock Y examples. If a total of $5,000 is invested, $3,000 in X and $2,000 in Y, the standard deviation of this two-asset portfolio may be calculated as follows:

$$= \sqrt{(3 \div 5)^2(\sigma_x^2) + (2 \div 5)^2(\sigma_y^2) + 2(3 \div 5)(2 \div 5)(r_{xy})(\sigma_x)(\sigma_y)}$$

$$= \sqrt{(.36)(27.72) + (.16)(56.22) + 2(.6)(.4)(.69)(5.26)(7.5)}$$

$$= 5.66$$

2.   **Portfolio management.** An investor wants to **maximize return and minimize risk** when choosing a portfolio of investments. A feasible portfolio that offers the highest expected return for a given risk or the least risk for a given expected return is an **efficient portfolio**. A portfolio that is selected from the efficient set of portfolios because it is tangent to the investor's highest indifference curve is the **optimal portfolio**.

a.   An **indifference curve** represents combinations of portfolios having equal utility to the investor. Given that risk and returns are plotted on the horizontal and vertical axes, respectively, and that the investor is risk averse, the curve has an increasingly positive slope. As risk increases, the additional required return per unit of additional risk also increases.

   1)   The steeper the slope of an indifference curve, the more risk averse an investor is.

   2)   The higher the curve, the greater is the investor's level of utility.

   3)   In the diagram below, A, B, C, D, and E are indifference curves. A represents the highest level of utility and E the lowest. On a given curve, each point represents the same total utility to a risk-averse investor. For example, points 1, 2, and 3 are different combinations of risk and return that yield the same utility. The investor is indifferent as to which combination is chosen.

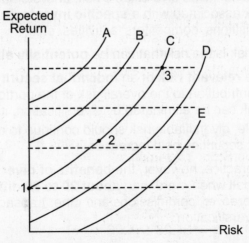

b.   Two important decisions are involved in managing a company's portfolio:

   1)   The amount of money to invest
   2)   The securities in which to invest

c. The investment in securities should be based on **expected net cash flows** and **cash flow uncertainty evaluations**.

1) Arranging a portfolio so that the maturity of funds will coincide with the need for funds will maximize the average return on the portfolio and provide increased flexibility.

a) **Maturity matching** ensures that securities will not have to be sold unexpectedly.

2) If its cash flows are relatively uncertain, a security's marketability and market risk are important factors to be considered. Transaction costs are also a consideration.

a) Higher-yield long-term securities provide less certainty.

3) When cash flows are relatively certain, the maturity date is a paramount concern.

3. Stop and review! You have completed the outline for this subunit. Study multiple-choice questions 19 and 20 on page 212.

7.5 DIVERSIFICATION

1. **Portfolio theory** concerns the composition of an investment portfolio that is efficient in balancing the risk with the rate of return of the portfolio.

a. **Asset allocation** is a key concept in financial planning and money management. It is the process of dividing investments among different kinds of assets, such as stocks, bonds, real estate, and cash, to optimize the risk-reward tradeoff based on specific situations and goals. The rationale is that the returns on different types of assets are not perfectly positively correlated. Asset allocation is especially useful for such institutional investors as pension fund managers, who have a duty to invest with prudence.

b. The **expected rate of return of a portfolio** is the weighted average of the expected returns of the individual assets in the portfolio.

c. The **variability (risk) of a portfolio's return** is determined by the correlation of the returns of individual portfolio assets.

1) To the extent the returns are not perfectly positively correlated, variability is decreased.

d. **Specific risk**, also called diversifiable risk, unsystematic risk, residual risk, and unique risk, is the risk associated with **a specific investee's operations**: new products, patents, acquisitions, competitors' activities, etc.

1) Specific risk is the risk that can be **potentially eliminated by diversification**.

a) The **relevant risk** of an **individual security** held in a portfolio is its contribution to the overall risk of the portfolio. When much of a security's risk can be eliminated by diversification, its relevant risk is low.

2) In principle, diversifiable risk should continue to decrease as the number of different securities held increases.

a) In practice, however, the **benefits of diversification** become extremely small when more than **about 20 to 30 different securities** are held. Moreover, commissions and other transaction costs increase with greater diversification.

e. **Market risk**, also called undiversifiable risk and systematic risk, is the risk of **the stock market as a whole**. Some conditions in the national economy affect all businesses, which is why equity prices so often move together.

1) The effect of an individual security on the volatility of a portfolio is measured by its sensitivity to movements by the overall market. This sensitivity is stated in terms of a stock's **beta coefficient**.

a) An **average-risk** stock has a **beta of 1.0** because its returns are perfectly positively correlated with those on the market portfolio. For example, if the market return increases by 20%, the return on the security increases by 20%.

b) A beta of **less than 1.0** means that the security is **less volatile than the market**; e.g., if the market return increases by 20% and the security's return increases only 10%, the security has a beta of .5.

c) A **beta over 1.0** indicates a **volatile security**; e.g., if the return increases 30% when the market return increases by 15%, the security has a beta of 2.0.

2) The word **beta** is derived from the regression equation for regressing the return of an individual security (the dependent variable) to the overall market return. The beta coefficient is the **slope of the regression line**.

a) The beta for a security may also be calculated by dividing the covariance of the return on the market and the return on the security by the variance of the return on the market.

3) Beta is the best measure of the risk of an individual security held in a diversified portfolio because it determines how the security affects the risk of the portfolio.

4) The **beta of a portfolio** is the weighted average of the betas of the individual securities.

a) **Portfolio insurance** is a strategy of hedging a stock portfolio against market risk by selling stock index futures short or buying stock index put options. A stock index futures contract is an agreement to deliver the cash equivalent of a group of stocks on a specified date. This cash equivalent equals a given stock index value, for example, the S&P 500, times a cash amount. Thus, if the stock index falls (rises), a seller of stock index futures gains (loses) and a buyer loses (gains).

f. The **value-at-risk (VAR) model** uses statistical analysis of historical market trends and volatilities to estimate the likelihood that a given portfolio's losses will exceed a certain amount. It is preferable to sensitivity analysis because it states the probability (stated at a specific confidence level) that a given change in a variable (e.g., a foreign currency exchange rate or an interest rate) will result in a given loss. Simulation and variance-covariance methods are among the techniques used to calculate VAR, sometimes called the maximum normal loss.

2. Stop and review! You have completed the outline for this subunit. Study multiple-choice questions 21 through 23 on page 213.

7.6 CAPM, APT, AND HEDGING

1.   The **Capital Asset Pricing Model (CAPM)** relates the risk of a security, as measured by its beta coefficient, to the rate of return expected on that security.

   a.   The **required rate of return on equity capital (R)** can be estimated by adding the risk-free rate (determined by government securities) to the product of the beta coefficient (a measure of the firm's risk) and the difference between the market return and the risk-free rate. Below is the basic equilibrium equation for the CAPM.

$$R = R_F + \beta(R_M - R_F)$$

   1)   The graph of the above equation (with rate of return plotted on the vertical axis and betas on the horizontal axis) is the **security market line**. The slope of the SML equals the market risk premium and the y-intercept is the risk-free rate.

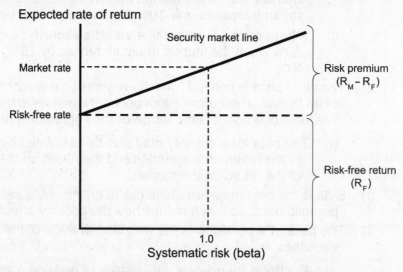

   2)   The **market risk premium** ($R_M - R_F$) is the amount above the risk-free rate required to induce average investors to enter the market.

   3)   The **beta coefficient** (β) of an individual stock is the correlation between the volatility (price variation) of the stock market and the volatility of the price of the individual stock.

      a)   EXAMPLE: If an individual stock rises 10% and the stock market 10%, the beta coefficient is 1.0. If the stock rises 15% and the market only 10%, beta is 1.5.

   4)   EXAMPLE: Assuming a beta of 1.20, a market rate of return of approximately 17%, and an expected risk-free rate of 12%, the required rate of return on equity capital is .12 + 1.20 (.17 − .12), or 18%.

   5)   The **risk premium** is the difference in expected rates of return on a risky asset and a less risky asset.

   b.   **Arbitrage pricing theory (APT)** is based on the assumption that an asset's return is a function of multiple systematic risk factors. In contrast, the CAPM is a model that uses just one systematic risk factor to explain the asset's return. That factor is the expected return on the market portfolio, i.e., the market-valued weighted-average return for all securities in the market.

   1)   The difference between actual and expected returns on an asset is attributable to systematic and unsystematic risks. Investors must be paid a risk premium to compensate for systematic (market) risk.

2) Accordingly, APT provides for a separate beta and a separate risk premium for each systematic risk factor identified in the model. Examples of the many potential systematic risk factors are the gross domestic product (GDP), inflation, and real interest rates. The APT for a three-factor model may be formulated as follows:

$$R = R_F + \beta_1 k_1 + \beta_2 k_2 + \beta_3 k_3$$

Where:
R = expected rate of return
R_F = risk-free rate
$\beta_{1,2,3}$ = individual factor beta coefficients
$k_{1,2,3}$ = individual factor risk premiums

3) EXAMPLE: Assume R_F = 9%
k_1 = 2% β_1 = .6
k_2 = 5% β_2 = .4
k_3 = 8% β_3 = .2

Applying these values to the formula, the expected rate of return is .09 + (.6)(.02) + (.4)(.05) + (.2)(.08), or 13.8%.

c. R also may be estimated by adding a percentage to the firm's long-term cost of debt. A 3% to 5% premium is frequently used.

2. **Hedging** is defined in *The CPA Letter* (October 2000) as "a defensive strategy designed to protect an entity against the risk of adverse price or interest-rate movements on certain of its assets, liabilities, or anticipated transactions. A hedge is used to avoid or reduce risks by creating a relationship by which losses on certain positions are expected to be counterbalanced in whole or in part by gains on separate positions in another market."

a. Thus, the purchase or sale of a derivative or other instrument is a hedge if it is expected to neutralize the risk of a recognized asset or liability, an unrecognized firm commitment, a forecasted transaction, etc. For example, if a flour company buys and uses 1 million bushels of wheat each month, it may wish to guard against increases in wheat costs when it has committed to sell at a price related to the current cost of wheat. If so, the company will purchase wheat futures contracts that will result in gains if the price of wheat increases (offsetting the actual increased costs).

b. **Long hedges** are futures contracts that are purchased to protect against price increases.

c. **Short hedges** are futures contracts that are sold to protect against price declines.

d. EXAMPLE: In the commodities market, a company may contract with a farmer to buy soybeans at a future date. The price is agreed upon as the current price. The company will lose money if the soybean prices decline before the soybeans are delivered. To avoid loss (or gain), the company may sell soybeans in the future at today's price. If the price of soybeans declines before the delivery date, the company will lose money on the soybeans bought from the farmer, but it will gain money on the soybeans sold through the futures contract by buying cheap soybeans in the future to cover the delivery.

1) Because commodities can be bought and sold **on margin**, considerable leverage is involved. Leverage is most beneficial to the speculator who is seeking large returns and is willing to bear proportionate risk. For hedgers, however, the small margin requirement is useful only because the risk can be hedged without tying up a large amount of cash.

3. **Interest rate futures contracts** involve risk-free securities such as Treasury bonds, T-bills, and money-market certificates.

   a. The quantity traded is either $100,000 or $1,000,000, depending on which market is used.

   b. EXAMPLE: If a corporation wants to borrow money in 6 months for a major project, but the lender refuses to commit itself to an interest rate, the interest rate futures market can be used to hedge the risk that interest rates might increase in the interim. The company agrees to sell Treasury bonds in 6 months. If interest rates do increase over the period, the value of the Treasury bonds will decline. The company can buy Treasury bonds in 6 months and use them to cover the delivery that it had promised in the futures contract. Because the price of Treasury bonds has declined over the period, the company will make a profit on their delivery. The interest rates that the company will have to pay on the upcoming loan will be higher, however. It has cost the company money to wait 6 months for the loan. The profit from the futures contract should approximately offset the loss resulting from the higher interest loan. If interest rates had declined, the company would have had the benefit of a lower interest loan but would have lost money on the Treasury bonds. The goal of any such hedging operation is to break even on the change in interest rates.

      1) By hedging, the financial manager need not worry about fluctuations in interest rates but can concentrate instead on the day-to-day operations of the company.

4. **Duration hedging** involves hedging interest-rate risk. **Duration** is the weighted average of the periods of time to interest and principal payments. If duration increases, the volatility of the price of the debt instrument increases.

   a. Duration is lower if the nominal rate on the instrument is higher because more of the return is received earlier. The following symbols are used in the formula for duration:

   C_T = Interest or principal payment
   T = Time to payment
   n = Time to maturity
   r = Yield to maturity
   V = Value of the instrument

   $$\sum_{T=1}^{n}\left(\frac{C_T \times T}{(1 + r)^T}\right) \div V$$

      1) $C_T \div (1 + r)^T$ is the present value of the cash flow.

   b. The goal of duration hedging is not to equate the duration of assets and the duration of liabilities but for the following relationship to apply:

   (Value of assets) × (Duration of assets) = (Value of liabilities) × (Duration of liabilities)

      1) The firm is immunized against interest-rate risk when the total price change for assets equals the total price change for liabilities

   c. Assets have positive duration numbers and liabilities have negative numbers. If the duration is positive, then we are exposed to rising interest rates. Likewise, if the duration is negative, we are exposed to falling interest rates.

   d. Duration hedging does not provide a perfect hedge. For example, Gator Company has $4,000,000 of net assets with a net duration of 4 years. This could be hedged by raising the duration of liabilities in any combination to achieve a duration match, such as $4,000,000 of 4.0 years net duration liabilities; or $8,000,000 of 2.0 year net duration liabilities or $2,000,000 of 8.0 year net duration liabilities, etc.

5. **Swaps** are contracts to hedge risk by exchanging cash flows. The simplest form, sometimes called a **plain vanilla swap**, is an exchange of interest rates without any change in the initial debt arrangement.

    a. In an **interest-rate swap**, one firm exchanges its fixed interest payments for a series of payments based on a floating rate. Such contracts are highly customized. If a firm has debt with fixed charges, but its revenues fluctuate with interest rates, it may prefer to swap for cash outflows based on a floating rate. The advantage is that revenues and the amounts of debt service will then move in the same direction and interest-rate risk will be reduced. The specified dollar amount on which the exchanged interest payments are based is called the **notional principal** amount.

        1) The **swap spread** is the market-determined additional yield that compensates counterparties who receive fixed payments in a swap for the credit risk involved in the swap. The swap spread will differ with the creditworthiness of the counterparty.

        2) Most swaps are priced to be **at-the-money** at inception, meaning that the value of the floating rate cash flows is the same as the value of the fixed rate cash flows. Naturally, as interest rates change, the values may change. Receiving the fixed rate flow will become more valuable than receiving the floating rate flow if interest rates drop or if credit spreads tighten.

    b. A **currency swap** is an exchange of an obligation to pay out cash flows denominated in one currency for an obligation to pay in another. For example, a U.S. firm with revenues in euros has to pay suppliers and workers in dollars, not euros. To minimize exchange-rate risk, it might agree to exchange euros for dollars held by a firm that needs euros. The exchange rate will be an average of the rates expected over the life of the agreement.

    c. A **swaption** is an option on a swap, usually on an interest-rate swap, that provides the holder with the right to enter into a swap at a specified future date at specified terms (freestanding option on a swap) or to extend or terminate the life of an existing swap (embedded option on a swap).

6. Interest Rate Caps, Floors, and Collars

    a. An **interest rate cap** is an option that limits the risk of interest rate increases. If interest rates rise above a certain level, the cap holder receives the excess of the actual interest rate over a designated interest rate (the strike or cap rate) based on the notional principal amount. The cap holder's loss is limited to the premium paid to the cap writer. The cap writer has unlimited risk from potential increases in interest rates above the specified rate.

    b. An **interest rate floor** is an option that limits the risk of interest rate decreases. If rates fall below a specified level, the floor holder receives cash payments equal to the excess of a designated rate (the strike or floor rate) over the actual rate based on the notional principal amount. The buyer pays the writer a premium to receive this right, and the floor writer faces significant risk from potential decreases in rates below the specified rate.

    c. A **collar** is an option that combines the strategies of a cap and a floor. The buyer acquires a cap and writes a floor. The writer writes a cap and buys a floor. Collars fix the rate a variable-rate lender will receive or a borrower will pay between the cap and floor rate levels. Collars help reduce the cost of buying outright a cap or floor. Because a borrower or lender is usually only interested in protecting against movements in interest rates in one direction, the premium received for writing a cap or floor serves to reduce the cost of the cap or floor purchased.

7. Stop and review! You have completed the outline for this subunit. Study multiple-choice questions 24 through 28 beginning on page 214.

7.7 CORE CONCEPTS

Calculating Return

- A **return** is the amount received by an investor as compensation for taking on the risk of the investment. The **rate of return** is the return stated as a percentage of the amount invested, calculated as follows: (amount received − amount invested) ÷ amount invested.

- The **expected rate of return** on an investment is determined using an **expected value** calculation. It is an average of the outcomes weighted according to their probabilities.

- The **greater the standard deviation** of the expected return, the **riskier the investment**.

- The **coefficient of variation** is useful when the rates of return and standard deviations of two investments differ. It measures the risk per unit of return because it divides the standard deviation by the expected return.

Types of Risk

- Specific **types of investment risks** include interest-rate risk, purchasing-power risk, default risk, market (systematic) risk, nonmarket (diversifiable) risk, portfolio risk, total risk, liquidity risk, business risk, exchange rate risk, commodities risk, and political risk.

- **Leverage** is the relative amount of the fixed cost of capital, principally debt, in a firm's capital structure.

- The **degree of financial leverage** is the ratio of operating income to net income.

- The **degree of operating leverage** is the ratio of contribution margin to operating income. It measures the extent to which a firm incurs fixed rather than variable costs in operations.

- The **degree of total leverage** is the degree of financial leverage times the degree of operating leverage. Firms with a high degree of operating leverage do not usually employ a high degree of financial leverage and vice versa. One of the most important considerations in the use of financial leverage is operating leverage.

Relationship Between Risk and Return

- **Riskier investments** have higher potential rates of return.

- A **risk averse** investor is one with a diminishing marginal utility for wealth, i.e., the potential gain is not worth the additional risk. A **risk neutral** investor adopts an expected value approach. A **risk-seeking** investor has an optimistic attitude toward risk.

Risk and Return in a Portfolio Context

- **Risk and return** should be evaluated for a firm's **entire portfolio**, not for individual assets.

- Thanks to the diversification effect, **combining securities** results in a **portfolio risk that is less** than the average of the standard deviations because the returns are imperfectly correlated.

- Given **perfect negative correlation** of the prices of two stocks, risk would in theory be eliminated.

- An important measurement used in portfolio analysis is the **covariance**. It measures the **volatility** of returns together with their correlation with the returns of other securities.

- A feasible portfolio that offers the highest expected return for a given risk or the least risk for a given expected return is an **efficient portfolio**. A portfolio that is selected from the efficient set of portfolios because it is tangent to the investor's highest indifference curve is the **optimal portfolio**.

- A company's investment in securities should be based on **expected net cash flows** and **cash flow uncertainty evaluations**. Arranging a portfolio so that the maturity of funds will coincide with the need for funds will maximize the average return on the portfolio and provide increased flexibility.

Diversification

- **Portfolio theory** concerns the composition of an investment portfolio that is efficient in balancing the risk with the rate of return of the portfolio. **Asset allocation** is a key concept in financial planning and money management.

- **Specific risk**, also called diversifiable risk, unsystematic risk, residual risk, and unique risk, is the risk associated with a specific investee's operations: new products, patents, acquisitions, competitors' activities, etc. Specific risk is the risk that can be **potentially eliminated by diversification**.

- **Market risk**, also called undiversifiable risk and systematic risk, is the risk of the stock market as a whole. Some conditions in the national economy **affect all businesses**, which is why equity prices so often move together.

- The effect of an individual security on the volatility of a portfolio is measured by its sensitivity to movements by the overall market. This sensitivity is stated in terms of a stock's **beta coefficient**.

- The stock can have the same **volatility** as the overall market (beta = 1.0), be more volatile than average (beta > 1.0), or be less volatile than average (beta < 1.0).

CAPM, APT, and Hedging

- The **capital asset pricing model** relates the risk of a security, as measured by its beta coefficient, to the rate of return expected on that security. The **security market line** graphically depicts market risk premium.

- **Arbitrage pricing theory** is based on the assumption that an asset's return is a function of multiple systematic risk factors. In contrast, the CAPM is a model that uses just one systematic risk factor to explain the asset's return.

- **Hedging** is defined in *The CPA Letter* as "a defensive strategy designed to protect an entity against the risk of adverse price or interest-rate movements on certain of its assets, liabilities, or anticipated transactions. A hedge is used to avoid or reduce risks . . ."

QUESTIONS

7.1 Calculating Return

1. An asset with high risk will have a(n)

    A. Low expected return.

    B. Lower price than an asset with low risk.

    C. Increasing expected rate of return.

    D. High standard deviation of returns.

Answer (D) is correct. *(Publisher, adapted)*
    REQUIRED: The characteristic of an asset with high risk.
    DISCUSSION: The greater the standard deviation of the expected return, the riskier the investment. A large standard deviation implies that the range of possible returns is wide; i.e., the probability distribution is broadly dispersed. Conversely, the smaller the standard deviation, the tighter the probability distribution and the lower the risk.
    Answer (A) is incorrect because an asset with high risk will have a high expected return to compensate for the additional risk. Answer (B) is incorrect because an asset with high risk will not necessarily have a lower price than an asset with low risk. For example, two bond issues with different risk levels might be sold at the same price but have different interest rates. Answer (C) is incorrect because an expected rate of return by definition is a constant expected return.

7.2 Types of Risk

2. Catherine & Co. has extra cash at the end of the year and is analyzing the best way to invest the funds. The company should invest in a project only if the

- A. Expected return on the project exceeds the return on investments of comparable risk.

- B. Return on investments of comparable risk exceeds the expected return on the project.

- C. Expected return on the project is equal to the return on investments of comparable risk.

- D. Return on investments of comparable risk equals the expected return on the project.

Answer (A) is correct. *(Publisher, adapted)*
REQUIRED: The rule for deciding whether to invest in a project.
DISCUSSION: Investment risk is analyzed in terms of the probability that the actual return on an investment will be lower than the expected return. Comparing a project's expected return with the return on an asset of similar risk helps determine whether the project is worth investing in. If the expected return on a project exceeds the return on an asset of comparable risk, the project should be pursued.

3. Which of the following are components of interest-rate risk?

- A. Purchasing-power risk and default risk.

- B. Price risk and market risk.

- C. Portfolio risk and reinvestment-rate risk.

- D. Price risk and reinvestment-rate risk.

Answer (D) is correct. *(Publisher, adapted)*
REQUIRED: The components of interest-rate risk.
DISCUSSION: Interest-rate risk is the risk of fluctuations in the value of an asset due to changes in interest rates. One component of interest-rate risk is price risk; for example, the value of bonds declines as interest rates increase. Reinvestment-rate risk is another component of interest-rate risk. If interest rates decline, lower returns will be available for reinvestment of interest and principal payments received.
Answer (A) is incorrect because purchasing-power risk concerns inflation, and default risk concerns nonpayment by the debtor. Answer (B) is incorrect because market risk concerns price changes in the overall securities markets. Answer (C) is incorrect because portfolio risk is the risk remaining in a portfolio after diversifying investments.

4. The type of risk that is not diversifiable and affects the value of a portfolio is

- A. Purchasing-power risk.

- B. Market risk.

- C. Nonmarket risk.

- D. Interest-rate risk.

Answer (B) is correct. *(Publisher, adapted)*
REQUIRED: The term for the type of risk that is not diversifiable.
DISCUSSION: Prices of all stocks, even the value of portfolios, are correlated to some degree with broad swings in the stock market. Market risk is the risk that changes in a stock's price will result from changes in the stock market as a whole. Market risk is commonly referred to as nondiversifiable risk.
Answer (A) is incorrect because purchasing-power risk is the risk that a general rise in the price level will reduce the quantity of goods that can be purchased with a fixed sum of money. Answer (C) is incorrect because nonmarket risk is the risk that is influenced by an individual firm's policies and decisions. Nonmarket risk is diversifiable since it is specific to each firm. Answer (D) is incorrect because interest-rate risk is the risk that the value of an asset will fluctuate due to changes in the interest rate.

5. The risk that securities cannot be sold at a reasonable price on short notice is called

- A. Default risk.

- B. Interest-rate risk.

- C. Purchasing-power risk.

- D. Liquidity risk.

Answer (D) is correct. *(CIA, adapted)*
REQUIRED: The term for the risk that securities cannot be sold at a reasonable price on short notice.
DISCUSSION: An asset is liquid if it can be converted to cash on short notice. Liquidity (marketability) risk is the risk that assets cannot be sold at a reasonable price on short notice. If an asset is not liquid, investors will require a higher return than for a liquid asset. The difference is the liquidity premium.
Answer (A) is incorrect because default risk is the risk that a borrower will not pay the interest or principal on a loan. Answer (B) is incorrect because interest-rate risk is the risk to which investors are exposed because of changing interest rates. Answer (C) is incorrect because purchasing-power risk is the risk that inflation will reduce the purchasing power of a given sum of money.

6. When purchasing temporary investments, which one of the following best describes the risk associated with the ability to sell the investment in a short period of time without significant price concessions?

    A. Interest-rate risk.

    B. Purchasing-power risk.

    C. Financial risk.

    D. Liquidity risk.

Answer (D) is correct. *(CMA, adapted)*
    REQUIRED: The risk associated with the ability to sell investments in a short period of time without significant price concessions.
    DISCUSSION: Liquidity risk is the possibility that an asset cannot be sold on short notice for its market value. If an asset must be sold at a high discount, it is said to have a substantial amount of liquidity risk.
    Answer (A) is incorrect because interest-rate risk is caused by fluctuations in the value of an asset as interest rates change. Its components are price risk and reinvestment-rate risk. Answer (B) is incorrect because purchasing-power risk is the risk that a general rise in the price level (inflation) will reduce what can be purchased with a fixed sum of money. Answer (C) is incorrect because financial risk is the risk borne by shareholders, in excess of basic business risk that arises from use of financial leverage (issuance of fixed income securities, i.e., debt and preferred stock).

7. Prior to the introduction of the euro, O & B Company, a U.S. corporation, is in possession of accounts receivable denominated in German deutsche marks. To what type of risk are they exposed?

    A. Liquidity risk.

    B. Business risk.

    C. Exchange-rate risk.

    D. Price risk.

Answer (C) is correct. *(Publisher, adapted)*
    REQUIRED: The risk to which a business is exposed when accounts receivable are denominated in a foreign currency.
    DISCUSSION: Exchange-rate risk is the risk that a foreign currency transaction will be negatively exposed to fluctuations in exchange rates. Because O & B Company sells goods to German customers and records accounts receivable denominated in deutsche marks, O & B Company is exposed to exchange-rate risk.
    Answer (A) is incorrect because liquidity risk is the possibility that an asset cannot be sold on short notice for its market value. Answer (B) is incorrect because business risk is the risk of fluctuations in earnings before interest and taxes or in operating income when the firm uses no debt. Answer (D) is incorrect because price risk is a component of interest-rate risk.

8. A firm must select from among several methods of financing arrangements when meeting its capital requirements. To acquire additional growth capital while attempting to maximize earnings per share, a firm should normally

    A. Attempt to increase both debt and equity in equal proportions, which preserves a stable capital structure and maintains investor confidence.

    B. Select debt over equity initially, even though increased debt is accompanied by interest costs and a degree of risk.

    C. Select equity over debt initially, which minimizes risk and avoids interest costs.

    D. Discontinue dividends and use current cash flow, which avoids the cost and risk of increased debt and the dilution of EPS through increased equity.

Answer (B) is correct. *(CIA, adapted)*
    REQUIRED: The financing arrangement that should be selected to acquire additional growth capital while attempting to maximize earnings per share.
    DISCUSSION: Earnings per share will ordinarily be higher if debt is used to raise capital instead of equity, provided that the firm is not over-leveraged. The reason is that the cost of debt is lower than the cost of equity because interest is tax deductible. However, the prospect of higher EPS is accompanied by greater risk to the firm resulting from required interest costs, creditors' liens on the firm's assets, and the possibility of a proportionately lower EPS if sales volume fails to meet projections.
    Answer (A) is incorrect because EPS is not a function of investor confidence and is not maximized by concurrent proportional increases in both debt and equity. EPS is usually higher if debt is used instead of equity to raise capital, at least initially. Answer (C) is incorrect because equity capital is initially more costly than debt. Answer (D) is incorrect because using only current cash flow to raise capital is usually too conservative an approach for a growth-oriented firm. Management is expected to be willing to take acceptable risks to be competitive and attain an acceptable rate of growth.

Questions 9 through 11 are based on the following information. Carlisle Company currently sells 400,000 bottles of perfume each year. Each bottle costs $.84 to produce and sells for $1.00. Fixed costs are $28,000 per year. The firm has annual interest expense of $6,000, preferred stock dividends of $2,000 per year, and a 40% tax rate. Carlisle uses the following formulas to determine the company's leverage:

$$Operating\ leverage = \frac{Q\ (S - VC)}{Q\ (S - VC) - FC}$$

$$Financial\ leverage = \frac{EBIT}{EBIT - I - [P \div (1 - T)]}$$

$$Total\ leverage = \frac{Q\ (S - VC)}{Q\ (S - VC) - FC - I - [P \div (1 - T)]}$$

Where:
- Q = Quantity
- FC = Fixed cost
- VC = Variable cost
- S = Selling price
- I = Interest expense
- P = Preferred dividends
- T = Tax rate
- EBIT = Earnings before interest and taxes

9. The degree of operating leverage for Carlisle Company is

- A. 2.4
- B. 1.78
- C. 1.35
- D. 1.2

Answer (B) is correct. *(CMA, adapted)*
REQUIRED: The degree of operating leverage.
DISCUSSION: Operating leverage is the percentage change in operating income resulting from a percentage change in sales. It measures how a change in volume affects profits. Companies with larger investments and greater fixed costs ordinarily have higher contribution margins and more operating leverage. The degree of operating leverage measures the extent to which fixed assets are used in the production process. A company with a high percentage of fixed costs is more risky than a firm in the same industry that relies more on variable costs to produce. Based on a contribution margin of $.16 per unit ($1 – $.84 variable cost), the degree of operating leverage is (400,000 × $.16) ÷ [(400,000 × $.16) – 28,000] = 1.78.
Answer (A) is incorrect because 2.4 could be obtained only by overstating the contribution margin or the fixed costs. Answer (C) is incorrect because 1.35 includes a nonoperating expense (interest) and dividends on preferred stock as fixed costs. It is the degree of financial leverage, not operating leverage. Answer (D) is incorrect because 1.2 is obtained by understating the $64,000 contribution margin or understating the $28,000 of fixed costs.

10. If Carlisle Company did not have preferred stock, the degree of total leverage would

- A. Decrease in proportion to a decrease in financial leverage.
- B. Increase in proportion to an increase in financial leverage.
- C. Remain the same.
- D. Decrease but not be proportional to the decrease in financial leverage.

Answer (A) is correct. *(CMA, adapted)*
REQUIRED: The true statement about the degree of total leverage if the company did not have preferred stock.
DISCUSSION: The degree of total leverage is equal to the degree of operating leverage times the degree of financial leverage. Thus, a decrease in either of these ratios results in a decrease in total leverage. If the company had no preferred stock, the DFL and the DTL would be lower because the pretax income necessary to pay the preferred dividends [P ÷ (1 – T)] is subtracted from the denominator of the DFL.
Answer (B) is incorrect because the increases would not be proportional. Answer (C) is incorrect because the elimination of preferred stock would change the equation. Answer (D) is incorrect because the decrease would be proportional.

11. The degree of financial leverage for Carlisle Company is

A. 2.4

B. 1.78

C. 1.35

D. 2.3

Answer (C) is correct. *(CMA, adapted)*
REQUIRED: The degree of financial leverage.
DISCUSSION: The degree of financial leverage is the percentage change in earnings available to common shareholders that is associated with a given percentage change in net operating income. Operating income equals earnings before interest and taxes. The more financial leverage employed, the greater the degree of financial leverage, and the riskier the firm. Earnings before interest and taxes equal $36,000 [$400,000 sales − (400,000 units × $.84) VC − $28,000 FC]. Using the given formula, the calculation is as follows:

$$\frac{\$36,000}{\$36,000 \ - \ \$6,000 \ - \ (\$2,000 \ \div \ .6)} = \frac{\$36,000}{\$26,667} = 1.35$$

Answer (A) is incorrect because 2.4 could be obtained only by overstating the contribution margin or the fixed costs. **Answer (B) is incorrect** because 1.78 is the degree of operating leverage, not financial leverage. **Answer (D) is incorrect** because 2.3 is derived by overstating the $64,000 contribution margin or the $28,000 of fixed costs.

Question 12 is based on the following information. Presented below are partial year-end financial statement data for companies A and B.

	Company A	Company B		Company A	Company B
Cash	$100	$200	Sales	$600	$5,800
Accounts Receivable	unknown	100	Cost of Goods Sold	300	5,000
Inventories	unknown	100	Administrative Expenses	100	500
Net Fixed Assets	200	100	Depreciation Expense	100	100
Accounts Payable	100	50	Interest Expense	20	10
Long-Term Debt	200	50	Income Tax Expense	40	95
Common Stock	100	200	Net Income	40	95
Retained Earnings	150	100			

---

12. The degree of financial leverage of Company B, to two decimal places, is

A. 1.03

B. 1.05

C. 1.12

D. 1.25

Answer (B) is correct. *(CIA, adapted)*
REQUIRED: The degree of financial leverage for Company B.
DISCUSSION: The degree of financial leverage for Company B may be calculated as earnings before interest and taxes, divided by EBIT minus interest. EBIT is $200 ($95 NI + $10 interest + $95 tax expense). Thus, the DFL is 1.05 [$200 ÷ ($200 − $10)].
Answer (A) is incorrect because 1.03 results if depreciation expense is omitted from the calculation of EBIT. **Answer (C) is incorrect** because 1.12 results if net income is used instead of EBIT. **Answer (D) is incorrect** because 1.25 is the degree of financial leverage for Company A.

---

13. A firm's financial risk is a function of how it manages and maintains its debt. Which one of the following sets of ratios characterizes the firm with the greatest amount of financial risk?

A. High debt-to-equity ratio, high interest-coverage ratio, volatile return on equity.

B. High debt-to-equity ratio, high interest-coverage ratio, stable return on equity.

C. Low debt-to-equity ratio, low interest-coverage ratio, volatile return on equity.

D. High debt-to-equity ratio, low interest-coverage ratio, volatile return on equity.

Answer (D) is correct. *(CMA, adapted)*
REQUIRED: The set of ratios that characterizes the firm with the greatest financial risk.
DISCUSSION: A firm with high risk will have a higher debt-to-equity ratio than a low-risk firm, a lower interest coverage, and a volatile return on equity. A higher debt-to-equity ratio poses a greater risk of insolvency. Debtholders must be paid regardless of whether the firm is profitable. Low interest coverage means that the margin of safety of earnings before interest and taxes is small. A volatile return on equity signifies that earnings are unpredictable. Lack of predictability increases risk.
Answer (A) is incorrect because high interest coverage suggests lower risk. Also, stable returns on equity indicate a low level of risk. **Answer (B) is incorrect** because high interest coverage suggests lower risk. Also, stable returns on equity indicate a low level of risk. **Answer (C) is incorrect** because a low debt-to-equity ratio indicates a low level of risk.

14. Business risk is the risk inherent in a firm's operations that excludes financial risk. It depends on all of the following factors except the

    A. Amount of financial leverage.

    B. Sales price variability.

    C. Demand variability.

    D. Input price variability.

Answer (A) is correct. *(Publisher, adapted)*
    REQUIRED: The factor not affecting business risk of a firm.
    DISCUSSION: Business risk is the risk of fluctuations in earnings before interest and taxes or in operating income when the firm uses no debt. It depends on factors such as demand variability, sales price variability, input price variability, and the amount of operating leverage. Financial leverage affects financial risk and is not a factor affecting business risk.
    Answer (B) is incorrect because sales price variability is a factor affecting business risk. Answer (C) is incorrect because demand variability is a factor affecting business risk. Answer (D) is incorrect because input price variability is a factor affecting business risk.

15. A higher degree of operating leverage compared with the industry average implies that the firm

    A. Has higher variable costs.

    B. Has profits that are more sensitive to changes in sales volume.

    C. Is more profitable.

    D. Is less risky.

Answer (B) is correct. *(CMA, adapted)*
    REQUIRED: The effect of a higher degree of operating leverage (DOL).
    DISCUSSION: Operating leverage is a measure of the degree to which fixed costs are used in the production process. A company with a higher percentage of fixed costs (higher operating leverage) has greater risk than one in the same industry that relies more heavily on variable costs. The DOL equals the percentage change in net operating income divided by the percentage change in sales. Thus, profits become more sensitive to changes in sales volume as the DOL increases.
    Answer (A) is incorrect because a firm with higher operating leverage has higher fixed costs and lower variable costs. Answer (C) is incorrect because a firm with higher leverage will be relatively more profitable than a firm with lower leverage when sales are high. The opposite is true when sales are low. Answer (D) is incorrect because a firm with higher leverage is more risky. Its reliance on fixed costs is greater.

7.3 Relationship Between Risk and Return

16. The marketable securities with the least amount of default risk are

    A. Federal government agency securities.

    B. U.S. Treasury securities.

    C. Repurchase agreements.

    D. Commercial paper.

Answer (B) is correct. *(CMA, adapted)*
    REQUIRED: The marketable securities with the least default risk.
    DISCUSSION: The marketable securities with the lowest default risk are those issued by the federal government because they are backed by the full faith and credit of the U.S. government and are therefore the least risky form of investment.
    Answer (A) is incorrect because securities issued by a federal agency are first backed by that agency and secondarily by the U.S. government. Agency securities are issued by agencies and corporations created by the federal government, such as the Federal Housing Administration. Answer (C) is incorrect because repurchase agreements could become worthless if the organization agreeing to make the repurchase goes bankrupt. Answer (D) is incorrect because commercial paper is unsecured.

17. From the viewpoint of the investor, which of the following securities provides the least risk?

    A. Mortgage bond.

    B. Subordinated debenture.

    C. Income bond.

    D. Debentures.

Answer (A) is correct. *(CIA, adapted)*

REQUIRED: The least risky security from the viewpoint of the investor.

DISCUSSION: A mortgage bond is secured with specific fixed assets, usually real property. Thus, under the rights enumerated in the bond indenture, creditors will be able to receive payments from liquidation of the property in case of default. In a bankruptcy proceeding, these amounts are paid before any transfers are made to other creditors, including those preferences. Hence, mortgage bonds are less risky than the others listed.

Answer (B) is incorrect because a debenture is long-term debt that is not secured (collateralized) by specific property. Subordinated debentures have a claim on the debtor's assets that may be satisfied only after senior debt has been paid in full. Debentures of either kind are therefore more risky than mortgage bonds. Answer (C) is incorrect because an income bond pays interest only if the debtor earns it. Such bonds are also more risky than secured debt. Answer (D) is incorrect because unsecured debt is riskier than a mortgage bond.

18. Which of the following classes of securities are listed in order from lowest risk/opportunity for return to highest risk/opportunity for return?

    A. U.S. Treasury bonds; corporate first mortgage bonds; corporate income bonds; preferred stock.

    B. Corporate income bonds; corporate mortgage bonds; convertible preferred stock; subordinated debentures.

    C. Common stock; corporate first mortgage bonds; corporate second mortgage bonds; corporate income bonds.

    D. Preferred stock; common stock; corporate mortgage bonds; corporate debentures.

Answer (A) is correct. *(CIA, adapted)*

REQUIRED: The correct listing of classes of securities from lowest to highest risk/opportunity for return.

DISCUSSION: The general principle is that risk and return are directly correlated. U.S. Treasury securities are backed by the full faith and credit of the federal government and are therefore the least risky form of investment. However, their return is correspondingly lower. Corporate first mortgage bonds are less risky than income bonds or stock because they are secured by specific property. In the event of default, the bondholders can have the property sold to satisfy their claims. Holders of first mortgages have rights paramount to those of any other parties, such as holders of second mortgages. Income bonds pay interest only in the event the corporation earns income. Thus, holders of income bonds have less risk than shareholders because meeting the condition makes payment of interest mandatory. Preferred shareholders receive dividends only if they are declared, and the directors usually have complete discretion in this matter. Also, shareholders have claims junior to those of debtholders if the enterprise is liquidated.

Answer (B) is incorrect because the proper listing is mortgage bonds, subordinated debentures, income bonds, and preferred stock. Debentures are unsecured debt instruments. Their holders have enforceable claims against the issuer even if no income is earned or dividends declared. Answer (C) is incorrect because the proper listing is first mortgage bonds, second mortgage bonds, income bonds, and common stock. The second mortgage bonds are secured, albeit junior, claims. Answer (D) is incorrect because the proper listing is mortgage bonds, debentures, preferred stock, and common stock. Holders of common stock cannot receive dividends unless the holders of preferred stock receive the stipulated periodic percentage return, in addition to any averages if the preferred stock is cumulative.

7.4 Risk and Return in a Portfolio Context

19. A feasible portfolio that offers the highest expected return for a given risk or the least risk for a given expected return is a(n)

    A. Optimal portfolio.

    B. Desirable portfolio.

    C. Efficient portfolio.

    D. Effective portfolio.

Answer (C) is correct. *(Publisher, adapted)*
    REQUIRED: The term for a portfolio that offers the highest expected return for a given risk.
    DISCUSSION: A feasible portfolio that offers the highest expected return for a given risk or the least risk for a given expected return is called an efficient portfolio.
    Answer (A) is incorrect because an optimal portfolio is a portfolio selected from the efficient set of portfolios because it is tangent to the investor's highest indifference curve. Answer (B) is incorrect because a desirable portfolio is a nonsense term. Answer (D) is incorrect because an effective portfolio is a nonsense term.

20. A U.S. company currently has domestic operations only. It is considering an equal-size investment in either Canada or Britain. The data on expected rate of return and the risk associated with each of these proposed investments are given below.

Proposed Investment	Mean Return	Standard Deviation
British Investment	22%	10%
Canadian Investment	28%	15%

The mean return on the company's current, domestic only, business is 20% with a standard deviation of 15%. Using the above data and the correlation coefficients, the company calculated the following portfolio risk and return (based on a ratio of 50% U.S. domestic operations and 50% international operations).

Proposed Investment	Mean Return	Standard Deviation
U.S. and Britain	21%	3%
U.S. and Canada	24%	15%

The company plans to select the optimal combination of countries based on risk and return for the domestic and international investments taken together. Because the company is new to the international business environment, it is relatively risk averse. Based on the above data, which one of the following alternatives provides the best risk-adjusted return to the firm?

    A. Undertake the British investment.

    B. Undertake the Canadian investment.

    C. Do not undertake either investment.

    D. Unable to determine based on data given.

Answer (A) is correct. *(Publisher, adapted)*
    REQUIRED: The investment that should be chosen by a risk-averse company.
    DISCUSSION: A risk-averse company will select the investment with the lesser risk. Thus, by choosing to invest in Britain, the overall rate of return will increase from 20% to 21%, and risk, based on the standard deviation, will decline from 15% to 3%. This gives a better return per unit of risk as compared to the Canadian investment.
    Answer (B) is incorrect because the Canadian investment would increase the return to 24% but would not change the degree of risk. Answer (C) is incorrect because to invest in Britain is more desirable than the status quo in terms of both return (21% versus 20%) and risk (3% versus 15%). Answer (D) is incorrect because the standard deviations and mean rates of return are adequate information upon which to base a decision.

7.5 Diversification

21. A measure that describes the risk of an investment project relative to other investments in general is the

    A. Coefficient of variation.

    B. Beta coefficient.

    C. Standard deviation.

    D. Expected return.

Answer (B) is correct. *(CIA, adapted)*
    REQUIRED: The measure of the risk of an investment relative to investments in general.
    DISCUSSION: The required rate of return on equity capital in the capital asset pricing model is the risk-free rate (determined by government securities), plus the product of the market risk premium times the beta coefficient (beta measures the firm's risk). The market risk premium is the amount above the risk-free rate that will induce investment in the market. The beta coefficient of an individual stock is the correlation between the volatility (price variation) of the stock market and that of the price of the individual stock. For example, if an individual stock goes up 15% and the market only 10%, beta is 1.5.
    Answer (A) is incorrect because the coefficient of variation compares risk with expected return (standard deviation ÷ expected return). Answer (C) is incorrect because standard deviation measures dispersion (risk) of project returns. Answer (D) is incorrect because expected return does not describe risk.

22. The benefits of diversification decline to near zero when the number of securities held increases beyond

    A. 4

    B. 6

    C. 10

    D. 40

Answer (D) is correct. *(Publisher, adapted)*
    REQUIRED: The number of securities beyond which the benefits of diversification decline to near zero.
    DISCUSSION: The benefits of diversification become extremely small when more than 20 to 30 different securities are held. Moreover, commissions and other transaction costs increase with greater diversification.

23. What is the formula for the beta coefficient of a security?

    A. Covariance of the returns on the market and on the security ÷ Variance of the return on the market.

    B. Covariance of the returns on the market and on the security × Variance of the return on the market.

    C. Variance of the return on the market ÷ Variance of the return on the security.

    D. Variance of the return on the market × Variance of the return on the security ÷ Covariance of the returns on the market and on the security.

Answer (A) is correct. *(Publisher, adapted)*
    REQUIRED: The formula for the beta coefficient.
    DISCUSSION: The word beta is derived from the regression equation for regressing the return of an individual security (the dependent variable) to the overall market return. The beta coefficient is the slope of the regression line. The beta for a security may also be calculated by dividing the covariance of the return on the market and the return on the security by the variance of the return on the market.

7.6 CAPM, APT, and Hedging

24. When a firm finances each asset with a financial instrument of the same approximate maturity as the life of the asset, it is applying

    A. Working capital management.

    B. Return maximization.

    C. Financial leverage.

    D. A hedging approach.

Answer (D) is correct. *(CMA, adapted)*
    REQUIRED: The technique used when a firm finances a specific asset with a financial instrument having the same approximate maturity as the life of the asset.
    DISCUSSION: Maturity matching, or equalizing the life of an asset and the debt instrument used to finance that asset, is a hedging approach. The basic concept is that the company has the entire life of the asset to recover the amount invested before having to pay the lender.
    Answer (A) is incorrect because working capital management is short-term asset management. Answer (B) is incorrect because return maximization is more aggressive than maturity matching. It entails using the lowest cost forms of financing. Answer (C) is incorrect because financial leverage is the relationship between debt and equity financing.

25. A company has recently purchased some stock of a competitor as part of a long-term plan to acquire the competitor. However, it is somewhat concerned that the market price of this stock could decrease over the short run. The company could hedge against the possible decline in the stock's market price by

    A. Purchasing a call option on that stock.

    B. Purchasing a put option on that stock.

    C. Selling a put option on that stock.

    D. Obtaining a warrant option on that stock.

Answer (B) is correct. *(CIA, adapted)*
    REQUIRED: The means of hedging against the possible decline in the stock's market price.
    DISCUSSION: A put option is the right to sell stock at a given price within a certain period. If the market price falls, the put option may allow the sale of stock at a price above market, and the profit of the option holder will be the difference between the price stated in the put option and the market price, minus the cost of the option, commissions, and taxes. The company that issues the stock has nothing to do with put (and call) options.
    Answer (A) is incorrect because a call option is the right to purchase shares at a given price within a specified period. Answer (C) is incorrect because selling a put option could force the company to purchase additional stock if the option is exercised. Answer (D) is incorrect because a warrant gives the holder a right to purchase stock from the issuer at a given price (it is usually distributed along with debt).

26. An interest swap covers a 3-year period with annual payments on a $1 million notional principal amount. Party X agrees to pay a fixed rate of 8.5% to Party Z, who will in return pay to X a floating rate equal to the London Interbank Offered Rate (LIBOR) in effect. LIBOR is the rate offered by major London banks on large dollar deposits. The contract is initiated on January 1, Year 1. The first payment is due on December 21, Year 1. The following are the floating rates on LIBOR over the 3-year period:

Time	LIBOR
1/1/Year 1	8.00%
1/1/Year 2	9.00%
1/1/Year 3	9.50%
1/1/Year 4	8.50%

What is the net payment made to the party that recognized a net gain on the contract?

    A. $0

    B. $10,000 to X.

    C. $15,000 to X.

    D. $15,000 to Z.

Answer (B) is correct. *(Publisher, adapted)*
    REQUIRED: The net payment to the party recognizing a gain on an interest-rate swap.
    DISCUSSION: Party X owed $85,000 ($1,000,000 × .085) for each of 3 years, a total of $255,000 ($85,000 × 3). Party Z owed $80,000 ($1,000,000 × .08) for Year 1, $90,000 ($1,000,000 × .09) for Year 2, and $95,000 ($1,000,000 × .095) for Year 3, a total of $265,000. Consequently, Party X received a net cash inflow of $10,000.
    Answer (A) is incorrect because the cash payments were not equal over the 3-year period. Answer (C) is incorrect because a net payment of $15,000 to X assumes that the LIBOR was 9.00% at all times. Answer (D) is incorrect because Party X had a net cash inflow, not Party Z.

Question 27 is based on the following information. DQZ Telecom is considering a project for the coming year that will cost $50 million. DQZ plans to use the following combination of debt and equity to finance the investment.

- Issue $15 million of 20-year bonds at a price of $101, with a coupon rate of 8%, and flotation costs of 2% of par.
- Use $35 million of funds generated from earnings.
- The equity market is expected to earn 12%. U.S. Treasury bonds are currently yielding 5%. The beta coefficient for DQZ is estimated to be .60. DQZ is subject to an effective corporate income tax rate of 40%.

27. The capital asset pricing model (CAPM) computes the expected return on a security by adding the risk-free rate of return to the incremental yield of the expected market return, which is adjusted by the company's beta. Compute DQZ's expected rate of return.

A. 9.20%

B. 12.20%

C. 7.20%

D. 12.00%

Answer (A) is correct. *(CMA, adapted)*
REQUIRED: The expected rate of return using the capital asset pricing model (CAPM).
DISCUSSION: The market return (R_M), given as 12%, minus the risk-free rate (R_F), given as 5%, is the market risk premium. It is the rate at which investors must be compensated to induce them to invest in the market. The beta coefficient (β) of an individual stock, given as 60%, is the correlation between volatility (price variation) of the stock market and the volatility of the price of the individual stock. Consequently, the expected rate of return is 9.20% [$R_F + \beta (R_M - R_F) = .05 + .6(.12 - .05)$].
Answer (B) is incorrect because 12.20% equals the risk-free rate plus 60% of market rate. Answer (C) is incorrect because 7.20% results from multiplying both the market rate premium and the risk-free rate by 60%. Answer (D) is incorrect because 12.00% is the market rate.

28. Which of the following is the major difference between the capital asset pricing model (CAPM) and arbitrage pricing theory (APT)?

A. CAPM uses discounted cash flows whereas APT does not.

B. CAPM uses a single systematic risk factor to explain an asset's return whereas APT uses multiple systematic factors.

C. APT uses a single systematic risk factor to explain an asset's return whereas CAPM uses multiple systematic factors.

D. Under CAPM, the beta coefficient of the risk-free rate of return is assumed to be higher than that of any asset in the portfolio. Under APT, the beta coefficient of every asset in the portfolio is individually compared to the beta of the risk-free rate.

Answer (B) is correct. *(Publisher, adapted)*
REQUIRED: The major difference between CAPM and APT.
DISCUSSION: CAPM uses a single systematic risk factor to explain an asset's return whereas APT uses multiple systematic factors.
Answer (A) is incorrect because all calculations of rates of return use discounted cash flows. Answer (C) is incorrect because CAPM uses a single systematic risk factor to explain an asset's return whereas APT uses multiple systematic factors. Answer (D) is incorrect because it is a nonsense answer.

Use Gleim's *CMA Test Prep* for interactive testing with **over 2,000 additional multiple-choice questions**!

STUDY UNIT EIGHT
FINANCIAL INSTRUMENTS

(22 pages of outline)

This study unit is the **second of five** on **corporate finance**. The relative weight assigned to this major topic in Part 3 of the exam is **25%** at **skill level B** (four skill types required). The five study units are

Study Unit 7: Risk and Return
Study Unit 8: Financial Instruments
Study Unit 9: Cost of Capital
Study Unit 10: Managing Current Assets
Study Unit 11: Financing Current Assets

After studying the outline and answering the multiple-choice questions, you will have the skills necessary to address the following topics listed in the IMA's Learning Outcome Statements:

Part 3 – Section C.2. Financial instruments

The candidate should be able to:

a. define and identify characteristics of bonds, common stock, and preferred stock

b. identify and describe the basic features of a bond such as maturity, par value, coupon rate, provisions for redeeming, covenants, options granted to the issuer or investor, indentures, and restrictions

c. define the different types of dividends, including cash dividends, stock dividends, and stock splits

d. identify and discuss the factors that influence the dividend policy of a firm

e. demonstrate an understanding of the dividend payment process for both common and preferred stock

f. value bonds, common stock, and preferred stock using discounted cash flow methods

g. demonstrate an understanding of the dividend discount model

h. demonstrate an understanding of relative or comparable valuation methods, such as price/earnings (P/E) ratios, market/book ratios, and price/sales ratios

i. demonstrate an understanding of duration as a measure of bond interest rate sensitivity

j. demonstrate an understanding of how income taxes impact financing decisions

k. define and demonstrate an understanding of derivatives, their payoff structures, and their uses

l. distinguish between futures and forwards

m. demonstrate an understanding of options

n. demonstrate a basic understanding of the Black-Scholes and the binomial option-valuation models and how a change in one variable will affect the value of the option (calculation not required)

o. define and identify characteristics of other sources of long-term financing, such as leases, convertible securities, warrants, and retained earnings

8.1 SOURCES OF LONG-TERM FINANCING

1. A firm may have long-term financing requirements that it cannot or does not want to meet using retained earnings. It must therefore issue equity or debt securities.

   a. Certain hybrid forms of available financing include convertible issues and warrants. These are also used to attract long-term financing.

   b. The **primary market** is the market for new stocks and bonds; investment money flows directly to the company that will use the funds to increase productive capacity.

      1) Existing securities are traded in **secondary markets**, such as stock exchanges.

   c. The **underwriting spread** is the difference between the price that an investment banker pays the issuer for a new security issue and the price at which that security is resold.

   d. The principal issues regarding financing are the cost of each type of financing (including the question of risk) and the lender's (the investor's) view of the financing device. The following discussion highlights principal components of the decision.

2. **Common stock.** The common shareholders are the owners of the corporation, and their rights as owners, although reasonably uniform, depend on the laws of the state in which the firm is incorporated. Equity ownership involves risk because holders of common stock are not guaranteed a return and are last in priority in a liquidation. Shareholders' capital provides the cushion for creditors if any losses occur on liquidation.

   a. **Advantages to the Issuer**

      1) Common stock does not require a fixed dividend; dividends are paid from profits when available.

      2) There is no fixed maturity date for repayment of the capital.

      3) The sale of common stock increases the creditworthiness of the firm by providing more equity.

      4) Common stock is frequently more attractive to investors than debt because it grows in value with the success of the firm.

         a) The higher the common stock value, the more advantageous equity financing is compared with debt financing.

   b. **Disadvantages to the Issuer**

      1) Control (voting rights) is usually diluted as more common stock is sold. (While this aspect is disadvantageous to existing shareholders, management of the corporation may view it as an advantage.)

      2) New common stock sales dilute earnings available to existing shareholders because of the greater number of shares outstanding.

      3) Underwriting costs are typically higher for common stock issues.

      4) Too much equity may raise the average cost of capital of the firm above its optimal level.

      5) Cash dividends on common stock are not deductible as an expense and are after-tax cash deductions to the firm.

   c. Common shareholders ordinarily have **preemptive rights**.

      1) Preemptive rights give common shareholders the right to purchase any additional stock issuances in proportion to their current ownership percentages.

      2) If applicable state law or the corporate charter does not provide preemptive rights, the firm may nevertheless sell to the existing common shareholders in a **rights** offering. Each shareholder is issued a certificate or warrant that is an option to buy a certain number of shares at a fixed price.

a) Until the rights are actually issued, the stock trades **rights-on**; that is, the stock and the rights are not separable. After the rights are received, the stock trades **ex-rights** because the rights can be sold separately. The formula for the value of a stock right when the stock price is rights-on is

$$\frac{P - S}{N + 1}$$

Where: P = value of a share rights-on
S = subscription price of a share
N = number of rights needed to buy a share

b) The amount recorded for stock rights is based on an allocation of the cost of the shares owned based on the relative market values of the shares and the rights.

d. **Stock warrants** (certificates evidencing options to buy stock at a given price within a certain period) may be given to employees as compensation, or they may be issued with bonds or preferred stock.

1) The proceeds of securities issued with **detachable warrants** are allocated between the warrants and the securities based on their relative market values. If the fair value of one but not the other is known, the proceeds are allocated incrementally. If warrants are not detachable, they are not accounted for separately.

e. A stock's **par value** represents legal capital. It is an arbitrary value assigned to stock before the stock is issued. It also represents the maximum liability of a shareholder.

3. **Preferred stock** is a hybrid of debt and equity. It has a fixed charge and increases leverage, but payment of dividends is not an obligation. Also, preferred shareholders stand ahead of common shareholders in priority in the event of corporate bankruptcy.

a. **Advantages to the Issuer**

1) It is a form of equity and therefore builds the creditworthiness of the firm.
2) Control is still held by common shareholders.
3) Superior earnings of the firm are usually still reserved for the common shareholders.

b. **Disadvantages to the Issuer**

1) Cash dividends on preferred stock are not deductible as a tax expense and are paid with taxable income. The result is a substantially greater cost relative to bonds.
2) In periods of economic difficulty, accumulated dividends (dividends in arrears) may create major managerial and financial problems for the firm.

c. Typical Provisions of Preferred Stock Issues

1) **Priority in assets and earnings.** If the firm goes bankrupt, the preferred shareholders have priority over common shareholders.
2) **Accumulation of dividends.** If preferred dividends are cumulative, dividends in arrears must be paid before any common dividends can be paid.
3) **Convertibility.** Preferred stock issues may be convertible into common stock at the option of the shareholder.
4) **Participation.** Preferred stock may participate with common in excess earnings of the company. For example, 8% participating preferred stock might pay a dividend each year greater than 8% when the corporation is extremely profitable, but nonparticipating preferred stock will receive no more than is stated on the face of the stock.

5) **Par value.** Par value is the liquidation value, and a percentage of par equals the preferred dividend.

6) **Redeemability.** Some preferred stock may be redeemed at a given time or at the option of the holder or otherwise at a time not controlled by the issuer. This feature makes preferred stock more nearly akin to debt, particularly in the case of **transient preferred stock**, which must be redeemed within a short time (e.g., 5 to 10 years). The SEC requires a separate presentation of redeemable preferred, nonredeemable preferred, and common stock.

7) **Voting rights.** These may be conferred if preferred dividends are in arrears for a stated period.

8) **Callability.** The issuer may have the right to repurchase the stock. For example, the stock may be noncallable for a stated period, after which it may be called if the issuer pays a call premium (an amount exceeding par value).

9) **Maturity.** Preferred stock may have a sinking fund that allows for the purchase of a given annual percentage of the outstanding shares.

d. Holding preferred stock rather than bonds provides corporations a major tax advantage. At least 70% of the dividends received from preferred stock is tax deductible, but all bond interest received is taxable.

1) The **dividends-received deduction** also applies to common stock.

4. **Bonds** are long-term debt instruments. They are similar to term loans except that they are usually offered to the public and sold to many investors.

a. Bonds are sold at the sum of the present values of the maturity amount and the interest payments (if interest-bearing). The difference between the face amount and the selling price of bonds is either a discount or a premium.

1) Bonds are sold at a discount when they sell for less than face amount, that is, when the contract (stated) interest rate is less than the market (effective) interest rate.

2) Bonds are sold at a premium (in excess of face amount) when the stated rate exceeds the effective rate.

3) A bond discount or premium appears as a direct deduction from or addition to the face amount of the bond payable.

b. **Advantages of Bonds to the Issuer**

1) Basic control of the firm is not shared with the debtholder.

2) Cost of debt is limited. Bondholders usually do not participate in the superior earnings of the firm.

3) Ordinarily, the expected yield of bonds is lower than the cost of common stock.

4) Interest paid on debt is tax deductible as an expense.

5) Debt may add substantial flexibility in the financial structure of the corporation through the insertion of call provisions in the bond indenture.

c. **Disadvantages of Bonds to the Issuer**

1) Debt has a fixed charge. Thus, if earnings fluctuate, the firm risks not meeting its fixed interest obligations, which could lead to its demise.

2) Debt adds risk to a firm. Shareholders will consequently demand higher capitalization rates on equity earnings, which may result in a decline in the market price of stock.

3) Debt usually has a maturity date.

4) Debt is a long-term commitment, a factor that can affect risk profiles. Debt originally appearing to be profitable may become a burden and drive the firm into bankruptcy.

5) Certain managerial prerogatives are usually given up in the contractual relationship outlined in the bond's indenture contract.

    a) For example, specific ratios must be kept above a certain level during the term of the loan.

6) The amount of debt financing available to the individual firm is limited. Generally accepted standards of the investment community will usually dictate a certain debt-equity ratio for an individual firm. Beyond this limit, the cost of debt may rise rapidly, or debt may not be available.

    d. **Types of Bonds**

1) A **mortgage bond** is a pledge of certain assets for a loan. It is usually secured by real property as a condition of the loan.

2) A **debenture bond** is a long-term bond not secured by specific property. It is a general obligation of the borrower. Only companies with the best credit ratings can issue debentures because holders will be general creditors. They will have a status inferior to that of secured parties and creditors with priorities in bankruptcy.

3) An **income bond** pays interest only if the issuing company has earnings. Such bonds are riskier than other bonds.

4) **Serial bonds** have staggered maturities. These bonds permit investors to choose the maturity dates that meet their needs.

5) **Zero-coupon bonds** pay no interest but sell at a deep discount from their face amount. Although a relatively new type of bond, these instruments are very useful to investors and investees.

    a) The need to reinvest the periodic payments renders the final return available from normal coupon bonds uncertain because future reinvestment rates are uncertain. However, the investors know the exact return on a zero-coupon bond. Investors might therefore be willing to pay a premium for them, which in turn might lead firms to issue them.

    b) The lack of interest payments means the firm faces no additional insolvency risk from the issue until it matures.

6) **Junk bonds** are very high-risk, high-yield securities issued to finance leveraged buyouts and mergers. They are also issued by troubled companies. They exploit the large tax deductions for interest payments made by entities with high debt ratios.

7) **International bonds** are of two types: foreign bonds and Eurobonds. **Foreign bonds** are denominated in the currency of the nation in which they are sold. **Eurobonds** are denominated in a currency other than that of the nation where they are sold.

    a) Foreign bonds issued in the United States and denominated in dollars must be registered with the SEC, but such extensive disclosure is not required in most foreign nations. Thus, an American company may elect to issue Eurobonds denominated in dollars in a foreign nation because of the convenience of not having to comply with governmental registration requirements.

8) **Registered bonds** are issued in the name of the owner. Interest payments are sent directly to the owner. When the owner sells registered bonds, the bond certificates must be surrendered and new certificates issued.

    a) They differ from **coupon (bearer) bonds**, which can be freely transferred and have a detachable coupon for each interest payment.

9) **Participating bonds** participate in excess earnings of the debtor as defined in the indenture.

10) **Indexed bonds** (purchasing power bonds) pay interest that is indexed to a measure of general purchasing power, such as the Consumer Price Index.

11) **Subordinated debentures** possess a feature undesirable to investors. They are subordinated to (inferior to) the claims of other general creditors as well as secured parties and persons with priorities in bankruptcy. The indenture specifies the claims (senior debt) to which these bonds are subordinate. They are usually issued only when the company has some debt instrument outstanding that prohibits the issuance of additional regular bonds. Subordinated debentures will normally pay a higher rate of interest than secured bonds.

e.   **Restrictive covenants** in bond **indentures** (bond contracts) are intended to prevent the issuer from taking actions not in the bondholders' best interests. A trustee may be appointed to monitor compliance.

1) **Call provisions** give the corporation the right to call in the bond for redemption. This feature is an advantage to the firm but not the investor. If interest rates decline, the company can call in the high-interest bonds and replace them with low-interest bonds. However, bonds may be **putable**, or redeemable, at the holder's option.

   a)   Bonds are putable if the holder has the right to exchange them for cash. This option is usually not activated unless the issuer takes a stated action, for example, greatly increasing its debt or being acquired by another entity.

2) **Sinking fund** requirements provide that the firm retire a certain portion of its bonds each year or that money be set aside for repayment in the future. It increases the probability of repayment for bondholders but requires the use of capital by the firm.

3) The issuer may be required to maintain certain financial ratios, limit dividends, or restrict new bonds to a percentage of fixed assets.

4) An **acceleration clause** may allow lenders to demand early payment of the entire balance or additional collateral in some cases, for example, failing to make timely payments, filing for bankruptcy, or violating another term of the indenture.

f.   **Bond ratings** play a role in bond yields. The correlation between the bond rating (based on risk) and the interest rate that is attractive to an investor tends to be inverse. A high rating (low risk) will lead to a lower interest rate.

1) The two largest bond-rating agencies are Standard and Poor's and Moody's. The bond-rating agencies base their evaluations on the profitability of the issuing corporation, stability of the industry, competitive position, and the usual financial ratios.

   a)   **Investment-grade bonds** are the safest and receive the highest ratings. Some fiduciary organizations (such as banks and insurance companies) are only allowed to invest in investment-grade bonds.

   b)   **Speculative-grade bonds** are riskier than investment grade bonds.

5.   Stop and review! You have completed the outline for this subunit. Study multiple-choice questions 1 through 24 beginning on page 239.

8.2 DIVIDEND POLICY

1. **Dividend policy** determines **what portion** of a corporation's net income **is distributed** to shareholders and **what portion is retained** for reinvestment.

   a. A high dividend rate means a slower rate of growth. A high growth rate usually means a low dividend rate.

   b. Because both a high growth rate and a high dividend rate are desirable, the financial manager attempts to achieve the balance that maximizes the firm's share price.

   c. Normally, corporations try to maintain a stable level of dividends, even though profits may fluctuate considerably, because many shareholders buy stock with the expectation of receiving a certain dividend every year. Hence, management tends not to raise dividends if the payout cannot be sustained.

      1) The desire for stability has led theorists to propound the **information content** or **signaling hypothesis**, which states that a change in dividend policy is a signal to the market regarding management's forecast of future earnings. Thus, firms generally have an active policy strategy with respect to dividends.

   d. This stability often results in a stock that sells at a higher market price because shareholders perceive less risk in receiving their dividends.

2. Various factors influence a company's dividend policy.

   a. **Legal restrictions.** Dividends ordinarily cannot be paid out of paid-in capital. A corporation must have a balance in its retained earnings account before dividends can be paid.

   b. **Stability of earnings.** A company whose earnings fluctuate greatly from year to year will tend to pay out a smaller dividend during good years so that the same dividend can be paid even if profits are much lower. For example, a company with fluctuating earnings might pay out $1 every year whether earnings per share are $10 (10% payout rate) or $1 (100% payout rate).

   c. **Rate of growth.** A company with a faster growth rate will have a greater need to finance that growth with **retained earnings**. Thus, growth companies usually have lower dividend payout ratios.

      1) Shareholders hope to be able to obtain larger capital gains in the future.

   d. **Cash position.** Regardless of a firm's earnings record, cash must be available before a dividend can be paid. No dividend can be declared if all of a firm's earnings are tied up in receivables and inventories.

   e. **Restrictions in debt agreements.** Restrictive covenants in bond indentures and other debt agreements often limit the dividends that a firm can declare.

   f. **Tax position of shareholders.** In corporations, the shareholders may not want regular dividends because the individual owners are in such high tax brackets. They may want to forgo dividends in exchange for future capital gains or wait to receive dividends in future years when they are in lower tax brackets.

   g. However, an **accumulated earnings tax** is assessed on a corporation if it has accumulated retained earnings beyond its reasonably expected needs.

   h. **Residual theory of dividends.** The amount (residual) of earnings paid as dividends depends on the available investment opportunities and the debt-equity ratio at which cost of capital is minimized. The rational investor should prefer reinvestment of retained earnings when the return exceeds what the investor could earn on investments of equal risk. However, the firm may prefer to pay dividends when investment opportunities are poor and the use of internal equity financing would move the firm away from its ideal capital structure.

3.   **Important Dates Concerning the Declaration of Dividends**

    a.   The **date of declaration** is the date the directors meet and formally vote to declare a dividend. On this date, the dividend becomes a liability of the corporation.

    b.   The **date of record** is the date as of which the corporation determines the shareholders who will receive the declared dividend. Essentially, the corporation closes its shareholder records on this date. Only those shareholders who own the stock on the date of record will receive the dividend. It typically falls from 2 to 6 weeks after the declaration date.

    c.   The **date of payment** is the date on which the dividend is actually paid (when the checks are put into the mail to the investors). The payment date is usually from 2 to 4 weeks after the date of record.

    d.   The **ex-dividend date** is a date established by the stock exchanges, such as 4 business days before the date of record. Unlike the other dates previously mentioned, it is not established by the corporate board of directors. The period between the ex-dividend date and the date of record gives the stock exchange members time to process any transactions so that new shareholders will receive the dividends to which they are entitled. An investor who buys a share of stock before the ex-dividend date will receive the dividend that has been previously declared. An investor who buys the stock after the ex-dividend date (but before the date of record or payment date) will not receive the declared dividend. Instead, the individual who sold the stock will receive the dividend because (s)he owned it on the ex-dividend date.

        1)   Usually, a stock price will drop on the ex-dividend date by the amount of the dividend because the new investor will not receive it.

4.   Although the **cash dividend** is the most common type, other types are available. Stock dividends and splits involve issuance of additional shares to existing shareholders.

    a.   Stock shareholders do not really receive any increase in the value of their holdings. The previous holdings are simply divided into more pieces (additional shares).

    b.   A **stock dividend** is an issuance of stock and entails the transfer of a sum from the retained earnings account to a paid-in capital account.

        1)   Usually, the corporation wants to give something to the shareholders but without paying out a cash dividend because the funds are needed in the business.

        2)   Casual investors may believe they are receiving something of value when in essence their previous holdings are merely being divided into more pieces.

        3)   Stock dividends are often used by growing companies that wish to retain earnings in the business while placating shareholders.

    c.   A **stock split** does not involve any accounting entries. Instead, the existing shares are divided into more pieces so that the market price per share will be reduced.

        1)   EXAMPLE: If a corporation has 1 million shares outstanding, each of which sells for $90, a 2-for-1 stock split will result in 2 million shares outstanding, each of which sells for about $45.

        2)   **Reverse stock splits** reduce the shares outstanding.

    d.   **Advantages of Issuing Stock Splits and Dividends**

        1)   Because more shares will be outstanding, the price per share will be lower. The lower price per share will induce more small investors to purchase the company's stock. Thus, because demand for the stock is greater, the price may increase.

            a)   EXAMPLE: In the example above, the additional investors interested in the company at the lower price may drive the price up to $46 or $47, or slightly higher than the theoretically correct price of $45. Consequently, current shareholders will benefit from the split (or dividend) after all.

2)   A dividend or split can be a publicity gesture. Because shareholders may believe they are receiving something of value (and may be indirectly), they will have a better opinion of their company.

3)   Moreover, the more shares a corporation has outstanding, the larger the number of shareholders, who are usually good customers for their own company's products.

e.   On rare occasions, a firm may use a reverse stock split to raise the market price per share. For example, a 1-for-10 stock split would require shareholders to turn in ten old shares to receive one new share.

5.   Stop and review! You have completed the outline for this subunit. Study multiple-choice questions 25 through 34 beginning on page 246.

8.3 VALUATION METHODS

1.   Investors generally expect to receive **two distinct payment streams**:

a.   Periodic receipts of interest (for debt) or dividends (for equities) and
b.   A lump sum of the principal (for debt) or market value (for equities).

2.   A quantity of money to be received or paid in the future is worth less than the same amount now. The difference, called **the time value of money**, is measured in terms of interest calculated using the appropriate **discount rate**.

a.   The present value of any investment is the **sum of the discounted expected cash flows**.

b.   Standard tables have been developed to facilitate the calculation of present values. Each entry in one of these tables represents the factor by which any dollar amount can be modified to obtain its present value.

3.   **The Time Value of Money**

a.   The **present value (PV) of an amount** is the value today of some future payment.

1)   It equals the future payment times the present value of $1 (a factor found in a standard table) for the given number of periods and interest rate.

	Present Value		
No. of Periods	6%	8%	10%
1	0.943	0.926	0.909
2	0.890	0.857	0.826
3	0.840	0.794	0.751
4	0.792	0.735	0.683
5	0.747	0.681	0.621

2)   EXAMPLE:

a)   An investor owns 100 shares of stock. (S)he expects the price of the stock to be $52 per share at the end of 3 years.

b)   The investor expects the prevailing rate of return in the market for the next 3 years to be 8%.

c)   The expected present value of the stock itself is therefore equal to $5,200 to be received in 3 years discounted at 8%, or $4,128.80 ($5,200 × 0.794).

b. An **ordinary annuity (annuity in arrears)** is a series of payments occurring at the end of each period. In an **annuity due (annuity in advance)** the payments are made (received) at the beginning of each period.

1) The **PV of an ordinary annuity** is the value today of a series of equal payments extending into the future. Note that these values are simply the aggregates of the values in the single-amount table.

	Present Value		
No. of Periods	6%	8%	10%
1	0.943	0.926	0.909
2	1.833	1.783	1.736
3	2.673	2.577	2.487
4	3.465	3.312	3.170
5	4.212	3.993	3.791

2) EXAMPLE:

a) The investor expects the stock to pay a steady annual dividend of 10% of its par value which is $50 per share.

b) The present value of the dividend stream is therefore equal to an ordinary annuity of three payments of $500 each [(100 shares × ($50 × 10%)] discounted at 8%, or $1,243.50 ($500 × 2.487).

c. The expected present value of an investment is derived by adding the present values of the expected cash flows.

1) EXAMPLE:

Present value of stock ($5,200 × 0.794)	$4,128.80
Present value of dividend stream ($500 × 2.487)	1,243.50
Present value of investment	$5,372.30

4. The **dividend discount model** is another method of arriving at the present value of an equity investment:

$$\frac{Dividend\ per\ share}{Discount\ rate\ -\ Dividend\ growth\ rate}$$

5. **Per-share ratios** relate company financial information to the market price per share.

a. **Earnings per share (EPS)** equals net income available to common shareholders divided by the average number of shares outstanding for the period.

$$\frac{Net\ income\ available\ to\ common\ shareholders}{Average\ shares\ outstanding}$$

1) Net income available to common shareholders is usually net income minus preferred dividends.

2) Under SFAS 128, basic and diluted EPS must be presented.

b. **Book value per share** equals the amount of net assets available to the shareholders of a given type of stock divided by the number of those shares outstanding.

$$\frac{Shareholders'\ equity}{Shares\ outstanding}$$

1) When a company has preferred as well as common stock outstanding, the computation of book value per common share must consider potential claims by preferred shareholders, such as whether the preferred stock is cumulative and in arrears, or participating. It must also take into account whether the call price (or possibly the liquidation value) exceeds the carrying amount of the preferred stock.

c. **Dividend yield** equals the annual dividend payment divided by the market value per share.

$$\frac{Dividends\ per\ share}{Market\ value\ per\ share}$$

1) A related ratio is the **dividend payout**, which equals dividends per common share divided by EPS.

d. The **price-earnings (P-E) ratio** equals the market price per share of common stock divided by EPS.

$$\frac{Market\ Price}{EPS}$$

1) Most analysts prefer to use diluted EPS. The diluted EPS is usually a more accurate reflection of a company's earning power. **Earning power** is defined as a company's ability to generate income from normal operations.

2) Growth companies are likely to have high P-E ratios. A high ratio may also indicate that the firm is relatively low risk or that its choice of accounting methods results in a conservative EPS.

3) Because of the widespread use of the P-E ratio and other measures, the relationship between accounting data and stock prices is crucial. Thus, managers have an incentive to "manage earnings," sometimes by fraudulent means.

e. **Price-book ratio** (also called the market-to-book ratio).

$$\frac{Market\ price\ per\ share}{Book\ Value\ per\ share}$$

1) Well-managed firms should sell at high multiples of their book value, which reflects historical cost.

f. **Price-sales ratio** is preferred by some analysts over profit ratios.

$$\frac{Market\ price\ per\ share}{Sales\ per\ share}$$

1) Analysts who use the price-sales ratio believe that strong sales are the basic ingredient of profits and that sales are the item on the financial statements least subject to manipulation.

6. **Bond Duration and Volatility**

a. Interest-bearing or serial bonds consist of **multiple payments over time** to the bondholder. A bond's **duration** is the average time until each payment, weighted for the proportion of the total stream that each payment constitutes.

1) The duration of a 6%, 5-year $10,000 bond sold to yield 8% can be calculated as follows:

(1) Year	(2) Cash Payment	(3) PV Factor	(4) PV of Payment Stream	(5) Proportion of Total Stream	(1) × (5) Duration of Stream
1	$ 600	0.9259	$ 555.54	6.04%	0.0604
2	600	0.8573	514.38	5.59%	0.1118
3	600	0.7940	476.40	5.18%	0.1553
4	600	0.7350	441.00	4.79%	0.1917
5	10,600	0.6806	7,214.36	78.40%	3.9201
			$9,201.68	100.00%	4.4393

This bond's duration is thus 4.4393 years.

b.   The longer a bond's term, the more sensitive is its price to interest rate changes. The graph below depicts this relationship:

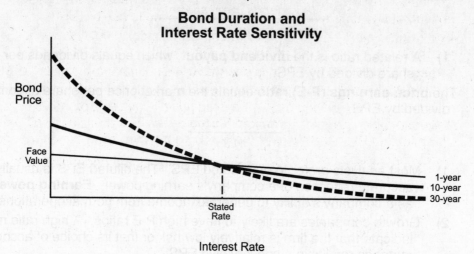

7.   Stop and review! You have completed the outline for this subunit. Study multiple-choice questions 35 through 45 beginning on page 249.

8.4 DERIVATIVES AND OTHER FINANCIAL INSTRUMENTS

1.   A **derivative** is defined informally as an investment transaction in which the buyer purchases the right to a potential gain with a commitment for a potential loss. It is a wager on whether the value of something will go up or down. The purpose of the transaction is either to **speculate** (incur risk) or to **hedge** (avoid risk).

a.   Thus, a derivative is an executory contract that results in cash flow between two **counterparties** based on the change in some other indicator of value. Examples of these indicators include prices of financial instruments, such as common shares or government bonds; currency exchange rates; interest rates; commodity prices; and indexes, such as the S&P 500 or the Dow Jones Industrial Average.

b.   Derivative instruments (derivatives) should be contrasted with financial instruments, which include cash, accounts receivable, notes receivable, bonds, preferred shares, common shares, etc.

2.   **Options and futures** are derivative securities. They are not claims on business assets, such as those represented by equity securities. Instead, they are created by the parties who trade in them.

a.   An **American option** is a contractual arrangement that gives the owner the right to buy or sell an asset at a fixed price at any moment in time before or on a specified date. A **European option** is exercisable only at the expiration date.

b.   Exercising the option is the act of buying or selling the asset underlying the option contract. An **open interest** is the total number of option or futures contracts that have not expired, been exercised, or been fulfilled by delivery.

c.   An option is a right of the owner, not an obligation.

d.   The **exercise or striking price** is the price at which the owner can purchase the asset underlying the option contract. The **option price**, also called **option premium**, is the amount paid to acquire an option.

1)   The **bid-ask spread** is the difference between what a buyer is willing to bid and what a seller is asking.

    e.   An option usually has an expiration date after which it can no longer be exercised.

    f.   The longer the time before its expiration, the more valuable the option. The reason is the increased time available for the asset's price to rise or fall.

    g.   A **covered option** is one that is written against stock held in the option writer's portfolio.

    h.   A **naked (uncovered) option** is one that does not have the backing of stock.

    i.   A **call option** is the most common type of option. It gives the owner the right to purchase the underlying asset at a fixed price. Thus, it represents a long position because the owner gains from a price increase. The profit is the difference between the price paid and the value at the closing date, minus the brokerage fee.

        1)   Call options usually involve common stock as the underlying asset; however, any type of asset may underlie an option.

        2)   If the value of the asset underlying a call option is less than the exercise price of the option, the option is "out-of-the-money," or not worth exercising. If the value of the asset underlying the option is greater than the exercise price, it is "in-the-money" and can earn the owner a profit.

        3)   A call option's expiration value equals the excess of the current price of the asset over the exercise price. If the exercise price exceeds the current price, the option is worthless.

        4)   **Net Gain or Loss on a Call Option**

            a)   For the purchaser (long position), the gain or loss is the following:
[(# of shares) × (Market price – Exercise price)] – Amount paid for option

            b)   For the seller (short position), the loss or gain is the following:
[(# of shares) × (Exercise price – Market price)] + Amount option sold for

            c)   The call option will not be exercised unless the market price is greater than the exercise price. The seller profits only when

                i)   The option is not exercised, and

                ii)   The price paid for the option exceeds the difference between the exercise price and the market price.

            d)   EXAMPLE: If the exercise price is $100, the market price is $105, and 100 options were sold for $3 each, the purchaser has a gain of $200 {[100 options × ($105 – $100)] – (100 options × $3)}. The seller has a loss of $200 {[100 options × ($100 – $105)] + (100 options × $3)}.

    j.   A **put option** gives the owner the right to sell the underlying asset for a fixed price. It represents a short position because the owner benefits from a price decrease.

        1)   If the value of the asset underlying a put option is greater than its exercise price, the put option is worthless or "out-of-the-money."

        2)   If the value of the asset underlying the put option is less than the exercise price of the put option, the put is "in-the-money." **Intrinsic value** is the difference between the exercise price and the market price of the underlying security.

        3)   A put option's expiration value equals either zero or the excess of the exercise price over the current market price.

4) **Net Gain or Loss on a Put Option**

a) For the purchaser (long position), the gain or loss is the following:
[(# of shares) × (Exercise price – Market price)] – Amount paid for option

b) For the seller (short position), the loss or gain is the following:
[(# of shares) × (Market price – Exercise price)] + Amount option sold for

c) The put option will not be exercised unless the exercise price is greater than the market price. The seller profits only when

i)   The option is not exercised, and

ii) The price paid for the option exceeds the difference between the market price and the exercise market price.

d) EXAMPLE: If the exercise price is $105, the market price is $100, and 100 options were sold for $3 each, the purchaser has a gain of $200 {[100 options × ($105 – $100)] – (100 options × $3)}. The seller has a loss of $200 {[100 options × ($100 – $105)] + (100 options × $3)}.

k. A **stock option** is an option to buy a specific stock at some future time. An **index option** is an option whose underlying security is an index. If exercised, settlement is made by cash payment because physical delivery is not possible. **Long-Term Equity Anticipation Securities (LEAPS)** are examples of long-term stock options or index options, with expiration dates up to three years away. **Foreign currency options** give the holder the right to buy a specific foreign currency at a designated exchange rate.

l. **Put-call parity.** For European options, given market equilibrium for all relevant prices (no arbitrage possibilities), equal exercise prices for the put and the call, and the same expiration date, the put-call parity theorem states that a fixed relationship applies to the market values of the put and call options on a security.

1) For example, a strategy of selling one call option, buying one share of the stock, and buying one put option should result in a risk-free return. The gain (loss) from the stock and the put should equal the gain (loss) on the call.

2) If V_S is the value of the stock, V_P is the value of the put, V_C is the value of the call, and PV_E is the present value of the exercise price (the time interval is the time to expiration), the formula for put-call parity may be stated as follows:

$$V_S + V_P - V_C = PV_E$$

m. The value of a call option is based on its exercise price, its expiration date, the price of the underlying asset, the variability of that asset, and the risk-free interest rate. The well-known **Black-Scholes Option-Pricing Model** uses these factors.

1) The following are the symbols used in this complex equation:

C = Current value of a call option
t = Years until expiration
S = Current stock price
$N(d_1)$ = Cumulative probability that a deviation less than d_1 will occur in a standardized normal distribution.
E = Exercise price of the option
e = A constant - approximately 2.7183
r = Annualized continuous risk-free rate of return
ln(S/E) = Natural logarithm of S/E
σ^2 = Variance of rate of return of the stock
$SN(d_1)$ ≈ Expected present value of the final stock price
$Ee^{-rt}N(d_2)$ ≈ Present value of exercise price

*$N(d_1)$ and $N(d_2)$ represent areas under a standard normal distribution function.

$$C = SN(d_1) - Ee^{-rt}N(d_2) \qquad d_1 = \frac{ln(S/E) + [r + (\sigma^2 \div 2)]t}{\sigma\sqrt{t}} \qquad d_2 = d_1 - \sigma\sqrt{t}$$

a) In effect, the first term of the equation for C is the expected present value of the final stock price, and the second term is essentially the present value of the exercise price.

2) The **binomial methods** are based on upward and downward stock price movements comparable to the standard deviation in the Black-Scholes formula. The formula below applies to given percentage movements in the stock price and given maximum and minimum payoffs for a 1-period call option. The following symbols are used in this version of the binomial method:

CU = Call option payoff when stock price rises
CD = Call option payoff when stock price declines
U = Factor for upward movement [U>(1+r)>1]
D = Factor for downward movement (D<1)
r = The risk-free rate

$$\left[CU\left(\frac{1 + r - D}{U - D}\right) + CD\left(\frac{U - 1 - r}{U - D}\right) \right] \div (1 + r)$$

a) EXAMPLE: If the stock price is $50, the exercise price is $46, and the stock price may increase to $65 with a given probability of q or decrease to $35 with a given probability of 1 − q, the option has a maximum payoff of $19 ($65 − $46) and a minimum payoff of $0.

b)   EXAMPLE: Based on the facts given in the previous example and assuming a 4% risk-free rate, U is 1.3 ($65 ÷ $50), D is .70 ($35 ÷ $50), CU is $19 ($65 – $46), and CD is $0 (the absolute minimum value of a call option is $0). Thus, the value of the call option for these parameters is $10.35.

$$\left[\$19 \left(\frac{1 + .04 - .70}{1.3 - .70} \right) + \$0 \left(\frac{1.3 - 1 - .04}{1.3 - .70} \right) \right] \div [1 + .04]$$

$$\left(\$19 \times \frac{.34}{.60} \right) \div 1.04 = \$10.35$$

3)   Of interest is the issuance by the FASB of SFAS 123 (R), *Share-Based Payment*. Under that pronouncement, public entities must account for share-based payments using the fair-value-based method and must apply an option-pricing model.

4)   Candidates should be aware that option pricing is a complex subject and that the derivation of the formulas and an understanding of their theoretical basis are beyond the scope of this text.

3.   A futures contract is a specific kind of **forward contract**, which is simply an executory contract. The parties to a forward contract agree to the terms of a purchase and sale, but performance, that is, payment by the buyer and delivery by the seller, is deferred. A **futures contract** is a definite agreement that allows a trader to purchase or sell an asset at a fixed price during a specific future month. Futures contracts for agricultural commodities, metals, oil, and financial assets are traded on numerous exchanges.

a.   One characteristic of a futures contract is that it may be highly leveraged. The initial **margin** paid may be a very small percentage of the price. Thus, the risk of either gain or loss to a speculator may be great.

b.   A futures contract differs from a forward contract in part because it is traded on an exchange. The result is a liquid market in futures that permits buyers and sellers to net out their positions. For example, a party who has sold a contract can net out his/her position by buying a futures contract.

c.   Because futures contracts are for delivery during a given month, not a specific day, they are more flexible arrangements than forward contracts. The seller notifies the exchange clearinghouse when delivery is to be made, and the clearinghouse randomly matches the seller with a buyer who has purchased a contract for the same month.

1)   A forward contract typically results in an actual delivery. However, a futures contract usually results in net settlement rather than a physical delivery. Thus, the two parties simply exchange the difference between the contracted price and the market price at the expiration date.

d.   A futures contract is entered into as either a **speculation** or a **hedge**. A financial manager can protect a company against adverse changes in prices and interest rates by hedging in the futures market. See Subunit 7.6.

4.   Stop and review! You have completed the outline for this subunit. Study multiple-choice questions 46 through 56 beginning on page 253.

8.5 OTHER SOURCES OF LONG-TERM FINANCING

1. Numerous financing arrangements are used by corporate management to increase investor interest in corporate securities. The objective is a lower interest rate on bonds or a higher selling price for stocks.

    a. **Stock rights** evidenced by **warrants** are options that are distributed with debt or preferred stock. They permit a holder to share in a company's prosperity through a future purchase of stock at a special low price. They should be distinguished from **pure options**, which are created by parties outside of the company and are traded in option markets. These options include puts and calls.

        1) A **put option** is a right to sell stock at a given price within a specified period.
        2) A **call option** is a right to purchase stock at a given price within a specified period.

    b. **Convertibility.** Bonds or preferred stock may be exchangeable by the investor for common stock under certain conditions.

        1) The **conversion price** is calculated by dividing the face amount of the bond by the number of shares received in a conversion. For example, a $1,000 bond that is convertible into 40 shares has a conversion price of $25 per share. The current selling price of the bond in the aftermarket has no effect on the conversion price. The conversion price is normally higher than the market price of the stock at the date the bonds are issued.

    c. Both the issuance of rights and a conversion feature offer a corporation a means of delayed equity financing when market prices are unfavorable. When the market price rises above the conversion price, holders will presumably exercise the warrants or convert the securities.

2. **Employee stock ownership plans (ESOPs)** are established by a corporation under federal income tax laws. Under such a plan, an employee stock ownership trust (ESOT) acquires qualifying employer securities, which may be outstanding shares, treasury shares, or newly issued shares. It holds the stock in the name of the company's employees. In a typical arrangement, the trust obtains the cash to buy the stock by borrowing from a bank, and the corporation cosigns the note to the bank. Each year, the corporation makes contributions to the ESOT as deductible contributions to a qualified retirement plan. The employees may also make deposits to the ESOT.

    a. The corporation receives the benefit of the bank loan by selling stock to the ESOT. Moreover, the corporation in effect repays the bank loan through deductible contributions (with pretax dollars) to the ESOT. Thus, use of a leveraged ESOP allows the corporation to obtain a deduction for the principal as well as the interest on the loan.

    b. Another advantage of an ESOP is that employees should be motivated to perform better because they have a financial interest in the success of the company (although, if the market price of the stock declines, morale may be harmed).

    c. Some small business owners have found that an ESOP is an effective way to transfer ownership (to employees) when no other buyer can be found.

3. **American depository receipts (ADRs)** are ownership rights in foreign corporations.

    a. Foreign stocks are deposited with a large U.S. bank, which in turn issues ADRs representing ownership in the foreign shares. The ADR shares then trade on a U.S. stock exchange, whereas the company's original shares trade on a foreign stock market.

    b. ADRs permit foreign companies to increase their development of a U.S. shareholder base.

c. Foreign companies want to participate in the U.S. equity market for a number of reasons, including a desire to increase liquidity of stocks, to raise equity capital without putting pressure on the stock price in the home market, and to develop a U.S. shareholder base.

4. **Dividend reinvestment plans (DRPs or DRIPs).** Any dividends due to shareholders are automatically reinvested in shares of the same corporation's common stock. Broker's fees on such purchases of stock are either zero (the costs absorbed by the corporation) or only a few cents per shareholder because only one purchase is made and the total fee is divided among all shareholders participating.

   a. Initially, dividends were reinvested in stock bought by a trustee (typically a large bank) on the open market. Many plans are still of this type.

   b. More recently, corporations have seen the opportunity to use DRPs as a source of financing. Thus, many plans now involve a sale of newly issued stock to the trustee to fulfill the requirements of the plan. The corporation benefits because it can issue stock at the current market value without incurring underwriting and issue costs.

5. **Intermediate-term financing** refers to debt issues having approximate maturities of greater than 1 but less than 10 years. The principal types of intermediate-term financing are term loans and lease financing. Major lenders under term agreements are commercial banks, life insurance companies, and, to some extent, pension funds.

   a. **Term loans.** One possible feature of term loans is tying the interest payable on the loan to a variable rate of interest. This **floating rate**, usually stated as some percentage over the prime, creates the potential for extremely high borrowing costs.

      1) This risk must be traded off against

         a) The need of the firm to obtain the loan
         b) The flexibility inherent in term borrowing
         c) The ability of the firm to borrow in the capital market
         d) Other available types of debt financing
         e) The amount of privacy desired

      2) Term loans are private contracts between private firms, whereas long-term debt securities usually involve the SEC and massive disclosure.

      3) Variable or floating rate loans are advantageous to lenders because they permit better matching of interest costs and revenues. Their market values tend to be more stable than those for fixed rate loans.

         a) The disadvantages include a heightened risk of default, losses of expected revenues if interest rates decline or if market rates rise above the ceiling specified in the agreement, and the difficulty of working with a more complex product.

      4) Borrowers may benefit from lower initial costs of these loans but must accept increased interest rate risk, difficulty in forecasting cash flow, a possible loss of creditworthiness if interest rates are expected to rise, and the burden of more complex financing arrangements.

      5) If the interest rate is variable but the monthly loan payment is fixed, an increase in the rate means that the interest component of the payment and the total interest for the loan term will be greater.

         a) The term of the loan will also be extended, and the principal balance will increase because amortization is diminished. Indeed, negative amortization may occur if the interest rate increase is great enough.

         b) Floating or variable rate loans have an impact on monetary policy because they render analyses more complex. These loans give the Federal Reserve less control over the money supply and credit. The economy is now more sensitive to interest rate fluctuations, and political pressure to avoid rate increases will become greater.

    b. **Lease financing** must be analyzed by comparing the cost of owning to the cost of leasing. Leasing is a major means of financing because it offers a variety of tax and other benefits. If leases are not accounted for as installment purchases, they provide off-balance-sheet financing. Thus, under an operating lease, the lessee need not record an asset or a liability, and rent expense (not rent) is recognized. The three principal forms of leases are discussed below:

        1) A **sale-leaseback** is a financing method. A firm seeking financing sells an asset to an investor (creditor) and leases the asset back, usually on a noncancelable lease. The lease payments consist of principal and interest paid by the lessee to the lessor.

        2) **Service or operating leases** usually include both financing and maintenance services.

        3) **Financial leases**, which do not provide for maintenance services, are noncancelable and fully amortize the cost of the leased asset over the term of the basic lease contract. They are installment purchases.

6. **Maturity matching.** The desirability of maturity matching (equalizing the life of an asset acquired with the debt instrument used to finance it) is an important factor in choosing the source of funds. Financing long-term assets with long-term debt allows the company to generate sufficient cash flows from the assets to satisfy obligations as they mature.

7. **Venture capital.** Venture capital firms invest in new enterprises that might not be able to obtain funds in the usual capital markets due to the riskiness of new products. Placements of securities with venture capital firms are usually "private placements" and not subject to SEC regulation.

    a. Venture capitalists risk low liquidity for their investments and high risk.

    b. The payoff may be substantial if the company does succeed.

8. **Initial Public Offerings (IPOs).** A firm's first issuance of securities to the public is an IPO. The process by which a closely held corporation issues new securities to the public is called **going public**. When a firm goes public, it issues its securities on a **new issue** or **IPO market** (a primary market).

    a. **Advantages of Going Public**

        1) The ability to raise additional funds

        2) The establishment of the firm's value in the market

        3) An increase in the liquidity of the firm's stock

    b. **Disadvantages of Going Public**

        1) Costs of the reporting requirements of the SEC and other agencies

        2) Access to the firm's operating data by competing firms

        3) Access to net worth information of major shareholders

        4) Limitations on self-dealing by corporate insiders

        5) Pressure from outside shareholders for earnings growth

        6) Stock prices that do not accurately reflect the true net worth of the firm

        7) Loss of control by management as ownership is diversified

        8) Need for improved management control as operations expand

        9) Increased shareholder servicing costs

    c. To have its stock listed (have it traded on a stock exchange), the firm must apply to a stock exchange, pay a fee, and fulfill the exchange's requirements for membership.

        1) Included in the requirements for membership is disclosure of the firm's financial data.

d.   Once the decision to make an IPO has been made, the questions are similar to those for **seasoned issues**: the amount to be raised, the type of securities to sell, and the method of sale. For example, the following matters should be considered in selecting the type of securities to issue:

1)   Should fixed charges be avoided? Debt creates fixed charges.
2)   Is a maturity date on the security preferable?
3)   Does the firm want a cushion to protect itself from losses to creditors?
4)   How quickly and easily does the firm want to raise the capital?
5)   Are there concerns about loss of control of the firm?
6)   How does the cost of underwriting differ among the types of securities?

e.   The firm's next step is to prepare and file an SEC registration statement and prospectus, unless an exemption is available.

1)   A **registration statement** is a complete disclosure to the SEC of all material information with respect to the issuance of the specific securities.

a)   The SEC does not make any judgment on the financial health of an investment or guarantee the accuracy of the information contained in the registration statement.

2)   A **prospectus** must be furnished to any interested investor. Its purpose is to supply sufficient facts to make an informed investment decision. The prospectus contains material information (financial and otherwise) with respect to the offering and the issuer.

3)   The entire allotment of securities ordinarily is made available for purchase on the effective date of the registration statement. An exception is a **shelf registration**. Under the SEC's Rule 415, a master registration statement is filed for securities that the company reasonably expects to sell within 2 years. However, they are put "on the shelf" until the most opportune time for offering is determined.

a)   Shelf registrations allow large, well-established issuers to respond rapidly in volatile markets and to reduce flotation costs.

f.   In an IPO, the value of a stock is determined by an underwriter on the basis of a number of factors, including general market conditions, book value of the stock, earning potential of the firm, and the P-E ratios of competing firms. Nevertheless, such arbitrary assignments of value are rarely accurate, and a major change in stock price often occurs in the week of the IPO.

g.   A **roll-up** is sometimes used to combine several small "mom-and-pop" businesses into a single corporation large enough to enter the IPO market.

1)   The original owners of individual firms that have been rolled up often remain as managers of the individual branches.

2)   The objective of a roll-up is to use the IPO market as an outlet to sell stock in firms that would ordinarily not be large enough to warrant a public offering.

9.   Stop and review! You have completed the outline for this subunit. Study multiple-choice questions 57 through 63 beginning on page 256.

8.6 CORE CONCEPTS

Sources of Long-Term Financing

- A firm may have long-term financing requirements that it cannot, or does not want to, meet using retained earnings. A firm must in such cases issue **debt**, **common stock**, or **preferred stock** (a hybrid of the first two).

- **Advantages** of issuing **common stock** include the fact that common stock does not require a fixed dividend and that there is no fixed maturity date for repayment of the capital. **Disadvantages** include the dilution of control (voting rights), the dilution of earnings available for distribution, and high underwriting costs.

- **Preferred stock** is a hybrid of debt and equity. It has a fixed charge and increases leverage, but payment of dividends is not an obligation. Also, preferred shareholders stand ahead of common shareholders in priority in the event of corporate bankruptcy.

- **Bonds** are long-term debt instruments. They are similar to term loans except that they are usually offered to the public and sold to many investors. **Advantages** include not having to share basic control of the firm with debtholders and that the interest paid on debt is tax deductible as an expense. **Disadvantages** include the fact that debt has a fixed charge and that debt adds risk to a firm.

Dividend Policy

- **Dividend policy** determines what portion of a corporation's net income is distributed to shareholders and what portion is retained for reinvestment.

- The desire for stability has led theorists to propound the **information content** or **signaling hypothesis**, which states that "a change in dividend policy is a signal to the market regarding management's forecast of future earnings."

- **Important dates** concerning the declaration of dividends are: (1) the date of declaration, (2) the date of record, (3) the date of payment, and (4) the ex-dividend date.

- Dividends can take the form of **cash** or **stock**.

Valuation Methods

- A quantity of money to be received or paid in the future is worth less than the same amount now. The difference, called **the time value of money**, is measured in terms of interest calculated using the appropriate **discount rate**.

- **Per-share ratios** relate company financial information to the market price per share.

- **Earnings per share** equals net income available to common shareholders divided by the average number of shares outstanding for the period.

- **Book value per share** equals the amount of net assets available to the shareholders of a given type of stock divided by the number of those shares outstanding.

- **Dividend yield** equals the annual dividend payment divided by the market value per share.

- The **price-earnings (P-E)** ratio equals the market price per share of common stock divided by EPS.

- **Price-book ratio** equals the market price per share of common stock divided by the book value per share.

- **Price-sales ratio** equals the market price per share of common stock divided by sales per share.

- A bond's **duration** is the average time until each payment, weighted for the proportion of the total stream that each payment constitutes.

Derivatives and Other Financial Instruments

- A **derivative** is defined informally as an investment transaction in which the buyer purchases the right to a potential gain with a commitment for a potential loss. It is a wager on whether the value of something will go up or down. The purpose of the transaction is either to **speculate** (incur risk) or to **hedge** (avoid risk).

- **Options** and **futures** are derivative securities. They are not claims on business assets, such as those represented by equity securities. Instead, they are created by the parties who trade in them.

- A **call option** is the most common type of option. It gives the owner the right to purchase the underlying asset at a fixed price. Thus, it represents a long position because the owner gains from a price increase.

- A **put option** gives the owner the right to sell the underlying asset for a fixed price. It represents a short position because the owner benefits from a price decrease.

- The value of a call option is based on its exercise price, its expiration date, the price of the underlying asset, the variability of that asset, and the risk-free interest rate. The well-known **Black-Scholes Option-Pricing Model** uses these factors.

- The **binomial methods** are based on upward and downward stock price movements comparable to the standard deviation in the Black-Scholes formula.

- A futures contract is a specific kind of **forward contract**, which is simply an executory contract. The parties to a forward contract agree to the terms of a purchase and sale, but performance, that is, payment, by the buyer and delivery by the seller is deferred.

- A **futures contract** is a definite agreement that allows a trader to purchase or sell an asset at a fixed price during a specific future month. Futures contracts for agricultural commodities, metals, oil, and financial assets are traded on numerous exchanges.

Other Sources of Long-Term Financing

- Corporations have certain methods of making their debt and equity issues more **attractive to investors**.

- **Stock rights** evidenced by **warrants** are options that are distributed with debt or preferred stock. They permit a holder to share in a company's prosperity through a future purchase of stock at a special low price.

- **Convertible bonds** or **convertible preferred stock** may be exchangeable by the investor for common stock under certain conditions.

- **Employee stock ownership plans** acquire shares in the company's stock and hold them in the name of the company's employees.

- Under a **dividend reinvestment plan**, any dividends due to shareholders are automatically reinvested in shares of the same corporation's common stock.

- A firm's first issuance of securities to the public is called an initial public offering, known as **going public**. When a firm goes public, it issues its securities on a new issue or IPO market (a primary market).

QUESTIONS

8.1 Sources of Long-Term Financing

1. If Brewer Corporation's bonds are currently yielding 8% in the marketplace, why is the firm's cost of debt lower?

- A. Market interest rates have increased.

- B. Additional debt can be issued more cheaply than the original debt.

- C. There should be no difference; cost of debt is the same as the bonds' market yield.

- D. Interest is deductible for tax purposes.

Answer (D) is correct. *(CMA, adapted)*
REQUIRED: The reason a firm's cost of debt is lower than its current market yield.
DISCUSSION: Because interest is deductible for tax purposes, the actual cost of debt capital is the net effect of the interest payment and the offsetting tax deduction. The actual cost of debt equals the interest rate times (1 – the marginal tax rate). Thus, if a firm with an 8% market rate is in a 40% tax bracket, the net cost of the debt capital is 4.8% [8% × (1 − .4)].
Answer (A) is incorrect because the tax deduction always causes the market yield rate to be higher than the cost of debt capital. Answer (B) is incorrect because additional debt may or may not be issued more cheaply than earlier debt, depending upon the interest rates in the market place. Answer (C) is incorrect because the cost of debt is less than the yield rate given that bond interest is tax deductible.

2. In general, it is more expensive for a company to finance with equity capital than with debt capital because

- A. Long-term bonds have a maturity date and must therefore be repaid in the future.

- B. Investors are exposed to greater risk with equity capital.

- C. Equity capital is in greater demand than debt capital.

- D. Dividends fluctuate to a greater extent than interest rates.

Answer (B) is correct. *(CMA, adapted)*
REQUIRED: The reason equity financing is more expensive than debt financing.
DISCUSSION: Providers of equity capital are exposed to more risk than are lenders because the firm is not obligated to pay them a return. Also, in case of liquidation, creditors are paid before equity investors. Thus, equity financing is more expensive than debt because equity investors require a higher return to compensate for the greater risk assumed.
Answer (A) is incorrect because the obligation to repay at a specific maturity date reduces the risk to investors and thus the required return. Answer (C) is incorrect because the demand for equity capital is directly related to its greater cost to the issuer. Answer (D) is incorrect because dividends are based on managerial discretion and may rarely change; interest rates, however, fluctuate daily based upon market conditions.

3. A firm is planning to issue a callable bond with an 8% coupon rate and 10 years to maturity. A straight bond with a similar rate is priced at $1,000. If the value of the issuer's call option is estimated to be $50, what is the value of the callable bond?

- A. $1,000

- B. $950

- C. $1,050

- D. $900

Answer (B) is correct. *(Publisher, adapted)*
REQUIRED: The value of a callable bond.
DISCUSSION: A callable bond is not as valuable to an investor as a straight bond. Thus, the $50 call option is subtracted from the $1,000 value of a straight bond to arrive at a $950 value for the callable bond.

4. In capital markets, the primary market is concerned with the provision of new funds for capital investments through

- A. New issues of bond and stock securities.

- B. Exchanges of existing bond and stock securities.

- C. The sale of forward or future commodities contracts.

- D. New issues of bond and stock securities and exchanges of existing bond and stock securities.

Answer (A) is correct. *(CMA, adapted)*
REQUIRED: The purpose of the primary market.
DISCUSSION: The primary market is the market for new stocks and bonds. In this market, wherein investment money flows directly to the issuer, securities are initially sold by investment bankers who purchase them from issuers and sell them through an underwriting group. Later transactions occur on securities exchanges or other markets.
Answer (B) is incorrect because existing securities are traded on a secondary market (e.g., securities exchanges). Answer (C) is incorrect because the futures market is where commodities contracts are sold, not the capital market. Answer (D) is incorrect because exchanges of existing securities do not occur in the primary market.

5. The term "underwriting spread" refers to the

   A. Commission percentage an investment banker receives for underwriting a security issue.

   B. Discount investment bankers receive on securities they purchase from the issuing company.

   C. Difference between the price the investment banker pays for a new security issue and the price at which the securities are resold.

   D. Commission a broker receives for either buying or selling a security on behalf of an investor.

Answer (C) is correct. *(CMA, adapted)*
REQUIRED: The definition of underwriting spread.
DISCUSSION: An investment banker performs an underwriting or insurance function when it purchases an issue of securities and then resells them. The risk of price fluctuations during the distribution period is borne entirely by the investment banker. Investment banking is also an efficient vehicle for marketing the securities because investment bankers are specialists in such activities. The profit earned is the underwriting spread, or the difference between the purchase and resale prices of the securities (effectively, the wholesale and retail prices).
Answer (A) is incorrect because the underwriting spread is not based on a commission. The underwriter actually buys the new securities and resells them at a price that is expected to result in a profit. Answer (B) is incorrect because the underwriting spread is not a genuine discount; it is simply the difference between the price paid and the price received for a new security. Answer (D) is incorrect because the underwriting spread is not based on a commission. The underwriter actually buys the new securities and resells them at a price that is expected to result in a profit.

6. In general, it is more expensive for a company to finance with equity capital than with debt capital because

   A. Long-term bonds have a maturity date and must therefore be repaid in the future.

   B. Investors are exposed to greater risk with equity capital.

   C. The interest on debt is a legal obligation.

   D. Equity capital is in greater demand than debt capital.

Answer (B) is correct. *(CMA, adapted)*
REQUIRED: The reason equity financing is more expensive than debt financing.
DISCUSSION: Providers of equity capital are exposed to more risk than are lenders because the firm is not obligated to pay them a return. Also, in case of liquidation, creditors are paid before equity investors. Thus, equity financing is more expensive than debt because equity investors require a higher return to compensate for the greater risk assumed.
Answer (A) is incorrect because the obligation to repay at a specific maturity date reduces the risk to investors and thus the required return. Answer (C) is incorrect because the existence of a legal obligation is but one reason that debt poses less risk to investors. Thus, it is a more limited answer than "investors are exposed to greater risk with equity capital." Answer (D) is incorrect because the demand for equity capital is directly related to its greater cost to the issuer.

7. The equity section of Smith Corporation's Statement of Financial Position is presented below.

Preferred stock, $100 par	$12,000,000
Common stock, $5 par	10,000,000
Paid-in capital in excess of par	18,000,000
Retained earnings	9,000,000
Net worth	$49,000,000

The common shareholders of Smith Corporation have preemptive rights. If Smith Corporation issues 400,000 additional shares of common stock at $6 per share, a current holder of 20,000 shares of Smith Corporation's common stock must be given the option to buy

   A. 1,000 additional shares.

   B. 3,774 additional shares.

   C. 4,000 additional shares.

   D. 3,333 additional shares.

Answer (C) is correct. *(CMA, adapted)*
REQUIRED: The new shares that a shareholder may buy given preemptive rights.
DISCUSSION: Common shareholders usually have preemptive rights, which means they have first right to purchase any new issues of stock in proportion to their current ownership percentages. The purpose of a preemptive right is to allow stockholders to maintain their current percentages of ownership. Given that Smith had 2,000,000 shares outstanding ($10,000,000 ÷ $5 par), an investor with 20,000 shares has a 1% ownership. Hence, this investor must be allowed to purchase 4,000 (400,000 shares × 1%) of the additional shares.
Answer (A) is incorrect because the investor would be allowed to purchase 1% of any new issues. Answer (B) is incorrect because preferred shareholders do not share in preemptive rights. Answer (D) is incorrect because preferred shareholders do not share in preemptive rights.

8. The formula for determining the value of one stock right when the price of the stock is rights-on is

$$R_{on} = \frac{P_{on} - S}{N + 1}$$

Where: R_{on} = market value of one right when the stock is selling rights-on.

P_{on} = market value of one share of stock with rights-on.

N = number of rights necessary to purchase one share of stock.

S = subscription price per share.

If the market price of a stock is $50 per share, the subscription price is $40 per share, and three rights are necessary to buy an additional share of stock, the theoretical market value of one right used to buy the stock prior to the ex-rights date is

A. $2.00

B. $2.50

C. $10.00

D. $40.00

Answer (B) is correct. *(CMA, adapted)*
REQUIRED: The theoretical value of one right prior to the ex-rights date.
DISCUSSION: Plugging the amounts into the formula produces a theoretical value of $2.50 per right:

$$(\$50 - \$40) \div (3 + 1) = \$2.50$$

To check the answer, assume that an investor purchases three rights at $2.50 each (a total of $7.50) and uses them to buy a share of stock for $40. The total investment is $47.50. Similarly, a person holding a $50 share of stock before the rights are issued will have a basis of $47.50 after selling the right for $2.50. Thus, the value of the stock ex-rights is $47.50, and the value of the right is $2.50.
Answer (A) is incorrect because the right is worth $2.50. Answer (C) is incorrect because $10 is the difference between the price of the stock with rights ($50) and the exercise price ($40). Answer (D) is incorrect because $40 is the exercise price of the new issue.

Questions 9 and 10 are based on the following information. A company's stock trades rights-on for $50.00 and ex-rights for $48.00. The subscription price for rights holders is $40.00, and four rights are required to purchase one share of stock.

---

9. The value of a right while the stock is still trading rights-on is

A. $0.40

B. $0.50

C. $1.60

D. $2.00

Answer (D) is correct. *(CMA, adapted)*
REQUIRED: The value of a right when the stock is still trading rights-on.
DISCUSSION: Until rights are actually issued, the stock trades rights-on, meaning that the stock and rights are inseparable. If P is the value of a share rights-on, S is the subscription price of a new share, and N is the number of rights needed to buy a new share, the value of a right when the stock is selling rights-on is (P – S) ÷ (N + 1). Thus, the value of a right when the stock is selling rights-on is $2.00 [($50 – $40) ÷ (4 + 1)].
Answer (A) is incorrect because $0.40 is the rights-on value if P is $50 and S is $48. Answer (B) is incorrect because $0.50 is the ex-rights value if P is $50 and S is $48. Answer (C) is incorrect because $1.60 is the rights-on value if P is $48 and S is $40.

---

10. The value of a right when the stock is trading ex-rights is

A. $0.40

B. $0.50

C. $2.00

D. $2.50

Answer (C) is correct. *(CMA, adapted)*
REQUIRED: The value of a right when the stock is trading ex-rights.
DISCUSSION: If a stock can be purchased for $48 on the open market, or for $40 with four rights, each right must be worth $2.00 ($8 savings ÷ 4 rights).
Answer (A) is incorrect because $0.40 is the rights-on value if P is $50 and S is $48. Answer (B) is incorrect because $0.50 is the ex-rights value if P is $50 and S is $48. Answer (D) is incorrect because $2.50 is the ex-rights value if P is $50 and S is $40.

11. The market value of a share of stock is $50, and the market value of one right prior to the ex-rights date is $2.00 after the offering is announced but while the stock is still selling rights-on. The offer to the shareholder is that it will take three rights to buy an additional share of stock at a subscription price of $40 per share. If the theoretical value of the stock when it goes ex-rights is $47.50, then the shareholder

   A. Does not receive any additional benefit from a rights offering.

   B. Receives an additional benefit from a rights offering.

   C. Merely receives a return of capital.

   D. Should redeem the right and purchase the stock before the ex-rights date.

Answer (A) is correct. *(CMA, adapted)*
   REQUIRED: The true statement about the effect on the value of stock when it goes ex-rights.
   DISCUSSION: Plugging the amounts into the formula given in the preceding question produces a theoretical value of $2.50 per right, which leaves a theoretical value of $47.50 for the stock:

$$(\$50 - \$40) \div (3 + 1) = \$2.50$$

However, if the stock declines to $47.50 when the right is worth only $2, the original investor is worse off then before the rights issuance; i.e., the investor would have only $49.50 worth of investments. Hence, the original shareholder receives no benefit from the issuance of the rights.
   Answer (B) is incorrect because the stockholder would be worse off after the rights offering ($49.50) than before the rights offering ($50). Answer (C) is incorrect because the shareholder receives only a certificate granting the right to make an additional investment. Answer (D) is incorrect because an investor cannot redeem a right before the ex-rights date, i.e., while the stock is still rights-on.

12. Growl Corporation's $1,000 par value convertible debentures are selling at $1,040 when its stock is selling for $46.00 per share. If the conversion ratio is 20, what will be the conversion price?

   A. $22.61

   B. $46.00

   C. $50.00

   D. $52.00

Answer (C) is correct. *(Publisher, adapted)*
   REQUIRED: The conversion price.
   DISCUSSION: The conversion price is the assumed price of the stock, which was set at the time the bonds were issued. Dividing the $1,000 face value by the 20 shares results in a conversion price of $50.
   Answer (A) is incorrect because it is the ratio of stock price to bond price, not the conversion price. Answer (B) is incorrect because $46 is the market price. Answer (D) is incorrect because $52 is the effective price that a bond holder would pay in the event of a conversion.

13. On January 1 of the current year, Bongo Company issued convertible bonds with $1,000 par value and a conversion ratio of 50. Which of the following should be the market price per share of the company's common stock on January 1?

   A. Under $20.

   B. $20

   C. Between $20 and $50.

   D. Above $50.

Answer (A) is correct. *(Publisher, adapted)*
   REQUIRED: The probable market price of stock at the date convertible bonds are issued.
   DISCUSSION: The conversion price, in this case $20 ($1,000 ÷ 50 shares), is normally greater than the market price at the time the bonds are issued. Therefore, the market price must be less than $20.
   Answer (B) is incorrect because a conversion price equal to market price would be of little benefit to the issuer. Answer (C) is incorrect because the market price cannot be greater than the conversion price; otherwise, investors would immediately convert for a short-term gain. Answer (D) is incorrect because the market price cannot be greater than the conversion price; otherwise, investors would immediately convert for a short-term gain.

14. The par value of a common stock represents

   A. The estimated market value of the stock when it was issued.

   B. The liability ceiling of a shareholder when a company undergoes bankruptcy proceedings.

   C. The total value of the stock that must be entered in the issuing corporation's records.

   D. A theoretical value of $100 per share of stock with any differences entered in the issuing corporation's records as discount or premium on common stock.

Answer (B) is correct. *(CMA, adapted)*
   REQUIRED: The amount represented by the par value of common stock.
   DISCUSSION: Par value represents a stock's legal capital. It is an arbitrary value assigned to stock before it is issued. Par value represents a shareholder's liability ceiling because, as long as the par value has been paid in to the corporation, the shareholders obtain the benefits of limited liability.
   Answer (A) is incorrect because par value is rarely the same as market value. Normally, market value will be equal to or greater than par value, but there is no relationship between the two. Answer (C) is incorrect because all assets received for stock must be entered into a corporation's records. The amount received is very rarely the par value. Answer (D) is incorrect because par value can be any amount more or less than $100.

15. Each share of nonparticipating, 8%, cumulative preferred stock in a company that meets its dividend obligations has all of the following characteristics except

A. Voting rights in corporate elections.

B. Dividend payments that are not tax deductible by the company.

C. No principal repayments.

D. A superior claim to common stock equity in the case of liquidation.

Answer (A) is correct. *(CMA, adapted)*
REQUIRED: The item that is not characteristic of nonparticipating, cumulative preferred stock.
DISCUSSION: Dividends on cumulative preferred stock accrue until declared; that is, the book value of the preferred stock increases by the amount of any undeclared dividends. Participating preferred stock participates with common shareholders in excess earnings of the company. In other words, 8% participating preferred stock might pay a dividend each year greater than 8% when the corporation is extremely profitable. Therefore, nonparticipating preferred stock will receive no more than is stated on the face of the stock. Preferred shareholders rarely have voting rights. Voting rights are exchanged for preferences regarding dividends and liquidation of assets.
Answer (B) is incorrect because a corporation does not receive a tax deduction for making dividend payments on any type of stock. Answer (C) is incorrect because preferred stock normally need not be redeemed as long as the corporation remains in business. Answer (D) is incorrect because preferred shareholders do have priority over common shareholders in a liquidation.

16. If a $1,000 bond sells for $1,125, which of the following statements are true?

I. The market rate of interest is greater than the coupon rate on the bond.

II. The coupon rate on the bond is greater than the market rate of interest.

III. The coupon rate and the market rate are equal.

IV. The bond sells at a premium.

V. The bond sells at a discount.

A. I and IV.

B. I and V.

C. II and IV.

D. II and V.

Answer (C) is correct. *(CMA, adapted)*
REQUIRED: The true statement(s) about a bond that sells at more than its face value.
DISCUSSION: The excess of the price over the face value is a premium. A premium is paid because the coupon rate on the bond is greater than the market rate of interest. In other words, because the bond is paying a higher rate than other similar bonds, its price is bid up by investors.
Answer (A) is incorrect because, if a bond sells at a premium, the market rate of interest is less than the coupon rate. Answer (B) is incorrect because a bond sells at a discount when the price is less than the face amount. Answer (D) is incorrect because a bond sells at a discount when the price is less than the face amount.

17. Debentures are

A. Income bonds that require interest payments only when earnings permit.

B. Subordinated debt and rank behind convertible bonds.

C. Bonds secured by the full faith and credit of the issuing firm.

D. A form of lease financing similar to equipment trust certificates.

Answer (C) is correct. *(CMA, adapted)*
REQUIRED: The true statement about debentures.
DISCUSSION: Debentures are unsecured bonds. Although no assets are mortgaged as security for the bonds, debentures are secured by the full faith and credit of the issuing firm. Debentures are a general obligation of the borrower. Only companies with the best credit ratings can issue debentures because only the company's credit rating and reputation secure the bonds.
Answer (A) is incorrect because debentures must pay interest regardless of earnings levels. Answer (B) is incorrect because debentures are not subordinated except to the extent of assets mortgaged against other bond issues. Debentures are a general obligation of the borrower and rank equally with convertible bonds. Answer (D) is incorrect because debentures have nothing to do with lease financing. Debentures are not secured by assets.

18. Which one of the following characteristics distinguishes income bonds from other bonds?

   A. The bondholder is guaranteed an income over the life of the security.

   B. By promising a return to the bondholder, an income bond is junior to preferred and common stock.

   C. Income bonds are junior to subordinated debt but senior to preferred and common stock.

   D. Income bonds pay interest only if the issuing company has earned the interest.

Answer (D) is correct. *(CMA, adapted)*
   REQUIRED: The characteristic of income bonds.
   DISCUSSION: An income bond is one that pays interest only if the issuing company has earned the interest, although the principal must still be paid on the due date. Such bonds are riskier than normal bonds.
   Answer (A) is incorrect because bondholders will receive an income only if the issuing company earns sufficient income to pay the interest. Answer (B) is incorrect because all bonds have priority over preferred and common stock. Answer (C) is incorrect because subordinated debt is junior to nonsubordinated debt.

19. Serial bonds are attractive to investors because

   A. All bonds in the issue mature on the same date.

   B. The yield to maturity is the same for all bonds in the issue.

   C. Investors can choose the maturity that suits their financial needs.

   D. The coupon rate on these bonds is adjusted to the maturity date.

Answer (C) is correct. *(CMA, adapted)*
   REQUIRED: The reason serial bonds are attractive to investors.
   DISCUSSION: Serial bonds have staggered maturities; that is, they mature over a period (series) of years. Thus, investors can choose the maturity date that meets their investment needs. For example, an investor who will have a child starting college in 16 years can choose bonds that mature in 16 years.
   Answer (A) is incorrect because serial bonds mature on different dates. Answer (B) is incorrect because bonds maturing on different dates may have different yields, or they may be the same. Usually, the earlier date maturities carry slightly lower yields than the later maturities. Answer (D) is incorrect because the coupon rate is the same for all bonds; only the selling price and yield differ.

20. The best advantage of a zero-coupon bond to the issuer is that the

   A. Bond requires a low issuance cost.

   B. Bond requires no interest income calculation to the holder or issuer until maturity.

   C. Interest can be amortized annually by the APR method and need not be shown as an interest expense to the issuer.

   D. Interest can be amortized annually on a straight-line basis but is a noncash outlay.

Answer (D) is correct. *(CMA, adapted)*
   REQUIRED: The best advantage of a zero-coupon bond to the issuer.
   DISCUSSION: Zero-coupon bonds do not pay periodic interest. The bonds are sold at a discount from their face value, and the investors do not receive interest until the bonds mature. The issuer does not have to make annual cash outlays for interest. However, the discount must be amortized annually and reported as interest expense.
   Answer (A) is incorrect because the issuance costs are no lower than for any other bond issue. Answer (B) is incorrect because interest income and expense must be calculated annually based on the amount of the initial discount that is amortized. Answer (C) is incorrect because the annual amortization must be shown as interest expense. APR means "annual percentage rate."

21. Junk bonds are

   A. Securities rated at less than investment grade.

   B. Worthless securities.

   C. Securities that are highly risky but offer only low yields.

   D. Considered illegal since the collapse of the Drexel Burnham Lambert firm.

Answer (A) is correct. *(CMA, adapted)*
   REQUIRED: The definition of junk bonds.
   DISCUSSION: Junk bonds are high-risk and therefore high-yield securities that are normally issued when the debt ratio is very high. Thus, the bondholders have as much risk as the holders of equity securities. Such bonds are not highly rated by credit evaluation companies. Junk bonds have become accepted because of the tax deductibility of the interest paid.
   Answer (B) is incorrect because junk bonds are not yet worthless; they simply bear high interest rates and high risk. Answer (C) is incorrect because junk bonds typically offer high yields. Answer (D) is incorrect because Drexel Burnham was not the only underwriter to package junk bonds, and they were never illegal.

22. The best reason corporations issue Eurobonds rather than domestic bonds is that

A. These bonds are denominated in the currency of the country in which they are issued.

B. These bonds are normally a less expensive form of financing because of the absence of government regulation.

C. Foreign buyers more readily accept the issues of both large and small U.S. corporations than do domestic investors.

D. Eurobonds carry no foreign exchange risk.

Answer (B) is correct. *(CMA, adapted)*
REQUIRED: The best reason for issuing Eurobonds instead of domestic bonds.
DISCUSSION: International bonds are of two types: foreign bonds and Eurobonds. Foreign bonds are denominated in the currency of the nation in which they are sold. Eurobonds are denominated in a currency other than that of the nation where they are sold. Foreign bonds issued in the United States and denominated in dollars must be registered with the SEC, but such extensive disclosure is not required in most European nations. Thus, an American company may elect to issue Eurobonds denominated in dollars in a foreign nation because of the convenience of not having to comply with governmental registration requirements.
Answer (A) is incorrect because Eurobonds are not denominated in the currency of the nation in which they are sold. The difference is a possible disadvantage because of exchange rate risk. Nevertheless, many foreign bonds are denominated in U.S. dollars. Answer (C) is incorrect because foreign nationals are often hesitant about buying bonds issued by small companies with which they are not familiar. Answer (D) is incorrect because Eurobonds carry foreign exchange risk. The foreign lender may suffer a loss if the dollar declines relative to its domestic currency.

23. Which one of the following statements is true when comparing bond financing alternatives?

A. A bond with a call provision typically has a lower yield to maturity than a similar bond without a call provision.

B. A convertible bond must be converted to common stock prior to its maturity.

C. A call provision is generally considered detrimental to the investor.

D. A call premium requires the investor to pay an amount greater than par at the time of purchase.

Answer (C) is correct. *(CMA, adapted)*
REQUIRED: The true statement comparing bond financing alternatives.
DISCUSSION: A callable bond can be recalled by the issuer prior to maturity. A call provision is detrimental to the investor because the issuer can recall the bond when market interest rates decline. It is usually exercised only when a company wishes to refinance high-interest debt.
Answer (A) is incorrect because callable bonds sometimes pay a slightly higher rate of interest. Investors may demand a greater return because of the uncertainty over the true maturity date. Answer (B) is incorrect because conversion is at the option of the investor. Answer (D) is incorrect because the call premium is the amount in excess of par that the issuer must pay when bonds are called.

24. All of the following may reduce the coupon rate on a bond issued at par except a

A. Sinking fund.

B. Call provision.

C. Change in rating from Aa to Aaa.

D. Conversion option.

Answer (B) is correct. *(CMA, adapted)*
REQUIRED: The item that will not reduce the coupon rate on a bond issued at par.
DISCUSSION: A bond issued at par may carry a lower coupon rate than other similar bonds in the market if it has some feature that makes it more attractive to investors. For example, a sinking fund reduces default risk. Hence, investors may require a lower risk premium and be willing to accept a lower coupon rate. Other features attractive to investors include covenants in the bond indenture that restrict risky undertakings by the issuer and an option to convert the debt instruments to equity securities. The opportunity to profit from appreciation of the firm's stock justifies a lower coupon rate. An improvement in a bond's rating from Aa to Aaa (the highest possible) also justifies reduction in the risk premium and a lower coupon rate. However, a call provision is usually undesirable to investors. The issuer may take advantage of a decline in interest rates to recall the bond and stop paying interest before maturity.

8.2 Dividend Policy

25. The Dawson Corporation projects the following for the year:

Earnings before interest and taxes	$35 million
Interest expense	$5 million
Preferred stock dividends	$4 million
Common stock dividend-payout ratio	30%
Common shares outstanding	2 million
Effective corporate income tax rate	40%

The expected common stock dividend per share for Dawson Corporation is

- A. $2.34
- B. $2.70
- C. $1.80
- D. $2.10

Answer (D) is correct. *(CMA, adapted)*
REQUIRED: The expected common stock dividend per share.
DISCUSSION: The company's net income is $18,000,000 [($35,000,000 EBIT – $5,000,000 interest) × (1.0 – .4 tax rate)]. Thus, the earnings available to common shareholders equal $14,000,000 ($18,000,000 – $4,000,000 preferred dividends), and EPS is $7 ($14,000,000 ÷ 2,000,000 common shares). Given a dividend-payout ratio of 30%, the dividend to common shareholders is expected to be $2.10 per share ($7 × 30%).
Answer (A) is incorrect because $2.34 results from treating preferred dividends as tax deductible. Answer (B) is incorrect because $2.70 ignores the effect of preferred dividends. Answer (C) is incorrect because $1.80 is based on a 60% effective tax rate and ignores the effect of preferred dividends.

26. In practice, dividends

- A. Usually exhibit greater stability than earnings.
- B. Fluctuate more widely than earnings.
- C. Tend to be a lower percentage of earnings for mature firms.
- D. Are usually changed every year to reflect earnings changes.

Answer (A) is correct. *(CMA, adapted)*
REQUIRED: The true statement about dividends and their relation to earnings.
DISCUSSION: Dividend policy determines the portion of net income distributed to stockholders. Corporations normally try to maintain a stable level of dividends, even though profits may fluctuate considerably, because many stockholders buy stock with the expectation of receiving a certain dividend every year. Thus, management tends not to raise dividends if the payout cannot be sustained. The desire for stability has led theorists to propound the information content or signaling hypothesis: a change in dividend policy is a signal to the market regarding management's forecast of future earnings. This stability often results in a stock that sells at a higher market price because stockholders perceive less risk in receiving their dividends.
Answer (B) is incorrect because most companies try to maintain stable dividends. Answer (C) is incorrect because mature firms have less need of earnings to reinvest for expansion; thus, they tend to pay a higher percentage of earnings as dividends. Answer (D) is incorrect because most companies try to maintain stable dividends.

27. Residco, Inc. expects net income of $800,000 for the next fiscal year. Its targeted and current capital structure is 40% debt and 60% common equity. The director of capital budgeting has determined that the optimal capital spending for next year is $1.2 million. If Residco follows a strict residual dividend policy, what is the expected dividend-payout ratio for next year?

- A. 90.0%
- B. 66.7%
- C. 40.0%
- D. 10.0%

Answer (D) is correct. *(CMA, adapted)*
REQUIRED: The expected dividend-payout ratio assuming a strict residual dividend policy.
DISCUSSION: Under the residual theory of dividends, the residual of earnings paid as dividends depends on the available investments and the debt-equity ratio at which cost of capital is minimized. The rational investor should prefer reinvestment of retained earnings when the return exceeds what the investor could earn on investments of equal risk. However, the firm may prefer to pay dividends when investment returns are poor and the internal equity financing would move the firm away from its ideal capital structure. If Residco wants to maintain its current structure, 60% of investments should be financed from equity. Hence, it needs $720,000 ($1,200,000 × 60%) of equity funds, leaving $80,000 of net income ($800,000 NI – $720,000) available for dividends. The dividend-payout ratio is therefore 10% ($80,000 ÷ $800,000 NI).
Answer (A) is incorrect because 90% is the reinvestment ratio. Answer (B) is incorrect because 66.7% is the ratio between earnings and investment. Answer (C) is incorrect because 40% is the ratio of debt in the ideal capital structure.

Questions 28 and 29 are based on the following information. A firm's dividend policy may treat dividends either as the residual part of a financing decision or as an active policy strategy.

28. Treating dividends as the residual part of a financing decision assumes that

A. Earnings should be retained and reinvested as long as profitable projects are available.

B. Dividends are important to shareholders, and any earnings left over after paying dividends should be invested in high-return assets.

C. Dividend payments should be consistent.

D. Dividends are relevant to a financing decision.

Answer (A) is correct. *(CMA, adapted)*
REQUIRED: The assumption made when dividends are treated as a residual part of a financing decision.
DISCUSSION: According to the residual theory of dividends, the amount (residual) of earnings paid as dividends depends on the available investment opportunities and the debt-equity ratio at which cost of capital is minimized. The rational investor should prefer reinvestment of retained earnings when the return exceeds what the investor could earn on investments of equal risk. However, the firm may prefer to pay dividends when investment opportunities are poor and the use of internal equity financing would move the firm away from its ideal capital structure.
Answer (B) is incorrect because a residual theory assumes that investors want the company to reinvest earnings in worthwhile projects, not pay dividends. Answer (C) is incorrect because dividend payments will not be consistent under a residual theory. The corporation will pay dividends only when internal investment options are unacceptable. Answer (D) is incorrect because dividends would not be important to a financing decision under the residual theory.

29. Treating dividends as an active policy strategy assumes that

A. Dividends provide information to the market.

B. The firm should pay dividends only after investing in all investment opportunities having an expected return greater than the cost of capital.

C. Dividends are irrelevant.

D. Dividends are costly, and the firm should retain earnings and issue stock dividends.

Answer (A) is correct. *(CMA, adapted)*
REQUIRED: The assumption made when dividends are treated as an active policy strategy.
DISCUSSION: Stock prices often move in the same direction as dividends. Moreover, companies dislike cutting dividends. They tend not to raise dividends unless anticipated future earnings will be sufficient to sustain the higher payout. Thus, some theorists have proposed the information content or signaling hypothesis. According to this view, a change in dividend policy is a signal to the market regarding management's forecast of future earnings. Consequently, the relation of stock price changes to changes in dividends reflects not an investor preference for dividends over capital gains but rather the effect of the information conveyed.
Answer (B) is incorrect because the residual theory of dividends assumes that the firm should pay dividends only after investing in all investment opportunities having an expected return greater than the cost of capital. Answer (C) is incorrect because an active dividend policy suggests management assumes that dividends are relevant to investors. Answer (D) is incorrect because an active dividend policy recognizes that investors want dividends.

30. A stock dividend

A. Increases the debt-to-equity ratio of a firm.

B. Decreases future earnings per share.

C. Decreases the size of the firm.

D. Increases shareholders' wealth.

Answer (B) is correct. *(CMA, adapted)*
REQUIRED: The true statement about a stock dividend.
DISCUSSION: A stock dividend is a transfer of equity from retained earnings to paid-in capital. The debit is to retained earnings and the credits are to common stock and additional paid-in capital. Additional shares are outstanding following the stock dividend, but every shareholder maintains the same percentage of ownership. In effect, a stock dividend divides the pie (the corporation) into more pieces, but the pie is still the same size. Hence, a corporation will have a lower EPS and a lower book value per share following a stock dividend, but every shareholder will be just as well off as previously. A stock dividend has no effect except on the composition of the shareholders' equity section of the balance sheet.

31. Brady Corporation has 6,000 shares of 5% cumulative, $100 par value preferred stock outstanding and 200,000 shares of common stock outstanding. Brady's board of directors last declared dividends for the year ended May 31, Year 1, and there were no dividends in arrears. For the year ended May 31, Year 3, Brady had net income of $1,750,000. The board of directors is declaring a dividend for common shareholders equivalent to 20% of net income. The total amount of dividends to be paid by Brady at May 31, Year 3, is

A. $350,000

B. $380,000

C. $206,000

D. $410,000

Answer (D) is correct. *(CMA, adapted)*
REQUIRED: The total amount of dividends to be paid given cumulative preferred stock.
DISCUSSION: If a company has cumulative preferred stock, all preferred dividends for the current and any unpaid prior years must be paid before any dividends can be paid on common stock. The total preferred dividends that must be paid equal $60,000 (6,000 shares × $100 par × 5% × 2 years), and the common dividend is $350,000 ($1,750,000 × 20%), for a total of $410,000.
Answer (A) is incorrect because $350,000 is the common stock dividend. Answer (B) is incorrect because $380,000 omits the $30,000 of cumulative dividends for Year 2. Answer (C) is incorrect because $206,000 is based on a flat rate of $1 per share of stock.

32. A 10% stock dividend most likely

A. Increases the size of the firm.

B. Increases shareholders' wealth.

C. Decreases future earnings per share.

D. Decreases net income.

Answer (C) is correct. *(CMA, adapted)*
REQUIRED: The most likely effect of a stock dividend.
DISCUSSION: A stock dividend is a transfer of equity from retained earnings to paid-in capital. The debit is to retained earnings, and the credits are to common stock and additional paid-in capital. Additional shares are outstanding following the stock dividend, but every shareholder maintains the same percentage of ownership. In effect, a stock dividend divides the pie (the corporation) into more pieces, but the pie is still the same size. Hence, a corporation will have a lower EPS and a lower book value per share following a stock dividend, but every shareholder will be just as well off as previously. A stock dividend has no effect except on the composition of the shareholders' equity section of the balance sheet.

33. When a company desires to increase the market value per share of common stock, the company will implement

A. The sale of treasury stock.

B. A reverse stock split.

C. The sale of preferred stock.

D. A stock split.

Answer (B) is correct. *(CMA, adapted)*
REQUIRED: The transaction that increases the market value per share of common stock.
DISCUSSION: A reverse stock split decreases the number of shares outstanding, thereby increasing the market price per share. A reverse stock split may be desirable when a stock is selling at such a low price that management is concerned that investors will avoid the stock because it has an undesirable image.
Answer (A) is incorrect because a sale of treasury stock increases the supply of shares and could lead to a decline in market price. Answer (C) is incorrect because a sale of preferred stock will take dollars out of investors' hands, thereby reducing funds available to invest in common stock; therefore, market price per share of common stock will not increase. Answer (D) is incorrect because a stock split increases the shares issued and outstanding. The market price per share is likely to decline as a result.

34. Arch, Inc. has 200,000 shares of common stock outstanding. Net income for the recently ended fiscal year was $500,000, and the stock has a price-earnings ratio of eight. The board of directors has just declared a three-for-two stock split. For an investor who owns 100 shares of stock before the split, the approximate value (rounded to the nearest dollar) of the investment in Arch stock immediately after the split is

A. $250

B. $1,333

C. $2,000

D. $3,000

Answer (C) is correct. *(CMA, adapted)*
REQUIRED: The value of an investment after a stock split given the P-E ratio.
DISCUSSION: EPS equals $2.50 ($500,000 NI ÷ 200,000 pre-split shares). Thus, 100 shares had a value of $2,000 (100 shares × $2.50 EPS × 8 P-E ratio) before the split. This value is unchanged by the stock split. Although the stockholder has more shares, the total value of the investment is the same.
Answer (A) is incorrect because $250 represents the annual earnings on 100 shares. Answer (B) is incorrect because $1,333 assumes that the value of the total investment declines after the split. Answer (D) is incorrect because $3,000 assumes that the value of the investment as well as the number of shares increases by 50%.

8.3 Valuation Methods

35. A company had 150,000 shares outstanding on January 1. On March 1, 75,000 additional shares were issued through a stock dividend. Then on November 1, the company issued 60,000 shares for cash. The number of shares to be used in the denominator of the EPS calculation for the year is

  A. 222,500 shares.

  B. 225,000 shares.

  C. 235,000 shares.

  D. 285,000 shares.

Answer (C) is correct. *(CIA, adapted)*
  REQUIRED: The number of shares to be used in the denominator of the EPS calculation.
  DISCUSSION: The weighted-average of shares outstanding during the year is used in the EPS denominator. Shares issued in a stock dividend are assumed to have been outstanding as of the beginning of the earliest accounting period presented. Thus, the 75,000 shares issued on March 1 are deemed to have been outstanding on January 1. The EPS denominator equals 235,000 shares {[150,000 × (12 months ÷ 12 months)] + [75,000 × (12 months ÷ 12 months)] + [60,000 × (2 months ÷ 12 months)]}.
  Answer (A) is incorrect because 222,500 is the weighted-average number of shares if the stock dividend is not treated as retroactive. Answer (B) is incorrect because 225,000 ignores the November 1 issuance. Answer (D) is incorrect because 285,000 is the year-end number of outstanding shares.

36. Everything else being equal, a <List A> highly leveraged firm will have <List B> earnings per share.

	List A	List B
A.	More	Lower
B.	More	Less volatile
C.	Less	Less volatile
D.	Less	Higher

Answer (C) is correct. *(CIA, adapted)*
  REQUIRED: The effect of leverage on EPS.
  DISCUSSION: Earnings per share is less volatile in less highly leveraged firms. Lower fixed costs result in less variable earnings when sales fluctuate.
  Answer (A) is incorrect because higher leverage is associated with higher, not lower, EPS when sales exceed the breakeven point. Answer (B) is incorrect because earnings per share is more volatile in more highly leveraged firms. Answer (D) is incorrect because less leverage is associated with lower, not higher, EPS when sales exceed the breakeven point.

37. In calculating diluted earnings per share when a company has convertible bonds outstanding, the number of common shares outstanding must be <List A> to adjust for the conversion feature of the bonds, and the net income must be <List B> by the amount of interest expense on the bonds, net of tax.

	List A	List B
A.	Increased	Increased
B.	Increased	Decreased
C.	Decreased	Increased
D.	Decreased	Decreased

Answer (A) is correct. *(CIA, adapted)*
  REQUIRED: The appropriate calculation of diluted EPS.
  DISCUSSION: The weighted-average number of shares outstanding must be increased to reflect the shares into which the bonds could be converted. Also, the effect of the bond interest on net income must be eliminated. In this way, earnings per share is calculated as if the bonds had been converted into common shares as of the start of the year.

38. All else being equal, a company with a higher dividend-payout ratio will have a <List A> debt-to-assets ratio and a <List B> current ratio.

	List A	List B
A.	Higher	Higher
B.	Higher	Lower
C.	Lower	Higher
D.	Lower	Lower

Answer (B) is correct. *(CIA, adapted)*
  REQUIRED: The implications of a higher dividend payout ratio.
  DISCUSSION: A company with a higher dividend payout ratio is distributing more of its earnings as dividends to common shareholders. It will have less cash and less total assets than a comparable firm with a lower payout ratio. The debt-to-assets ratio will be higher because total assets are lower, and the current ratio will be lower because cash is lower.
  Answer (A) is incorrect because the current ratio will be lower. Answer (C) is incorrect because the debt-to-assets ratio will be higher and the current ratio will be lower. Answer (D) is incorrect because the debt-to-assets ratio will be higher.

Question 39 is based on the following information. Alberto Corp. has common and preferred shares outstanding with the following characteristics:

	Common Shares	Preferred Shares
Number of shares outstanding	50,000	25,000
Dividends paid during the year	$100,000	$50,000
Year-end market price per share	$10	$5
Book value of equity	$500,000	$250,000

For the year just ended, the company had the following statement of income:

Sales revenue	$1,000,000
Cost of goods sold	(300,000)
Depreciation expense	(100,000)
Earnings before interest and tax	$ 600,000
Interest expense	(100,000)
Earnings before tax	$ 500,000
Tax expense	(250,000)
Net income	$ 250,000

39. Alberto Corp. has earnings per share of

A. $2.67

B. $3.33

C. $4.00

D. $5.00

Answer (C) is correct. *(CIA, adapted)*
REQUIRED: The company's EPS.
DISCUSSION: EPS equals the income available for distribution to common shareholders divided by the number of common shares outstanding, or $4.00 [($250,000 NI – $50,000 preferred dividends) ÷ 50,000 common shares].
Answer (A) is incorrect because $2.67 includes all outstanding shares, common and preferred, in the denominator. Answer (B) is incorrect because $3.33 fails to deduct the preferred dividends from the numerator and includes all outstanding shares in the denominator. Answer (D) is incorrect because $5.00 fails to deduct the preferred dividends from the numerator.

Question 40 is based on the following information. Presented below are partial year-end financial statement data for companies A and B.

	Company A	Company B		Company A	Company B
Cash	$100	$200	Sales	$600	$5,800
Accounts Receivable	unknown	100	Cost of Goods Sold	300	5,000
Inventories	unknown	100	Administrative Expenses	100	500
Net Fixed Assets	200	100	Depreciation Expense	100	100
Accounts Payable	100	50	Interest Expense	20	10
Long-Term Debt	200	50	Income Tax Expense	40	95
Common Stock	100	200	Net Income	40	95
Retained Earnings	150	100			

40. If Company A has 60 common shares outstanding, then it has a book value per share, to the nearest cent, of

A. $1.67

B. $2.50

C. $4.17

D. $5.00

Answer (C) is correct. *(CIA, adapted)*
REQUIRED: The book value per share of Company A.
DISCUSSION: The book value per share for Company A equals the sum of common stock and retained earnings, divided by the number of shares, or $4.17 [($100 + $150) ÷ 60].
Answer (A) is incorrect because $1.67 results if retained earnings is omitted from the numerator. Answer (B) is incorrect because $2.50 results if common stock is omitted from the numerator. Answer (D) is incorrect because $5.00 is the book value per share for Company B.

41. A company has 100,000 outstanding common shares with a market value of $20 per share. Dividends of $2 per share were paid in the current year and the company has a dividend payout ratio of 40%. The price to earnings ratio of the company is

   A. 2.5

   B. 4

   C. 10

   D. 50

Answer (B) is correct. *(CIA, adapted)*
   REQUIRED: The P-E ratio.
   DISCUSSION: The P-E ratio equals the share price divided by EPS. If the dividends per share equaled $2 and the dividend-payout ratio was 40%, EPS must have been $5 ($2 ÷ .4). Accordingly, the P-E ratio is 4 ($20 share price ÷ $5 EPS).
   Answer (A) is incorrect because 2.5 equals EPS divided by dividends per share. Answer (C) is incorrect because 10 equals share price divided by dividends per share. Answer (D) is incorrect because 50 equals price per share divided by the dividend-payout percentage.

42. The equity section of Smith Corporation's Statement of Financial Position is presented below.

Preferred stock, $100 par	$12,000,000
Common stock, $5 par	10,000,000
Paid-in capital in excess of par	18,000,000
Retained earnings	9,000,000
Net worth	$49,000,000

The book value per share of Smith Corporation's common stock is

   A. $18.50

   B. $5.00

   C. $14.00

   D. $100

Answer (A) is correct. *(CMA, adapted)*
   REQUIRED: The book value per share of common stock.
   DISCUSSION: The book value per common share equals the net assets (equity) attributable to common shareholders divided by the common shares outstanding, or $18.50 [($10,000,000 common stock + $18,000,000 additional paid-in capital + $9,000,000 RE) ÷ ($10,000,000 ÷ $5 par)].
   Answer (B) is incorrect because $5 is the par value per share. Answer (C) is incorrect because $14.00 fails to include retained earnings in the portion of equity attributable to common shareholders. Answer (D) is incorrect because $100 is the par value of a preferred share.

43. The Dawson Corporation projects the following for the year:

Earnings before interest and taxes	$35 million
Interest expense	$5 million
Preferred stock dividends	$4 million
Common stock dividend-payout ratio	30%
Common shares outstanding	2 million
Effective corporate income tax rate	40%

If Dawson Corporation's common stock is expected to trade at a price-earnings ratio of eight, the market price per share (to the nearest dollar) would be

   A. $104

   B. $56

   C. $72

   D. $68

Answer (B) is correct. *(CMA, adapted)*
   REQUIRED: The market price per share given the P-E ratio.
   DISCUSSION: Net income is $18,000,000 [($35,000,000 EBIT – $5,000,000 interest) × (1.0 – .4 tax rate)], and EPS is $7 [($18,000,000 NI – $4,000,000 preferred dividends) ÷ 2,000,000 common shares]. Consequently, the market price is $56 ($7 EPS × 8 P-E ratio).
   Answer (A) is incorrect because $104 ignores income taxes. Answer (C) is incorrect because $72 ignores the effect of preferred dividends. Answer (D) is incorrect because $68 ignores the deductibility of interest.

44. A company has purchased a $1,000, 7%, 5-year bond at par that pays interest annually. The discount factors for the present value of $1 at 7% for five periods are as follows:

Period	Factor
1	.935
2	.873
3	.816
4	.763
5	.713

For purposes of duration hedging, the duration of the bond is

A. 5.39 years.

B. 5.00 years.

C. 4.39 years.

D. 3.81 years.

Answer (C) is correct.   *(Publisher, adapted)*
REQUIRED: The duration of the bond.
DISCUSSION: Duration hedging involves hedging interest-rate risk by matching the duration and value of assets with the duration and value of liabilities. Duration is the weighted average of the times to interest and principal payments. If duration increases, the volatility of the price of the debt instrument increases. Duration is lower if the nominal rate on the instrument is higher because more of the return is received earlier. The formula for duration is as follows if C_T is the interest or principal payment, T is the time to the payment, n is the time to maturity, r is the yield to maturity, and V is the value of the instrument:

$$\sum_{t=1}^{n} \left[\frac{C_T \times T}{(1 + r)^T} \right] \div V$$

Because the expression $1 \div (1 + r)^T$ is the present value of $1, the weighted present values of the payments can be calculated as follows: $65.45 (1 period × $1,000 × 7% × .935), $122.22 (2 periods × $1,000 × 7% × .873), $171.36 (3 periods × $1,000 × 7% × .816), $213.64 (4 periods × $1,000 × 7% × .763), and $3,814.55 (5 periods × $1,000 × 107% × .713). The total is $4,387.22. The value of the bond is $1,000 {[[$70 × (.935 + .873 + .816 + .763 + .713)] + ($1,000 × .713)}}. Thus, the duration is approximately 4.39 years ($4,387.22 ÷ $1,000).
Answer (A) is incorrect because 5.39 years results from adding $1,000 to the numerator of the calculation. Answer (B) is incorrect because 5.00 years is the term of the bond. Answer (D) is incorrect because 3.81 years equals the weighted present value of the final payment divided by $1,000.

45. Essex Corporation is evaluating a lease that takes effect on March 1. The company must make eight equal payments, with the first payment due on March 1. The concept most relevant to the evaluation of the lease is the

A. Present value of an annuity due.

B. Present value of an ordinary annuity.

C. Future value of an annuity due.

D. Future value of an ordinary annuity.

Answer (A) is correct.   *(CMA, adapted)*
REQUIRED: The concept most relevant to evaluating a long-term lease given that the first payment is due at the inception of the lease.
DISCUSSION: An annuity is a series of cash flows or other economic benefits occurring at fixed intervals, ordinarily as a result of an investment. Present value is the value at a specified time of an amount or amounts to be paid or received later, discounted at some interest rate. In an annuity due, the payments occur at the beginning, rather than at the end, of the periods. Thus, the present value of an annuity due includes the initial payment at its undiscounted amount. Evaluation of an investment decision, e.g., a lease, that involves multi-period cash payments (an annuity) requires an adjustment for the time value of money. Because of the interest factor, a dollar today is worth more than a dollar in the future. Consequently, comparison of different investments requires restating their future benefits and costs in terms of present values. This lease should therefore be evaluated using the present value of an annuity due.
Answer (B) is incorrect because an ordinary annuity assumes that each payment occurs at the end of a period. Answer (C) is incorrect because future value is the converse of a present value. It is an amount accumulated in the future. Evaluation of a lease, however, necessitates calculation of a present value. Answer (D) is incorrect because future value is the converse of a present value. It is an amount accumulated in the future. Evaluation of a lease, however, necessitates calculation of a present value.

8.4 Derivatives and Other Financial Instruments

46. If a call option is "out-of-the-money,"

A. It is not worth exercising.

B. The value of the underlying asset is less than the exercise price.

C. The option no longer exists.

D. It is not worth exercising, and the value of the underlying asset is less than the exercise price.

Answer (D) is correct. *(Publisher, adapted)*
REQUIRED: The definition of "out-of-the-money."
DISCUSSION: When the value of the asset underlying a call option is less than the exercise price of the option, the option is "out-of-the-money," which means it is not worth exercising.
Answer (A) is incorrect because, although the call option is not worth exercising, the value of the underlying asset is also less than the exercise price. Answer (B) is incorrect because, although the value of the underlying asset is less than the exercise price, it is also not worth exercising. Answer (C) is incorrect because the option does exist; it is just not worth exercising.

47. The type of option that does not have the backing of stock is called a(n)

A. Covered option.

B. Unsecured option.

C. Naked option.

D. Put option.

Answer (C) is correct. *(Publisher, adapted)*
REQUIRED: The type of option that does not have the backing of stock.
DISCUSSION: A naked or uncovered option is a call option that does not have the backing of stock. Thus, the option writer will have to purchase the underlying stock if the call option is exercised.
Answer (A) is incorrect because a covered option is one that is written against stock held in the option writer's portfolio. Answer (B) is incorrect because an unsecured option is a nonsense term. Answer (D) is incorrect because a put option is an option that gives the owner the right to sell the underlying asset for a fixed price.

48. A contractual arrangement that gives the owner the right to buy or sell an asset at a fixed price at any moment in time before or on a specified date is a(n)

A. European option.

B. Foreign option.

C. Future option.

D. American option.

Answer (D) is correct. *(Publisher, adapted)*
REQUIRED: The type of option that can be exercised at any time before or on a specified date.
DISCUSSION: An American option is a contractual arrangement that gives the owner the right to buy or sell an asset at a fixed price at any moment in time before or on a specified date.
Answer (A) is incorrect because a European option is exercisable only at the expiration date. Answer (B) is incorrect because a foreign option is a nonsense term. Answer (C) is incorrect because, although an option can be exercised in the future, it is not called a future option.

49. The use of derivatives to either hedge or speculate results in

A. Increased risk regardless of motive.

B. Decreased risk regardless of motive.

C. Offsetting risk when hedging and increased risk when speculating.

D. Offsetting risk when speculating and increased risk when hedging.

Answer (C) is correct. *(Publisher, adapted)*
REQUIRED: The effects on risk of hedging and speculating.
DISCUSSION: Derivatives, including options and futures, are contracts between the parties who contract. Unlike stocks and bonds, they are not claims on business assets. A futures contract is entered into as either a speculation or a hedge. Speculation involves the assumption of risk in the hope of gaining from price movements. Hedging is the process of using offsetting commitments to minimize or avoid the impact of adverse price movements.
Answer (A) is incorrect because hedging decreases risk by using offsetting commitments that avoid the impact of adverse price movements. Answer (B) is incorrect because speculation involves the assumption of risk in the hope of gaining from price movements. Answer (D) is incorrect because speculating increases risk while hedging offsets risk.

50. A forward contract involves a commitment today to purchase a product

A. On a specific future date at a price to be determined some time in the future.

B. At some time during the current day at its present price.

C. On a specific future date at a price determined today.

D. Only when its price increases above its current exercise price.

Answer (C) is correct. *(Publisher, adapted)*
REQUIRED: The terms of a forward contract.
DISCUSSION: A forward contract is an executory contract in which the parties involved agree to the terms of a purchase and a sale, but performance is deferred. Accordingly, a forward contract involves a commitment today to purchase a product on a specific future date at a price determined today.
Answer (A) is incorrect because the price of a future contract is determined on the day of commitment, not some time in the future. Answer (B) is incorrect because performance is deferred in a future contract, and the price of the product is not necessarily its present price. The price can be any price determined on the day of commitment. Answer (D) is incorrect because a forward contract is a firm commitment to purchase a product. It is not based on a contingency. Also, a forward contract does not involve an exercise price (exercise price is in an option contract).

Questions 51 and 52 are based on the following information. AA Company has purchased one share of QQ Company common stock and one put option. It has also sold one call option. The options are written on one share of QQ Company common stock and have the same maturity date and exercise price. The exercise price ($40) is the same as the share price. Moreover, the options are exercisable only at the expiration date.

51. Assume that the value of a share of QQ Company common stock at the expiration date is either $30 or $45. The difference in the net payoff on the portfolio because of a difference in the stock price at the maturity date is

A. $10.00

B. $7.50

C. $5.00

D. $0

Answer (D) is correct. *(Publisher, adapted)*
REQUIRED: The difference in the net payoff on the portfolio because of a difference in the stock price at the maturity date.
DISCUSSION: If the stock price at the maturity date is $30, AA Company will have a share of stock worth $30 and a put option worth $10 ($40 exercise price – $30 stock price). The call option will be worthless. Hence, the net payoff is $40 ($30 + $10). If the stock price at the maturity date is $45, the share of stock will be worth $45, the put will be worthless, and the loss on the call will be $5 ($45 – $40). Thus, the net payoff will be $40 ($45 – $5). Consequently, the difference in the net payoff on the portfolio because of a difference in the stock price at the maturity date is $0 ($40 – $40). The portfolio has the same value at the maturity date regardless of the price of the stock.

52. Assuming the present value of the exercise price is $36 and the value of the call is $4.50, the value of the put in accordance with the put-call parity theorem is

A. $4.50

B. $4.00

C. $.50

D. $0

Answer (C) is correct. *(Publisher, adapted)*
REQUIRED: The value of the put in accordance with the put-call parity theorem.
DISCUSSION: For European options, given market equilibrium for all relevant prices (no arbitrage possibilities), equal exercise prices for the put and the call, and the same expiration date, the put-call parity theorem states that a fixed relationship applies to the market values of the put and call options on a security. For example, a strategy of selling one call option, buying one share of the stock, and buying one put option should result in a risk-free return. The gain (loss) from the stock and the put should equal the gain (loss) on the call. If VS is the value of the stock, VP is the value of the put, VC is the value of the call, and PVE is the present value of the exercise price (the time interval is the time to expiration), the formula for put-call parity may be stated as follows:

$$V_S + V_P - V_C = PV_E$$

Accordingly, the value of the put is $.50 ($36 + $4.50 – $40).
Answer (A) is incorrect because $4.50 is the value of the call. Answer (B) is incorrect because $4.00 is the difference between the exercise price and its present value. Answer (D) is incorrect because the put has a value of $.50.

53. An automobile company that uses the futures market to set the price of steel to protect a profit against price increases is an example of

A. A short hedge.

B. A long hedge.

C. Selling futures to protect the company from loss.

D. Selling futures to protect against price declines.

Answer (B) is correct. *(Publisher, adapted)*

REQUIRED: The example of the use of the futures market to protect a profit.

DISCUSSION: A change in prices can be minimized or avoided by hedging. Hedging is the process of using offsetting commitments to minimize or avoid the impact of adverse price movements. The automobile company desires to stabilize the price of steel so that its cost to the company will not rise and cut into profits. Accordingly, the automobile company uses the futures market to create a long hedge, which is a futures contract that is purchased to protect against price increases.

Answer (A) is incorrect because a short hedge is a futures contract that is sold to protect against price declines. The automobile company wishes to protect itself against price increases. Answer (C) is incorrect because the automobile company needs to purchase futures in order to protect itself from loss, not sell futures. Selling futures protects against price declines. Answer (D) is incorrect because it is the definition of a short hedge, which is used for avoiding price declines. The automobile company wants to protect itself against price increases.

54. If a corporation holds a forward contract for the delivery of U.S. Treasury bonds in 6 months and, during those 6 months, interest rates decline, at the end of the 6 months the value of the forward contract will have

A. Decreased.

B. Increased.

C. Remained constant.

D. Any of the answers may be correct, depending on the extent of the decline in interest rates.

Answer (B) is correct. *(Publisher, adapted)*

REQUIRED: The impact of an interest rate decline on the value of a forward contract.

DISCUSSION: Interest rate futures contracts involve risk-free bonds, such as U.S. Treasury bonds. When interest rates decrease over the period of a forward contract, the value of the bonds and the forward contract increase.

Answer (A) is incorrect because the value of the forward contract will increase when interest rates decrease. Answer (C) is incorrect because the value of the forward contract will increase when interest rates decrease. Answer (D) is incorrect because any decline in interest rates increases the value of the bonds.

55. A company wishes to price a call option written on a nondividend-paying stock. The current stock price is $50, the exercise price is $48, the risk-free interest rate is 5.0%, the option expires in 1 year, and the cumulative probabilities used to calculate the present values of the final stock price and the exercise price are .65 and .58, respectively. The company uses the Black-Scholes Option Pricing Model. If $e^{(-rt)}$ is .9515, the current value of the call option is

A. $6.02

B. $4.66

C. $4.02

D. $2.00

Answer (A) is correct. *(Publisher, adapted)*

REQUIRED: The current value of the call option according to the Black-Scholes Option Pricing Model.

DISCUSSION: The basic formula is

$$C = SN(d_1) - Ee^{(-rt)}N(d_2)$$

C is the current value of a call option with time t in years until expiration, S is the current stock price, N (d_i) is the cumulative probability that an i deviation less than d will occur in a standardized i normal distribution [N (d_i) is an area to the left i of d under the curve for the standard normal distribution], E is the call's exercise price, e is a constant (approximately 2.7183), and r is the annualized continuous risk-free rate of return. Thus, the value of the call is

$$
\begin{aligned}
C &= (\$50 \times .65) - \$48 \times 2.7183^{(-.05 \times 1)} \times .58 \\
&= \$32.50 - (\$48 \times .9515 \times .58) \\
&= \$32.50 - \$26.48 \\
&= \$6.02
\end{aligned}
$$

Answer (B) is incorrect because $4.66 results from omitting the term $e^{(-rt)}$ from the equation. Answer (C) is incorrect because $4.02 equals the estimated call price minus the difference between the current stock price and the exercise price. Answer (D) is incorrect because $2.00 is the difference between the current stock price and the exercise price.

56. How much must the stock be worth at expiration in order for a call holder to break even if the exercise price is $60 and the call premium was $3?

A. $57.00

B. $60.00

C. $61.50

D. $63.00

Answer (D) is correct. *(Publisher, adapted)*
    REQUIRED: The value of a stock that would result in a breakeven situation for the option holder.
    DISCUSSION: Because the call premium is $3, the stock price must be at least $63 ($60 exercise price + $3 call premium).
    Answer (A) is incorrect because $57 is the result of deducting the call premium from the exercise price. Answer (B) is incorrect because $60 is the result of failing to consider the impact of the call premium. Answer (C) is incorrect because the full call premium must be added to the exercise price.

8.5 Other Sources of Long-Term Financing

Questions 57 and 58 are based on the following information. The market price of Flesher Corporation's common stock is $100 per share, and each share gives its owner one subscription right. Five rights are required to purchase an additional share of common stock at the subscription price of $91 per share.

57. If the common stock is currently selling "rights-on," the value of a right is closest to, in theory,

A. $1.50

B. $1.80

C. $2.25

D. $9.00

Answer (A) is correct. *(Publisher, adapted)*
    REQUIRED: The theoretical value of a right.
    DISCUSSION: The formula for the value of a stock right when the stock price is rights-on follows.

$$\frac{P - S}{N + 1}$$

If P is the value of a share rights-on, S is the subscription price, and N is the number of rights needed to buy a share, the value of a right is

$$\frac{\$100 - \$91}{6} = \$1.50$$

Answer (B) is incorrect because $1.80 results from a failure to adjust for the decline in share value once the rights are issued. Answer (C) is incorrect because $2.25 is based on deducting 1 from N rather than adding 1. Answer (D) is incorrect because $9.00 results from a failure to consider that five rights are needed to purchase one share.

58. The value of one share of Flesher's common stock when it goes "ex-rights," in theory, is closest to

A. $91.00

B. $98.20

C. $98.50

D. $100.00

Answer (C) is correct. *(Publisher, adapted)*
    REQUIRED: The theoretical value of a share after the rights distribution.
    DISCUSSION: The stock will decline in value by the value of the right. The theoretical value of a right is $1.50. Thus, the value of the stock should decline to $98.50 ($100.00 – $1.50).
    Answer (A) is incorrect because $91 is the subscription price. Answer (B) is incorrect because $98.20 is based on the assumption that a right is worth $1.80, as a result of dividing by N instead of N + 1. Answer (D) is incorrect because the value of the stock will decline with the distribution of the rights.

59. A major use of warrants in financing is to

A. Lower the cost of debt.

B. Avoid dilution of earnings per share.

C. Maintain managerial control.

D. Permit the buy-back of bonds before maturity.

Answer (A) is correct. *(CMA, adapted)*
REQUIRED: The major use of warrants in financing.
DISCUSSION: Warrants are long-term options that give holders the right to buy common stock in the future at a specific price. If the market price goes up, the holders of warrants will exercise their rights to buy stock at the special price. If the market price does not exceed the exercise price, the warrants will lapse. Issuers of debt sometimes attach stock purchase warrants to debt instruments as an inducement to investors. The investor then has the security of fixed-return debt plus the possibility for large gains if stock prices increase significantly. If warrants are attached, debt can sell at an interest rate slightly lower than the market rate.
Answer (B) is incorrect because outstanding warrants dilute earnings per share. They are included in the denominator of the EPS calculation even if they have not been exercised.
Answer (C) is incorrect because warrants can, if exercised, result in a dilution of management's holdings. Answer (D) is incorrect because a call provision in a bond indenture, not the use of warrants, permits the buyback of bonds.

60. A technique used by stock promoters to combine several small businesses in the same industry into a company large enough to initiate an initial public offering (IPO) is a

A. Sale-leaseback.

B. Roll-up.

C. DRIP.

D. ESOP.

Answer (B) is correct. *(Publisher, adapted)*
REQUIRED: The technique used to combine several small companies for purposes of an IPO.
DISCUSSION: A roll-up is a technique used by an underwriter to combine several mom-and-pop type businesses in the same industry into a company large enough for an IPO.
Answer (A) is incorrect because a sale-leaseback involves a sale of individual assets--not an entire company. Answer (C) is incorrect because DRIP is an acronym for a dividend reinvestment plan. Answer (D) is incorrect because an ESOP is used to give employees an ownership interest in a corporation.

61. Gulf Coast Magnetic Corporation (GCMC) is negotiating an intermediate-term loan to finance a joint project with another company. GCMC intends to sell its share of the venture to its partner after 6 years. The lending bank has therefore agreed to structure the loan with a balloon payment at that time. The amount of the loan is $100,000. GCMC will make level quarterly payments at an annual rate of 8%. Because the loan is to be only partially amortized, the payments are based on a full amortization life of 10 years. Which one of the following statements in regard to this loan is true? (Round your answer to the nearest dollar.)

A. The quarterly payment is $3,726.

B. The quarterly payment is $5,288.

C. The balloon payment is $12,107.

D. The balloon payment is $49,636.

Answer (D) is correct. *(CMA, adapted)*
REQUIRED: The true statement about a loan with a balloon payment.
DISCUSSION: The level quarterly payments based on a full-amortization life of 10 years constitute an annuity with a present value of $100,000. Assuming payments are due at the end of each quarter, the payment equals $100,000 divided by the present value interest factor for an ordinary annuity of 40 periods (4 × 10 years) at 2% (8% ÷ 4), or $3,655.64 ($100,000 ÷ 27.355). The balloon payment is the present value of the remaining payments. It equals the quarterly payment times the present value interest factor for an ordinary annuity of 16 periods [(10 years – 6 years) × 4] at 2% (8% ÷ 4), or $49,636 ($3,655.64 × 13.578).
Answer (A) is incorrect because the quarterly payment is $3,655.64. Answer (B) is incorrect because the quarterly payment is $3,655.64. Answer (C) is incorrect because $12,107 equals the quarterly payment times the present value interest factor for 4 periods at 8%.

62. The characteristics of venture capital include all of the following except

- A. Initial private placement for the majority of issues.
- B. A minimum holding period of 5 years for new securities.
- C. The use of common stock for most placements.
- D. A lack of liquidity for a period of time.

Answer (B) is correct. *(CMA, adapted)*
REQUIRED: The item that is not a characteristic of venture capital.
DISCUSSION: The concept of venture (risk) capital applies to new enterprises that might not be able to obtain funds in the usual capital markets because of the riskiness of new products. Such companies sometimes try to place securities, normally common stock, with venture capital firms. These are normally private placements of the securities and thus not subject to SEC regulation. The venture capitalists risk low liquidity for their investments until the young corporation becomes successful. The payoff may be substantial if the company does succeed. There is no minimum holding period for venture capital investments.
Answer (A) is incorrect because venture capital investments are typically private placements. Answer (C) is incorrect because common stock is usually a part of most venture capital deals. Venture capitalists want large payoffs in exchange for the risk assumed. Answer (D) is incorrect because venture capital investments typically are not liquid for a substantial time after the investment is made.

63. Shelf registration of a security is a procedure allowing a firm to

- A. Register an issue price on its securities for a specified period of time.
- B. Control both the issue price and the secondary market price of its securities by registering these prices for a specified period of time.
- C. Register a security for a specified period of time and then sell the securities on a piecemeal basis.
- D. Freeze the market price of its new issues of securities for a specified period of time.

Answer (C) is correct. *(CMA, adapted)*
REQUIRED: The purpose of shelf registration.
DISCUSSION: SEC Rule 415 allows corporations to file registration statements covering a stipulated amount of securities that may be issued over the 2-year effective period of the statement. The securities are placed on the shelf and issued at an opportune moment without the necessity of filing a new registration statement, observing a 20-day waiting period, or preparing a new prospectus. The issuer is required only to provide updating amendments or to refer investors to quarterly and annual statements filed with the SEC. Shelf registration is most advantageous to large corporations that frequently offer securities to the public.
Answer (A) is incorrect because prices are not registered. Answer (B) is incorrect because prices are not registered. Answer (D) is incorrect because the market price of securities is not frozen by shelf registration.

Use Gleim's ***CMA Test Prep*** for interactive testing with **over 2,000 additional multiple-choice questions**!

STUDY UNIT NINE
COST OF CAPITAL

(6 pages of outline)

This study unit is the **third of five** on **corporate finance**. The relative weight assigned to this major topic in Part 3 of the exam is **25%** at **skill level B** (four skill types required). The five study units are

Study Unit 7:   Risk and Return
Study Unit 8:   Financial Instruments
Study Unit 9:   Cost of Capital
Study Unit 10:   Managing Current Assets
Study Unit 11:   Financing Current Assets

After studying the outline and answering the multiple-choice questions, you will have the skills necessary to address the following topics listed in the IMA's Learning Outcome Statements:

Part 3 – Section C.3. Cost of capital

The candidate should be able to:

    a.   define the cost of capital and demonstrate an understanding of its applications in capital structure decisions

    b.   determine the weighted average (historical) cost of capital and the cost of its individual components

    c.   calculate the marginal cost of capital and demonstrate an understanding of the significance of using the marginal cost as opposed to the historical cost

    d.   demonstrate an understanding of the use of the cost of capital in capital investment decisions

    e.   demonstrate an understanding of how income taxes impact capital structure and capital investment decisions

9.1 COST OF CAPITAL AND ITS COMPONENTS

    1.   A firm's **cost of capital** is the price, in both dollar terms and opportunity cost, of raising funds. SMA 4A, *Cost of Capital*, defines it as "a composite of the cost of various sources of funds comprising a firm's capital structure."

        a.   Managers must know the firm's cost of capital when making investment (long-term funding) decisions because investments with a return higher than the cost of capital will increase the value of the firm (shareholders' wealth).

        b.   The theory underlying the cost of capital applies to new, long-term funding because long-term funds finance **long-term investments**. Long-term investment decisions are typically made using the cost of capital to discount future cash flows.

            1)   Working capital and other temporary needs are met with short-term funds. Thus, cost of capital is of less concern for short-term funding.

2.   The **weighted-average cost of capital (WACC)** weights the cost of each debt and equity component by the percentage of that component in the financial structure.

   a.   The **cost of debt** is the after-tax interest rate of the debt.

   Interest rate × (1 - Marginal tax rate)

   1)   The after-tax rate is used because interest paid is a tax deduction to the firm. Hence, as tax rates go up, debt becomes a more attractive financing option.

   b.   The **cost of preferred stock** includes flotation costs necessary to offer the stock to the investing public.

   Dividend per share ÷ Net issuance cost per share

   1)   Because preferred dividends paid are not deductible by the firm, the tax rate is not taken into account.

   c.   The **cost of new external common equity** factors in the return that potential shareholders expect.

   Dollar return demanded by investors ÷ Net issuance cost per share

   1)   An issue of new common stock is used mostly by young, growing companies. Mature firms rarely issue new common stock to the general public because of the issue costs involved and the depressing influence a new issue can have on the stock's price.

   d.   The **cost of retained earnings** is an opportunity cost, i.e., the rate that investors can earn elsewhere on investments of comparable risk.

   1)   If the firm is not able to generate a shareholder's required rate of return, the retained earnings should be paid out in the form of dividends so that the shareholders can find their own, higher-return investments.

   e.   **Providers of equity capital** are exposed to **more risk** than are lenders because the firm is not obligated to pay them a return. Also, in case of liquidation, equity investors trail creditors in priority.

   1)   Thus, **equity financing is more expensive than debt** because equity investors require a higher return to compensate for the greater risk assumed.

   f.   EXAMPLE: Note that short-term debt is not part of a firm's capital structure.

	(1)	(2)	(3)	(4)	(5)	(3) × (5)
					Weight	
		Interest or	After-Tax Rate		(Proportion of	Weighted-
	Carrying	Dividend	or Expected	Market	Total Market	Average Cost
Component	Amount	Rate	Return	Value	Value)	of Capital
Bonds Payable	$ 2,000,000	8.5%	7.4%	$ 2,200,000	0.1000	0.7400%
Preferred Stock	4,000,000	14.0%	10.0%	4,600,000	0.2091	2.0909%
Common Stock	12,000,000		16.0%	14,000,000	0.6364	10.1818%
Retained Earnings	1,200,000		16.0%	1,200,000	0.0545	0.8727%
Totals	$19,200,000			$22,000,000	1.0000	13.8855%

3.   Standard financial theory provides a model for the **optimal capital structure** of every firm. This model holds that shareholder wealth-maximization results from **minimizing the weighted-average cost of capital**.

   a.   Thus, the focus of management should **not** be on **maximizing earnings per share**. EPS can be increased by taking on debt, but debt increases risk.

   1)   The optimal capital structure usually involves some debt but not 100% debt.

b. The relevant relationships are depicted below:

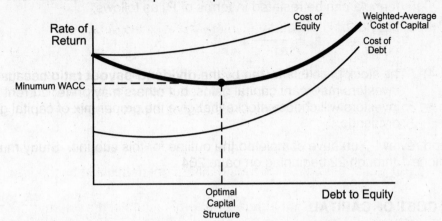

c. Ordinarily, firms cannot identify this optimal point precisely. Thus, they should attempt to find an optimal range for the capital structure.

d. The **economic value of a firm** is expressed by the following formula:

$$V = \sum_{t=1}^{n} \frac{CF_t}{(1 + k)^t}$$

Where:
V = Value
CF = Net cash flow
k = The discount rate
t = Time

e. The **dividend growth model** estimates the **cost of retained earnings** using the dividends per share, the expected growth rate, and the market price. To justify retention of earnings, management must expect a return at least equal to the dividend yield plus a growth rate.

1) The formula for calculating the cost of retained earnings is

$$R = \frac{D_1}{P_0} + G$$

Where:
P_0 = current price
D_1 = next dividend
R = required rate of return
G = growth rate in dividends per share (but the model assumes that the dividend-payout ratio, retention rate, and therefore the EPS growth rate are constant).

   a) EXAMPLE: If a company's dividend is expected to be $4 while the market price is $50 and the dividend is expected to grow at a constant rate of 6%, the required rate of return would be ($4 ÷ $50) + .06, or 14%.

2) To determine the **cost of new common stock** (external equity), the model is altered to incorporate the **flotation cost**. As the flotation cost rises, R increases accordingly.

$$R = \frac{D_1}{P_0(1 - Flotation\ cost)} + G$$

3) The dividend growth model is also used for **stock price evaluation**. The formula can be restated in terms of P_0 as follows:

$$P_0 = \frac{D_1}{R - G}$$

4) The stock price is affected by the **dividend-payout ratio** because some investors may want capital gains, but others may prefer current income. Thus, investors will choose stocks that give the proper mix of capital gains and dividends.

4. Stop and review! You have completed the outline for this subunit. Study multiple-choice questions 1 through 22 beginning on page 264.

9.2 MARGINAL COST OF CAPITAL

1. A firm cannot continue to raise unlimited amounts of new funds at its historical cost of capital. At some point, the costs of servicing new sources of funding will increase a firm's cost of capital.

   a. The **marginal cost of capital (MCC)** is the cost to a firm of the next dollar of new capital raised.

   b. EXAMPLE: The company depicted in the schedule in item 2.f. in Subunit 9.1 has determined that it requires $2,000,000 of new funding to fulfill its plans.

      1) The simplest source of new funding is retained earnings, but they are insufficient. The additional $800,000 will have to come from another source.

         a) If the company issues new bonds, the firm's debt-to-equity ratio will be increased, revealing the company to be a riskier investment, forcing a higher interest rate than the one on the currently outstanding bonds.

         b) If the company issues new preferred stock, the investors will demand a priority dividend.

         c) If the company issues new preferred or common stock, issue costs will be involved.

      2) Clearly, the company's cost of capital will be its current marginal rate of 13.8855% for the $1,200,000 of retained earnings, but will shift to a higher marginal rate for the next dollar after that.

   c. This phenomenon can be depicted as follows:

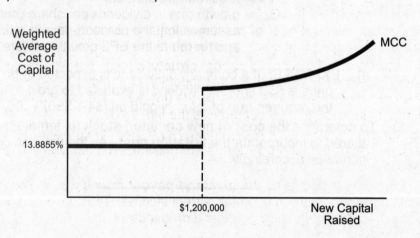

2.   The **marginal efficiency of investment** is the decrease in return on additional dollars of
capital investment because the most profitable investments are made initially.

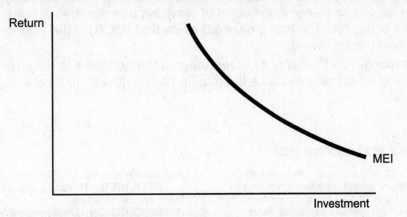

a.   Combining the MCC and MEI curves highlights the equilibrium investment level for the
firm (Q*) at a particular interest rate (I) and given capital budget.

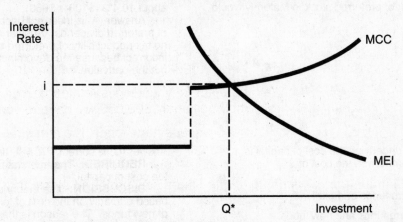

3.   Stop and review! You have completed the outline for this subunit. Study multiple-choice
questions 23 through 27 on page 272.

9.3 CORE CONCEPTS

Cost of Capital and Its Components

- The **weighted-average cost of capital** weights the cost of each debt and equity component
  by the percentage of that component in the financial structure.

- Each **component of the firm's capital structure** (debt, preferred stock, common stock,
  retained earnings) is weighted for its proportion of the total. These weights are then
  applied to each component's after-tax rate (for debt) or expected rate of return (for equity).
  The total of the resulting percentages is the firm's WACC.

- Standard financial theory provides a model for the **optimal capital structure** of every firm.
  This model holds that shareholder wealth-maximization results from minimizing the
  weighted-average cost of capital.

- The stock price is affected by the **dividend-payout ratio** because some investors may want
  capital gains, but others may prefer current income. Thus, investors will choose stocks that
  give the proper mix of capital gains and dividends.

Marginal Cost of Capital

- A firm cannot continue to raise unlimited amounts of new funds at its historical cost of capital. At some point, the costs of servicing new sources of funding will increase a firm's cost of capital. The **marginal cost of capital (MCC)** is the cost to a firm of the next dollar of new capital raised.

- The **marginal efficiency of investment** is the decrease in return on additional dollars of capital investment because the most profitable investments are made initially.

QUESTIONS

9.1 Cost of Capital and Its Components

1. Maloney, Inc.'s $1,000 par value preferred stock paid its $100 per share annual dividend on April 4 of the current year. The preferred stock's current market price is $960 a share on the date of the dividend distribution. Maloney's marginal tax rate (combined federal and state) is 40%, and the firm plans to maintain its current capital structure relationship. The component cost of preferred stock to Maloney would be closest to

A. 6%

B. 6.25%

C. 10%

D. 10.4%

Answer (D) is correct. *(Publisher, adapted)*
REQUIRED: The component cost of preferred stock in the firm's capital structure.
DISCUSSION: Dividends on preferred stock are not deductible for tax purposes; therefore, there is no adjustment for tax savings. The annual dividend on preferred stock is $100 when the price of the stock is $960. This results in a cost of about 10.4% ($100 ÷ $960).
Answer (A) is incorrect because there is no tax deductibility of preferred dividends. Answer (B) is incorrect because there is no tax deductibility of preferred dividends. Answer (C) is incorrect because the denominator is the current market price, not the par value.

2. The theory underlying the cost of capital is primarily concerned with the cost of

A. Long-term funds and old funds.

B. Short-term funds and new funds.

C. Long-term funds and new funds.

D. Short-term funds and old funds.

Answer (C) is correct. *(CMA, adapted)*
REQUIRED: The true statement about the theory underlying the cost of capital.
DISCUSSION: The theory underlying the cost of capital is based primarily on the cost of long-term funds and the acquisition of new funds. The reason is that long-term funds are used to finance long-term investments. For an investment alternative to be viable, the return on the investment must be greater than the cost of the funds used. The objective in short-term borrowing is different. Short-term loans are used to meet working capital needs and not to finance long-term investments.
Answer (A) is incorrect because the concern is with the cost of new funds; the cost of old funds is a sunk cost and of no relevance for decision-making purposes. Answer (B) is incorrect because the cost of short-term funds is not usually a concern for investment purposes. Answer (D) is incorrect because the cost of old funds is a sunk cost and of no relevance for decision-making purposes. Similarly, short-term funds are used for working capital or other temporary purposes, and there is less concern with the cost of capital and the way it compares with the return earned on the assets borrowed.

3. When calculating the cost of capital, the cost assigned to retained earnings should be

A. Zero.

B. Lower than the cost of external common equity.

C. Equal to the cost of external common equity.

D. Higher than the cost of external common equity.

Answer (B) is correct. *(CIA, adapted)*
REQUIRED: The cost assigned to retained earnings when calculating cost of capital.
DISCUSSION: Newly issued or external common equity is more costly than retained earnings. The company incurs issuance costs when raising new, outside funds.
Answer (A) is incorrect because the cost of retained earnings is the rate of return shareholders require on equity capital the firm obtains by retaining earnings. The opportunity cost of retained funds will be positive. Answer (C) is incorrect because retained earnings will always be less costly than external equity financing. Earnings retention does not require the payment of issuance costs. Answer (D) is incorrect because retained earnings will always be less costly than external equity financing. Earnings retention does not require the payment of issuance costs.

4. A preferred stock is sold for $101 per share, has a face value of $100 per share, underwriting fees of $5 per share, and annual dividends of $10 per share. If the tax rate is 40%, the cost of funds (capital) for the preferred stock is

A. 4.2%

B. 6.2%

C. 10.0%

D. 10.4%

Answer (D) is correct. *(CMA, adapted)*
REQUIRED: The cost of capital for a preferred stock issue.
DISCUSSION: Because the dividends on preferred stock are not deductible for tax purposes, the effect of income taxes is ignored. Thus, the relevant calculation is to divide the $10 annual dividend by the quantity of funds received at the time the stock is issued. In this case, the funds received equal $96 ($101 selling price – $5 underwriting fee). Thus, the cost of capital is 10.4% ($10 ÷ $96).
Answer (A) is incorrect because the 4.2% figure can be obtained only by incorrectly treating the dividends as deductible. Answer (B) is incorrect because the 6.2% figure can be obtained only by treating the dividends as deductible. Answer (C) is incorrect because 10% can be obtained only by basing the calculation on par value instead of funds received.

5. Osgood Products has announced that it plans to finance future investments so that the firm will achieve an optimum capital structure. Which one of the following corporate objectives is consistent with this announcement?

A. Maximize earnings per share.

B. Minimize the cost of debt.

C. Maximize the net worth of the firm.

D. Minimize the cost of equity.

Answer (C) is correct. *(CMA, adapted)*
REQUIRED: The consistent corporate objective.
DISCUSSION: Financial structure is the composition of the financing sources of the assets of a firm. Traditionally, the financial structure consists of current liabilities, long-term debt, retained earnings, and stock. For most firms, the optimum structure includes a combination of debt and equity. Debt is cheaper than equity, but excessive use of debt increases the firm's risk and drives up the weighted-average cost of capital.
Answer (A) is incorrect because the maximization of EPS may not always suggest the best capital structure. Answer (B) is incorrect because the minimization of debt cost may not be optimal; as long as the firm can earn more on debt capital than it pays in interest, debt financing may be indicated. Answer (D) is incorrect because minimizing the cost of equity may signify overly conservative management.

6. In referring to the graph of a firm's cost of capital, if e is the current position, which one of the following statements best explains the saucer or U-shaped curve?

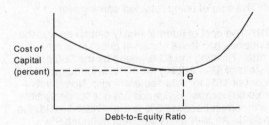

A. The composition of debt and equity does not affect the firm's cost of capital.

B. The cost of capital is almost always favorably influenced by increases in financial leverage.

C. The cost of capital is almost always negatively influenced by increases in financial leverage.

D. Use of at least some debt financing will enhance the value of the firm.

Answer (D) is correct. *(CMA, adapted)*
REQUIRED: The best explanation of the U-shaped curve in a cost-of-capital graph.
DISCUSSION: The U-shaped curve indicates that the cost of capital is quite high when the debt-to-equity ratio is quite low. As debt increases, the cost of capital declines as long as the cost of debt is less than that of equity. Eventually, the decline in the cost of capital levels off because the cost of debt ultimately rises as more debt is used. Additional increases in debt (relative to equity) will then increase the cost of capital. The implication is that some debt is present in the optimal capital structure because the cost of capital initially declines when debt is added. However, a point is reached at which debt becomes excessive and the cost of capital begins to rise.
Answer (A) is incorrect because the composition of the capital structure affects the cost of capital since the components have different costs. Answer (B) is incorrect because the cost of debt does not remain constant as financial leverage increases. Eventually, that cost also increases. Answer (C) is incorrect because increased leverage is initially favorable.

Questions 7 through 12 are based on the following information. The FLF Corporation is preparing to evaluate capital expenditure proposals for the coming year. Because the firm employs discounted cash flow methods, the cost of capital for the firm must be estimated. The following information for FLF Corporation is provided:

- The market price of common stock is $60 per share.
- The dividend next year is expected to be $3 per share.
- Expected growth in dividends is a constant 10%.
- New bonds can be issued at face value with a 10% coupon rate.

- The current capital structure of 40% long-term debt and 60% equity is considered to be optimal.
- Anticipated earnings to be retained in the coming year are $3 million.
- The firm has a 40% marginal tax rate.

7. The after-tax cost to FLF Corporation of the new bond issue is

A. 4%

B. 6%

C. 10%

D. 14%

Answer (B) is correct. *(Publisher, adapted)*
REQUIRED: The after-tax cost of issuing bonds.
DISCUSSION: Because the bonds are issued at their face value, the pretax effective rate is 10%. However, interest is deductible for tax purposes, so the government absorbs 40% of the cost, leaving a 6% after-tax cost.
Answer (A) is incorrect because 4% assumes a 60% tax rate. Answer (C) is incorrect because 10% is the before-tax rate. Answer (D) is incorrect because the after-tax cost will be less than the effective before-tax rate.

8. If FLF Corporation must assume a 20% flotation cost on new stock issuances, what is the cost of new common stock?

A. 6.25%

B. 15%

C. 16.25%

D. 10%

Answer (C) is correct. *(Publisher, adapted)*
REQUIRED: The cost of new issuances of common stock given flotation costs.
DISCUSSION: The company will receive only 80% of the $60 market price, or $48. Consequently, the dividend yield is 6.25% ($3 ÷ $48). Adding the 10% growth rate produces a cost of new equity capital of 16.25%.
Answer (A) is incorrect because 6.25% ignores the dividend growth rate. Answer (B) is incorrect because 15% ignores the flotation costs. Answer (D) is incorrect because 10% is the dividend growth rate.

9. The cost of using FLF Corporation retained earnings for financing is

A. 5%

B. 9%

C. 10%

D. 15%

Answer (D) is correct. *(Publisher, adapted)*
REQUIRED: The cost of using retained earnings for financing.
DISCUSSION: The cost of internal equity capital equals the dividend yield (dividends per share ÷ market price) plus the dividend growth rate. Dividing the $3 dividend by the $60 market price results in a yield of 5%. Adding the 10% dividend growth rate produces a cost of 15% for retained earnings. No adjustment is made for taxes because dividends are not tax deductible.
Answer (A) is incorrect because 5% is the dividend yield; the growth rate is ignored. Answer (B) is incorrect because 9% would be the after-tax cost if dividends were deductible. Answer (C) is incorrect because 10% is the dividend growth rate; it ignores the dividend yield.

10. The maximum capital expansion that FLF Corporation can support in the coming year without resorting to external equity financing is

A. $2 million.

B. $3 million.

C. $5 million.

D. Cannot determine from the information given.

Answer (C) is correct. *(Publisher, adapted)*
REQUIRED: The maximum capital expansion that can be supported without resorting to external equity financing.
DISCUSSION: The current optimal capital structure is 40% debt and 60% equity. The $3 million to be retained from earnings in the coming year represents the equity portion of the maximum new capital outlay. To retain the optimal capital structure, $2 million of debt must be added to the $3 million of retained earnings. Hence, the maximum capital expansion is $5 million.
Answer (A) is incorrect because $2 million is the amount of debt that must be added to maintain the optimal structure. Answer (B) is incorrect because $3 million is the amount of earnings retained. Answer (D) is incorrect because the amount of $5 million can be calculated.

11. Without prejudice to your answers from any other questions, assume that the after-tax cost of debt financing is 10%, the cost of retained earnings is 14%, and the cost of new common stock is 16%. If capital expansion needs to be $7 million for the coming year, what is the after-tax weighted-average cost of capital to FLF Corporation?

    A. 11.14%

    B. 12.74%

    C. 13.6%

    D. 16%

Answer (B) is correct. *(Publisher, adapted)*
    REQUIRED: The after-tax weighted-average cost of capital given the amount of the budget.
    DISCUSSION: To maintain a capital structure of 40% debt and 60% equity, the $7 million total must consist of $2.8 million of debt and $4.2 million of equity. The equity will consist of $3 million of retained earnings and $1.2 million of new stock. The weighted-average cost of the three sources of new capital is determined as follows:

$3,000,000 ÷ $7,000,000 × 14% =   6.00%
$1,200,000 ÷ $7,000,000 × 16% =   2.74%
$2,800,000 ÷ $7,000,000 × 10% =   4.00%
                                    12.74%

    Answer (A) is incorrect because 11.14% assumes a tax adjustment for the cost of debt, but the 10% rate is an after-tax amount. Answer (C) is incorrect because 13.6% assumes the equity consists solely of new common stock. Answer (D) is incorrect because 16% is the cost of new common stock.

12. Without prejudice to your answers from any other questions, assume that the after-tax cost of debt financing is 10%, the cost of retained earnings is 14%, and the cost of new common stock is 16%. What is the marginal cost of capital to FLF Corporation for any projected capital expansion in excess of $7 million?

    A. 10%

    B. 12.74%

    C. 13.6%

    D. 16%

Answer (C) is correct. *(Publisher, adapted)*
    REQUIRED: The marginal cost of capital after projects exceed the capital budget.
    DISCUSSION: For this calculation, the weighted-average cost of capital is based on the 16% cost of new common stock and the 10% cost of debt. Retained earnings will not be considered because the amount available has been exhausted. Thus, the weighted average of any additional capital required will be 13.6% [(60% × 16% cost of new equity) + (40% × 10% cost of new debt)].
    Answer (A) is incorrect because 10% is the cost of debt capital. Answer (B) is incorrect because 12.74% is the weighted-average cost of capital calculated for a $7 million budget. Answer (D) is incorrect because 16% is the cost of new common stock.

13. Global Company Press has $150 par value preferred stock with a market price of $120 a share. The organization pays a $15 per share annual dividend. Global's current marginal tax rate is 40%. Looking to the future, the company anticipates maintaining its current capital structure. What is the component cost of preferred stock to Global?

    A. 4%

    B. 5%

    C. 10%

    D. 12.5%

Answer (D) is correct. *(Publisher, adapted)*
    REQUIRED: The cost of preferred stock.
    DISCUSSION: The cost of preferred stock is the preferred dividend divided by the price. No tax adjustment is necessary because dividends are not deductible. If the market price is $120 when the dividend is $15, the cost of preferred capital is 12.5% ($15 ÷ $120).
    Answer (A) is incorrect because the preferred stock dividend is not deductible for tax purposes. Answer (B) is incorrect because the preferred stock dividend is not deductible for tax purposes. Answer (C) is incorrect because the denominator is the market price, not the par value.

Questions 14 through 17 are based on the following information.

Williams, Inc. is interested in measuring its overall cost of capital and has gathered the following data. Under the terms described as follows, the company can sell unlimited amounts of all instruments.

- Williams can raise cash by selling $1,000, 8%, 20-year bonds with annual interest payments. In selling the issue, an average premium of $30 per bond would be received, and the firm must pay flotation costs of $30 per bond. The after-tax cost of funds is estimated to be 4.8%.

- Williams can sell $8 preferred stock at par value, $105 per share. The cost of issuing and selling the preferred stock is expected to be $5 per share.

- Williams' common stock is currently selling for $100 per share. The firm expects to pay cash dividends of $7 per share next year, and the dividends are expected to remain constant. The stock will have to be underpriced by $3 per share, and flotation costs are expected to amount to $5 per share.

- Williams expects to have available $100,000 of retained earnings in the coming year; once these retained earnings are exhausted, the firm will use new common stock as the form of common stock equity financing.

- Williams' preferred capital structure is

Long-term debt	30%
Preferred stock	20%
Common stock	50%

14. The cost of funds from the sale of common stock for Williams, Inc. is

A. 7.0%

B. 7.6%

C. 7.4%

D. 8.1%

Answer (B) is correct. *(CMA, adapted)*
REQUIRED: The percentage cost of capital from the sale of common stock.
DISCUSSION: According to the Gordon growth model, the three elements required to calculate the cost of equity capital are (1) the dividends per share, (2) the expected growth rate, and (3) the market price of the stock. If flotation costs are incurred when issuing new stock, they are deducted from the market price to arrive at the amount of capital the corporation will actually receive. Accordingly, the $100 selling price is reduced by the $3 discount and the $5 flotation costs to arrive at the $92 to be received for the stock. Because the dividend is not expected to increase in future years, no growth factor is included in the calculation. Thus, the cost of the common stock is 7.6% ($7 dividend ÷ $92).
Answer (A) is incorrect because the 7.0% figure would be correct only if $100 were received from the sale of the stock. Answer (C) is incorrect because 7.4% would be correct only if the stock could be sold without giving a $3 discount. Answer (D) is incorrect because 8.1% would be correct only if the amount received were about $86 or if some growth factor were assumed.

15. The cost of funds from retained earnings for Williams, Inc. is

A. 7.0%

B. 7.6%

C. 7.4%

D. 8.1%

Answer (A) is correct. *(CMA, adapted)*
REQUIRED: The percentage cost of funds from using retained earnings as a capital source.
DISCUSSION: The three elements required to calculate the cost of equity capital are (1) the dividends per share, (2) the expected growth rate, and (3) the market price of the stock. Because growth is not expected, the calculation is simply to divide the dividend of $7 by the $100 market price of the stock to arrive at a cost of equity capital of 7%.
Answer (B) is incorrect because 7.6% would be the cost of new equity capital from selling stock if the stock resulted in proceeds of $92 per share. Answer (C) is incorrect because 7.4% would be correct only if new stock were sold and resulted in proceeds of $95 per share. Answer (D) is incorrect because dividing the $7 dividend by the $100 market price of the stock produces a ratio of 7%, not 8.1%.

16. If Williams, Inc. needs a total of $200,000, the firm's weighted-average cost of capital would be

A. 19.8%

B. 4.8%

C. 6.5%

D. 6.8%

Answer (C) is correct.   *(CMA, adapted)*
REQUIRED: The weighted-average cost of capital assuming that the firm needs a total of $200,000.
DISCUSSION: Williams' preferred capital structure is 50% common stock. However, $100,000 of retained earnings (50% of the required $200,000 of capital) will be used before any common stock is issued. Thus, the weighted-average cost of capital will be determined based on the respective costs of the bonds, preferred stock, and retained earnings. The cost of the bonds is given as 4.8%, the cost of the preferred stock is 8%, and the cost of the retained earnings is 7% ($7 dividend ÷ $100 market price of the common stock). These three costs are then weighted by the preferred capital structure ratios:

30% × 4.8%	=	1.44%
20% × 8.0%	=	1.60%
50% × 7.0%	=	3.50%
Total		6.54%

Rounding to the nearest tenth produces the correct answer of 6.5%.
Answer (A) is incorrect because 19.8% represents the unweighted sum of each of the three elements of cost. Answer (B) is incorrect because 4.8% is the cost of the long-term debt. All funding will not be obtained from debt because the firm wants to maintain a capital structure in which debt represents only 30% of the total capital. Answer (D) is incorrect because the 6.8% figure can only be obtained if new stock is sold. New stock will not be sold because the retained earnings can be used at a lower cost, and there is no need to sell stock when the total capital required is only $200,000.

17. If Williams, Inc. needs a total of $1,000,000, the firm's weighted-average cost of capital would be

A. 6.8%

B. 4.8%

C. 6.5%

D. 27.4%

Answer (A) is correct.   *(CMA, adapted)*
REQUIRED: The weighted-average cost of capital if the firm needs $1,000,000 in total capital.
DISCUSSION: The cost of the bonds is given as 4.8%. The cost of the preferred stock is 8% ($8 dividend ÷ $100), the cost of new common stock is 7.6% ($7 dividend ÷ $92 proceeds), and the cost of the retained earnings is 7% ($7 dividend ÷ $100 market price). These four costs are then weighted by the preferred capital structure ratios, a process that requires subdividing the common stock portion into retained earnings of $100,000 (10% of capital) and new common stock of $400,000 (40% of capital):

30% × 4.8%	=	1.44%
20% × 8.0%	=	1.60%
40% × 7.6%	=	3.04%
10% × 7.0%	=	.70%
Total		6.78%

Rounding to the nearest tenth results in the correct answer of 6.8%.
Answer (B) is incorrect because 4.8% is the cost of the long-term debt. Answer (C) is incorrect because 6.5% would be correct only if the equity capital were obtained totally from retained earnings. Because only $100,000 of retained earnings is available, the remainder of equity capital must come from sales of new stock. Answer (D) is incorrect because 27.4% represents the unweighted total of each of the four elements of cost.

Questions 18 and 19 are based on the following information. DQZ Telecom is considering a project for the coming year that will cost $50 million. DQZ plans to use the following combination of debt and equity to finance the investment.

- Issue $15 million of 20-year bonds at a price of $101, with a coupon rate of 8%, and flotation costs of 2% of par.
- Use $35 million of funds generated from earnings.
- The equity market is expected to earn 12%. U.S. Treasury bonds are currently yielding 5%. The beta coefficient for DQZ is estimated to be .60. DQZ is subject to an effective corporate income tax rate of 40%.

18. The before-tax cost of DQZ's planned debt financing, net of flotation costs, in the first year is

A. 11.80%

B. 8.08%

C. 10.00%

D. 7.92%

Answer (B) is correct. *(CMA, adapted)*
REQUIRED: The before-tax cost of the planned debt financing, net of flotation costs.
DISCUSSION: Proceeds are $14,850,000 [(1.01 × $15,000,000) − (.02 × $15,000,000)]. The annual interest is $1.2 million (.08 coupon rate × $15,000,000). Thus, the company is paying $1.2 million annually for the use of $14,850,000, a rate of 8.08% ($1,200,000 ÷ $14,850,000).
Answer (A) is incorrect because the contract rate is 8% annually. Answer (C) is incorrect because 10.00% is the sum of the coupon rate and the flotation rate. Answer (D) is incorrect because 7.92% ignores the 2% flotation costs.

19. Assume that the after-tax cost of debt is 7% and the cost of equity is 12%. Determine the weighted-average cost of capital to DQZ.

A. 10.50%

B. 8.50%

C. 9.50%

D. 6.30%

Answer (A) is correct. *(CMA, adapted)*
REQUIRED: The weighted-average cost of capital given the costs of debt and equity.
DISCUSSION: The 7% debt cost and the 12% equity cost should be weighted by the proportions of the total investment represented by each source of capital. The total project costs $50 million, of which debt is $15 million, or 30% of the total. Equity capital is the other 70%. Consequently, the weighted-average cost of capital is 10.5% [(7%)(30%) + (12%)(70%)].
Answer (B) is incorrect because 8.50% reverses the weights. Answer (C) is incorrect because 9.50% assumes debt and equity are equally weighted. Answer (D) is incorrect because the weighted-average cost cannot be less than any of its components.

20. The difference between the required rate of return on a given risky investment and that on a riskless investment with the same expected return is the

A. Risk premium.

B. Coefficient of variation.

C. Standard deviation.

D. Beta coefficient.

Answer (A) is correct. *(CIA, adapted)*
REQUIRED: The difference between the required rate of return on a given risky investment and that on a riskless investment with the same expected return.
DISCUSSION: The required rate of return on equity capital in the capital asset pricing model is the risk-free rate (determined by government securities) plus the product of the market risk premium times the beta coefficient (beta measures the firm's risk). The market risk premium is the amount above the risk-free rate that will induce investment in the market. The beta coefficient of an individual stock is the correlation between the volatility (price variation) of the stock market and that of the price of the individual stock.
Answer (B) is incorrect because the coefficient of variation is the standard deviation of an investment's returns divided by the mean return. Answer (C) is incorrect because the standard deviation is a measure of the variability of an investment's returns. Answer (D) is incorrect because the beta coefficient measures the sensitivity of the investment's returns to market volatility.

21. The common stock of the Nicolas Corporation is currently selling at $80 per share. The leadership of the company intends to pay a $4 per share dividend next year. With the expectation that the dividend will grow at 5% perpetually, what will the market's required return on investment be for Nicolas common stock?

A. 5%

B. 5.25%

C. 7.5%

D. 10%

22. A firm's new financing will be in proportion to the market value of its current financing shown below.

	Carrying Amount ($000 Omitted)
Long-term debt	$7,000
Preferred stock (100,000 shares)	1,000
Common stock (200,000 shares)	7,000

The firm's bonds are currently selling at 80% of par, generating a current market yield of 9%, and the corporation has a 40% tax rate. The preferred stock is selling at its par value and pays a 6% dividend. The common stock has a current market value of $40 and is expected to pay a $1.20 per share dividend this fiscal year. Dividend growth is expected to be 10% per year, and flotation costs are negligible. The firm's weighted-average cost of capital is (round calculations to tenths of a percent)

A. 13.0%

B. 8.3%

C. 9.6%

D. 9.0%

Answer (D) is correct. *(Publisher, adapted)*
REQUIRED: The market's required return.
DISCUSSION: The dividend growth model estimates the cost of retained earnings using the dividends per share, the expected growth rate, and the market price. The current dividend yield is 5% ($4 ÷ $80). Adding the growth rate of 5% to the yield of 5% results in a required return of 10%.

Answer (A) is incorrect because 5% represents only half of the return elements (either yield or growth). Answer (B) is incorrect because the growth rate is based on market value, not yield. Answer (C) is incorrect because the yield and growth rate are 5% each, a total of 10%.

Answer (C) is correct. *(CMA, adapted)*
REQUIRED: The weighted-average cost of capital.
DISCUSSION: The first step is to determine the after-tax cost of the long-term debt. Multiplying the current yield of 9% times one minus the tax rate (1 − .4 = .6) results in an after-tax cost of debt of 5.4% (9% × .6). The cost of the preferred stock is 6% (the annual dividend rate). The dividend growth model for measuring the cost of equity capital is a frequently used method that combines the dividend yield with the growth rate. Dividing the $1.20 dividend by the $40 market price produces a dividend yield of 3%. Adding the 3% dividend yield and the 10% growth rate gives a 13% cost of common equity capital.

Once the costs of the three types of capital have been computed, the next step is to weight them according to the market values of the elements of the current capital structure. The $1,000,000 of preferred stock is selling at par. The market value of the long-term debt is 80% of its carrying amount, or $5,600,000 ($7,000,000 × 80%). The common stock has a current market price of $8,000,000 (200,000 shares × $40). Thus, the weighted-average cost of capital is 9.6% ($1,402,000 ÷ $14,600,000), as shown below.

Debt	.054 × $ 5,600,000	=	$ 302,400
Preferred	.06 × $ 1,000,000	=	$ 60,000
Common	.13 × $ 8,000,000	=	$1,040,000
Total	$14,600,000		$1,402,400

Answer (A) is incorrect because 13% is the cost of equity. Answer (B) is incorrect because 8.3% is the simple average. Answer (D) is incorrect because 9% is based on carrying amounts.

9.2 Marginal Cost of Capital

Questions 23 through 26 are based on the following information.

Rogers, Inc. operates a chain of restaurants located in the Southeast. The company has steadily grown to its present size of 48 restaurants. The board of directors recently approved a large-scale remodeling of the restaurant, and the company is now considering two financing alternatives.

● The first alternative would consist of

  ● Bonds that would have a 9% coupon rate and reissued at their base amount would net $19.2 million after flotation costs
  ● Preferred stock with a stated rate of 6% that would yield $4.8 million after a 4% flotation cost
  ● Common stock that would yield $24 million after a 5% flotation cost

● The second alternative would consist of a public offering of bonds that would have an 11% coupon rate and would net $48 million after flotation costs.

Rogers' current capital structure, which is considered optimal, consists of 40% long-term debt, 10% preferred stock, and 50% common stock. The current market value of the common stock is $30 per share, and the common stock dividend during the past 12 months was $3 per share. Investors are expecting the growth rate of dividends to equal the historical rate of 6%. Rogers is subject to an effective income tax rate of 40%.

---

23. The after-tax cost of the common stock proposed in Rogers' first financing alternative would be

  A. 16.00%

  B. 16.53%

  C. 16.60%

  D. 17.16%

Answer (D) is correct. *(CFM, adapted)*
REQUIRED: The after-tax cost of a proposed common stock issuance.
DISCUSSION: To determine the cost of new common stock, the dividend growth model is adjusted to include flotation cost as follows:

$$R = \frac{D_1}{P_0(1 - Flotation)} + G = \frac{\$3.18}{\$30.00(.95)} + .06 = 17.16\%$$

Answer (A) is incorrect because 16% ignores the increase in dividends and flotation costs. Answer (B) is incorrect because 16.53% ignores the increase in the next dividend. Answer (C) is incorrect because 16.6% ignores the flotation costs.

---

24. Assuming the after-tax cost of common stock is 15%, the after-tax weighted marginal cost of capital for Rogers' first financing alternative consisting of bonds, preferred stock, and common stock would be

  A. 7.285%

  B. 8.725%

  C. 10.375%

  D. 11.700%

Answer (C) is correct. *(CFM, adapted)*
REQUIRED: The weighted marginal cost of the first financing alternative.
DISCUSSION: In the calculation below, the cost of preferred stock equals the preferred dividend divided by the net issuance price. The preferred stock will yield $4,800,000 after subtracting the 4% flotation cost, so it must sell for $5,000,000 ($4,800,000 ÷ .96). The annual dividend on the preferred stock is $300,000 ($5,000,000 × 6%). Consequently, the cost of capital raised by issuing preferred stock is 6.25% ($300,000 dividend ÷ $4,800,000 net issuance price). The flotation cost operates, in effect, as a discount. Thus, the before-tax rate of return must exceed the coupon (nominal) rate of 9%. Assuming that the market rate for instruments with similar risk is 9%, the bonds were issued at par with proceeds at $19.2 million after payment of $800,000 of flotation costs. The before-tax rate of return on the debt is therefore .09375 [($20,000,000 × 9%) ÷ $19,200,000]. The weighted after-tax cost of debt is .0225 [.4 × .09375 × (1.0 – .4)], and the weighted marginal cost of the first financing alternative is 10.375% (2.25% + .625% + 7.5%).

	Weight		
Bonds	40% × 9.375% × (1.0 – .4)	=	2.250%
Preferred stock	10% × 6.25%	=	.625
Common stock	50% × 15%	=	7.500
			10.375%

25. The after-tax weighted marginal cost of capital for Rogers' second financing alternative consisting solely of bonds would be

A. 5.13%

B. 5.40%

C. 6.27%

D. 6.60%

Answer (D) is correct. *(CFM, adapted)*
REQUIRED: The weighted marginal cost of the second financing alternative.
DISCUSSION: The cost of the bonds equals the interest rate times one minus the tax rate, or 6.60% [11% × (100% – 40%)].
Answer (A) is incorrect because 5.13% is 5.40% reduced by the 5% stock flotation costs. Answer (B) is incorrect because 5.40% is 60% of 9%. Answer (C) is incorrect because 6.27% is 6.60% reduced by the 5% stock flotation costs.

26. The interest rate on the bonds is greater to Rogers, Inc. for the second alternative consisting of pure debt than it is for the first alternative consisting of both debt and equity because the

A. Diversity of the combination alternative creates greater risk for the investor.

B. Pure debt alternative would flood the market and be more difficult to sell.

C. Pure debt alternative carries the risk of increasing the probability of default.

D. Combination alternative carries the risk of increasing dividend payments.

Answer (C) is correct. *(CFM, adapted)*
REQUIRED: The reason increases in debt financing relative to equity financing increase the interest rate.
DISCUSSION: As a larger proportion of an entity's capital is provided by debt, the debt becomes riskier and more expensive. Hence, it requires a higher interest rate.
Answer (A) is incorrect because the diversity decreases, not increases, risk. Answer (B) is incorrect because $50,000,000 is minuscule in the debt markets. Answer (D) is incorrect because the combination alternative maintains the same debt-equity mixture, which would not warrant a rate increase in the cost of debt or equity.

27. A firm seeking to optimize its capital budget has calculated its marginal cost of capital and projected rates of return on several potential projects. The optimal capital budget is determined by

A. Calculating the point at which marginal cost of capital meets the projected rate of return, assuming that the most profitable projects are accepted first.

B. Calculating the point at which average marginal cost meets average projected rate of return, assuming the largest projects are accepted first.

C. Accepting all potential projects with projected rates of return exceeding the lowest marginal cost of capital.

D. Accepting all potential projects with projected rates of return lower than the highest marginal cost of capital.

Answer (A) is correct. *(CIA, adapted)*
REQUIRED: The determinant of the optimal capital budget.
DISCUSSION: In economics, a basic principle is that a firm should increase output until marginal cost equals marginal revenue. Similarly, the optimal capital budget is determined by calculating the point at which marginal cost of capital (which increases as capital requirements increase) and marginal efficiency of investment (which decreases if the most profitable projects are accepted first) intersect.
Answer (B) is incorrect because the intersection of average marginal cost with average projected rates of return when the largest (not most profitable) projects are accepted first offers no meaningful capital budgeting conclusion. Answer (C) is incorrect because the optimal capital budget may exclude profitable projects as lower-cost capital goes first to projects with higher rates of return. Answer (D) is incorrect because accepting projects with rates of return lower than the cost of capital is not rational.

Use Gleim's ***CMA Test Prep*** for interactive testing with **over 2,000 additional multiple-choice questions**!

STUDY UNIT TEN
MANAGING CURRENT ASSETS

(15 pages of outline)

This study unit is the **fourth of five** on **corporate finance**. The relative weight assigned to this major topic in Part 3 of the exam is **25%** at **skill level B** (four skill types required). The five study units are

Study Unit 7: Risk and Return
Study Unit 8: Financial Instruments
Study Unit 9: Cost of Capital
Study Unit 10: Managing Current Assets
Study Unit 11: Financing Current Assets

After studying the outline and answering the multiple-choice questions, you will have the skills necessary to address the following topics listed in the IMA's Learning Outcome Statements:

Part 3 – Section C.4. Managing current assets

The candidate should be able to:

a. define working capital and identify its components
b. explain the benefit of short-term financial forecasts in the management of working capital
c. identify factors influencing the levels of cash
d. identify and explain the three motives for holding cash
e. demonstrate an understanding of how firms monitor cash inflows and outflows and prepare forecasts of future cash flows
f. identify methods of speeding up cash collections
g. calculate the net benefit of a lockbox system
h. define concentration banking and discuss how firms utilize it
i. demonstrate an understanding of the uses of compensating balances
j. identify methods of slowing down disbursements
k. define payable through draft and zero balance account
l. demonstrate an understanding of disbursement float and overdraft systems
m. define electronic commerce and discuss its use by firms
n. define the different types of marketable securities, including money market instruments, T-bills, Treasury notes, Treasury bonds, repurchase agreements, Federal agency securities, bankers' acceptances, commercial paper, negotiable CDs, Eurodollars, and other marketable securities
o. demonstrate an understanding of the variables in marketable security selections, including safety, marketability, yield, maturity, and taxability
p. demonstrate an understanding of the risk and return trade-off in the selection of marketable securities
q. list reasons for holding marketable securities

r.   identify reasons for carrying accounts receivable and the factors influencing the level of receivables

s.   demonstrate an understanding of the impact of changes in credit terms

t.   define default risk

u.   demonstrate an understanding of the factors involved in determining an optimal credit policy

v.   calculate the average collection period

w.   identify reasons for carrying inventory and the factors influencing its level

x.   identify and calculate the costs related to inventory

y.   define lead time and safety stock

z.   demonstrate an understanding of economic order quantity (EOQ) and how a change in one variable would affect the EOQ (calculation not required)

aa.   define just-in-time and kanban inventory management systems

10.1 FINANCIAL MANAGEMENT

1.   The **objective of the firm** is to maximize the shareholders' wealth in the long term, i.e., to maximize the price per share of common stock. The market price of the stock is the result of the firm's investment and financing decisions within the context of legal and ethical bounds, including those relating to

   a.   Product safety
   b.   Minority hiring
   c.   Pollution control
   d.   Fair competition
   e.   Fair advertising

2.   **Other objectives** of the firm are less beneficial to shareholders than maximization of the per-share price of stock.

   a.   **Profit maximization** is not the optimal objective when it is not consistent with the maximization of stock price. For example,

      1)   Investing in high-risk projects may increase profits but returns may not be commensurate with the additional risk borne by the firm.

      2)   Increasing equity investment (resulting in a lower return on equity) will lower EPS and the stock price.

      3)   Delaying needed maintenance may increase accounting profits, but damage to capital assets may more than offset this increase in short-term profit.

   b.   **Sales maximization** is a nonoptimal objective when it does not maximize shareholders' wealth.

      1)   A firm wants to increase sales only when the marginal revenue from the sale is greater than (or equal to) the marginal cost of the sale. Only at this output (sales) level is shareholders' wealth maximized.

   c.   **Social responsibility** is an important issue, but if it were the only objective of the firm, the firm's existence would be short.

      1)   However, some mutual funds invest only in socially responsible firms. Consequently, social responsibility can increase the demand for a corporation's stocks and bonds and thus increase shareholder wealth.

3.   Management must make **investment decisions** to obtain a proper mix of productive assets. Also, it must secure financing for these assets with the objective of maximizing shareholders' wealth.

   a.   This is a dynamic process over time and requires adjusting to changes in the factors of production and finished-goods markets.

        b.   It is a multifaceted process because of the large number of markets in which most businesses deal.

             1)   The interrelationships among these many markets are complex.

4.   The **investing and financing** decisions are not independent.

        a.   The amount and composition of assets are directly related to the amount and composition of financing.

        b.   Given current and expected industry and overall economic conditions, the resulting mix of assets, liabilities, and capital determines the business risk.

             1)   Managerial decisions and their outcomes are related to and dependent on many external **(exogenous)** variables:

                  a)   Technological developments

                  b)   Weather

                  c)   National fiscal policies

                  d)   National monetary policies

                  e)   International relations and their effect on particular industries

                  f)   Competitors' actions (may not be exogenous if they are affected by the company's decisions)

5.   **Taxes** (federal, state, local, and foreign) are an important consideration because they are frequently 25% to 50% of all costs.

        a.   They include income, use, excise, property, legal document, payroll, and others.

        b.   Thus, **governmental services** (national defense, fire, police, etc.) are an important and costly factor of production.

        c.   **Tax planning** is very important in investment and financing decisions.

             1)   **Investment tax credits** have at times provided direct reductions of taxes when assets were purchased for use in the business.

                  a)   The net effect is to decrease the cost of the asset.

                  b)   The amount of the credit and limitations on the tax credit on used equipment affect investment decisions.

                  c)   Investment tax credits are currently available for solar and geothermal property (business energy credit), for rehabilitation of historic structures, and for certain reforestation property.

             2)   **Accelerated depreciation** is permitted on many types of business assets.

                  a)   Accordingly, in the early periods of an asset's life, depreciation is higher, taxable income is lower, and the rate of return on investment is higher.

             3)   **Corporate capital gains** are taxed at regular rates. For sales after May 5, 2003, the capital gains of individuals are taxed at a maximum rate of 15% (5% for individuals in a 10% or 15% bracket).

             4)   Special **loss carryforward and carryback** rules permit businesses to deduct net operating losses incurred in one period against income earned in other periods.

             5)   A **dividends-received deduction** makes tax free 70% to 100% of dividends received by one company from investments in the stock of another company.

                  a)   This prevents or reduces double taxation.

                  b)   It also encourages (does not discourage) one company to invest in the stock of another company.

             6)   **Interest** is a tax-deductible expense of the debtor company.

                  a)   But dividends on common or preferred stock are not deductible by the issuer.

d. Federal tax policy is **fiscal policy** that affects the overall economy, which in turn affects production and the finished-goods markets in which the company operates.

e. Government **monetary policy** determines the availability and cost of capital, which affect financing and investing decisions.

    1) Monetary policy also affects overall economic activity.

6. **Growth and expansion** are important to attract both personnel and capital.

a. Growth can be either **internal or external**.

    1) Internal growth arises from earnings retained in the business.
    2) External growth occurs through issuance of equity or debt securities.

b. **Expansion** occurs through

    1) New product lines
    2) Purchase of other companies
    3) Investments in other companies
    4) Franchising

c. The **financial perspective** on growth is the most important, encompassing all the legal, tax, and accounting perspectives.

    1) Additional factors determining the terms of **business combinations**

        a) Earnings levels and growth rates
        b) Sales levels and growth rates
        c) Dividends
        d) Market values
        e) Book values
        f) Net current assets

    2) The **exchanges of stock** in business combinations involving public companies often result in a greater market value than the sum of the market values of the individual companies.

        a) Qualitative considerations not reflected in the historical financial data may operate to create a synergistic effect.

            i) For example, a firm needing stronger management expertise, a better distribution network, or a research and development capacity may seek a complementary merger partner.

7. **Working capital finance** concerns the optimal level, mix, and use of current assets and current liabilities. The objective is to minimize the cost of maintaining liquidity while guarding against the possibility of technical insolvency.

a. From a financial analyst's perspective, **working capital** equals **current assets**. Its components include cash, marketable securities, receivables, and inventory. From the accounting perspective, working capital equals current assets minus current liabilities.

    1) Assets are current if they are reasonably expected to be realized in cash or sold or consumed during the normal operating cycle of the business.

    2) **Current liabilities** include trade accounts payable, taxes payable, unearned revenues, other accrued operating costs, short-term debt, and the currently due component of long-term debt. Liabilities are current if their liquidation will require the use of current assets or the incurrence of other current liabilities.

3) **Permanent working capital** is a concept reflecting the observation that a firm always maintains a minimum level of current assets. **Temporary working capital**, however, fluctuates seasonally.

a) Hence, permanent working capital is akin to the firm's fixed assets and should increase as the firm grows. It differs in that the terms included in working capital turn over relatively rapidly, although their minimum total is maintained or increased over the long term.

b. A company that adopts a **conservative working capital policy** seeks to minimize **liquidity risk** by increasing working capital. The result is that it forgoes the potentially higher returns available from using the additional working capital to acquire long-term assets.

c. An **aggressive policy** reduces the current ratio and liquidity and accepts a higher risk of short-term cash flow problems in an effort to increase profits.

8. **Financial Ratios to Evaluate Working Capital Management**

a. **Ratio analysis** is a means of evaluating the financing and investing decisions of a business. Common ratios may be categorized as follows:

1) Solvency ratios measure the firm's ability to meet short-term obligations.
2) Activity ratios measure how effectively the firm is using its resources.
3) Leverage ratios measure the extent of debt financing.
4) Profitability ratios measure the firm's earning power.
5) Per-share ratios include EPS, yield, and book value ratios.

b. Solvency and activity ratios are relevant to working capital finance. Leverage, profitability, and per-share data are relevant to capital structure finance.

c. Ratio analysis is based on **norms and trends**.

1) Normal or average ratios are computable for broad industrial categories.
2) Ratios for individual firms can be compared with those of competitors.
3) Changes in ratios through time provide insight about the future.

a) Comparisons of trends in ratios of competitors are also useful.

4) Benchmarks have evolved concerning ratios.

d. **Solvency ratios** measure the short-term viability of the business, i.e., the firm's ability to continue in the short term by paying its obligations.

1) The **current ratio** equals current assets divided by current liabilities.

a) $$\frac{Current\ assets}{Current\ liabilities}$$

b) The most commonly used measure of near-term solvency, it relates current assets to the claims of short-term creditors.

c) Benchmark: The current ratio should not be less than 2.0.

i) Companies with an aggressive financing policy will have a low current ratio.
ii) Conservative financing policies result in a higher current ratio.

d) The current ratio may be too high. Working capital is not a productive asset. Effective working capital management requires that working capital be kept as low as possible given a particular management's threshold for risk. The optimal level is not the highest possible level.

e) The current ratio is improved by paying off current liabilities.

2)   The **acid test or quick ratio** is a more conservative measure than the current ratio because it does not include inventory in the numerator.

a) $$\frac{Cash\ +\ Net\ receivables\ +\ Marketable\ securities}{Current\ liabilities}$$

b)   It measures the firm's ability to pay its short-term debts from its most liquid assets.

c)   Benchmark: The quick ratio should be greater than 1.0.

i)   Liquidity is usually obtained at the cost of profitability. Liquid investments usually do not provide as high a return as productive assets.

3)   **Working capital** equals current assets minus current liabilities.

a)   *Current assets – Current liabilities*

b)   This calculation does not facilitate comparisons because it measures an absolute difference.

e.   **Activity ratios** measure the firm's use of assets to generate revenue and income.

1)   The **inventory turnover ratio** equals cost of sales divided by average inventories.

a) $$\frac{Cost\ of\ sales}{Average\ inventory}$$

b)   A high turnover implies that the firm does not hold excessive stocks of inventories that are unproductive and lessen the firm's profitability.

c)   A high turnover also implies that the inventory is truly marketable and does not contain obsolete goods.

d)   An average inventory figure should be used.

i)   If average annual inventory is cyclical, a monthly average should be used.

2)   The **number of days of inventory** equals the number of days in the year divided by the inventory turnover ratio.

a) $$\frac{365,\ 360,\ or\ 300}{Inventory\ turnover}$$

b)   It measures the average number of days inventory is held before sale.

i)   It reflects the efficiency of inventory management.

c)   The number of days in a year may be 365, 360 (a banker's year), or 300 (number of business days).

d)   The lower the number of days, the better.

3)   The **receivables turnover ratio** equals net credit sales divided by average accounts receivable (but with net sales often used because of unavailability of credit sales data).

a) $$\frac{Net\ credit\ sales}{Average\ accounts\ receivable}$$

b)   It indicates the efficiency of accounts receivable collection.

4) The **number of days of receivables** equals the number of days in the year divided by the receivables turnover ratio.

a) $$\frac{365,\ 360,\ or\ 300}{Receivables\ turnover}$$

b) It is the average number of days to collect a receivable **(average collection period)**.

c) It may also be computed as average accounts receivable divided by average daily sales.

i) Average daily sales equals net credit sales divided by the number of days in a year.

d) **Average gross receivables** equals average daily sales times the average collection period.

e) This ratio should be compared with the seller's credit terms to determine whether most customers are paying on time.

5) The **operating cycle** equals number of days of inventory plus number of days of receivables.

a) *Number of days of inventory + Number of days of receivables.*

b) The operating cycle represents the time between the acquisition of inventory and the receipt of cash from sales of inventory.

9. Stop and review! You have completed the outline for this subunit. Study multiple-choice questions 1 through 13 beginning on page 289.

10.2 CASH MANAGEMENT

1. The following are the three motives for **holding cash**:

a. As a **medium of exchange**. Cash is still needed for some business transactions.

b. As a **precautionary measure**. Cash or a money-market fund can be held for emergencies. Normally, investment in high-grade, short-term securities is a better alternative to holding cash.

1) Long ago, given cash shortages, money was literally held as a precaution against bank closings.

2) Today, if the banks fail, paper money will be worthless; thus, there is no precautionary reason to hoard U.S. paper dollars.

c. For **speculation**. Cash may be held to take advantage of bargain-purchase opportunities. However, short-term, highly liquid securities are also preferable for this purpose.

2. The **cash budget** details projected receipts and disbursements, preferably for planning the synchronization of inflows and outflows.

a. It is based on the projected sales and credit terms, collection percentages, and estimated purchases and payment terms.

b. Cash outflows are budgeted based on the level of sales.

c. Cash budgeting is an ongoing, cumulative activity.

1) The starting point is a beginning balance.

2) Budgets must be for a specified period of time.

a) The units of time must be short enough to assure that all cash obligations can be met.

3. **Cash collections** should be expedited.

   a. Invoices should be mailed promptly.

   b. Credit terms must be competitive but should encourage prompt payment.

      1) See also Receivables Management in Subunit 10.4.

   c. A **lockbox system** may be used to expedite the receipt of funds. A company maintains mailboxes, often in numerous locations around the country, to which customers send payments. A bank checks these mailboxes several times a day, and funds received are immediately deposited to the company's account without first being processed by the company's accounting system. This process hastens availability of the funds. In addition, having several lockboxes throughout the country reduces the time a payment is in the postal system.

      1) **Concentration banking** may be useful in this context. Regional concentration banks may serve as centers for the transfer of lockbox receipts. A disbursement account at the regional center will then expedite the use of the receipts for payments in that region. Such use might be delayed if all receipts were transmitted to a national central bank.

      2) Sometimes banks require a borrower to leave a **compensating balance** on deposit in lieu of a fee for the bank's services. This raises the effective interest rate of the loan.

   d. Transfer of monies by wire expedites cash management. A **wire transfer** is any electronic funds transfer by means of a two-way system, for example, the Federal Reserve Wire Transfer System (Fedwire).

   e. **Electronic Data Interchange (EDI)** is the communication of electronic documents directly from one computer to another. **Electronic funds transfer (EFT)** and customer debit cards are applications of EDI that expedite cash inflows. With the widespread growth of **electronic commerce** (the buying and selling of products and services by electronic means, such as EDI, email, and the Internet) by individuals, the use of electronic funds transfer has mushroomed. Companies such as PayPal enable individuals to transfer funds to each other at little or no cost.

   f. **Automated clearing houses (ACHs)** are electronic networks that facilitate the reading of data among banks. The 32 regional ACH associations guarantee 1-day clearing of checks. Except for the New York ACH, they are operated by the Federal Reserve.

4. **Slowing cash disbursements** increases available cash.

   a. **Trade payables** usually come with terms to encourage creditors to pay early.

      1) Typical **terms** are 2/10 net 30, which means the creditor can take a 2% discount if (s)he pays within 10 days of the invoice and must pay the full balance within 30 days.

      2) Creditors strike a balance between the desire to pay less by paying early and the need to conserve cash flow by paying after the **discount period**.

      3) Paying after the 30-day deadline creates vendor ill will and often generates interest charges, creating a worse cash flow problem in the future.

   b. Payment by **draft** (a three-party instrument in which the drawer orders the drawee to pay money to the payee) is a means of slowing cash outflows. A **check** is the most common form of draft.

      1) **Check float** arises from the delay between an expenditure or receipt by check and the clearing of the check. The effect is an interest-free loan to the payor.

         a) Accordingly, companies attempt to **maximize disbursements float,** the period from when checks are written to when they are deducted from the bank balance.

        b)   Also, they attempt to **minimize collections float**, the sum of the time checks are in the mail, internal processing time, and the time required for clearing through the banking system.

      2)   **Payable through drafts (PTDs)** are also drafts, but they differ from checks because they are not payable on demand, and the drawee is the payor, not a bank. After presentment to a bank, a PTD must be presented to the issuer. If the latter chooses to accept the instrument, it will deposit the necessary funds. Consequently, use of PTDs allows a firm to postpone the deposit of funds and therefore to maintain lower cash balances.

          a)   The drawbacks of PTDs are that suppliers prefer checks. Furthermore, banks impose greater charges for processing PTDs.

  c.   Banks offer **overdraft protection** when a check is presented against an account with insufficient funds. The bank automatically transfers enough into the account to cover the check.

      1)   An interest rate is charged on the overdraft coverage just as on any other loan. The effective rate can be calculated as follows:

          a) $\dfrac{Total\ interest\ cost}{Total\ principal}$

  d.   **Zero-balance accounts (ZBAs)** are disbursement accounts (for example, payroll) offered by some banks. The account balance is maintained at zero until a check is presented for payment. The resulting overdraft is covered by a transfer from a master (parent) account earning interest.

      1)   The disadvantage is that the bank may charge a fee for this service, and the amount needed in the master account still needs to be estimated.

5.   The amount of cash to keep on hand should be determined by **cost-benefit analysis**.

  a.   The reduction in average cash times the interest rate (cost of capital or investment yield rate) is the benefit.

  b.   Costs of having insufficient cash include incremental personnel cost, lost discounts, and lost vendor goodwill.

  c.   The economic order quantity (EOQ) model is applicable to cash management.

      1)   It can be stated in terms of the following assumptions:

          a)   A known demand for cash

          b)   A given carrying (interest) cost

          c)   The flat amount (cost) of converting other assets to cash, such as the broker's fee for sale of marketable securities (assumed to be constant regardless of the transaction size)

      2)   One such EOQ-type model is the **Baumol cash management model**. The Baumol model attempts to minimize the total of the costs of securities transactions and the opportunity costs of holding cash (the return forgone by not investing in marketable securities or the cost of borrowing cash).

$$OC = \sqrt{\frac{2bT}{i}}$$

Where: OC = the optimal cash level
           b = the cost per transaction
           T = the total demand for cash for the period
           i = the interest rate on marketable equity securities or the cost of borrowing cash

3) The Baumol model, like the EOQ model, is deterministic and relies on simplifying assumptions. For example, the demand for cash must be known.

   a) If such information is not known, the **Miller-Orr cash management model** can be used. The Miller-Orr model assumes uncertain cash flows that are random in amount and direction and are normally distributed as the number of periods increases.

   b) It derives the most cost efficient cash balance by determining an upper limit and lower limit for cash balances. The target cash balance is between these two limits. As long as cash is between the two limits, no transaction to replenish or invest the cash balance occurs.

   c) The diagram below illustrates the Miller-Orr Model. At points A, B, and D, the cash balance reaches the upper limit, and the excess over the return point is immediately invested in short-term securities. At point C, the lower limit is reached, and sufficient securities are sold to make the balance of cash equal the return point.

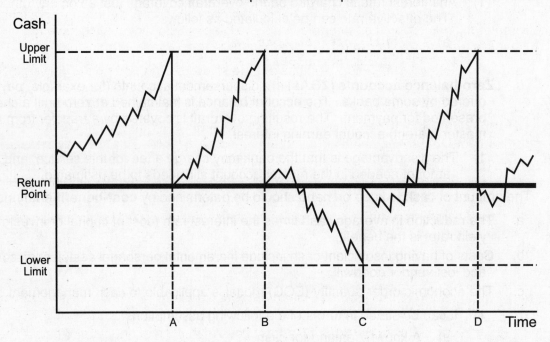

6. Stop and review! You have completed the outline for this subunit. Study multiple-choice questions 14 through 31 beginning on page 294.

10.3 MARKETABLE SECURITIES MANAGEMENT

1. Short-term marketable securities are sometimes held as **substitutes** for cash but are more likely to be acquired as temporary investments.

   a. Most companies avoid large cash balances and prefer borrowing to meet short-term needs.

   b. As **temporary investments**, marketable securities may be purchased with **maturities** timed to meet seasonal fluctuations, to pay off a bond issue, to make tax payments, or otherwise to satisfy anticipated needs.

   c. Marketable securities should be chosen with a view to their degree of safety, that is, their **default risk**.

      1) U.S. government securities are the least risky.

2. **Interest-rate risk** should be minimized given the reasons for holding marketable securities.

   a. Long-term securities are more likely than short-term securities to fluctuate in price because of changes in the general level of interest rates.

   b. Interest rate expectation theory states that long-term interest rates are usually a geometric average of expected future short-term interest rates.

3. **Changes in the general price level** (usually inflationary) determine the **purchasing power** of payments on investments (principal and interest) and thus the types of securities chosen and the rates charged.

4. The degree of **marketability** of a security determines its **liquidity**, that is, the ability to resell at the quoted market price.

5. The firm's **tax position** will influence its choice of securities. For example, a firm with net loss carryforwards may prefer a higher-yielding taxable security to a tax-exempt municipal bond.

6. Short-term marketable securities are usually chosen for reasons that make high-yield, high-risk investments unattractive. Hence, a higher return may be forgone in exchange for greater safety. Given the various options available, a company should have an **investment policy statement** to provide continuing guidance to management.

   a. Thus, speculative tactics, such as **selling short** (borrowing and selling securities in the expectation that their price will decline by the time they must be replaced) and **margin trading** (borrowing from a broker to buy securities) are avoided.

7. The **money market** is the market for short-term investments where companies invest their temporary surpluses of cash.

   a. The money market is not formally organized, but consists of many financial institutions, companies, and government agencies offering a wide array of instruments of various risk levels and short- to medium-range maturities.

   b. Some **common money market instruments** are described below and on the next page.

      1) **U.S. Treasury obligations** are offered in three maturity ranges. They are all exempt from state and local taxation and are highly liquid.

         a) **Treasury bills (T-bills)** have maturities of one year or less. Rather than bear interest, they are sold on a discount basis.

         b) **Treasury notes (T-notes)** have maturities of one to ten years. They provide the lender with a coupon (interest) payment every six months.

         c) **Treasury bonds (T-bonds)** have maturities of ten years or longer. They provide the lender with a coupon (interest) payment every six months.

            i) The U.S. government stopped issuing the famous 30-year Treasury bond (the "long bond") in October 2001 as efforts to pay off the national debt accelerated. The long bond became available again starting in February 2006.

      2) **Repurchase agreements (repos)** involve sales by a dealer in government securities who agrees to repurchase at a given time for a specific price. Maturities may be very short-term. This arrangement is in essence a secured loan.

      3) **Federal agency securities** are issued by individual government agencies, such as the Federal Home Loan Mortgage Corporation (Freddie Mac) and the Federal National Mortgage Association (Fannie Mae), which issue mortgage-backed securities. Agency securities may be long- or short-term.

         a) Obligations of federal agencies are not guaranteed by the U.S. government but only by the agency itself.

4) **Bankers' acceptances** are drafts drawn by a nonfinancial firm on deposits at a bank. The acceptance by the bank is a guarantee of payment at maturity.

5) **Commercial paper** consists of unsecured, short-term notes issued by large companies that are very good credit risks.

6) **Certificates of deposit (CDs)** are a form of savings deposit that cannot be withdrawn before maturity without a high penalty. CDs often yield a lower return than commercial paper because they are less risky.

   a) **Negotiable CDs** are traded under the regulation of the Federal Reserve System.

7) **Eurodollars** are time deposits of U.S. dollars in banks located abroad.

8) **Others**

   a) **Money-market mutual funds** invest in short-term, low-risk securities. In addition to paying interest, these funds allow investors to write checks on their balances.

   b) **State and local governments** issue short-term securities exempt from taxation.

8. Stop and review! You have completed the outline for this subunit. Study multiple-choice questions 32 through 35 beginning on page 299.

10.4 RECEIVABLES MANAGEMENT

1. The **objective** of managing accounts receivable is to have both the optimal amount of receivables outstanding and the optimal amount of bad debts.

   a. This balance requires a trade-off between the benefits of credit sales, such as more sales, and the costs of accounts receivable, e.g., collection, interest, and bad debt costs.

   b. The **optimal credit policy** does not seek merely to maximize sales (for example, by lowering credit standards, offering longer discount periods, or charging lower interest) or to minimize **default risk**. Thus, a company should extend credit until the marginal benefit (profit) of an additional sale is zero (considering opportunity costs of alternative investments).

2. Credit standards, credit periods, collection policies, discounts, and other terms are frequently determined by **competitive factors**. A company often must match inducements offered by rivals to make sales.

3. Companies often use a statistical technique called **credit scoring** to determine whether to extend credit to a specific customer. Credit scoring assigns numerical values to the elements of credit worthiness, such as income, length of employment in the borrower's current job, occupation, and home ownership.

4. Receivables management seeks to maximize the **accounts-receivable-turnover ratio**, that is, to shorten the average time receivables are held.

   a. A common analytical tool is an **aging schedule** developed from a company's accounts receivable ledger. It stratifies the accounts depending on how long they have been outstanding.

5. The following are different types of credit instruments used in receivables management:

   a. An **invoice** is a bill issued by a company that has provided goods or services to a customer. It includes the prices, terms, and types of goods. In asset-based lending (such as factoring), an invoice means an account receivable.

   b. A **promissory note** is a two-party negotiable instrument that contains an unconditional promise to pay a fixed sum of money at a definite time.

c. A **conditional sales contract** is a financing method often used by sellers of equipment. The buyer receives possession and use of the goods. The seller initially receives a promissory note but retains title until the installment debt is paid. Retention of title facilitates repossession.

6. Other tools of credit such as bank charge cards should be evaluated as an alternative to charge accounts.

   a. Banks charge a fee equal to 3% to 5% of charge sales.
   b. Charge tickets can be deposited at a bank in the same way as customer checks.
   c. Money is instantly available to the seller.

7. Stop and review! You have completed the outline for this subunit. Study multiple-choice questions 36 through 45 beginning on page 300.

10.5 INVENTORY MANAGEMENT

1. The firm should minimize total inventory costs. They include

   a. **Ordering costs**, the costs of placing and receiving orders.
   b. **Carrying costs**, the costs of
      1) Storage,
      2) Insurance,
      3) Security,
      4) Inventory taxes,
      5) Depreciation or rent of facilities,
      6) Interest,
      7) Obsolescence and spoilage, and
      8) The opportunity cost of inventory investment.

2. The firm must also minimize the sum of the costs of stockouts and safety stock.

   a. **Stockout costs** are incurred when an entity does not have products demanded by customers. Lost sales and customer goodwill are stockout costs. Expediting costs (additional ordering and transportation costs) may be incurred to avoid loss of sales.
   b. **Safety stock** is the quantity held for sale during the lead time.
      1) **Lead time** is the period between when an order is placed and when it is received.

3. The **order point** is the time an order should be placed to insure receiving the inventory before stockout occurs.

   a. For example, if the firm uses 20 units per day and the lead time is 3 days, an order should, in the absence of safety stock, be placed when the inventory level reaches 60 units.
   b. In practice, firms often allow for disruptions in delivery by carrying some safety stock. If the safety stock were 25 units, the order would be placed when the inventory level is reduced to 85 units [(3 days × 20 units) + 25 units of safety stock].

4.   The traditional inventory management approach uses the basic **economic order quantity (EOQ)** model to minimize the sum of ordering and carrying costs.

   a.   Demand is assumed to be known and constant throughout the period. Order cost per order and unit carrying costs are also assumed to be constant. Because demand is assumed to be deterministic, there are no stockout costs.

$$EOQ = \sqrt{\frac{2aD}{k}}$$

Where: a = the variable cost per purchase order
        D = the periodic demand in units
        k = the periodic carrying cost per unit

5.   **Just-in-time** and **kanban systems** are addressed in Study Unit 2.1.

6.   Modern inventory management is often accomplished in the context of **automated manufacturing**, whether involving one piece of equipment, a cell, or an integrated plant. See Study Unit 2.4 for outlines that cover automated methods.

7.   Stop and review! You have completed the outline for this subunit. Study multiple-choice questions 46 through 54 beginning on page 304.

10.6   CORE CONCEPTS

Financial Management

   ■   Management must make **investment decisions** to obtain a proper mix of productive assets. Also, it must secure financing for these assets with the objective of maximizing shareholders' wealth.

   ■   The **investing and financing** decisions are not independent. The amount and composition of assets are directly related to the amount and composition of financing.

   ■   **Taxes** (federal, state, local, and foreign) are an important consideration because they are frequently 25% to 50% of all costs.

   ■   **Working capital finance** concerns the optimal level, mix, and use of current assets and current liabilities. The objective is to minimize the cost of maintaining liquidity while guarding against the possibility of technical insolvency.

   ■   **Solvency ratios**, such as the current ratio and quick ratio, measure the short-term viability of the business, i.e., the firm's ability to continue in the short term by paying its obligations.

   ■   **Activity ratios**, such as the inventory turnover ratio and receivables turnover ratio, measure the firm's use of assets to generate revenue and income.

Cash Management

   ■   **Three motives** for holding cash are: as a medium of exchange, as a precautionary measure, and for speculation.

   ■   **Cash collections** should be **expedited**. Thus, invoices should be mailed promptly; credit terms must be competitive but should encourage prompt payment; and a lockbox system may be used.

   ■   **Slowing cash disbursements** increases available cash. Cash flow considerations sometimes make it necessary to forgo the discounts offered for early settlement of trade payables. Payment by draft (usually in the form of a check) is a means of slowing cash outflows.

   ■   **Models for cash management**, such as the Baumol and Miller-Orr models, provide a firm with guidelines for holding the correct amount of cash, such that enough is available to pay current liabilities but not so much that interest revenue is forgone.

Marketable Securities Management

- As temporary investments, marketable securities may be purchased with **maturities timed** to meet seasonal fluctuations, to pay off a bond issue, to make tax payments, or otherwise to satisfy anticipated needs. Marketable securities should be chosen with a view to their degree of safety, that is their default risk.
- The **money market** is the market for short-term investments where companies invest their temporary surpluses of cash.
- Some **common money market instruments** are: U.S. Treasury obligations, repurchase agreements, federal agency securities, bankers' acceptances, commercial paper, and certificates of deposit.

Receivables Management

- The objective of managing accounts receivable is to have both the **optimal amount** of receivables outstanding and the optimal amount of bad debts. This balance requires a trade-off between the benefits of credit sales, such as more sales, and the costs of accounts receivable, e.g., collection, interest, and bad debt costs.
- Receivables management seeks to maximize the accounts-receivable-turnover ratio, that is, to **shorten the average time receivables are held**. A common analytical tool is an aging schedule.

Inventory Management

- The firm should **minimize total inventory costs**. These include ordering costs (the costs of placing and receiving orders) and carrying costs (the costs of storage, insurance, security, etc.).
- The firm must also **minimize stockout costs** (the lost sales and lost goodwill incurred when an entity does not have products demanded by customers) and **safety stock** (the quantity held for sale during the lead time).
- The **order point** is the time an order should be placed to insure receiving the inventory before stockout occurs.
- The traditional inventory management approach uses the basic **economic order quantity model** to minimize the sum of ordering and carrying costs.

QUESTIONS

10.1 Financial Management

1. Net working capital is the difference between

   A. Current assets and current liabilities.

   B. Fixed assets and fixed liabilities.

   C. Total assets and total liabilities.

   D. Shareholders' investment and cash.

Answer (A) is correct. *(CMA, adapted)*
   REQUIRED: The definition of net working capital.
   DISCUSSION: Net working capital is defined by accountants as the difference between current assets and current liabilities. Working capital is a measure of short-term solvency.
   Answer (B) is incorrect because working capital refers to the difference between current assets and current liabilities; fixed assets are not a component. Answer (C) is incorrect because total assets and total liabilities are not components of working capital; only current items are included. Answer (D) is incorrect because shareholders' equity is not a component of working capital; only current items are included in the concept of working capital.

2. Determining the appropriate level of working capital for a firm requires

    A. Changing the capital structure and dividend policy of the firm.

    B. Maintaining short-term debt at the lowest possible level because it is generally more expensive than long-term debt.

    C. Offsetting the benefit of current assets and current liabilities against the probability of technical insolvency.

    D. Maintaining a high proportion of liquid assets to total assets in order to maximize the return on total investments.

Answer (C) is correct. *(CMA, adapted)*
    REQUIRED: The requirement for determining the appropriate level of working capital.
    DISCUSSION: Working capital finance concerns the determination of the optimal level, mix, and use of current assets and current liabilities. The objective is to minimize the cost of maintaining liquidity, while guarding against the possibility of technical insolvency. Technical insolvency is defined as the inability to pay debts as they come due.
    Answer (A) is incorrect because capital structure and dividends relate to capital structure finance, not working capital finance. Answer (B) is incorrect because short-term debt is usually less expensive than long-term debt. Answer (D) is incorrect because liquid assets do not ordinarily earn high returns relative to long-term assets, so holding the former will not maximize the return on total assets.

3. All of the following statements in regard to working capital are true except

    A. Current liabilities are an important source of financing for many small firms.

    B. Profitability varies inversely with liquidity.

    C. The hedging approach to financing involves matching maturities of debt with specific financing needs.

    D. Financing permanent inventory buildup with long-term debt is an example of an aggressive working capital policy.

Answer (D) is correct. *(CMA, adapted)*
    REQUIRED: The false statement about working capital.
    DISCUSSION: Financing permanent inventory buildup, which is essentially a long-term investment, with long-term debt is a moderate or conservative working capital policy. An aggressive policy uses short-term, relatively low-cost debt to finance the inventory buildup. It focuses on high profitability potential, despite high risk and low liquidity. An aggressive policy reduces the current ratio and accepts a higher risk of short-term lack of liquidity. Financing inventory with long-term debt increases the current ratio and accepts higher borrowing costs in exchange for greater liquidity and lower risk.
    Answer (A) is incorrect because current liabilities, e.g., trade credit, is a major source of funds for small firms. Answer (B) is incorrect because liquid investments tend to have low returns. Answer (C) is incorrect because matching of asset and liability maturities is a moderate policy that minimizes risk. The expectation is that cash flows from the assets will be available to meet obligations for the liabilities.

4. Which one of the following transactions would increase the current ratio and decrease net profit?

    A. A federal income tax payment due from the previous year is paid.

    B. A stock dividend is declared.

    C. Uncollectible accounts receivable are written off against the allowance account.

    D. Vacant land is sold for less than the net book value.

Answer (D) is correct. *(CMA, adapted)*
    REQUIRED: The transaction that would increase the current ratio and decrease net profit.
    DISCUSSION: The current ratio is calculated by dividing current assets by current liabilities. Thus, any transaction that will either increase current assets or decrease current liabilities will increase the current ratio. Selling vacant land for less than its book value (at a loss) would increase current assets (cash) and decrease net profit.
    Answer (A) is incorrect because paying the federal tax liability from the previous year has no effect on the current year's net profit. Answer (B) is incorrect because a stock dividend (debit retained earnings, credit common stock) has no impact on either the current ratio or net profit. Answer (C) is incorrect because writing off receivables against an allowance account does not change total current assets. The allowance account is a contra account in the current asset section of the balance sheet.

5. Which one of the following transactions does not change either the current ratio or the total current assets?

A. A cash advance is made to a divisional office.

B. A cash dividend is declared.

C. Short-term notes payable are retired with cash.

D. A fully depreciated asset is sold for cash.

Answer (A) is correct. *(CMA, adapted)*
REQUIRED: The transaction not affecting the current ratio or total current assets.
DISCUSSION: The current ratio is calculated by dividing current assets by current liabilities. Thus, any transaction that changes current assets or current liabilities changes the current ratio. A cash advance to a divisional office does not change current assets because the cash (a current asset) will be replaced by a receivable (a current asset). Current liabilities are also unaffected, so the cash advance affects neither the current ratio nor total current assets.
Answer (B) is incorrect because the declaration of a cash dividend creates a current liability, which reduces the current ratio. Answer (C) is incorrect because retiring short-term notes with cash reduces current assets and current liabilities. Answer (D) is incorrect because selling a fully depreciated asset increases cash, a current asset.

6. A company has a current ratio of 1.9 and a quick ratio of .5. Which of the following transactions will increase both ratios?

A. Pay off $10,000 of current liabilities.

B. Borrow $10,000 on a short-term note.

C. Transfer $10,000 of inventory to a vendor in full payment of a $10,000 account payable.

D. Sell inventory for cash at a loss.

Answer (C) is correct. *(Publisher, adapted)*
REQUIRED: The transaction that will increase both the current ratio and the quick ratio.
DISCUSSION: This question is somewhat tricky because one of the ratios is less than 1.0, while the other is greater than 1.0. If the current ratio is greater than 1.0, then paying off a current liability will increase the ratio. Thus, both answers (A) and (C) will increase the current ratio. However, transferring cash to a creditor will decrease the quick ratio if the present ratio is less than 1.0. Thus, only the transfer of a non-quick asset to a creditor will increase the quick ratio. For example, if the total of current assets was $190,000 and quick assets totaled $50,000, then current liabilities would have been $100,000. Transferring $10,000 of inventory would change the totals to $180,000 for current assets and $90,000 for current liabilities. Quick assets would remain at $50,000. The new current ratio would be 2.0 ($180,000 ÷ $90,000), and the new quick ratio would be .556 ($50,000 ÷ $90,000).
Answer (A) is incorrect because using cash to pay the creditor will cause a decline in the quick ratio. Answer (B) is incorrect because the current ratio will decline. Answer (D) is incorrect because selling goods at a loss will cause the current ratio to decline.

7. During the year, Mason Company's current assets increased by $120, current liabilities decreased by $50, and net working capital

A. Increased by $70.

B. Did not change.

C. Decreased by $170.

D. Increased by $170.

Answer (D) is correct. *(Publisher, adapted)*
REQUIRED: The effect on net working capital of an increase in current assets and a decrease in current liabilities.
DISCUSSION: Net working capital is the excess of current assets over current liabilities. An increase in current assets or a decrease in current liabilities increases working capital. Thus, net working capital increased by $170 ($120 + $50).
Answer (A) is incorrect because both the increase in current assets and the decrease in current liabilities increase working capital. Answer (B) is incorrect because net working capital did change. Answer (C) is incorrect because net working capital increased.

8. MFC Corporation has 100,000 shares of stock outstanding. Below is part of MFC's Statement of Financial Position for the last fiscal year.

MFC Corporation
Statement of Financial Position - Selected Items
December 31

Cash	$455,000
Accounts receivable	900,000
Inventory	650,000
Prepaid assets	45,000
Accrued liabilities	285,000
Accounts payable	550,000
Current portion, long-term notes payable	65,000

What is the maximum amount MFC can pay in cash dividends per share and maintain a minimum current ratio of 2 to 1? Assume that all accounts other than cash remain unchanged.

A. $2.05

B. $2.50

C. $3.35

D. $3.80

Answer (B) is correct. *(CMA, adapted)*
REQUIRED: The maximum dividends consistent with a specified minimum current ratio.
DISCUSSION: Before the dividend, total current assets equal $2,050,000 ($455,000 cash + $900,000 receivables + $650,000 inventory + $45,000 prepaid assets). Current liabilities total $900,000 ($285,000 accrued liabilities + $550,000 accounts payable + $65,000 current portion of long-term debt). The payment of the cash dividend will not change current liabilities, so a current ratio of 2 to 1 requires that current assets be maintained at a minimum of $1,800,000 (2 × $900,000). Thus, cash can decrease by $250,000 ($2,050,000 – $1,800,000). The maximum per-share rate is $2.50 ($250,000 ÷ 100,000 shares).
Answer (A) is incorrect because $2.05 fails to include prepaid assets (prepaid expenses) as current assets.
Answer (C) is incorrect because $3.35 fails to include the current portion of long-term debt as a current liability. Answer (D) is incorrect because $3.80 fails to consider prepaid assets as a current asset and the current portion of long-term debt as a current liability.

9. Spotech Co.'s budgeted sales and budgeted cost of sales for the coming year are $212,000,000 and $132,500,000, respectively. Short-term interest rates are expected to average 5%. If Spotech could increase inventory turnover from its current 8.0 times per year to 10.0 times per year, its expected cost savings in the current year would be

A. $165,625

B. $0

C. $3,312,500

D. $828,125

Answer (A) is correct. *(CMA, adapted)*
REQUIRED: The expected cost savings from increasing the inventory turnover rate from eight to ten times per year.
DISCUSSION: If cost of sales is $132,500,000, and the inventory turnover rate is 8.0 times per year, the average inventory is $16,562,500 ($132,500,000 ÷ 8). If the turnover increases to 10.0 times annually, the average inventory will decline to $13,250,000 ($132,500,000 ÷ 10), a decrease of $3,312,500. At a 5% rate, reducing working capital by $3,312,500 will save the company $165,625 ($3,312,500 × .05).
Answer (B) is incorrect because the faster turnover reduces working capital and releases funds for other uses. Answer (C) is incorrect because $3,312,500 is the decrease in average inventory. Answer (D) is incorrect because $828,125 is 5% of $16,562,500.

10. A change in credit policy has caused an increase in sales, an increase in discounts taken, a reduction in the investment in accounts receivable, and a reduction in the number of doubtful accounts. Based upon this information, we know that

A. Net profit has increased.

B. The average collection period has decreased.

C. Gross profit has declined.

D. The size of the discount offered has decreased.

Answer (B) is correct. *(CMA, adapted)*
REQUIRED: The true statement about a change in credit policy that has resulted in greater sales and a reduction in accounts receivable.
DISCUSSION: An increase in discounts taken accompanied by declines in receivables balances and doubtful accounts all indicate that collections on the increased sales have been accelerated. Accordingly, the average collection period must have declined. The average collection period is a ratio calculated by dividing the number of days in a year (365) by the receivable turnover. Thus, the higher the turnover, the shorter the average collection period. The turnover increases when either sales (the numerator) increase, or receivables (the denominator) decrease. Accomplishing both higher sales and a lower receivables increases the turnover and results in a shorter collection period.
Answer (A) is incorrect because no statement can be made with respect to profits without knowing costs. Answer (C) is incorrect because no statement can be made with respect to profits without knowing costs. Answer (D) is incorrect because the discount may have been increased, which has led to quicker payments.

11. Which one of the following statements is most likely to be true if a seller extends credit to a purchaser for a period of time longer than the purchaser's operating cycle? The seller

    A. Will have a lower level of accounts receivable than those companies whose credit period is shorter than the purchaser's operating cycle.

    B. Is, in effect, financing more than just the purchaser's inventory needs.

    C. Can be certain that the purchaser will be able to convert the inventory into cash before payment is due.

    D. Has no need for a stated discount rate or credit period.

Answer (B) is correct. *(CMA, adapted)*
    REQUIRED: The true statement about extending credit for a period longer than the purchaser's operating cycle.
    DISCUSSION: The normal operating cycle is defined as the period from the acquisition of inventory to the collection of the account receivable. If trade credit is for a period longer than the normal operating cycle, the seller must therefore be financing more than just the purchase of inventory.
    Answer (A) is incorrect because a seller who extends long-term credit will have a higher level of receivables than a firm with a shorter credit period. Answer (C) is incorrect because the seller is not guaranteed that a purchaser will resell the merchandise. Answer (D) is incorrect because offering a discount may accelerate payment.

12. Clauson, Inc. grants credit terms of 1/15, net 30 and projects gross sales for next year of $2,000,000. The credit manager estimates that 40% of their customers pay on the discount date, 40% on the net due date, and 20% pay 15 days after the net due date. Assuming uniform sales and a 360-day year, what is the projected days' sales outstanding (rounded to the nearest whole day)?

    A. 20 days.

    B. 24 days.

    C. 27 days.

    D. 30 days.

Answer (C) is correct. *(CMA, adapted)*
    REQUIRED: The projected days' sales outstanding.
    DISCUSSION: Given that 40% of sales will be collected on the 15th day, 40% on the 30th day, and 20% on the 45th day, the days' sales outstanding can be determined by weighting the collection period for each group of receivables by its collection percentage. Hence, the projected days' sales outstanding equal 27 days [(40% × 15) + (40% × 30) + (20% × 45)].
    Answer (A) is incorrect because average receivables are outstanding for much more than 20 days. Answer (B) is incorrect because 24 days assumes 40% of receivables are collected after 15 days and 60% after 30 days. Answer (D) is incorrect because more receivables are collected on the 15th day than on the 45th day; thus, the average must be less than 30 days.

13. Management of a firm does not want to violate a working capital restriction contained in its bond indenture. If the firm's current ratio falls below 2.0 to 1, technically it will have defaulted. The firm's current ratio is now 2.2 to 1. If current liabilities are $200 million, the maximum new commercial paper that can be issued to finance inventory expansion is

    A. $20 million.

    B. $40 million.

    C. $240 million.

    D. $180 million.

Answer (B) is correct. *(Publisher, adapted)*
    REQUIRED: The amount of commercial paper that can be issued to finance inventory without violating the bond indenture.
    DISCUSSION: If current liabilities are $200 million and the current ratio (current assets ÷ current liabilities) is 2.2, current assets must be $440 million (2.2 × $200 million). If X amount of commercial paper is issued to finance inventory (current assets), thereby increasing both current assets and current liabilities by X, the level of current assets at which the new current ratio will be 2.0 is $480 million ($440 million + $40 million of commercial paper).

$$(\$440 + X) \div (\$200 + X) = 2.0$$
$$\$440 + X = 2(\$200 + X)$$
$$\$440 + X = \$400 + 2X$$
$$\$440 = \$400 + X$$
$$X = \$40$$

    Answer (A) is incorrect because $20 million ignores the increase in current assets. This answer would be appropriate if noncurrent assets were being financed. Answer (C) is incorrect because $240 million is the amount of working capital both before and after the issuance of commercial paper. Answer (D) is incorrect because $180 million is a nonsense answer.

10.2 Cash Management

14. The most direct way to prepare a cash budget for a manufacturing firm is to include

    A. Projected sales, credit terms, and net income.

    B. Projected net income, depreciation, and goodwill amortization.

    C. Projected purchases, percentages of purchases paid, and net income.

    D. Projected sales and purchases, percentages of collections, and terms of payments.

Answer (D) is correct. *(CMA, adapted)*
    REQUIRED: The most direct way of preparing a cash budget for a manufacturing firm.
    DISCUSSION: The most direct way of preparing a cash budget requires incorporation of sales projections and credit terms, collection percentages, estimated purchases and payment terms, and other cash receipts and disbursements. In other words, preparation of the cash budget requires consideration of both inflows and outflows.
    Answer (A) is incorrect because net income includes noncash elements, e.g., goodwill impairment and depreciation. Answer (B) is incorrect because net income includes noncash elements, e.g., goodwill impairment and depreciation. Answer (C) is incorrect because collection percentages must be considered, and net income includes noncash elements.

15. RLF Corporation had income before taxes of $60,000 for the year. Included in this amount were depreciation of $5,000, a charge of $6,000 for the amortization of bond discounts, and $4,000 for interest expense. The estimated cash flow for the period is

    A. $60,000

    B. $66,000

    C. $49,000

    D. $71,000

Answer (D) is correct. *(CMA, adapted)*
    REQUIRED: The estimated cash flow for the period.
    DISCUSSION: To determine cash flow for the period, all noncash expenses should be added back to net income. Adding the $5,000 of depreciation and the $6,000 of discount amortization to the $60,000 of net income produces a cash flow of $71,000.
    Answer (A) is incorrect because the cash flow for the period is greater than net income given noncash expenses in the form of depreciation and bond discount amortization. Answer (B) is incorrect because $66,000 does not reflect the noncash expense for depreciation. Answer (C) is incorrect because the $5,000 of depreciation and the $6,000 for amortization should be added back to, not subtracted from, income.

16. Shown below is a forecast of sales for Cooper Inc. for the first 4 months of the year (all amounts are in thousands of dollars).

	January	February	March	April
Cash sales	$ 15	$ 24	$18	$14
Sales on credit	100	120	90	70

On average, 50% of credit sales are paid for in the month of sale, 30% in the month following the sale, and the remainder is paid 2 months after the month of sale. Assuming there are no bad debts, the expected cash inflow for Cooper in March is

    A. $138,000

    B. $122,000

    C. $119,000

    D. $108,000

Answer (C) is correct. *(CMA, adapted)*
    REQUIRED: The expected cash inflows for March.
    DISCUSSION: Cash inflows for March would consist of 50% of March credit sales ($90 × 50% = $45), plus 30% of February credit sales ($120 × 30% = $36), plus 20% of January credit sales ($100 × 20% = $20), plus cash sales for March of $18. Consequently, total collections equal $119,000.
    Answer (A) is incorrect because $138,000 equals the sum of February credit sales and March cash sales. Answer (B) is incorrect because $122,000 equals 50% of January credit sales, 30% of February credit sales, 20% of March credit sales, and 100% of March cash sales. Answer (D) is incorrect because $108,000 is the total sales for March, not the total cash collections for March.

17. A firm has daily cash receipts of $100,000 and collection time of 2 days. A bank has offered to reduce the collection time on the firm's deposits by 2 days for a monthly fee of $500. If money market rates are expected to average 6% during the year, the net annual benefit (loss) from having this service is

    A. $3,000

    B. $12,000

    C. $0

    D. $6,000

Answer (D) is correct. *(CMA, adapted)*
    REQUIRED: The net annual benefit or loss.
    DISCUSSION: If collection time is 2 days, and average daily receipts are $100,000, the average cash balance will increase by $200,000 if the bank's system is adopted. At a 6% interest rate, $200,000 will generate $12,000 of interest revenue annually. The $500 monthly charge by the bank will result in an annual expense of $6,000. Thus, the net annual benefit is $6,000 ($12,000 – $6,000).
    Answer (A) is incorrect because $3,000 miscalculates the annual service charge. Answer (B) is incorrect because $12,000 fails to deduct the annual service charge from the interest earned. Answer (C) is incorrect because $0 results from figuring the interest earned for only one day, not two.

18. The treasury analyst for Garth Manufacturing has estimated the cash flows for the first half of next year (ignoring any short-term borrowings) as follows:

	Cash (millions)	
	Inflows	Outflows
January	$2	$1
February	2	4
March	2	5
April	2	3
May	4	2
June	5	3

Garth has a line of credit of up to $4 million on which it pays interest monthly at a rate of 1% of the amount utilized. Garth is expected to have a cash balance of $2 million on January 1 and no amount utilized on its line of credit. Assuming all cash flows occur at the end of the month, approximately how much will Garth pay in interest during the first half of the year?

A. $0

B. $61,000

C. $80,000

D. $132,000

Answer (B) is correct. *(CMA, adapted)*
REQUIRED: The interest expense for six months.
DISCUSSION: The sum of the beginning balance and inflows exceeds the outflows for the first 2 months. At the end of March, however, Garth must use $2,000,000 of its line of credit ($2,000,000 beginning balance + $6,000,000 inflows – $10,000,000 outflows). Thus, interest for April is $20,000 ($2,000,000 × 1%). The net cash outflow for April (ignoring short-term borrowings) is $1,000,000 of an additional $1,000,000 of the line of credit. However, the $20,000 of interest for April must also be paid, so the amount of the line of credit used in May is $3,020,000 ($2,000,000 + $1,000,000 + $20,000). Interest for May is therefore $30,200 ($3,020,000 × 1%). Given the net cash inflow for May of $2,000,000 (again ignoring short-term borrowings) and the borrowing of $30,200 to pay the interest for May, the amount of the line of credit used in June is $1,050,200. Interest in June is $10,502 ($1,050,200 × 1%), and total interest is $60,702 ($20,000 + $30,200 + $10,502). Consequently, the closest answer is $61,000.
Answer (A) is incorrect because interest must be paid monthly when the credit line is used in April, May, and June. Answer (C) is incorrect because the company would repay the credit line at the end of months with a positive cash flow. Answer (D) is incorrect because the company would repay the credit line at the end of months with a positive cash flow.

19. Kemple is a newly established janitorial firm, and the owner is deciding what type of checking account to open. Kemple is planning to keep a $500 minimum balance in the account for emergencies and plans to write roughly 80 checks per month. The bank charges $10 per month plus a $0.10 per check charge for a standard business checking account with no minimum balance. Kemple also has the option of a premium business checking account that requires a $2,500 minimum balance but has no monthly fees or per check charges. If Kemple's cost of funds is 10%, which account should Kemple choose?

A. Standard account, because the savings is $34 per year.

B. Premium account, because the savings is $34 per year.

C. Standard account, because the savings is $16 per year.

D. Premium account, because the savings is $16 per year.

Answer (D) is correct. *(CMA, adapted)*
REQUIRED: The checking account that should be chosen.
DISCUSSION: The standard account will cost $10 per month plus $8 in check charges (80 checks × $.10), for a total of $18 per month or $216 per year. The premium account has no check charges, but it will require the depositor to maintain a balance of $2,000 more than desired. At a 10% cost of capital, the incremental $2,000 minimum deposit will cost $200 per year. Thus, the premium account should be selected because it is cheaper by $16 per year.
Answer (A) is incorrect because the relevant cost of the minimum premium account deposit is based on the $2,000 incremental deposit, not the full $2,500. Answer (B) is incorrect because the savings on the premium account is $16. Answer (C) is incorrect because the savings on the premium account is $16.

20. Newman Products has received proposals from several banks to establish a lockbox system to speed up receipts. Newman receives an average of 700 checks per day averaging $1,800 each, and its cost of short-term funds is 7% per year. Assuming that all proposals will produce equivalent processing results and using a 360-day year, which one of the following proposals is optimal for Newman?

A. A $0.50 fee per check.

B. A flat fee of $125,000 per year.

C. A fee of 0.03% of the amount collected.

D. A compensating balance of $1,750,000.

Answer (D) is correct. *(CMA, adapted)*
REQUIRED: The optimal fee structure for a lockbox system.
DISCUSSION: Multiplying 700 checks times 360 days results in a total of 252,000 checks per year. Accordingly, under (A), total annual cost is $126,000 (252,000 × $.50), which is less desirable than the $125,000 flat fee in (B). Given that the annual collections equal $453,600,000 (700 checks × $1,800 × 360 days), (C) is also less desirable because the annual fee would be $136,080 ($453,600,000 × .03%). The best option is therefore to maintain a compensating balance of $1,750,000 when the cost of funds is 7%, resulting in a total cost of $122,500 ($1,750,000 × .07).
Answer (A) is incorrect because the annual cost is $126,000. Answer (B) is incorrect because the annual cost is $125,000. Answer (C) is incorrect because the annual cost is $136,080.

21. Cleveland Masks and Costumes, Inc. (CMC) has a majority of its customers located in the states of California and Nevada. Keystone National Bank, a major west coast bank, has agreed to provide a lockbox system to CMC at a fixed fee of $50,000 per year and a variable fee of $0.50 for each payment processed by the bank. On average, CMC receives 50 payments per day, each averaging $20,000. With the lockbox system, the company's collection float will decrease by 2 days. The annual interest rate on money market securities is 6%. If CMC makes use of the lockbox system, what would be the net benefit to the company? Use 365 days per year.

A. $59,125

B. $60,875

C. $50,000

D. $120,000

Answer (B) is correct. *(CMA, adapted)*
REQUIRED: The net benefit to the company if a lockbox system is adopted.
DISCUSSION: If payments are collected 2 days earlier, the company can earn $120,000 (50 payments per day × 2 days × $20,000 × .06) at a cost of $59,125 [$50,000 + (50 payments × $.50 × 365 days)], a gain of $60,875.
Answer (A) is incorrect because $59,125 is the annual lockbox cost. Answer (C) is incorrect because $50,000 is the annual fixed fee. Answer (D) is incorrect because $120,000 is the annual savings without regard to costs.

22. A firm has daily cash receipts of $300,000 and is interested in acquiring a lockbox service in order to reduce collection time. Bank 1's lockbox service costs $3,000 per month and will reduce collection time by 3 days. Bank 2's lockbox service costs $5,000 per month and will reduce collection time by 4 days. Bank 3's lockbox service costs $500 per month and will reduce collection time by 1 day. Bank 4's lockbox service costs $1,000 per month and will reduce collection time by 2 days. If money market rates are expected to average 6% during the year, and the firm wishes to maximize income, which bank should the firm choose?

A. Bank 1.

B. Bank 2.

C. Bank 3.

D. Bank 4.

Answer (D) is correct. *(Publisher, adapted)*
REQUIRED: The amount gained by using a lockbox service to process cash collections.
DISCUSSION: Because collections made using Bank 4's lockbox service will be accelerated by 2 days at a rate of $300,000 per day, the firm will have an additional $600,000 to invest. At a rate of 6%, the interest earned will be $36,000 per year. However, the bank will charge $12,000 ($1,000 per month × 12 months) for its services. Thus, the firm will gain $24,000 ($36,000 − $12,000).
Answer (A) is incorrect because Bank 1 will increase the firm's income by only $18,000. Answer (B) is incorrect because Bank 2 will increase the firm's income by only $12,000. Answer (C) is incorrect because Bank 3 will increase the firm's income by only $12,000.

23. If the average age of inventory is 60 days, the average age of the accounts payable is 30 days, and the average age of accounts receivable is 45 days, the number of days in the cash flow cycle is

A. 135 days.

B. 90 days.

C. 75 days.

D. 105 days.

Answer (C) is correct. *(Publisher, adapted)*
REQUIRED: The length of the cash flow cycle.
DISCUSSION: The cash flow cycle begins when the firm pays for merchandise it has purchased and ends when the firm receives cash from the sale of the merchandise. Inventory is held for an average of 60 days prior to sale, but the average age of accounts payable is 30 days. Consequently, the average time between outlay and sale is 30 days. Receivables are collected an average of 45 days after sale, so the length of the cash flow cycle is 75 days (30 + 45).
Answer (A) is incorrect because the age of payables should be deducted from the sum of the other items. Answer (B) is incorrect because the payables are not added to the inventory period. They are deducted. Answer (D) is incorrect because 105 days equals the sum of the inventory cycle and the receivables cycle.

24. DLF is a retail mail order firm that currently uses a central collection system that requires all checks to be sent to its Boston headquarters. An average of 6 days is required for mailed checks to be received, 3 days for DLF to process them, and 2 days for the checks to clear through its bank. A proposed lockbox system would reduce the mailing and processing time to 2 days and the check clearing time to 1 day. DLF has an average daily collection of $150,000. If DLF adopts the lockbox system, its average cash balance will increase by

    A. $1,200,000

    B. $750,000

    C. $600,000

    D. $450,000

Answer (A) is correct. *(Publisher, adapted)*
    REQUIRED: The average increase in cash after the adoption of a lockbox system.
    DISCUSSION: Checks are currently tied up for 11 days (6 for mailing, 3 for processing, and 2 for clearing). If that period were reduced to 3 days, DLF's cash balance would increase by $1,200,000 ($150,000 per day × 8 days).
    Answer (B) is incorrect because the decrease is 8 days, not 5. Answer (C) is incorrect because $600,000 represents only a 4-day savings. Answer (D) is incorrect because the lockbox system will result in an additional 8 days of savings, not 3.

25. Troy Toys is a retailer operating in several cities. The individual store managers deposit daily collections at a local bank in a non-interest bearing checking account. Twice per week, the local bank issues a depository transfer check (DTC) to the central bank at headquarters. The controller of the company is considering using a wire transfer instead. The additional cost of each transfer would be $25; collections would be accelerated by 2 days; and the annual interest rate paid by the central bank is 7.2% (0.02% per day). At what amount of dollars transferred would it be economically feasible to use a wire transfer instead of the DTC? Assume a 350-day year.

    A. It would never be economically feasible.

    B. $125,000 or above.

    C. Any amount greater than $173.

    D. Any amount greater than $62,500.

Answer (D) is correct. *(CMA, adapted)*
    REQUIRED: The amount at which wire transfers are preferable.
    DISCUSSION: Given a $25 fee and an interest rate of 0.02% per day for 2 days, the breakeven amount is $62,500 [$25 transfer fee ÷ (2 × .02% interest rate)]. Thus, the interest earned on a transfer of any amount greater than $62,500 would exceed the $25 fee.
    Answer (A) is incorrect because the $25 transfer fee is covered by the interest on $62,500 for 2 days. Answer (B) is incorrect because $125,000 is required if collections are accelerated by only one day. Answer (C) is incorrect because the interest on $173 for 2 days is less than $.07.

26. A working capital technique that increases the payable float and therefore delays the outflow of cash is

    A. Concentration banking.

    B. A draft.

    C. Electronic Data Interchange (EDI).

    D. A lockbox system.

Answer (B) is correct. *(CMA, adapted)*
    REQUIRED: The working capital technique to increase the payable float and delay the outflow of cash.
    DISCUSSION: Payment by draft, a three-party instrument in which the drawer orders the drawee to pay money to the payee, is a means of slowing cash outflows. A check is the most common type of draft. Check float arises from the delay between an expenditure and the clearing of the check through the banking system.
    Answer (A) is incorrect because concentration banking, a lockbox system, and the use of a local post office box are techniques used to accelerate cash receipts. Answer (C) is incorrect because EDI is the communication of electronic documents directly from a computer in one entity to a computer in another entity. Thus, EDI expedites cash payments. The payee receives the money almost instantaneously. Answer (D) is incorrect because concentration banking, a lockbox system, and the use of a local post office box are techniques used to accelerate cash receipts.

27. Assume that each day a company writes and receives checks totaling $10,000. If it takes 5 days for the checks to clear and be deducted from the company's account, and only 4 days for the deposits to clear, what is the float?

A. $10,000

B. $0

C. $(10,000)

D. $50,000

Answer (A) is correct. *(CMA, adapted)*
REQUIRED: The net float when checks clear more slowly than deposits.
DISCUSSION: The float period is the time between when a check is written and when it clears the payor's checking account. Check float results in an interest-free loan to the payor because of the delay between payment by check and its deduction from the bank account. If checks written require one more day to clear than checks received, the net float equals one day's receipts. The company will have free use of the money for one day. In this case, the amount is $10,000.
Answer (B) is incorrect because the company enjoys one day's net float because its checks clear more slowly than its deposits. Answer (C) is incorrect because the net float is positive. The company can write checks (up to $10,000) even when it has no money because the checks do not clear until a day after deposits clear. Answer (D) is incorrect because the net float represents the difference between when deposits clear and when disbursements clear.

28. A compensating balance

A. Compensates a financial institution for services rendered by providing it with deposits of funds.

B. Is used to compensate for possible losses on a marketable securities portfolio.

C. Is a level of inventory held to compensate for variations in usage rate and lead time.

D. Is the amount of prepaid interest on a loan.

Answer (A) is correct. *(CMA, adapted)*
REQUIRED: The true statement about compensating balances.
DISCUSSION: Banks sometimes require a borrower to keep a certain percentage of the face amount of a loan in a noninterest-bearing checking account. This requirement raises the effective rate of interest paid by the borrower. This greater rate compensates a bank for services provided and results in greater profitability for the financial institution. Funds kept as a compensating balance can often be withdrawn if a certain average balance is maintained.
Answer (B) is incorrect because, in financial accounting, a valuation allowance is used to reflect losses on marketable securities. Answer (C) is incorrect because safety stock is held for such purposes. Answer (D) is incorrect because interest deducted in advance is discount interest.

29. A company uses the following formula in determining its optimal level of cash.

$$OC = \sqrt{\frac{2bT}{i}}$$

Where: b = fixed cost per transaction
T = total demand for cash over a period of time
i = interest rate on marketable securities

This formula is a modification of the economic order quantity (EOQ) formula used for inventory management. Assume that the fixed cost of selling marketable securities is $10 per transaction and the interest rate on marketable securities is 6% per year. The company estimates that it will make cash payments of $12,000 over a one-month period. What is the average cash balance (rounded to the nearest dollar)?

A. $1,000

B. $2,000

C. $3,464

D. $6,928

Answer (C) is correct. *(CMA, adapted)*
REQUIRED: The average cash balance.
DISCUSSION: The EOQ for inventory is a function of ordering cost per order, inventory demand, and carrying cost. In the cash model, the fixed cost per sale of securities is equivalent to the ordering cost, the demand for cash is similar to the demand for inventory, and the interest rate is effectively the cost of carrying a dollar of cash for the period. Substituting in the formula yields an optimal cash balance of about $6,928. Thus, the average cash balance is $3,464 ($6,928 ÷ 2).

$$\sqrt{\frac{2bT}{i}} = \sqrt{\frac{2 \times \$10 \times \$12,000}{6\% \div 12 \text{ months}}} = \sqrt{\frac{\$240,000}{.005}} = \$6,928$$

Answer (A) is incorrect because $1,000 results from using 24% in the denominator. Answer (B) is incorrect because $2,000 results from using 6% in the denominator. Answer (D) is incorrect because $6,928 is the optimal cash balance.

30. Which one of the following is not a characteristic of a negotiable certificate of deposit? Negotiable certificates of deposit

A. Have a secondary market for investors.

B. Are regulated by the Federal Reserve System.

C. Are usually sold in denominations of a minimum of $100,000.

D. Have yields considerably greater than bankers' acceptances and commercial paper.

Answer (D) is correct. *(CMA, adapted)*
REQUIRED: The item not a characteristic of a negotiable certificate of deposit.
DISCUSSION: A certificate of deposit (CD) is a form of savings deposit that cannot be withdrawn before maturity without incurring a high penalty. A negotiable CD can be traded. CDs usually have a fairly high rate of return compared with other savings instruments because they are for fixed, usually long-term periods. However, their yield is less than that of commercial paper and bankers' acceptances because they are less risky.
Answer (A) is incorrect because negotiable CDs do have a secondary market (i.e., they are negotiable). Answer (B) is incorrect because negotiable CDs are regulated. Answer (C) is incorrect because negotiable CDs are typically issued in a denomination of $100,000.

31. A firm has daily cash receipts of $300,000. A bank has offered to provide a lockbox service that will reduce the collection time by 3 days. The bank requires a monthly fee of $2,000 for providing this service. If money market rates are expected to average 6% during the year, the additional annual income (loss) of using the lockbox service is

A. ($24,000)

B. $12,000

C. $30,000

D. $54,000

Answer (C) is correct. *(Publisher, adapted)*
REQUIRED: The amount a company will gain or lose by hiring a bank lockbox service to process cash collections.
DISCUSSION: Because collections will be accelerated by 3 days at a rate of $300,000 per day, the company will have an additional $900,000 to invest. At a rate of 6%, the interest earned will be $54,000 per year. However, the bank will charge $24,000 (12 months × $2,000 per month) for its services. Thus, the firm will increase its income by $30,000 ($54,000 – $24,000).
Answer (A) is incorrect because ($24,000) ignores the additional interest revenue from investing the increased funds. Answer (B) is incorrect because $12,000 is based on 2 days of accelerated inflows rather than 3. Answer (D) is incorrect because $54,000 ignores the $24,000 bank service charge.

10.3 Marketable Securities Management

32. When managing cash and short-term investments, a corporate treasurer is primarily concerned with

A. Maximizing rate of return.

B. Minimizing taxes.

C. Investing in Treasury bonds since they have no default risk.

D. Liquidity and safety.

Answer (D) is correct. *(CMA, adapted)*
REQUIRED: The primary concern when managing cash and short-term investments.
DISCUSSION: Cash and short-term investments are crucial to a firm's continuing success. Sufficient liquidity must be available to meet payments as they come due. At the same time, liquid assets are subject to significant control risk. Therefore, liquidity and safety are the primary concerns of the treasurer when dealing with highly liquid assets. Cash and short-term investments are held because of their ability to facilitate routine operations of the company. These assets are not held for purposes of achieving investment returns.
Answer (A) is incorrect because most companies are not in business to earn high returns on liquid assets (i.e., they are held to facilitate operations). Answer (B) is incorrect because the holding of cash and cash-like assets is not a major factor in controlling taxes. Answer (C) is incorrect because investments in Treasury bonds do not have sufficient liquidity to serve as short-term assets.

33. The term short-selling is the

A. Selling of a security that was purchased by borrowing money from a broker.

B. Selling of a security that is not owned by the seller.

C. Selling of all the shares you own in a company in anticipation that the price will decline dramatically.

D. Betting that a stock will increase by a certain amount within a given period of time.

Answer (B) is correct. *(CMA, adapted)*
REQUIRED: The definition of short-selling.
DISCUSSION: Short-selling is accomplished by borrowing securities from a broker and selling those securities. At a later time, the loan is repaid by buying securities on the open market and returning them to the broker. The seller speculates that the stock's market price will decline.
Answer (A) is incorrect because margin trading involves buying securities by borrowing from a broker. Answer (C) is incorrect because the investor does not own the shares sold in a short-sale. Answer (D) is incorrect because the short-seller is betting that the stock will decrease in price.

34. All of the following are alternative marketable securities suitable for investment except

    A. U.S. Treasury bills.

    B. Eurodollars.

    C. Commercial paper.

    D. Convertible bonds.

Answer (D) is correct. *(CMA, adapted)*
    REQUIRED: The item that is not a marketable security.
    DISCUSSION: Marketable securities are near-cash items used primarily for short-term investment. Examples include U.S. Treasury bills, Eurodollars, commercial paper, money-market mutual funds with portfolios of short-term securities, bankers' acceptances, floating rate preferred stock, and negotiable CDs of U.S. banks. A convertible bond is not a short-term investment because its maturity date is usually more than one year in the future and its price can be influenced substantially by changes in interest rates or by changes in the investee's stock price.
    Answer (A) is incorrect because U.S. Treasury bills are short-term marketable securities. Answer (B) is incorrect because Eurodollars are short-term marketable securities. Answer (C) is incorrect because commercial paper is a short-term marketable security.

35. Garo Company, a retail store, is considering forgoing sales discounts to delay using its cash. Supplier credit terms are 2/10, net 30. Assuming a 360-day year, what is the annual cost of credit if the cash discount is not taken and Garo pays net 30?

    A. 24.0%

    B. 24.5%

    C. 36.0%

    D. 36.7%

Answer (D) is correct. *(CMA, adapted)*
    REQUIRED: The annual cost of credit if cash discounts are not taken.
    DISCUSSION: On a $1,000 invoice, the company could save $20 by paying within the discount period. Thus, an immediate payment of $980 would save the company $20, and the interest rate charged for holding $980 an additional 20 days (30 – 10) is 2.04% ($20 ÷ $980). Because the number of 20-day periods in a year is 18 (360 ÷ 20), the annual rate is 36.7% (18 × 2.04%).
    Answer (A) is incorrect because the length of the extra credit period is 20 days, not 30 days. Answer (B) is incorrect because the length of the extra credit period is 20 days, not 30 days. Answer (C) is incorrect because 36.0% calculates the interest rate based on the full invoice price.

10.4 Receivables Management

36. The sales manager at Ryan Company feels confident that, if the credit policy at Ryan's were changed, sales would increase and, consequently, the company would utilize excess capacity. The two credit proposals being considered are as follows:

	Proposal A	Proposal B
Increase in sales	$500,000	$600,000
Contribution margin	20%	20%
Bad debt percentage	5%	5%
Increase in operating profits	$75,000	$90,000
Desired return on sales	15%	15%

Currently, payment terms are net 30. The proposed payment terms for Proposal A and Proposal B are net 45 and net 90, respectively. An analysis to compare these two proposals for the change in credit policy would include all of the following factors except the

    A. Cost of funds for Ryan.

    B. Current bad debt experience.

    C. Impact on the current customer base of extending terms to only certain customers.

    D. Bank loan covenants on days' sales outstanding.

Answer (B) is correct. *(CMA, adapted)*
    REQUIRED: The factor not considered in an analysis of proposed credit policies.
    DISCUSSION: All factors should be considered that differ between the two policies. Factors that do not differ, such as the current bad debt experience, are not relevant. Ryan must estimate the expected bad debt losses under each new policy.
    Answer (A) is incorrect because the cost of funds is an obvious element in the analysis of any investment. Answer (C) is incorrect because the impact on the current customer base of extending terms to only certain customers is relevant. The current customers may demand the same terms. Answer (D) is incorrect because existing loan agreements may require Ryan to maintain certain ratios at stated levels. Thus, Ryan's ability to increase receivables and possible bad debt losses may be limited.

37. Jackson Distributors sells to retail stores on credit terms of 2/10, net 30. Daily sales average 150 units at a price of $300 each. Assuming that all sales are on credit and 60% of customers take the discount and pay on day 10 while the rest of the customers pay on day 30, the amount of Jackson's accounts receivable is

A. $1,350,000

B. $990,000

C. $900,000

D. $810,000

Answer (D) is correct. *(CMA, adapted)*
REQUIRED: The amount of accounts receivable if some customers take cash discounts.
DISCUSSION: The firm has daily sales of $45,000 consisting of 150 units at $300 each. For 30 days, sales total $1,350,000. Forty percent of these sales, or $540,000, will be uncollected because customers do not take their discounts. The remaining 60%, or $810,000, will be paid within the discount period. However, by the end of 30 days, only 2/3 of the $810,000 will be collected because the sales from days 21 through 30 are still within the discount period. Therefore, an additional $270,000 ($810,000 – $540,000) will still be uncollected after the 30th day, but will be subject to a discount. In total, the average receivable balance is $810,000, consisting of $540,000 on which no discount will be taken and $270,000 that will be paid within the discount period.
Answer (A) is incorrect because 60% of the sales will be paid for within the 10-day discount period. Answer (B) is incorrect because $990,000 is based on a sales total of $1,650,000 for 30 days rather than $1,350,000. Answer (C) is incorrect because $900,000 is based on a sales total of $1,650,000 for 30 days rather than $1,350,000.

38. The average collection period for a firm measures the number of days

A. After a typical credit sale is made until the firm receives the payment.

B. For a typical check to "clear" through the banking system.

C. Beyond the end of the credit period before a typical customer payment is received.

D. Before a typical account becomes delinquent.

Answer (A) is correct. *(CMA, adapted)*
REQUIRED: The meaning of a firm's average collection period.
DISCUSSION: The average collection period measures the number of days between the date of sale and the date of collection. It should be related to a firm's credit terms. For example, a firm that allows terms of 2/15, net 30, should have an average collection period of somewhere between 15 and 30 days.
Answer (B) is incorrect because it describes the concept of float. Answer (C) is incorrect because the average collection period includes the total time before a payment is received, including the periods both before and after the end of the normal credit period. Answer (D) is incorrect because it describes the normal credit period.

39. A change in credit policy has caused an increase in sales, an increase in discounts taken, a decrease in the amount of bad debts, and a decrease in the investment in accounts receivable. Based upon this information, the company's

A. Average collection period has decreased.

B. Percentage discount offered has decreased.

C. Accounts receivable turnover has decreased.

D. Working capital has increased.

Answer (A) is correct. *(CMA, adapted)*
REQUIRED: The true statement about a change in credit policy that has resulted in greater sales and a reduction in accounts receivable.
DISCUSSION: An increase in discounts taken accompanied by declines in receivables balances and doubtful accounts all indicate that collections on the increased sales have been accelerated. Accordingly, the average collection period must have declined. The average collection period is a ratio calculated by dividing the number of days in a year (365) by the receivable turnover. Thus, the higher the turnover, the shorter the average collection period. The turnover increases when either sales (the numerator) increase, or receivables (the denominator) decrease. Accomplishing both higher sales and a lower receivables increases the turnover and results in a shorter collection period.
Answer (B) is incorrect because a decrease in the percentage discount offered provides no incentive for early payment. Answer (C) is incorrect because accounts receivable turnover (sales ÷ average receivables) has increased. Answer (D) is incorrect because no information is given relative to working capital elements other than receivables. Both receivables and cash are elements of working capital, so an acceleration of customer payments will have no effect on working capital.

40. A company plans to tighten its credit policy. The new policy will decrease the average number of days in collection from 75 to 50 days and will reduce the ratio of credit sales to total revenue from 70% to 60%. The company estimates that projected sales will be 5% less if the proposed new credit policy is implemented. If projected sales for the coming year are $50 million, calculate the dollar impact on accounts receivable of this proposed change in credit policy. Assume a 360-day year.

    A. $3,819,445 decrease.

    B. $6,500,000 decrease.

    C. $3,333,334 decrease.

    D. $18,749,778 increase.

Answer (C) is correct. *(CMA, adapted)*
    REQUIRED: The dollar impact on accounts receivable of a change in credit policy.
    DISCUSSION: If sales are $50 million, 70% of which are on credit, total credit sales will be $35 million. The receivables turnover equals 4.8 times per year (360 days ÷ 75-day collection period). Receivables turnover equals net credit sales divided by average receivables. Accordingly, average receivables equal $7,291,667 ($35,000,000 ÷ 4.8). Under the new policy, sales will be $47.5 million ($50,000,000 × 95%), and credit sales will be $28.5 million ($47,500,000 × 60%). The collection period will be reduced to 50 days, resulting in a turnover of 7.2 times per year (360 ÷ 50). The average receivables balance will therefore be $3,958,333 ($28,500,000 ÷ 7.2), a reduction of $3,333,334 ($7,291,667 − $3,958,333).
    Answer (A) is incorrect because $3,819,445 is calculated using total, not credit, sales. Answer (B) is incorrect because $6,500,000 is the decrease in total credit sales. Answer (D) is incorrect because receivables will decrease.

41. A company with $4.8 million in credit sales per year plans to relax its credit standards, projecting that this will increase credit sales by $720,000. The company's average collection period for new customers is expected to be 75 days, and the payment behavior of the existing customers is not expected to change. Variable costs are 80% of sales. The firm's opportunity cost is 20% before taxes. Assuming a 360-day year, what is the company's benefit (loss) on the planned change in credit terms?

    A. $0

    B. $28,800

    C. $144,000

    D. $120,000

Answer (D) is correct. *(CMA, adapted)*
    REQUIRED: The annual benefit or loss resulting from a change in credit terms.
    DISCUSSION: The incremental sales will produce an increased contribution margin of $144,000 ($720,000 × 20%). However, that amount must be offset by the cost of funds invested in receivables. The variable costs associated with the incremental sales are $576,000 ($720,000 × 80%). Given a 75-day credit period, the average investment in receivables equals $120,000 [$576,000 × (75 ÷ 360)]. Accordingly, the cost of the investment in additional receivables is $24,000 ($120,000 × 20% opportunity cost), and the net benefit of the planned change in credit terms is $120,000 ($144,000 − $24,000).
    Answer (A) is incorrect because the company benefits from the change in credit terms. Answer (B) is incorrect because $28,800 results from multiplying the contribution margin by the 20% interest rate. Answer (C) is incorrect because $144,000 overlooks the costs created by having funds invested in receivables for 75 days.

42. Which of the following represents a firm's average gross receivables balance?

I.   Days' sales in receivables × accounts receivable turnover.

II. Average daily sales × average collection period.

III. Net sales ÷ average gross receivables.

    A. I only.

    B. I and II only.

    C. II only.

    D. II and III only.

Answer (C) is correct. *(CMA, adapted)*
    REQUIRED: The calculation of the average gross receivables balance.
    DISCUSSION: A firm's average gross receivables balance can be calculated by multiplying average daily sales by the average collection period (days' sales outstanding). Alternatively, annual credit sales can be divided by the accounts-receivable turnover (net credit sales ÷ average accounts receivable) to obtain the average balance in receivables.
    Answer (A) is incorrect because Alternative I cannot be correct. Neither of the multiplicands is a dollar figure, so the product could not be the dollar balance of receivables.
Answer (B) is incorrect because Alternative I cannot be correct. Neither of the multiplicands is a dollar figure, so the product could not be the dollar balance of receivables. Answer (D) is incorrect because Alternative III cannot be correct. It contains average gross receivables, the amount being calculated.

43. The high cost of short-term financing has recently caused a company to reevaluate the terms of credit it extends to its customers. The current policy is 1/10, net 60. If customers can borrow at the prime rate, at what prime rate must the company change its terms of credit in order to avoid an undesirable extension in its collection of receivables?

A. 2%

B. 5%

C. 7%

D. 8%

Answer (D) is correct. *(Publisher, adapted)*
REQUIRED: The prime rate at which a vendor must change its terms to avoid an undesirable extension in the collection of its receivables.
DISCUSSION: Terms of 1/10, net 60 mean that a buyer can save 1% of the purchase price by paying 50 days early. In essence, not taking the discount results in the buyer's borrowing 99% of the invoice price for 50 days at a total interest charge of 1% of the invoice price. Because a year has 7.3 50-day periods (365 ÷ 50), the credit terms 1/10, net 60 yield an effective annualized interest charge of approximately 7.37% [(1% ÷ 99%) × 7.3]. If the prime rate were higher than 7.37%, the buyer would prefer to borrow from the vendor (i.e., not pay within the discount period) rather than from a bank. Consequently, an 8% prime rate could cause the vendor's receivables to increase.
Answer (A) is incorrect because the prime rate must be greater than 7.37% to make the company's terms preferable to those of a bank. Answer (B) is incorrect because the prime rate must be greater than 7.37% to make the company's terms preferable to those of a bank. Answer (C) is incorrect because the prime rate must be greater than 7.37% to make the company's terms preferable to those of a bank.

44. A firm averages $4,000 in sales per day and is paid, on an average, within 30 days of the sale. After they receive their invoice, 55% of the customers pay by check, while the remaining 45% pay by credit card. Approximately how much would the company show in accounts receivable on its balance sheet on any given date?

A. $4,000

B. $120,000

C. $48,000

D. $54,000

Answer (B) is correct. *(CMA, adapted)*
REQUIRED: The average balance in accounts receivable given the average payment period and sales per day.
DISCUSSION: If sales are $4,000 per day, and customers pay in 30 days, 30 days of sales are outstanding, or $120,000. Whether customers pay by credit card or cash, collection requires 30 days.
Answer (A) is incorrect because $4,000 is only one day's sales. Answer (C) is incorrect because invoices are outstanding for 30 days, not 12 days. Answer (D) is incorrect because $54,000 is based on the 45% of collections via credit card.

45. Best Computers believes that its collection costs could be reduced through modification of collection procedures. This action is expected to result in a lengthening of the average collection period from 28 days to 34 days; however, there will be no change in uncollectible accounts. The company's budgeted credit sales for the coming year are $27,000,000, and short-term interest rates are expected to average 8%. To make the changes in collection procedures cost beneficial, the minimum savings in collection costs (using a 360-day year) for the coming year would have to be

A. $30,000

B. $360,000

C. $180,000

D. $36,000

Answer (D) is correct. *(CMA, adapted)*
REQUIRED: The minimum savings in collection costs that would be necessary to make the lengthened credit period beneficial.
DISCUSSION: Given sales of $27,000,000, the average amount of daily sales must be $75,000 ($27,000,000 ÷ 360 days). The increased accounts receivable balance is therefore $450,000 ($75,000 × 6 days). With an additional $450,000 of capital invested in receivables, the company's interest cost will increase by $36,000 per year ($450,000 × 8%). Thus, the company must save at least $36,000 per year to justify the change in procedures.

10.5 Inventory Management

46. Which one of the following would not be considered a carrying cost associated with inventory?

    A. Insurance costs.

    B. Cost of capital invested in the inventory.

    C. Cost of obsolescence.

    D. Shipping costs.

Answer (D) is correct. *(CMA, adapted)*
    REQUIRED: The item that is not a carrying cost of inventory.
    DISCUSSION: Carrying costs are incurred to hold inventory. Examples include such costs as warehousing, insurance, the cost of capital invested in inventories, inventory taxes, and the cost of obsolescence and spoilage. Neither shipping costs nor the initial cost of the inventory are carrying costs.

47. An example of a carrying cost is

    A. Disruption of production schedules.

    B. Quantity discounts lost.

    C. Handling costs.

    D. Spoilage.

Answer (D) is correct. *(CMA, adapted)*
    REQUIRED: The inventory carrying cost.
    DISCUSSION: Inventory costs fall into three categories: order or set-up costs, carrying (holding) costs, and stockout costs. Carrying costs include storage costs for inventory items plus opportunity cost (i.e., the cost incurred by investing in inventory rather than making an income-earning investment). Examples are insurance, spoilage, interest on invested capital, obsolescence, and warehousing costs.
    Answer (A) is incorrect because disruption of production schedules may result from a stockout. Answer (B) is incorrect because quantity discounts lost are related to ordering costs or inventory acquisition costs. Answer (C) is incorrect because shipping and handling costs are included in acquisition costs.

48. The ordering costs associated with inventory management include

    A. Insurance costs, purchasing costs, shipping costs, and spoilage.

    B. Obsolescence, setup costs, quantity discounts lost, and storage costs.

    C. Purchasing costs, shipping costs, setup costs, and quantity discounts lost.

    D. Shipping costs, obsolescence, setup costs, and capital invested.

Answer (C) is correct. *(CMA, adapted)*
    REQUIRED: The items included in ordering costs.
    DISCUSSION: Ordering costs are costs incurred when placing and receiving orders. Ordering costs include purchasing costs, shipping costs, setup costs for a production run, and quantity discounts lost.
    Answer (A) is incorrect because insurance costs are a carrying cost. Answer (B) is incorrect because obsolescence, spoilage, interest on invested capital, and storage costs are carrying costs. Answer (D) is incorrect because obsolescence, spoilage, interest on invested capital, and storage costs are carrying costs.

49. The amount of inventory that a company would tend to hold in stock would increase as the

    A. Sales level falls to a permanently lower level.

    B. Cost of carrying inventory decreases.

    C. Variability of sales decreases.

    D. Cost of running out of stock decreases.

Answer (B) is correct. *(CMA, adapted)*
    REQUIRED: The reason for an increase in inventory.
    DISCUSSION: Inventory management attempts to minimize the total costs of ordering, carrying inventory, and stockouts. Thus, a firm incurs carrying costs to reduce ordering and stockout costs. If the cost of carrying inventory declines, the inventory level must increase to minimize total inventory costs.
    Answer (A) is incorrect because permanently lower sales, more predictable sales, decreased stockout costs, and decreased inventory transit time are reasons for decreasing inventory. Answer (C) is incorrect because permanently lower sales, more predictable sales, decreased stockout costs, and decreased inventory transit time are reasons for decreasing inventory. Answer (D) is incorrect because permanently lower sales, more predictable sales, decreased stockout costs, and decreased inventory transit time are reasons for decreasing inventory.

50. In inventory management, the safety stock will tend to increase if the

    A. Carrying cost increases.

    B. Cost of running out of stock decreases.

    C. Variability of the lead time increases.

    D. Variability of the usage rate decreases.

Answer (C) is correct. *(CMA, adapted)*
    REQUIRED: The factor that will cause safety stocks to increase.
    DISCUSSION: A company maintains safety stocks to protect itself against the losses caused by stockouts. These can take the form of lost sales or lost production time. Safety stock is necessary because of the variability in lead time and usage rates. As the variability in lead time increases, a company will tend to carry larger safety stocks.
    Answer (A) is incorrect because an increase in inventory carrying costs makes it less economical to carry safety stocks. Thus, safety stocks will be reduced. Answer (B) is incorrect because, if the cost of stockouts declines, the incentive to carry large safety stocks is reduced. Answer (D) is incorrect because a decline in the variability of usage makes it easier to plan orders, and safety stocks will be less necessary.

51. The result of the economic order quantity formula indicates the

    A. Annual quantity of inventory to be carried.

    B. Annual usage of materials during the year.

    C. Safety stock plus estimated inventory for the year.

    D. Quantity of each individual order during the year.

Answer (D) is correct. *(CMA, adapted)*
    REQUIRED: The indication given by the EOQ formula.
    DISCUSSION: The EOQ model is a deterministic model that calculates the ideal order (or production lot) quantity given specified demand, ordering or setup costs, and carrying costs. The model minimizes the sum of inventory carrying costs and either ordering or production setup costs.
    Answer (A) is incorrect because the annual quantity of inventory demanded is an input into the formula, not the result. Answer (B) is incorrect because annual usage is a determinant of annual demand, which is an input into the formula. Answer (C) is incorrect because safety stock is not reflected in the basic EOQ formula.

52. The Stewart Co. uses the economic order quantity (EOQ) model for inventory management. A decrease in which one of the following variables would increase the EOQ?

    A. Annual sales.

    B. Cost per order.

    C. Safety stock level.

    D. Carrying costs.

Answer (D) is correct. *(CMA, adapted)*
    REQUIRED: The variable for which a decrease will lead to an increase in the economic order quantity (EOQ).
    DISCUSSION: The EOQ model minimizes the total of ordering and carrying costs. The EOQ is calculated as follows:

$$\sqrt{\frac{2\,(Demand)\,(Order\ costs)}{Carrying\ costs\ per\ unit}}$$

Increases in the numerator (demand or ordering costs) will increase the EOQ, whereas decreases in demand or ordering costs will decrease the EOQ. Similarly, a decrease in the denominator (carrying costs) will increase the EOQ.
    Answer (A) is incorrect because a decrease in demand (annual sales), which is in the numerator, will decrease the EOQ. Answer (B) is incorrect because a decrease in ordering costs will encourage more orders, or a decrease in the EOQ. Answer (C) is incorrect because a decrease in safety stock levels will not affect the EOQ, although it might lead to a different ordering point.

53. Edwards Manufacturing Corporation uses the standard economic order quantity (EOQ) model. If the EOQ for Product A is 200 units and Edwards maintains a 50-unit safety stock for the item, what is the average inventory of Product A?

    A. 250 units.

    B. 150 units.

    C. 125 units.

    D. 100 units.

Answer (B) is correct. *(CMA, adapted)*
    REQUIRED: The average inventory of a product.
    DISCUSSION: If safety stock is 50 units, the receipt of an order should increase the inventory to 250. That amount will decline to 50 just prior to the receipt of the next order. Thus, the average inventory would be the average of 250 and 50 [(250 + 50) ÷ 2], or 150 units.
    Answer (A) is incorrect because 250 is the maximum inventory level. Answer (C) is incorrect because 125 units assumes an EOQ of 250 units and no safety stock. Answer (D) is incorrect because 100 units assumes no safety stock.

54. A major supplier has offered Alpha Corporation a year-end special purchase whereby Alpha could purchase 180,000 cases of sport drink at $10 per case. Alpha normally orders 30,000 cases per month at $12 per case. Alpha's cost of capital is 9%. In calculating the overall opportunity cost of this offer, the cost of carrying the increased inventory would be

A. $32,400

B. $40,500

C. $64,800

D. $81,000

Answer (A) is correct. *(CMA, adapted)*
REQUIRED: The cost of carrying the increased inventory.
DISCUSSION: If Alpha makes the special purchase of 6 months of inventory (180,000 cases ÷ 30,000 cases per month), the average inventory for the 6-month period will be $900,000 [(180,000 × $10) ÷ 2]. If the special purchase is not made, the average inventory for the same period will be the average monthly inventory of $180,000 [(30,000 × $12) ÷ 2]. Accordingly, the incremental average inventory is $720,000 ($900,000 – $180,000), and the interest cost of the incremental 6-month investment is $32,400 [($720,000 × 9%) ÷ 2].
Answer (B) is incorrect because $40,500 is the result of assuming an incremental average inventory of $900,000. Answer (C) is incorrect because $64,800 is the interest cost for 12 months. Answer (D) is incorrect because $81,000 is the result of assuming an incremental average inventory of $900,000 and a 12-month period.

Use Gleim's **CMA Test Prep** for interactive testing with **over 2,000 additional multiple-choice questions**!

STUDY UNIT ELEVEN
FINANCING CURRENT ASSETS

(4 pages of outline)

This study unit is the **last of five** on **corporate finance**. The relative weight assigned to this major topic in Part 3 of the exam is **25%** at **skill level B** (four skill types required). The five study units are

Study Unit 7:   Risk and Return
Study Unit 8:   Financial Instruments
Study Unit 9:   Cost of Capital
Study Unit 10: Managing Current Assets
Study Unit 11: Financing Current Assets

After studying the outline and answering the multiple-choice questions, you will have the skills necessary to address the following topics listed in the IMA's Learning Outcome Statements:

Part 3 – Section C.5. Financing current assets

The candidate should be able to:

   a.   demonstrate an understanding of how risk affects a firm's approach to its current asset financing policy (aggressive, conservative, etc.)

   b.   describe the different types of short-term credit, including trade credit, short-term bank loans, commercial paper, lines of credit, and bankers' acceptances and identify their advantages and disadvantages

   c.   estimate the annual cost and effective annual interest rate of not taking a cash discount

   d.   calculate the effective annual interest rate of a bank loan with a compensating balance requirement and/or a commitment fee

   e.   describe the different types of secured short-term credit, including accounts receivable financing and inventory financing

   f.   demonstrate an understanding of factoring accounts receivable and calculate the cost of factoring

   g.   demonstrate an understanding of the maturity matching or hedging approach to financing

11.1 SHORT-TERM CREDIT

1.   Short-term credit is debt scheduled to be **repaid within 1 year**. It often involves a lower interest rate and is more readily available than long-term credit.

2.   The major sources of short-term credit are described below and on the next page.

   a.   **Accrued expenses** such as salaries, wages, interest, dividends, and taxes constitute an interest-free method of financing because no interest accumulates until the due date.

      1)   EXAMPLES: Employees work five, six, or seven days a week but are only paid every two weeks. A company carries on operations constantly but must only remit federal income taxes every quarter.

      2)   Accruals have the additional advantage of fluctuating directly with operating activity.

b.   **Trade credit** is spontaneous financing because it arises automatically as part of the purchase transaction. The terms of payment are set by suppliers.

1)   Payment should be made within the discount period if the cost of not taking the discount exceeds the firm's cost of capital.

c.   **Short-term bank loans** provide money that appears on the balance sheet of the borrower as a note payable. The term is usually less than a year, which requires the firm to roll over the debt frequently at uncertain interest rates.

1)   A **promissory note** states the terms of the loan and repayment policy.
2)   Banks may require a borrower to keep a certain percentage of the face amount of the loan, called a compensating balance, in his/her account, which raises the real (effective) rate of interest to the borrower.

d.   **Commercial paper** consists of short-term, unsecured notes payable issued in large denominations ($100,000 or more) by large companies with high credit ratings to other companies and institutional investors, such as pension funds, banks, and insurance companies.

1)   Maturities of commercial paper are at most 270 days. No general secondary market exists for commercial paper. Commercial paper is a lower cost source of funds than bank loans and is usually issued at below the prime rate.

2)   **Advantages**

a)   Provides broad and efficient distribution
b)   Provides a large amount of funds (at a given cost)
c)   Avoids costly financing arrangements

3)   **Disadvantages**

a)   Impersonal market
b)   Total amount of funds available limited to the excess liquidity of big corporations

e.   A **line of credit** is the maximum amount that a bank agrees to lend the borrower in a certain period. It is the most practical form of financing for most small retail businesses.

1)   EXAMPLE: On January 1, a bank official may tell Firm X that it may borrow up to $100,000 in the coming year. A **revolving line of credit** allows the amount borrowed to be repaid and then borrowed again.

f.   If a firm's credit is questionable, a creditor may ask the company to obtain a **banker's acceptance**. The payor arranges for a bank to accept the payor's time draft, thereby guaranteeing that the draft will be good.

3.   The **annual cost of not taking a discount** (not considering compounding effects) is approximately

$$\frac{360}{Total\ payment\ period - Discount\ period} \times \frac{Discount\ \%}{100\% - Discount\ \%}$$

a.   EXAMPLE: Given terms of 2/10, net 30 (see item 4.a. under subunit 10 for an explanation), the annualized cost of not taking the discount can be calculated as follows:

$$\frac{360}{30-10} \times \frac{2\%}{100\% - 2\%} = \frac{360}{20} \times \frac{2\%}{98\%} = 18 \times .0204 = 36.72\%$$

b.   A more accurate calculation of the cost of not taking discounts considers the effects of **compounding**. In the example on the previous page, annualizing this cost means that 18 payments (360 ÷ 20) are deemed to occur during the year. The annual effective rate is

$$
\begin{aligned}
Rate &= [1.0 + (Discount\ \% \div (100\% - Discount\ \%)]^{Number\ of\ periods} - 1.0 \\
&= [1.0 + (2\% \div (100\% - 2\%)]^{18} - 1.0 \\
&= [1.0 + .0204]^{18} - 1.0 \\
&= 1.0204^{18} - 1.0 \\
&= 1.4384 - 1.0 \\
&= 43.84\%
\end{aligned}
$$

4.   The **prime interest rate** is the rate charged by commercial banks to their best (the largest and financially strongest) business customers. It is traditionally the lowest rate charged by banks. However, in recent years, banks have been making loans at still lower rates in response to competition from the commercial paper market.

a.   The **cost of a bank loan** is calculated based on its terms.

1)   **Regular (simple) interest** loan (principal and interest paid at maturity):

$$\frac{Interest}{Borrowed\ amount}$$

a)   The denominator is the borrowed proceeds net of any compensating balance.

2)   **Discounted (paid in advance) interest:**

$$\frac{Interest}{Borrowed\ amount - Interest}$$

3)   **Installment (add-on) interest** (principal plus interest equals the sum of installments):

$$\frac{Interest}{Average\ borrowed\ amount}$$

5.   **Secured Forms of Short-Term Credit**

a.   Loans can be secured by **pledging receivables**, i.e., committing the proceeds of the receivables to paying off the loan. A bank will often lend up to 80% of outstanding receivables.

b.   **Warehouse financing** uses **inventory** as security for the loan.

1)   A third party, such as a public warehouse, holds the collateral and serves as the creditor's agent, and the creditor receives the **terminal warehouse receipts** evidencing its rights in the collateral. A **field warehouse** is established when the warehouser takes possession of the inventory on the debtor's property. The inventory is released (often from a fenced-in area) as needed for sale.

2)   Warehouse receipts may be **negotiable or nonnegotiable**. A nonnegotiable receipt is issued to a named party, e.g., the lender, and does not state that the goods are deliverable to bearer or to the order of a named person. A negotiable warehouse receipt meets all of the requirements of the Uniform Commercial Code for negotiability and is transferable by endorsement.

c.   **Trust receipts** are used in inventory financing. The creditor purchases and holds title to the inventory. The debtor is considered a trustee for purposes of selling the inventory and bears the risk of loss.

6. **Factoring receivables.** A factor purchases accounts receivable and assumes the risk of collection. The seller of the receivables receives money immediately to reinvest in new inventories. The financing cost is usually high -- about two points or more above prime, plus a fee for collection.

    a. A firm that uses a factor can eliminate its credit department and accounts receivable staff. Also, bad debts are eliminated. These reductions in costs can more than offset the fee charged by the factor.

    b. The factor can often operate more efficiently than its clients because of the specialized nature of its service.

    c. Before the advent of computers, factoring was often considered a last-resort source of financing used only when bankruptcy was imminent. However, the factor's computerization of receivables means it can operate a receivables department more economically than most small manufacturers. Factoring is no longer viewed as an undesirable source of financing.

    d. EXAMPLE: A typical CMA question concerns the cost to the firm of a proposed factoring agreement. Assume a factor charges a 2% fee plus an interest rate of 18% on all monies advanced. Monthly sales are $100,000, and the factor advances 90% of the receivables submitted after deducting the 2% fee and the interest. Credit terms are net 60 days. What is the cost of this arrangement?

Amount of receivables submitted	$100,000
Minus: 10% reserve	(10,000)
Minus: 2% factor's fee	(2,000)
Amount accruing to the firm	$ 88,000
Minus: 18% interest for 60 days (on $88,000)	(2,640)
Amount to be received immediately	$ 85,360

       1) The firm will also receive the $10,000 reserve at the end of the 60-day period if it has not been absorbed by sales returns and allowances. Thus, the total cost to the firm to factor the sales for the month is $4,640 ($2,000 factor's fee + interest of $2,640). Assuming that the factor has approved the customers' credit in advance, the seller will not absorb any bad debts.

       2) The previously listed costs should be compared with the cost of operating a credit and collection department and also the cost of borrowing monies otherwise advanced by the factor.

7. Stop and review! You have completed the outline for this subunit. Study multiple-choice questions 1 through 22 beginning on page 311.

11.2 CORE CONCEPTS

Short-Term Credit

- Short-term credit is debt scheduled to be **repaid within 1 year**. It often involves a lower interest rate and is more readily available than long-term credit.

- The major **sources of short-term credit** are: accrued expenses, trade credit, short-term bank loans, commercial paper, lines of credit, and bankers' acceptances.

- Before deciding whether to take a **trade discount**, the firm should have calculated the annualized cost of not taking the discount. The cost of a bank loan can be calculated using simple formulas.

- **Secured** forms of short-term credit include pledged receivables, warehouse financing, and trust receipts.

- Cash gain can be obtained by **factoring** (selling) receivables to a third party.

QUESTIONS

11.1 Short-Term Credit

1. Which one of the following provides a spontaneous source of financing for a firm?

A. Accounts payable.

B. Mortgage bonds.

C. Accounts receivable.

D. Debentures.

Answer (A) is correct. *(CMA, adapted)*
REQUIRED: The item that provides a spontaneous source of financing.
DISCUSSION: Trade credit is a spontaneous source of financing because it arises automatically as part of a purchase transaction. Because of its ease in use, trade credit is the largest source of short-term financing for many firms both large and small.
Answer (B) is incorrect because mortgage bonds and debentures do not arise automatically as a result of a purchase transaction. Answer (C) is incorrect because the use of receivables as a financing source requires an extensive factoring arrangement and often involves the creditor's evaluation of the credit ratings of the borrower's customers. Answer (D) is incorrect because mortgage bonds and debentures do not arise automatically as a result of a purchase transaction.

2. Assuming a 360-day year, the current price of a $100 U.S. Treasury bill due in 180 days on a 6% discount basis is

A. $97.00

B. $94.00

C. $100.00

D. $93.00

Answer (A) is correct. *(CMA, adapted)*
REQUIRED: The current price of a Treasury bill.
DISCUSSION: The 6% discount rate is multiplied times the face amount of the Treasury bill to determine the amount of interest the lender will earn. The interest on this Treasury bill is $3 ($100 × 6% × .5 year), thus the purchase price is $97 ($100 – $3).
Answer (B) is incorrect because the interest is for 180 days, not a full year. Answer (C) is incorrect because the purchase price will always be less than the face value when the Treasury bill is sold at a discount. Answer (D) is incorrect because the interest rate is 6% per year.

3. Which one of the following responses is not an advantage to a corporation that uses the commercial paper market for short-term financing?

A. This market provides more funds at lower rates than other methods provide.

B. The borrower avoids the expense of maintaining a compensating balance with a commercial bank.

C. There are no restrictions as to the type of corporation that can enter into this market.

D. This market provides a broad distribution for borrowing.

Answer (C) is correct. *(CMA, adapted)*
REQUIRED: The item not an advantage of using commercial paper for short-term financing.
DISCUSSION: Commercial paper is a short-term, unsecured note payable issued in large denominations by major companies with excellent credit ratings. Maturities usually do not exceed 270 days. Commercial paper is a lower cost source of funds than bank loans, and no compensating balances are required. Commercial paper provides a broad and efficient distribution of debt, and costly financing arrangements are avoided. The market is not open to all companies because only major corporations with high credit ratings can participate.
Answer (A) is incorrect because lower rates are an advantage of commercial paper. Answer (B) is incorrect because avoidance of compensating balance requirements is an advantage of commercial paper. Answer (D) is incorrect because broad debt distribution is an advantage of commercial paper.

Questions 4 through 7 are based on the following information. The Frame Supply Company has just acquired a large account and needs to increase its working capital by $100,000. The controller of the company has identified the four sources of funds given below.

1. Pay a factor to buy the company's receivables, which average $125,000 per month and have an average collection period of 30 days. The factor will advance up to 80% of the face value of receivables at 10% and charge a fee of 2% on all receivables purchased. The controller estimates that the firm would save $24,000 in collection expenses over the year. Assume the fee and interest are not deductible in advance.
2. Borrow $110,000 from a bank at 12% interest. A 9% compensating balance would be required.
3. Issue $110,000 of 6-month commercial paper to net $100,000. (New paper would be issued every 6 months.)
4. Borrow $125,000 from a bank on a discount basis at 20%. No compensating balance would be required.

Assume a 360-day year in all of your calculations.

4. The cost of Alternative 1. to Frame Supply Company is

A. 10.0%

B. 12.0%

C. 13.2%

D. 16.0%

Answer (D) is correct. *(CMA, adapted)*
REQUIRED: The annual percentage cost of factoring receivables.
DISCUSSION: The factor will advance $100,000 ($125,000 × 80%). This amount is the average balance outstanding throughout the year. Thus, annual interest will be $10,000 ($100,000 × 10%). In addition, the company will pay an annual fee of $30,000 ($125,000 per month × 2% × 12 months), so the total annual net cost is $16,000 ($10,000 + $30,000 − $24,000 savings). Hence, the annual cost is 16% ($16,000 ÷ $100,000 loan).
Answer (A) is incorrect because 10% is the interest rate on the amount advanced. Answer (B) is incorrect because 12% is the sum of the interest rate and the fee percentage. Answer (C) is incorrect because 13.2% is the cost of Alternative 2.

5. The cost of Alternative 2. to Frame Supply Company is

A. 9.0%

B. 12.0%

C. 13.2%

D. 21.0%

Answer (C) is correct. *(CMA, adapted)*
REQUIRED: The annual percentage cost of borrowing with a compensating balance requirement.
DISCUSSION: Even though the company will borrow $110,000, it will have use of only $100,100 because a 9% compensating balance, or $9,900, must be maintained at all times. Consequently, the effective annual interest rate is 13.2% [($110,000 × 12%) ÷ $100,100].
Answer (A) is incorrect because 9% is the compensating balance requirement. Answer (B) is incorrect because 12% is the contract rate. Answer (D) is incorrect because 21% is the sum of the contract rate and the compensating balance requirement.

6. The cost of Alternative 3. to Frame Supply Company is

A. 9.1%

B. 10.0%

C. 18.2%

D. 20.0%

Answer (D) is correct. *(CMA, adapted)*
REQUIRED: The annual percentage cost of issuing commercial paper.
DISCUSSION: By issuing commercial paper, the company will receive $100,000 and repay $110,000 every six months. Thus, for the use of $100,000 in funds, the company pays $10,000 in interest each six-month period, or a total of $20,000 per year. The annual percentage rate is therefore 20% ($20,000 ÷ $100,000).
Answer (A) is incorrect because 9.1% is the 6-month rate based on the face amount of the paper. Answer (B) is incorrect because 10% is the rate for six months. Answer (C) is incorrect because 18.2% is based on the face amount of the commercial paper.

7. The cost of Alternative 4. to Frame Supply Company is

A. 20.0%

B. 25.0%

C. 40.0%

D. 50.0%

Answer (B) is correct. *(CMA, adapted)*
REQUIRED: The annual percentage cost of a discounted note.
DISCUSSION: The company will receive $100,000 ($125,000 × 80%) at an annual cost of $25,000, so the annual interest rate is 25% ($25,000 ÷ $100,000).
Answer (A) is incorrect because the effective rate must exceed the contract rate of 20%. Answer (C) is incorrect because 40% assumes no discount and a 6-month loan term. Answer (D) is incorrect because 50% assumes a 6-month loan term.

8. If a firm purchases raw materials from its supplier on a 2/10, net 40, cash discount basis, the equivalent annual interest rate (using a 360-day year) of forgoing the cash discount and making payment on the 40th day is

A. 2%

B. 18.36%

C. 24.49%

D. 36.72%

Answer (C) is correct. *(Publisher, adapted)*
REQUIRED: The equivalent annual interest charge for not taking the discount.
DISCUSSION: The buyer could satisfy the $100 obligation by paying $98 on the 10th day. By choosing to wait until the 40th day, the buyer is effectively paying a $2 interest charge for the use of $98 for 30 days (40-day credit period – 10-day discount period). The interest rate on what is essentially a 30-day loan is 2.04081% ($2 ÷ $98). Extrapolating this 30-day rate to a yearly rate involves multiplying by the number of periods in a year. Thus, the effective annual rate is about 24.49% [2.04081% × (360 ÷ 30 days)].
Answer (A) is incorrect because 2% is the discount rate. Answer (B) is incorrect because 18.36% is based on the 40-day credit period. Answer (D) is incorrect because 36.72% is based on a 20-day credit period.

9. Commercial paper

A. Has a maturity date greater than 1 year.

B. Is usually sold only through investment banking dealers.

C. Ordinarily does not have an active secondary market.

D. Has an interest rate lower than Treasury bills.

Answer (C) is correct. *(CMA, adapted)*
REQUIRED: The true statement about commercial paper.
DISCUSSION: Commercial paper is a form of unsecured note that is sold by only the most creditworthy companies. It is issued at a discount from its face value and has a maturity period of 270 days or less. Commercial paper usually carries a low interest rate in comparison to other means of financing. SMA 4M, *Understanding Financial Instruments*, observes that no general (active) secondary market exists for commercial paper, but that "most dealers or organizations will repurchase an issue that they have sold."
Answer (A) is incorrect because commercial paper usually has a maturity date of 270 days or less to avoid securities registration requirements. Answer (B) is incorrect because commercial paper is often issued directly by the borrowing firm. Answer (D) is incorrect because interest rates must be higher than those of Treasury bills to entice investors. Commercial paper is more risky than Treasury bills.

10. A company enters into an agreement with a firm that will factor the company's accounts receivable. The factor agrees to buy the company's receivables, which average $100,000 per month and have an average collection period of 30 days. The factor will advance up to 80% of the face value of receivables at an annual rate of 10% and charge a fee of 2% on all receivables purchased. The controller of the company estimates that the company would save $18,000 in collection expenses over the year. Fees and interest are not deducted in advance. Assuming a 360-day year, what is the annual cost of financing?

A. 10.0%

B. 12.0%

C. 14.0%

D. 17.5%

Answer (D) is correct. *(CMA, adapted)*
REQUIRED: The annual percentage cost of financing under a factoring agreement.
DISCUSSION: In an average month, the company will receive $80,000 at the time the receivables are sent to the factor. Over a year's time, the interest on this average advance of $80,000 would be $8,000 at 10% interest. In addition, the factor will charge a 2% factor fee, or $24,000 ($100,000 × .02 × 12) over the course of a year. However, this $24,000 fee is offset by the $18,000 savings in collection expenses, producing a net outlay of only $6,000. Adding the $6,000 to the $8,000 of interest produces an annual net cost of $14,000. Dividing the $14,000 cost by the $80,000 of advanced funds results in a cost of 17.5%.
Answer (A) is incorrect because 10% overlooks the factor fee. Answer (B) is incorrect because 12% overlooks the fact that the 2% fee recurs every month. Answer (C) is incorrect because 14% miscalculates the factor fee and the savings from reduced collection costs.

Questions 11 through 13 are based on the following information. Morton Company needs to pay a supplier's invoice of $60,000 and wants to take a cash discount of 2/10, net 40. The firm can borrow the money for 30 days at 11% per annum with a 9% compensating balance. Assume a 360-day year.

11. The amount Morton Company must borrow to pay the supplier within the discount period and cover the compensating balance is

   A. $60,000

   B. $65,934

   C. $64,615

   D. $58,800

Answer (C) is correct. *(Publisher, adapted)*
REQUIRED: The amount the company must borrow to pay the supplier within the discount period and cover the compensating balance requirement.
DISCUSSION: The company will need $58,800 ($60,000 × 98%) to pay the invoice. In addition, it will need a compensating balance equal to 9% of the loan. The equation is

$$Loan = \$58,800 + .09\ Loan$$

Thus, the loan amount needed is $64,615 ($58,800 ÷ .91).
Answer (A) is incorrect because $60,000 is the invoice amount. Answer (B) is incorrect because $65,934 assumes the amount paid to the supplier is $60,000. Answer (D) is incorrect because $58,800 is the amount to be paid to the supplier.

12. Assuming Morton Company borrows the money on the last day of the discount period and repays it 30 days later, the effective interest rate on the loan is

   A. 11%

   B. 10%

   C. 12.09%

   D. 9.90%

Answer (C) is correct. *(Publisher, adapted)*
REQUIRED: The effective interest rate when a company borrows to take a discount when the terms are 2/10, net 40.
DISCUSSION: The interest at 11% annually on a 30-day loan of $64,615 is $592.30 [$64,615 × 11% × (30 ÷ 360)]. However, the company has access to only $58,800. The interest expense on usable funds is therefore at an annual rate of 12.09% [($592.30 ÷ $58,800) × 12 months].
Answer (A) is incorrect because 11% is the contract rate of interest. Answer (B) is incorrect because the effective rate is greater than the contract rate. The usable funds are less than the face amount of the note. Answer (D) is incorrect because the effective rate is greater than the contract rate. The usable funds are less than the face amount of the note.

13. If Morton fails to take the discount and pays on the 40th day, what effective rate of annual interest is it paying the vendor?

   A. 2%

   B. 24%

   C. 24.49%

   D. 36.73%

Answer (C) is correct. *(Publisher, adapted)*
REQUIRED: The effective interest rate paid when a discount is not taken.
DISCUSSION: By failing to take the discount, the company is essentially borrowing $58,800 for 30 days. Thus, at a cost of $1,200, the company acquires the use of $58,800, resulting in a rate of 2.04081% ($1,200 ÷ $58,800) for 30 days. Assuming a 360-day year, the effective annual rate is 24.489% [2.04081% × (360 days ÷ 30 days)].
Answer (A) is incorrect because 2% is the discount rate for a 30-day period. Answer (B) is incorrect because 24% assumes that the available funds equal $60,000. Answer (D) is incorrect because 36.73% assumes a 20-day discount period.

14. A company has just borrowed $2 million from a bank. The stated rate of interest is 10%. If the loan is discounted and is repayable in one year, the effective rate on the loan is approximately

   A. 8.89%

   B. 9.09%

   C. 10.00%

   D. 11.11%

Answer (D) is correct. *(Publisher, adapted)*
REQUIRED: The effective rate of interest on a discounted loan.
DISCUSSION: If the loan is discounted, the borrower receives the face amount minus the prepaid interest. Thus, the borrower will receive proceeds of $1,800,000 [$2,000,000 – ($2,000,000 × 10%)]. The effective interest rate is 11.11% ($200,000 ÷ $1,800,000).
Answer (A) is incorrect because the prepayment of interest reduces the funds available, resulting in an effective interest rate greater than the contract rate. Answer (B) is incorrect because the prepayment of interest reduces the funds available, resulting in an effective interest rate greater than the contract rate. Answer (C) is incorrect because 10% is the contract rate. The effective rate is higher because the full $2 million face amount of the note will not be available to the borrower.

15. The following forms of short-term borrowing are available to a firm:

- Floating lien
- Factoring
- Revolving credit
- Chattel mortgages
- Bankers' acceptances
- Lines of credit
- Commercial paper

The forms of short-term borrowing that are unsecured credit are

A. Floating lien, revolving credit, chattel mortgage, and commercial paper.

B. Factoring, chattel mortgage, bankers' acceptances, and line of credit.

C. Floating lien, chattel mortgage, bankers' acceptances, and line of credit.

D. Revolving credit, bankers' acceptances, line of credit, and commercial paper.

Answer (D) is correct. *(CMA, adapted)*
REQUIRED: The forms of short-term borrowing that are unsecured credit.
DISCUSSION: An unsecured loan is a loan made by a bank based on credit information about the borrower and the ability of the borrower to repay the obligation. The loan is not secured by collateral, but is made on the signature of the borrower. Revolving credit, bankers' acceptances, lines of credit, and commercial paper are all unsecured means of borrowing.
Answer (A) is incorrect because a chattel mortgage is a loan secured by personal property (movable property such as equipment or livestock). Also, a floating lien is secured by property, such as inventory, the composition of which may be constantly changing. Answer (B) is incorrect because a chattel mortgage is a loan secured by personal property (movable property such as equipment or livestock). Also, factoring is a form of financing in which receivables serve as security. Answer (C) is incorrect because a chattel mortgage is a loan secured by personal property (movable property such as equipment or livestock). Also, a floating lien is secured by property, such as inventory, the composition of which may be constantly changing.

16. A firm often factors its accounts receivable. Its finance company requires a 6% reserve and charges a 1.4% commission on the amount of the receivables. The remaining amount to be advanced is further reduced by an annual interest charge of 15%. What proceeds (rounded to the nearest dollar) will the firm receive from the finance company at the time a $100,000 account due in 60 days is factored?

A. $92,600

B. $96,135

C. $90,285

D. $85,000

Answer (C) is correct. *(Publisher, adapted)*
REQUIRED: The proceeds of factoring.
DISCUSSION: The factor will withhold $6,000 ($100,000 × 6%) as a reserve against returns and allowances and $1,400 ($100,000 × 1.4%) as a commission. The remaining $92,600 will be reduced by interest at the rate of 15% annually. The interest charge should be $2,315, assuming a 360-day year [($92,600 × .15) × (60-day payment period ÷ 360 days)]. The proceeds to be received by the seller equal $90,285 ($92,600 – $2,315).
Answer (A) is incorrect because $92,600 ignores interest. Answer (B) is incorrect because $96,135 fails to deduct the 6% reserve. Answer (D) is incorrect because $85,000 assumes that the only amount withheld is a full year's interest on $100,000.

17. On January 1, Scott Corporation received a $300,000 line of credit at an interest rate of 12% from Main Street Bank and drew down the entire amount on February 1. The line of credit agreement requires that an amount equal to 15% of the loan be deposited into a compensating balance account. What is the effective annual cost of credit for this loan arrangement?

A. 11.00%

B. 12.00%

C. 12.94%

D. 14.12%

Answer (D) is correct. *(CMA, adapted)*
REQUIRED: The effective annual cost of credit.
DISCUSSION: Annual interest is $36,000 ($300,000 × 12%), and the amount available is $255,000 [$300,000 – ($300,000 × 15%)]. Thus, the effective interest rate is 14.12% ($36,000 ÷ $255,000).
Answer (A) is incorrect because 11.00% is the nominal rate for 11 months. Answer (B) is incorrect because 12.00% is the nominal rate of interest. Answer (C) is incorrect because 12.94% equals $33,000 (11 months of interest) divided by $255,000.

Questions 18 and 19 are based on the following information.

CyberAge Outlet, a relatively new store, is a cafe that offers customers the opportunity to browse the Internet or play computer games at their tables while they drink coffee. The customer pays a fee based on the amount of time spent signed on to the computer. The store also sells books, tee-shirts, and computer accessories. CyberAge has been paying all of its bills on the last day of the payment period, thus forfeiting all supplier discounts. Shown below are data on CyberAge's two major vendors, including average monthly purchases and credit terms.

Vendor	Average Monthly Purchases	Credit Terms
Web Master	$25,000	2/10, net 30
Softidee	50,000	5/10, net 90

---

18. Assuming a 360-day year and that CyberAge continues paying on the last day of the credit period, the company's weighted-average annual interest rate for trade credit (ignoring the effects of compounding) for these two vendors is

A. 27.0%

B. 25.2%

C. 28.0%

D. 30.2%

Answer (B) is correct. *(CMA, adapted)*
    REQUIRED: The weighted-average annual interest rate.
    DISCUSSION: If the company pays Web Master within 10 days, it will save $500 ($25,000 × 2%). Thus, the company is effectively paying $500 to retain $24,500 ($25,000 – $500) for 20 days (30 – 10). The annualized interest rate on this borrowing is 36.7346% [($500 ÷ $24,500) × (360 days ÷ 20 days)]. Similarly, the company is, in effect, paying Softidee $2,500 ($50,000 × 5%) to hold $47,500 ($50,000 – $2,500) for 80 days (90 – 10). The annualized rate on this borrowing is 23.6842% [($2,500 ÷ $47,500) × (360 days ÷ 80 days)]. The average amount borrowed from Web Master is $16,333.33 [$24,500 × 1 month × (20 days ÷ 30 days)], and the average amount borrowed from Softidee is $126,666.67 [$47,500 × 3 months × (80 days ÷ 90 days)]. Thus, the weighted average of these two rates based on average borrowings is 25.2% {[($16,333.33 × 36.7346%) + ($126,666.67 × 23.6842%)] ÷ ($16,333.33 + $126,666.67)}. This calculation, however, understates the true cost of not taking the discount because it does not consider the effects of compounding.
    Answer (A) is incorrect because 27.0% is based on weights of $25,000 and $50,000. Answer (C) is incorrect because 28.0% is based on weights of $24,500 and $47,500. Answer (D) is incorrect because 30.2% is an unweighted average of the two interest rates.

---

19. Should CyberAge use trade credit and continue paying at the end of the credit period?

A. Yes, if the cost of alternative short-term financing is less.

B. Yes, if the firm's weighted-average cost of capital is equal to its weighted-average cost of trade credit.

C. No, if the cost of alternative long-term financing is greater.

D. Yes, if the cost of alternative short-term financing is greater.

Answer (D) is correct. *(CMA, adapted)*
    REQUIRED: The true statement about the decision to use trade credit and pay at the end of the credit period.
    DISCUSSION: The company is currently paying an annual rate of 25.2% (see previous question) to obtain trade credit and pay at the end of the credit period. This policy should be continued if trade credit is the only source of financing, or if other sources are available only at a higher rate.
    Answer (A) is incorrect because the company should continue the current practice unless alternative short-term financing is available at a lower rate. Answer (B) is incorrect because the weighted-average cost of capital is usually a concern in capital budgeting and is not as important in the decision process as the marginal cost of capital. Furthermore, trade credit is just one element in the firm's financing structure. An optimal mix of financing sources may require that trade credit be obtained at less than the weighted-average cost of capital. Answer (C) is incorrect because the company should maintain its current practice if the cost of alternative long-term financing is higher.

20. Gatsby, Inc. is going to begin factoring its accounts receivable and has collected information on the following four finance companies:

	Required Reserves	Commissions	Annual Interest Charge
Company A	6%	1.4%	15%
Company B	7%	1.2%	12%
Company C	5%	1.7%	20%
Company D	8%	1.0%	5%

Which company will give Gatsby the highest proceeds from a $100,000 account due in 60 days? Assume a 360-day year.

A. Company A.

B. Company B.

C. Company C.

D. Company D.

Answer (A) is correct. *(Publisher, adapted)*
REQUIRED: The highest proceeds from factoring.
DISCUSSION: Company A will withhold $6,000 ($100,000 × 6%) as a reserve against returns and allowances and $1,400 ($100,000 × 1.4%) as a commission. The remaining $92,600 will be reduced by interest at the rate of 15% annually. The interest charge will be $2,315, assuming a 360-day year [($92,600 × .15) ÷ (60-day payment period ÷ 360 days)]. The proceeds to be received by Gatsby equal $90,285 ($92,600 – $2,315).

Answer (B) is incorrect because Company B will produce proceeds of only $89,964. Answer (C) is incorrect because Company C will produce proceeds of only $90,190. Answer (D) is incorrect because Company D will produce proceeds of only $90,241.

21. Hagar Company's bank requires a compensating balance of 20% on a $100,000 loan. If the stated interest on the loan is 7%, what is the effective cost of the loan?

A. 5.83%

B. 7.00%

C. 8.40%

D. 8.75%

Answer (D) is correct. *(CMA, adapted)*
REQUIRED: The effective cost of a loan when a compensating balance is required.
DISCUSSION: Interest on the loan is $7,000 ($100,000 × 7%). Given that the borrower has to maintain a 20% compensating balance, only $80,000 [$100,000 – ($100,000 × 20%)] is available for use. Thus, the company is paying $7,000 for the use of $80,000 in funds at an effective cost of 8.75% ($7,000 ÷ $80,000).

Answer (A) is incorrect because the borrower has access to less, not more, than the face amount of the loan. Answer (B) is incorrect because the effective rate is higher than the contract rate as a result of the compensating balance requirement. Answer (C) is incorrect because 8.40% is 120% of the contract rate.

22. A company obtained a short-term bank loan of $250,000 at an annual interest rate of 6%. As a condition of the loan, the company is required to maintain a compensating balance of $50,000 in its checking account. The company's checking account earns interest at an annual rate of 2%. Ordinarily, the company maintains a balance of $25,000 in its checking account for transaction purposes. What is the effective interest rate of the loan?

A. 6.44%

B. 7.00%

C. 5.80%

D. 6.66%

Answer (A) is correct. *(CMA, adapted)*
REQUIRED: The effective interest rate on a loan that requires a compensating balance of $25,000 above the company's normal working balance.
DISCUSSION: The $50,000 compensating balance requirement is partially satisfied by the company's practice of maintaining a $25,000 balance for transaction purposes. Thus, only $25,000 of the loan will not be available for current use, leaving $225,000 of the loan usable. At 6% interest, the $250,000 loan would require an interest payment of $15,000 per year. This is partially offset by the 2% interest earned on the $25,000 incremental balance, or $500. Subtracting the $500 interest earned from the $15,000 of expense results in net interest expense of $14,500 for the use of $225,000 in funds. Dividing $14,500 by $225,000 produces an effective interest rate of 6.44%.

Answer (B) is incorrect because 7.00% fails to consider that the $25,000 currently being maintained counts toward the compensating balance requirement. Answer (C) is incorrect because 5.8% fails to consider the compensating balance requirement. Answer (D) is incorrect because 6.66% fails to consider the interest earned on the incremental balance being carried.

STUDY UNIT TWELVE
THE DECISION PROCESS

(7 pages of outline)

Decision analysis is an important element of the management accountant's job. Therefore, the CMA Examination puts heavy emphasis on the logical steps to reach a decision, relevant data concepts, cost-volume-profit analysis, marginal analysis, cost-based pricing, and the income tax implications for operational decision analysis.

This study unit is the **first of five** on **decision analysis**. The relative weight assigned to this major topic in Part 3 of the exam is **25%** at **skill level C** (all six skill types required). The five study units are

Study Unit 12: The Decision Process
Study Unit 13: Data Concepts Relevant to Decision Making
Study Unit 14: Cost-Volume-Profit Analysis
Study Unit 15: Marginal Analysis
Study Unit 16: Cost-Based Pricing

After studying the outline and answering the multiple-choice questions, you will have the skills necessary to address the following topics listed in the IMA's Learning Outcome Statements:

Part 3 – Section D.1. Decision process

The candidate should be able to:

a. identify and demonstrate an understanding of the steps needed to reach a decision, i.e., (i) obtain and analyze information, (ii) identify alternative courses of action, (iii) make predictions about future scenarios, (iv) choose and justify an alternative, (v) implement a decision, and (vi) evaluate performance to provide feedback

b. demonstrate an understanding of how management should evaluate decision results

12.1 THE DECISION-MAKING PROCESS

1. The **consideration of choices** and the selection of the choice expected to give the best results are key parts of the planner's job.

   a. Rational decision making involves

      1) Defining the problem
      2) Obtaining information
      3) Identifying alternative courses of action
      4) Making predictions about future costs
      5) Choosing and justifying an alternative
      6) Implementing the decision
      7) Evaluating performance to provide feedback

   b. Management accountants provide qualitative information as well as quantitative financial and nonfinancial information useful in applying a **decision model**, which is a formal means of choosing future courses of action.

      1) The **programmed decision process** is used for routine or repetitive decisions. This process is based upon decision rules. They are the parameters within which a routine decision is based.

2) The **nonprogrammed decision process** is used for complex, nonroutine situations calling for the use of the problem-solving process. Four questions need to be answered before making a nonprogrammed decision.

    a) What decision needs to be made?
    b) When does it need to be made?
    c) Who makes the decision?
    d) Who needs to be consulted before implementation of the decision?

2. **Defining the Problem**

    a. Defining the problem is the most common difficulty in problem solving. Pitfalls in defining problems include

        1) Defining the problem according to a solution

            a) Do not rule out other solutions.
            b) Focus on "bringing the actual situation closer to the desired situation."

        2) Concentrating on nonpertinent areas

            a) Define minor problems.
            b) Concentrate on problems that are important.
            c) Rank the priority of the problems in an organized manner.

        3) Defining problems by their symptoms

            a) Focus on the causes of the gap between "the actual and the desired situations."

    b. Awareness of the existence of a problem, i.e., realization that a gap exists between planned results and reality (between where the enterprise is and where it wants to be), precedes defining the problem.

        1) **Bounded rationality** (the inability to see all aspects of the situation) may prevent accurate problem definition. Faulty perception may preclude the decision maker from seeing the correct problem.

            a) We see what we **expect** to see.
            b) We see what we are **trained** to see.
            c) Our **needs** influence what we observe.
            d) **Group pressure** may influence what problems we perceive or how we define them.

3. **Obtaining Information**

    a. In this step, the decision maker determines what issues must be addressed, for example, whether to make a component, outsource the component, or redesign the product to eliminate the component.

    b. The decision maker also considers the objectives of the desired course of action, for example, to increase return on investment or to enter a new market.

    c. These objectives furnish the criteria by which the decision will be evaluated. Hence, the information obtained must pertain to the issues to be resolved and the objectives to be achieved.

4. **Identifying Alternative Courses of Action**

    a. The search can be primary (e.g., surveys, samples, attitude questionnaires) or secondary (e.g., reading scholarly papers).

    b. It can be creative.

        1) **Attribute listing** is applied primarily to improve a tangible object. It lists the parts and essential features of the object and systematically analyzes modifications intended as improvements.

2) **Blast! then refine** is a U.S. Navy problem-solving methodology. It completely disregards (blasts out of one's consciousness) any existing approach. An entirely new problem solution is then sought that will attain the original objectives.

3) **Brainstorming** is an unstructured approach that relies on the spontaneous contribution of ideas from all members of a group. This technique breaks down broadly based problems into their essentials.

4) **Creative leap** is a process that formulates an ideal solution and then works back to a feasible one.

5) **Delphi technique** is an approach in which the manager solicits opinions on a problem from experts in the field, summarizes the opinions, and feeds the summaries back to the experts (without revealing any of the participants to each other). The process is reiterated until the opinions converge on an optimal solution. This method attempts to avoid **groupthink** (the tendency of individuals to conform to what they perceive to be the consensus).

6) The **Edisonian approach** is a trial-and-error experimental method. It should usually not be applied unless other approaches have been unsuccessful.

7) **Forced relationship** is a structured adaptation of free association. The elements of a problem are analyzed, and the associations among them are identified so as to detect patterns that may suggest new ideas.

8) **Free association** is a method of idea generation that reports the first thought to come to mind in response to a given stimulus, for example, a symbol or analogy pertaining to a product for which an advertising slogan is sought. The objective is to express the content of consciousness without censorship or control.

9) **Morphological matrix analysis** is a structured technique that plots decision variables along the axes of a matrix. The relationships of these variables are found in the squares within the chart.

10) **Synectics** is a highly structured group approach to problem statement and solution based on creative thinking. It involves free use of analogies and metaphors in informal exchange within a carefully selected small group of individuals of diverse personality and areas of specialization.

11) **Trial-and-error** generates new ideas based on failed ones.

12) **Value analysis** is a methodical approach primarily designed to optimize performance of an activity at a minimum cost. Emphasis is on the cost-benefit criterion.

   c. In open systems, the search cannot feasibly consider all possibilities.

   d. The search ordinarily ends for most people when they find a solution they consider not optimal but good enough (satisficing).

   e. Information processing for decision making is characterized by two styles.

1) The thinking or **analytic** style is objective, deductive, precise, detailed, logical, and repetitive. It tends to prevail in the traditional, pyramidal organization.

2) The **intuitive** style is subjective, inductive, nonroutine, and unstructured. Intuitive people may rely on hunches and reach decisions without explicitly applying a formal process.

   f. **Limiting factor principle.** The crucial factor is the one that limits or prevents achievement of the desired goal. The mass of alternative choices can be reduced if managers can identify the limiting factors to a problem.

1) EXAMPLE: If a company directs a division to turn a loss into a profit, the immediate means might be purchasing new equipment, and a limiting factor might be lack of cash or good credit.

    a) Seeking alternative sources for the equipment may reveal someone willing to swap, take a lien, etc.

    b) Alternatives calling for purchases and loans can be discarded.

2) This limiting factor principle is sometimes known as the **theory of constraints** (see Subunit 2.3).

    a) The objective is to identify the constraints (i.e., slow machines) that inhibit productivity and eliminate them.

5. **Making Predictions about Future Costs**

    a. To be **relevant** to a decision, a cost must

        1) Be paid or incurred in the future and
        2) Vary between alternatives.

    b. One of the most **common errors** in decision making is taking **sunk costs** into account. Because sunk costs have already been incurred, they can play no role in rational decision making.

        1) EXAMPLE: In deciding whether to attend college for a fourth year, the money already expended for the first three years is not relevant because it occurred in the past and remains spent regardless of further attendance. Only the tuition, fees, etc., for the fourth year (i.e., the incremental costs) and the forgone wages of not working full time (i.e., the opportunity costs) have any relevance.

    c. Only costs that are **different** from one alternative to the next should be taken into account.

        1) EXAMPLE: Tuition is not a factor in deciding whether to major in accounting or chemistry. The cost of attending classes is the same in either case. (Other costs, such as textbooks, computer time, and lab fees, may be relevant, however.)

6. **Evaluation of solutions.** The analysis of facts and the development of solutions have been improved in recent years through the adoption of mathematical techniques. These techniques are not a panacea -- they will not provide useful solutions for poorly formulated problems -- but they will provide valuable results for well-defined quantitative problems. Some of these quantitative tools or approaches are defined below and on the following pages.

    a. **Operations research** is an overall approach that applies a variety of scientific and mathematical techniques. It involves the

        1) Recognition of the complete system, including interrelationships, in which the problem operates
        2) Formulation of a mathematical model
        3) Testing of the model
        4) Implementation of the optimal solution as produced by the model

    b. **Simulation** is an approach that is economically feasible because of the availability of high-speed computers.

        1) Simulation is used when an optimization model is not possible.

            a) For example, the number of variables may exceed the number of equations describing the variables.

        2) Simulation requires the construction of a quantitative model that incorporates most of the features of the problem situation.

        3) The model is then tested in a variety of hypothetical situations.

            a) For example, if certain conditions hold true, what performance can be expected from the system being modeled?

        4) The modeled response to the situations can then be measured.

c. **Linear programming** is a tool for allocating scarce resources in the presence of **resource constraints**.

    1) The problem must be described by a system of linear equations. An objective function (usually cost or revenue) is maximized or minimized subject to constraint equations. This description is seldom strictly accurate but provides useful approximations.

    2) The simultaneous solution to the system of equations maximizes profit (or minimizes cost).

d. **Cost-benefit analysis** is a simple test for possible solutions. Cost should be less than the benefits realized.

e. **Queuing theory** is a technique to analyze waiting-line problems through the use of probability theory. It minimizes the sum of the cost of waiting lines and the cost of reducing or eliminating queues.

f. **Decision trees (decision theory)** map out possible actions given probabilistic events. Probabilities are assigned, and the expected value (payoff or loss) for each decision choice and the events that might follow from that choice is calculated.

    1) A current decision may entail a choice among multiple options, each of which may lead to different future events (states of nature).

        a) EXAMPLE: If one invests in a fast-food franchise and the economy improves, investing in the franchise is the action, and the improvement in the economy is the future event.

g. **Monte Carlo method.** Random behavior may be added to otherwise deterministic models to simulate the uncertainty inherent in real-world situations. The model is then run a large number of times, and the variance of the probability distribution of the results and the average performance are determined.

h. **Certainty, risk, and uncertainty.** Assigning probabilities or assuming away uncertainty with precise mathematical formulas is not always feasible.

    1) **Certainty** is a condition in which a decision maker can predict the outcome of a decision with perfect accuracy.

    2) One common definition of **risk** is that it is a condition in which a decision maker, using incomplete but reliable information, can estimate the probability of a given outcome of a decision.

        a) **Probability** is a number between 0 and 1 inclusive that measures the likelihood of the occurrence of some event. The less likely the event, the closer the number is to 0. The two types of probabilities are objective and subjective.

            i) Objective probabilities are derived mathematically from historical data.

            ii) Subjective probabilities are estimated based on past experience and judgment.

    3) **Uncertainty** may be used in two senses. It is most often defined as an absence of certainty. Some technical writers, however, define it narrowly as the condition in which no reliable factual evidence is available to support a probability estimate. Thus, an objective probability cannot be stated for a given outcome of a decision. Intuition and creative decision making may be necessary.

    i.   **Portfolio analysis.** Business units may be treated as elements of an investment portfolio. A portfolio should be efficient in balancing risk and returns.

        1)   The expected rate of return of a portfolio is the weighted average of the expected returns of the individual assets in the portfolio.

        2)   The variability (risk) of a portfolio's return is determined by the correlation of the returns of individual portfolio assets.

            a)   To the extent the returns are not perfectly positively correlated, variability is decreased.

    j.   **Generic competitive strategies.** Michael Porter's model of competitive strategies has two variables: competitive advantage and competitive scope. The strategy adopted depends on whether the advantage sought is based on lower cost or product differentiation and on whether the scope is broad or narrow.

    k.   **Scenario development.** Scenario development is a qualitative forecasting method that requires preparation of conceptual scenarios of future events given carefully defined assumptions. It entails writing multiple alternative but equally likely descriptions of future states. A longitudinal scenario indicates how the current circumstances may develop, and a cross-sectional scenario describes possible future states at a designated time.

    l.   **Situational analysis.** Situational analysis is a method of determining an organization's direction by systematically matching its strengths and weaknesses with its environmental opportunities and threats (referred to as a SWOT analysis).

7.   **Making the choice.** The selection of the best available solution is the objective of the decision-making process.

    a.   The optimal solution is selected.

        1)   If the complete decision-making process has been followed, the result will be profit-maximizing behavior rather than satisficing behavior.

            a)   This result should be attained if cost-benefit analysis is applied to the overall decision-making process as well as to its individual steps.

    b.   The choice involves not only comparing the future cash flows of the potential courses of action but also considering **qualitative factors**, for example, relationships with employees, suppliers, and customers; and **nonfinancial quantitative factors**, for example, rate of defective output or manufacturing lead time.

    c.   Human aspects of the choice must be considered. A decision is useful only if those responsible for its implementation are convinced of its value.

        1)   Decisions are made in a multidimensional environment and therefore have many, sometimes unexpected, effects.

        2)   An otherwise optimal solution may fail if the opinion and attitudes of the people involved are not considered in the decision-making process.

        3)   The multistep process of decision making must be followed when making organizational changes.

            a)   Implementing change is a critical part of the decision-making process because people are crucial to the effectiveness of the choice.

8.   **Implementing the Decision**

9.   **Evaluating performance and giving feedback.** This step is vital to improve future execution of the prior steps or even the decision model itself.

    a.   The proper delegation of authority is made to the individual responsible for implementing the action to be taken. Performance measurement is then provided for.

b. This process puts the solution into a feasible framework, which assures it will be carried out.

c. The failure to provide for practical implementation causes many otherwise correct decisions to fail to produce the desired results.

d. Decisions cannot be fully implemented until they are effectively communicated.

10. **Three Decision-Making Problems**

a. **Framing error** is the human tendency to judge positively presented information favorably and negatively presented information unfavorably.

b. **Escalation** is the human tendency to become committed to failing courses of action instead of quitting or admitting error.

c. **Overconfidence** can expose the decision maker to unreasonable risks.

11. Stop and review! You have completed the outline for this subunit. Study multiple-choice questions 1 through 47 beginning below.

12.2 CORE CONCEPTS

The Decision-Making Process

- Rational decision making involves these **steps**: defining the problem, obtaining information, identifying alternative courses of action, making predictions about future costs, choosing and justifying an alternative, implementing the decision, and evaluating performance to provide feedback.

- The most common difficulty in problem solving is **defining the problem**.

- Among the **methods** that can be used to **search for a solution** are attribute listing, blast! then refine, brainstorming, creative leap, and Delphi technique.

- Among the **models** that can be used for **evaluating alternatives** are simulation, linear programming, and the Monte Carlo method.

- Choosing a course of action involves not only comparing the **future cash flows** of the potential courses of action, but also considering **qualitative factors**, such as relationships with employees, and **nonfinancial quantitative factors**, such as the rate of defective output.

- **Three problems** in decision making are framing error, escalation, and overconfidence.

QUESTIONS

12.1 The Decision-Making Process

1. An organization's executive committee, meeting to solve an important problem, spent 30 minutes analyzing data and debating the cause of the problem. Finally, they agreed and could move onto the next step. Possible steps in the creative problem-solving process are listed below. Which step should the committee perform next?

A. Select a solution.

B. Generate alternative solutions.

C. Identify the problem.

D. Consider the reaction of competitors to various courses of action.

Answer (B) is correct. *(CIA, adapted)*
REQUIRED: The next step in the creative problem-solving process.
DISCUSSION: Robert Kreitner [*Management*, 9th ed., Houghton-Mifflin (2004), page 268] states that "managerial problem solving consists of a four-step sequence: (1) identifying the problem, (2) generating alternative solutions, (3) selecting a solution, and (4) implementing and evaluating the solution." In the first step, management determines what the actual situation is, what the desired situation is, and the reason for the difference.
Answer (A) is incorrect because selecting a solution is the third step in the process. Answer (C) is incorrect because identifying the problem is the first step in the process. Answer (D) is incorrect because considering the reaction of competitors is part of the fourth step of implementing and evaluating the solution.

2. The rational decision-making process is most often typified by

A. Perfect information.

B. Bounded rationality.

C. Selection of optimum decisions.

D. Choice of the least risky solution.

Answer (B) is correct. *(Publisher, adapted)*
REQUIRED: The condition typical of rational decision making.
DISCUSSION: Rarely can decision makers know all possible courses of action, the variables that will affect them, and their precise outcomes. Decision makers face limitations of time, money, technical methods, and creativity. Accordingly, they are restricted to a bounded rationality. Because rationality is inherently limited, decisions invariably entail some risk.
Answer (A) is incorrect because perfect information is a result of complete (unbounded) rationality. Answer (C) is incorrect because optimum solutions are result of complete (unbounded) rationality. Answer (D) is incorrect because choosing the least risky solution is a possible consequence of bounded rationality.

3. A company has recently introduced total quality management (TQM). The company's top management wants to determine a new and innovative approach to foster total participation throughout the company. Management should

A. Seek isolation from all distractions in order to think the problem through.

B. Bring the employees together for a brainstorming session.

C. Rely on themselves to develop a new approach.

D. Use a disciplined problem-solving approach.

Answer (B) is correct. *(CIA, adapted)*
REQUIRED: The way to develop a new and innovative approach to group participation.
DISCUSSION: Group decisions tend to be more creative than individual decisions. One creative approach is brainstorming, which breaks down broadly based problems into their essentials. It is an unstructured approach that relies on the spontaneous contribution of ideas from all members of a group.
Answer (A) is incorrect because group decisions tend to be more creative than individual decisions. They bring many points of view to bear on the problem. Answer (C) is incorrect because group decisions tend to be more creative than individual decisions. They bring many points of view to bear on the problem. Answer (D) is incorrect because the best way to enhance creativity is to involve other people.

4. Which of the following is not an assumption that is made when assuming rationality on the part of the company?

A. The company chooses the decision that results in the maximum economic payoff.

B. The criteria and alternatives can be ranked according to their importance.

C. Specific decision criteria are constant and the weights assigned to them are stable over time.

D. The company seeks solutions that minimize conflict.

Answer (D) is correct. *(CIA, adapted)*
REQUIRED: The assumption that does not underlie rationality.
DISCUSSION: According to Robbins, *Organizational Behavior* (6th ed. Prentice-Hall, 1993), rationality has the same assumptions as the optimizing (outcome maximizing) model for decision making. Rational decision making is fully objective and logical. The model assumes that a single, well-defined goal is to be maximized; that all relevant criteria and feasible options are known; that the criteria and options can be assigned numerical values and ranked; that preferences are constant (criteria and their assigned weights do not change); and that the decision maker will choose the option with the highest rank (the maximum benefits). However, rationality does not require an assumption about the avoidance of conflict.
Answer (A) is incorrect because the choice of the maximum payoff is an assumption of rationality. Answer (B) is incorrect because the ranking of criteria and options is an assumption of rationality. Answer (C) is incorrect because the constancy of the criteria and their weights is an assumption of rationality.

5. A highly risk-averse decision maker will often react to bounded rationality by

A. Satisficing.

B. Ignoring the limiting factor.

C. Attempting to find the optimum solution.

D. Increasing the number of solutions considered.

Answer (A) is correct. *(Publisher, adapted)*
REQUIRED: The reaction to bounded rationality by a risk-averse decision maker.
DISCUSSION: Rational decision making is almost always subject to limitations that make the certain determination of the optimal decision impossible. A very risk-averse decision maker may react to such uncertainty by satisficing, that is, choosing an adequate course of action that is perceived to be safe. Satisficing thus leads to decisions that are not only less than optimal but also less than the best available.
Answer (B) is incorrect because a limiting factor should never be ignored since overcoming it is essential to attainment of the decision maker's goals. Answer (C) is incorrect because optimum solutions are rarely possible. Answer (D) is incorrect because the tendency is to choose the first solution that is "good enough."

6. A chief executive officer (CEO) believes that a major competitor may be planning a new campaign. The CEO sends a questionnaire to key personnel asking for original thinking concerning what the new campaign may be. The CEO selects the best possibilities then sends another questionnaire asking for the most likely option. The process employed by the CEO is called the

    A. Least squares technique.

    B. Delphi technique.

    C. Maximum likelihood technique.

    D. Optimizing of expected payoffs.

Answer (B) is correct. *(CIA, adapted)*

    REQUIRED: The process employed by the CEO to encourage original thinking.

    DISCUSSION: The Delphi Technique is a forecasting or decision making approach that attempts to avoid groupthink (the tendency of individuals to conform to what they perceive to be the consensus). The technique allows only written, anonymous communication among group members. Each member takes a position on the problem at hand. A summary of these positions is communicated to each member. The process is repeated for several iterations as the members move toward a consensus. Thus, the Delphi technique is a qualitative, not quantitative, technique.

    Answer (A) is incorrect because least squares refers to regression analysis and involves specified variables. Answer (C) is incorrect because the maximum likelihood technique is a complex alternative to least squares. Answer (D) is incorrect because optimizing expected payoffs is used in the analysis of decision-making alternatives, which relies on historical information.

7. A company has a computer that it no longer needs because of a discontinued operation. Currently, there are several computer projects that may be able to use the machine but some modification will be necessary if such new application is to be successful. Which of the following techniques is most appropriate to use?

    A. Attribute listing.

    B. Operations research.

    C. Morphological matrix analysis.

    D. Synectics.

Answer (A) is correct. *(CIA, adapted)*

    REQUIRED: The technique useful in developing new uses for a computer.

    DISCUSSION: Attribute listing is applied primarily to improve a tangible object. It lists the parts and essential features of the object and systematically analyzes modifications intended as improvements.

    Answer (B) is incorrect because operations research attempts to find optimal solutions using classical concepts such as statistics, simulation, logical thinking, and other scientific and mathematical techniques to develop and test hypotheses. This application closely fits the problem and charge given. Answer (C) is incorrect because morphological matrix analysis is a structured technique that plots decision variables along the axes of a matrix. The relationships of these variables are found in the squares within the chart. Answer (D) is incorrect because synectics is a highly structured group approach to problem statement and solution based on creative thinking. It involves free use of analogies and metaphors in informal exchange within a carefully selected small group of individuals of diverse personality and areas of specialization.

8. A company is about to introduce a new service and wishes to develop a new slogan and logo to be used in advertising and on company publications. You have been chosen to participate in this process and to look at past slogans, logos, and suggestions given by the advertising agency. You are not limited to the suggested ideas and have been encouraged to suggest original ideas of your own. Which of the following techniques is most appropriate to use?

    A. Brainstorming.

    B. Value analysis.

    C. Free association.

    D. Attribute listing.

Answer (C) is correct. *(CIA, adapted)*

    REQUIRED: The technique that considers suggested ideas but also encourages original thinking.

    DISCUSSION: Free association is an approach to idea generation that reports the first thought to come to mind in response to a given stimulus, for example, a symbol or analogy pertaining to a product for which an advertising slogan is sought. The objective is to express the content of consciousness without censorship or control.

    Answer (A) is incorrect because brainstorming breaks down broadly-based problems into their essentials. It is an unstructured approach that relies on the spontaneous contribution of ideas from all members of a group. Answer (B) is incorrect because value analysis is a methodical approach primarily designed to optimize performance of an activity at a minimum cost. Emphasis is on the cost-benefit criterion. Answer (D) is incorrect because attribute listing is applied primarily to improve a tangible object. It lists the parts and essential features of the object and systematically analyzes modifications intended as improvements.

9. A company wishes to determine what advertising mix of radio, television, and newspapers offers the optimal desired result in increased sales and improved public image. Which of the following techniques is most appropriate to use?

    A. Synectics.

    B. Value analysis.

    C. Brainstorming.

    D. Forced relationship.

Answer (B) is correct. *(CIA, adapted)*
    REQUIRED: The technique to determine the optimal advertising mix.
    DISCUSSION: Value analysis is a methodical approach primarily designed to optimize performance of an activity at a minimum cost. Emphasis is on the cost-benefit criterion.
    Answer (A) is incorrect because synectics is a highly structured group approach to problem statement and solution based on creative thinking. It involves free use of analogies and metaphors in informal exchange within a carefully selected small group of individuals of diverse personality and areas of specialization. Answer (C) is incorrect because brainstorming breaks down broadly based problems into their essentials. It is an unstructured approach that relies on the spontaneous contribution of ideas from all members of a group. Answer (D) is incorrect because forced relationship is a structured adaptation of free association. The elements of a problem are analyzed and the associations among them are identified so as to detect patterns that may suggest new ideas.

10. A company is concerned that spare parts inventories are too large. It has attempted to keep critical parts for its fleet in stock so that equipment will have minimal downtime. Management wants to know what the optimal spare parts inventory should be if downtime is estimated to cost $150 per day. Carrying cost and order cost have not been measured. You have been asked to make a formal recommendation on spare parts stocking levels. Which of the following techniques is most appropriate to use?

    A. Operations research.

    B. Value analysis.

    C. Attribute listing.

    D. Brainstorming.

Answer (A) is correct. *(CIA, adapted)*
    REQUIRED: The technique for determining the optimal spare parts inventory.
    DISCUSSION: Operations research attempts to find optimal solutions using classical concepts such as statistics, simulation, logical thinking, and other scientific and mathematical techniques to develop and test hypotheses. This application closely fits the problem and charge given.
    Answer (B) is incorrect because value analysis is a methodical approach primarily designed to optimize performance of an activity at a minimum cost. Emphasis is on the cost-benefit criterion. Answer (C) is incorrect because attribute listing is applied primarily to improve a tangible object. It lists the parts and essential features of the object and systematically analyzes modifications intended as improvements. Answer (D) is incorrect because brainstorming breaks down broadly based problems into their essentials. It is an unstructured approach that relies on the spontaneous contribution of ideas from all members of a group.

11. A company is deciding whether to purchase an automated machine to manufacture one of its products. Cash flows from this decision depend on several factors, interactions among those factors, and the probabilities associated with different levels of those factors. The method that the company should use to evaluate the distribution of net cash flows from this decision and changes in net cash flows resulting from changes in levels of various factors is

    A. Simulation and sensitivity analysis.

    B. Linear programming.

    C. Correlation analysis.

    D. Differential analysis.

Answer (A) is correct. *(CIA, adapted)*
    REQUIRED: The technique used to evaluate cash flows from the purchase of a machine.
    DISCUSSION: Simulation is a technique used to describe the behavior of a real-world system over time. This technique usually employs a computer program to perform the simulation computations. Sensitivity analysis examines how outcomes change as the model parameters change.
    Answer (B) is incorrect because linear programming is a mathematical technique for optimizing a given objective function subject to certain constraints. Answer (C) is incorrect because correlation analysis is a statistical procedure for studying the relation between variables. Answer (D) is incorrect because differential analysis is used for decision making that compares differences in costs (revenues) of two or more options.

12. A company is designing a new regional distribution warehouse. To minimize delays in loading and unloading trucks, an adequate number of loading docks must be built. The most relevant technique to assist in determining the proper number of docks is

- A. Correlation and regression analysis.
- B. Cost-volume-profit analysis.
- C. PERT/cost analysis.
- D. Queuing theory.

Answer (D) is correct. *(CMA, adapted)*
REQUIRED: The technique to assist in determining the proper number of docks.
DISCUSSION: Queuing theory is a group of mathematical models for systems involving waiting lines. In general, a queuing system consists of a waiting line and a service facility (loading docks in this case). The objective of queuing theory is to minimize the total cost of the system, including both service and waiting costs, for a given rate of arrivals.
Answer (A) is incorrect because correlation and regression analysis is a means of determining the degree of the relationship among two or more variables. Answer (B) is incorrect because CVP analysis is used to analyze the relationship among fixed costs, variable costs, sales volume, and profit or loss. Answer (C) is incorrect because PERT/cost is a means of network analysis that assigns costs to all activities so that the effect of any change in a given task on cost as well as on time may be estimated.

13. Managers must make decisions in many different situations. A manager must make a subjective decision when the environment is one in which

- A. Uncertainty exists.
- B. Risk exists.
- C. Certainty may be achieved.
- D. Probabilities can be calculated.

Answer (A) is correct. *(Publisher, adapted)*
REQUIRED: The situation in which intuition must be used to make a decision.
DISCUSSION: Uncertainty exists when the results of possible outcomes cannot even be estimated using the tools of statistical probability. This environment is the most difficult for decision making because objective mathematical analyses cannot be made. Hence, creativity is required in the decision-making process, and reliance on the educated guess rather than the probabilistically calculated estimate is necessary.
Answer (B) is incorrect because risk implies uncertainty that can be alleviated by quantitative analysis. Under conditions of risk, probabilities of various outcomes can be objectively determined and a decision maker need not rely solely on hunches. Answer (C) is incorrect because, under conditions of certainty, outcome of each choice is known with a probability of 1.0. The decision process can thus be a purely objective one. Answer (D) is incorrect because risk implies uncertainty that can be alleviated by quantitative analysis. Under conditions of risk, probabilities of various outcomes can be objectively determined, and a decision maker need not rely solely on hunches.

14. Behavioral scientists have identified human tendencies that can erode the quality of decision making. Which of the following best describes a behavioral decision error referred to as "framing error"?

- A. Evaluating positive information favorably and negative information unfavorably.
- B. Getting locked into losing courses of action because of personal commitment.
- C. Evaluating the probabilities of outcomes as point estimates instead of ranges.
- D. Becoming overconfident because of past successes.

Answer (A) is correct. *(CIA, adapted)*
REQUIRED: The best description of a framing error.
DISCUSSION: How information is presented influences both its interpretation and the resulting behavior. Framing error is the tendency to evaluate positively presented information favorably and negatively presented information unfavorably.
Answer (B) is incorrect because getting locked into losing courses of action because of personal commitment is escalation of commitment. Answer (C) is incorrect because a framing error is defined as evaluating positive information favorably and negative information unfavorably. Answer (D) is incorrect because overconfidence does not relate to framing errors.

15. The term "escalation of commitment" refers to

A. The process of continuing to fund old projects because of inadequate information or time to formally analyze the costs and benefits associated with continued investment.

B. The decision maker increasing the resources to a new course of action if the employee can recommend alternatives such that the decision the new course of action as his/her own initiative.

C. Committing to projects that have been shown to be successful and limiting the additional commitment of resources to projects that have been unsuccessful.

D. The decision maker increasing the resources to the previous course of action in an effort to demonstrate that the previous course of action was appropriate.

Answer (D) is correct. *(CIA, adapted)*
REQUIRED: The definition of escalation of commitment.
DISCUSSION: Consistency may be dysfunctional because it may result in inflexibility. The desire to avoid the inner conflict resulting from inconsistency may have adverse effects on decision making. For example, when a decision maker feels responsible for the failure of a course of action, (s)he may want to prove that the original decision was sound despite increasing evidence to the contrary. Thus, his/her commitment to a failed policy may escalate, and additional resources may be squandered.
Answer (A) is incorrect because escalation of commitment is a psychological phenomenon unrelated to availability of information or time. Answer (B) is incorrect because increasing resources to a new course of action is antithetical to escalation of commitment. Answer (C) is incorrect because limiting resources to unsuccessful projects is antithetical to escalation of commitment.

16. Rational decision making is a multistep process. In which stage of this process will effective communication to persons affected by the decision be most important?

A. Evaluating possible solutions.

B. Defining the problem.

C. Following up.

D. Gathering relevant information.

Answer (C) is correct. *(Publisher, adapted)*
REQUIRED: The decision step in which communication is most important.
DISCUSSION: A decision cannot be communicated to affected parties until it has been made. Effective communication is vital to successful implementation of the change resulting from the decision. Follow-up to evaluate the decision will determine whether the decision was correct. One reason desired results may not be obtained is lack of effective communication.
Answer (A) is incorrect because evaluating solutions precedes implementation, which is an aspect of the follow-up to the decision choice. Answer (B) is incorrect because defining the problem precedes implementation, which is an aspect of the follow-up to the decision choice. Answer (D) is incorrect because gathering data precedes implementation, which is an aspect of the follow-up to the decision choice.

17. Rational decision making involves all of the following steps except

A. Defining the problem.

B. Taking sunk costs into account.

C. Choosing an alternative.

D. Implementing the decision.

Answer (B) is correct. *(Publisher, adapted)*
REQUIRED: The step not involved in rational decision making.
DISCUSSION: The consideration of choices and the selection of the choice expected to give the best results are key parts of the planner's job. Rational decision making involves the following steps: defining the problem, obtaining information, identifying alternative courses of action, making predictions about future costs, choosing and justifying an alternative, implementing the decision, and evaluating performance to provide feedback. One of the most common errors in decision making is taking sunk costs into account. Because sunk costs have already been incurred, they can play no role in rational decision making.
Answer (A) is incorrect because defining the problem is one of the steps involved in rational decision making. Answer (C) is incorrect because choosing an alternative is one of the steps involved in rational decision making. Answer (D) is incorrect because implementing the decision is one of the steps involved in rational decision making.

18. The most common difficulty in problem solving is

   A. Obtaining information.

   B. Identifying alternative courses of action.

   C. Defining the problem.

   D. Being aware of the existence of a problem.

Answer (C) is correct. *(Publisher, adapted)*
   REQUIRED: The most common difficulty in problem solving.
   DISCUSSION: Defining the problem is the most common difficulty in problem solving. Pitfalls in defining problems include defining the problem according to a solution, concentrating on nonpertinent areas, and defining problems by their symptoms.
   Answer (A) is incorrect because obtaining information follows defining the problem in the problem-solving process. Answer (B) is incorrect because identifying alternative courses of action results from defining the problem and obtaining information about the problem. Answer (D) is incorrect because awareness of the existence of a problem precedes defining the problem. The awareness leads to the problem solving.

19. In the decision-making process, identifying alternative courses of action can be accomplished by many methods. Which of the following is a method of idea generation that reports the first thought to come to mind in response to a given stimulus?

   A. Creative leap.

   B. Brainstorming.

   C. Forced relationship.

   D. Free association.

Answer (D) is correct. *(Publisher, adapted)*
   REQUIRED: The method of idea generation that reports the first thought to come to mind in response to a given stimulus.
   DISCUSSION: Identifying alternative courses of action can be primary or secondary, or it can be creative. One of the creative methods is free association. Free association is a method of idea generation that reports the first thought to come to mind in response to a given stimulus. The objective is to express the content of consciousness without censorship or control.
   Answer (A) is incorrect because creative leap is a process that formulates an ideal solution and then works back to a feasible one. Answer (B) is incorrect because brainstorming is an unstructured approach that relies on spontaneous contribution of ideas from all members of a group. Answer (C) is incorrect because forced relationship is a structured adaptation of free association. The elements of a problem are analyzed, and the associations among them are identified to detect patterns that may suggest new ideas.

20. The evaluation technique of linear programming involves all of the following except

   A. Linear equations.

   B. Scarce resources.

   C. Accurate results.

   D. Objective function.

Answer (C) is correct. *(Publisher, adapted)*
   REQUIRED: The item not involved with linear programming.
   DISCUSSION: Linear programming is a tool for allocating scarce resources in the presence of resource constraints. The problem must be described by a system of linear equations. An objective function (usually cost or revenue) is maximized or minimized subject to constraint equations. The simultaneous solution to the system of equations maximizes profit (or minimizes cost). This description is seldom strictly accurate but provides useful approximations.
   Answer (A) is incorrect because linear programming uses linear equations. Answer (B) is incorrect because linear programming is a tool for allocating scarce resources. Answer (D) is incorrect because linear programming utilizes an objective function (usually cost or revenue), which is maximized or minimized subject to constraint equations.

21. The human tendency to judge positively-presented information favorably and negatively-presented information unfavorably is known as

   A. Bounded rationality.

   B. Framing error.

   C. Escalation.

   D. Overconfidence.

Answer (B) is correct. *(Publisher, adapted)*
   REQUIRED: The name of the described decision-making problem.
   DISCUSSION: Three problems that arise in decision making are framing error, escalation, and overconfidence. Framing error is the human tendency to judge positively-presented information favorably and negatively-presented information unfavorably.
   Answer (A) is incorrect because bounded rationality is the inability to sell all aspects of a situation. This occurs during the phase of defining a problem. Answer (C) is incorrect because the decision-making problem of escalation is the human tendency to become committed to failing courses of action instead of quitting or admitting error. Answer (D) is incorrect because the decision-making problem of overconfidence can expose the decision maker to unreasonable risks.

22. All of the following are tools used to evaluate solutions except

- A. Value analysis.
- B. Simulation.
- C. Linear programming.
- D. Decision theory.

Answer (A) is correct. *(Publisher, adapted)*
REQUIRED: The tool not used to evaluate problem solutions.
DISCUSSION: The analysis of facts and the development of solutions have been improved through the adoption of mathematical techniques. Although they will not provide useful solutions for poorly formulated problems, they will provide valuable results for well-defined quantitative problems. Some of these tools include simulation, linear programming, and decision theory. Value analysis is a technique utilized to identify alternative courses of action, not for evaluation of problem solutions.

Answer (B) is incorrect because simulation is an approach used to evaluate solutions. Answer (C) is incorrect because linear programming is used to evaluate solutions by allocating scarce resources in the presence of resource constraints. Answer (D) is incorrect because decision theory, also called decision trees, maps out possible actions given probabilistic events.

23. The Delphi technique is used during which step of the decision-making process?

- A. Defining the problem.
- B. Obtaining information.
- C. Identifying alternative courses of action.
- D. Evaluating the different problem solutions.

Answer (C) is correct. *(Publisher, adapted)*
REQUIRED: The step in the decision-making process in which the Delphi technique is used.
DISCUSSION: The Delphi technique is used in identifying alternative courses of action. It is an approach in which the manager solicits opinions on a problem from experts in the field, summarizes the opinions, and feeds the summaries back to the experts.

Answer (A) is incorrect because the Delphi technique is not used to define the problem. Answer (B) is incorrect because obtaining information involves determining which issues to address and the objectives to be achieved. The Delphi technique is not used for this purpose. Answer (D) is incorrect because evaluating solutions utilizes quantitative tools or approaches. The Delphi technique is a creative method of identifying alternative courses of action, not evaluating solutions.

24. Under the Monte Carlo method,

- A. The model is run once.
- B. Uncertainty is simulated.
- C. Total performance is determined.
- D. Probability distribution is not used.

Answer (B) is correct. *(Publisher, adapted)*
REQUIRED: The correct statement regarding the Monte Carlo method.
DISCUSSION: The Monte Carlo method is a tool used to evaluate problem solutions. Random behavior may be added to otherwise deterministic models to simulate the uncertainty inherent in real-world situations. The model is run a large number of times, and the variance of the probability distribution of the results and the average performance are determined.

Answer (A) is incorrect because the Monte Carlo method is run a large number of times. Answer (C) is incorrect because, when using the Monte Carlo method, average, not total performance, is determined. Answer (D) is incorrect because the Monte Carlo method does use the probability distribution. This model is run a large number of times, and the variance of the probability distribution of the results and the average performance are determined.

25. Faulty perception may preclude the decision maker from seeing the correct problem. Which of the following is an example of faulty perception?

- A. A person's needs do not influence what is observed.
- B. A person does not see what (s)he is trained to see.
- C. Group pressure may influence which problems are perceived.
- D. A person does not see what (s)he expects to see.

Answer (C) is correct. *(Publisher, adapted)*
REQUIRED: The example of faulty perception.
DISCUSSION: The inability to see all aspects of a situation may prevent accurate problem definition. This inability may be caused by faulty perception. Faulty perception includes group pressure influencing which problems are perceived or how the problems are defined.

Answer (A) is incorrect because a person's needs do influence what the person observes. Answer (B) is incorrect because a person does see what (s)he is trained to see. Answer (D) is incorrect because a person sees what the person expects to see.

26. When choosing the best available solution to a problem, human aspects of the choice must be considered. Which is a true statement regarding human aspects of the choice?

    A. The opinions and attitudes of the people involved do not require consideration.

    B. The people involved do not have to be convinced of the decision's value.

    C. Decisions do not have unexpected effects.

    D. Implementing change is a critical part of the decision-making process.

Answer (D) is correct. *(Publisher, adapted)*
    REQUIRED: The true statement regarding the human aspects of choosing the best available solution.
    DISCUSSION: The selection of the best available solution is the objective of the decision-making process. Human aspects of the choice must be considered. The multistep process of decision making must be followed when making organizational changes. Implementing change is a critical part of the decision-making process because people are crucial to the effectiveness of the choice.
    Answer (A) is incorrect because the opinions and attitudes of the people involved do require consideration in the process. If these are not considered, an otherwise optimal solution may fail. Answer (B) is incorrect because a decision is only useful if those responsible for its implementation are convinced of its value. Answer (C) is incorrect because decisions are made in a multidimensional environment and therefore have many, sometimes unexpected, effects.

27. A decision maker is operating in an environment in which all the facts surrounding a decision are known exactly, and each alternative is associated with only one possible outcome. The environment is known as

    A. Certainty.

    B. Risk.

    C. Uncertainty.

    D. Probability.

Answer (A) is correct. *(CMA, adapted)*
    REQUIRED: The name of the described environment.
    DISCUSSION: The less the variability of the future results of a decision, the smaller the risk involved. If each choice is associated with only one possible outcome, no variability exists. Such a condition is one of certainty (zero variance).
    Answer (B) is incorrect because there would be no risk or uncertainty if all facts were known and there was only one possible outcome for each alternative. Answer (C) is incorrect because uncertainty is the absence of certainty. There would be no uncertainty if all facts were known and there was only one possible outcome for each alternative. Answer (D) is incorrect because probability is a number between 0 and 1 inclusive that measures the likelihood of the occurrence of some event. The less likely the event, the closer the number is to zero.

28. The use of a decision tree is appropriate for decision making under conditions of

    A. Uncertainty and risk.

    B. Uncertainty and subjective likelihoods.

    C. Certainty.

    D. Risk.

Answer (D) is correct. *(CMA, adapted)*
    REQUIRED: The conditions under which the use of a decision tree is appropriate.
    DISCUSSION: Decision tree analysis is used when various options of certainty, their consequences, and the probabilities of those consequences can be ascertained with a high degree of confidence. Under conditions of uncertainty, however, probabilities are unknown.
    Answer (A) is incorrect because uncertainty does not allow probabilities to be assigned to possible actions. Answer (B) is incorrect because certainty, not uncertainty, is necessary for using decision tree analysis. Answer (C) is incorrect because, under a condition of certainty, a decision tree would be unnecessary.

29. The modeling technique to be used for situations involving a sequence of events with several possible outcomes associated with each event is

    A. Queuing theory.

    B. Simulation.

    C. Linear programming.

    D. Decision tree analysis.

Answer (D) is correct. *(CMA, adapted)*
    REQUIRED: The described modeling technique.
    DISCUSSION: Decision tree analysis is useful when the most beneficial series of decisions is to be chosen. The possible decisions for each decision point, the events that might follow from each decision, the probabilities of these events, and the quantified outcomes should be known.
    Answer (A) is incorrect because queuing theory is a technique used to analyze waiting-line problems through the use of probability theory. Answer (B) is incorrect because simulation requires the construction of a quantitative model that incorporates most of the features of the problem situation. It is used when an optimization model is not possible, such as when the number of variables exceeds the number of equations describing the variables. Answer (C) is incorrect because linear programming is a tool for allocating scarce resources in the presence of resource constraints. The problem is described using a system of linear equations.

30. Which of the following statements is/are true about choosing a course of action?

I.   Future cash flows of the potential courses of action must be compared.

II.   Qualitative factors must be considered.

III. Nonfinancial quantitative factors do not have to be considered.

    A. I only.

    B. I and II.

    C. III only.

    D. I, II, and III.

Answer (B) is correct. *(Publisher, adapted)*
    REQUIRED: The true statement(s) about choosing a course of action.
    DISCUSSION: The selection of the best available solution is the objective of the decision-making process. The choice involves not only comparing the future cash flows of the potential courses of action, but also considering qualitative and nonfinancial quantitative factors. Qualitative factors include relationships with employees, suppliers, and customers. Nonfinancial quantitative factors include rate of defective output and manufacturing lead time.
    Answer (A) is incorrect because qualitative factors, such as relationships with employees, suppliers, and customers, must also be considered. Answer (C) is incorrect because nonfinancial quantitative factors, such as rate of defective output and manufacturing lead time, must be considered when choosing a course of action. Answer (D) is incorrect because nonfinancial quantitative factors must also be considered when choosing a course of action.

31. Simulation, a widely used technique in decision modeling, is a

    A. Process of modeling in which real activities are represented in mathematical form.

    B. Tool used for allocating scarce resources.

    C. Technique used to add random behavior to simulate uncertainty.

    D. Technique used to map out possible actions given probabilistic events.

Answer (A) is correct. *(CMA, adapted)*
    REQUIRED: The correct description of simulation.
    DISCUSSION: Computer simulation is used when an optimization model cannot be developed, e.g., because the variables exceed the equations describing them. Simulation involves constructing a mathematical/logical model incorporating most of the features of the problem. This model is tested in a variety of hypothetical situations, and the modeled responses can then be measured.
    Answer (B) is incorrect because linear programming is a tool used for allocating scarce resources in the presence of resource constraints. Answer (C) is incorrect because the Monte Carlo method adds random behavior to simulate the uncertainty inherent in real-world situations. Answer (D) is incorrect because decision tree analysis maps out possible actions given probabilistic events.

32. A company experiences both variable usage rates and variable lead times for its inventory items. The probability distributions for both usage and lead times are known. A technique the company could use for determining the optimal safety stock levels for an inventory item is

    A. Queuing theory.

    B. Linear programming.

    C. Decision tree analysis.

    D. The Monte Carlo method.

Answer (D) is correct. *(CMA, adapted)*
    REQUIRED: The technique the company could use to determine optimal safety stock levels.
    DISCUSSION: Simulation is a technique for experimenting with mathematical models using a computer. The Monte Carlo method is a technique used to generate the individual values for a random variable. This simulates the uncertainty inherent in real-world situations. The model is then run a large number of times, and the variance of the probability distribution of the results and the average performance are determined.
    Answer (A) is incorrect because queuing theory is used to minimize the costs of waiting lines. Answer (B) is incorrect because linear programming is used to minimize a cost function or maximize a profit function using given constraints. Answer (C) is incorrect because decision tree analysis analyzes sequences of probabilistic decisions, the events that may follow each decision, and their outcomes.

33. Decisions are frequently classified as those made under certainty and those made under uncertainty. Certainty exists when

    A. The probability of the event is less than 1.

    B. There is absolutely no doubt that an event will occur.

    C. There is more than one outcome for each possible action.

    D. There is risk involved.

Answer (B) is correct. *(Publisher, adapted)*
    REQUIRED: The statement describing when certainty exists.
    DISCUSSION: An event is certain if there is no doubt that it will occur. The probability is 1 if an event is certain to occur and 0 if it is certain not to occur. Under conditions of certainty, consequences are therefore deterministic, not probabilistic or unknown.
    Answer (A) is incorrect because a probability of less than 1 would not be certainty. Answer (C) is incorrect because certainty implies a specific outcome. Answer (D) is incorrect because risk is a condition in which a decision maker, using incomplete but reliable information, can estimate the probability of a given outcome of a decision.

34. Which of the following is not an attribute of a probability distribution?

    A. The total probability associated with all possible occurrences equals 1.

    B. It can be modeled by means that provide the probability for every possible outcome.

    C. Only one outcome is possible.

    D. It concerns a random variable.

Answer (C) is correct. *(Publisher, adapted)*
    REQUIRED: The item that is not an attribute of a probability distribution.
    DISCUSSION: In a probability distribution, the probability of any event(s) is bounded by 0 (no chance) and 1 (certainty). The total probability of all possible outcomes must add up to 1. Also, a probability distribution models a random variable through the use of a formula or graph that provides the probability associated with the occurrence of certain values of the random variable. If only one outcome is possible, the variable is not random but rather constant and known with certainty.
    Answer (A) is incorrect because the total probability associated with all possible occurrences does equal 1. Answer (B) is incorrect because a probability can be modeled by means of a formula or graph that provides the probability for every possible outcome. Answer (D) is incorrect because a probability distribution does concern a random variable.

35. The modeling technique to be employed in a situation involving a sequence of events with several possible outcomes associated with each event is

    A. Cost-benefit analysis.

    B. Decision tree analysis.

    C. The Monte Carlo method.

    D. Linear programming.

Answer (B) is correct. *(CMA, adapted)*
    REQUIRED: The described modeling technique.
    DISCUSSION: Decision trees may be used to describe complex decision situations. Each branch of the tree represents a different decision, and each twig extending from each branch represents several possible outcomes of the decision.
    Answer (A) is incorrect because cost-benefit analysis is a simple test for possible solutions. Cost should be less than the benefits realized. Answer (C) is incorrect because the Monte Carlo method is a technique for experimenting with mathematical models using a computer, which generates random values for each variable. Answer (D) is incorrect because linear programming is a means of allocating scarce resources given a specified objective and a variety of constraints.

36. When making predictions about costs, what makes a cost relevant to a decision?

    A. Cost has already been paid.

    B. Cost must vary between alternatives.

    C. Cost must be paid in the future.

    D. Cost must both vary between alternatives and be paid in the future.

Answer (D) is correct. *(Publisher, adapted)*
    REQUIRED: The condition that makes a cost relevant to a decision.
    DISCUSSION: To be relevant to a decision, a cost must vary between alternatives and be paid or incurred in the future.
    Answer (A) is incorrect because a cost that has already been paid is a sunk cost. It has already been incurred and can play no role in rational decision making. Answer (B) is incorrect because the cost also must be paid in the future. Answer (C) is incorrect because the cost also must vary between alternatives.

37. A chief executive officer (CEO) believes that a major competitor may be planning a new marketing campaign. The CEO sends a questionnaire to key personnel asking for original thinking concerning what the new campaign may be. The CEO selects the best possibilities and then sends another questionnaire asking for the most likely option. The process employed by the CEO is called

    A. Forced relationship.

    B. The Delphi technique.

    C. Morphological matrix analysis.

    D. Synectics.

Answer (B) is correct. *(CIA, adapted)*
    REQUIRED: The process employed by the CEO.
    DISCUSSION: The Delphi technique is a decision-making approach that attempts to avoid groupthink (the tendency of individuals to conform to what they perceive to be the consensus). The technique allows only written, anonymous communication among group members. Each member takes a position on the problem at hand. A summary of these positions is communicated to each member. The process is repeated several times as the members move toward a consensus.
    Answer (A) is incorrect because forced relationship is a structured adaptation of free association. The elements of a problem are analyzed, and the associations among them are identified to detect patterns that may suggest new ideas. Answer (C) is incorrect because morphological matrix analysis is a structured technique that plots decision variables along the axes of a matrix. The relationships of these variables are found in the squares within the chart. Answer (D) is incorrect because synectics involves free use of analogies and metaphors in informal exchange within a carefully selected small group of individuals of diverse personalities and areas of specialization.

38. A company is designing a new regional distribution warehouse. To minimize delays in loading and unloading trucks, an adequate number of loading docks must be built. The most relevant technique to assist in determining the proper number of docks is

    A. Linear programming.

    B. Decision trees.

    C. The Monte Carlo method.

    D. Queuing theory.

Answer (D) is correct. *(CMA, adapted)*
    REQUIRED: The relevant technique to determine the proper number of docks.
    DISCUSSION: Queuing theory is a group of mathematical models for systems involving waiting lines. In general, a queuing system consists of a waiting line and a service facility (loading docks in this case). The objective of queuing theory is to minimize the total cost of the system, including both service and waiting costs, for a given rate of arrivals.
    Answer (A) is incorrect because linear programming is a tool for allocating scarce resources in the presence of resource constraints. Answer (B) is incorrect because decision trees map out possible actions given probabilistic events. Answer (C) is incorrect because the Monte Carlo method adds random behavior to otherwise deterministic models to simulate the uncertainty inherent in real-world situations.

39. A decision model is a formal means of choosing future courses of action. The programmed decision process and the nonprogrammed decision process are used for making decisions. What is the difference between the two?

    A. The programmed decision process is used for complex situations.

    B. The programmed decision process is not based upon decision rules.

    C. The nonprogrammed decision process requires answers to four questions.

    D. No difference exists between the two.

Answer (C) is correct. *(Publisher, adapted)*
    REQUIRED: The difference between the programmed decision process and the nonprogrammed decision process.
    DISCUSSION: Management accountants provide qualitative information as well as quantitative financial and nonfinancial information useful in applying a decision model. The programmed decision process is used for routine or repetitive decisions. The nonprogrammed decision process is used for complex, nonroutine situations calling for the use of the problem-solving process. Four questions need to be answered before making a nonprogrammed decision.
    Answer (A) is incorrect because the programmed decision process is used for routine or repetitive decisions. Answer (B) is incorrect because the programmed decision process is based upon decision rules. They are the parameters within which a routine decision is based. Answer (D) is incorrect because differences do exist between programmed and nonprogrammed decision processes.

40. Information processing for decision making is characterized by two styles: analytic and intuitive. Which of the following is a characteristic of the intuitive style?

    A. Unstructured.

    B. Objective.

    C. Detailed.

    D. Deductive.

Answer (A) is correct. *(Publisher, adapted)*
    REQUIRED: The characteristic of the intuitive style of information processing.
    DISCUSSION: The intuitive style of information processing for decision making is subjective, inductive, nonroutine, and unstructured. Intuitive people may rely on hunches and reach decisions without explicitly applying a formal process. The thinking or analytic style of decision making is objective, deductive, precise, detailed, logical, and repetitive. It tends to prevail in the traditional organization.
    Answer (B) is incorrect because the thinking or analytic style of decision making is objective. Answer (C) is incorrect because the analytic style of decision making is detailed. Answer (D) is incorrect because the analytic style of decision making is deductive.

41. The limiting factor principle

    A. Applies to identifying alternative courses of action.

    B. Defines the problem.

    C. Justifies an alternative.

    D. Predicts future costs.

Answer (A) is correct. *(Publisher, adapted)*
    REQUIRED: The true statement regarding the limiting factor principle.
    DISCUSSION: The limiting factor principle is used in the decision-making process during the step involving identifying alternative courses of action. The crucial factor is the one that limits or prevents achievement of the desired goal. The mass of alternative choices can be reduced if managers can identify the limiting factors to a problem.
    Answer (B) is incorrect because defining the problem is done as the first step in the decision-making process. The limiting factor principle occurs later in the process. Answer (C) is incorrect because justifying an alternative takes place after the identification of alternative courses of action, where the limiting factor principle is utilized. Answer (D) is incorrect because the limiting factor principle does not predict future costs.

42. Determining what issues must be addressed and considering the objectives of the desired course of action are accomplished during which step of the decision-making process?

    A. Defining the problem.

    B. Obtaining information.

    C. Evaluating solutions.

    D. Implementing the decision.

Answer (B) is correct. *(Publisher, adapted)*
    REQUIRED: The described step in the decision-making process.
    DISCUSSION: During the step in the decision-making process of obtaining information, the decision maker determines which issues must be addressed, for example, whether to make or outsource a component. The decision maker also considers the objectives of the desired course of action, for example, to increase return on investment or to enter a new market.
    Answer (A) is incorrect because defining the problem is the first step in the decision-making process. During this step, issues are not yet addressed. Answer (C) is incorrect because evaluating solutions involves the analysis of facts in determining a solution. Answer (D) is incorrect because implementing the decision occurs after addressing issues and considering objectives of the desired course of action.

43. Scenario development

    A. Is a quantitative forecasting method.

    B. Is a method of determining an organization's direction.

    C. Is used to identify courses of action.

    D. Requires preparation of future event scenarios.

Answer (D) is correct. *(Publisher, adapted)*
    REQUIRED: The true statement regarding scenario development.
    DISCUSSION: Scenario development is a qualitative forecasting method that requires preparation of conceptual scenarios of future events given carefully defined assumptions. It entails writing multiple different but equally likely descriptions of future states.
    Answer (A) is incorrect because scenario development is a qualitative, not quantitative, forecasting method. Answer (B) is incorrect because situational analysis is a method of determining an organization's direction by systematically matching its strengths and weaknesses with its environmental opportunities and threats. Answer (C) is incorrect because scenario development is used to evaluate solutions during the decision-making process.

44. Which method of identifying alternative courses of action is primarily designed to optimize performance of an activity at a minimum cost?

    A. Edisonian approach.

    B. Value analysis.

    C. Brainstorming.

    D. Attribute listing.

Answer (B) is correct. *(Publisher, adapted)*
    REQUIRED: The described method of identifying alternative courses of action.
    DISCUSSION: Value analysis is a methodical approach primarily designed to optimize performance of an activity at a minimum cost. Emphasis is on the cost-benefit criterion.
    Answer (A) is incorrect because the Edisonian approach is a trial-and-error experimental method. Answer (C) is incorrect because brainstorming is an unstructured approach that relies on the spontaneous contribution of ideas from all members of a group. Answer (D) is incorrect because attribute listing is applied primarily to improve a tangible object. It lists the parts and essential features of the object and systematically analyzes modifications intended as improvements.

45. The operations research approach to evaluating solutions includes all of the following except:

    A. Testing of a mathematical model.

    B. Formulating a mathematical model.

    C. Constructing a quantitative model.

    D. Recognizing the complete system in which the problem operates.

Answer (C) is correct. *(Publisher, adapted)*
    REQUIRED: The incorrect statement regarding the operations research approach.
    DISCUSSION: Operations research is an overall approach that applies a variety of scientific and mathematical techniques. It involves the following: recognition of the complete system, including interrelationships, in which the problem operates; formulation of a mathematical model; testing of the model; and implementation of the optimal solution as produced by the model. Simulation requires the construction of a quantitative model.
    Answer (A) is incorrect because testing the model is one of the steps in the operations research approach. Answer (B) is incorrect because formulation of a mathematical model is one of the steps in the operations research approach. Answer (D) is incorrect because recognition of the complete system in which the problem operates is one of the steps in the operations research approach.

46. When a decision maker is faced with a decision and the probabilities of various outcomes are known, the situation is said to be decision making

- A. Under risk.
- B. Under uncertainty.
- C. Under certainty.
- D. Through satisficing.

Answer (A) is correct. *(CIA, adapted)*

REQUIRED: The described situation for decision making.

DISCUSSION: Decision making under risk entails consideration of multiple possible future states of nature for each choice. The decision is under risk if a probability distribution for these states can be estimated. Thus, the states of nature will be mutually exclusive, and the sum of their probabilities will equal 1.0. Risk increases as the variability of outcomes becomes greater. In practice, however, the terms risk and uncertainty are often treated as synonyms.

Answer (B) is incorrect because, under uncertainty, the probabilities of the possible states of nature are unknown. Answer (C) is incorrect because, under certainty, that is, with perfect information, the outcome of each decision choice is known; that is, its probability is 1.0. Answer (D) is incorrect because satisficing decisions are satisfactory or sufficient but not optimal.

47. Evaluating performance and giving feedback is the final step in the decision-making process. This step involves

I. Proper delegation of authority.

II. Placement of the solution in a feasible framework.

III. Effective communication of the decision.

- A. I only.
- B. I and II.
- C. II only.
- D. I, II, and III.

Answer (D) is correct. *(Publisher, adapted)*

REQUIRED: The true statement(s) about the step in the decision-making process of evaluating performance and giving feedback.

DISCUSSION: The step of evaluating performance and giving feedback is vital to improve future execution of the prior steps or even the decision model itself. The proper delegation of authority is made to the individual responsible for implementing the action to be taken. Performance measurement is then provided for. This process puts the solution into a feasible framework, which assures it will be carried out. Finally, decisions cannot be fully implemented until they are effectively communicated.

Answer (A) is incorrect because putting the solution into a feasible framework and effectively communicating the decision are also involved in this step. Answer (B) is incorrect because effective communication of the decision is also involved in evaluating performance and giving feedback. Answer (C) is incorrect because properly delegating authority and putting the solution into a feasible framework are also involved in this step.

Use Gleim's *CMA Test Prep* for interactive testing with **over 2,000 additional multiple-choice questions!**

STUDY UNIT THIRTEEN
DATA CONCEPTS RELEVANT
TO DECISION MAKING

(4 pages of outline)

This study unit is the **second of five** on **decision analysis**. The relative weight assigned to this major topic in Part 3 of the exam is **25%** at **skill level C** (all six skill types required). The five study units are

Study Unit 12: The Decision Process
Study Unit 13: Data Concepts Relevant to Decision Making
Study Unit 14: Cost-Volume-Profit Analysis
Study Unit 15: Marginal Analysis
Study Unit 16: Cost-Based Pricing

After studying the outline and answering the multiple-choice questions, you will have the skills necessary to address the following topics listed in the IMA's Learning Outcome Statements:

Part 3 – Section D.2. Relevant data concepts

The candidate should be able to:

a.   differentiate between economic concepts of revenues and costs and accounting concepts of revenues and costs

b.   define relevant revenues (expected future revenues) and relevant costs (expected future costs)

c.   identify cost behavior patterns, define cost traceability, and demonstrate an understanding of cost relevance as it relates to various cost objects for which decisions are to be made

d.   demonstrate an understanding of various costs incurred in the value chain and the composition of such costs for decisions such as pricing, alternative operating options, contract negotiations, and outsourcing decisions

e.   differentiate between costs that are avoidable or unavoidable in a decision process setting

f.   identify relevant costs as the incremental, marginal, or differential costs among alternative courses of action and calculate the relevant costs given a numerical scenario

g.   define sunk costs and explain why they are not relevant

h.   distinguish between quantitative factors (e.g., cost of direct labor) and qualitative factors (e.g., reduction in new-product development time)

i.   define qualitative factors as outcomes that cannot be measured in numerical terms, e.g., employee morale

j.   demonstrate an understanding of opportunity costs as the contribution to income that is forgone by not using a limited resource in its best alternative use

k.   demonstrate an understanding of the impact of income taxes on the relevant revenue and cost data employed in the decision process

13.1 COST AND REVENUE RELEVANCE

1. In business decision making, revenues and costs must be projected from two standpoints.

   a. The **accounting concept** of costs includes **only explicit costs**, i.e., those that represent actual outlays of cash, the allocation of outlays of cash, or commitments to pay cash. Examples include the incurrence of payables, the satisfaction of payables, and the recognition of depreciation.

   b. The **economic concept** of costs includes **both explicit and implicit costs**.

      1) **Implicit** in any business decision is **opportunity cost**, defined as "the contribution to income that is forgone by not using a limited resource in its best alternative use."

   c. EXAMPLE: A manufacturer's accounting cost for a new product line consists only of the costs associated with the new machinery and personnel, but the economic cost includes the 4.75% return the company could make by simply investing the money in certificates of deposit.

2. In decision making, an organization must focus on only **relevant revenues and costs**. To be relevant, the revenues and costs must

   a. Be made in the **future**.

      1) Costs which have already been incurred or to which the organization is committed, called **sunk costs**, have no bearing on any future decisions.

      2) EXAMPLE: A manufacturer is considering upgrading its production equipment owing to the obsolescence of its current machinery. The amounts paid for the existing equipment are sunk costs; they make no difference in the decision to modernize.

   b. **Differ** among the possible alternative courses of action.

      1) EXAMPLE: The relevant revenue in the above manufacturer's decision is not total sales, but only the additional sales that can be generated with more modern equipment.

3. A vital concept in decision making is that of **relevant range**, i.e., the range of activity over which fixed costs remain fixed. Relevant range is synonymous with **the short run**.

   a. **Cost behavior** is therefore an important factor in decision making.

      1) **Fixed costs in total** remain unchanged in the short run regardless of production level, e.g., the amount paid for an assembly line is the same even if production is halted entirely.

         a) **Fixed cost per unit**, however, varies indirectly with the activity level.

      2) **Variable costs in total** vary directly and proportionally with changes in volume, e.g., direct materials.

         a) **Variable cost per unit**, however, remains constant regardless of changes in activity.

      3) **Mixed (semivariable) costs** combine fixed and variable elements, e.g., rental on a car that carries a flat fee per month plus an additional fee for each mile driven.

   b. Note that cost behavior **does not necessarily determine the relevance** of costs.

      1) If decision makers commit the organization to a level of production that is above the current relevant range, fixed costs become relevant. If all decision alternatives are within the relevant range, only variable costs are relevant.

    c.   **Incremental (differential) costs** are inherent in the concept of relevant range.

        1)   Throughout the relevant range, the incremental cost of an additional unit of output is the same. Once a certain level of output is reached, however, the current production capacity is insufficient and another increment of fixed costs must be incurred.

    d.   Another pitfall in relevant cost determination is the use of **unit revenues and costs**. The emphasis should be on **total relevant revenues and costs** because unit data may include irrelevant amounts or may have been computed for an output level different from the one for which the analysis is being made.

4.   A **cost object** is any business phenomenon to which costs can be applied, e.g., a product, a service, or a project.

    a.   **Cost traceability** allows decision makers to associate costs with a cost object in an economically feasible way. For example, direct materials are traceable costs of automobiles, but insurance on the factory is not.

        1)   Costs which **cannot be traced** must be **allocated**. As the case of the factory shows, **an allocated cost may still be relevant**.

            a)   EXAMPLE: If central administrative costs are allocated to segments of a firm and one segment decides to discontinue a major customer, the decrease in those costs that will result is relevant even if the allocation to the segment does not change. Conversely, if the cost allocated to the segment changes but the total does not, the allocated cost is not relevant to the decision.

5.   The composition of **costs in the value chain** are relevant to decision making. Refer to the diagram in item 2. in Subunit 3.1.

    a.   Support activities can be relevant costs under some circumstances. Changes in production levels or product mix involve changes in the inventory management function. New manufacturing setups involve the plant maintenance department. New sources of supply or the decision to outsource certain functions involve contract management.

6.   Only **avoidable costs** are relevant.

    a.   An **avoidable cost** may be saved by not adopting a particular option. Avoidable costs might include variable raw material costs and direct labor costs.

    b.   An **unavoidable cost** is one that cannot be avoided if a particular action is taken. For example, if a company has a long-term lease on a building, closing out the business in that building will not eliminate the need to pay rent. Thus, the rent is an unavoidable cost.

7.   Both quantitative and qualitative factors are considered.

    a.   **Quantitative factors** fall into two categories, **financial** (e.g., stock price, earnings per share, cost of capital) and **nonfinancial** (e.g., number of employees, rate of defective output, manufacturing lead time).

    b.   **Qualitative factors** are those which must be considered but cannot be objectively measured, e.g., relationships with suppliers and customer satisfaction.

8.   The **impact of income taxes** on a company's earnings must be considered in any business decision.

    a.   For instance, investing in new equipment could allow the company to reduce taxable income considerably in the first few years under the Modified Accelerated Cost Recovery System (MACRS). At the same time, increased revenues from new product lines will increase the company's taxable income.

9. **Additional cost terms** applicable to decision analysis situations.

    a. An **imputed cost** is not recognized in the accounting records but must be considered in an investment decision to give recognition to economic reality. Required returns on investment and opportunity costs are examples.

    b. A **postponable cost** may be shifted to the future with little effect on the efficiency of current operations. Routine maintenance is an example.

10. Stop and review! You have completed the outline for this subunit. Study multiple-choice questions 1 through 15 beginning below.

13.2 CORE CONCEPTS

Cost and Revenue Relevance

- The **accounting concept** of costs includes only explicit costs, i.e., those that represent actual outlays of cash, the allocation of outlays of cash, or commitments to pay cash. The **economic concept** of costs includes both explicit and implicit (i.e., opportunity) costs.
- In decision making, an organization must focus on only **relevant revenues and costs**. To be relevant, revenues and costs must be made in the future and differ among the possible alternative courses of action.
- A vital concept in decision making is that of **relevant range**, i.e., the range of activity over which fixed costs remain fixed. Relevant range is synonymous with the short run.
- **Cost behavior** does not necessarily determine the relevance of costs.
- **Cost traceability** allows decision makers to associate costs with a cost object in an economically feasible way. Costs which cannot be traced must be allocated. An allocated cost may still be relevant.
- The **impact of income taxes** on a company's earnings must be considered in any business decision.

QUESTIONS

13.1 Cost and Revenue Relevance

1. In a decision analysis situation, which one of the following costs is not likely to contain a variable cost component?

    A. Labor.

    B. Overhead.

    C. Depreciation.

    D. Selling.

Answer (C) is correct. *(CMA, adapted)*
    REQUIRED: The cost not likely to contain a variable component.
    DISCUSSION: Most types of costs either are variable or contain some mix of fixed and variable components. For example, labor and materials are primarily variable. Their amounts fluctuate with the relevant cost drivers. Selling expenses and overhead costs can be either fixed or variable. Depreciation, however, is strictly a fixed cost when viewed in a decision analysis situation because it requires no cash outlay. Instead, the initial acquisition of the long-lived asset requires the cash outlay.

2. An important concept in decision making is described as "the contribution to income that is forgone by not using a limited resource in its best alternative use." This concept is called

    A. Marginal cost.

    B. Incremental cost.

    C. Potential cost.

    D. Opportunity cost.

Answer (D) is correct. *(CMA, adapted)*
    REQUIRED: The contribution to income that is forgone by not adopting the best alternative use of a limited resource.
    DISCUSSION: An opportunity cost is the maximum benefit sacrificed by employing a scarce productive resource in a specified manner. In other words, it is the value or worth of that resource in its next best alternative use.
    Answer (A) is incorrect because marginal cost is an incremental or differential cost. Answer (B) is incorrect because incremental cost is the difference in total cost between two decision choices. Answer (C) is incorrect because a potential cost may arise in the future.

3. American Coat Company estimates that 60,000 special zippers will be used in the manufacture of men's jackets during the next year. Reese Zipper Company has quoted a price of $.60 per zipper. American would prefer to purchase 5,000 units per month, but Reese is unable to guarantee this delivery schedule. In order to ensure availability of these zippers, American is considering the purchase of all 60,000 units at the beginning of the year. Assuming American can invest cash at 8%, the company's opportunity cost of purchasing the 60,000 units at the beginning of the year is

A. $1,320

B. $1,440

C. $1,500

D. $2,640

Answer (A) is correct. *(CMA, adapted)*
REQUIRED: The opportunity cost of purchasing the total annual requirement at the beginning of the year instead of in monthly increments.
DISCUSSION: The cost of 60,000 zippers is $36,000 (60,000 × $.60). The monthly cost is $3,000 (5,000 × $.60). Because the company wants to purchase the items monthly, it will invest at least $3,000 in January. Accordingly, the zippers to be used in January will be purchased at the first of the year even if no special purchase is made. Thus, the incremental advance purchase will be only $33,000, not $36,000. The incremental investment will decline at a constant rate of $3,000 per month, so the amount for February will be $30,000, for March $27,000, etc. Hence, the incremental investment for December will be $0. Accordingly, assuming consumption is uniform, the average incremental investment during the year will be $16,500 ($33,000 ÷ 2) if the onetime purchase is made. Total opportunity cost is therefore $1,320 ($16,500 × 8% cost of capital).

4. In a decision analysis situation, which one of the following costs is generally not relevant to the decision?

A. Incremental cost.

B. Differential cost.

C. Avoidable cost.

D. Historical cost.

Answer (D) is correct. *(CMA, adapted)*
REQUIRED: The cost ordinarily not relevant to a decision.
DISCUSSION: Management decision analysis is based on the concept of relevant costs. Relevant costs differ among decision choices. Thus, incremental (differential or avoidable) costs are always relevant. Opportunity cost is also relevant because it is the benefit forgone by selecting one choice instead of another. Historical costs, because they occurred in the past, are sunk costs and not relevant to most management decisions.
Answer (A) is incorrect because incremental cost is relevant to management decision analysis. Answer (B) is incorrect because differential cost is relevant to management decision analysis. Answer (C) is incorrect because avoidable cost is relevant to management decision analysis.

5. All of the following costs are relevant to a decision to accept or reject an order except

A. Differential costs.

B. Out-of-pocket costs.

C. Replacement costs.

D. Sunk costs.

Answer (D) is correct. *(CMA, adapted)*
REQUIRED: The irrelevant costs.
DISCUSSION: A sunk cost cannot be avoided because either the expenditure has occurred, or an irrevocable decision to incur the cost has been made. Sunk costs are irrelevant to management decision-making because they cannot vary with the option selected.
Answer (A) is incorrect because a differential (incremental) cost is relevant. It is the difference in total cost between two decisions. Answer (B) is incorrect because out-of-pocket costs (outlay costs) are relevant. They require negative cash flows (expenditures) currently or in the future. Answer (C) is incorrect because a replacement cost is relevant. It is the cash or equivalent that would be paid for a current acquisition of the same or an equivalent asset.

6. A cost that can be saved by not adopting a particular option is a(n)

A. Imputed cost.

B. Avoidable cost.

C. Unavoidable cost.

D. Postponable cost.

Answer (B) is correct. *(Publisher, adapted)*
REQUIRED: The term for a cost that can be saved by not adopting a particular course of action.
DISCUSSION: An avoidable cost is one that can be saved by not adopting a particular alternative.
Answer (A) is incorrect because an imputed cost is an unstated cost, such as an opportunity cost. Answer (C) is incorrect because an unavoidable cost cannot be eliminated. Answer (D) is incorrect because a postponable cost is one that can be shifted to the future.

7. Which one of the following is most relevant to a manufacturing equipment replacement decision?

    A. Original cost of the old equipment.

    B. Disposal price of the old equipment.

    C. Gain or loss on the disposal of the old equipment.

    D. A lump-sum write-off amount from the disposal of the old equipment.

Answer (B) is correct. *(CMA, adapted)*
REQUIRED: The item most relevant to a manufacturing equipment replacement decision.
DISCUSSION: Management decision analysis is based on the concept of relevant costs. Relevant costs differ among decision choices. Thus, incremental or differential costs are always relevant. Because they were incurred in the past, historical costs, such as the original cost of the equipment, are not relevant. Similarly, any gain or loss on the old equipment is not relevant because this amount is based on the historical cost. However, the disposal price of the old equipment is relevant because it involves a future cash inflow that will not occur unless the equipment is disposed of.
Answer (A) is incorrect because the original cost of the old equipment is a sunk cost with no relevance to future decision making. Answer (C) is incorrect because gain or loss is based on historical cost, which is a sunk cost. Answer (D) is incorrect because a lump-sum write-off of a sunk cost is not relevant to a future decision.

8. The terms direct cost and indirect cost are commonly used in accounting. A particular cost might be considered a direct cost of a manufacturing department but an indirect cost of the product produced in the manufacturing department. Classifying a cost as either direct or indirect depends upon

    A. The behavior of the cost in response to volume changes.

    B. Whether the cost is expensed in the period in which it is incurred.

    C. The cost objective to which the cost is being related.

    D. Whether an expenditure is unavoidable because it cannot be changed regardless of any action taken.

Answer (C) is correct. *(CMA, adapted)*
REQUIRED: The factor that influences whether a cost is classified as direct or indirect.
DISCUSSION: A direct cost can be specifically associated with a single cost object in an economically feasible way. An indirect cost cannot be specifically associated with a single cost object. Thus, the specific cost object influences whether a cost is direct or indirect. For example, a cost might be directly associated with a single plant. The same cost, however, might not be directly associated with a particular department in the plant.
Answer (A) is incorrect because behavior in response to volume changes is a factor only if the cost object is a product. Answer (B) is incorrect because the timing of an expense is not a means of classifying a cost as direct or indirect. Answer (D) is incorrect because both direct and indirect costs can be either avoidable or unavoidable, depending upon the cost object.

9. An assembly plant accumulates its variable and fixed manufacturing overhead costs in a single cost pool, which is then applied to work in process using a single application base. The assembly plant management wants to estimate the magnitude of the total manufacturing overhead costs for different volume levels of the application activity base using a flexible budget formula. If there is an increase in the application activity base that is within the relevant range of activity for the assembly plant, which one of the following relationships regarding variable and fixed costs is true?

    A. The variable cost per unit is constant, and the total fixed costs decrease.

    B. The variable cost per unit is constant, and the total fixed costs increase.

    C. The variable cost per unit and the total fixed costs remain constant.

    D. The variable cost per unit increases, and the total fixed costs remain constant.

Answer (C) is correct. *(CIA, adapted)*
REQUIRED: The effect on variable and fixed costs of a change in activity within the relevant range.
DISCUSSION: Total variable cost changes when changes in the activity level occur within the relevant range. The cost per unit for a variable cost is constant for all activity levels within the relevant range. Thus, if the activity volume increases within the relevant range, total variable costs will increase. A fixed cost does not change when volume changes occur in the activity level within the relevant range. If the activity volume increases within the relevant range, total fixed costs will remain unchanged.

10. The difference between variable costs and fixed costs is

A. Variable costs per unit fluctuate and fixed costs per unit remain constant.

B. Variable costs per unit are fixed over the relevant range and fixed costs per unit are variable.

C. Total variable costs are variable over the relevant range and fixed in the long term, while fixed costs never change.

D. Variable costs per unit change in varying increments, while fixed costs per unit change in equal increments.

Answer (B) is correct. *(CMA, adapted)*
REQUIRED: The difference between variable and fixed costs.
DISCUSSION: Fixed costs remain unchanged within the relevant range for a given period despite fluctuations in activity, but per unit fixed costs do change as the level of activity changes. Thus, fixed costs are fixed in total but vary per unit as activity changes. Total variable costs vary directly with activity. They are fixed per unit, but vary in total.
Answer (A) is incorrect because variable costs are fixed per unit; they do not fluctuate. Fixed costs per unit change as production changes. Answer (C) is incorrect because all costs are variable in the long term. Answer (D) is incorrect because unit variable costs are fixed in the short term.

11. "Committed costs" are

A. Costs which management decides to incur in the current period to enable the company to achieve objectives other than the filling of orders placed by customers.

B. Costs which are likely to respond to the amount of attention devoted to them by a specified manager.

C. Costs which are governed mainly by past decisions that established the present levels of operating and organizational capacity and which only change slowly in response to small changes in capacity.

D. Amortization of costs which were capitalized in previous periods.

Answer (C) is correct. *(CMA, adapted)*
REQUIRED: The definition of committed costs.
DISCUSSION: Committed costs are those which are required as a result of past decisions.
Answer (A) is incorrect because costs incurred in a current period to achieve objectives other than the filling of orders by customers are known as discretionary costs. Answer (B) is incorrect because costs which are likely to respond to the amount of attention devoted to them by a specified manager are controllable costs. Answer (D) is incorrect because amortization of costs capitalized in previous periods is depreciation.

12. "Discretionary costs" are

A. Costs which management decides to incur in the current period to enable the company to achieve objectives other than the filling of orders placed by customers.

B. Costs which are likely to respond to the amount of attention devoted to them by a specified manager.

C. Costs which are governed mainly by past decisions that established the present levels of operating and organizational capacity and which only change slowly in response to small changes in capacity.

D. Costs which will be unaffected by current managerial decisions.

Answer (A) is correct. *(CMA, adapted)*
REQUIRED: The definition of discretionary costs.
DISCUSSION: Discretionary costs are those that are incurred in the current period at the "discretion" of management and are not required to fill orders by customers.
Answer (B) is incorrect because costs which are likely to respond to the amount of attention devoted to them by a specified manager are controllable costs. Answer (C) is incorrect because costs required as a result of past decisions are committed costs. Answer (D) is incorrect because costs unaffected by managerial decisions are costs such as committed costs and depreciation that were determined by decisions of previous periods.

13. "Controllable costs" are

A. Costs which management decides to incur in the current period to enable the company to achieve objectives other than the filling of orders placed by customers.

B. Costs which are likely to respond to the amount of attention devoted to them by a specified manager.

C. Costs which fluctuate in total in response to small changes in the rate of utilization of capacity.

D. Costs which will be unaffected by current managerial decisions.

Answer (B) is correct. *(CMA, adapted)*
REQUIRED: The definition of controllable costs.
DISCUSSION: Controllable costs can be affected by the efforts of a manager.
Answer (A) is incorrect because costs incurred in a current period to achieve objectives other than the filling of orders by customers are known as discretionary costs. Answer (C) is incorrect because costs that fluctuate with small changes in volume are variable costs. Answer (D) is incorrect because costs that are unaffected by managerial decisions are costs such as committed costs and depreciation that was determined by decisions of previous periods.

14. Which of the following is the best example of a variable cost?

A. The corporate president's salary.

B. Cost of raw material.

C. Interest charges.

D. Property taxes.

Answer (B) is correct. *(CMA, adapted)*
REQUIRED: The item that is a variable cost.
DISCUSSION: Variable costs vary directly with the level of production. As production increases or decreases, material cost increases or decreases, usually in a direct relationship.
Answer (A) is incorrect because the president's salary usually does not vary with production levels. Answer (C) is incorrect because interest charges are independent of production levels. They are called "fixed" costs and are elements of overhead. Answer (D) is incorrect because property taxes are independent of production levels. They are called "fixed" costs and are elements of overhead.

15. The sum of the costs necessary to effect a one-unit increase in the activity level is a(n)

A. Differential cost.

B. Opportunity cost.

C. Marginal cost.

D. Incremental cost.

Answer (C) is correct. *(Publisher, adapted)*
REQUIRED: The cost accounting term.
DISCUSSION: A marginal cost is the sum of the costs necessary to effect a one-unit increase in the activity level.
Answer (A) is incorrect because differential (or incremental) cost is the difference in total cost between two decisions. Answer (B) is incorrect because opportunity cost is the maximum benefit forgone by using a scarce resource for a given purpose. It is the benefit, for example, the contribution to income, provided by the best alternative use of that resource. Answer (D) is incorrect because differential (or incremental) cost is the difference in total cost between two decisions.

Use Gleim's **CMA Test Prep** for interactive testing with **over 2,000 additional multiple-choice questions**!

STUDY UNIT FOURTEEN
COST-VOLUME-PROFIT ANALYSIS

(7 pages of outline)

This study unit is the **third of five** on **decision analysis**. The relative weight assigned to this major topic in Part 3 of the exam is **25%** at **skill level C** (all six skill types required). The five study units are

Study Unit 12: The Decision Process
Study Unit 13: Data Concepts Relative to Decision Making
Study Unit 14: Cost-Volume-Profit Analysis
Study Unit 15: Marginal Analysis
Study Unit 16: Cost-Based Pricing

After studying the outlines and answering the multiple-choice questions, you will have the skills necessary to address the following topics listed in the IMA's Learning Outcome Statements:

Part 3 – Section D.3. Cost-volume-profit analysis

The candidate should be able to:

a.   demonstrate an understanding of how cost-volume-profit (CVP) analysis (breakeven analysis) is used to examine the behavior of total revenues, total costs, and operating income as changes occur in output levels, selling prices, variable costs per unit, or fixed costs

b.   differentiate between costs that are fixed and costs that are variable with respect to levels of output

c.   demonstrate an understanding of the behavior of total revenues and total costs in relation to output within a relevant range

d.   explain why the classification of fixed vs. variable costs is affected by the time frame being considered

e.   demonstrate an understanding of how contribution margin per unit is used in CVP analysis

f.   calculate contribution margin per unit and total contribution margin

g.   calculate the breakeven point in units and dollar sales to achieve targeted operating income or targeted net income

h.   demonstrate an understanding of how changes in unit sales mix affect operating income in multiple-product situations

i.   demonstrate an understanding of why there is no unique breakeven point in multiple-product situations

j.   analyze and recommend a course of action using CVP analysis

k.   demonstrate an understanding of the impact of income taxes on CVP analysis

14.1 COST-VOLUME-PROFIT (CVP) ANALYSIS

1.   **Cost-volume-profit (CVP) analysis** (also called breakeven analysis) is a tool for understanding the interaction of revenues with fixed and variable costs. It illuminates how changes in assumptions about cost behavior and the relevant ranges in which those assumptions are valid may affect the relationships among revenues, variable costs, and fixed costs at various production levels. Thus, CVP analysis allows management to discern the probable effects of changes in sales volume, sales price, product mix, etc.

2.   The inherent simplifying **assumptions** of CVP analysis are the following:

   a.   Cost and revenue relationships are predictable and linear. These relationships are true over the **relevant range** of activity and specified time span. For example, reductions in prices are not necessary to increase revenues, and no learning curve effect operates to reduce unit variable labor costs at higher output levels.

   b.   Total **variable costs** change proportionally with volume, but unit variable costs are constant over the relevant range. Raw materials and direct labor are typically variable costs.

   c.   Changes in inventory are insignificant in amount.

   d.   **Fixed costs** remain constant over the relevant range of volume, but unit fixed costs vary indirectly with volume. The classification of fixed versus variable can be affected by the time frame being considered.

   e.   Unit selling prices and market conditions are constant.

   f.   Production equals sales.

   g.   The **revenue (sales) mix** is constant, or the firm makes and sells only one product.

   h.   All costs are either fixed or variable relative to a given cost object for a given time span. The longer the time span, the more likely the cost is variable.

   i.   Technology and productive efficiency are constant.

   j.   Revenues and costs vary only with changes in physical unit volume. Hence, volume is the sole revenue driver and cost driver.

   k.   The breakeven point is directly related to costs and inversely related to the budgeted margin of safety and the contribution margin.

   l.   The time value of money is ignored.

3.   The assumptions under which CVP analysis operates primarily hinge on **certainty**. However, many decisions must be made even though uncertainty exists. Assigning probabilities to the various outcomes and sensitivity ("what-if") analysis are important approaches to dealing with uncertainty.

4.   **Definitions**

   a.   The **breakeven point** is the level of output at which total revenues equal total expenses, that is, the point at which operating income is zero.

   b.   The **margin of safety** is a measure of risk. It is the excess of budgeted revenues over breakeven revenues (or budgeted units over breakeven units).

   c.   **Mixed costs (or semivariable costs)** are costs with both fixed and variable elements.

   d.   The **revenue (sales) mix** is the composition of total revenues in terms of various products, i.e., the percentages of each product included in total revenues. It is maintained for all volume changes.

   e.   **Sensitivity analysis** examines the effect on the outcome of not achieving the original forecast or of changing an assumption.

   f.   **Unit contribution margin (UCM)** is the unit selling price minus the unit variable cost. It is the contribution from the sale of one unit to cover fixed costs (and possibly a targeted profit).

   1)   It is expressed as either a percentage of the selling price **(contribution margin ratio)** or a dollar amount.

   2)   The UCM is the slope of the total cost curve plotted so that volume is on the x-axis and dollar value is on the y-axis.

5.   The general formula for operating income can be stated as follows:

$$Operating\ income\ =\ Sales\ -\ Variable\ costs\ -\ Fixed\ costs$$

   a.   The **breakeven point** can be determined by setting **operating income equal to zero** and solving the equation.

   b.   EXAMPLE: A product is sold for $.60 per unit, with variable costs of $.20 per unit and fixed costs of $10,000. What is the breakeven point?

$$
\begin{aligned}
Operating\ income &= Sales - Variable\ costs - Fixed\ costs \\
\$0 &= (\$.60 \times Q) - (\$.20 \times Q) - \$10,000 \\
\$.40 \times Q &= \$10,000 \\
Q &= 25,000\ units
\end{aligned}
$$

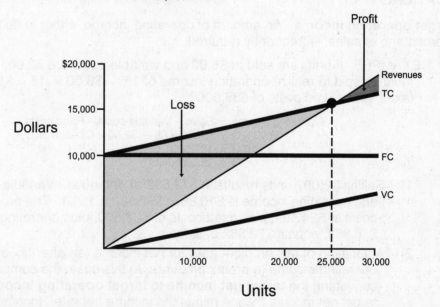

   c.   A simpler calculation is to divide fixed costs by the unit contribution margin (the unit contribution to coverage of fixed costs).

$$Breakeven\ point\ in\ units\ =\ \frac{Fixed\ costs}{UCM}$$

   1)   The UCM is $.40 ($.60 sales price – $.20 variable cost). Thus, to cover $10,000 of fixed costs, 25,000 units ($10,000 ÷ $.40 UCM) must be sold to break even.

   d.   The breakeven point in dollars can be calculated by dividing fixed costs by the contribution margin ratio {[$10,000 ÷ ($.40 ÷ $.60)] = $15,000}.

6. The **contribution income statement with per unit amounts** is an integral part of breakeven analysis.

    a. EXAMPLE:

	In Total	Per Unit	Percent
Sales (40,000 units)	$ 24,000	$ 0.60	100%
Less: variable costs	(8,000)	(0.20)	(33%)
Contribution margin	$ 16,000	$ 0.40	67%
Less: fixed costs	(10,000)		
Operating income	$ 6,000		

    b. Every unit sold **contributes** a certain percentage of its sales revenue to **covering fixed costs**, in this case 67%. Management can conclude that every unit sold in the relevant range will contribute $.40 to covering fixed costs.

    c. Once fixed costs are fully covered, all additional revenue becomes **profit**.

7. Stop and review! You have completed the outline for this subunit. Study multiple-choice questions 1 through 17 beginning on page 353.

14.2 APPLICATIONS

1. **Target operating income.** An amount of operating income, either in dollars or as a percentage of sales, is frequently required.

    a. EXAMPLE: If units are sold at $6.00 and variable costs are $2.00, how many units must be sold to realize operating income of 15% ($6.00 × .15 = $.90 per unit) before taxes, given fixed costs of $37,500?

    $$\text{Operating income} = \text{Sales} - \text{Variable costs} - \text{Fixed costs}$$
    $$\$0.90 \times Q = (\$6.00 \times Q) - (\$2.00 \times Q) - \$37,500$$
    $$\$3.10\,Q = \$37,500$$
    $$Q = 12,097 \text{ units}$$

    1) Selling 12,097 units results in $72,582 of revenues. Variable costs are $24,194, and operating income is $10,888 ($72,582 × 15%). The proof is that variable costs of $24,194, plus fixed costs of $37,500, plus operating income of $10,888, equals $72,582 of sales.

    2) A variation of this problem asks for net income (an after-tax amount) instead of operating income (a pretax amount). In this case, the computation requires converting the **target net income** to **target operating income** by dividing the target net income by one minus the income tax rate. Income tax liability does not change the breakeven point because, at that output level, operating income and therefore income tax expense are zero. However, other taxes, such as sales tax, do change the breakeven point.

    3) Thus, to incorporate taxes into the calculation, the basic CVP formula is adjusted as follows:

    Sales = [Target net income ÷ (1 − tax rate)] + Variable costs + Fixed costs

    4) EXAMPLE: If variable costs are $1.20, fixed costs are $10,000, and selling price is $2, and the company targets a $5,000 after-tax profit when the tax rate is 30%, the calculation is as follows:

    $$\$ 2Q = [\$5,000 \div (1 - .3)] + \$1.20Q + \$10,000$$
    $$\$.8Q = \$7,142.86 + \$10,000$$
    $$\$.8Q = \$17,142.86$$
    $$Q = \$17,142.86 \div .8$$
    $$Q = 21,428.575 \text{ units}$$

a) If the company plans to sell 21,428.575 units at $2 each, revenue will be $42,857.15. The following is the pro forma income statement for the target net income:

Sales (21,428.575 × $2)	$ 42,857.15
Less: variable costs (21,428.575 × $1.20)	(25,714.29)
Contribution margin	$ 17,142.86
Less: fixed costs	(10,000.00)
Operating income	$ 7,142.86
Income taxes (30%)	(2,142.86)
Net income	$ 5,000.00

2. **Multiple products (or services)** may be involved in calculating a breakeven point.

   a. EXAMPLE: A and B account for 60% and 40% of total sales, respectively. The variable costs of A and B are 60% and 85% of individual product sales, respectively. What is the breakeven point, given fixed costs of $150,000?

$$S = FC + VC$$
$$S = \$150{,}000 + .6\,(.6\,S) + .85\,(.4\,S)$$
$$S = \$150{,}000 + .36\,S + .34\,S$$
$$.30\,S = \$150{,}000$$
$$S = \$500{,}000$$

     1) In effect, the result is obtained by calculating a weighted-average contribution margin ratio (100% − 36% − 34% = 30%) and dividing it into the fixed costs to arrive at the breakeven point in sales dollars.

     2) Another approach to multiproduct breakeven problems is to divide fixed costs by the UCM for a composite unit (when unit prices are known) to determine the number of composite units. The number of individual units can then be calculated based on the stated mix.

       a) EXAMPLE: If 150,000 units of X and 300,000 units of Y are expected to be sold, the composite unit consists of 1 unit of X and 2 units of Y. If X and Y have UCMs of $5 and $7, respectively, the composite UCM is $19 ($5 + $7 + $7). Dividing $19 into fixed costs gives the breakeven point in composite units. The units of X and Y equal the number of composite units and twice the number of composite units, respectively.

       b) In a multiple product (or service) problem, the breakeven point in total units varies with the sales mix. The BEP in units will be lower (higher) when the proportion of high (low) CM items is greater. Thus, there is no unique breakeven point in multiple-product situations. The breakeven point depends upon the specific mix of products.

3. **Choice of product.** When resources are limited, a company may produce only a single product. A breakeven analysis of the point where the same operating income or loss will result, regardless of the product selected, is calculated by setting the breakeven formulas of the individual products equal to each other.

   a. EXAMPLE: Assume a lessor can rent property to either of two lessees. One lessee offers a rental fee of $100,000 per year plus 2% of revenues. The other lessee offers $20,000 per year plus 5% of revenues. The optimal solution depends on the level of revenues. A typical CMA question asks at what level the lessor will be indifferent. The solution is to equate the two formulas as follows:

$$\$100{,}000 + .02\,R = \$20{,}000 + .05\,R$$
$$.03\,R = \$80{,}000$$
$$R = \$80{,}000 \div .03$$
$$R = \$2{,}666{,}667$$

Where: R = revenues

Thus, if revenues are expected to be less than $2,666,667, the lessor would prefer the larger fixed rental of $100,000 and the smaller variable rental.

4.   Sometimes CVP analysis is applied to **special orders**. This application is essentially contribution margin analysis.

   a.   EXAMPLE: What is the effect of accepting a special order for 10,000 units at $8.00, given the following operating data?

	Gross Approach	Per Unit
Sales		$12.50
Less: manufacturing costs		
Variable	$6.25	
Fixed	1.75	(8.00)
Gross profit		$ 4.50
Less: selling expenses		
Variable	$1.80	
Fixed	1.45	(3.25)
Operating income		$ 1.25

   1)   Because the variable cost of manufacturing is $6.25, the UCM is $1.75 ($8.00 – $6.25), and the increase in operating income resulting from accepting the special order is $17,500 (10,000 units × $1.75).

   2)   The assumptions are that idle capacity is sufficient to manufacture 10,000 extra units, that sale at $8.00 per unit will not affect the price or quantity of other units sold, and that no additional selling expenses are incurred.

5.   The foregoing discussion of breakeven applications assumes that **variable costing** is used. Under variable costing, the breakeven level of unit sales does not vary with production. It is a function solely of total fixed costs and the UCM.

   a.   Under **absorption costing**, however, the breakeven level of unit sales also depends on units produced and the amount of the denominator value used to assign fixed manufacturing costs to inventory. Then, no unique breakeven level of unit sales exists because the amounts of the elements of the formula may be varied to produce the same result. Moreover, as the formula below indicates, the greater the number of units produced, the lower the breakeven point in units sold. This inverse relationship arises because some fixed manufacturing costs are inventoried under absorption costing. This amount is reflected in the second term of the numerator in the formula below. Accordingly, the breakeven point (BEP) in units sold under absorption costing equals total fixed costs (TFC) plus the product of the fixed manufacturing cost application rate (FMCAR) and the difference between the BEP in units sold and total units produced (UP), all divided by the UCM:

$$BEP = \frac{TFC + \left[FMCAR(BEP - UP)\right]}{UCM}$$

   1)   If the target operating income is not zero, the formula is adjusted by adding its amount to the numerator.

6.   The **degree of operating leverage (DOL)** is the change in operating income (earnings before interest and taxes) resulting from a percentage change in sales. It measures the extent to which a firm incurs fixed rather than variable costs in operations.

$$Operating\ leverage = \frac{Percentage\ change\ in\ operating\ income}{Percentage\ change\ in\ sales}$$

   a.   The assumption is that companies with larger investments (and greater fixed costs) will have higher contribution margins and more operating leverage.

   1)   Thus, as companies invest in better and more expensive equipment, their variable production costs should decrease.

2) EXAMPLE: If sales increase by 40% and operating income increases by 50%, the operating leverage is 1.25 (50% ÷ 40%).

b. Given that Q equals the number of units sold, P is unit price, VC is unit variable cost, and FC is fixed cost, the DOL can also be calculated from the formula below, which equals total contribution margin divided by operating income (total contribution margin minus fixed cost). This formula is derived from the operating leverage formula on the previous page, but the derivation procedure is not given.

$$\frac{Q(P - VC)}{Q(P - VC) - FC}$$

c. The DOL is calculated with respect to a given base level of sales. The significance of the DOL is that a given percentage increase in sales yields a percentage increase in operating income equal to the DOL for the base sales level times the percentage increase in sales.

7. Stop and review! You have completed the outline for this subunit. Study multiple-choice questions 18 through 36 beginning on page 359.

14.3 CORE CONCEPTS

Cost-Volume-Profit (CVP) Analysis

- **Cost-volume-profit analysis** (also called breakeven analysis) is a tool for understanding the interaction of revenues with fixed and variable costs.

- The **breakeven point** is the level of output at which total revenues equal total expenses; that is, the point at which operating income is zero.

- The **contribution income statement** with per unit amounts is an integral part of breakeven analysis. Every unit sold contributes a certain percentage of its sales revenue to covering fixed costs. Once fixed costs are fully covered, all additional revenue contributes to profit.

Applications

- The breakeven model can be used to find **target operating income**, or to find the breakeven point for **multiple products**, or to determine the profitability of a **special order**.

QUESTIONS

14.1 Cost-Volume-Profit (CVP) Analysis

1. Cost-volume-profit (CVP) analysis is a key factor in many decisions, including choice of product lines, pricing of products, marketing strategy, and use of productive facilities. A calculation used in a CVP analysis is the breakeven point. Once the breakeven point has been reached, operating income will increase by the

A. Gross margin per unit for each additional unit sold.

B. Contribution margin per unit for each additional unit sold.

C. Fixed costs per unit for each additional unit sold.

D. Variable costs per unit for each additional unit sold.

Answer (B) is correct. *(CMA, adapted)*
REQUIRED: The amount by which operating income will increase once the breakeven point has been reached.
DISCUSSION: At the breakeven point, total revenue equals the fixed cost plus the variable cost. Beyond the BEP, each unit sale will increase operating income by the unit contribution margin (unit sales price – unit variable cost) because fixed cost will already have been recovered.
Answer (A) is incorrect because the gross margin equals sales price minus cost of goods sold, including fixed cost. Answer (C) is incorrect because operating income will increase by the UCM. Answer (D) is incorrect because operating income will increase by the UCM.

2. If inventories are expected to change, the type of costing that provides the best information for breakeven analysis is

A. Job order costing.

B. Variable (direct) costing.

C. Joint costing.

D. Absorption (full) costing.

Answer (B) is correct. *(CMA, adapted)*
REQUIRED: The type of costing system that provides the best information for breakeven analysis if inventories are expected to change.
DISCUSSION: A variable (direct) costing system is best for providing the information needed for CVP analysis because both techniques separate the fixed costs from variable costs. CVP analysis calculates a variable cost per unit and deducts it from unit sales price to determine the unit contribution margin. The total contribution margin from a given level of unit sales measures the extent of recovery of fixed costs and the profit earned. Direct costing is likewise oriented toward determination of the contribution margin because it treats fixed manufacturing overhead as a period, not a product, cost. Thus, it facilitates CVP analysis by isolating variable manufacturing costs.
Answer (A) is incorrect because job order costing does not separate fixed costs from variable costs. Answer (C) is incorrect because joint costing does not separate fixed costs from variable costs. Answer (D) is incorrect because absorption (full) costing does not separate fixed costs from variable costs.

3. One of the major assumptions limiting the reliability of breakeven analysis is that

A. Efficiency and productivity will continually increase.

B. Total variable costs will remain unchanged over the relevant range.

C. Total fixed costs will remain unchanged over the relevant range.

D. The cost of production factors varies with changes in technology.

Answer (C) is correct. *(CMA, adapted)*
REQUIRED: The major assumption limiting the use of breakeven analysis.
DISCUSSION: The inherent simplifying assumptions used in CVP analysis are the following: Costs and revenues are predictable and are linear over the relevant range; variable costs change proportionally with activity level; changes in inventory are insignificant in amount; fixed costs remain constant over the relevant range of volume; prices remain fixed; production equals sales; there is a relevant range in which the various relationships are true for a given time span; all costs are either fixed or variable; productive efficiency is constant; costs vary only with changes in sales volume; and there is a constant mix of products (or only one product).
Answer (A) is incorrect because breakeven analysis assumes no changes in efficiency and productivity. Answer (B) is incorrect because one limiting assumption is that unit variable cost, not total variable cost, is constant. Answer (D) is incorrect because the cost of production factors is assumed to be stable.

4. In working on a CVP analysis, the accountant is unsure of the exact results and/or assumptions under which to operate. What can the accountant do to help management in this CVP decision?

A. Nothing. It is not the responsibility of the accountant to be concerned with the ambiguity of the results and/or assumptions.

B. Ascertain the probabilities of various outcomes and work with management on understanding those probabilities in reference to the CVP decision.

C. Calculate the probabilities of various outcomes and make the decision for management.

D. Use a random number table to generate a decision model and make the decision for management.

Answer (B) is correct. *(Publisher, adapted)*
REQUIRED: The approach to take in a probabilistic CVP decision.
DISCUSSION: The assumptions under which CVP analysis operates primarily hinge on certainty. Once uncertainty enters the situation, the results are not so clear. Thus, the accountant should make an appropriate effort to ascertain the probabilities of various outcomes. The accountant can then work with management to help make the appropriate decision.
Answer (A) is incorrect because it is the responsibility of the accountant to be involved with management and aid in their decision making. Answer (C) is incorrect because it is not appropriate for the accountant to make the decision. Management should make the decision with the accountant's advice and help. Answer (D) is incorrect because, although using a random number table or a simulation may be part of the decision process, the decision should not rest with the accountant alone.

5. The margin of safety is a key concept of CVP analysis. The margin of safety is the

A. Contribution margin rate.

B. Difference between budgeted contribution margin and breakeven contribution margin.

C. Difference between budgeted sales and breakeven sales.

D. Difference between the breakeven point in sales and cash flow breakeven.

Answer (C) is correct. *(CMA, adapted)*
REQUIRED: The definition of the margin of safety.
DISCUSSION: The margin of safety measures the amount by which sales may decline before losses occur. It is the excess of budgeted or actual sales over sales at the BEP. It may be stated in either units sold or sales revenue.
Answer (A) is incorrect because the contribution margin rate is computed by dividing contribution margin by sales. The contribution margin equals sales minus total variable costs. Answer (B) is incorrect because the margin of safety is expressed in revenue or units, not contribution margin. Answer (D) is incorrect because cash flow is not relevant.

6. When used in cost-volume-profit analysis, sensitivity analysis

A. Determines the most profitable mix of products to be sold.

B. Allows the decision maker to introduce probabilities in the evaluation of decision alternatives.

C. Is done through various possible scenarios and computes the impact on profit of various predictions of future events.

D. Is limited because, in cost-volume-profit analysis, costs are not separated into fixed and variable components.

Answer (C) is correct. *(CMA, adapted)*
REQUIRED: The true statement about sensitivity analysis.
DISCUSSION: Sensitivity analysis permits the decision maker to measure the effects of errors in certainty equivalents, which are estimated amounts developed by the best means available and assumed for purposes of a given decision model to be certain. The decision model then may be evaluated by changing certain data variables (certainty equivalents) critical to the success of the entity and observing the outcomes. This analysis allows the decision maker to quantify the effects of forecasting or prediction errors and to identify the most critical variables. For example, with respect to breakeven analysis, a firm might make computations using several different estimates of what fixed costs are expected to be. These calculations indicate how sensitive the results are to changes in fixed costs.
Answer (A) is incorrect because CVP analysis assumes a constant product mix or only one product. Answer (B) is incorrect because expected value analysis allows the decision maker to introduce probabilities in the evaluation of decision alternatives. Answer (D) is incorrect because, in cost-volume-profit analysis, costs are separated into fixed and variable components.

7. Which of the following would decrease unit contribution margin the most?

A. A 15% decrease in selling price.

B. A 15% increase in variable expenses.

C. A 15% decrease in variable expenses.

D. A 15% decrease in fixed expenses.

Answer (A) is correct. *(CMA, adapted)*
REQUIRED: The change in a CVP variable causing the greatest decrease in UCM.
DISCUSSION: The plausible options are a decrease in selling price or an increase in variable expenses because UCM equals unit sales price minus unit variable cost. However, a given percentage change in unit sales price must have a greater effect than an equal but opposite percentage change in unit variable cost because the former is greater than the latter. The example below demonstrates this point.

Original:	SP =	$100
	VC =	50
	CM =	$ 50
SP – 15%:	SP =	$ 85
	VC =	50
	CM =	$ 35 ($15 decrease)
VC + 15%:	SP =	$100.00
	VC =	57.50
	CM =	$ 42.50 ($7.50 decrease)

Answer (B) is incorrect because a 15% increase in variable expenses will not decrease the CM as much as a 15% decrease in sales price. Answer (C) is incorrect because a decrease in variable expenses would increase UCM. Answer (D) is incorrect because a decrease in fixed expenses has no effect on the UCM.

8. Marston Enterprises sells three chemicals: petrol, septine, and tridol. Petrol is the company's most profitable product; tridol is the least profitable. Which one of the following events will definitely decrease the firm's overall breakeven point for the upcoming accounting period?

A. The installation of new computer-controlled machinery and subsequent layoff of assembly-line workers.

B. A decrease in tridol's selling price.

C. An increase in the overall market for septine.

D. An increase in anticipated sales of petrol relative to sales of septine and tridol.

Answer (D) is correct.   *(CMA, adapted)*
REQUIRED: The event that will decrease the firm's overall breakeven point.
DISCUSSION: A company's breakeven point will be reduced if fixed costs are lowered or the average unit contribution margin is increased. Given that petrol is the company's most profitable product, and assuming that it has a higher unit contribution margin than septine and tridol, an increase in sales of petrol relative to the other products will result in a higher average unit contribution margin and a lower breakeven point (fixed costs ÷ average UCM).
Answer (A) is incorrect because the acquisition of new machinery will result in greater fixed costs and the possibility of a higher breakeven point. Answer (B) is incorrect because a decrease in selling price reduces the unit contribution margin, which in turn increases the breakeven point. Answer (C) is incorrect because an increase in the market for septine has an indeterminate effect. The facts given do not indicate whether its unit contribution margin is greater or less than the average unit contribution margin for all products.

9. Product A accounts for 75% of a company's total sales revenue and has a variable cost equal to 60% of its selling price. Product B accounts for 25% of total sales revenue and has a variable cost equal to 85% of its selling price. What is the breakeven point given fixed costs of $150,000?

A. $375,000

B. $444,444

C. $500,000

D. $545,455

Answer (B) is correct.   *(Publisher, adapted)*
REQUIRED: The breakeven point in a multiproduct firm.
DISCUSSION: Sales = VC + FC. The proportion of each product's sales must be considered.

$$S = 0.75S(0.60) + 0.25S(0.85) + \$150,000$$
$$S = 0.45S + 0.2125S + \$150,000$$
$$S - 0.6625S = \$150,000$$
$$0.3375S = \$150,000$$
$$S = \$444,444$$

Answer (A) is incorrect because $375,000 is based on the contribution margin of Product A only rather than a weighted average. Answer (C) is incorrect because $500,000 is based on half of the required sales at B's contribution margin. Answer (D) is incorrect because $545,455 is based on an unweighted average of the two contribution margins.

10. Which of the following will result in raising the breakeven point?

A. A decrease in the variable cost per unit.

B. An increase in the semivariable cost per unit.

C. An increase in the contribution margin per unit.

D. A decrease in income tax rates.

Answer (B) is correct.   *(CIA, adapted)*
REQUIRED: The change in a CVP factor that will raise the breakeven point.
DISCUSSION: The BEP equals fixed cost divided by the UCM (selling price – unit variable cost). An increase in semivariable costs increases fixed costs and/or variable costs. An increase in either will raise the BEP. If fixed costs increase, more units must be sold, assuming the same UCM, to cover the greater fixed costs. If variable costs increase, the UCM will decrease and again more units must be sold to cover the fixed costs.
Answer (A) is incorrect because, if other factors are constant, an increase in sales price or a decrease in unit variable cost increases the CM and lowers the BEP. Answer (C) is incorrect because an increase in the CM decreases the BEP. Answer (D) is incorrect because, if income taxes are taken into account, they are treated as variable costs. A decrease in variable costs lowers the BEP.

11. A company's breakeven point in sales dollars may be affected by equal percentage increases in both selling price and variable cost per unit (assume all other factors are constant within the relevant range). The equal percentage changes in selling price and variable cost per unit will cause the breakeven point in sales dollars to

A. Decrease by less than the percentage increase in selling price.

B. Decrease by more than the percentage increase in the selling price.

C. Increase by the percentage change in variable cost per unit.

D. Remain unchanged.

Answer (D) is correct. *(CIA, adapted)*
REQUIRED: The effect of equal percentage changes in selling price and variable cost on the breakeven point in sales dollars.
DISCUSSION: The BEP in sales dollars is equal to the fixed cost divided by the CMR. Accordingly, equal percentage changes in selling price and variable cost per unit will not affect the BEP in sales dollars. For example, assume the unit price of a product is $1 and its unit variable cost is $.60. The CMR equals 40% [($1 – $.60)UCM ÷ $1 unit price]. If fixed cost is $100, the BEP in sales dollars is $250 ($100 ÷ 40%). Raising the selling price and variable cost by 20% to $1.20 and $.72, respectively, leaves the CMR at 40% ($.48 ÷ $1.20). Similarly, lowering the selling price and variable cost to $.80 and $.48, respectively, also leaves the CMR at 40% ($.32 ÷ $.80).
Answer (A) is incorrect because the breakeven point in sales dollars will not change. Answer (B) is incorrect because the CMR will remain the same. Therefore, the breakeven point in sales dollars will remain unchanged. Answer (C) is incorrect because the breakeven point in sales dollars will not change.

12. Two companies produce and sell the same product in a competitive industry. Thus, the selling price of the product for each company is the same. Company 1 has a contribution margin ratio of 40% and fixed costs of $25 million. Company 2 is more automated, making its fixed costs 40% higher than those of Company 1. Company 2 also has a contribution margin ratio that is 30% greater than that of Company 1. By comparison, Company 1 will have the <List A> breakeven point in terms of dollar sales volume and will have the <List B> dollar profit potential once the indifference point in dollar sales volume is exceeded.

	List A	List B
A.	Lower	Lesser
B.	Lower	Greater
C.	Higher	Lesser
D.	Higher	Greater

Answer (A) is correct. *(CIA, adapted)*
REQUIRED: The breakeven points and dollar profit potentials for two manufacturers.
DISCUSSION: Company 1's breakeven point is lower because its fixed costs are lower. Company 1's breakeven point is $62,500,000 ($25,000,000 ÷ 40%). Company 2's breakeven point is $67,307,692 [($25,000,000 × 1.4) ÷ (40% × 1.3)]. The indifference point, at which dollar profits are equal, is $83,000,000 ($25,000,000 + .60X = $35,000,000 + .48X). Once the indifference point is passed, Company 1 will make lower profits than Company 2 because Company 2 has a higher contribution margin.

13. Which of the following is a characteristic of a contribution income statement?

A. Fixed and variable expenses are combined as one line.

B. Fixed expenses are listed separately from variable expenses.

C. Fixed and variable manufacturing costs are combined as one line item, but fixed operating expenses are shown separately from variable operating expenses.

D. Fixed and variable operating expenses are combined as one line item, but fixed manufacturing expenses are shown separately from variable manufacturing expenses.

Answer (B) is correct. *(CIA, adapted)*
REQUIRED: The characteristic of a contribution income statement.
DISCUSSION: The contribution income statement emphasizes the distinction between fixed and variable costs. Making this distinction facilitates determination of CVP relationships and the effects of changes in sales volume on income. Thus, fixed manufacturing costs and other fixed costs are separated from variable manufacturing costs and other variable costs. The basic categories in the contribution income statement are variable costs, contribution margin, fixed costs, and operating income.
Answer (A) is incorrect because the contribution income statement shows the contribution margin (sales – variable costs) before it subtracts the fixed costs. Fixed costs are not combined with variable costs. Answer (C) is incorrect because fixed costs are not combined with variable costs on contribution income statements. Answer (D) is incorrect because fixed costs are not combined with variable costs on contribution income statements.

14. The breakeven point in units increases when unit costs

    A. Increase and sales price remains unchanged.

    B. Decrease and sales price remains unchanged.

    C. Remain unchanged and sales price increases.

    D. Decrease and sales price increases.

Answer (A) is correct. *(CMA, adapted)*
    REQUIRED: The event that causes the breakeven point in units to increase.
    DISCUSSION: The breakeven point in units is calculated by dividing the fixed costs by the contribution margin per unit. If selling price is constant and costs increase, the unit contribution margin will decline, resulting in an increase of the breakeven point.
    Answer (B) is incorrect because a decrease in costs will lower the breakeven point. The unit contribution margin will increase. Answer (C) is incorrect because an increase in the selling price will also increase the unit contribution margin, resulting in a lower breakeven point. Answer (D) is incorrect because both a cost decrease and a sales price increase will increase the unit contribution margin, resulting in a lower breakeven point.

15. For a profitable company, the amount by which sales can decline before losses occur is known as the

    A. Sales volume variance.

    B. Hurdle rate.

    C. Variable sales ratio.

    D. Margin of safety.

Answer (D) is correct. *(CMA, adapted)*
    REQUIRED: The amount by which sales can decline before losses occur.
    DISCUSSION: The margin of safety measures the amount by which sales may decline before losses occur. It equals budgeted or actual sales minus sales at the BEP. It may be stated in either units sold or sales revenue.
    Answer (A) is incorrect because the sales quantity (volume) variance focuses on the firm's aggregate results. It assumes a constant product mix and an average contribution margin for the composite unit. The sales volume variance equals the budgeted average UCM calculated for the composite unit multiplied by the difference between the actual and budgeted unit sales. Answer (B) is incorrect because it is the rate of return a potential investment must earn before it is acceptable to management. Answer (C) is incorrect because it is a nonsense term.

16. Which one of the following is true regarding a relevant range?

    A. Total variable costs will not change.

    B. Total fixed costs will not change.

    C. Actual fixed costs usually fall outside the relevant range.

    D. The relevant range cannot be changed after being established.

Answer (B) is correct. *(CMA, adapted)*
    REQUIRED: The true statement about a relevant range.
    DISCUSSION: The relevant range is the range of activity over which unit variable costs and total fixed costs are constant. The incremental cost of one additional unit of production will be equal to the variable cost.
    Answer (A) is incorrect because variable costs will change in total, but unit variable costs will be constant. Answer (C) is incorrect because actual fixed costs should not vary greatly from budgeted fixed costs for the relevant range. Answer (D) is incorrect because the relevant range can change whenever production activity changes; the relevant range is merely an assumption used for budgeting and control purposes.

17. The breakeven point in units sold for Tierson Corporation is 44,000. If fixed costs for Tierson are equal to $880,000 annually and variable costs are $10 per unit, what is the contribution margin per unit for Tierson Corporation?

    A. $0.05

    B. $20.00

    C. $44.00

    D. $88.00

Answer (B) is correct. *(Publisher, adapted)*
    REQUIRED: The contribution margin per unit.
    DISCUSSION: The breakeven point in units is equal to the fixed costs divided by the contribution margin per unit. Thus, the UCM is $20.00 ($880,000 ÷ 44,000 units).
    Answer (A) is incorrect because $.05 results from inverting the numerator and denominator in the calculation. Answer (C) is incorrect because $44.00 results from using variable cost as part of the calculation. Answer (D) is incorrect because $88.00 results from dividing by an erroneous denominator.

14.2 Applications

Questions 18 and 19 are based on the following information.

Delphi Company has developed a new project that will be marketed for the first time during the next fiscal year. Although the Marketing Department estimates that 35,000 units could be sold at $36 per unit, Delphi's management has allocated only enough manufacturing capacity to produce a maximum of 25,000 units of the new product annually. The fixed costs associated with the new product are budgeted at $450,000 for the year, which includes $60,000 for depreciation on new manufacturing equipment.

Data associated with each unit of product are presented as follows. Delphi is subject to a 40% income tax rate.

	Variable Costs
Direct material	$ 7.00
Direct labor	3.50
Manufacturing overhead	4.00
Total variable manufacturing cost	$14.50
Selling expenses	1.50
Total variable cost	$16.00

18. The maximum after-tax profit that can be earned by Delphi Company from sales of the new product during the next fiscal year is

A. $30,000

B. $50,000

C. $110,000

D. $66,000

Answer (A) is correct. *(CMA, adapted)*
REQUIRED: The maximum after-tax profit.
DISCUSSION: The maximum output (maximum sales level) is 25,000 units (given). Thus, the breakeven point in units is 22,500 ($450,000FC ÷ $20). The unit contribution margin is $20 ($36 selling price – $16 unit VC). At the breakeven point, all fixed costs have been recovered. Hence, pretax profit equals the unit contribution margin times unit sales in excess of the breakeven point, or $50,000 [(25,000 unit sales – 22,500 BEP) × $20 UCM]. After-tax profit is $30,000 [$50,000 × (1.0 – .4 tax rate)].

Answer (B) is incorrect because $50,000 is the pre-tax profit. Answer (C) is incorrect because $110,000 fails to include depreciation as a fixed cost and ignores income taxes. Answer (D) is incorrect because $66,000 fails to include depreciation as a fixed cost.

19. Delphi Company's management has stipulated that it will not approve the continued manufacture of the new product after the next fiscal year unless the after-tax profit is at least $75,000 the first year. The unit selling price to achieve this target profit must be at least

A. $37.00

B. $36.60

C. $34.60

D. $39.00

Answer (D) is correct. *(CMA, adapted)*
REQUIRED: The unit selling price to achieve a targeted after-tax profit.
DISCUSSION: If X represents the necessary selling price, 25,000 equals maximum sales volume, $16 is the variable cost per unit, $450,000 is the total fixed cost, and $125,000 [$75,000 target after-tax profit ÷ (1.0 – .4 tax rate)] is the desired pre-tax profit, the following formula may be solved to determine the requisite unit price:

$$25,000 (X - \$16) - \$450,000 = \$125,000$$
$$25,000X - \$400,000 - \$450,000 = \$125,000$$
$$25,000X = \$975,000$$
$$X = \$39$$

Answer (A) is incorrect because $37.00 does not consider income taxes. Answer (B) is incorrect because $36.60 excludes depreciation. Answer (C) is incorrect because $34.60 does not include depreciation or taxes.

Questions 20 through 22 are based on the following information. Bruell Electronics Co. is developing a new product, surge protectors for high-voltage electrical flows. The cost information below relates to the product:

	Unit Costs
Direct materials	$3.25
Direct labor	4.00
Distribution	.75

The company will also be absorbing $120,000 of additional fixed costs associated with this new product. A corporate fixed charge of $20,000 currently absorbed by other products will be allocated to this new product.

20. If the selling price is $14 per unit, the breakeven point in units (rounded to the nearest hundred) for surge protectors is

A. 8,500 units.

B. 10,000 units.

C. 15,000 units.

D. 20,000 units.

Answer (D) is correct. *(CMA, adapted)*
REQUIRED: The breakeven point in units.
DISCUSSION: The breakeven point in units equals total additional fixed costs divided by the unit contribution margin. Unit variable costs total $8 ($3.25 + $4.00 + $.75). Thus, UCM is $6 ($14 unit selling price – $6 unit VC), and the breakeven point is 20,000 units ($120,000 FC ÷ $6).
Answer (A) is incorrect because a breakeven point of 8,500 units ignores variable costs. Answer (B) is incorrect because the breakeven point is 20,000 units when the contribution margin is $6 per unit. Answer (C) is incorrect because 15,000 units equals fixed costs divided by unit variable cost.

21. How many surge protectors (rounded to the nearest hundred) must Bruell Electronics sell at a selling price of $14 per unit to gain $30,000 additional income before taxes?

A. 10,700 units.

B. 12,100 units.

C. 20,000 units.

D. 25,000 units.

Answer (D) is correct. *(CMA, adapted)*
REQUIRED: The number of units to be sold to generate a targeted pre-tax income.
DISCUSSION: The number of units to be sold to generate a specified pre-tax income equals the sum of total fixed costs and the targeted pre-tax income, divided by the unit contribution margin. Unit variable costs total $8 ($3.25 + $4.00 + $.75), and UCM is $6 ($14 unit selling price – $8). Thus, the desired unit sales level equals 25,000 units [($120,000 + $30,000) ÷ $6].
Answer (A) is incorrect because 10,700 units is based on a UCM equal to selling price. Answer (B) is incorrect because a contribution margin of $6 per unit necessitates sales of 25,000 units to produce a $30,000 before-tax profit. Answer (C) is incorrect because 20,000 units is the breakeven point.

22. How many surge protectors (rounded to the nearest hundred) must Bruell Electronics sell at a selling price of $14 per unit to increase after-tax income by $30,000? Bruell Electronics' effective income tax rate is 40%.

A. 10,700 units.

B. 12,100 units.

C. 20,000 units.

D. 28,300 units.

Answer (D) is correct. *(CMA, adapted)*
REQUIRED: The number of units to be sold to generate a specified after-tax income.
DISCUSSION: The number of units to be sold to generate a specified pre-tax income equals the sum of total fixed costs and the targeted pre-tax income, divided by the unit contribution margin. Given a desired after-tax income of $30,000 and a tax rate of 40%, the targeted pre-tax income must be $50,000 [$30,000 ÷ (1.0 – .4)]. Unit variable costs total $8 ($3.25 + $4.00 + $.75), and UCM is $6 ($14 unit selling price – $8). Hence, the desired unit sales level is 28,333 [($120,000 + $50,000) ÷ $6]. Rounded to the nearest hundred, the answer is $28,300.
Answer (A) is incorrect because 10,700 units is based on a UCM equal to selling price and $30,000 of pretax income. Answer (B) is incorrect because a $6 UCM necessitates sales of 28,300 units to produce a $30,000 after-tax profit. Answer (C) is incorrect because 20,000 units is the breakeven point.

23. BE&H Manufacturing is considering dropping a product line. It currently produces a multi-purpose woodworking clamp in a simple manufacturing process that uses special equipment. Variable costs amount to $6.00 per unit. Fixed overhead costs, exclusive of depreciation, have been allocated to this product at a rate of $3.50 a unit and will continue whether or not production ceases. Depreciation on the special equipment amounts to $20,000 a year. If production of the clamp is stopped, the special equipment can be sold for $18,000; if production continues, however, the equipment will be useless for further production at the end of 1 year and will have no salvage value. The clamp has a selling price of $10 a unit. Ignoring tax effects, the minimum number of units that would have to be sold in the current year to break even on a cash flow basis is

A. 4,500 units.

B. 5,000 units.

C. 20,000 units.

D. 36,000 units.

Answer (A) is correct. *(CMA, adapted)*
REQUIRED: The breakeven point in units on a cash flow basis.
DISCUSSION: The BEP in units is equal to fixed costs divided by the difference between unit selling price and unit variable cost (UCM). The $18,000 salvage value, the cash flow to be received if production is discontinued, is treated here as a fixed cost. Hence, continuation of the product line will permit the firm to break even or make a profit only if the total CM is $18,000 or more.

$$BEP = \frac{\$18,000}{\$10 - \$6} = 4,500 \ units$$

Fixed overhead allocated is not considered in this calculation because it is not a cash flow and will continue regardless of the decision.
Answer (B) is incorrect because the BEP is equal to the salvage value (not depreciation) divided by the UCM of $4 ($10 – $6). Depreciation is a non-cash flow and therefore should not be considered in the cash flow breakeven point calculation. Answer (C) is incorrect because the BEP is equal to the salvage value (not depreciation) divided by the UCM of $4 ($10 – $6). Depreciation is a non-cash flow and therefore should not be considered in the cash flow breakeven point calculation. Answer (D) is incorrect because unit fixed costs should not be subtracted in determining the unit contribution margin. The fixed costs will continue regardless so they are not included in the calculation. Therefore, the $18,000 salvage value will be divided by the $4 unit contribution margin in determining the cash flow breakeven point in units.

24. Austin Manufacturing, which is subject to a 40% income tax rate, had the following operating data for the period just ended.

Selling price per unit	$60
Variable cost per unit	$22
Fixed costs	$504,000

Management plans to improve the quality of its sole product by (1) replacing a component that costs $3.50 with a higher-grade unit that costs $5.50, and (2) acquiring a $180,000 packing machine. Austin will depreciate the machine over a 10-year life with no estimated salvage value by the straight-line method of depreciation. If the company wants to earn after-tax income of $172,800 in the upcoming period, it must sell

A. 19,300 units.

B. 21,316 units.

C. 22,500 units.

D. 23,800 units.

Answer (C) is correct. *(CMA, adapted)*
REQUIRED: The number of units to be sold to generate a targeted after-tax profit given that variable costs and fixed costs increase.
DISCUSSION: The units to be sold equal fixed costs plus the desired pretax profit, divided by the unit contribution margin. In the preceding year, the unit contribution margin was $38 ($60 price – $22 unit VC). That amount will decrease by $2 to $36 in the upcoming year because of use of a higher-grade component. Fixed costs will increase from $504,000 to $522,000 as a result of the $18,000 ($180,000 ÷ 10 years) increase in fixed costs attributable to depreciation on the new machine. Dividing the $172,800 of desired after-tax income by 60% (the complement of the tax rate) produces a desired before-tax income of $288,000. Hence, the breakeven point in units is 22,500 [($522,000 + $288,000) ÷ $36].
Answer (A) is incorrect because 19,300 units does not take income taxes into consideration. Answer (B) is incorrect because 21,316 units fails to consider the increased variable costs from the introduction of the higher-priced component. Answer (D) is incorrect because 23,800 units does not take income taxes into consideration, and it includes the entire cost of the new machine as a fixed cost.

Questions 25 through 27 are based on the following information. Siberian Ski Company recently expanded its manufacturing capacity, which will allow it to produce up to 15,000 pairs of cross-country skis of the mountaineering model or the touring model. The Sales Department assures management that it can sell between 9,000 pairs and 13,000 pairs of either product this year. Because the models are very similar, Siberian Ski will produce only one of the two models. The following information was compiled by the Accounting Department:

	Per-Unit (Pair) Data	
	Mountaineering	Touring
Selling price	$88.00	$80.00
Variable costs	52.80	52.80

Fixed costs will total $369,600 if the mountaineering model is produced but will be only $316,800 if the touring model is produced. Siberian Ski is subject to a 40% income tax rate.

25. The total sales revenue at which Siberian Ski Company would make the same profit or loss regardless of the ski model it decided to produce is

A. $880,000

B. $422,400

C. $924,000

D. $686,400

Answer (A) is correct. *(CMA, adapted)*
REQUIRED: The sales revenue resulting in the same profit or loss regardless of which model is produced.
DISCUSSION: The sales revenue at which the same profit or loss will be made equals the unit price times the units sold for each kind of skis. Accordingly, if M is the number of units sold of mountaineering skis and T is the number of units sold of touring skis, this level of sales revenue may be stated as $88M or $80T, and M is therefore equal to ($80 ÷ $88)T. Moreover, given the same profit or loss, the difference between sales revenue and total costs (variable + fixed) will also be the same for the two kinds of skis. Solving the equation below by substituting for M yields sales revenue of $880,000 [(11,000 × $80) or (10,000 × $88)].

$$Sales_M - VC_M - FC_M = Sales_T - VC_T - FC_T$$
$$\$88M - \$52.80M - \$369,600 = \$80T - \$52.80T - \$316,800$$
$$\$35.2M - \$52,800 = \$27.2T$$
$$\$35.2(\$80 \div \$88)T = \$27.2T + \$52,800$$
$$T = 11,000 \text{ units}$$
$$M = 10,000 \text{ units}$$

26. If the Siberian Ski Company Sales Department could guarantee the annual sale of 12,000 pairs of either model, Siberian Ski would

A. Produce 12,000 pairs of touring skis because they have a lower fixed cost.

B. Be indifferent as to which model is sold because each model has the same variable cost per unit.

C. Produce 12,000 pairs of mountaineering skis because they have a lower breakeven point.

D. Produce 12,000 pairs of mountaineering skis because they are more profitable.

Answer (D) is correct. *(CMA, adapted)*
REQUIRED: The model that should be produced if sales are exactly 12,000 pairs.
DISCUSSION: Preparing income statements determines which model will produce the greater profit at a sales level of 12,000 pairs. Thus, as indicated below, the mountaineering skis should be produced.

	Mountain	Touring
Sales	$1,056,000	$960,000
Variable costs	(633,600)	(633,600)
Fixed costs	(369,600)	(316,800)
Net Income	$ 52,800	$ 9,600

Answer (A) is incorrect because, at a sales volume of 12,000 pairs, the higher contribution margin of the mountaineering skis results in a greater profit. Answer (B) is incorrect because the lower selling price of the touring skis results in a lower contribution margin per unit sold. Answer (C) is incorrect because breakeven point is not a consideration. A sales volume of 12,000 units is above the breakeven point for both models.

27. If Siberian Ski Company desires an after-tax net income of $24,000, how many pairs of touring model skis will the company have to sell?

A. 13,118 pairs.

B. 12,529 pairs.

C. 13,853 pairs.

D. 4,460 pairs.

Answer (A) is correct. *(CMA, adapted)*
REQUIRED: The units of touring model skis the company will have to sell to produce a given after-tax profit.
DISCUSSION: The breakeven sales volume equals total fixed costs divided by the unit contribution margin (UCM). In the breakeven formula, the desired profit should be treated as a fixed cost. Because the UCM is stated in pretax dollars, the targeted profit must be adjusted for taxes. Hence, the targeted after-tax net income of $24,000 is equivalent to a pretax profit of $40,000 [$24,000 ÷ (1.0 − .4 tax rate)]. The sum of the pretax profit and the fixed costs is $356,800 ($316,800 + $40,000). Consequently, the desired sales volume is 13,118 pairs of touring skis [$356,800 ÷ ($80 price − $52.80 unit VC)].

28. Mason Enterprises has prepared the following budget for the month of July:

	Selling Price Per Unit	Variable Cost Per Unit	Unit Sales
Product A	$10.00	$4.00	15,000
Product B	15.00	8.00	20,000
Product C	18.00	9.00	5,000

Assuming that total fixed costs will be $150,000 and the mix remains constant, the breakeven point (rounded to the next higher whole unit) will be

A. 20,455 units.

B. 21,429 units.

C. 21,819 units.

D. 6,818 units.

Answer (C) is correct. *(CMA, adapted)*
REQUIRED: The breakeven point in units given fixed costs and a constant product mix.
DISCUSSION: Given the constant product mix of 3:4:1 established by the budgeted unit sales, a composite unit consists of eight individual units (3 of A, 4 of B, and 1 of C). The unit contribution margins for A, B, and C are $6 ($10 price − $4 VC), $7 ($15 − $8 VC), and $9 ($18 price − $9 VC), respectively. Hence, the contribution margin for a composite unit is $55 [(3 × $6) + (4 × $7) + (1 × $9)], and the breakeven point is 2,727.2727 composite units ($150,000 FC ÷ $55). This amount equals 21,819 (rounded up) individual units (8 × 2,727.2727).
Answer (A) is incorrect because the breakeven point is 21,819 units. Answer (B) is incorrect because the breakeven point is 21,819 units. Answer (D) is incorrect because 6,818 is based on an average contribution margin of $22 per unit.

Questions 29 through 31 are based on the following information.

Moorehead Manufacturing Company produces two products for which the following data have been tabulated. Fixed manufacturing cost is applied at a rate of $1.00 per machine hour. The sales manager has had a $160,000 increase in the budget allotment for advertising and wants to apply the money to the most profitable product. The products are not substitutes for one another in the eyes of the company's customers.

Per Unit	XY-7	BD-4
Selling price	$4.00	$3.00
Variable manufacturing cost	$2.00	$1.50
Fixed manufacturing cost	$ .75	$ .20
Variable selling cost	$1.00	$1.00

29. Suppose the sales manager chooses to devote the entire $160,000 to increased advertising for XY-7. The minimum increase in sales units of XY-7 required to offset the increased advertising is

A. 640,000 units.

B. 160,000 units.

C. 128,000 units.

D. 80,000 units.

Answer (B) is correct. *(CMA, adapted)*
REQUIRED: The minimum increase in sales units to offset increased advertising costs.
DISCUSSION: The contribution margin (CM) for XY-7 is $1 per unit ($4 sales price – $3 variable costs). Thus, 160,000 units of XY-7 will generate an additional $160,000 of CM, which is sufficient to cover the increase in advertising costs.
Answer (A) is incorrect because 640,000 units would be the result if the UCM for XY-7 were $.25 instead of $1.00 (640,000 × $.25 = $160,000). Fixed manufacturing costs are not included in determining UCM. Answer (C) is incorrect because 128,000 units implies a $1.25 UCM. Variable selling costs are included and fixed manufacturing costs are not included in determining UCM. Answer (D) is incorrect because 80,000 units implies a $2.00 UCM. The correct UCM of $1.00 is found by subtracting all variable costs from the selling price.

30. Suppose the sales manager chooses to devote the entire $160,000 to increased advertising for BD-4. The minimum increase in sales dollars of BD-4 required to offset the increased advertising would be

A. $160,000

B. $320,000

C. $960,000

D. $1,600,000

Answer (C) is correct. *(CMA, adapted)*
REQUIRED: The minimum increase in sales dollars to offset increased advertising costs.
DISCUSSION: Sales dollars must increase sufficiently to cover the $160,000 increase in advertising. The unit contribution margin for BD-4 is $.50 ($3 – $2.50 variable costs), and the CMR is 1/6 (UCM ÷ $3 sales price). Dividing the $160,000 by 1/6 gives the sales dollars necessary to generate a CM of $960,000 ($160,000 ÷ 1/6 = $960,000).
Answer (A) is incorrect because a $1 increase in sales does not result in a $1 increase in profits. Variable costs of producing the units must be deducted in order to determine the contribution margin derived from each unit sold. Answer (B) is incorrect because 320,000 is the number of sales units, not sales dollars, needed to offset the increased advertising costs. Answer (D) is incorrect because fixed manufacturing costs are not included in determining unit contribution margin.

31. Suppose Moorehead has only 100,000 machine hours that can be made available to produce additional units of XY-7 and BD-4. If the potential increase in sales units for either product resulting from advertising is far in excess of this production capacity, which product should be advertised and what is the estimated increase in contribution margin earned?

A. Product XY-7 should be produced, yielding a contribution margin of $75,000.

B. Product XY-7 should be produced, yielding a contribution margin of $133,333.

C. Product BD-4 should be produced, yielding a contribution margin of $187,500.

D. Product BD-4 should be produced, yielding a contribution margin of $250,000.

Answer (D) is correct. *(CMA, adapted)*
REQUIRED: The more profitable product and the estimated increase in contribution margin.
DISCUSSION: The machine hours are a scarce resource that must be allocated to the product(s) in a proportion that maximizes the total CM. Given that potential additional sales of either product are in excess of production capacity, only the product with the greater CM per unit of scarce resource should be produced. XY-7 requires .75 hours; BD-4 requires .2 hours of machine time (given fixed manufacturing cost applied at $1 per machine hour of $.75 for XY-7 and $.20 for BD-4).
XY-7 has a CM of $1.33 per machine hour ($1 UCM ÷ .75 hours), and BD-4 has a CM of $2.50 per machine hour ($.50 ÷ .2 hours). Thus, only BD-4 should be produced, yielding a CM of $250,000 (100,000 × $2.50). The key to the analysis is CM per unit of scarce resource.
Answer (A) is incorrect because product XY-7 actually has a CM of $133,333, which is lower than the $250,000 CM for product BD-4. Answer (B) is incorrect because product BD-4 has a higher CM at $250,000. Answer (C) is incorrect because product BD-4 has a CM of $250,000.

Questions 32 through 34 are based on the following information. MultiFrame Company has the following revenue and cost budgets for the two products it sells:

	Plastic Frames	Glass Frames
Sales price	$10.00	$15.00
Direct materials	(2.00)	(3.00)
Direct labor	(3.00)	(5.00)
Fixed overhead	(3.00)	(4.00)
Net income per unit	$ 2.00	$ 3.00
Budgeted unit sales	100,000	300,000

The budgeted unit sales equal the current unit demand, and total fixed overhead for the year is budgeted at $975,000. Assume that the company plans to maintain the same proportional mix. In numerical calculations, MultiFrame rounds to the nearest cent and unit.

32. The total number of units MultiFrame needs to produce and sell to break even is

A. 150,000 units.

B. 354,545 units.

C. 177,273 units.

D. 300,000 units.

Answer (A) is correct. *(CMA, adapted)*
   REQUIRED: The total units sold at the breakeven point.
   DISCUSSION: The calculation of the breakeven point is to divide the fixed costs by the contribution margin per unit. This determination is more complicated for a multi-product firm. If the same proportional product mix is maintained, one unit of plastic frames is sold for every three units of glass frames. Accordingly, a composite unit consists of four frames: one plastic and three glass. For plastic frames, the unit contribution margin is $5 ($10 – $2 – $3). For glass frames, the unit contribution margin is $7 ($15 – $3 – $5). Thus, the composite unit contribution margin is $26 ($5 + $7 + $7 + $7), and the breakeven point is 37,500 packages ($975,000 FC ÷ $26). Because each composite unit contains four frames, the total units sold equal 150,000.

33. The total number of units needed to break even if the budgeted direct labor costs were $2 for plastic frames instead of $3 is

A. 154,028 units.

B. 144,444 units.

C. 156,000 units.

D. 146,177 units.

Answer (B) is correct. *(CMA, adapted)*
   REQUIRED: The breakeven point in units if labor costs for the plastic frames are reduced.
   DISCUSSION: If the labor costs for the plastic frames are reduced by $1, the composite unit contribution margin will be $27 [($10 – $2 – $3) + (3)($15 – $3 – $5)]. Hence, the new breakeven point is 144,444 units [4 units × ($975,000 FC ÷ $27)].

34. The total number of units needed to break even if sales were budgeted at 150,000 units of plastic frames and 300,000 units of glass frames with all other costs remaining constant is

A. 171,958 units.

B. 418,455 units.

C. 153,947 units.

D. 365,168 units.

Answer (C) is correct. *(CMA, adapted)*
   REQUIRED: The total number of units needed to break even if the product mix is changed.
   DISCUSSION: The unit contribution margins for plastic frames and glass frames are $5 ($10 – $2 – $3) and $7 ($15 – $3 – $5), respectively. If the number of plastic frames sold is 50% of the number of glass frames sold, a composite unit will contain one plastic frame and two glass frames. Thus, the composite unit contribution margin will be $19 ($5 + $7 + $7), and the breakeven point in units will be 153,947 [3 units × ($975,000 ÷ $19)].

Questions 35 and 36 are based on the following information.

Barnes Corporation manufactures skateboards and is in the process of preparing next year's budget. The pro forma income statement for the current year is presented in the next column.

Sales		$1,500,000
Cost of sales:		
Direct materials	$250,000	
Direct labor	150,000	
Variable overhead	75,000	
Fixed overhead	100,000	575,000
Gross profit		$ 925,000
Selling and G&A:		
Variable	$200,000	
Fixed	250,000	450,000
Operating income		$ 475,000

35. The breakeven point (rounded to the nearest dollar) for Barnes Corporation for the current year is

A. $146,341

B. $636,364

C. $729,730

D. $181,818

Answer (B) is correct. *(CMA, adapted)*
REQUIRED: The breakeven point in dollars.
DISCUSSION: Fixed costs total $350,000. Variable costs total $675,000. Given sales of $1,500,000, the contribution margin is $825,000 ($1,500,000 – $675,000). Thus, the contribution margin percentage is 55% ($825,000 ÷ $1,500,000). Dividing the $350,000 of fixed costs by 55% produces a breakeven point of $636,363.64.
Answer (A) is incorrect because $146,341 does not even cover fixed costs. Answer (C) is incorrect because $729,730 of sales result in a small profit. Answer (D) is incorrect because $181,818 does not cover the $350,000 of fixed costs.

36. For the coming year, the management of Barnes Corporation anticipates a 10% increase in sales, a 12% increase in variable costs, and a $45,000 increase in fixed expenses. The breakeven point for next year will be

A. $729,027

B. $862,103

C. $214,018

D. $474,000

Answer (A) is correct. *(CMA, adapted)*
REQUIRED: The breakeven point following an increase in sales, variable costs, and fixed expenses.
DISCUSSION: Sales are expected to be $1,650,000 ($1,500,000 × 1.10), variable costs $756,000 ($675,000 × 1.12), and fixed expenses $395,000 ($350,000 + $45,000). Thus, the contribution margin will be $894,000 ($1,650,000 – $756,000), and the contribution margin percentage is 54.1818%. The breakeven point is therefore $729,027 ($395,000 fixed expenses ÷ 54.1818%).
Answer (B) is incorrect because the contribution margin percentage is computed by dividing the contribution margin (total sales – total variable costs) by total sales, not by dividing the total variable costs by total sales. Answer (C) is incorrect because $214,018 does not cover fixed costs. Answer (D) is incorrect because $474,000 barely covers fixed costs.

Use Gleim's ***CMA Test Prep*** for interactive testing with **over 2,000 additional multiple-choice questions**!

STUDY UNIT FIFTEEN
MARGINAL ANALYSIS

(4 pages of outline)

This study unit is the **fourth of five** on **decision analysis**. The relative weight assigned to this major topic in Part 3 of the exam is **25%** at **skill level C** (all six skill types required). The five study units are

Study Unit 12: The Decision Process
Study Unit 13: Data Concepts Relevant to Decision Making
Study Unit 14: Cost-Volume-Profit Analysis
Study Unit 15: Marginal Analysis
Study Unit 16: Cost-Based Pricing

After studying the outline and answering the multiple-choice questions, you will have the skills necessary to address the following topics listed in the IMA's Learning Outcome Statements:

Part 3 – Section D.4. Marginal analysis

The candidate should be able to:

a. demonstrate proficiency in the use of marginal analysis for decisions such as (a) introducing a new product or changing output levels of existing products, (b) accepting or rejecting special orders, (c) making or buying a product or service, (d) selling a product or performing additional processes and selling a more value-added product, and (e) adding or dropping a segment

b. identify such relevant information as the future revenues and future costs that will differ between the decisions in any type of marginal analysis

c. explain why any cost, including any allocated costs, that does not differ between alternatives, should be ignored in marginal decision analyses

d. demonstrate an understanding of opportunity cost in marginal analysis

e. calculate the effect of opportunity cost in a marginal analysis decision

f. recommend a course of action using marginal analysis

g. calculate the effect on operating income when changes in output levels occur

h. calculate the effect on operating income of a decision to accept or reject a special order when there is idle capacity and the order has no long-run implications

i. identify qualitative factors in make-or-buy decisions, such as product quality and dependability of suppliers

j. calculate the effect on operating income of a decision to make or buy a product or service

k. differentiate between avoidable and unavoidable costs in the decision to drop or add a segment

l. demonstrate an understanding of the impact of income taxes on marginal analysis decisions

15.1 DECISION MAKING AND MARGINAL ANALYSIS

1.   The typical problem for which **marginal (differential or incremental) analysis** can be used involves choices among courses of action.

   a.   **Quantitative analysis** emphasizes the ways in which revenues and costs vary with the option chosen. Thus, the focus is on **incremental revenues and costs**, not the totals of all revenues and costs for the given option.

   b.   EXAMPLE: A firm produces a product for which it incurs the following unit costs:

Direct materials	$2.00
Direct labor	3.00
Variable overhead	.50
Fixed overhead	.50
Total cost	$6.00

   1)   The product normally sells for $10 per unit. An application of marginal analysis is necessary if a foreign buyer, who has never before been a customer, offers to pay $5.60 per unit for a **special order** of the firm's product.

      a)   The immediate reaction might be to refuse the offer because the selling price is less than the average cost of production.

   2)   However, **marginal analysis** results in a different decision. Assuming that the firm has idle capacity, only the additional costs should be considered.

      a)   In this example, the only marginal costs are for direct materials, direct labor, and variable overhead. No additional fixed overhead costs would be incurred.

      b)   Because **marginal revenue** (the $5.60 selling price) **exceeds marginal costs** ($2 materials + $3 labor + $.50 variable OH = $5.50 per unit), accepting the special order will be profitable.

   3)   **If a competitor bids** $5.80 per unit, the firm can still profitably accept the special order while underbidding the competitor by setting a price below $5.80 per unit but above $5.50 per unit.

2.   Caution always must be used in applying marginal analysis because of the many qualitative factors involved.

   a.   **Qualitative factors** include

   1)   Special price concessions place the firm in violation of the **price discrimination** provisions of the Robinson-Patman Act of 1936.

   2)   Government contract pricing regulations apply.

   3)   Sales to a special customer affect sales in the firm's regular market.

   4)   Regular customers learn of a special price and demand equal terms.

   5)   Disinvestment, such as by dropping a product line, will hurt sales in the other product lines (e.g., the dropped product may have been an unintended loss leader).

   6)   An outsourced product's quality is acceptable and the supplier is reliable.

   7)   Employee morale may be affected. If employees are laid off or asked to work too few or too many hours, morale may be affected favorably or unfavorably.

3.   **Make-or-Buy Decisions** (Insourcing vs. Outsourcing)

   a.   The firm should use **available resources** as efficiently as possible before outsourcing. Often, an array of products can be produced efficiently if production capacity is available.

      1)   If not enough capacity is available to produce all products, those that are produced **least efficiently should be outsourced** (or capacity should be expanded).

      2)   Support services such as computer processing, legal work, accounting, and training, may also be outsourced.

      3)   Moreover, both products and services may be outsourced internationally. Thus, computer programming, information processing, customer service via telephone, etc., as well as manufacturing tasks, may be not only outsourced but outsourced offshore.

   b.   In a **make-or-buy** decision, the manager considers only the costs relevant to the investment decision. If the total relevant costs of production are less than the cost to buy the item, it should be insourced.

      1)   The **key variable** is **total relevant costs**, not all total costs.

      2)   **Sunk costs are irrelevant.** Hence, a production plant's cost of repairs last year is irrelevant to this year's make-or-buy decision. The carrying amount of old equipment is another example.

      3)   **Costs that do not differ** between two alternatives should be **ignored** because they are not relevant to the decision being made.

      4)   **Opportunity costs** must be considered when **idle capacity** is not available. They are of primary importance because they represent the forgone opportunities of the firm.

   c.   EXAMPLE: Should a company make or buy an item?

	Make	Buy
Total variable cost	$10	
Allocation of fixed cost	5	
Total unit costs	$15	$13

      1)   If the plant has excess capacity, the decision should be to produce the item. Total variable cost ($10) is less than the purchase price.

         a)   However, if the plant is running at capacity, the opportunity cost of displaced production becomes a relevant cost that might alter the decision in favor of purchasing the item from a supplier.

      2)   The firm also should consider the qualitative aspects of the decision. For example, will product quality be as high if a component is outsourced than if produced internally? Also, how reliable are the suppliers?

4.   **Capacity Constraints and Product Mix**

   a.   Marginal analysis also applies to decisions about which products and services to sell and in what quantities given the known demand and resource limitations.

      1)   For example, if the firm can sell as much as it can produce and has a single resource constraint, the decision rule is to **maximize the contribution margin per unit** of the constrained resource.

         a)   However, given multiple constraints, the decision is more difficult. In that case, sophisticated techniques such as **linear programming** must be used.

5.   **Disinvestment** decisions are the opposite of capital budgeting decisions, i.e., to terminate an operation, product or product line, business segment, branch, or major customer rather than start one.

   a.   In general, if the **marginal cost** of a project **exceeds the marginal revenue**, the firm should disinvest.

   b.   **Four steps** should be taken in making a disinvestment decision:

   1)   **Identify fixed costs** that will be eliminated by the disinvestment decision, e.g., insurance on equipment used.

   2)   Determine the **revenue needed to justify continuing operations**. In the short run, this amount should at least equal the variable cost of production or continued service.

   3)   Establish the **opportunity cost of funds** that will be received upon disinvestment (e.g., salvage value).

   4)   Determine whether the **carrying amount of the assets** is equal to their economic value. If not, reevaluate the decision using current fair value rather than the carrying amount.

   c.   When a firm disinvests, excess capacity exists unless another project uses this capacity immediately. The **cost of idle capacity** should be treated as a **relevant cost**.

6.   **Sell-or-Process Decisions**

   a.   In determining whether to sell a product at the split-off point or process the item further at additional cost, the **joint cost** of the product is **irrelevant** because it is a sunk cost.

   b.   The sell-or-process decision should be based on the relationship between the **incremental costs** (the cost of additional processing) and the **incremental revenues** (the benefits received).

7.   Stop and review! You have completed the outline for this subunit. Study multiple-choice questions 1 through 26 beginning on page 371.

15.2 CORE CONCEPTS

Decision Making and Marginal Analysis

■   The typical problem for which **marginal (differential or incremental) analysis** can be used involves choices among courses of action. The focus is on incremental revenues and costs, not the totals of all revenues and costs for the given option.

■   A special order which might at first be rejected could turn out to be profitable after marginal analysis. Marginal analysis emphasizes incremental costs, highlighting the ability of marginal revenue to **cover fixed costs**.

■   The key variable in a **make-or-buy** (insource vs. outsource) decision is total relevant costs, not total costs.

■   Marginal analysis also applies to decisions regarding **which products and services** to sell and in what quantities to sell them given the known demand and resource limitations.

■   In general, if the marginal cost of a project exceeds the marginal revenue, the firm should **disinvest** in a particular operation or product line.

QUESTIONS

15.1 Decision Making and Marginal Analysis

Questions 1 through 3 are based on the following information. Kator Co. is a manufacturer of industrial components. One of their products that is used as a subcomponent in auto manufacturing is KB-96. This product has the following financial structure per unit:

Selling price	$150
Direct materials	$ 20
Direct labor	15
Variable manufacturing overhead	12
Fixed manufacturing overhead	30
Shipping and handling	3
Fixed selling and administrative	10
Total costs	$ 90

1. Kator Co. has received a special, one-time order for 1,000 KB-96 parts. Assuming Kator has excess capacity, the minimum price that is acceptable for this one-time special order is in excess of

   A. $47

   B. $50

   C. $60

   D. $77

Answer (B) is correct. *(CMA, adapted)*
   REQUIRED: The minimum acceptable price.
   DISCUSSION: A company must cover the incremental costs of a special order when it has excess capacity. The incremental costs for product KB-96 are $50 ($20 direct materials + $15 direct labor + $12 variable overhead + $3 shipping and handling). The fixed costs will not change as a result of the special order, so they are not relevant. Thus, any price in excess of $50 per unit is acceptable.
   Answer (A) is incorrect because $47 ignores the shipping and handling costs. Answer (C) is incorrect because $60 includes fixed selling and administrative costs. Answer (D) is incorrect because $77 includes fixed manufacturing overhead but omits shipping and handling costs.

2. During the next year, KB-96 sales are expected to be 10,000 units. All of the costs will remain the same except that fixed manufacturing overhead will increase by 20% and direct materials will increase by 10%. The selling price per unit for next year will be $160. Based on this data, the contribution margin from KB-96 for next year will be

   A. $620,000

   B. $750,000

   C. $1,080,000

   D. $1,110,000

Answer (C) is correct. *(CMA, adapted)*
   REQUIRED: The contribution margin for next year.
   DISCUSSION: Contribution margin equals sales minus variable costs. All variable costs will remain the same except that direct materials will increase to $22 per unit (1.1 × $20). Thus, total unit variable costs will be $52 ($22 + $15 + $12 + $3), and the contribution margin will be $1,080,000 [10,000 units ($160 unit selling price – $52)].
   Answer (A) is incorrect because $620,000 includes all fixed costs. Answer (B) is incorrect because $750,000 includes all manufacturing costs. Answer (D) is incorrect because $1,110,000 assumes that the fixed costs and shipping and handling are the only relevant costs.

3. Kator Co. has received a special, one-time order for 1,000 KB-96 parts. Assume that Kator is operating at full capacity and that the contribution margin of the output that would be displaced by the special order is $10,000. Using the original data, the minimum price that is acceptable for this one-time special order is in excess of

   A. $60

   B. $70

   C. $87

   D. $100

Answer (A) is correct. *(CMA, adapted)*
   REQUIRED: The minimum acceptable price.
   DISCUSSION: Given no excess capacity, the price must cover the incremental costs. The incremental costs for KB-96 equal $50 ($20 direct materials + $15 direct labor + $12 variable overhead + $3 shipping and handling). Opportunity cost is the benefit of the next best alternative use of scarce resources. Because acceptance of the special order would cause the company to forgo a contribution margin of $10,000, that amount must be reflected in the price. Hence, the minimum unit price is $60 [$50 unit incremental cost + ($10,000 lost CM ÷ 1,000 units)].
   Answer (B) is incorrect because $70 includes fixed selling and administrative costs. Answer (C) is incorrect because $87 includes fixed manufacturing overhead but omits shipping and handling costs. Answer (D) is incorrect because $100 is based on full absorption cost.

4. In joint-product costing and analysis, which one of the following costs is relevant when deciding the point at which a product should be sold to maximize profits?

A. Separable costs after the split-off point.

B. Joint costs to the split-off point.

C. Sales salaries for the period when the units were produced.

D. Purchase costs of the materials required for the joint products.

Answer (A) is correct. *(CMA, adapted)*
REQUIRED: The cost relevant to deciding when a joint product should be sold.
DISCUSSION: Joint products are created from processing a common input. Common costs are incurred prior to the split-off point and cannot be identified with a particular joint product. As a result, common costs are irrelevant to the timing of sale. However, separable costs incurred after the split-off point are relevant because, if incremental revenues exceed the separable costs, products should be processed further, not sold at the split-off point.
Answer (B) is incorrect because joint costs (common costs) have no effect on the decision as to when to sell a product. Answer (C) is incorrect because sales salaries for the production period do not affect the decision. Answer (D) is incorrect because purchase costs are joint costs.

5. A firm produces two joint products (A and B) from one unit of raw material, which costs $1,000. Product A can be sold for $700 and product B can be sold for $500 at the split-off point. Alternatively, both A and/or B can be processed further and sold for $900 and $1,200, respectively. The additional processing costs are $100 for A and $750 for B. Should the firm process products A and B beyond the split-off point?

A. Both A and B should be processed further.

B. Only B should be processed further.

C. Only A should be processed further.

D. Neither product should be processed further.

Answer (C) is correct. *(CIA, adapted)*
REQUIRED: The best decision regarding additional processing.
DISCUSSION: The incremental costs ($100) for A are less than the incremental revenue ($200). However, the incremental costs of B ($750) exceed the incremental revenue ($700). Consequently, the firm should process A further and sell B at the split-off point.

6. Copeland Inc. produces X-547 in a joint manufacturing process. The company is studying whether to sell X-547 at the split-off point or upgrade the product to become Xylene. The following information has been gathered:

I.   Selling price per pound of X-547
II. Variable manufacturing costs of upgrade process
III. Avoidable fixed costs of upgrade process
IV. Selling price per pound of Xylene
V.   Joint manufacturing costs to produce X-547

Which items should be reviewed when making the upgrade decision?

A. I, II, and IV only.

B. I, II, III, and IV only.

C. I, II, IV, and V only.

D. II and III only.

Answer (B) is correct. *(CMA, adapted)*
REQUIRED: The items reviewed when making a sell-or-process decision.
DISCUSSION: Common, or joint, costs cannot be identified with a particular joint product. By definition, joint products have common costs until the split-off point. Costs incurred after the split-off point are separable costs. The decision to continue processing beyond split-off is made separately for each product. The costs relevant to the decision are the separable costs because they can be avoided by selling at the split-off point. They should be compared with the incremental revenues from processing further. Thus, items I. (revenue from selling at split-off point), II. (variable costs of upgrade), III. (avoidable fixed costs of upgrade), and IV. (revenue from selling after further processing) are considered in making the upgrade decision.

Questions 7 and 8 are based on the following information.

N-Air Corporation uses a joint process to produce three products: A, B, and C, all derived from one input. The company can sell these products at the point of split-off (end of the joint process) or process them further. The joint production costs during October were $10,000. N-Air allocates joint costs to the products in proportion to the relative physical volume of output. Additional information is presented in the opposite column.

| | | | If Processed Further | |
Product	Units Produced	Unit Sales Price at Split-off	Unit Sales Price	Unit Additional Cost
A	1,000	$4.00	$5.00	$ .75
B	2,000	2.25	4.00	1.20
C	1,500	3.00	3.75	.90

7. Assuming that all products were sold at the split-off point during October, the gross profit from the production process would be

A. $13,000

B. $10,000

C. $8,625

D. $3,000

Answer (D) is correct. *(CIA, adapted)*
REQUIRED: The gross profit from the production process if all products are sold at the split-off point.
DISCUSSION: If all products are sold at split-off, the gross profit is computed as follows:

Product A (1,000 × $4.00)	$ 4,000
Product B (2,000 × $2.25)	4,500
Product C (1,500 × $3.00)	4,500
Total sales	$ 13,000
Joint costs	(10,000)
Gross profit	$ 3,000

Answer (A) is incorrect because $13,000 is the total sales if all products are sold at split-off. Answer (B) is incorrect because $10,000 is the joint production cost during October. Answer (C) is incorrect because, if all products were sold at split-off, total sales are determined by multiplying units produced by the unit sales price at split-off, not the unit sales price if processed further.

8. Assuming sufficient demand exists, N-Air could sell all the products at the prices previously mentioned at either the split-off point or after further processing. To maximize its profits, N-Air Corporation should

A. Sell product A at split-off and perform additional processing on products B and C.

B. Sell product B at split-off and perform additional processing on products C and A.

C. Sell product C at split-off and perform additional processing on products A and B.

D. Sell products A, B, and C at split-off.

Answer (C) is correct. *(CIA, adapted)*
REQUIRED: The product(s) that should be processed further to maximize profits.
DISCUSSION: To maximize profits, it must be determined whether each product's incremental revenues will exceed its incremental costs. Joint costs are irrelevant because they are sunk costs.

	A	B	C
Unit sales price if processed further	$5.00	$4.00	$3.75
Minus unit sales price at split-off	(4.00)	(2.25)	(3.00)
Incremental revenue per unit	$1.00	$1.75	$ .75
Minus incremental unit cost	(.75)	(1.20)	(.90)
Excess unit revenue over unit cost	$ .25	$ .55	$ (.15)

It is most profitable for N-Air to process products A and B further and to sell product C at the split-off point.

Questions 9 and 10 are based on the following information. Whitehall Corporation produces chemicals used in the cleaning industry. During the previous month, Whitehall incurred $300,000 of joint costs in producing 60,000 units of AM-12 and 40,000 units of BM-36. Whitehall uses the units-of-production method to allocate joint costs. Currently, AM-12 is sold at split-off for $3.50 per unit. Flank Corporation has approached Whitehall to purchase all of the production of AM-12 after further processing. The further processing will cost Whitehall $90,000.

9. Concerning AM-12, which one of the following alternatives is most advantageous?

A. Whitehall should process further and sell to Flank if the total selling price per unit after further processing is greater than $3.00, which covers the joint costs.

B. Whitehall should continue to sell at split-off unless Flank offers at least $4.50 per unit after further processing, which covers Whitehall's total costs.

C. Whitehall should process further and sell to Flank if the total selling price per unit after further processing is greater than $5.00.

D. Whitehall should process further and sell to Flank if the total selling price per unit after further processing is greater than $5.25, which maintains the same gross profit percentage.

Answer (C) is correct. *(CMA, adapted)*
REQUIRED: The processing and selling alternative that is most advantageous.
DISCUSSION: The unit price of the product at the split-off point is known to be $3.50, so the joint costs are irrelevant. The additional unit cost of further processing is $1.50 ($90,000 ÷ 60,000 units). Consequently, the unit price must be at least $5.00 ($3.50 opportunity cost + $1.50).
Answer (A) is incorrect because the joint costs are irrelevant. Answer (B) is incorrect because the unit price must cover the $3.50 opportunity cost plus the $1.50 of additional costs. Answer (D) is incorrect because any price greater than $5 will provide greater profits, in absolute dollars, even though the gross profit percentage declines.

10. Assume that Whitehall Corporation agreed to sell AM-12 to Flank Corporation for $5.50 per unit after further processing. During the first month of production, Whitehall sold 50,000 units with 10,000 units remaining in inventory at the end of the month. With respect to AM-12, which one of the following statements is true?

A. The operating profit last month was $50,000, and the inventory value is $15,000.

B. The operating profit last month was $50,000, and the inventory value is $45,000.

C. The operating profit last month was $125,000, and the inventory value is $30,000.

D. The operating profit last month was $200,000, and the inventory value is $30,000.

Answer (B) is correct. *(CMA, adapted)*
REQUIRED: The operating profit and inventory value after specified sales of a product.
DISCUSSION: Joint costs are allocated based on units of production. Accordingly, the unit joint cost allocated to AM-12 is $3.00 [$300,000 ÷ (60,000 units of AM-12 + 40,000 units of BM-36)]. The unit cost of AM-12 is therefore $4.50 [$3.00 joint cost + ($90,000 additional cost ÷ 60,000 units)]. Total inventory value is $45,000 (10,000 units × $4.50), and total operating profit is $50,000 [50,000 units sold × ($5.50 unit price – $4.50 unit cost)].
Answer (A) is incorrect because the $3 unit joint cost should be included in the inventory value. Answer (C) is incorrect because the $1.50 unit additional cost should be included in total unit cost. Answer (D) is incorrect because the $3 unit joint cost should be included in the cost of goods sold, and inventory should include the $1.50 unit additional cost.

11. When a multiproduct plant operates at full capacity, quite often decisions must be made as to which products to emphasize. These decisions are frequently made with a short-run focus. In making such decisions, managers should select products with the highest

A. Sales price per unit.

B. Individual unit contribution margin.

C. Sales volume potential.

D. Contribution margin per unit of the constraining resource.

Answer (D) is correct. *(CMA, adapted)*
REQUIRED: The products to be made in the short run.
DISCUSSION: In the short run, many costs are fixed. Hence, contribution margin (revenues – all variable costs) becomes the best measure of profitability. Moreover, certain resources are also fixed. Accordingly, when deciding which products to produce at full capacity, the criterion should be the contribution margin per unit of the most constrained resource. This approach maximizes total contribution margin.
Answer (A) is incorrect because the highest sales price does not consider costs and constraints. Answer (B) is incorrect because the product with the highest UCM may require greater usage of the constrained resource than another product contributing a lesser amount per unit. Answer (C) is incorrect because the highest sales volume does not consider costs and constraints.

Questions 12 through 14 are based on the following information.

Condensed monthly operating income data for Korbin, Inc. for May follows:

	Urban Store	Suburban Store	Total
Sales	$80,000	$120,000	$200,000
Variable costs	32,000	84,000	116,000
Contribution margin	$48,000	$ 36,000	$ 84,000
Direct fixed costs	20,000	40,000	60,000
Store segment margin	$28,000	$ (4,000)	$ 24,000
Common fixed cost	4,000	6,000	10,000
Operating income	$24,000	$ (10,000)	$ 14,000

Additional information regarding Korbin's operations follows:

- One-fourth of each store's direct fixed costs would continue if either store is closed.
- Korbin allocates common fixed costs to each store on the basis of sales dollars.
- Management estimates that closing the Suburban Store would result in a 10% decrease in the Urban Store's sales, while closing the Urban Store would not affect the Suburban Store's sales.
- The operating results for May are representative of all months.

12. A decision by Korbin to close the Suburban Store would result in a monthly increase (decrease) in Korbin's operating income of

A. $(10,800)

B. $(6,000)

C. $(1,200)

D. $4,000

Answer (A) is correct. *(CMA, adapted)*
REQUIRED: The effect on operating income of closing the Suburban Store.
DISCUSSION: If the Suburban Store is closed, one-fourth of its direct fixed costs will continue. Thus, the segment margin that should be used to calculate the effect of its closing on Korbin's operating income is $6,000 {$36,000 contribution margin – [$40,000 direct fixed costs × (1.0 – .25)]}. In addition, the sales (and contribution margin) of the Urban Store will decline by 10% if the Suburban store closes. A 10% reduction in Urban's $48,000 contribution margin will reduce income by $4,800. Accordingly, the effect of closing the Suburban Store is to decrease operating income by $10,800 ($6,000 + $4,800).
Answer (B) is incorrect because $(6,000) overlooks the decline in profitability at the Urban Store. Answer (C) is incorrect because $(1,200) assumes that the effect on the Urban Store is a $4,800 increase in contribution margin. Answer (D) is incorrect because profits will decline.

13. Korbin is considering a promotional campaign at the Suburban Store that would not affect the Urban Store. Increasing annual promotional expense at the Suburban Store by $60,000 in order to increase this store's sales by 10% would result in a monthly increase (decrease) in Korbin's operating income during the year (rounded) of

A. $(5,000)

B. $(1,400)

C. $487

D. $7,000

Answer (B) is correct. *(CMA, adapted)*
REQUIRED: The effect on monthly income of an advertising campaign.
DISCUSSION: The $60,000 advertising campaign will increase direct fixed costs by $5,000 per month ($60,000 ÷ 12). Sales and contribution margin will also increase by 10%. Hence, the contribution margin for the Suburban Store will increase by $3,600 ($36,000 × 10%), and income will decline by $1,400 ($5,000 – $3,600).
Answer (A) is incorrect because $(5,000) is the monthly advertising cost. Answer (C) is incorrect because the contribution margin of the Suburban Store will increase by $3,600, which is $1,400 less than the increased advertising cost. Answer (D) is incorrect because $7,000 omits the 10% increase in variable costs from the calculation.

14. One-half of the Suburban Store's dollar sales are from items sold at variable cost to attract customers to the store. Korbin is considering the deletion of these items, a move that would reduce the Suburban Store's direct fixed expenses by 15% and result in a 20% loss of Suburban Store's remaining sales volume. This change would not affect the Urban Store. A decision by Korbin to eliminate the items sold at cost would result in a monthly increase (decrease) in Korbin's operating income of

A. $(5,200)

B. $(1,200)

C. $(7,200)

D. $2,000

Answer (B) is correct. *(CMA, adapted)*
REQUIRED: The effect on monthly income of eliminating sales made at variable cost.
DISCUSSION: If 50% of the Suburban Store's sales are at variable cost, its contribution margin (sales – variable costs) must derive wholly from sales of other items. However, eliminating sales at variable cost reduces other sales by 20%. Thus, the effect is to reduce the contribution margin to $28,800 ($36,000 × .8). Moreover, fixed costs will be reduced by 15% to $34,000 ($40,000 × .85). Consequently, the new segment margin is $(5,200) ($34,000 direct fixed costs – $28,800 contribution margin), a decrease of $1,200 [$(5,200) – $(4,000)].
Answer (A) is incorrect because $(5,200) is the new segment margin. Answer (C) is incorrect because $(7,200) is the reduction in the Suburban Store's contribution margin. Answer (D) is incorrect because operating income must decrease.

15. Polar Company sells refrigeration components both in the U.S. and to a subsidiary located in France. One of the components, Part No. 456, has a variable manufacturing cost of $30. The part can be sold domestically or shipped to the French subsidiary for use in the manufacture of a residential sub-assembly. Relevant data with regard to Part No. 456 are shown below.

Part No. 456

Domestic selling price	$65
Shipping charges to France	15
Cost of acquiring Part No. 456 in France	75
French residential subassembly:	
Sales price	170
Other additional manufacturing costs	55
Units shipped to France	150,000*

*If deemed preferable, these units could be sold in the U.S.

Polar's applicable income tax rates are 40% in the U.S. and 70% in France.

Polar will transfer Part No. 456 to the French subsidiary at either variable manufacturing cost or the domestic market price. On the basis of this information, which one of the following strategies should be recommended to Polar's management?

A. Transfer 150,000 units at $30 and the French subsidiary pays the shipping costs.

B. Transfer 150,000 units at $65 and the French subsidiary pays the shipping costs.

C. Sell 150,000 units in the U.S. and the French subsidiary obtains Part No. 456 in France.

D. Transfer 150,000 units at $65 and have the U.S. company absorb the shipping costs.

Answer (C) is correct. *(CMA, adapted)*
REQUIRED: The best strategy for use of a component if a company has the option of selling it domestically or including it in a product sold by a foreign subsidiary.
DISCUSSION: If the 150,000 components are sold separately in the U.S., the after-tax profit per unit will be $21 [($65 – $30) × .6]. The French subsidiary will then purchase 150,000 components domestically to include in the subassembly. The per-unit profit on sales of the subassembly will be $12 [($170 – $75 – $55) × .3]. The total per-unit profit for the consolidated entity from these transactions will therefore be $33 ($21 + $12).
Answer (A) is incorrect because, if the components are transferred at cost, no tax will be paid in the U.S., and the per-unit tax on French sales of the subassembly will be $49 [($170 – $30 – $15 – $55) × .7]. Thus, the consolidated entity's per-unit profit will be $21 ($170 – $30 – $15 – $55 – $49). Answer (B) is incorrect because, if the transfer is at $65, U.S. tax per unit will be $14 [($65 – $30) × .4], and the French tax per unit will be $24.50 [($170 – $65 – $15 – $55) × .7]. The consolidated entity's per-unit profit will therefore be $31.50 ($170 – $30 – $15 – $55 – $14 – $24.50). Answer (D) is incorrect because, if the transfer is at $65 and the U.S. parent pays the shipping costs, the U.S. tax per unit will be $8 [($65 – $30 – $15) × .4], and the French tax per unit will be $35 [($170 – $65 – $55) × .7]. The consolidated entity's per-unit profit will be $27 ($170 – $30 – $15 – $55 – $8 – $35).

16. Listed below are a company's monthly unit costs to manufacture and market a particular product.

Manufacturing costs:	
Direct materials	$2.00
Direct labor	2.40
Variable indirect	1.60
Fixed indirect	1.00
Marketing costs:	
Variable	2.50
Fixed	1.50

The company must decide to continue making the product or buy it from an outside supplier. The supplier has offered to make the product at the same level of quality that the company can make it. Fixed marketing costs would be unaffected, but variable marketing costs would be reduced by 30% if the company were to accept the proposal. What is the maximum amount per unit that the company can pay the supplier without decreasing operating income?

A. $8.50

B. $6.75

C. $7.75

D. $5.25

Answer (B) is correct. *(CMA, adapted)*
REQUIRED: The maximum amount paid to an outside supplier without decreasing operating income.
DISCUSSION: The company's avoidable unit costs total $6.75 [($2.00 DM + $2.40 DL + $1.60 VOH) + ($2.50 variable marketing costs × .3)]. Hence, it will at least break even by paying no more than $6.75.
Answer (A) is incorrect because $8.50 assumes that all variable marketing costs are avoidable. Answer (C) is incorrect because $7.75 assumes that fixed manufacturing costs of $1 are avoidable. Answer (D) is incorrect because $5.25 results from subtracting the savings in marketing costs from the manufacturing savings.

17. In a make-versus-buy decision, the relevant costs include variable manufacturing costs as well as

- A. Factory management costs.
- B. General office costs.
- C. Avoidable fixed costs.
- D. Depreciation costs.

Answer (C) is correct. *(CMA, adapted)*
REQUIRED: The relevant costs in a make-versus-buy decision.
DISCUSSION: The relevant costs in a make-versus-buy decision are those that differ between the two decision choices. These costs include any variable costs plus any avoidable fixed costs. Avoidable fixed costs will not be incurred if the "buy" decision is selected.
Answer (A) is incorrect because factory management costs are unlikely to differ regardless of which decision is selected. Answer (B) is incorrect because general office costs are unlikely to differ regardless of which decision is selected. Answer (D) is incorrect because depreciation costs are unlikely to differ regardless of which decision is selected.

18. Laurel Corporation has its own cafeteria with the following annual costs:

Food	$100,000
Labor	75,000
Overhead	110,000
Total	$285,000

The overhead is 40% fixed. Of the fixed overhead, $25,000 is the salary of the cafeteria supervisor. The remainder of the fixed overhead has been allocated from total company overhead. Assuming the cafeteria supervisor will remain and Laurel will continue to pay his/her salary, the maximum cost Laurel will be willing to pay an outside firm to service the cafeteria is

- A. $285,000
- B. $175,000
- C. $219,000
- D. $241,000

Answer (D) is correct. *(CMA, adapted)*
REQUIRED: The maximum that could be paid.
DISCUSSION: Given that overhead is 40% fixed, $66,000 ($110,000 × 60%) is variable, and $44,000 is fixed. Of the latter amount, $25,000 is attributable to the supervisor's salary. The $19,000 remainder is allocated from total company overhead and is unavoidable. Assuming the company will continue to pay the supervisor's salary if an outside firm services the cafeteria, the total fixed overhead is not an avoidable (incremental) cost. Thus, the total avoidable cost of the cafeteria's operation is $241,000 ($100,000 food + $75,000 labor + $66,000 VOH). This amount is the savings from hiring an outside firm. Accordingly, it is also the maximum that Laurel should be willing to pay the outside firm.
Answer (A) is incorrect because $285,000 is greater than the avoidable cost of operating the cafeteria. Answer (B) is incorrect because the company can pay more than $175,000. Its overhead costs are avoidable. Answer (C) is incorrect because the company can pay more than $219,000.

19. Power Systems, Inc. manufactures jet engines for the United States armed forces on a cost-plus basis. The cost of a particular jet engine the company manufactures is shown as follows:

Direct materials	$200,000
Direct labor	150,000
Overhead:	
Supervisor's salary	20,000
Fringe benefits on direct labor	15,000
Depreciation	12,000
Rent	11,000
Total cost	$408,000

If production of this engine were discontinued, the production capacity would be idle, and the supervisor would be laid off. When asked to bid on the next contract for this engine, the minimum unit price that Power Systems should bid is

- A. $408,000
- B. $365,000
- C. $397,000
- D. $385,000

Answer (D) is correct. *(CMA, adapted)*
REQUIRED: The minimum unit price that should be bid.
DISCUSSION: The company will need to cover its variable costs and any other incremental costs. Thus, direct materials ($200,000), direct labor ($150,000), the supervisor's salary ($20,000), and fringe benefits on direct labor ($15,000) are the incremental unit costs of manufacturing the engines. The breakeven price is therefore $385,000 ($200,000 + $150,000 + $20,000 + $15,000).
Answer (A) is incorrect because depreciation and rent are allocated costs that will be incurred even if the contract is lost. Answer (B) is incorrect because the supervisor's salary will have to be covered. The $20,000 salary is an avoidable cost. Answer (C) is incorrect because depreciation is a cost that cannot be avoided.

Questions 20 and 21 are based on the following information. Geary Manufacturing has assembled the data appearing in the next column pertaining to two products. Past experience has shown that the unavoidable fixed manufacturing factory overhead included in the cost per machine hour averages $10. Geary has a policy of filling all sales orders, even if it means purchasing units from outside suppliers.

	Blender	Electric Mixer
Direct materials	$ 6	$11
Direct labor	4	9
Manufacturing overhead at $16 per hour	16	32
Cost if purchased from an outside supplier	20	38
Annual demand (units)	20,000	28,000

20. If 50,000 machine hours are available, and Geary Manufacturing desires to follow an optimal strategy, it should produce

A. 25,000 electric mixers and purchase all other units as needed.

B. 20,000 blenders and 15,000 electric mixers, and purchase all other units as needed.

C. 20,000 blenders and purchase all other units as needed.

D. 28,000 electric mixers and purchase all other units as needed.

Answer (B) is correct. *(CMA, adapted)*
REQUIRED: The optimal strategy with respect to producing or purchasing two products.
DISCUSSION: Sales (20,000 blenders and 28,000 mixers) and total revenue are constant, so the strategy is to minimize total variable cost. Each blender requires 1 machine hour ($16 OH ÷ $16 per hour), and each mixer requires 2 machine hours ($32 OH ÷ $16 per hour). For blenders, the unit variable cost is $16 ($6 DM + $4 DL + $6 VOH). For each blender made, the company saves $4 ($20 – $16), or $4 ($4 ÷ 1 hr.) per unit of the constrained resource. The unit variable cost to make a mixer is $32 ($11 DM + $9 DL + $12 VOH). The savings is $6 per mixer ($38 – $32), or $3 ($6 ÷ 2 hours) per unit of the constrained resource. Thus, as many blenders as possible should be made. If 20,000 hours (20,000 units × 1 hour) are used for blenders, 30,000 hours are available for 15,000 mixers. Total variable cost will be $1,294,000 [(20,000 blenders × $16) + (15,000 mixers × $32) + (13,000 mixers × $38)].
Answer (A) is incorrect because producing 25,000 mixers results in a total variable cost of $1,314,000. Answer (C) is incorrect because producing 20,000 blenders and no mixers increases costs by $90,000 (15,000 units × $6). Answer (D) is incorrect because the company can produce at most 25,000 mixers.

21. With all other things constant, if Geary Manufacturing is able to reduce the direct materials for an electric mixer to $6 per unit, the company should

A. Produce 25,000 electric mixers and purchase all other units as needed.

B. Produce 20,000 blenders and 15,000 electric mixers, and purchase all other units as needed.

C. Produce 20,000 blenders and purchase all other units as needed.

D. Purchase all units as needed.

Answer (A) is correct. *(CMA, adapted)*
REQUIRED: The optimal strategy if direct materials costs for a product are reduced.
DISCUSSION: Reducing unit direct materials cost for mixers from $11 to $6 decreases unit variable cost to $27 ($6 DM + $9 DL + $12 VOH) and increases the cost savings of making a mixer from $6 to $11, or $5.50 per hour ($11 ÷ 2 hours per unit). Given a cost savings per hour for blenders of $4, the company can minimize total variable cost by making 25,000 mixers (50,000 hours capacity ÷ 2). Total variable cost will be $1,189,000 [(25,000 mixers × $27) + (3,000 mixers × $38) + (20,000 blenders × $20)].
Answer (B) is incorrect because producing 20,000 blenders and 15,000 mixers results in a total variable cost of $1,219,000. Answer (C) is incorrect because producing 20,000 blenders results in a total variable cost of $1,384,000. Answer (D) is incorrect because the variable cost of making these items is less than the cost of purchase.

Questions 22 and 23 are based on the following information. Pontotoc Industries manufactures a product that is used as a subcomponent by other manufacturers. It has the following price and cost structure:

Selling price		$ 300
Costs		
Direct materials	40	
Direct labor	30	
Variable manufacturing overhead	24	
Fixed manufacturing overhead	60	
Variable selling	6	
Fixed selling and administrative	20	(180)
Operating margin		$ 120

22. Pontotoc received a special, one-time order for 1,000 of the above parts. Assuming Pontotoc has excess capacity, the minimum unit price for this special, one-time order is in excess of

A. $180

B. $120

C. $100

D. $160

Answer (C) is correct. *(Publisher, adapted)*
REQUIRED: The minimum unit price for a special order when a company has excess manufacturing capacity.
DISCUSSION: In a special order situation, a company with excess capacity has a $0 opportunity cost of filling the special order. Accordingly, it should be willing to sell the product at a price that exceeds its incremental costs. The incremental (relevant) costs for Pontotoc equal the variable costs of $100 ($40 direct materials + $30 direct labor + $24 variable overhead + $6 variable selling costs). Thus, if the selling price is in excess of $100, the company should be willing to accept the order.
Answer (A) is incorrect because, given excess capacity, the total absorption cost of $180 per unit is not relevant. Answer (B) is incorrect because $120 is the normal operating margin, not a cost. Answer (D) is incorrect because $160 includes the fixed manufacturing overhead, an irrelevant cost.

23. Pontotoc received a special, one-time order for 1,000 units of its product. However, Pontotoc has an alternative use for this capacity that will result in a contribution of $20,000. The minimum unit price for this special, one time order is in excess of

A. $200

B. $180

C. $140

D. $120

Answer (D) is correct. *(Publisher, adapted)*
REQUIRED: The minimum unit price for a special order when the company does not have idle capacity.
DISCUSSION: Incremental (relevant) costs include the variable costs of $100 ($40 direct materials + $30 direct labor + $24 variable overhead + $6 variable selling costs). Furthermore, if the company does not have idle capacity, the unit price must cover the opportunity costs as well as the variable costs. Given that the alternative use will generate a $20,000 contribution, the 1,000 special-order units will have to generate at least $20 per unit ($20,000 ÷ 1,000 units) above their variable costs, a total of $120 per unit.
Answer (A) is incorrect because $200 is based on a $20 increment over the total cost on an absorption costing basis. Answer (B) is incorrect because $180 is the total absorption cost. Answer (C) is incorrect because $140 is based on a $20 increment over the operating margin.

24. A company has 7,000 obsolete toys carried in inventory at a manufacturing cost of $6 per unit. If the toys are reworked for $2 per unit, they could be sold for $3 per unit. If the toys are scrapped, they could be sold for $1.85 per unit. Which alternative is more desirable (rework or scrap), and what is the total dollar amount of the advantage of that alternative?

A. Scrap, $5,950.

B. Rework, $36,050.

C. Scrap, $47,950.

D. Rework, $8,050.

Answer (A) is correct. *(CIA, adapted)*
REQUIRED: The total dollar amount of the advantage of the more desirable option.
DISCUSSION: The original manufacturing cost of $6 per unit is a sunk cost that is not relevant to this decision. The relevant costs are the amounts that must be expended now. Hence, selling the toys for scrap has a $5,950 advantage because rework will produce an additional $7,000 [7,000 × ($3 – $2)], whereas the alternative generates an additional $12,950 (7,000 × $1.85).
Answer (B) is incorrect because the original manufacturing cost of $6 should not be added to the sales price. Answer (C) is incorrect because the original manufacturing cost of $6 should not be added to the sales price. Answer (D) is incorrect because $8,050 (rework) does not include the cost of the rework.

25. The ABC Company manufactures components for use in producing one of its finished products. When 12,000 units are produced, the full cost per unit is $35, separated as follows:

Direct materials	$ 5
Direct labor	15
Variable overhead	10
Fixed overhead	5

The XYZ Company has offered to sell 12,000 components to ABC for $37 each. If ABC accepts the offer, some of the facilities currently being used to manufacture the components can be rented as warehouse space for $40,000. However, $3 of the fixed overhead currently applied to each component would have to be covered by ABC's other products. What is the differential cost to the ABC Company of purchasing the components from the XYZ Company?

   A. $8,000

   B. $20,000

   C. $24,000

   D. $44,000

Answer (B) is correct. *(CIA, adapted)*
   REQUIRED: The differential cost of purchasing the components.
   DISCUSSION: Differential (incremental) cost is the difference in total cost between two decisions. The relevant costs do not include unavoidable costs, such as the $3 of fixed overhead. It would cost ABC an additional $20,000 to purchase, rather than manufacture, the components.

Cost to purchase (12,000 × $37)	$444,000
Minus rental income	(40,000)
	$404,000
Cost to manufacture (12,000 × $32)	$384,000
Cost differential	$ 20,000

   Answer (A) is incorrect because $8,000 assumes that $3 of fixed overhead is avoidable. Answer (C) is incorrect because $24,000 compares the full cost of manufacturing with cost to purchase. Answer (D) is incorrect because $44,000 ignores the opportunity cost.

26. American Coat Company estimates that 60,000 special zippers will be used in the manufacture of men's jackets during the next year. Reese Zipper Company has quoted a price of $.60 per zipper. American would prefer to purchase 5,000 units per month, but Reese is unable to guarantee this delivery schedule. To ensure availability of these zippers, American is considering the purchase of all 60,000 units at the beginning of the year. Assuming American can invest cash at 8%, the company's opportunity cost of purchasing the 60,000 units at the beginning of the year is

   A. $1,320

   B. $1,440

   C. $2,640

   D. $2,880

Answer (A) is correct. *(CMA, adapted)*
   REQUIRED: The opportunity cost of purchasing the total annual requirement at the beginning of the year.
   DISCUSSION: The cost of 60,000 zippers is $36,000 (60,000 × $.60). The monthly cost is $3,000 (5,000 × $.60). The company would like to purchase the items monthly, so it will invest at least $3,000 in January. Accordingly, the zippers to be used in January will be purchased at the first of the year even if no special purchase is made. Thus, the incremental advance purchase is only $33,000. Because the alternative arrangement involves a constant monthly expenditure of $3,000, the incremental investment declines by that amount each month. The result is that the average incremental investment for the year is $16,500 ($33,000 ÷ 2), and the opportunity cost of purchasing 60,000 units at the beginning of the year is $1,320 ($16,500 × 8%).
   Answer (B) is incorrect because $1,440 is 8% of $18,000 ($36,000 ÷ 2). Answer (C) is incorrect because $2,640 equals 8% of $33,000. Answer (D) is incorrect because $2,880 equals 8% of $36,000.

Use Gleim's ***CMA Test Prep*** for interactive testing with **over 2,000 additional multiple-choice questions!**

STUDY UNIT SIXTEEN
COST-BASED PRICING

(6 pages of outline)

This study unit is the **last of five** on **decision analysis**. The relative weight assigned to this major topic in Part 3 of the exam is **25%** at **skill level C** (all six skill types required). The five study units are

Study Unit 12: The Decision Process
Study Unit 13: Data Concepts Relevant to Decision Making
Study Unit 14: Cost-Volume-Profit Analysis
Study Unit 15: Marginal Analysis
Study Unit 16: Cost-Based Pricing

After studying the outline and answering the multiple-choice questions, you will have the skills necessary to address the following topics listed in the IMA's Learning Outcome Statements:

Part 3 – Section D.5. Cost-based pricing
The candidate should be able to:

a. demonstrate an understanding of cost-behavior patterns, cost traceability, cost drivers, and cost relevance in measuring the costs of products

b. demonstrate an understanding of how the pricing of a product or service is affected by the demand for the product or service, as well as the supply availability

c. discuss how pricing decisions in the short-run can differ from pricing decisions in the long-run

d. calculate the relevant costs associated with short-run special product purchase orders

e. discuss the importance of stable and predictable costs over an extended time period for long-run pricing decisions

f. demonstrate an understanding of the market-based approach to the pricing decision

g. differentiate between a cost-based approach and a market-based approach to setting prices

h. explain why market-based pricing strategies are generally used when operating in a competitive commodities type market

i. define and demonstrate an understanding of target pricing and target costing

j. identify techniques used to set prices based on understanding customers' perceptions of value, competitors' technologies, products, costs, and financial conditions

k. identify the main steps in developing target prices and target costs

l. define value engineering

m. calculate the target operating income per unit and target cost per unit

n. define and distinguish between a value-added cost and a nonvalue-added cost

o. define the pricing technique of cost plus target rate of return

p. define a product life cycle and life-cycle costing

q. define peak-load pricing

r. evaluate and recommend pricing strategies under specific market conditions or opportunities

16.1 PRICING

1. **Pricing Objectives**

   a. **Profit maximization.** Classical economic theory assumes all firms always select the price that results in the highest profit.

   b. **Target margin maximization.** This objective is stated as a percentage ratio of profits to sales.

   c. **Volume-oriented objectives** set prices to meet target sales volumes or market shares.

   d. **Image-oriented objectives** set prices to enhance the consumer's perception of the firm's merchandise mix.

   e. **Stabilization objectives** set prices to maintain a stable relationship between the firm's prices and the industry leader's prices.

2. **Price-Setting Factors**

   a. **Supply** of and **demand** for products and services are determined by customers' demand, the actions of competitors, and costs.

   b. **Internal Factors**

      1) Marketing objectives may include survival, current profit maximization, market-share leadership, or product-quality leadership.

      2) Marketing-mix strategy.

      3) All relevant costs (variable, fixed, and total costs) in the value chain from R&D to customer service affect the amount of a product that the company is willing to supply. Thus, the lower costs are in relation to a given price, the greater the amount supplied.

      4) Organizational locus of pricing decisions.

      5) Capacity.

         a) For example, under **peak-load pricing**, prices vary directly with capacity usage. Thus, when idle capacity is available, that is, when demand falls, the price of a product or service tends to be lower given a peak-load pricing approach. When demand is high, the price charged will be higher. Peak-load pricing is often used by public utilities.

   c. **External Factors**

      1) The **type of market** (pure competition, monopolistic competition, oligopolistic competition, or pure monopoly) affects the price. For example, a monopolist is usually able to charge a higher price because it has no competitors. However, a company selling a relatively undifferentiated product in a highly competitive market may have no control over price.

      2) Customer perceptions of price and value.

      3) The price-demand relationship.

         a) The demand curve for **normal goods** is ordinarily downward sloping to the right (quantity demanded increases as the price decreases).

         b) However, over some intermediate range of prices, the reaction to a price increase for **prestige goods** is an increase, not a decrease, in the quantity demanded. Within this range, the demand curve is upward sloping. The reason is that consumers interpret the higher price to indicate a better or more desirable product. Above some price level, the relation between price and quantity demanded will again become negatively sloped.

           c)   **Price elasticity of demand.** If demand is price elastic (inelastic), the ratio of the percentage change in quantity demanded to the percentage change in price is greater (less) than 1.0. For example, if customer demand is price elastic, a price increase will result in the reduction of the seller's total revenue.

           4)   Competitors' products, costs, prices, and amounts supplied.

   d.   The **time dimension** for price setting is important. Whether the decision is for the short-term (generally, less than 1 year) or the long-term determines which costs are relevant and whether prices are set to achieve tactical goals or to earn a targeted return on investment. For example, short-term fixed costs may be variable in the long-term, and short-term prices may be raised (lowered) when customer demand is strong (weak).

       1)   From the long-term perspective, maintaining price stability may be preferable to responding to short-term fluctuations in demand. A policy of predictable prices is desirable when the company wishes to cultivate long-term customer relationships. This policy is only feasible, however, when the company can predict its long-term costs.

3.   **General Pricing Approaches**

   a.   **Cost-Based Pricing** (See item 4.)

   b.   **Market-based pricing** involves basing prices on the product's perceived value and competitors' actions rather than on the seller's cost. Nonprice variables in the marketing mix augment the perceived value. For example, a cup of coffee may have a higher price at an expensive restaurant than at a fast-food outlet. Market-based pricing is typical when there are many competitors and the product is undifferentiated, as in many commodities markets, e.g., agricultural products or natural gas.

       1)   For a significant type of market-based pricing, see item 5.

   c.   **Competition-Based Pricing**

       1)   Going-rate pricing bases price largely on competitors' prices.
       2)   Sealed-bid pricing bases price on a company's perception of its competitors' prices.

   d.   **New Product Pricing**

       1)   Price skimming is the practice of setting an introductory price relatively high to attract buyers who are not concerned about price and to recover research and development costs.
       2)   Penetration pricing is the practice of setting an introductory price relatively low to gain deep market penetration quickly.

   e.   **Pricing by Intermediaries**

       1)   Using markups tied closely to the price paid for a product.
       2)   Using markdowns -- a reduction in the original price set on a product.

   f.   **Price Adjustments**

       1)   Geographical Pricing

           a)   FOB-origin pricing charges each customer its actual freight costs.

           b)   A seller that uses uniform delivered pricing charges the same price, inclusive of shipping, to all customers regardless of their location.

               i)   This policy is easy to administer, permits the company to advertise one price nationwide, and facilitates marketing to faraway customers.

      c)   Zone pricing sets differential freight charges for customers on the basis of their location. Customers are not charged actual average freight costs.

      d)   Basing-point pricing charges each customer the freight costs incurred from a specified city to the destination regardless of the actual point of origin of the shipment.

      e)   A seller that uses freight-absorption pricing absorbs all or part of the actual freight charges. Customers are not charged actual delivery costs.

    2)   Discounts and Allowances

      a)   Cash discounts encourage prompt payment, improve cash flows, and avoid bad debts.

      b)   Quantity discounts encourage large volume purchases.

      c)   Trade (functional) discounts are offered to other members of the marketing channel for performing certain services, such as selling.

      d)   Seasonal discounts are offered for sales out of season. They help smooth production.

      e)   Allowances (e.g., trade-in and promotional allowances) reduce list prices.

    3)   Discriminatory pricing adjusts for differences among customers, the forms of a product, or locations.

    4)   Psychological pricing is based on consumer psychology. For example, consumers who cannot judge quality may assume higher prices correlate with higher quality.

    5)   Promotional pricing temporarily reduces prices below list or even cost to stimulate sales.

    6)   Value pricing entails redesigning products to improve quality without raising prices or offering the same quality at lower prices.

    7)   International pricing adjusts prices to local conditions.

  g. **Product-Mix Pricing**

    1)   Product-line pricing sets price steps among the products in the line based on costs, consumer perceptions, and competitors' prices.

    2)   Optional-product pricing requires the firm to choose which products to offer as accessories and which as standard features of a main product.

    3)   Captive-product pricing involves products that must be used with a main product, such as razor blades with a razor. Often the main product is relatively cheap, but the captive products have high markups.

    4)   By-product pricing usually sets prices at any amount in excess of storing and delivering by-products. Such prices allow the seller to reduce the costs and therefore the prices of the main products.

    5)   Product-bundle pricing entails selling combinations of products at a price lower than the combined prices of the individual items. This strategy promotes sales of items consumers might not otherwise buy if the price is low enough. An example is season tickets for sports events.

  h. Certain pricing tactics are illegal. For example, pricing products below cost to destroy competitors **(predatory pricing)** is illegal.

    1)   The U.S. Supreme Court has held that a price is predatory if it is below an appropriate measure of costs and the seller has a reasonable prospect of recovering its losses in the future through higher prices or greater market share.

2) Also illegal is **price discrimination** among customers. The **Robinson-Patman Act of 1936** makes such pricing illegal if it has the effect of lessening competition, although price discrimination may be permissible if the competitive situation requires it and if costs of serving some customers are lower. The Robinson-Patman Act applies to manufacturers, not service entities.

3) Another improper form of pricing is **collusive pricing**. Companies may not conspire to restrict output and set artificially high prices. Such behavior violates antitrust laws.

4) Still another inappropriate pricing tactic is selling below cost in other countries **(dumping)**, which may trigger retaliatory tariffs and other sanctions.

4. **Cost-based pricing** begins with a cost determination followed by setting a price that will recover the value chain costs and provide the desired return on investment. When an industry is characterized by significant product differentiation, e.g., the automobile industry, cost-based and market-based pricing approaches are combined.

   a. Basing prices on cost assumes that costs can be correctly determined. Thus, cost-behavior patterns, cost traceability, and cost drivers become important determinants of profitability.

   b. A **cost-plus price** equals the cost plus a markup. Cost may be defined in many ways. Most companies use either absorption manufacturing cost or total cost when calculating the price. Variable costs may be used as the basis for cost, but then fixed costs must be covered by the markup.

      1) Following are four commonly used cost-plus pricing formulas:

         a) $Price = Total\ cost + (Total\ cost \times Markup\ percentage)$

         b) $Price = Abs.\ mfg.\ cost + (Abs.\ mfg.\ cost \times Markup\ percentage)$

         c) $Price = Var.\ mfg.\ cost + (Var.\ mfg.\ cost \times Markup\ percentage)$

         d) $Price = Tot.\ var.\ cost + (Tot.\ var.\ cost \times Markup\ percentage)$

      2) The costs of unused capacity in production facilities, distribution channels, marketing organizations, etc., are ordinarily not assignable to products or services on a cause-and-effect basis, so their inclusion in overhead rates may distort pricing decisions. Including the fixed costs of unused capacity in a cost-based price results in higher prices and in what is known as the **downward (black hole) demand spiral**.

         a) As higher prices depress demand, unused capacity costs and the fixed costs included in prices will increase. As a result of still higher prices, demand will continue to spiral downward. One way to avoid this problem is not to assign unused capacity costs to products or services. The result should be better operating decisions and better evaluation of managerial performance.

5. A **target price** is the expected market price for a product or service, given the company's knowledge of its consumers' perceptions of value and competitors' responses.

   a. The company's contacts with its customers and its market research studies provide information about consumers' perceptions of value.

   b. The company must also gain information about competitors' potential responses by learning about their technological expertise, products, costs, and financial positions. This information may be obtained from competitors' customers, suppliers, employees, and financial reports. Reverse engineering of their products is also possible.

   c. Subtracting the unit target operating income determines the long-term unit **target cost**. Relevant costs are all future value-chain costs whether variable or fixed.

1) Because it may be lower than the full cost of the product, the target cost may not be achievable unless the company adopts comprehensive cost-reduction measures.

2) The Japanese concept of **kaizen** is relevant to target costing. A policy of seeking continuous improvement in all phases of company activities facilitates cost reduction, often through numerous minor changes.

3) **Value engineering** is a means of reaching targeted cost levels. It is a systematic approach to assessing all aspects of the **value chain** cost buildup for a product: R&D, design of products, design of processes, production, marketing, distribution, and customer service. The purpose is to minimize costs without sacrificing customer satisfaction.

   a) Value engineering requires identifying value-added and nonvalue-added costs. **Value-added costs** are costs of activities that cannot be eliminated without reducing the quality, responsiveness, or quantity of the output required by a customer or the organization.

   b) Value engineering also requires distinguishing between cost incurrence and locked-in costs. **Cost incurrence** is the actual use of resources, whereas **locked-in (designed-in) costs** will result in use of resources in the future as a result of past decisions. Traditional cost accounting focuses on budget comparisons, but value engineering emphasizes controlling costs at the design stage before they are locked in.

6. The **product life cycle** begins with R&D, proceeds through the introduction and growth stages, continues into the product's mature stage, and finally ends with the harvest or decline stage and the final provision of customer support. **Life-cycle costing** is sometimes used as a basis for cost planning and product pricing. Life-cycle costing estimates a product's revenues and expenses over its expected life cycle. The result is to highlight upstream and downstream costs in the cost planning process that often receive insufficient attention. Emphasis is on the need to price products to cover all costs, not just production costs.

   a. A concept related to life-cycle cost that is relevant to pricing is **whole-life cost**, which equals life-cycle costs plus after-purchase costs (operating, support, repair, and disposal) incurred by customers. Reduction of whole-life costs is a strong competitive weapon. Customers may pay a premium for a product with low after-purchase costs.

7. Stop and review! You have completed the outline for this subunit. Study multiple-choice questions 1 through 36 beginning on page 387.

16.2 CORE CONCEPTS

Pricing

- **Pricing objectives** include profit maximization, target margin maximization, volume-oriented objectives, image-oriented objectives, and stabilization objectives.

- **Factors** to consider in pricing decisions are: supply and demand; internal factors, such as marketing-mix strategy and relevant costs; and external factors, such as market type (pure competition, monopolistic competition, etc.) and customer perceptions.

- **Pricing approaches** include cost-based pricing, market-based pricing, competition-based pricing, new product pricing, pricing by intermediaries, and product-mix pricing.

- A **target price** is the expected market price for a product or service, given the company's knowledge of its consumers' perceptions of value and competitors' responses.

- **Life-cycle costing** estimates a product's revenues and expenses over its expected life cycle, from R&D all the way through product phaseout.

QUESTIONS

16.1 Pricing

1. Which one of the graphs depicts the demand curve for prestige goods?

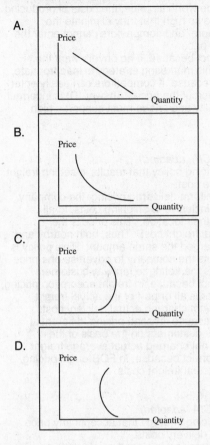

A.

Price

Quantity

B.

Price

Quantity

C.

Price

Quantity

D.

Price

Quantity

Answer (C) is correct. *(CIA, adapted)*
REQUIRED: The graph depicting the demand curve for prestige goods.
DISCUSSION: Over some intermediate range of prices, the reaction to a price increase for prestige goods is an increase, not a decrease, in the quantity demanded. Within this range, the demand curve is upward sloping. The reason is that consumers interpret the higher price to indicate a better or more desirable product. Above some price level, the relation between price and quantity demanded will again become negatively sloped.
Answer (A) is incorrect because this graph describes the familiar, negatively sloped relation between price charged and the resulting demand level for normal goods. Answer (B) is incorrect because the demand curve can be linear or curvilinear. Answer (D) is incorrect because this demand curve has the same basic shape as the demand curve for prestige goods, but it bends the wrong way. As prices increase, quantity demanded first falls and then rises in this graph.

2. Buyer-based pricing involves

A. Adding a standard markup to the cost of the product.

B. Determining the price at which the product will earn a target profit.

C. Basing prices on the product's perceived value.

D. Basing prices on competitors' prices.

Answer (C) is correct. *(CIA, adapted)*
REQUIRED: The definition of buyer-based pricing.
DISCUSSION: Buyer-based pricing involves basing prices on the product's perceived value rather than on the seller's cost. Nonprice variables in the marketing mix augment the perceived value. For example, a cup of coffee may have a higher price at an expensive restaurant than at a fast food outlet.
Answer (A) is incorrect because adding a standard markup to the cost of the product is cost-plus pricing. Answer (B) is incorrect because determining the price at which the product will earn a target profit is target profit pricing. Answer (D) is incorrect because basing prices on competitors' prices is going-rate pricing.

3. Which of the following price adjustment strategies is designed to stabilize production for the selling firm?

A. Cash discounts.

B. Quantity discounts.

C. Functional discounts.

D. Seasonal discounts.

Answer (D) is correct. *(CIA, adapted)*
REQUIRED: The price adjustment strategy intended to stabilize production.
DISCUSSION: Seasonal discounts are designed to smooth production by the selling firm. For example, a ski manufacturer offers seasonal discounts to retailers in the spring and summer to encourage early ordering.
Answer (A) is incorrect because cash discounts encourage prompt payment. Answer (B) is incorrect because quantity discounts encourage large volume purchases. Answer (C) is incorrect because functional or trade discounts are provided to channel members in return for the performance of certain functions, such as selling, storing, and record keeping.

4. Market-skimming pricing strategies could be appropriate when

    A. No buyers want the product at a high price.

    B. The costs of producing a small volume are low.

    C. Competitors can easily enter the market.

    D. The product is of poor quality.

Answer (B) is correct. *(CIA, adapted)*
   REQUIRED: The circumstances under which market-skimming pricing strategies are appropriate.
   DISCUSSION: Market-skimming pricing is used when a new product is introduced at the highest price possible given the benefits of the product. For market skimming to work, the product must appear to be worth its price, the costs of producing a small volume cannot be so high that they eliminate the advantage of charging more, and competitors cannot enter the market and undercut the price.
   Answer (A) is incorrect because, if no buyers want the product at a high price, this marketing strategy is inappropriate. Answer (C) is incorrect because, if competitors can easily enter the market, they can undercut the price. Answer (D) is incorrect because the product quality and image must support a high price.

5. Which of the following pricing policies involves the selling company setting freight charges to customers at the actual average freight cost?

    A. Freight absorption pricing.

    B. Uniform delivered pricing.

    C. Zone pricing.

    D. FOB-origin pricing.

Answer (B) is correct. *(CIA, adapted)*
   REQUIRED: The pricing policy that results in setting freight charges at actual average cost.
   DISCUSSION: In uniform delivered pricing, the company charges the same price, inclusive of shipping costs, to all customers regardless of their location. This price is the company's average actual freight cost. Thus, both nearby and distant customers are charged the same amount. This policy is easy to administer, permits the company to advertise one price nationwide, and facilitates marketing to faraway customers.
   Answer (A) is incorrect because, in freight absorption pricing, the selling company absorbs all or part of the actual freight charges. Customers are not charged actual delivery costs. Answer (C) is incorrect because, in zone pricing, differential freight charges are set for customers on the basis of their location. Customers are not charged actual average freight costs. Answer (D) is incorrect because, in FOB-origin pricing, each customer pays its actual freight costs.

6. In which product-mix pricing strategy is it appropriate for the seller to accept any price that exceeds the storage and delivery costs for the product?

    A. By-product pricing.

    B. Optional-product pricing.

    C. Captive-product pricing.

    D. Product-bundle pricing.

Answer (A) is correct. *(CIA, adapted)*
   REQUIRED: The pricing strategy that accepts any price greater than storage and delivery costs.
   DISCUSSION: A by-product is a product of relatively minor importance generated during the production of one or more other products. Its production entails no additional costs. Any amount received above the storage and delivery costs for a by-product allows the seller to reduce the main product's price to make it more competitive.
   Answer (B) is incorrect because optional products are offered for sale along with the main product. They are unlikely to have a zero production cost, so the seller must receive a price above their storage and delivery costs. Answer (C) is incorrect because captive products must be used along with the main product, such as film for use with a camera. Sellers often make their profits on the captive products rather than on the main product, which is sold at a low price. The captive products therefore will be priced well above the storage and delivery costs. Answer (D) is incorrect because product bundles are combinations of products sold together at a reduced price, such as season tickets for a theater. Products are bundled to promote the sale of certain items that consumers might not otherwise purchase. The combined price of the bundle must be low enough to encourage consumers to buy the bundle but must recover production costs and provide some profit for the seller, so the price must exceed storage and delivery costs.

7. Several surveys point out that most managers use full product costs, including unit fixed costs and unit variable costs, in developing cost-based pricing. Which one of the following is least associated with cost-based pricing?

    A. Price stability.

    B. Price justification.

    C. Target pricing.

    D. Fixed-cost recovery.

Answer (C) is correct. *(CMA, adapted)*
    REQUIRED: The concept least associated with cost-based pricing.
    DISCUSSION: A target price is the expected market price of a product, given the company's knowledge of its customers and competitors. Hence, under target pricing, the sales price is known before the product is developed. Subtracting the unit target profit margin determines the long-term unit target cost. If cost-cutting measures do not permit the product to be made at or below the target cost, it will be abandoned.
    Answer (A) is incorrect because full-cost pricing promotes price stability. It limits the ability to cut prices. Answer (B) is incorrect because full-cost pricing provides evidence that the company is not violating antitrust laws against predatory pricing. Answer (D) is incorrect because full-cost pricing has the advantage of recovering the full long-term costs of the product. In the long term, all costs are relevant.

8. If a U.S. manufacturer's price in the U.S. market is below an appropriate measure of costs and the seller has a reasonable prospect of recovering the resulting loss in the future through higher prices or a greater market share, the seller has engaged in

    A. Collusive pricing.

    B. Dumping.

    C. Predatory pricing.

    D. Price discrimination.

Answer (C) is correct. *(Publisher, adapted)*
    REQUIRED: The pricing strategy characterized by charging a price that is below an appropriate measure of costs when the seller reasonably expects to recover the loss through higher prices or a greater market share.
    DISCUSSION: Predatory pricing is intentionally pricing below cost to eliminate competition and reduce supply. Federal statutes and many state laws prohibit the practice. The U.S. Supreme Court has held that pricing is predatory when two conditions are met: (1) The seller's price is below "an appropriate measure of its costs," and (2) it has a reasonable prospect of recovering the resulting loss through higher prices or greater market share.
    Answer (A) is incorrect because collusive pricing involves a conspiracy to set higher prices. Answer (B) is incorrect because dumping is defined under U.S. law as sale by a non-U.S. company in the U.S. market of a product below its market value in the country where it was produced. Such sale is illegal if it threatens material injury to a U.S. industry. Answer (D) is incorrect because price discrimination entails charging different prices to different customers for essentially the same product if the effect is to lessen competition substantially; to tend to create a monopoly; or to injure, destroy, or prevent competition.

9. Fulford Company applies the target pricing and costing approach. The following information about costs and revenues of Fulford's product are available for the year just ended:

Unit sales	60,000
Unit selling price	$ 400
Cost of goods sold	13,200,000
Value-chain operating costs excluding production	7,920,000

Fulford plans to increase unit sales to 80,000 by reducing the product's unit price to $320. If Fulford desires a unit target operating income of 12%, by what amount must it reduce the full cost per unit?

    A. $32.00

    B. $38.40

    C. $70.40

    D. $80.00

Answer (C) is correct. *(Publisher, adapted)*
    REQUIRED: The necessary reduction in the full cost per unit.
    DISCUSSION: Unit target operating income is $38.40 ($320 unit target price × 12%). Hence, the unit target full cost is $281.60 ($320 – $38.40). The current full cost per unit is $352.00 [($13,200,000 CGS + $7,920,000 other value chain operating costs) ÷ 60,000 units sold], so the necessary reduction in the full cost per unit is $70.40 ($352.00 – $281.60).
    Answer (A) is incorrect because $32.00 equals the current full cost per unit minus the new unit target price. Answer (B) is incorrect because $38.40 is the unit target operating income. Answer (D) is incorrect because $80.00 equals the change in the unit price.

10. A company's product has an expected 4-year life cycle from research, development, and design through its withdrawal from the market. Budgeted costs are

Upstream costs (R&D, design)	$2,000,000
Manufacturing costs	3,000,000
Downstream costs (marketing, distribution, customer service)	1,200,000
After-purchase costs	1,000,000

The company plans to produce 200,000 units and price the product at 125% of the whole-life unit cost. Thus, the budgeted unit selling price is

A. $15

B. $31

C. $36

D. $45

Answer (D) is correct. *(Publisher, adapted)*
REQUIRED: The unit selling price.
DISCUSSION: Whole-life costs include after-purchase costs (operating, support, repair, and disposal) incurred by customers as well as life-cycle costs (R&D, design, manufacturing, marketing, distribution, and research). Hence, the budgeted unit whole-life cost is $36 [($2,000,000 + $3,000,000 + $1,200,000 + $1,000,000) ÷ 200,000 units], and the budgeted unit selling price is $45 ($36 × 125%).
Answer (A) is incorrect because $15 is the budgeted unit manufacturing cost. Answer (B) is incorrect because $31 is the budgeted unit life-cycle cost. Answer (C) is incorrect because $36 is the budgeted unit whole-life cost.

11. The primary difference between centralization and decentralization is

A. Separate offices for all managers.

B. Geographical separation of divisional headquarters and central headquarters.

C. The extent of freedom of decision making by many levels of management.

D. The relative size of the firm.

Answer (C) is correct. *(Publisher, adapted)*
REQUIRED: The primary difference between centralization and decentralization.
DISCUSSION: The primary distinction is in the degree of freedom of decision making by managers at many levels. In decentralization, decision making is at as low a level as possible. The premise is that the local manager can make more informed decisions than a centralized manager. Centralization assumes decision making must be consolidated so that activities throughout the organization may be more effectively coordinated. In most organizations, a mixture of these approaches is best.
Answer (A) is incorrect because whether all managers have separate offices is a trivial issue. Answer (B) is incorrect because geographical separation is possible in a centralized environment. Answer (D) is incorrect because relative size is a secondary factor in determining whether to centralize.

12. Which of the following is most likely to be a disadvantage of decentralization?

A. Lower-level employees will develop less rapidly than in a centralized organization.

B. Lower-level employees will complain of not having enough to do.

C. Top management will have less time available to devote to unique problems.

D. Lower-level managers may make conflicting decisions.

Answer (D) is correct. *(CIA, adapted)*
REQUIRED: The item most likely to be a disadvantage of decentralization.
DISCUSSION: The disadvantages of decentralization include a tendency to focus on short-run results to the detriment of the long-term health of the entity, an increased risk of loss of control by top management, the increased difficulty of coordinating interdependent units, and less cooperation and communication among competing decentralized unit managers.
Answer (A) is incorrect because decentralization encourages development of lower-level managers. They will have greater responsibilities and authority. Answer (B) is incorrect because more tasks will be delegated to lower-level employees. Answer (C) is incorrect because top managers will be freed from operating problems.

13. Which of the following is not a cost of decentralization?

A. Dysfunctional decision making owing to disagreements of managers regarding overall goals and subgoals of the individual decision makers.

B. A decreased understanding of the overall goals of the organization.

C. Increased costs for developing the information system.

D. Decreased costs of corporate-level staff services and management talent.

Answer (D) is correct. *(Publisher, adapted)*
REQUIRED: The item not a cost of decentralization.
DISCUSSION: The costs of centralized staff may actually decrease under decentralization. On the other hand, the corporate staff and the various services they provide may have to be duplicated in various divisions, thereby increasing overall costs. Suboptimal decisions may result from disharmony among organizational goals, subgoals of the division, and the individual goals of managers. The overall goals of the firm may more easily be misunderstood because individual managers may not see the larger picture. Moreover, the information system necessary for adequate reporting in a decentralized mode will tend toward redundancy, which increases costs.
Answer (A) is incorrect because dysfunctional decision making is a cost of decentralization. Answer (B) is incorrect because a decreased understanding of the overall goals of an organization is a cost of decentralization. Answer (C) is incorrect because increased costs for developing the information system is a cost of decentralization.

14. The CEO of a rapidly growing high-technology firm has exercised centralized authority over all corporate functions. Because the company now operates in four states, the CEO is considering the advisability of decentralizing operational control over production and sales. Which of the following conditions probably will result from and be a valid reason for decentralizing?

A. Greater local control over compliance with federal regulations.

B. More efficient use of headquarters staff officials and specialists.

C. Quicker and better operating decisions.

D. Greater economies in purchasing.

Answer (C) is correct. *(CIA, adapted)*
REQUIRED: The condition that would be a valid reason for decentralizing.
DISCUSSION: Decentralization results in greater speed in making operating decisions because they are made by lower-level managers instead of being referred to top management. The quality of operating decisions should also be enhanced, assuming proper training of managers, because those closest to the problems should be the most knowledgeable about them.
Answer (A) is incorrect because compliance with governmental regulations is probably more easily achieved by centralization. A disadvantage of decentralization is the difficulty of assuring uniform action by units of the entity that have substantial autonomy. Answer (B) is incorrect because decentralization may result in duplication of efforts, resulting in less efficient use of headquarters staff officials and specialists. Answer (D) is incorrect because decentralization usually results in a duplication of purchasing efforts.

15. Which one of the following will not occur in an organization that gives managers throughout the organization maximum freedom to make decisions?

A. Individual managers regarding the managers of other segments as they do external parties.

B. Two divisions of the organization having competing models that aim for the same market segments.

C. Delays in securing approval for the introduction of new products.

D. Greater knowledge of the marketplace and improved service to customers.

Answer (C) is correct. *(CMA, adapted)*
REQUIRED: The event that will not occur in a decentralized organization.
DISCUSSION: Decentralization is beneficial because it creates greater responsiveness to the needs of local customers, suppliers, and employees. Managers at lower levels are more knowledgeable about local markets and the needs of customers, etc. A decentralized organization is also more likely to respond flexibly and quickly to changing conditions, for example, by expediting the introduction of new products. Furthermore, greater authority enhances managerial morale and development. Disadvantages of decentralization include duplication of effort and lack of goal congruence.
Answer (A) is incorrect because, when segments are autonomous, other segments are regarded as external parties, e.g., as suppliers, customers, or competitors. Answer (B) is incorrect because autonomous segments may have the authority to compete in the same markets. Answer (D) is incorrect because decentralizing decision making results in improved service. The managers closest to customers are making decisions about customer service.

16. The price that one division of a company charges another division for goods or services provided is called the

A. Market price.

B. Transfer price.

C. Outlay price.

D. Distress price.

Answer (B) is correct.   *(CIA, adapted)*
REQUIRED: The price that one division of a company charges another for goods or services provided.
DISCUSSION: A transfer price is the price charged by one segment of an organization for a product or service supplied to another segment of the same organization.
Answer (A) is incorrect because market price is an approach to determine a transfer price. Answer (C) is incorrect because outlay price is an approach to determine a transfer price. Answer (D) is incorrect because distress price is an approach to determine a transfer price.

17. The most fundamental responsibility center affected by the use of market-based transfer prices is a(n)

A. Production center.

B. Investment center.

C. Cost center.

D. Profit center.

Answer (D) is correct.   *(CMA, adapted)*
REQUIRED: The most fundamental responsibility center affected by the use of market-based transfer prices.
DISCUSSION: Transfer prices are often used by profit centers and investment centers. Profit centers are the more fundamental of these two centers because investment centers are responsible not only for revenues and costs but also for invested capital.
Answer (A) is incorrect because a production center may be a cost center, a profit center, or even an investment center. Transfer prices are not used in a cost center. Transfer prices are used to compute profitability, but a cost center is responsible only for cost control. Answer (B) is incorrect because an investment center is not as fundamental as a profit center. Answer (C) is incorrect because transfer prices are not used in a cost center.

18. Transfer pricing should encourage goal congruence and managerial effort. In a decentralized organization, it should also encourage autonomous decision making. Managerial effort is the

A. Desire and the commitment to achieve a specific goal.

B. Sharing of goals by supervisors and subordinates.

C. Extent to which individuals have the authority to make decisions.

D. Extent of the attempt to accomplish a specific goal.

Answer (D) is correct.   *(Publisher, adapted)*
REQUIRED: The definition of managerial effort.
DISCUSSION: Managerial effort is the extent to which a manager attempts to accomplish a goal. Managerial effort may include psychological as well as physical commitment to a goal.
Answer (A) is incorrect because motivation is the desire and the commitment to achieve a specific goal. Answer (B) is incorrect because goal congruence is the sharing of goals by supervisors and subordinates. Answer (C) is incorrect because autonomy is the extent to which individuals have the authority to make decisions.

19. Goal congruence is the

A. Desire and the commitment to achieve a specific goal.

B. Sharing of goals by supervisors and subordinates.

C. Extent to which individuals have the authority to make decisions.

D. Extent of the attempt to accomplish a specific goal.

Answer (B) is correct.   *(Publisher, adapted)*
REQUIRED: The definition of goal congruence.
DISCUSSION: Goal congruence is agreement on the goals of the organization and/or the segment by both supervisors and subordinates. Performance is assumed to be optimized when the parties understand that personal and segmental goals should be consistent with those of the organization.
Answer (A) is incorrect because motivation is the desire and the commitment to achieve a specific goal. Answer (C) is incorrect because autonomy is the extent to which individuals have the authority to make decisions. Answer (D) is incorrect because managerial effort is the extent of the attempt to accomplish a specific goal.

20. Motivation is the

A. Desire and the commitment to achieve a specific goal.

B. Sharing of goals by supervisors and subordinates.

C. Extent to which individuals have the authority to make decisions.

D. Extent of the attempt to accomplish a specific goal.

Answer (A) is correct. *(Publisher, adapted)*
REQUIRED: The definition of motivation.
DISCUSSION: Motivation is the desire to attain a specific goal (goal congruence) and the commitment to accomplish the goal (managerial effort). Managerial motivation is therefore a combination of managerial effort and goal congruence.
Answer (B) is incorrect because goal congruence is the sharing of goals by supervisors and subordinates. Answer (C) is incorrect because autonomy is the extent to which individuals have the authority to make decisions. Answer (D) is incorrect because managerial effort is the extent of the attempt to accomplish a specific goal.

21. A proposed transfer price may be based upon the outlay cost. Outlay cost plus opportunity cost is the

A. Retail price.

B. Price representing the cash outflows of the supplying division plus the contribution to the supplying division from an outside sale.

C. Price usually set by an absorption-costing calculation.

D. Price set by charging for variable costs plus a lump sum or an additional markup, but less than full markup.

Answer (B) is correct. *(Publisher, adapted)*
REQUIRED: The definition of outlay cost plus opportunity cost.
DISCUSSION: At this price, the supplying division is indifferent as to whether it sells internally or externally. Outlay cost plus opportunity cost therefore represents a minimum acceptable price for a seller. However, no transfer price formula is appropriate in all circumstances.
Answer (A) is incorrect because the retail price is the definition of the market price, assuming an arm's-length transaction. Answer (C) is incorrect because full cost is the price usually set by an absorption-costing calculation. Answer (D) is incorrect because the variable-cost-plus price is the price set by charging for variable costs plus a lump sum or an additional markup, but less than full markup.

22. A proposed transfer price may be a cost-plus price. Variable-cost-plus price is the price

A. On the open market.

B. Representing the cash outflows of the supplying division plus the contribution to the supplying division from an outside sale.

C. Usually set by an absorption-costing calculation.

D. Set by charging for variable costs plus a lump sum or an additional markup, but less than full markup.

Answer (D) is correct. *(Publisher, adapted)*
REQUIRED: The definition of variable-cost-plus price.
DISCUSSION: The variable-cost-plus price is the price set by charging for variable cost plus either a lump sum or an additional markup but less than the full markup price. This permits top management to enter the decision process and dictate that a division transfer at variable cost plus some appropriate amount.
Answer (A) is incorrect because the price on the open market is the definition of the market price. Answer (B) is incorrect because outlay cost plus opportunity cost is the price representing the cash outflows of the supplying division plus the contribution to the supplying division from an outside sale. Answer (C) is incorrect because the full-cost price is the price usually set by an absorption-costing calculation.

23. A proposed transfer price may be based upon the full-cost price. Full-cost price is the price

A. On the open market.

B. Representing the cash outflows of the supplying division plus the contribution to the supplying division from an outside sale.

C. Usually set by an absorption-costing calculation.

D. Set by charging for variable costs plus a lump sum or an additional markup, but less than full markup.

Answer (C) is correct. *(Publisher, adapted)*
REQUIRED: The definition of full-cost price.
DISCUSSION: Full-cost price is the price usually set by an absorption-costing calculation and includes materials, labor, and a full allocation of manufacturing O/H. This full-cost price may lead to dysfunctional behavior by the supplying and receiving divisions, e.g., purchasing from outside sources at a slightly lower price that is substantially above the variable costs of internal production.
Answer (A) is incorrect because the market price is the price on the open market. Answer (B) is incorrect because the outlay cost plus opportunity cost is the price representing the cash outflows of the supplying division plus the contribution to the supplying division from an outside sale. Answer (D) is incorrect because the variable-cost-plus price is the price set by charging for variable costs plus a lump sum or an additional markup, but less than full markup.

24. A limitation of transfer prices based on actual cost is that they

    A. Charge inefficiencies to the department that is transferring the goods.

    B. Can lead to suboptimal decisions for the company as a whole.

    C. Must be adjusted by some markup.

    D. Lack clarity and administrative convenience.

Answer (B) is correct. *(CIA, adapted)*
    REQUIRED: The limitation of transfer prices based on actual cost.
    DISCUSSION: The optimal transfer price of a selling division should be set at a point that will have the most desirable economic effect on the firm as a whole while at the same time continuing to motivate the management of every division to perform efficiently. Setting the transfer price based on actual costs rather than standard costs would give the selling division little incentive to control costs.
    Answer (A) is incorrect because inefficiencies are charged to the buying department. Answer (C) is incorrect because, by definition, cost-based transfer prices are not adjusted by some markup. Answer (D) is incorrect because cost-based transfer prices provide the advantages of clarity and administrative convenience.

25. Brent Co. has intracompany service transfers from Division Core, a cost center, to Division Pro, a profit center. Under stable economic conditions, which of the following transfer prices is likely to be most conducive to evaluating whether both divisions have met their responsibilities?

    A. Actual cost.

    B. Standard variable cost.

    C. Actual cost plus markup.

    D. Negotiated price.

Answer (B) is correct. *(CPA, adapted)*
    REQUIRED: The transfer price likely to be most useful for evaluating both divisions.
    DISCUSSION: A cost center is responsible for costs only. A profit center is responsible for costs and revenues. Hence, the transfer from the cost center must, by definition, be at a cost-based figure. The transfer should be at standard variable cost so as to isolate any variance resulting from Core's operations. Assuming fixed costs are not controllable in the short run, the relevant variance is the difference between actual cost and the standard variable cost.
    Answer (A) is incorrect because actual cost is not appropriate for a transfer price from a cost center to a profit center. Answer (C) is incorrect because, as a cost center, Core will use cost as a transfer price. Answer (D) is incorrect because, as a cost center, Core will use cost as a transfer price.

26. Which of the following is the most significant disadvantage of a cost-based transfer price?

    A. Requires internally developed information.

    B. Imposes market effects on company operations.

    C. Requires externally developed information.

    D. May not promote long-term efficiencies.

Answer (D) is correct. *(CIA, adapted)*
    REQUIRED: The most significant disadvantage of a cost-based transfer price.
    DISCUSSION: A cost-based transfer price is a price charged in an intracompany transaction that covers only the selling subunit's costs. However, by ignoring relevant alternative market prices, a company may pay more than is necessary to produce goods and services internally.
    Answer (A) is incorrect because internally developed information should be developed whether or not transfer prices are used. Answer (B) is incorrect because market effects on company operations are characteristic of a market-based transfer price. Answer (C) is incorrect because externally developed information is needed for a market-based transfer price.

27. A large manufacturing company has several autonomous divisions that sell their products in perfectly competitive external markets as well as internally to the other divisions of the company. Top management expects each of its divisional managers to take actions that will maximize the organization's goals as well as their own goals. Top management also promotes a sustained level of management effort of all of its divisional managers. Under these circumstances, for products exchanged between divisions, the transfer price that will generally lead to optimal decisions for the manufacturing company would be a transfer price equal to the

A. Full cost of the product.

B. Full cost of the product plus a markup.

C. Variable cost of the product plus a markup.

D. Market price of the product.

Answer (D) is correct. *(CIA, adapted)*
REQUIRED: The optimal transfer price.
DISCUSSION: A market-based transfer price promotes goal congruence and sustained management effort. It is also consistent with divisional autonomy. A market transfer price is most appropriate when the market is competitive, interdivisional dependency is low, and buying in the market involves no marginal costs or benefits.
Answer (A) is incorrect because a transfer at full cost means that the selling division will not make a profit. In addition, the selling division may be forgoing profits that could be obtained by selling to outside customers. Thus, full-cost transfer prices can lead to suboptimal decisions. Answer (B) is incorrect because a transfer at full cost plus markup results in no incentive for the selling division to control its costs. Hence, a sustained level of management effort may not be maintained. Answer (C) is incorrect because a transfer at variable cost plus markup has the same weaknesses as full cost plus markup.

28. The Eastern division sells goods internally to the Western division of the same company. The quoted external price in industry publications from a supplier near Eastern is $200 per ton plus transportation. It costs $20 per ton to transport the goods to Western. Eastern's actual market cost per ton to buy the direct materials to make the transferred product is $100. Actual per-ton direct labor is $50. Other actual costs of storage and handling are $40. The company president selects a $220 transfer price. This is an example of

A. Market-based transfer pricing.

B. Cost-based transfer pricing.

C. Negotiated transfer pricing.

D. Cost plus 20% transfer pricing.

Answer (A) is correct. *(CIA, adapted)*
REQUIRED: The type of transfer price.
DISCUSSION: A transfer price is the price charged by one segment of an organization for a product or service supplied to another segment of the same organization. The three basic criteria that the transfer pricing system in a decentralized company should satisfy are to (1) provide information allowing central management to evaluate divisions with respect to total company profit and each division's contribution to profit, (2) stimulate each manager's efficiency without losing each division's autonomy, and (3) motivate each divisional manager to achieve his/her own profit goal in a manner contributing to the company's success. Because the $220 transfer price selected is based on the quoted external price (market), it is an example of market-based transfer pricing.
Answer (B) is incorrect because the cost-based price would be $210 ($100 + $50 + $40 + $20). Answer (C) is incorrect because no negotiations took place. Answer (D) is incorrect because cost plus 20% would be $252 ($210 × 1.20).

29. Which of the following is false about international transfer prices for a multinational firm?

A. Allows firms to attempt to minimize worldwide taxes.

B. Allows the firm to evaluate each division.

C. Provides each division with a profit-making orientation.

D. Allows firms to correctly price products in each country in which it operates.

Answer (D) is correct. *(CIA, adapted)*
REQUIRED: The false statement about international transfer prices.
DISCUSSION: The calculation of transfer prices should be unique to each country. A scheme for calculating transfer prices for a firm may correctly price the firm's product in Country A but not in Country B. The product may be overpriced in Country B, and sales will be lower than anticipated. Alternatively, the product may be underpriced in Country B, and the authorities may allege that the firm is dumping its product there.
Answer (A) is incorrect because properly chosen transfer prices allow firms to minimize taxes by producing various parts of the products in different countries and strategically transferring the parts at various systematically calculated prices. Answer (B) is incorrect because properly chosen transfer prices allocate revenues and expenses to divisions in various countries. These numbers are used as part of the input for the performance evaluation of each division. Answer (C) is incorrect because transfer prices motivate division managers to buy parts and products (from either internal or external suppliers) at the lowest possible prices and to sell their products (to either internal or external customers) at the highest possible prices.

30. A company has two divisions, A and B, each operated as a profit center. A charges B $35 per unit for each unit transferred to B. Other data follow:

A's variable cost per unit	$ 30
A's fixed costs	10,000
A's annual sales to B	5,000 units
A's sales to outsiders	50,000 units

A is planning to raise its transfer price to $50 per unit. Division B can purchase units at $40 each from outsiders, but doing so would idle A's facilities now committed to producing units for B. Division A cannot increase its sales to outsiders. From the perspective of the company as a whole, from whom should Division B acquire the units, assuming B's market is unaffected?

A. Outside vendors.

B. Division A, but only at the variable cost per unit.

C. Division A, but only until fixed costs are covered, then from outside vendors.

D. Division A, despite the increased transfer price.

31. An appropriate transfer price between two divisions of The Stark Company can be determined from the following data:

Fabricating Division

Market price of subassembly	$50
Variable cost of subassembly	$20
Excess capacity (in units)	1,000

Assembling Division

Number of units needed	900

What is the natural bargaining range for the two divisions?

A. Between $20 and $50.

B. Between $50 and $70.

C. Any amount less than $50.

D. $50 is the only acceptable price.

32. Division A of a company is currently operating at 50% capacity. It produces a single product and sells all its production to outside customers for $13 per unit. Variable costs are $7 per unit, and fixed costs are $6 per unit at the current production level. Division B, which currently purchases this product from an outside supplier for $12 per unit, would like to purchase the product from Division A. Division A will operate at 80% capacity to meet outside customers' and Division B's demand. What is the minimum price that Division A should charge Division B for this product?

A. $7.00 per unit.

B. $10.40 per unit.

C. $12.00 per unit.

D. $13.00 per unit.

Answer (D) is correct. *(CIA, adapted)*
REQUIRED: The purchasing decision benefiting the company.
DISCUSSION: Opportunity costs are $0 because A's facilities would be idle if B did not purchase from A. Assuming fixed costs are not affected by the decision, the intracompany sale is preferable from the company's perspective because A's $30 variable unit cost is less than the outside vendor's price of $40.

Answer (A) is incorrect because outside purchase will increase the company's cost of sales by $10 per unit. Answer (B) is incorrect because the transfer price is irrelevant to the decision. It does not affect overall profits. Answer (C) is incorrect because the company is initially concerned with covering variable rather than fixed costs.

Answer (A) is correct. *(CMA, adapted)*
REQUIRED: The appropriate transfer price.
DISCUSSION: An ideal transfer price should permit each division to operate independently and achieve its goals while functioning in the best interest of the overall company. Transfer prices can be determined in a number of ways, including normal market price, negotiated price, variable costs, or full absorption costs. The capacity of the selling division is often a determinant of the ideal transfer price. If the Fabricating Division had no excess capacity, it would charge the Assembling Division the regular market price. However, given excess capacity of 1,000 units, negotiation is possible because any transfer price greater than the variable cost of $20 would absorb some fixed costs and result in increased divisional profits. Thus, any price between $20 and $50 is acceptable to the Fabricating Division. Any price under $50 is acceptable to the Assembling Division because that is the price that would be paid to an outside supplier.

Answer (B) is incorrect because Assembling will not pay more than $50. Answer (C) is incorrect because Fabricating will not be willing to accept less than $20. Answer (D) is incorrect because Fabricating should be willing to accept any price between $20 and $50.

Answer (A) is correct. *(CIA, adapted)*
REQUIRED: The minimum price that should be charged by one division of a company to another.
DISCUSSION: From the seller's perspective, the price should reflect at least its incremental cash outflow (outlay cost) plus the contribution from an outside sale (opportunity cost). Because A has idle capacity, the opportunity cost is $0. Thus, the minimum price Division A should charge Division B is $7.00.

Answer (B) is incorrect because $7.00 is the minimum that should be charged. Answer (C) is incorrect because Division A should not include any fixed costs in its transfer price because Division A has idle capacity. Answer (D) is incorrect because, since Division A has idle capacity, the minimum transfer price should recover Division A's variable (outlay) costs.

Questions 33 through 35 are based on the following information.

Parkside, Inc. has several divisions that operate as decentralized profit centers. Parkside's Entertainment Division manufactures video arcade equipment using the products of two of Parkside's other divisions. The Plastics Division manufactures plastic components, one type that is made exclusively for the Entertainment Division, while other less complex components are sold to outside markets. The products of the Video Cards Division are sold in a competitive market; however, one video card model is also used by the Entertainment Division. The actual costs per unit used by the Entertainment Division are presented in the next column.

	Plastic Components	Video Cards
Direct material	$1.25	$2.40
Direct labor	2.35	3.00
Variable overhead	1.00	1.50
Fixed overhead	.40	2.25
Total cost	$5.00	$9.15

The Plastics Division sells its commercial products at full cost plus a 25% markup and believes the proprietary plastic component made for the Entertainment Division would sell for $6.25 per unit on the open market. The market price of the video card used by the Entertainment Division is $10.98 per unit.

---

33. A per-unit transfer price from the Video Cards Division to the Entertainment Division at full cost, $9.15, would

A. Allow evaluation of both divisions on a competitive basis.

B. Satisfy the Video Cards Division's profit desire by allowing recovery of opportunity costs.

C. Provide no profit incentive for the Video Cards Division to control or reduce costs.

D. Encourage the Entertainment Division to purchase video cards from an outside source.

Answer (C) is correct. *(CMA, adapted)*
REQUIRED: The effect of a full-cost transfer price.
DISCUSSION: A transfer price is the amount one segment of an organization charges another segment for a product. The selling division should be allowed to recover its incremental cost plus the opportunity cost of the transfer. Hence, in a competitive market, the seller should be able to charge the market price. Using full cost as a transfer price provides no incentive to the seller to control production costs.
Answer (A) is incorrect because evaluating the seller is difficult if it can pass along all costs to the buyer. Answer (B) is incorrect because transfers at full cost do not allow for a seller's profit. Answer (D) is incorrect because a full-cost transfer is favorable to the buyer. It is lower than the market price.

34. Assume that the Entertainment Division is able to purchase a large quantity of video cards from an outside source at $8.70 per unit. The Video Cards Division, having excess capacity, agrees to lower its transfer price to $8.70 per unit. This action would

A. Optimize the profit goals of the Entertainment Division while subverting the profit goals of Parkside.

B. Allow evaluation of both divisions on the same basis.

C. Subvert the profit goals of the Video Cards Division while optimizing the profit goals of the Entertainment Division.

D. Optimize the overall profit goals of Parkside.

Answer (D) is correct. *(CMA, adapted)*
REQUIRED: The impact of lowering the transfer price to match an outside seller's price.
DISCUSSION: If the seller has excess capacity, it should lower its transfer price to match the outside offer. This decision optimizes the profits of the company as a whole by allowing for use of capacity that would otherwise be idle.
Answer (A) is incorrect because this action is congruent with the goals of Parkside. The use of idle capacity enhances profits. Answer (B) is incorrect because the transfer is at a loss (relative to full cost) to the seller, although the company as a whole will benefit. Answer (C) is incorrect because the buyer is indifferent as to whether to purchase internally or externally.

35. Assume that the Plastics Division has excess capacity and it has negotiated a transfer price of $5.60 per plastic component with the Entertainment Division. This price will

A. Cause the Plastics Division to reduce the number of commercial plastic components it manufactures.

B. Motivate both divisions as estimated profits are shared.

C. Encourage the Entertainment Division to seek an outside source for plastic components.

D. Demotivate the Plastics Division causing mediocre performance.

Answer (B) is correct. *(CMA, adapted)*
REQUIRED: The effect of using a negotiated transfer price that is greater than full cost but less than market price.
DISCUSSION: Given that the Plastics Division (the seller) has excess capacity, transfers within the company entail no opportunity cost. Accordingly, the transfer at the negotiated price will improve the performance measures of the transferor. Purchasing internally at below the market price also benefits the transferee, so the motivational purpose of transfer pricing is achieved. The goal congruence purpose is also achieved because the internal transaction benefits the company.
Answer (A) is incorrect because this arrangement creates no disincentive for the seller. It will make a profit on every unit transferred. Answer (C) is incorrect because the market price charged by outside sources is higher than the negotiated price. Answer (D) is incorrect because, given idle capacity, selling at any amount in excess of variable cost should motivate the seller.

36. The Alpha Division of a company, which is operating at capacity, produces and sells 1,000 units of a certain electronic component in a perfectly competitive market. Revenue and cost data are as follows:

Sales	$50,000
Variable costs	34,000
Fixed costs	12,000

The minimum transfer price that should be charged to the Beta Division of the same company for each component is

A. $12

B. $34

C. $46

D. $50

Answer (D) is correct.   *(CIA, adapted)*

REQUIRED: The minimum transfer price that should be charged to another division of the same company.

DISCUSSION: In a perfectly competitive market, market price is ordinarily the appropriate transfer price. Because the market price is objective, using it avoids waste and maximizes efficiency. In a perfectly competitive market, the market price equals the minimum transfer price, which is the sum of outlay cost and opportunity cost. Outlay cost is the variable cost per unit, or $34 ($34,000 ÷ 1,000). Opportunity cost is the contribution margin forgone, or $16 ($50 – $34). Thus, the minimum transfer price is $50 ($34 + $16).

Answer (A) is incorrect because, given that Alpha Division has no idle capacity, the transfer price to Beta should be the market price of $50 per unit. Answer (B) is incorrect because the opportunity cost needs to be included. Answer (C) is incorrect because the minimum transfer price equals outlay (variable) costs plus opportunity cost, not variable costs plus fixed costs.

Use Gleim's **CMA Test Prep** for interactive testing with **over 2,000 additional multiple-choice questions**!

STUDY UNIT SEVENTEEN
THE CAPITAL BUDGETING PROCESS

(8 pages of outline)

Management accountants must be able to help management analyze decisions. This involves making cash flow estimates, calculating the time value of money, and being able to apply discounted cash flow concepts, such as net present value and internal rate of return. Non-discounting analysis techniques are also covered on the CMA examination, as are the income tax implications for investment decision analysis. Candidates will also be tested on such things as ranking investment projects, performing risk analysis, and evaluating real options.

This study unit is the **first of four** on **investment decisions**. The relative weight assigned to this major topic in Part 3 of the exam is **20%** at **skill level C** (all six skill types required). The four study units are

Study Unit 17: The Capital Budgeting Process
Study Unit 18: Discounted Cash Flow and Payback
Study Unit 19: Ranking Investment Projects
Study Unit 20: Risk Analysis and Real Options

After studying the outline and answering the multiple-choice questions, you will have the skills necessary to address the following topics listed in the IMA's Learning Outcome Statements:

Part 3 – Section E.1. Capital budgeting process

The candidate should be able to:

    a.   define capital budgeting

    b.   demonstrate an understanding of capital budgeting applications in making decisions for project investments

    c.   identify the steps or stages undertaken in developing and implementing a capital budget for a project

    d.   identify and calculate the relevant cash flows of a capital investment project on both a pretax and after-tax basis

    e.   demonstrate an understanding of how income taxes affect cash flows

    f.   distinguish between cash flows and accounting profits and discuss the relevance to capital budgeting of the following: incremental cash flow, sunk cost, and opportunity cost

    g.   explain the importance of changes in net working capital in the capital budgeting process

    h.   discuss how the effects of inflation are reflected in capital budgeting analysis

    i.   describe the role of the post-audit in the capital budgeting process

17.1 THE CAPITAL BUDGETING PROCESS

1. **Capital budgeting** is the process of planning and controlling investments for **long-term projects**.

    a. It is this long-term aspect of capital budgeting that presents the management accountant with specific challenges.

        1) Most financial and management accounting topics, such as calculating allowance for doubtful accounts or accumulating product costs, concern tracking and reporting activity for a **single accounting or reporting cycle**, such as one month or one year.

        2) By their nature, capital projects affect **multiple accounting periods** and will constrain the organization's financial planning well into the future. Once made, capital budgeting decisions tend to be relatively inflexible.

    b. Capital budgeting applications include:

        1) Buying equipment
        2) Building facilities
        3) Acquiring a business
        4) Developing a product or product line
        5) Expanding into new markets

    c. A firm must accurately **forecast future changes in demand** in order to have the necessary production capacity when demand for its product is strong, without having excess idle capacity when demand slackens.

    d. A capital project usually involves **substantial expenditures**.

        1) Planning is crucial because of possible **changes in capital markets, inflation, interest rates, and the money supply**.

2. **Types of Costs Considered in Capital Budgeting Analysis**

    a. An **avoidable cost** may be eliminated by ceasing an activity or by improving efficiency.

    b. A **common cost** is shared by all options and is not clearly allocable to any one of them.

    c. The **weighted-average cost of capital** is the weighted average of the interest cost of debt (net of tax) and the costs (implicit or explicit) of the components of equity capital to be invested in long-term assets. It represents a required minimum return of a new investment to prevent dilution of owners' interests.

        1) The **desired rate of return** is the minimum that the firm will accept. It may be the opportunity cost of funds, the weighted-average cost of capital, or some other minimum based on, for example, other investment options or the industry average.

    d. A **deferrable cost** may be shifted to the future with little or no effect on current operations.

    e. A **fixed cost** does not vary with the level of activity within the relevant range.

    f. An **imputed cost** may not entail a specified dollar outlay formally recognized by the accounting system, but it is nevertheless relevant to establishing the economic reality analyzed in the decision-making process.

    g. An **incremental cost** is the difference in cost resulting from selecting one option instead of another.

    h. An **opportunity cost** is the benefit forgone, such as the contribution to income, by not selecting the best alternative use of scarce resources.

    i.   **Relevant costs** vary with the action. Other costs are constant and therefore do not affect the decision.

    j.   A **sunk cost** cannot be avoided because an expenditure or an irrevocable decision to incur the cost has been made.

    k.   **Taxes**. As with every other business decision, the tax consequences of a new investment (and possible disinvestment of a replaced asset) must be considered.

        1)   All capital budgeting decisions need to be evaluated on an after-tax basis because taxes may affect decisions differently. Companies that operate in multiple tax jurisdictions may find the decision process more complex. Another possibility is that special tax concessions may be negotiated for locating an investment in a given locale.

3.   **Stages** in the capital budgeting process are:

    a.   **Identification and definition.** Those projects and programs that are needed to attain the entity's objectives are identified and defined.

        1)   For example, a firm that wishes to be the low-cost producer in its industry will be interested in investing in more efficient manufacturing machinery. A company that wishes to quickly expand into new markets will look at acquiring another established firm.

        2)   Defining the projects and programs determines their extent and facilitates cost, revenue, and cash flow estimation.

            a)   This stage is the most difficult.

    b.   **Search.** Potential investments are subjected to a preliminary evaluation by representatives from each function in the entity's value chain.

        1)   Dismal projects are dismissed at this point, while others are passed on for further evaluation.

    c.   **Information-acquisition.** The costs and benefits of the projects that passed the search phase are enumerated.

        1)   **Quantitative financial factors** are given the most scrutiny at this point.

            a)   These include initial investment and periodic cash inflow.

        2)   **Nonfinancial measures, both quantitative and qualitative**, are also identified and addressed.

            a)   Examples include the need for additional training on new equipment and higher customer satisfaction based on improved product quality.

            b)   Also to be considered are uncertainty about technological developments, demand, competitors' actions, governmental regulation, and economic conditions.

    d.   **Selection.** Employing one of the selection models (net present value, internal rate of return, etc.) and relevant nonfinancial measures, the project(s) that will increase shareholder value by the greatest margin are chosen for implementation.

    e.   **Financing.** Sources of funds for selected projects are identified. These can come from the company's operations, the issuance of debt, or the sale of the company's stock.

    f.   **Implementation and monitoring.** Once projects are underway, they must be kept on schedule and within budgetary constraints.

        1)   This step also involves determining whether previously unforeseen problems or opportunities have arisen and what changes in plans are appropriate.

4. Capital budgeting requires choosing among investment proposals. Thus, a ranking procedure for such decisions is needed. The following are **steps in the ranking procedure**:

    a. **Determine the asset cost or net investment.**

        1) The net investment is the net outlay, or gross cash requirement, minus cash recovered from the trade or sale of existing assets, with any necessary adjustments for applicable tax consequences. Cash outflows in subsequent periods also must be considered.

        2) Moreover, the investment required includes funds to provide for increases in **working capital**, for example, the additional receivables and inventories resulting from the acquisition of a new manufacturing plant. This investment in working capital is treated as an initial cost of the investment (a cash outflow) that will be recovered at the end of the project (i.e., the salvage value is equal to the initial cost).

    b. **Calculate estimated cash flows**, period by period, using the acquired assets.

        1) Reliable estimates of cost savings or revenues are necessary.

        2) Net cash flow is the economic benefit or cost, period by period, resulting from the investment.

        3) **Economic life** is the time period over which the benefits of the investment proposal are expected to be obtained, as distinguished from the physical or technical life of the asset involved.

        4) **Depreciable life** is the period used for accounting and tax purposes over which cost is to be systematically and rationally allocated. It is based upon permissible or standard guidelines and may have no particular relevance to economic life. Because depreciation is deductible for income tax purposes and it shields some revenue from taxation, the amount of depreciation is sometimes called a **depreciation tax shield.**

    c. **Relate the cash-flow benefits to their cost** by using one of several methods to evaluate the advantage of purchasing the asset.

    d. **Rank the investments.**

5. **Book rate of return.** A common misstep in regard to capital budgeting is the temptation to gauge the desirability of a project by using accrual accounting numbers instead of cash flows.

    a. Shareholders and financial analysts use GAAP-based numbers because they are readily available.

        1) The measure usually produced this way is called **book rate of return** or **accrual accounting rate of return**.

$$Book\ rate\ of\ return = \frac{GAAP\ net\ income\ from\ investment}{Book\ value\ of\ investment}$$

    b. However, net income and book value are **affected by the company's choices of accounting methods**.

        1) Accountants must choose which expenditures to capitalize versus which to expense immediately. They also choose how quickly to depreciate capitalized assets.

        2) A project's true rate of return cannot be dependent on such bookkeeping decisions.

   c.   Another distortion inherent in comparing a single project's book rate of return to the current one for the company as a whole is that the latter is an **average of all of a firm's capital projects**.

       1)   It reveals nothing about the performance of individual investment choices. Embedded in that number may be a handful of good projects making up for a large number of poor investments.

   d.   For these reasons, book rate of return is an **unsatisfactory guide** to selecting capital projects.

6.   **Relevant cash flows** are a much more reliable guide when judging capital projects, since only they provide a true measure of a project's potential to **affect shareholder value**.

   a.   The relevant cash flows can be divided into **three categories**:

       1)   **Net Initial Investment**

          a)   Purchase of new equipment
          b)   Initial working capital requirements
          c)   After-tax proceeds from disposal of old equipment

       2)   **Annual Net Cash Flows**

          a)   After-tax cash collections from operations (excluding depreciation effect)
          b)   Tax savings from depreciation deductions (depreciation tax shield)

       3)   **Project Termination Cash Flows**

          a)   After-tax proceeds from disposal of new equipment
          b)   After-tax proceeds from recovery of working capital

   b.   EXAMPLE: A company is determining the relevant cash flows for a **potential capital project**. The company has a 40% tax rate.

       1)   Net initial investment:

          a)   The project will require an initial outlay of $500,000 for new equipment.

          b)   The company expects to commit $12,000 of working capital for the duration of the project in the form of increased accounts receivable and inventories.

          c)   Calculating the after-tax proceeds from disposal of the existing equipment is a two-step process.

             i)   First, the book gain or loss is determined.

Disposal value	$ 5,000
Less: book value	(20,000)
Accrual-basis loss on disposal	**$(15,000)**

             ii)   The after-tax effect on cash can then be calculated.

Disposal value	$ 5,000
Add: tax savings on loss ($15,000 × .40)	6,000
After-tax cash inflow from disposal	**$11,000**

          d)   The cash outflow required for this project's net initial investment is therefore $(501,000) [$(500,000) + $(12,000) + $11,000].

2) Annual net cash flows:

    a) The project is expected to generate $100,000 annually from ongoing operations.

        i) However, 40% of this will have to be paid out in the form of income taxes.

Annual cash collections	$100,000
Less: income tax expense ($100,000 × .40)	(40,000)
After-tax cash inflow from operations	**$ 60,000**

    b) The project is slated to last 8 years.

        i) The new equipment will generate $62,500 per year in depreciation charges ($500,000 ÷ 8).

        ii) The old equipment was being depreciated at $20,000 per year and has four years of service life remaining.

        iii) Unlike the income from operations, the higher depreciation charges will generate a tax savings. This is referred to as the **depreciation tax shield**.

        iv) The tax savings generated by the higher depreciation for the first four years is $17,000 [($62,500 − $20,000) × .40] and for the last four years is $25,000 [($62,500 − $0) × .40].

    c) The annual net cash inflow from the project is thus $77,000 ($60,000 + $17,000) for the first four years and $85,000 ($60,000 + $25,000) for the last four years.

3) Project termination cash flows:

    a) The company expects the equipment acquired for the project to fetch $8,000 upon disposal. At that time, it will have a book value of $0.

        i) First, the book gain or loss is determined.

Disposal value	$8,000
Less: book value	0
Accrual-basis gain on disposal	**$8,000**

        ii) The after-tax effect on cash can then be calculated.

Disposal value	$8,000
Less: tax liability on gain ($8,000 × .40)	(3,200)
After-tax cash inflow from disposal	**$4,800**

    b) Once the project is over, the company will recover the $12,000 of working capital it committed to the project.

    c) The net cash inflow upon project termination is therefore $16,800 ($4,800 + $12,000).

c. As the above example indicates, **tax considerations are essential** when considering capital projects.

7. Other important concepts include the following:

  a. Three crucial terms.

    1) An **incremental cash flow** is the difference in cash received or disbursed resulting from selecting one option instead of another.

    2) A **sunk cost** is one that is either already paid or irrevocably committed to incur. Because it is unavoidable and will therefore not vary with the option chosen, it is not relevant to future decisions.

      a) An example is the amount already spent on manufacturing equipment.

    3) An **opportunity cost** is the maximum benefit forgone by using a scarce resource for a given purpose and not for the next-best alternative.

      a) In capital budgeting, the most basic application of this concept is the desire to place the company's limited funds in the most promising capital project(s).

      b) An even more important application is the **shareholders' opportunity cost of capital**. This is the rate of return the company's shareholders could earn by taking their funds and investing them **elsewhere at a similar level of risk**.

        i) Shareholders' opportunity cost of capital is one choice for a firm's hurdle rate.

  b. **Effects of inflation** on capital budgeting.

    1) Inflation raises the hurdle rate. In an inflationary environment, future dollars are worth less than today's dollars. Thus, the firm will require a higher rate of return to compensate.

  c. **Post-investment audits** should be conducted to serve as a control mechanism and to deter managers from proposing unprofitable investments.

    1) Actual-to-expected cash flow comparisons should be made, and unfavorable variances should be explained. The reason may be an inaccurate forecast or implementation problems.

    2) Individuals who supplied unrealistic estimates should have to explain differences. Knowing that a post-investment audit will be conducted may cause managers to provide more realistic forecasts in the future.

    3) The temptation to evaluate the outcome of a project too early must be overcome. Until all cash flows are known, the results can be misleading.

    4) Assessing the receipt of expected nonquantitative benefits is inherently difficult.

8. Stop and review! You have completed the outline for this subunit. Study multiple-choice questions 1 through 28 beginning on page 407.

17.2 CORE CONCEPTS

The Capital Budgeting Process

- Capital budgeting is the process of **planning and controlling** investments for **long-term projects**. By their nature, capital projects affect **multiple accounting periods** and will constrain the organization's financial planning well into the future. Once made, capital budgeting decisions tend to be relatively inflexible.

- **Stages** in the capital budgeting process are:

  - Identification and definition
  - Search for potential investments
  - Information acquisition
  - Selection
  - Financing
  - Implementation
  - Monitoring

- A **common misstep** in regard to capital budgeting is the temptation to gauge the desirability of a project by using accrual accounting numbers instead of cash flows. The measure usually produced this way is called **book rate of return** or accrual accounting rate of return. Book rate of return is considered an **unsatisfactory guide** to selecting capital projects for multiple reasons.

  GAAP net income from investment ÷ Book value of investment

- **Relevant cash flows** are a much more reliable guide when judging capital projects, since only they provide a true measure of a project's potential to affect shareholder value. The relevant cash flows can be divided into three categories:

  - **Net initial investment**

    - Purchase of new equipment
    - Initial working capital requirements
    - After-tax proceeds from disposal of old equipment

  - **Annual net cash flows**

    - After-tax cash collections from operations excluding depreciation effect
    - Tax savings from depreciation deductions

  - **Project termination cash flows**

    - After-tax proceeds from disposal of new equipment
    - After-tax proceeds from recovery of working capital

- Three crucial terms relevant to capital budgeting:

  - An **incremental cash flow** is the difference in cash received or disbursed resulting from selecting one option instead of another.

  - A **sunk cost** is one that is either already paid or irrevocably committed to be incurred. Because it is unavoidable and will therefore not vary with the option chosen, it is not relevant to future decisions.

  - An **opportunity cost** is the maximum benefit forgone by using a scarce resource for a given purpose and not for the next-best alternative. In capital budgeting, the most basic application of this concept is the desire to place the company's limited funds in the most promising capital project(s).

QUESTIONS

17.1 The Capital Budgeting Process

1. The relevance of a particular cost to a decision is determined by

A. Riskiness of the decision.

B. Number of decision variables.

C. Amount of the cost.

D. Potential effect on the decision.

Answer (D) is correct. *(CMA, adapted)*
REQUIRED: The determinant of relevance of a particular cost to a decision.
DISCUSSION: Relevance is the capacity of information to make a difference in a decision by helping users of that information to predict the outcomes of events or to confirm or correct prior expectations. Thus, relevant costs are those expected future costs that vary with the action taken. All other costs are constant and therefore have no effect on the decision.

2. Of the following decisions, capital budgeting techniques would least likely be used in evaluating the

A. Acquisition of new aircraft by a cargo company.

B. Design and implementation of a major advertising program.

C. Trade for a star quarterback by a football team.

D. Adoption of a new method of allocating nontraceable costs to product lines.

Answer (D) is correct. *(CMA, adapted)*
REQUIRED: The decision least likely to be evaluated using capital budgeting techniques.
DISCUSSION: Capital budgeting is the process of planning expenditures for investments on which the returns are expected to occur over a period of more than 1 year. Thus, capital budgeting concerns the acquisition or disposal of long-term assets and the financing ramifications of such decisions. The adoption of a new method of allocating nontraceable costs to product lines has no effect on a company's cash flows, does not concern the acquisition of long-term assets, and is not concerned with financing. Hence, capital budgeting is irrelevant to such a decision.
Answer (A) is incorrect because a new aircraft represents a long-term investment in a capital good. Answer (B) is incorrect because a major advertising program is a high cost investment with long-term effects. Answer (C) is incorrect because a star quarterback is a costly asset who is expected to have a substantial effect on the team's long-term profitability.

3. In equipment-replacement decisions, which one of the following does not affect the decision-making process?

A. Current disposal price of the old equipment.

B. Operating costs of the old equipment.

C. Original fair market value of the old equipment.

D. Cost of the new equipment.

Answer (C) is correct. *(CMA, adapted)*
REQUIRED: The irrelevant factor when making an equipment replacement decision.
DISCUSSION: All relevant costs should be considered when evaluating an equipment-replacement decision. These include the cost of the new equipment, the disposal price of the old equipment, and the operating costs of the old equipment versus the operating costs of the new equipment. The original cost or fair market value of the old equipment is a sunk cost and is irrelevant to future decisions.

4. The term that refers to costs incurred in the past that are not relevant to a future decision is

A. Discretionary cost.

B. Full absorption cost.

C. Underallocated indirect cost.

D. Sunk cost.

Answer (D) is correct. *(CMA, adapted)*
REQUIRED: The past costs not relevant to a future decision.
DISCUSSION: A sunk cost cannot be avoided because it represents an expenditure that has already been made or an irrevocable decision to incur the cost.
Answer (A) is incorrect because a discretionary cost is characterized by uncertainty about the input-output relationship; advertising and research are examples. Answer (B) is incorrect because full absorption costing includes in production costs materials, labor, and both fixed and variable overhead. Answer (C) is incorrect because underallocated indirect cost is a cost that has not yet been charged to production.

5. Which one of the following statements concerning cash flow determination for capital budgeting purposes is not correct?

A. Tax depreciation must be considered because it affects cash payments for taxes.

B. Book depreciation is relevant because it affects net income.

C. Sunk costs are not incremental flows and should not be included.

D. Net working capital changes should be included in cash flow forecasts.

Answer (B) is correct. *(CMA, adapted)*
   REQUIRED: The false statement about cash flow determination.
   DISCUSSION: Tax depreciation is relevant to cash flow analysis because it affects the amount of income taxes that must be paid. However, book depreciation is not relevant because it does not affect the amount of cash generated by an investment.

6. A depreciation tax shield is

A. An after-tax cash outflow.

B. A reduction in income taxes.

C. The cash provided by recording depreciation.

D. The expense caused by depreciation.

Answer (B) is correct. *(CMA, adapted)*
   REQUIRED: The definition of a depreciation tax shield.
   DISCUSSION: A tax shield is something that will protect income against taxation. Thus, a depreciation tax shield is a reduction in income taxes due to a company's being allowed to deduct depreciation against otherwise taxable income.
   Answer (A) is incorrect because a tax shield is not a cash flow, but a means of reducing outflows for income taxes. Answer (C) is incorrect because cash is not provided by recording depreciation; the shield is a result of deducting depreciation from taxable revenues. Answer (D) is incorrect because depreciation is recognized as an expense even if it has no tax benefit.

7. Lawson, Inc. is expanding its manufacturing plant, which requires an investment of $4 million in new equipment and plant modifications. Lawson's sales are expected to increase by $3 million per year as a result of the expansion. Cash investment in current assets averages 30% of sales; accounts payable and other current liabilities are 10% of sales. What is the estimated total investment for this expansion?

A. $3.4 million.

B. $4.3 million.

C. $4.6 million.

D. $5.2 million.

Answer (C) is correct. *(CMA, adapted)*
   REQUIRED: The estimated total cash investment.
   DISCUSSION: The investment required includes increases in working capital (e.g., additional receivables and inventories resulting from the acquisition of a new manufacturing plant). The additional working capital is an initial cost of the investment, but one that will be recovered (i.e., it has a salvage value equal to its initial cost). Lawson can use current liabilities to fund assets to the extent of 10% of sales. Thus, the total initial cash outlay will be $4.6 million {$4 million + [(30% − 10%) × $3 million sales]}.
   Answer (A) is incorrect because $3.4 million deducts the investment in working capital from the cost of equipment. Answer (B) is incorrect because $4.3 million equals $4 million plus 10% of $3 million. Answer (D) is incorrect because $5.2 million equals $4 million plus 30% of $4 million.

8. In equipment replacement decisions, which one of the following does not affect the decision-making process?

A. Current disposal price of the old equipment.

B. Operating costs of the old equipment.

C. Original fair value of the old equipment.

D. Operating costs of the new equipment.

Answer (C) is correct. *(CMA, adapted)*
   REQUIRED: The irrelevant factor when making an equipment replacement decision.
   DISCUSSION: All relevant costs should be considered when evaluating an equipment replacement decision. These include the initial investment in the new equipment, any required investment in working capital, the disposal price of the new equipment, the disposal price of the old equipment, the operating costs of the old equipment, and the operating costs of the new equipment. The original cost or fair value of the old equipment is a sunk cost and is irrelevant to future decisions.
   Answer (A) is incorrect because the current disposal price of the old equipment should be considered when evaluating an equipment replacement decision. Answer (B) is incorrect because the operating costs of the old equipment should be considered when evaluating an equipment replacement decision. Answer (D) is incorrect because the operating costs of the new equipment should be considered when evaluating an equipment replacement decision.

9. Kline Corporation is expanding its plant, which requires an investment of $8 million in new equipment. Kline's sales are expected to increase by $6 million per year as a result of the expansion. Cash investment in current assets averages 30% of sales, and accounts payable and other current liabilities are 10% of sales. What is the estimated total cash investment for this expansion?

A. $6.8 million.

B. $8.6 million.

C. $9.2 million.

D. $9.8 million.

Answer (C) is correct. *(Publisher, adapted)*
REQUIRED: The estimated total cash investment for the expansion.
DISCUSSION: For capital budgeting purposes, the net investment is the net outlay or cash requirement. This amount includes the cost of the new equipment, minus any cash recovered from the trade or sale of existing assets. The investment required also includes funds to provide for increases in working capital, for example, the additional receivables and inventories resulting from the acquisition of a new manufacturing plant. The investment in working capital is treated as an initial cost of the investment, although it will be recovered at the end of the project (its salvage value equals its initial cost). For Kline, the additional current assets will be 30% of sales, but current liabilities can be used to fund assets to the extent of 10% of sales. Thus, the initial investment in working capital will equal 20% of the $6 million in sales, or $1,200,000. The total initial cash outlay will consist of the $8 million in new equipment plus $1,200,000 in working capital, a total of $9.2 million.
Answer (A) is incorrect because $6.8 million subtracted the net investment in working capital from the cost of the equipment. Answer (B) is incorrect because $8.6 million assumes current assets will increase by 10% of new sales but that current liabilities will not change. Answer (D) is incorrect because $9.8 million ignores the financing of incremental current assets with accounts payable.

10. Regal Industries is replacing a grinder purchased 5 years ago for $15,000 with a new one costing $25,000 cash. The original grinder is being depreciated on a straight-line basis over 15 years to a zero salvage value; Regal will sell this old equipment to a third party for $6,000 cash. The new equipment will be depreciated on a straight-line basis over 10 years to a zero salvage value. Assuming a 40% marginal tax rate, Regal's net cash investment at the time of purchase if the old grinder is sold and the new one purchased is

A. $19,000

B. $15,000

C. $17,400

D. $25,000

Answer (C) is correct. *(CMA, adapted)*
REQUIRED: The net cash investment at the time of purchase of an old asset and the sale of a new one.
DISCUSSION: The old machine has a carrying amount of $10,000 [$15,000 cost – 5 ($15,000 cost ÷ 15 years) depreciation]. The loss on the sale is $4,000 ($10,000 – $6,000 cash received), and the tax savings from the loss is $1,600 ($4,000 × 40%). Thus, total inflows are $7,600. The only outflow is the $25,000 purchase price of the new machine. The net cash investment is therefore $17,400 ($25,000 – $7,600).
Answer (A) is incorrect because $19,000 overlooks the tax savings from the loss on the old machine. Answer (B) is incorrect because $15,000 is obtained by deducting the old book value from the purchase price. Answer (D) is incorrect because the net investment is less than $25,000 given sales proceeds from the old machine and the tax savings.

11. Garfield, Inc. is considering a 10-year capital investment project with forecasted revenues of $40,000 per year and forecasted cash operating expenses of $29,000 per year. The initial cost of the equipment for the project is $23,000, and Garfield expects to sell the equipment for $9,000 at the end of the tenth year. The equipment will be depreciated over 7 years. The project requires a working capital investment of $7,000 at its inception and another $5,000 at the end of Year 5. Assuming a 40% marginal tax rate, the expected net cash flow from the project in the tenth year is

A. $32,000

B. $24,000

C. $20,000

D. $11,000

Answer (B) is correct. *(CMA, adapted)*
REQUIRED: The expected net cash flow from the project in the tenth year.
DISCUSSION: The project will have an $11,000 before-tax cash inflow from operations in the tenth year ($40,000 – $29,000). Also, $9,000 will be generated from the sale of the equipment. The entire $9,000 will be taxable because the basis of the asset was reduced to zero in the 7th year. Thus, taxable income will be $20,000 ($11,000 + $9,000), leaving a net after-tax cash inflow of $12,000 [$20,000 × (1.0 – .4)]. To this $12,000 must be added the $12,000 tied up in working capital ($7,000 + $5,000). The total net cash flow in the 10th year will therefore be $24,000.
Answer (A) is incorrect because $32,000 omits the $8,000 outflow for income taxes. Answer (C) is incorrect because taxes will be $8,000, not $12,000. Answer (D) is incorrect because $11,000 is the net operating cash flow.

Questions 12 through 14 are based on the following information. The Moore Corporation is considering the acquisition of a new machine. The machine can be purchased for $90,000; it will cost $6,000 to transport to Moore's plant and $9,000 to install. It is estimated that the machine will last 10 years, and it is expected to have an estimated salvage value of $5,000. Over its 10-year life, the machine is expected to produce 2,000 units per year with a selling price of $500 and combined material and labor costs of $450 per unit. Federal tax regulations permit machines of this type to be depreciated using the straight-line method over 5 years with no estimated salvage value. Moore has a marginal tax rate of 40%.

12. What is the net cash outflow at the beginning of the first year that Moore Corporation should use in a capital budgeting analysis?

   A. $(85,000)

   B. $(90,000)

   C. $(96,000)

   D. $(105,000)

Answer (D) is correct. *(CMA, adapted)*
REQUIRED: The initial net cash outflow that should be used in a capital budgeting analysis.
DISCUSSION: Initially, the company must invest $105,000 in the machine, consisting of the invoice price of $90,000, the delivery costs of $6,000, and the installation costs of $9,000.
Answer (A) is incorrect because $(85,000) erroneously includes salvage value but ignores delivery and installation costs. Answer (B) is incorrect because $(90,000) ignores the outlays needed for delivery and installation costs, both of which are an integral part of preparing the new asset for use. Answer (C) is incorrect because $(96,000) fails to include installation costs in the total.

13. What is the net cash flow for the third year that Moore Corporation should use in a capital budgeting analysis?

   A. $68,400

   B. $68,000

   C. $64,200

   D. $79,000

Answer (A) is correct. *(CMA, adapted)*
REQUIRED: The net cash flows for the third year that would be used in a capital budgeting analysis.
DISCUSSION: The company will receive net cash inflows of $50 per unit ($500 selling price – $450 of variable costs), or a total of $100,000 per year. This amount will be subject to taxation, but, for the first 5 years, there will be a depreciation deduction of $21,000 per year ($105,000 cost divided by 5 years). Therefore, deducting the $21,000 of depreciation expense from the $100,000 of contribution margin will result in taxable income of $79,000. After income taxes of $31,600 ($79,000 × 40%), the net cash flow in the third year is $68,400 ($100,000 – $31,600).
Answer (B) is incorrect because $68,000 deducts salvage value when calculating depreciation expense, which is not required by the tax law. Answer (C) is incorrect because $64,200 assumes depreciation is deducted for tax purposes over 10 years rather than 5 years. Answer (D) is incorrect because $79,000 is taxable income.

14. What is the net cash flow for the tenth year of the project that Moore Corporation should use in a capital budgeting analysis?

A. $100,000

B. $81,000

C. $68,400

D. $63,000

Answer (D) is correct. *(CMA, adapted)*

REQUIRED: The net cash flow for the tenth year of the project that would be used in a capital budgeting analysis.

DISCUSSION: The company will receive net cash inflows of $50 per unit ($500 selling price – $450 of variable costs), or a total of $100,000 per year. This amount will be subject to taxation, as will the $5,000 gain on sale of the investment, bringing taxable income to $105,000. No depreciation will be deducted in the tenth year because the asset was fully depreciated after 5 years. Because the asset was fully depreciated (book value was zero), the $5,000 salvage value received would be fully taxable. After income taxes of $42,000 ($105,000 × 40%), the net cash flow in the tenth year is $63,000 ($105,000 – $42,000).

Answer (A) is incorrect because $100,000 overlooks the salvage proceeds and the taxes to be paid. Answer (B) is incorrect because $81,000 miscalculates income taxes. Answer (C) is incorrect because $68,400 assumes that depreciation is deducted; it also overlooks the receipt of the salvage proceeds.

15. Metrejean Industries is analyzing a capital investment proposal for new equipment to produce a product over the next 8 years. At the end of 8 years, the equipment must be removed from the plant and will have a net carrying amount of $0, a tax basis of $150,000, a cost to remove of $80,000, and scrap salvage value of $20,000. Metrejean's effective tax rate is 40%. What is the appropriate "end-of-life" cash flow related to these items that should be used in the analysis?

A. $90,000

B. $54,000

C. $24,000

D. $(36,000)

Answer (C) is correct. *(Publisher, adapted)*

REQUIRED: The appropriate end-of-life cash flow related to the investment.

DISCUSSION: The tax basis of $150,000 and the $80,000 cost to remove are deductible expenses, but the $20,000 scrap value is an offsetting cash inflow. Thus, the taxable loss is $210,000 ($150,000 + $80,000 – $20,000). At a 40% tax rate, the $210,000 loss will produce a tax savings (inflow) of $84,000. Accordingly, the final cash flows will consist of an outflow of $80,000 (cost to remove) and inflows of $20,000 (scrap) and $84,000 (tax savings), a net inflow of $24,000.

Answer (A) is incorrect because $90,000 assumes that the loss on disposal is a cash inflow. It also ignores income taxes. Answer (B) is incorrect because $54,000 assumes that the loss on disposal involves a cash inflow. Answer (D) is incorrect because $(36,000) assumes that the tax basis is $0.

16. Kore Industries is analyzing a capital investment proposal for new equipment to produce a product over the next 8 years. The analyst is attempting to determine the appropriate "end-of-life" cash flows for the analysis. At the end of 8 years, the equipment must be removed from the plant and will have a net book value of zero, a tax basis of $75,000, a cost to remove of $40,000, and scrap salvage value of $10,000. Kore's effective tax rate is 40%. What is the appropriate "end-of-life" cash flow related to these items that should be used in the analysis?

A. $45,000

B. $27,000

C. $12,000

D. $(18,000)

Answer (C) is correct. *(CMA, adapted)*

REQUIRED: The appropriate end-of-life cash flow related to the investment.

DISCUSSION: The tax basis of $75,000 and the $40,000 cost to remove can be written off. However, the $10,000 scrap value is a cash inflow. Thus, the taxable loss is $105,000 ($75,000 loss on disposal + $40,000 expense to remove – $10,000 of inflows). At a 40% tax rate, the $105,000 loss will produce a tax savings (inflow) of $42,000. The final cash flows will consist of an outflow of $40,000 (cost to remove) and inflows of $10,000 (scrap) and $42,000 (tax savings), or a net inflow of $12,000.

Answer (A) is incorrect because $45,000 ignores income taxes and assumes that the loss on disposal involves a cash inflow. Answer (B) is incorrect because $27,000 assumes that the loss on disposal involves a cash inflow. Answer (D) is incorrect because $(18,000) ignores the tax loss on disposal.

Questions 17 through 19 are based on the following information. The Dickins Corporation is considering the acquisition of a new machine at a cost of $180,000. Transporting the machine to Dickins' plant will cost $12,000. Installing the machine will cost an additional $18,000. It has a 10-year life and is expected to have a salvage value of $10,000. Furthermore, the machine is expected to produce 4,000 units per year with a selling price of $500 and combined direct materials and direct labor costs of $450 per unit. Federal tax regulations permit machines of this type to be depreciated using the straight-line method over 5 years with no estimated salvage value. Dickins has a marginal tax rate of 40%.

17. What is the net cash outflow at the beginning of the first year that Dickins should use in a capital budgeting analysis?

A. $(170,000)

B. $(180,000)

C. $(192,000)

D. $(210,000)

Answer (D) is correct. *(Publisher, adapted)*
REQUIRED: The net cash outflow at the beginning of the first year that should be used in a capital budgeting analysis.
DISCUSSION: Delivery and installation costs are essential to preparing the machine for its intended use. Thus, the company must initially pay $210,000 for the machine, consisting of the invoice price of $180,000, the delivery costs of $12,000, and the $18,000 of installation costs.
Answer (A) is incorrect because $(170,000) includes salvage value and ignores delivery and installation costs. Answer (B) is incorrect because $(180,000) ignores the outlays needed for delivery and installation. Answer (C) is incorrect because $(192,000) excludes installation costs.

18. What is the net cash flow for the third year that Dickins should use in a capital budgeting analysis?

A. $136,800

B. $136,000

C. $128,400

D. $107,400

Answer (A) is correct. *(Publisher, adapted)*
REQUIRED: The net cash flow for the third year.
DISCUSSION: The company will receive net cash inflows of $50 per unit ($500 selling price – $450 variable costs), a total of $200,000 per year for 4,000 units. This amount will be subject to taxation. However, for the first 5 years, a depreciation deduction of $42,000 per year ($210,000 cost ÷ 5 years) will be available. Thus, annual taxable income will be $158,000 ($200,000 – $42,000). At a 40% tax rate, income tax expense will be $63,200, and the net cash inflow will be $136,800 ($200,000 – $63,200).
Answer (B) is incorrect because $136,000 results from subtracting salvage value when calculating depreciation expense. Answer (C) is incorrect because $128,400 assumes depreciation is recognized over 10 years. Answer (D) is incorrect because $107,400 assumes that depreciation is recognized over 10 years and that it requires a cash outlay.

19. What is the net cash flow for the tenth year of the project that Dickins should use in a capital budgeting analysis?

A. $200,000

B. $158,000

C. $136,800

D. $126,000

Answer (D) is correct. *(Publisher, adapted)*
REQUIRED: The net cash flow for the tenth year of the project.
DISCUSSION: The company will receive net cash inflows of $50 per unit ($500 selling price – $450 of variable costs), a total of $200,000 per year for 4,000 units. This amount will be subject to taxation, as will the $10,000 gain on sale of the investment, resulting in taxable income of $210,000. No depreciation will be deducted in the tenth year because the asset was fully depreciated after 5 years. Because the asset was fully depreciated (book value was $0), the $10,000 received as salvage value is fully taxable. At 40%, the tax on $210,000 is $84,000. After subtracting $84,000 of tax expense from the $210,000 of inflows, the net inflows amount to $126,000.
Answer (A) is incorrect because $200,000 overlooks the salvage proceeds and the taxes to be paid. Answer (B) is incorrect because $158,000 equals annual taxable income for each of the first 5 years. Answer (C) is incorrect because $136,800 is the annual net cash inflow in the second through the fifth years.

Questions 20 and 21 are based on the following information. On January 1, Crane Company will acquire a new asset that costs $400,000 and is anticipated to have a salvage value of $30,000 at the end of 4 years. The new asset

- Qualifies as 3-year property under the Modified Accelerated Cost Recovery System (MACRS).
- Will replace an old asset that currently has a tax basis of $80,000 and can be sold now for $60,000.
- Will continue to generate the same operating revenues as the old asset ($200,000 per year). However, savings in operating costs will be experienced as follows: a total of $120,000 in each of the first 3 years and $90,000 in the fourth year.

Crane is subject to a 40% tax rate and rounds all computations to the nearest dollar. Assume that any gain or loss affects the taxes paid at the end of the year in which it occurred. The company uses the net present value method to analyze projects using the following factors and rates:

Period	Present Value of $1 at 14%	Present Value of $1 Annuity at 14%	MACRS
1	.88	.88	33%
2	.77	1.65	45
3	.68	2.33	15
4	.59	2.92	7

20. The present value of the depreciation tax shield for the fourth year MACRS depreciation of Crane Company's new asset is

A. $0.

B. $6,112.

C. $6,608.

D. $16,520.

Answer (C) is correct. *(CMA, adapted)*
REQUIRED: The present value of the depreciation tax shield for the 1995 MACRS depreciation deduction.
DISCUSSION: The firm will be able to deduct 7% of the asset's cost during the fourth year of the asset's life. The deduction is $28,000 ($400,000 × 7%), and the tax savings is $11,200 ($28,000 × 40%). The present value of this amount is $6,608 ($11,200 × .59 PV of $1 at 14% for four periods).
Answer (A) is incorrect because the depreciation tax shield in Year 4 does have a present value. Answer (B) is incorrect because $6,112 is calculated by using the cost of the asset less the salvage value to figure MACRS depreciation. Answer (D) is incorrect because $16,520 is the present value of the depreciation in Year 4.

21. The discounted net-of-tax amount that should be factored into Crane Company's analysis for the disposal transaction is

A. $45,760.

B. $60,000.

C. $67,040.

D. $68,000.

Answer (C) is correct. *(CMA, adapted)*
REQUIRED: The discounted net-of-tax amount included in the analysis of the disposal.
DISCUSSION: The old asset can be sold for $60,000, producing an immediate cash inflow of that amount. This sale will result in a $20,000 loss for tax purposes ($80,000 – $60,000). At a 40% tax rate, the loss, which is deemed to affect taxes paid at the end of the first year, will provide a tax savings (cash inflow) of $8,000. Because the $8,000 savings is treated as occurring at the end of the first year, it must be discounted. This discounted (present) value is $7,040 ($8,000 × .88 PV of $1 at 14% for one period). Combining the $60,000 initial inflow with the $7,040 of tax savings results in a net-of-tax amount of $67,040.
Answer (A) is incorrect because $45,760 is the present value of the cash from the sale of the old asset minus the tax savings from the loss on disposal. Answer (B) is incorrect because $60,000 does not include the tax effect of the loss on disposal of the old asset. Answer (D) is incorrect because $68,000 does not discount the tax savings. Because the $8,000 savings is treated as occurring at the end of the first year, it must be discounted.

22. The accounting rate of return

A. Is synonymous with the internal rate of return.

B. Focuses on income as opposed to cash flows.

C. Is inconsistent with the divisional performance measure known as return on investment.

D. Recognizes the time value of money.

Answer (B) is correct. *(CMA, adapted)*
REQUIRED: The true statement about the accounting rate of return.
DISCUSSION: The accounting rate of return (also called the unadjusted rate of return or book value rate of return) is calculated by dividing the increase in accounting net income by the required investment. Sometimes the denominator is the average investment rather than the initial investment. This method ignores the time value of money and focuses on income as opposed to cash flows.
Answer (A) is incorrect because the IRR is the rate at which the net present value is zero. Thus, it incorporates time value of money concepts, whereas the accounting rate of return does not. Answer (C) is incorrect because the accounting rate of return is similar to the divisional performance measure of return on investment. Answer (D) is incorrect because the accounting rate of return ignores the time value of money.

23. What is a challenge that the long-term aspect of capital budgeting presents to the management accountant?

A. Activity can be tracked for a single accounting period.

B. Capital projects affect multiple accounting periods.

C. The flexibility of the capital budgeting decision.

D. Freedom of the organization's financial planning.

Answer (B) is correct. *(Publisher, adapted)*
REQUIRED: The challenge presented to the management accountant by the long-term aspect of capital budgeting.
DISCUSSION: Capital budgeting is the process of planning and controlling investments for long-term projects. It is this long-term aspect of capital budgeting that presents the management accountant with specific challenges. Most financial and management accounting topics concern tracking and reporting activity for a single accounting or reporting cycle, such as one month or one year. By their nature, capital projects affect multiple accounting periods and will constrain the organization's financial planning well into the future. Once made, capital budgeting decisions tend to be relatively inflexible.
Answer (A) is incorrect because capital budgeting activity affects multiple accounting periods. Answer (C) is incorrect because, once made, capital budgeting decisions tend to be relatively inflexible. Answer (D) is incorrect because capital projects will constrain the organization's financial planning well into the future.

24. Which of the following is not a category of relevant cash flows?

A. Annual net cash flows.

B. Project termination cash flows.

C. Incremental cash flows.

D. Net initial investment.

Answer (C) is correct. *(Publisher, adapted)*
REQUIRED: The item that is not a category of relevant cash flows.
DISCUSSION: Relevant cash flows are a much more reliable guide when judging capital projects, since only they provide a true measure of a project's potential to affect shareholder value. The relevant cash flows can be divided into three categories: (1) net initial investment, (2) annual net cash flows, and (3) project termination cash flows. An incremental cash flow is the difference in cash received or disbursed resulting from selecting one option instead of another. It is not a category of relevant cash flows.

25. The capital budgeting process contains several stages. At which stage are financial and nonfinancial factors addressed?

    A. Identification and definition.

    B. Selection.

    C. Search.

    D. Information-acquisition.

Answer (D) is correct. *(Publisher, adapted)*
    REQUIRED: The stage in the capital budgeting process where financial and nonfinancial factors are addressed.
    DISCUSSION: During the information-acquisition stage of the capital budgeting process, quantitative financial factors are given the most scrutiny. These include initial investment and periodic cash inflow. Nonfinancial measures, both quantitative and qualitative, are also identified and addressed. Examples include the need for additional training on new equipment and uncertainty about technological developments and competitors' actions.
    Answer (A) is incorrect because the identification and definition stage involves identifying and defining those projects and programs that are needed to attain the entity's objectives. Answer (B) is incorrect because, during the selection stage, the project(s) which will increase shareholder value by the greatest margin are chosen for implementation. Answer (C) is incorrect because potential investments are subjected to a preliminary evaluation by representatives from each function in the entity's value chain during the search stage of the capital budgeting process.

26. Book rate of return is an unsatisfactory guide to selecting capital projects because

I.   It uses accrual accounting numbers.

II.   It compares a single project against the average of capital projects.

III. It uses cash flows to gauge the desirability of the project.

    A. I only.

    B. I & II.

    C. III only.

    D. I, II, & III.

Answer (B) is correct. *(Publisher, adapted)*
    REQUIRED: The reason(s) book rate of return is an unsatisfactory guide to selecting capital projects.
    DISCUSSION: A common misstep in regard to capital budgeting is the temptation to gauge the desirability of a project by using accrual accounting numbers instead of cash flows. Net income and book value are affected by the company's choices of accounting methods. A project's true rate of return cannot be dependent on bookkeeping decisions. Another distortion inherent in comparing a single project's book rate of return to the current one for the company as a whole is that the latter is an average of all of a firm's capital projects. Embedded in that average number may be a handful of good projects making up for a large number of poor investments.
    Answer (A) is incorrect because the comparison of a single project's book rate of return against an average of all of a firm's capital projects is also a reason that book rate of return is an unsatisfactory guide. Answer (C) is incorrect because the book rate of return does not use cash flows in determining the desirability of a capital project. Answer (D) is incorrect because book rate of return does not utilize cash flows in the determination.

27. The maximum benefit forgone by using a scarce resource for a given purpose and not for the next-best alternative is called

    A. Opportunity cost.

    B. Sunk cost.

    C. Incremental cash flow.

    D. Net initial investment.

Answer (A) is correct. *(Publisher, adapted)*
    REQUIRED: The name for the maximum benefit forgone by using a scarce resource for a given purpose and not for the next-best alternative.
    DISCUSSION: An opportunity cost is the maximum benefit forgone by using a scarce resource for a given purpose and not for the next-best alternative. In capital budgeting, the most basic application of this concept is the desire to place the company's limited funds in the most promising capital project(s).
    Answer (B) is incorrect because a sunk cost is one that is either already paid or irrevocably committed to incur. Because it is unavoidable and will therefore not vary with the option chosen, it is not relevant to future decisions. Answer (C) is incorrect because an incremental cash flow is the difference in cash received or disbursed resulting from selecting one option instead of another. Answer (D) is incorrect because net initial investment is one of the three categories of relevant cash flows.

28. Post-investment audits

A. Complete a stage in the capital budgeting process.

B. Serve as a control mechanism.

C. Allow the outcome of a project to be evaluated as soon as possible.

D. Deter managers from proposing profitable investments.

Answer (B) is correct.   *(Publisher, adapted)*
REQUIRED: The statement describing post-investment audits.
DISCUSSION: Post-investment audits should be conducted to serve as a control mechanism and to deter managers from proposing unprofitable investments. Actual-to-expected cash flow comparisons should be made, and unfavorable variances should be explained. Individuals who supplied unrealistic estimates should have to explain differences.
Answer (A) is incorrect because post-investment audits are not a stage in the capital budgeting process. Answer (C) is incorrect because the temptation to evaluate the outcome of a project too early must be overcome. Until all cash flows are known, the results can be misleading. Post-investment audits can reduce this possibility. Answer (D) is incorrect because the post-investment audits deter managers from proposing unprofitable investments.

Use Gleim's *CMA Test Prep* for interactive testing with **over 2,000 additional multiple-choice questions**!

STUDY UNIT EIGHTEEN
DISCOUNTED CASH FLOW AND PAYBACK

(11 pages of outline)

This study unit is the **second of four** on **investment decisions**. The relative weight assigned to this major topic in Part 3 of the exam is **20%** at **skill level C** (all six skill types required). The four study units are

Study Unit 17: The Capital Budgeting Process
Study Unit 18: Discounted Cash Flow and Payback
Study Unit 19: Ranking Investment Projects
Study Unit 20: Risk Analysis and Real Options

After studying the outline and answering the multiple-choice questions, you will have the skills necessary to address the following topics listed in the IMA's Learning Outcome Statements:

Part 3 – Section E.2. Discounted cash flow analysis

The candidate should be able to:

a. demonstrate an understanding of the two main discounted cash flow (DCF) methods, net present value (NPV), and internal rate of return (IRR)

b. demonstrate an understanding of the weighted average cost of capital approach to NPV calculations

c. calculate the NPV and IRR using time value of money tables

d. demonstrate an understanding of the decision criteria used in NPV and IRR analyses to determine acceptable projects

e. compare NPV and IRR, focusing on the relative advantages and disadvantages of each method, particularly with respect to independent versus mutually exclusive projects, the "multiple IRR problem" and the cash flow pattern that causes the problem, and why NPV and IRR methods can produce conflicting rankings for capital projects if not applied properly

f. identify assumptions of the different methods of evaluating capital investment projects

g. recommend project investments on the basis of DCF analysis

Part 3 – Section E.3. Payback and discounted payback

The candidate should be able to:

a. demonstrate an understanding of the payback method

b. identify the advantages and disadvantages/limitations of the payback method

c. calculate payback periods and discounted paybacks

d. identify the advantages and disadvantages/limitations of the discounted payback method

18.1 DISCOUNTED CASH FLOW ANALYSIS

1.   A dollar received in the future is worth less than a dollar received today. Thus, when analyzing capital projects, the management accountant must discount the relevant cash flows using the **time value of money**.

   a.   A firm's goal is for its **discount rate** to be **as low as possible**.

      1)   The lower the firm's discount rate, the lower the "hurdle" the company must clear to achieve profitability. For this reason, the rate is sometimes called the **hurdle rate**.

   b.   The **two most widely used rates** in capital budgeting are

      1)   The firm's weighted-average cost of capital and
      2)   The shareholders' opportunity cost of capital.

   c.   A **common pitfall** in capital budgeting is the tendency to use the company's current rate of return as the benchmark. This can lead to rejecting projects that should be accepted.

      1)   EXAMPLE: A firm's current rate of return on all projects is 12%. Its shareholders' opportunity cost of capital is 10%. The company incorrectly rejects a project earning 11%.

   d.   The **two principal methods** for projecting the profitability of an investment are net present value and internal rate of return.

2.   The **net present value (NPV) method** expresses a project's return in **dollar terms**.

   a.   NPV **nets the expected cash streams** related to a project (inflows and outflows), then discounts them at the hurdle rate, also called the **desired rate of return**.

      1)   If the NPV of a project is **positive**, the project is **desirable** because it has a higher rate of return than the company's desired rate.

   b.   EXAMPLE:

      1)   The company discounts the relevant net cash flows using a hurdle rate of 6% (its desired rate of return).

Period	Net Cash Flow	6% PV Factor	Discounted Cash Flows
Initial Investment	$(501,000)	1.00000	$(501,000)
Year 1	77,000	0.94340	72,642
Year 2	77,000	0.89000	68,530
Year 3	77,000	0.83962	64,651
Year 4	77,000	0.79209	60,991
Year 5	85,000	0.74726	63,517
Year 6	85,000	0.70496	59,922
Year 7	85,000	0.66506	56,530
Year 8	101,800	0.62741	63,870
Net Present Value			**$ 9,653**

      2)   Because the project has net present value > $0, it is profitable given the company's hurdle rate.

3.   The **internal rate of return (IRR)** expresses a project's return in **percentage terms**.

   a.   The IRR of an investment is the **discount rate** at which the investment's **NPV equals zero**. In other words, it is the rate that makes the present value of the expected cash inflows equal the present value of the expected cash outflows.

      1)   If the IRR is **higher** than the company's desired rate of return, the investment is **desirable**.

b.   EXAMPLE:

1)   The discounted cash flows used in the NPV exercise on the previous page can be recalculated using a higher discount rate (a higher rate will drive down the present value) in an attempt to get the solution closer to $0.

Period	Net Cash Flow	7% PV Factor	Discounted Cash Flows
Initial Investment	$(501,000)	1.00000	$(501,000)
Year 1	77,000	0.93458	71,963
Year 2	77,000	0.87344	67,255
Year 3	77,000	0.81630	62,855
Year 4	77,000	0.76290	58,743
Year 5	85,000	0.71299	60,604
Year 6	85,000	0.66634	56,639
Year 7	85,000	0.62275	52,934
Year 8	101,800	0.58201	59,249
Net Present Value			**$ (10,759)**

2)   The higher hurdle rate causes the NPV to be negative. Thus, the IRR of this project is somewhere around 6.5%.

3)   Because the company's desired rate of return is 6%, the project should be accepted, the same decision that was arrived at using the net present value method.

4.   **Cash Flows and Discounting**

a.   Conceptually, net present value is calculated using the following formula:

$$NPV = \frac{Cash\ Flow_0}{(1 + r)^0} + \frac{Cash\ Flow_1}{(1 + r)^1} + \frac{Cash\ Flow_2}{(1 + r)^2} + \frac{Cash\ Flow_3}{(1 + r)^3} + etc.$$

1)   The subscripts and exponents represent the discount periods. The variable *r* is the discount rate.

b.   Present value tables are available as a convenient way to discount cash flows.

5.   **Pitfalls of IRR.** IRR used in isolation is seldom the best route to a sound capital budgeting decision.

a.   **Direction of cash flows.** When the direction of the cash flows changes, focusing simply on IRR can be misleading.

1)   EXAMPLE: Below are the net cash flows for two potential capital projects.

	Initial	Period 1
Project X	$(222,222)	$ 240,000
Project Y	222,222	(240,000)

The cash flow amounts are the same in absolute value, but the directions differ. In choosing between the two, a decision maker might be tempted to select the project that has a cash inflow earlier and a cash outflow later.

2)   The IRR for both projects is 8%, which can be proved as follows:

Project X				Project Y			
$(222,222) ×	1.000	=	$(222,222)	$222,222 ×	1.000	=	$222,222
240,000 ×	0.926	=	222,222	(240,000) ×	0.926	=	(222,222)
			$ -0-				$ -0-

3) Discounting the cash flows at the company's hurdle rate of 6% reveals a different picture.

Project X			
$(222,222) ×	1.000	=	$(222,222)
240,000 ×	0.943	=	226,415
			$ 4,193

Project Y			
$222,222 ×	1.000	=	$222,222
(240,000) ×	0.943	=	(226,415)
			$ (4,193)

    a) It turns out that, given a hurdle rate lower than the rate at which the two projects have the same return, the project with the positive cash flow earlier is by far the less desirable of the two.

    b) Clearly, a decision maker can be seriously misled if (s)he uses the simple direction of the cash flows as the tiebreaker when two projects have the same IRR.

4) This effect is known as the **multiple IRR problem**. Essentially, there are **as many solutions** to the IRR formula as there are **changes in the direction** of the net cash flows.

b. **Mutually exclusive projects.** As with changing cash flow directions, focusing only on IRR when capital is limited can lead to unsound decisions.

1) EXAMPLE: Below are the cash flows for two potential capital projects.

	Initial	Period 1	IRR
Project S	$(178,571)	$ 200,000	12%
Project T	(300,000)	330,000	10%

2) If capital is available for only one project, using IRR alone would suggest that Project S be selected.

3) Once again, however, discounting both projects' net cash flows at the company's hurdle rate suggests a different decision.

Project S			
$(178,571) ×	1.000	=	$(178,571)
200,000 ×	0.943	=	188,679
			$ 10,108

Project T			
$(300,000) ×	1.000	=	$(300,000)
330,000 ×	0.943	=	311,321
			$ 11,321

    a) While Project S has the distinction of giving the company a higher internal rate of return, Project T is in fact preferable because it adds more to shareholder value.

c. **Varying rates of return.** A project's NPV can easily be determined using different desired rates of return for different periods. The IRR is limited to a single summary rate for the entire project.

d. **Multiple investments.** NPV amounts from different projects can be added, but IRR rates cannot. The IRR for the whole is not the sum of the IRRs for the parts.

6. **Comparing Cash Flow Patterns**

a. Often a decision maker must choose between two mutually exclusive projects, one whose **inflows are higher in the early years** but fall off drastically later and one whose **inflows are steady** throughout the project's life.

1) The **higher a firm's hurdle rate**, the more quickly a project must pay off.
2) Firms with **low hurdle rates** prefer a slow and steady payback.

b. **EXAMPLE:** Consider the net cash flows of these two projects:

	Initial	Year 1	Year 2	Year 3	Year 4
Project K	$(200,000)	$140,000	$100,000	–	–
Project L	(200,000)	65,000	65,000	$65,000	$65,000

1) A graphical representation of the two projects at various discount rates helps to illustrate the factors a decision maker must consider in such a situation.

NPV Profiles

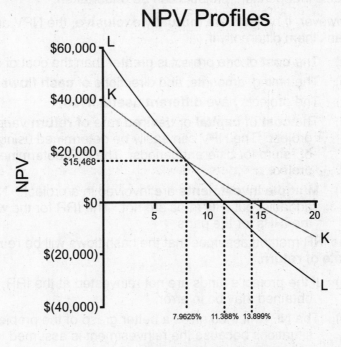

Discount Rate (%)

c. The NPV profile can be of great practical use to managers trying to make investment decisions. It gives the manager a clear insight into the following questions:

1) How sensitive is a project's profitability to changes in the discount rate?

a) At a hurdle rate of **exactly** 7.9625%, a decision maker is indifferent between the two projects. The net present value of both is $15,468 at that discount rate.

b) At hurdle rates **below** 7.9625%, the project whose **inflows last longer** into the future is the better investment (L).

c) At hurdle rates **above** 7.9625%, the project whose **inflows are "front-loaded"** is the better choice (K).

2) At what discount rates is an investment project still a profitable opportunity?

a) At any hurdle rate **above** 13.899%, Project K **loses money**. This is its IRR, i.e., the rate at which its NPV = $0 (Project L's is 11.388%).

7.   **Comparing NPV and IRR**

a.   The **reinvestment rate** becomes critical when choosing between the NPV and IRR methods. NPV assumes the cash flows from the investment can be reinvested at the particular project's discount rate, that is, the **desired rate of return**.

b.   The NPV and IRR methods give the same accept/reject decision if projects are independent. **Independent projects** have unrelated cash flows. Hence, all acceptable independent projects can be undertaken.

1)   However, if projects are **mutually exclusive**, the NPV and IRR methods may rank them differently if

a)   The **cost** of one project is greater than the cost of another.

b)   The timing, amounts, and directions of **cash flows** differ among projects.

c)   The projects have **different useful lives**.

d)   The **cost of capital** or **desired rate of return** varies over the life of a project. The NPV can easily be determined using different desired rates of return for different periods. The IRR determines one rate for the project.

e)   **Multiple investments** are involved in a project. NPV amounts are addable, but IRR rates are not. The IRR for the whole is not the sum of the IRRs for the parts.

2)   The IRR method assumes that the cash flows will be **reinvested at the internal rate of return.**

a)   If the project's funds are not reinvested at the IRR, the ranking calculations obtained may be in error.

b)   The NPV method gives a better grasp of the problem in many decision situations because the reinvestment is assumed to be in the **desired rate of return**.

c.   NPV and IRR are the soundest investment rules from a **shareholder wealth maximization** perspective.

1)   In some cases, NPV and IRR will rank projects differently.

a)   EXAMPLE:

Project	Initial Cost	Year-End Cash Flow	IRR	NPV (k=10%)
A	$1,000	$1,200	20%	$91
B	$ 50	$ 100	100%	$41

i)   IRR preference ordering: B, A
ii)   NPV preference ordering: A, B

d.   If one of two or more **mutually exclusive projects** is accepted, the others must be rejected.

1)   EXAMPLE: The decision to build a shopping mall on a piece of land eliminates placing an office building on the same land.

2)   When choosing between mutually exclusive projects, the ranking differences between NPV and IRR become very important. In the example above, a firm using IRR would accept B and reject A. A firm using NPV would make exactly the opposite choice.

e.   The problem can be seen more clearly using a **net present value profile**. The NPV profile is a plot of a project's NPV at different discount rates. The NPV is plotted on the vertical axis and the rate of return (k) on the horizontal axis.

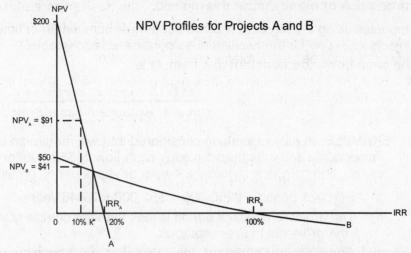

NPV Profiles for Projects A and B

1)   These profiles are downward sloping because a higher discount rate (desired rate of return) implies a lower NPV. The graph shows that, for all discount rates higher than k*, the firm should select project B over A because NPV$_B$ is greater than NPV$_A$. This preference ordering also results from applying the IRR criterion. Below k*, however, NPV$_A$ is greater than NPV$_B$, so A should be selected, even though IRR$_B$ is greater than IRR$_A$.

2)   These profiles show that IRR will always prefer B to A. NPV will prefer B to A only past some critical discount rate k*.

f.   The manager concerned with **shareholder wealth maximization** should choose the project with the **greatest NPV**, not the largest IRR. IRR is a percentage measure of wealth, but NPV is an absolute measure. Shareholder well-being is also measured in absolute amounts.

1)   The choice of NPV over IRR is easy to see with a simple example. Assume a choice between investing $1 and receiving $2 or investing $100,000 and receiving $150,000. The IRRs of the projects are 100% and 50%, respectively, which supports the first project. But assume instead that the interest rate is 10%. The NPVs of the projects are $.81 and $36,363, respectively. To select the first project because of the IRR criterion would lead to a return of $.81 instead of $36,363. Thus, the NPV is the better criterion when choosing between mutually exclusive projects.

g.   The NPV profile can be of great practical use to managers trying to make investment decisions. It gives the manager a clear insight into the following questions:

1)   At what interest rates is an investment project still a profitable opportunity?
2)   How sensitive is a project's profitability to changes in the discount rate?

8.   Stop and review! You have completed the outline for this subunit. Study multiple-choice questions 1 through 20 beginning on page 428.

18.2 PAYBACK AND DISCOUNTED PAYBACK

1. The **payback period** is the **number of years** required to return the original investment; that is, the time necessary for a new asset to pay for itself. Note that **no accounting is made for the time value of money** under this method.

   a. Companies using the payback method set a maximum length of time within which projects must pay for themselves to be considered acceptable.

   b. **If the cash flows are constant**, the formula is

   $$\text{Payback period} = \frac{\text{Initial net investment}}{\text{Annual expected cash flow}}$$

   1) EXAMPLE: A project is being considered that will require an outlay of $200,000 immediately and will return a steady cash flow of $52,000 for the next four years. The company requires a 4-year payback period on all capital projects.

      a) Payback period = $200,000 ÷ $52,000 = 3.846 years

      b) The project's payback period is less than the company's maximum, and the project is thus acceptable.

   c. **If the cash flows are not constant**, the calculation must be in cumulative form.

   1) EXAMPLE: Instead of the smooth inflows predicted above, the project's cash stream is expected to vary. The payback period is calculated as follows:

End of Year	Cash Inflow	Remaining Initial Investment
Year 0	$ 0	$200,000
Year 1	48,000	152,000
Year 2	54,000	98,000
Year 3	54,000	44,000
Year 4	42,000	2,000

      a) At the end of four years, the original investment has still not been recovered, so the project is rejected.

   d. The **strength** of the payback method is its simplicity.

   1) The payback method is sometimes used for foreign investments if foreign expropriation of firm assets is feared. Even in these circumstances, it is most often used in addition to a more sophisticated method.

   2) To some extent, the payback period measures risk. The longer the period, the more risky the investment.

   e. The payback method has two significant **weaknesses**:

   1) It disregards all cash inflows after the payback cutoff date. Applying a single cutoff date to every project results in accepting many marginal projects and rejecting good ones.

   2) It disregards the time value of money. Weighting all cash inflows equally ignores the fact that money has a cost.

2. The **discounted payback method** is sometimes used to overcome the second of the drawbacks inherent in the basic payback method.

    a. The net cash flows in the denominator are discounted to calculate the period required to recover the initial investment.

Period	Cash Inflow	6% PV Factor	Discounted Cash Flow	Remaining Initial Investment
Initial Investment	$ 0	1.00000	$ 0	$200,000
Year 1	48,000	0.94340	45,283	154,717
Year 2	54,000	0.89000	48,060	106,657
Year 3	54,000	0.83962	45,339	61,317
Year 4	42,000	0.79209	33,268	28,050

        1) After four years, the project is much further from paying off than under the basic method.

        2) Clearly then, this is a **more conservative** technique than the traditional payback method.

    b. The discounted payback method's advantage is that it acknowledges the time value of money.

        1) Its drawbacks are that it loses the simplicity of the basic payback method and still ignores cash flows after the arbitrary cutoff date.

3. **Other Payback Methods**

    a. The **bailout payback method** incorporates the salvage value of the asset into the calculation. It measures the length of the payback period when the periodic cash inflows are combined with the salvage value.

    b. The **payback reciprocal** (1 ÷ payback) is sometimes used as an estimate of the internal rate of return.

    c. The **breakeven time** is the period required for the discounted cumulative cash inflows on a project to equal the discounted cumulative cash outflows (usually but not always the initial cost).

        1) Thus, it is the time necessary for the present value of the discounted cash flows to equal zero. This period begins at the outset of a project, not when the initial cash outflow occurs.

        2) An alternative that results in a longer breakeven time is to consider the time required for the present value of the cumulative cash inflows to equal the present value of all the expected future cash outflows.

4. Stop and review! You have completed the outline for this subunit. Study multiple-choice questions 21 through 34 beginning on page 434.

18.3 CORE CONCEPTS

Discounted Cash Flow Analysis

- When analyzing capital projects, the management accountant must **discount the relevant cash flows** using the time value of money. A firm's goal is for its discount rate to be **as low as possible**. The lower the firm's discount rate, the lower the "hurdle" the company must clear to achieve profitability. For this reason, the rate is sometimes called the **hurdle rate**.

  - The two most widely used rates in capital budgeting are the firm's weighted-average cost of capital and the shareholders' opportunity cost of capital.

- A **common pitfall** in capital budgeting is the tendency to use the company's current rate of return as the benchmark. This can lead to rejecting projects that should be accepted.

  - For example, a firm's current rate of return on all projects is 12%. Its shareholders' opportunity cost of capital is 10%. The company incorrectly rejects a project earning 11%.

- The **net present value (NPV) method** for projecting the profitability of an investment expresses a project's return in dollar terms. NPV nets the expected cash streams related to a project (inflows and outflows), then discounts them at the hurdle rate, also called the desired rate of return.

  - If the NPV of a project is positive, the project is desirable because it has a higher rate of return than the company's desired rate.

- The **internal rate of return (IRR) method** expresses a project's return in percentage terms. The IRR of an investment is the discount rate at which the investment's NPV equals zero. In other words, it is the rate that makes the present value of the expected cash inflows equal the present value of the expected cash outflows.

  - If the IRR is higher than the company's desired rate of return, the investment is desirable.

- **IRR used in isolation** is seldom the best route to a sound capital budgeting decision.

  - When the **direction of the cash flows** changes, focusing simply on IRR can be misleading. This effect is known as the multiple IRR problem. Essentially, there are as many solutions to the IRR formula as there are changes in the direction of the net cash flows.

  - Focusing only on IRR **when capital is limited** can lead to unsound decisions. A project with a lower rate of return may actually add more shareholder value.

  - A project's NPV can easily be determined using different desired rates of return for different periods. The IRR is **limited to a single summary rate** for the entire project.

  - IRR rates **cannot simply be added** as NPV dollars can. The IRR for the whole is not the sum of the IRRs for the parts.

- Often a decision maker must choose between two mutually exclusive projects, one whose inflows are **higher in the early years** but fall off drastically later and one whose inflows are **steady throughout** the project's life.

  - The higher a firm's hurdle rate, the more quickly a project must pay off.
  - Firms with low hurdle rates prefer a slow and steady payback.

Payback and Discounted Payback

- The **payback period** is the number of years required to return the original investment; that is, the time necessary for a new asset to pay for itself. Note that no consideration is made for the time value of money under this method.

- Companies using the payback method set a maximum **length of time** within which projects must **pay for themselves** to be considered acceptable. If the cash flows are not constant, the calculation must be in cumulative form. If the cash flows are constant, this formula can be used:

  Payback period = Initial net investment ÷ Annual expected cash flow

- The strength of the payback method is its **simplicity**.

  - The payback method is sometimes used for foreign investments if foreign expropriation of firm assets is feared. Even in these circumstances, it is most often used in addition to a more sophisticated method.

  - To some extent, the payback period measures risk. The longer the period, the riskier the investment.

- The payback method has two significant **weaknesses**.

  - It disregards all cash inflows after the payback cutoff date. Applying a single cutoff date to every project results in accepting many marginal projects and rejecting good ones.

  - It disregards the time value of money. Weighting all cash inflows equally ignores the fact that money has a cost.

- The **discounted payback method** is sometimes used to overcome the second of the drawbacks inherent in the basic payback method. The net cash flows in the denominator are discounted to calculate the period required to recover the initial investment. Clearly, this is a more conservative technique than the traditional payback method.

  - The discounted payback method's advantage is that it acknowledges the time value of money.

  - Its drawbacks are that it loses the simplicity of the basic payback method and still ignores cash flows after the arbitrary cutoff date.

- The **bailout payback method** incorporates the salvage value of the asset into the calculation. It measures the length of the payback period when the periodic cash inflows are combined with the salvage value.

- The **payback reciprocal** (1 ÷ payback) is sometimes used as an estimate of the internal rate of return.

- The **breakeven time** is the period required for the discounted cumulative cash inflows on a project to equal the discounted cumulative cash outflows (usually but not always the initial cost).

QUESTIONS

18.1 Discounted Cash Flow Analysis

Questions 1 through 4 are based on the following information.

The following data pertain to a 4-year project being considered by Metro Industries:

- A depreciable asset that costs $1,200,000 will be acquired on January 1. The asset, which is expected to have a $200,000 salvage value at the end of 4 years, qualifies as 3-year property under the Modified Accelerated Cost Recovery System (MACRS).

- The new asset will replace an existing asset that has a tax basis of $150,000 and can be sold on the same January 1 for $180,000.

- The project is expected to provide added annual sales of 30,000 units at $20. Additional cash operating costs are: variable, $12 per unit; fixed, $90,000 per year.

- A $50,000 working capital investment that is fully recoverable at the end of the fourth year is required.

Metro is subject to a 40% income tax rate and rounds all computations to the nearest dollar. Assume that any gain or loss affects the taxes paid at the end of the year in which it occurred. The company uses the net present value method to analyze investments and will employ the following factors and rates.

Period	Present Value of $1 at 12%	Present Value of $1 Annuity at 12%	MACRS
1	0.89	0.89	33%
2	0.80	1.69	45
3	0.71	2.40	15
4	0.64	3.04	7

1. The discounted cash flow for the fourth year MACRS depreciation on the new asset is

A. $0

B. $17,920

C. $21,504

D. $26,880

Answer (C) is correct. *(CMA, adapted)*
REQUIRED: The discounted cash flow for the fourth year MACRS depreciation deduction on the new asset.
DISCUSSION: Tax law allows taxpayers to ignore salvage value when calculating depreciation under MACRS. Thus, the depreciation deduction is 7% of the initial $1,200,000 cost, or $84,000. At a 40% tax rate, the deduction will save the company $33,600 in taxes in the fourth year. The present value of this savings is $21,504 ($33,600 × 0.64 present value of $1 at 12% for four periods).
Answer (A) is incorrect because a tax savings will result in the fourth year from the MACRS deduction. Answer (B) is incorrect because $17,920 is based on a depreciation calculation in which salvage value is subtracted from the initial cost. Answer (D) is incorrect because the appropriate discount factor for the fourth period is 0.64, not 0.80.

2. The discounted, net-of-tax amount that relates to disposal of the existing asset is

A. $168,000

B. $169,320

C. $180,000

D. $190,680

Answer (B) is correct. *(CMA, adapted)*
REQUIRED: The discounted, net-of-tax amount relating to the disposal of the existing asset.
DISCUSSION: The cash inflow from the existing asset is $180,000, but that amount is subject to tax on the $30,000 gain ($180,000 – $150,000 tax basis). The tax on the gain is $12,000 ($30,000 × 40%). Because the tax will not be paid until year-end, the discounted value is $10,680 ($12,000 × .89 PV of $1 at 12% for one period). Thus, the net-of-tax inflow is $169,320 ($180,000 – $10,680). NOTE: This asset was probably a Section 1231 asset, and any gain on sale qualifies for the special capital gain tax rates. Had the problem not stipulated a 40% tax rate, the capital gains rate would be used. An answer based on that rate is not among the options.
Answer (A) is incorrect because $168,000 fails to discount the outflow for taxes. Answer (C) is incorrect because $180,000 ignores the impact of income taxes. Answer (D) is incorrect because the discounted present value of the income taxes is an outflow and is deducted from the inflow from the sale of the asset.

3. The expected incremental sales will provide a discounted, net-of-tax contribution margin over 4 years of

   A. $57,600

   B. $92,160

   C. $273,600

   D. $437,760

Answer (D) is correct. *(CMA, adapted)*
   REQUIRED: The expected net-of-tax contribution margin over 4 years.
   DISCUSSION: Additional annual sales are 30,000 units at $20 per unit. If variable costs are expected to be $12 per unit, the unit contribution margin is $8, and the total before-tax annual contribution margin is $240,000 (30,000 units × $8). The after-tax total annual contribution margin is $144,000 [$240,000 × (1.0 – .4)]. This annual increase in the contribution margin should be treated as an annuity. Thus, its present value is $437,760 ($144,000 × 3.04 PV of an annuity of $1 at 12% for four periods).
   Answer (A) is incorrect because $57,600 is based on only 1 year's results, not 4. Answer (B) is incorrect because $92,160 is based on only 1 year's results, not 4. Answer (C) is incorrect because $273,600 improperly includes fixed costs in the calculation of the contribution margin.

4. The overall discounted-cash-flow impact of the working capital investment on Metro's project is

   A. $(2,800)

   B. $(18,000)

   C. $(50,000)

   D. $(59,200)

Answer (B) is correct. *(CMA, adapted)*
   REQUIRED: The overall discounted-cash-flow impact of the working capital investment.
   DISCUSSION: The working capital investment is treated as a $50,000 outflow at the beginning of the project and a $50,000 inflow at the end of 4 years. Accordingly, the present value of the inflow after 4 years should be subtracted from the initial $50,000 outlay. The overall discounted-cash-flow impact of the working capital investment is $18,000 [$50,000 – ($50,000 × .64 PV of $1 at 12% for four periods)].
   Answer (A) is incorrect because the firm will have its working capital tied up for 4 years. Answer (C) is incorrect because the working capital investment is recovered at the end of the fourth year. Hence, the working capital cost of the project is the difference between $50,000 and the present value of $50,000 in 4 years. Answer (D) is incorrect because the answer cannot exceed $50,000, which is the amount of the cash outflow.

5. The net present value (NPV) method of investment project analysis assumes that the project's cash flows are reinvested at the

   A. Computed internal rate of return.

   B. Risk-free interest rate.

   C. Discount rate used in the NPV calculation.

   D. Firm's accounting rate of return.

Answer (C) is correct. *(CMA, adapted)*
   REQUIRED: The rate at which the NPV method assumes early cash inflows are reinvested.
   DISCUSSION: The NPV method is used when the discount rate is specified. It assumes that cash flows from the investment can be reinvested at the particular project's discount rate.
   Answer (A) is incorrect because the internal rate of return method assumes that cash flows are reinvested at the internal rate of return. Answer (B) is incorrect because the NPV method assumes that cash flows are reinvested at the NPV discount rate. Answer (D) is incorrect because the NPV method assumes that cash flows are reinvested at the NPV discount rate.

6. The rankings of mutually exclusive investments determined using the internal rate of return method (IRR) and the net present value method (NPV) may be different when

   A. The lives of the multiple projects are equal and the size of the required investments are equal.

   B. The required rate of return equals the IRR of each project.

   C. The required rate of return is higher than the IRR of each project.

   D. Multiple projects have unequal lives and the size of the investment for each project is different.

Answer (D) is correct. *(CMA, adapted)*
   REQUIRED: The circumstances in which IRR and NPV rankings of mutually exclusive projects may differ.
   DISCUSSION: The two methods ordinarily yield the same results, but differences can occur when the duration of the projects and the initial investments differ. The reason is that the IRR method assumes cash inflows from the early years will be reinvested at the internal rate of return. The NPV method assumes that early cash inflows are reinvested at the NPV discount rate.
   Answer (A) is incorrect because the two methods will give the same results if the lives and required investments are the same. Answer (B) is incorrect because, if the required rate of return equals the IRR, the two methods will yield the same decision. Answer (C) is incorrect because, if the required rate of return is higher than the IRR, both methods will yield a decision not to acquire the investment.

Questions 7 and 8 are based on the following information. A firm with an 18% desired rate of return is considering the following projects (on January 1, Year 1):

	January 1, Year 1 Cash Outflow (000's Omitted)	December 31, Year 5 Cash Inflow (000's Omitted)	Project Internal Rate of Return
Project A	$3,500	$7,400	16%
Project B	4,000	9,950	?

Present Value of $1 Due at the End of "N" Periods

N	12%	14%	15%	16%	18%	20%	22%
4	.6355	.5921	.5718	.5523	.5158	.4823	.4230
5	.5674	.5194	.4972	.4761	.4371	.4019	.3411
6	.5066	.4556	.4323	.4104	.3704	.3349	.2751

7. Using the net-present-value (NPV) method, Project A's net present value is

A. $316,920

B. $23,140

C. $(265,460)

D. $(316,920)

Answer (C) is correct. *(CIA, adapted)*
REQUIRED: The net present value of Project A.
DISCUSSION: The cash inflow occurs 5 years after the cash outflow, and the NPV method uses the firm's desired rate of return of 18%. The present value of $1 due at the end of 5 years discounted at 18% is .4371. Thus, the NPV of Project A is $(265,460) [($7,400,000 cash inflow × .4371) – $3,500,000 cash outflow].
Answer (A) is incorrect because $316,920 discounts the cash inflow over a 4-year period. Answer (B) is incorrect because $23,140 assumes a 16% discount rate. Answer (D) is incorrect because $(316,920) discounts the cash inflow over a 4-year period and also subtracts the present value of the cash inflow from the cash outflow.

8. Project B's internal rate of return is closest to

A. 15%

B. 16%

C. 18%

D. 20%

Answer (D) is correct. *(CIA, adapted)*
REQUIRED: The percentage closest to Project B's internal rate of return.
DISCUSSION: The internal rate of return is the discount rate at which the NPV is zero. Consequently, the cash outflow equals the present value of the inflow at the internal rate of return. The present value of $1 factor for Project B's internal rate of return is therefore .4020 ($4,000,000 cash outflow ÷ $9,950,000 cash inflow). This factor is closest to the present value of $1 for 5 periods at 20%.
Answer (A) is incorrect because 15% results in a positive NPV for Project B. Answer (B) is incorrect because 16% is the approximate internal rate of return for Project A. Answer (C) is incorrect because 18% is the company's cost of capital.

9. Amster Corporation has not yet decided on its hurdle rate for use in the evaluation of capital budgeting projects. This lack of information will prohibit Amster from calculating a project's

	Accounting Rate of Return	Net Present Value	Internal Rate of Return
A.	No	No	No
B.	Yes	Yes	Yes
C.	No	Yes	Yes
D.	No	Yes	No

Answer (D) is correct. *(CMA, adapted)*
REQUIRED: The capital budgeting technique(s), if any, that require determination of a hurdle rate.
DISCUSSION: A hurdle rate is not necessary in calculating the accounting rate of return. That return is calculated by dividing the net income from a project by the investment in the project. Similarly, a company can calculate the internal rate of return (IRR) without knowing its hurdle rate. The IRR is the discount rate at which the net present value is $0. However, the NPV cannot be calculated without knowing the company's hurdle rate. The NPV method requires that future cash flows be discounted using the hurdle rate.

10. All of the following items are included in discounted cash flow analysis except

    A. Future operating cash savings.

    B. The current asset disposal price.

    C. The future asset depreciation expense.

    D. The tax effects of future asset depreciation.

Answer (C) is correct. *(CMA, adapted)*
    REQUIRED: The item not included in discounted cash flow analysis.
    DISCUSSION: Discounted cash flow analysis, using either the internal rate of return (IRR) or the net present value (NPV) method, is based on the time value of cash inflows and outflows. All future operating cash savings are considered, as well as the tax effects on cash flows of future depreciation charges. The cash proceeds of future asset disposals are likewise a necessary consideration. Depreciation expense is a consideration only to the extent that it affects the cash flows for taxes. Otherwise, depreciation is excluded from the analysis because it is a noncash expense.

11. The use of an accelerated method instead of the straight-line method of depreciation in computing the net present value of a project has the effect of

    A. Raising the hurdle rate necessary to justify the project.

    B. Lowering the net present value of the project.

    C. Increasing the present value of the depreciation tax shield.

    D. Increasing the cash outflows at the initial point of the project.

Answer (C) is correct. *(CMA, adapted)*
    REQUIRED: The effect on NPV of using an accelerated depreciation method.
    DISCUSSION: Accelerated depreciation results in greater depreciation in the early years of an asset's life compared with the straight-line method. Thus, accelerated depreciation results in lower income tax expense in the early years of a project and higher income tax expense in the later years. By effectively deferring taxes, the accelerated method increases the present value of the depreciation tax shield.
    Answer (A) is incorrect because the hurdle rate can be reached more easily as a result of the increased present value of the depreciation tax shield. Answer (B) is incorrect because the greater depreciation tax shield increases the NPV. Answer (D) is incorrect because greater initial depreciation reduces the cash outflows for the taxes, but has no effect on the initial cash outflows.

12. The NPV of a project has been calculated to be $215,000. Which one of the following changes in assumptions would decrease the NPV?

    A. Decrease the estimated effective income tax rate.

    B. Decrease the initial investment amount.

    C. Extend the project life and associated cash inflows.

    D. Increase the discount rate.

Answer (D) is correct. *(CMA, adapted)*
    REQUIRED: The change in assumption that would decrease the net present value (NPV).
    DISCUSSION: An increase in the discount rate would lower the net present value, as would a decrease in cash flows or an increase in the initial investment.
    Answer (A) is incorrect because a decrease in the tax rate would decrease tax expense, thus increasing cash flows and the NPV. Answer (B) is incorrect because a decrease in the initial investment amount would increase the NPV. Answer (C) is incorrect because an extension of the project life and associated cash inflows would increase the NPV.

13. A disadvantage of the net present value method of capital expenditure evaluation is that it

    A. Is calculated using sensitivity analysis.

    B. Computes the true interest rate.

    C. Does not provide the true rate of return on investment.

    D. Is difficult to apply because it uses a trial-and-error approach.

Answer (C) is correct. *(CMA, adapted)*
    REQUIRED: The disadvantage of the NPV method.
    DISCUSSION: The NPV is broadly defined as the excess of the present value of the estimated net cash inflows over the net cost of the investment. A discount rate has to be stipulated by the person conducting the analysis. A disadvantage is that it does not provide the true rate of return for an investment, only that the rate of return is higher than a stipulated discount rate (which may be the cost of capital).
    Answer (A) is incorrect because the ability to perform sensitivity analysis is an advantage of the NPV method. Answer (B) is incorrect because the NPV method does not compute the true interest rate. Answer (D) is incorrect because the IRR method, not the NPV method, uses a trial-and-error approach when cash flows are not identical from year to year.

Questions 14 through 17 are based on the following information. In order to increase production capacity, Gunning Industries is considering replacing an existing production machine with a new technologically improved machine effective January 1. The following information is being considered by Gunning Industries:

- The new machine would be purchased for $160,000 in cash. Shipping, installation, and testing would cost an additional $30,000.

- The new machine is expected to increase annual sales by 20,000 units at a sales price of $40 per unit. Incremental operating costs include $30 per unit in variable costs and total fixed costs of $40,000 per year.

- The investment in the new machine will require an immediate increase in working capital of $35,000. This cash outflow will be recovered after 5 years.

- Gunning uses straight-line depreciation for financial reporting and tax reporting purposes. The new machine has an estimated useful life of 5 years and zero salvage value.

- Gunning is subject to a 40% corporate income tax rate.

Gunning uses the net present value method to analyze investments and will employ the following factors and rates:

Period	Present Value of $1 at 10%	Present Value of an Ordinary Annuity of $1 at 10%
1	.909	.909
2	.826	1.736
3	.751	2.487
4	.683	3.170
5	.621	3.791

14. Gunning Industries' net cash outflow in a capital budgeting decision is

A. $190,000

B. $195,000

C. $204,525

D. $225,000

Answer (D) is correct. *(CMA, adapted)*
REQUIRED: The net cash outflow in a capital budgeting decision.
DISCUSSION: The machine costs $160,000 and will require $30,000 to install and test. In addition, the company will have to invest in $35,000 of working capital to support the production of the new machine. Thus, the total investment necessary is $225,000.
Answer (A) is incorrect because $190,000 ignores the investment in working capital. Answer (B) is incorrect because $195,000 ignores the $30,000 of shipping, installation, and testing costs. Answer (C) is incorrect because $204,525 is the present value of $225,000 at 10% for 1 year.

15. Gunning Industries' discounted annual depreciation tax shield for the year of replacement is

A. $13,817

B. $16,762

C. $20,725

D. $22,800

Answer (A) is correct. *(CMA, adapted)*
REQUIRED: The discounted annual depreciation tax shield.
DISCUSSION: Gunning uses straight-line depreciation. Thus, the annual charge is $38,000 [($160,000 + $30,000) ÷ 5 years], and the tax savings is $15,200 ($38,000 × 40%). That benefit will be received in 1 year, so the present value is $13,817 ($15,200 tax savings × .909 present value of $1 for 1 year at 10%).
Answer (B) is incorrect because $16,762 is greater than the undiscounted tax savings. Answer (C) is incorrect because $20,725 assumes a 60% tax rate (the complement of the actual 40% rate). Answer (D) is incorrect because $22,800 assumes a 60% tax rate and no discounting.

16. The acquisition of the new production machine by Gunning Industries will contribute a discounted net-of-tax contribution margin of

A. $242,624

B. $303,280

C. $363,936

D. $454,920

Answer (D) is correct. *(CMA, adapted)*

REQUIRED: The discounted net-of-tax contribution margin from the new machine.

DISCUSSION: The new machine will increase sales by 20,000 units a year. The increase in the pretax total contribution margin will be $200,000 per year [20,000 units × ($40 SP – $30 VC)], and the annual increase in the after-tax contribution margin will be $120,000 [$200,000 × (1.0 – .4)]. The present value of the after-tax increase in the contribution margin over the 5-year useful life of the machine is $454,920 ($120,000 × 3.791 PV of an ordinary annuity for 5 years at 10%).

Answer (A) is incorrect because $242,624 deducts fixed costs from the pretax contribution margin and applies a 60% tax rate. Answer (B) is incorrect because $303,280 deducts fixed costs from the after-tax contribution margin before discounting. Answer (C) is incorrect because $363,936 deducts fixed costs from the contribution margin before calculating taxes and the present value.

17. The overall discounted cash flow impact of Gunning Industries' working capital investment for the new production machine would be

A. $(7,959)

B. $(10,080)

C. $(13,265)

D. $(35,000)

Answer (C) is correct. *(CMA, adapted)*

REQUIRED: The overall discounted cash flow impact of the working capital investment.

DISCUSSION: The $35,000 of working capital requires an immediate outlay for that amount, but it will be recovered in 5 years. Thus, the net discounted cash outflow is $13,265 [$35,000 initial investment – ($35,000 future inflow × .621 PV of $1 for 5 years at 10%)].

Answer (A) is incorrect because $(7,959) assumes the initial investment and its return are reduced by applying a 40% tax rate. Answer (B) is incorrect because $(10,080) assumes the initial investment was discounted for 1 year. Answer (D) is incorrect because $(35,000) fails to consider that the $35,000 will be recovered (essentially in the form of a salvage value) after the fifth year.

18. Jackson Corporation uses net present value techniques in evaluating its capital investment projects. The company is considering a new equipment acquisition that will cost $100,000, fully installed, and have a zero salvage value at the end of its five-year productive life. Jackson will depreciate the equipment on a straight-line basis for both financial and tax purposes. Jackson estimates $70,000 in annual recurring operating cash income and $20,000 in annual recurring operating cash expenses. Jackson's desired rate of return is 12% and its effective income tax rate is 40%. What is the net present value of this investment on an after-tax basis?

A. $28,840

B. $8,150

C. $36,990

D. $80,250

Answer (C) is correct. *(CMA, adapted)*

REQUIRED: The net present value on an after-tax basis.

DISCUSSION: Annual cash outflow for taxes is $12,000 {[$70,000 inflows – $20,000 cash operating expenses – ($100,000 ÷ 5) depreciation] × 40%}. The annual net cash inflow is therefore $38,000 ($70,000 – $20,000 – $12,000). The present value of these net inflows for a 5-year period is $136,990 ($38,000 × 3.605 present value of an ordinary annuity for 5 years at 12%), and the NPV of the investment is $36,990 ($136,990 – $100,000 investment).

Answer (A) is incorrect because $28,840 is the present value of the depreciation tax savings. Answer (B) is incorrect because $8,150 ignores the depreciation tax savings. Answer (D) is incorrect because $80,250 ignores taxes.

19. A weakness of the internal rate of return (IRR) approach for determining the acceptability of investments is that it

A. Does not consider the time value of money.

B. Is not a straightforward decision criterion.

C. Implicitly assumes that the firm is able to reinvest project cash flows at the firm's cost of capital.

D. Implicitly assumes that the firm is able to reinvest project cash flows at the project's internal rate of return.

Answer (D) is correct.   *(CMA, adapted)*
REQUIRED: The weakness of the internal rate of return approach.
DISCUSSION: The IRR is the rate at which the discounted future cash flows equal the net investment (NPV = 0). One disadvantage of the method is that inflows from the early years are assumed to be reinvested at the IRR. This assumption may not be sound. Investments in the future may not earn as high a rate as is currently available.
Answer (A) is incorrect because the IRR method considers the time value of money. Answer (B) is incorrect because the IRR provides a straightforward decision criterion. Any project with an IRR greater than the firm's desired rate of return is acceptable. Answer (C) is incorrect because the IRR method implicitly assumes reinvestment at the IRR; the NPV method implicitly assumes reinvestment at the cost of capital.

20. The internal rate of return (IRR) is the

A. Hurdle rate.

B. Rate of interest for which the net present value is greater than 1.0.

C. Rate of interest for which the net present value is equal to zero.

D. Rate of return generated from the operational cash flows.

Answer (C) is correct.   *(CMA, adapted)*
REQUIRED: The true statement about the internal rate of return (IRR).
DISCUSSION: The IRR is the interest rate at which the present value of the expected future cash inflows is equal to the present value of the cash outflows for a project. Thus, the IRR is the interest rate that will produce a net present value (NPV) equal to zero. The IRR method assumes that the cash flows will be reinvested at the internal rate of return.
Answer (A) is incorrect because the hurdle rate is a concept used to calculate the NPV of a project; it is determined by management prior to the analysis. Answer (B) is incorrect because the IRR is the rate of interest at which the NPV is zero. Answer (D) is incorrect because the IRR is a means of evaluating potential investment projects.

18.2 Payback and Discounted Payback

Questions 21 through 24 are based on the following information. Henderson, Inc. has purchased a new fleet of trucks to deliver its merchandise. The trucks have a useful life of 8 years and cost a total of $500,000. Henderson expects its net increase in after-tax cash flow to be $150,000 in Year 1, $175,000 in Year 2, $125,000 in Year 3, and $100,000 in each of the remaining years.

21. Ignoring the time value of money, how long will it take Henderson to recover the amount of investment?

A. 3.5 years.

B. 4.0 years.

C. 4.2 years.

D. 5 years.

Answer (A) is correct.   *(Publisher, adapted)*
REQUIRED: The payback period for an investment, ignoring the time value of money.
DISCUSSION: The payback period for an investment, ignoring the time value of money, can be found by accumulating each year's net cash flows until the initial investment is recovered. The amount accumulated after 3 years is $450,000. Thus, 50% of Year 4 cash flows is needed to recover the initial investment. The payback period is 3.5 years.
Answer (B) is incorrect because 4 years includes the additional $50,000 of Year 4. Answer (C) is incorrect because 4.2 years takes the average inflow of all 8 years and divides that into the $500,000 initial investment. Answer (D) is incorrect because 5 years uses only the cash flows from the remaining 5 years.

22. What is the payback reciprocal for Henderson's fleet of trucks?

    A. 29%

    B. 25%

    C. 24%

    D. 20%

Answer (A) is correct. *(Publisher, adapted)*
REQUIRED: The payback reciprocal for an investment.
DISCUSSION: The payback reciprocal for an investment is found by dividing 1 by the payback time. The payback time for this investment is 3.5 years, and the payback reciprocal is 1 divided by 3.5, or 29%.
Answer (B) is incorrect because 25% includes the additional $50,000 of Year 4 in the payback time. Answer (C) is incorrect because 24% takes the average inflow of all 8 years and divides that into the $500,000 initial investment in the payback time. Answer (D) is incorrect because 20% uses only the cash flows from the remaining 5 years in the payback time.

23. If the net cash flow is $130,000 a year, what is the payback time for Henderson's fleet of trucks?

    A. 3 years.

    B. 3.15 years.

    C. 3.85 years.

    D. 4 years.

Answer (C) is correct. *(Publisher, adapted)*
REQUIRED: The payback period for an investment, ignoring the time value of money.
DISCUSSION: The payback period for an investment, ignoring the time value of money, can be found by accumulating each year's net cash flows until the initial investment is recovered. Therefore, dividing the $500,000 initial investment by the annual $130,000 inflow gives a payback time of 3.85 years.
Answer (A) is incorrect because 3.85 years is the length of the payback period. Answer (B) is incorrect because 3.85 years is the length of the payback period. Answer (D) is incorrect because 4 years does not prorate the final $130,000.

24. Based on a 6% annual interest rate, what is the discounted payback period for Henderson's fleet of trucks?

    A. 3.5 years.

    B. 3.98 years.

    C. 4.25 years.

    D. 5.0 years.

Answer (C) is correct. *(Publisher, adapted)*
REQUIRED: The discounted payback period assuming a 6% discount rate.
DISCUSSION: The discounted payback period for an investment, assuming a 6% discount, can be found by accumulating each year's discounted net cash flows until the initial investment is recovered.

$150,000 × .94339 = $141,508.50
175,000 × .88999 = 155,748.25
125,000 × .83962 = 104,952.50
100,000 × .79209 = 79,209.00
$481,418.25

Thus, the answer is something greater than four years. After four years, an additional $18,581.75 ($500,000 – $481,418.25) is needed. The calculation for the fifth year is $74,726 ($100,000 × .74726). Consequently, the discounted payback period is approximately 4.25 years [4 + ($18,581.75 ÷ $74,726)].
Answer (A) is incorrect because 3.5 years is the undiscounted payback period. Answer (B) is incorrect because 3.98 years results from not discounting the cash flows in the fourth year. Answer (D) is incorrect because the full fifth year is not necessary.

25. The capital budgeting model that is generally considered the best model for long-range decision making is the

    A. Payback model.

    B. Accounting rate of return model.

    C. Unadjusted rate of return model.

    D. Discounted cash flow model.

Answer (D) is correct. *(CMA, adapted)*
REQUIRED: The best capital budgeting model for long-range decision making.
DISCUSSION: The capital budgeting methods that are generally considered the best for long-range decision making are the internal rate of return and net present value methods. These are both discounted cash flow methods.
Answer (A) is incorrect because the payback method gives no consideration to the time value of money or to returns after the payback period. Answer (B) is incorrect because the accounting rate of return does not consider the time value of money. Answer (C) is incorrect because the unadjusted rate of return does not consider the time value of money.

26. When evaluating projects, breakeven time is best described as

A. Annual fixed costs ÷ monthly contribution margin.

B. Project investment ÷ annual net cash inflows.

C. The point where cumulative cash inflows on a project equal total cash outflows.

D. The point at which discounted cumulative cash inflows on a project equal discounted total cash outflows.

Answer (D) is correct. *(CMA, adapted)*
REQUIRED: The definition of breakeven time.
DISCUSSION: Breakeven time is a capital budgeting tool that is widely used to evaluate the rapidity of new product development. It is the period required for the discounted cumulative cash inflows for a project to equal the discounted cumulative cash outflows. The concept is similar to the payback period, but it is more sophisticated because it incorporates the time value of money. It also differs from the payback method because the period covered begins at the outset of a project, not when the initial cash outflow occurs.
Answer (A) is incorrect because it is related to breakeven point, not breakeven time. Answer (B) is incorrect because the payback period equals investment divided by annual undiscounted net cash inflows. Answer (C) is incorrect because the payback period is the period required for total undiscounted cash inflows to equal total undiscounted cash outflows.

27. Irwinn Co. is considering an investment in a capital project. The sole outlay will be $800,000 at the outset of the project, and the annual net after-tax cash inflow will be $216,309.75 for 6 years. The present value factors at Irwinn's 8% cost of capital are

Year	PV Factors
1	.926
2	.857
3	.794
4	.735
5	.681
6	.630

What is the breakeven time (BET)?

A. 3.70 years.

B. 4.57 years.

C. 5.00 years.

D. 6.00 years.

Answer (B) is correct. *(Publisher, adapted)*
REQUIRED: The breakeven time.
DISCUSSION: Breakeven time is a more sophisticated version of the payback method. Breakeven time is defined as the period required for the discounted cumulative cash inflows on a project to equal the discounted cumulative cash outflows (usually the initial cost). Thus, it is the time necessary for the present value of the discounted cash flows to equal zero. This period begins at the outset of a project, not when the initial cash outflow occurs. Accordingly, the BET is calculated as follows:

Year	After-Tax Cash Flow	PV of Inflow	Cumulative PV
1	$216,309.75	$200,302.82	$200,302.82
2	216,309.75	185,377.45	385,680.27
3	216,309.75	171,749.94	557,430.21
4	216,309.75	158,987.66	716,417.87
5	216,309.75	147,306.93	

Amount required in Year 5:
$$\$800,000 - \$716,417.87 = \$83,582.13$$
$$BET = 4 \text{ years} + (\$83,582.13 \div \$147,306.93) = 4.57 \text{ years}$$

Answer (A) is incorrect because 3.70 years is the regular payback period. Answer (C) is incorrect because interpolation is necessary to determine the BET. Answer (D) is incorrect because the duration of net after-tax cash inflows is 6.00 years.

28. A characteristic of the payback method (before taxes) is that it

A. Incorporates the time value of money.

B. Neglects total project profitability.

C. Uses accrual accounting inflows in the numerator of the calculation.

D. Uses the estimated expected life of the asset in the denominator of the calculation.

Answer (B) is correct. *(CMA, adapted)*
REQUIRED: The characteristic of the payback method.
DISCUSSION: The payback method calculates the number of years required to complete the return of the original investment. This measure is computed by dividing the net investment required by the average expected cash flow to be generated, resulting in the number of years required to recover the original investment. Payback is easy to calculate but has two principal problems: it ignores the time value of money, and it gives no consideration to returns after the payback period. Thus, it ignores total project profitability.
Answer (A) is incorrect because the payback method does not incorporate the time value of money. Answer (C) is incorrect because the payback method uses the net investment in the numerator of the calculation. Answer (D) is incorrect because payback uses the net annual cash inflows in the denominator of the calculation.

29. Jasper Company has a payback goal of 3 years on new equipment acquisitions. A new sorter is being evaluated that costs $450,000 and has a 5-year life. Straight-line depreciation will be used; no salvage is anticipated. Jasper is subject to a 40% income tax rate. To meet the company's payback goal, the sorter must generate reductions in annual cash operating costs of

   A. $60,000

   B. $100,000

   C. $150,000

   D. $190,000

Answer (D) is correct. *(CMA, adapted)*
REQUIRED: The cash savings that must be generated to achieve a targeted payback period.
DISCUSSION: Given a periodic constant cash flow, the payback period is calculated by dividing cost by the annual cash inflows, or cash savings. To achieve a payback period of 3 years, the annual increment in net cash inflow generated by the investment must be $150,000 ($450,000 ÷ 3-year targeted payback period). This amount equals the total reduction in cash operating costs minus related taxes. Depreciation is $90,000 ($450,000 ÷ 5 years). Because depreciation is a noncash deductible expense, it shields $90,000 of the cash savings from taxation. Accordingly, $60,000 ($150,000 − $90,000) of the additional net cash inflow must come from after-tax net income. At a 40% tax rate, $60,000 of after-tax income equals $100,000 ($60,000 ÷ 60%) of pre-tax income from cost savings, and the outflow for taxes is $40,000. Thus, the annual reduction in cash operating costs required is $190,000 ($150,000 additional net cash inflow required + $40,000 tax outflow).
Answer (A) is incorrect because $60,000 is after-tax net income from the cost savings. Answer (B) is incorrect because $100,000 is the pre-tax income from the cost savings. Answer (C) is incorrect because $150,000 ignores the impact of depreciation and income taxes.

30. The length of time required to recover the initial cash outlay of a capital project is determined by using the

   A. Discounted cash flow method.

   B. Payback method.

   C. Weighted net present value method.

   D. Net present value method.

Answer (B) is correct. *(CMA, adapted)*
REQUIRED: The method of determining the time required to recover the initial cash outlay of a capital project.
DISCUSSION: The payback method measures the number of years required to complete the return of the original investment. This measure is computed by dividing the net investment by the average expected cash inflows to be generated, resulting in the number of years required to recover the original investment. The payback method gives no consideration to the time value of money, and there is no consideration of returns after the payback period.
Answer (A) is incorrect because the discounted cash flow method computes a rate of return. Answer (C) is incorrect because the net present value method is based on discounted cash flows; the length of time to recover an investment is not the result. Answer (D) is incorrect because the net present value method is based on discounted cash flows; the length of time to recover an investment is not the result.

31. Which one of the following statements about the payback method of investment analysis is correct? The payback method

   A. Does not consider the time value of money.

   B. Considers cash flows after the payback has been reached.

   C. Uses discounted cash flow techniques.

   D. Generally leads to the same decision as other methods for long-term projects.

Answer (A) is correct. *(CMA, adapted)*
REQUIRED: The true statement about the payback method of investment analysis.
DISCUSSION: The payback method calculates the amount of time required to complete the return of the original investment, i.e., the time it takes for a new asset to pay for itself. Although the payback method is easy to calculate, it has inherent problems. The time value of money and returns after the payback period are not considered.
Answer (B) is incorrect because the payback method ignores cash flows after payback. Answer (C) is incorrect because the payback method does not use discounted cash flow techniques. Answer (D) is incorrect because the payback method may lead to different decisions.

32. The payback reciprocal can be used to approximate a project's

A. Profitability index.

B. Net present value.

C. Accounting rate of return if the cash flow pattern is relatively stable.

D. Internal rate of return if the cash flow pattern is relatively stable.

Answer (D) is correct. *(CMA, adapted)*
REQUIRED: The item that can be approximated by a project's payback reciprocal.
DISCUSSION: The payback reciprocal (1 ÷ payback) has been shown to approximate the internal rate of return (IRR) when the periodic cash flows are equal and the life of the project is at least twice the payback period.
Answer (A) is incorrect because the payback reciprocal is not related to the profitability index. Answer (B) is incorrect because the payback reciprocal approximates the IRR, which is the rate at which the NPV is $0. Answer (C) is incorrect because the accounting rate of return is based on accrual-income based figures, not on discounted cash flows.

33. The bailout payback method

A. Incorporates the time value of money.

B. Equals the recovery period from normal operations.

C. Eliminates the disposal value from the payback calculation.

D. Measures the risk if a project is terminated.

Answer (D) is correct. *(CMA, adapted)*
REQUIRED: The true statement about the bailout payback method.
DISCUSSION: The payback period equals the net investment divided by the average expected cash flow, resulting in the number of years required to recover the original investment. The bailout payback incorporates the salvage value of the asset into the calculation. It determines the length of the payback period when the periodic cash inflows are combined with the salvage value. Hence, the method measures risk. The longer the payback period, the more risky the investment.
Answer (A) is incorrect because the bailout payback method does not consider the time value of money. Answer (B) is incorrect because the bailout payback includes salvage value as well as cash flow from operations. Answer (C) is incorrect because the bailout payback incorporates the disposal value in the payback calculation.

34. Whatney Co. is considering the acquisition of a new, more efficient press. The cost of the press is $360,000, and the press has an estimated 6-year life with zero salvage value. Whatney uses straight-line depreciation for both financial reporting and income tax reporting purposes and has a 40% corporate income tax rate. In evaluating equipment acquisitions of this type, Whatney uses a goal of a 4-year payback period. To meet Whatney's desired payback period, the press must produce a minimum annual before-tax operating cash savings of

A. $90,000

B. $110,000

C. $114,000

D. $150,000

Answer (B) is correct. *(CMA, adapted)*
REQUIRED: The minimum annual before-tax operating cash savings yielding a specified payback period.
DISCUSSION: Payback is the number of years required to complete the return of the original investment. Given a periodic constant cash flow, the payback period equals net investment divided by the constant expected periodic after-tax cash flow. The desired payback period is 4 years, so the constant after-tax annual cash flow must be $90,000 ($360,000 ÷ 4). Assuming that the company has sufficient other income to permit realization of the full tax savings, depreciation of the machine will shield $60,000 ($360,000 ÷ 6) of income from taxation each year, an after-tax cash savings of $24,000 ($60,000 × 40%). Thus, the machine must generate an additional $66,000 ($90,000 – $24,000) of after-tax cash savings from operations. This amount is equivalent to $110,000 [$66,000 ÷ (1.0 – .4)] of before-tax operating cash savings.
Answer (A) is incorrect because $90,000 is the total desired annual after-tax cash savings. Answer (C) is incorrect because $114,000 results from adding, not subtracting, the $24,000 of tax depreciation savings to determine the minimum annual after-tax operating savings. Answer (D) is incorrect because $150,000 assumes that depreciation is not tax deductible.

Use Gleim's **CMA Test Prep** for interactive testing with **over 2,000 additional multiple-choice questions!**

STUDY UNIT NINETEEN
RANKING INVESTMENT PROJECTS

(5 pages of outline)

This study unit is the **third of four** on **investment decisions**. The relative weight assigned to this major topic in Part 3 of the exam is **20%** at **skill level C** (all six skill types required). The four study units are

Study Unit 17: The Capital Budgeting Process
Study Unit 18: Discounted Cash Flow and Payback
Study Unit 19: Ranking Investment Projects
Study Unit 20: Risk Analysis and Real Options

After studying the outline and answering the multiple-choice questions, you will have the skills necessary to address the following topics listed in the IMA's Learning Outcome Statements:

Part 3 – Section E.4. Ranking investment projects

The candidate should be able to:

    a.   define capital rationing and mutually exclusive projects

    b.   rank capital investment projects and recommend optimal investments using the profitability index

    c.   determine when the profitability index would be recommended over the NPV rule (i.e., independent projects with capital rationing)

    d.   identify and discuss the problems inherent in comparing projects of unequal scale and/or unequal lives

    e.   demonstrate an understanding of the advantages and disadvantages of the different methods of evaluating alternate capital investment projects

    f.   identify alternative solutions to the ranking problem, including internal capital markets and linear programming

19.1 RANKING INVESTMENT PROJECTS

1.   **Capital rationing** exists when a firm sets a limit on the amount of funds to be invested during a given period. In such situations, a firm cannot afford to undertake all profitable projects.

    a.   Another way of stating this is that the firm cannot invest the entire amount needed to fund its theoretically optimal capital budget.

        1)   Only those projects that will return the **greatest NPV** for the limited capital available in the **internal capital market** can be undertaken.

    b.   **Reasons** for capital rationing include

        1)   A lack of nonmonetary resources (e.g., managerial or technical personnel)

        2)   A desire to control estimation bias (overly favorable projections of a project's cash flows)

        3)   An unwillingness to issue new equity (e.g., because of its cost or a reluctance to reveal data in regulatory filings)

2. The **profitability index** (or excess present value index) is a method for ranking projects to ensure that limited resources are placed with the investments that will return the highest NPV.

$$Profitability\ index = \frac{NPV\ of\ future\ cash\ flows}{Net\ investment}$$

a. EXAMPLE: A company has $200,000 to invest. It can therefore either invest in Project F below or in Projects G and H.

	Initial	Year 1	Year 2	Year 3	Year 4
Project F	$(200,000)	$140,000	$100,000	-	-
Project G	(100,000)	30,000	30,000	$30,000	$30,000
Project H	(100,000)	30,000	28,000	28,000	34,000

1) Discounting each project at 6% results in the following:

	NPV	Divided by: Initial Investment	Equals: Profitability Index
Project F	$21,075	$200,000	0.105
Project G	15,002	100,000	0.150
Project H	15,222	100,000	0.152

2) In an environment of capital rationing, the company can see that it should invest first in Project H, then in Project G, and, if new funding is found, last in Project F.

3. **Internal capital market** is a way of referring to the provision of funds by one division of a firm to another division. A division operating in a mature industry that generates a lot of cash can provide funding to another division that is in the cash-hungry development stage.

a. An advantage is the avoidance of stock issue costs or interest costs on new debt.

b. A disadvantage is that calling it a "market" is somewhat misleading. The dynamics of the process are more akin to centralized planning and budgeting than to the workings of a free marketplace.

4. **Linear programming** is a technique (now usually computerized) for optimizing resource allocations so as to select the most profitable or least costly way to use available resources.

a. It involves optimizing an objective function subject to the net of constraint equations.

b. For example, a linear programming application can maximize NPV for a group of projects in a capital rationing situation (expenditure constraint).

5. Stop and review! You have completed the outline for this subunit. Study multiple-choice questions 1 through 12 beginning on page 443.

19.2 COMPREHENSIVE EXAMPLES

1. **EXAMPLE:** Hazman Company plans to replace an old piece of equipment that is obsolete and expected to be unreliable under the stress of daily operations. The equipment is fully depreciated, and no salvage value can be realized upon its disposal. One piece of equipment being considered as a replacement will provide an annual cash savings of $7,000 before income taxes and without regard to the effect of depreciation. The equipment costs $18,000 and has an estimated useful life of 5 years. No salvage value will be used for depreciation purposes because the equipment is expected to have no value at the end of 5 years.

    Hazman uses the straight-line depreciation method on all equipment for both book and tax purposes. Hence, annual depreciation is $3,600. The company is subject to a 40% tax rate. Hazman's desired rate of return is 14%, so it will use the 14% column from a present value table.

    Analysis of cash flows

		Annual Before-Tax Cash Flow	Annual Tax Savings (Tax)	Annual After-Tax Cash Flow	Annual After-Tax Net Income
Investment	Year 0	$(18,000)	-0-	$(18,000)	-0-
Annual cash savings	Years 1-5	$ 7,000	$(2,800)	$ 4,200	$ 4,200
Depreciation tax shield	Years 1-5		1,440	1,440	(2,160)
Totals				$ 5,640	$ 2,040

    a. **Net present value** = (After-tax cash flows × Present value of an annuity)
        − Net investment
        = ($5,640 × 3.43) − $18,000
        = $19,345 − $18,000
        = **$1,345**

    b. **Internal rate of return.** The goal is to find the discount rate that most nearly equals the net investment.

Net present value at 16%:	$5,640 × 3.27 =	$18,443
Net present value at 18%:	$5,640 × 3.13 =	17,653
Difference		$ 790

Net present value at 16%:	$18,443
Initial investment	18,000
Difference	$ 443

Estimated increment ($443 ÷ $790) × 2% =	1.1%
Rate used	16.0
Internal rate of return	17.1%

    c. **Payback period** = Net investment ÷ After-tax cash flow
        = $18,000 ÷ $5,640
        = **3.19 years**

    d. **Profitability index** = NPV of future cash flows ÷ Net investment
        = ($5,640 × 3.43) ÷ $18,000
        = $19,345 ÷ $18,000
        = **1.07**

2.   EXAMPLE: The management of Flesher Farms is trying to decide whether to buy a new team of mules at a cost of $1,000 or a new tractor at a cost of $10,000. They will perform the same job. But because the mules require more laborers, the annual return is only $250 of net cash inflows. The tractor will return $2,000 of net cash inflows per year. The mules have a working life of 8 years and the tractor 10 years. Neither investment is expected to have a salvage value at the end of its useful life.

    a.   **Net Present Value**

	Mules	Tractor
Net cash inflows	$ 250	$ 2,000
Times: present value factor	6.209	7.360
Present value	1,552	14,720
Less: initial investment	(1,000)	(10,000)
Net present value	**$ 552**	**$ 4,720**

    b.   **Internal Rate of Return**

        1)   **Mules:** Initial investment ÷ Net cash inflows = $1,000 ÷ $250 = 4

            a)   On the 8-year line, a factor of 4 indicates a rate of return of approximately **18.7%**.

        2)   **Tractor:** Initial investment ÷ Net cash inflows = $10,000 ÷ $2,000 = 5

            a)   On the 10-year line, a factor of 5 indicates a rate of return of approximately **15.2%**.

    c.   **Payback Period**

        1)   **Mules:**   Initial investment ÷ Net cash inflows = $1,000 ÷ $250 = **4 years**

        2)   **Tractor:** Initial investment ÷ Net cash inflows = $10,000 ÷ $2,000 = **5 years**

    d.   **Profitability Index**

        1)   **Mules:** Present value of cash inflows ÷ Initial investment = $1,552 ÷ $1,000
                                                = **1.552**

        2)   **Tractor:** Present value of cash inflows ÷ Initial investment = $14,720 ÷ $10,000
                                                = **1.472**

    e.   The mule investment has the higher IRR, the quicker payback, and the better profitability index.

        1)   However, the tractor has the better net present value. The various methods thus give different answers to the investment question.

        2)   Either investment will be profitable. Management may decide to let noneconomic factors influence the decision.

            a)   For example, the mules will require the use of more laborers. If unemployment in the community is high, management might wish to achieve a social goal of providing more jobs.

            b)   Alternatively, a labor shortage might convince management to buy the tractor to reduce labor worries.

3.   Stop and review! You have completed the outline for this subunit. Study multiple-choice questions 13 through 27 beginning on page 447.

19.3 CORE CONCEPTS

Ranking Investment Projects

- **Capital rationing** exists when a firm sets a limit on the amount of funds to be invested during a given period. In such situations, a firm cannot afford to undertake all profitable projects. **Only those projects** that will return the greatest NPV for the limited capital available in the internal capital market can be undertaken.

- The **profitability index** (or excess present value index) is a method for ranking projects to ensure that limited resources are placed with the investments that will return the highest NPV.

  Profitability index = NPV of future cash flows ÷ Net investment

- **Internal capital market** is a way of referring to the provision of funds by one division of a firm to another division. A division operating in a mature industry that generates a lot of cash can provide funding to another division that is in the cash-hungry development stage.

  - An advantage is the avoidance of stock issue costs or interest costs on new debt.

  - A disadvantage is that calling it a "market" is somewhat misleading. The dynamics of the process are more akin to centralized planning and budgeting than to the workings of a free marketplace.

- **Linear programming** is a technique (now usually computerized) for optimizing resource allocations so as to select the most profitable or least costly way to use available resources. It involves optimizing an objective function subject to the net of constraint equations.

  - For example, a linear programming application can maximize NPV for a group of projects in a capital rationing situation (expenditure constraint).

QUESTIONS

19.1 Ranking Investment Projects

1. Barker, Inc. has no capital rationing constraint and is analyzing many independent investment alternatives. Barker should accept all investment proposals

- A. If debt financing is available for them.
- B. That have positive cash flows.
- C. That provide returns greater than the before-tax cost of debt.
- D. That have a positive net present value.

Answer (D) is correct. *(CMA, adapted)*

REQUIRED: The investment proposals that should be accepted by a company with no capital rationing constraints.

DISCUSSION: A company should accept any investment proposal, unless some are mutually exclusive, that has a positive net present value or an internal rate of return greater than the company's desired rate of return.

Answer (A) is incorrect because the mere availability of financing is not the only consideration; more important is the cost of the financing, which must be less than the rate of return on the proposed investment. Answer (B) is incorrect because an investment with positive cash flows may be a bad investment due to the time value of money; cash flows in later years are not as valuable as those in earlier years. Answer (C) is incorrect because returns should exceed the desired rate of return.

2. The profitability index approach to investment analysis

A. Fails to consider the timing of project cash flows.

B. Considers only the project's contribution to net income and does not consider cash flow effects.

C. Always yields the same accept/reject decisions for independent projects as the net present value method.

D. Always yields the same accept/reject decisions for mutually exclusive projects as the net present value method.

Answer (C) is correct. *(CMA, adapted)*
REQUIRED: The true statement about the profitability index.
DISCUSSION: The profitability index is the ratio of the present value of future net cash inflows to the initial net cash investment. It is a variation of the net present value (NPV) method and facilitates the comparison of different-sized investments. Because it is based on the NPV method, the profitability index will yield the same decision as the NPV for independent projects. However, decisions may differ for mutually exclusive projects of different sizes.
Answer (A) is incorrect because the profitability index, like the NPV method, discounts cash flows based on the cost of capital. Answer (B) is incorrect because the profitability index is cash based. Answer (D) is incorrect because the NPV and the profitability index may yield different decisions if projects are mutually exclusive and of different sizes.

3. If an investment project has a profitability index of 1.15, the

A. Project's internal rate of return is 15%.

B. Project's cost of capital is greater than its internal rate of return.

C. Project's internal rate of return exceeds its net present value.

D. Net present value of the project is positive.

Answer (D) is correct. *(CMA, adapted)*
REQUIRED: The meaning of a profitability index in excess of 1.0.
DISCUSSION: The profitability index is the ratio of the present value of future net cash inflows to the initial net cash investment. It is a variation of the NPV method that facilitates comparison of different-sized investments. A profitability index greater than 1.0 indicates a profitable investment or one that has a positive net present value.
Answer (A) is incorrect because the IRR is the discount rate at which the NPV is $0, which is also the rate at which the profitability index is 1.0. The IRR cannot be determined solely from the index. Answer (B) is incorrect because, if the index is 1.15 and the discount rate is the cost of capital, the NPV is positive, and the IRR must be higher than the cost of capital. Answer (C) is incorrect because the IRR is a discount rate, whereas the NPV is an amount.

4. The technique used to evaluate all possible capital projects of different dollar amounts and then rank them according to their desirability is the

A. Profitability index method.

B. Net present value method.

C. Payback method.

D. Discounted cash flow method.

Answer (A) is correct. *(CMA, adapted)*
REQUIRED: The technique used to evaluate and rank all possible capital projects of varying dollar amounts.
DISCUSSION: The profitability index is the ratio of the present value of future net cash inflows to the initial cash investment; that is, the figures are those used to calculate the net present value (NPV), but the numbers are divided rather than subtracted. This variation of the NPV method facilitates comparison of different-sized investments. It provides an optimal ranking in the absence of capital rationing.
Answer (B) is incorrect because the net present value method does not provide a return per dollar invested and is therefore not as effective as the profitability index in the absence of capital rationing. Answer (C) is incorrect because the payback method gives no consideration to the time value of money or to returns after the payback period. Answer (D) is incorrect because the profitability index method and the NPV method are discounted cash flow methods. However, the profitability index method is the variant that purports to calculate a return per dollar of investment.

5. The profitability index (present value index)

A. Represents the ratio of the discounted net cash outflows to cash inflows.

B. Is the relationship between the net discounted cash inflows less the discounted cash outflows divided by the discounted cash outflows.

C. Is calculated by dividing the discounted profits by the cash outflows.

D. Is the ratio of the discounted net cash inflows to discounted cash outflows.

Answer (D) is correct. *(CMA, adapted)*
REQUIRED: The true statement about the profitability index.
DISCUSSION: The profitability index, also known as the excess present value index, is the ratio of the present value of future net cash inflows to the initial net cash investment (discounted cash outflows). This tool is a variation of the NPV method that facilitates comparison of different-sized investments.
Answer (A) is incorrect because the cash inflows are also discounted in the profitability index. Answer (B) is incorrect because the numerator is the discounted net cash inflows. Answer (C) is incorrect because the profitability index is based on cash flows, not profits.

6. The method that divides a project's annual after-tax net income by the average investment cost to measure the estimated performance of a capital investment is the

    A. Internal rate of return method.

    B. Accounting rate of return method.

    C. Payback method.

    D. Net present value (NPV) method.

Answer (B) is correct. *(CMA, adapted)*
    REQUIRED: The capital budgeting method that divides annual after-tax net income by the average investment cost.
    DISCUSSION: The accounting rate of return uses undiscounted net income (not cash flows) to determine a rate of profitability. Annual after-tax net income is divided by the average carrying amount (or the initial value) of the investment in assets.
    Answer (A) is incorrect because the internal rate of return is the rate at which NPV is zero. The minimum desired rate of return is not used in the discounting. Answer (C) is incorrect because the payback period is the time required to complete the return of the original investment. This method gives no consideration to the time value of money or to returns after the payback period. Answer (D) is incorrect because the NPV method computes the discounted present value of future cash inflows to determine whether it is greater than the initial cash outflow.

7. If income tax considerations are ignored, how is depreciation handled by the following capital budgeting techniques?

	Internal Rate of Return	Accounting Rate of Return	Payback
A.	Excluded	Included	Excluded
B.	Included	Excluded	Included
C.	Excluded	Excluded	Included
D.	Included	Included	Included

Answer (A) is correct. *(CMA, adapted)*
    REQUIRED: The manner in which depreciation is handled by each capital budgeting technique.
    DISCUSSION: If taxes are ignored, depreciation is not a consideration in any of the methods based on cash flows because it is a non-cash expense. Thus, the internal rate of return, net present value, and payback methods would not consider depreciation because these methods are based on cash flows. However, the accounting rate of return is based on net income as calculated on an income statement. Because depreciation is included in the determination of accrual accounting net income, it would affect the calculation of the accounting rate of return.

8. Which one of the following capital investment evaluation methods does not take the time value of money into consideration?

    A. Net present value.

    B. Discounted payback.

    C. Internal rate of return.

    D. Accounting rate of return.

Answer (D) is correct. *(CMA, adapted)*
    REQUIRED: The capital investment evaluation method that does not discount cash flows.
    DISCUSSION: The accounting rate of return (unadjusted rate of return or rate of return on the carrying amount) equals accounting net income divided by the required initial or average investment. The accounting rate of return ignores the time value of money.
    Answer (A) is incorrect because the net present value is the sum of the present values of all the cash inflows and outflows associated with an investment. Answer (B) is incorrect because the discounted payback method calculates the payback period by determining the present values of the future cash flows. Answer (C) is incorrect because the internal rate of return is the discount rate at which the NPV is zero.

9. Which mutually exclusive project would you select if both are priced at $1,000 and your discount rate is 14%: Project A, with three annual cash flows of $1,000, Project B, with three years of zero cash flow followed by three years of $1,500 annually?

    A. Project A.

    B. Project B.

    C. The IRRs are equal, hence you are indifferent.

    D. The NPVs are equal, hence you are indifferent.

Answer (B) is correct. *(Publisher, adapted)*
    REQUIRED: The project with the highest NPV.
    DISCUSSION: Project A's NPV is calculated as follows:

$1,000 × 2.322	$2,322.00
– Original cost	(1,000.00)
NPV	$1,322.00

The second project's NPV is:

$1,500 × (3.889 – 2.322)	$2,350.00
– Original cost	(1,000.00)
NPV	$1,350.50

Since Project B has a slightly higher NPV, it should be selected.
    Answer (A) is incorrect because Project B has a slightly higher NPV and IRR. Answer (C) is incorrect because Project B has a slightly higher IRR. Answer (D) is incorrect because Project B has a slightly higher NPV.

Questions 10 through 12 are based on the following information. Maloney Company uses a 12% hurdle rate for all capital expenditures and has done the following analysis for four projects for the upcoming year:

	Project 1	Project 2	Project 3	Project 4
Initial outlay	$4,960,000	$5,440,000	$4,000,000	$5,960,000
Annual net cash inflows:				
Year 1	1,600,000	1,900,000	1,300,000	2,000,000
Year 2	1,900,000	2,500,000	1,400,000	2,700,000
Year 3	1,800,000	1,800,000	1,600,000	1,800,000
Year 4	1,600,000	1,200,000	800,000	1,300,000
Net present value	281,280	293,240	(75,960)	85,520
Profitability index	106%	105%	98%	101%
Internal rate of return	14%	15%	11%	13%

10. Which project(s) should Maloney undertake during the upcoming year assuming it has no budget restrictions?

A. All of the projects.

B. Projects 1, 2, and 3.

C. Projects 1, 2, and 4.

D. Projects 1 and 2.

Answer (C) is correct. *(Publisher, adapted)*
REQUIRED: The project(s) that should be undertaken given no capital rationing.
DISCUSSION: A company using the net present value (NPV) method should undertake all projects with positive NPVs that are not mutually exclusive. Given that Projects 1, 2, and 4 have positive NPVs, those projects should be undertaken. Furthermore, a company using the internal rate of return (IRR) as a decision rule ordinarily chooses projects with a return greater than the cost of capital. Given a 12% cost of capital, Projects 1, 2, and 4 should be chosen using an IRR criterion if they are not mutually exclusive. Use of the profitability index yields a similar decision because a project with an index greater than 100% should be undertaken.
Answer (A) is incorrect because Project 3 has a negative NPV. Answer (B) is incorrect because Project 3 has a negative NPV. Answer (D) is incorrect because Project 4 has a positive NPV and should be undertaken.

11. Which projects should Maloney undertake during the upcoming year if it has only $12,000,000 of investment funds available?

A. Projects 1 and 3.

B. Projects 1, 2, and 4.

C. Projects 1 and 4.

D. Projects 1 and 2.

Answer (D) is correct. *(Publisher, adapted)*
REQUIRED: The project(s) that should be undertaken given a capital rationing limitation of $12,000,000.
DISCUSSION: With only $12,000,000 available and each project costing $4,000,000 or more, no more than two projects can be undertaken. Accordingly, projects should be selected because they have the greatest NPVs and profitability indexes.
Answer (A) is incorrect because Project 3 has a negative NPV. Answer (B) is incorrect because choosing three projects violates the $12,000,000 limitation. Answer (C) is incorrect because the combined NPV of Projects 1 and 4 is less than the combined NPV of Projects 1 and 2.

12. Which project(s) should Maloney undertake during the upcoming year if it has only $6,000,000 of funds available?

A. Project 3.

B. Projects 1 and 2.

C. Project 1.

D. Project 2.

Answer (C) is correct. *(Publisher, adapted)*
REQUIRED: The project(s) that should be undertaken given a capital rationing limitation of $6,000,000.
DISCUSSION: With only $6,000,000 available and each project costing $4,000,000 or more, no more than one project can be undertaken. Project 1 should be chosen because it has a positive NPV and the highest profitability index. The high profitability index means that the company will achieve the highest NPV per dollar of investment with Project 1. The profitability index facilitates comparison of different-sized investments.
Answer (A) is incorrect because Project 3 has a negative NPV and should not be selected regardless of the capital available. Answer (B) is incorrect because selecting two projects violates the $6,000,000 limitation on funds. Answer (D) is incorrect because, despite having the highest NPV, Project 2 has a lower profitability index than Project 1. Consequently, Project 1 offers the greater return per dollar of investment.

19.2 Comprehensive Examples

Questions 13 through 16 are based on the following information. MS Trucking is considering the purchase of a new piece of equipment that has a net initial investment with a present value of $300,000. The equipment has an estimated useful life of 3 years. For tax purposes, the equipment will be fully depreciated at rates of 30%, 40%, and 30% in years one, two, and three, respectively. The new machine is expected to have a $20,000 salvage value. The machine is expected to save the company $170,000 per year in operating expenses. MS Trucking has a 40% marginal income tax rate and a 16% cost of capital. Discount rates for a 16% rate are:

	Present Value of an Ordinary Annuity of $1	Present Value of $1
Year 1	.862	.862
Year 2	1.605	.743
Year 3	2.246	.641

13. What is the net present value of this project?

A. $31,684

B. $26,556

C. $94,640

D. $18,864

Answer (B) is correct. *(Publisher, adapted)*
REQUIRED: The net present value (NPV) of the new machine.
DISCUSSION: The NPV method discounts the expected cash flows from a project using the required rate of return. A project is acceptable if its NPV is positive. The future cash inflows consist of $170,000 of saved expenses per year minus income taxes after deducting depreciation. In the first year, the after-tax cash inflow is $170,000 minus taxes of $32,000 {[$170,000 − ($300,000 × 30%) depreciation] × 40%}, or $138,000. In the second year, the after-tax cash inflow is $170,000 minus taxes of $20,000 {[$170,000 − ($300,000 × 40%) depreciation] × 40%}, or $150,000. In the third year, the after-tax cash inflow (excluding salvage value) is again $138,000. Also in the third year, the after-tax cash inflow from the salvage value is $12,000 [$20,000 × (1.0 − .40)]. Accordingly, the total for the third year is $150,000 ($138,000 + $12,000). The sum of these cash flows discounted using the factors for the present value of $1 at a rate of 16% is $326,556.

$138,000 × .862	=	$118,956
$150,000 × .743	=	111,450
$150,000 × .641	=	96,150
Discounted cash inflows		$326,556

Thus, the NPV is $26,556 ($326,556 − $300,000 initial outflow).
Answer (A) is incorrect because $31,684 does not consider the income taxes on the salvage value. The asset was fully depreciated, so any sales receipts would be taxable income. Answer (C) is incorrect because $94,640 does not consider income taxes. Answer (D) is incorrect because $18,864 does not consider the salvage value.

14. What is the profitability index for the project?

A. 1.089

B. 1.106

C. 1.315

D. 1.063

Answer (A) is correct. *(Publisher, adapted)*
REQUIRED: The profitability index.
DISCUSSION: The profitability index is the present value of the future net cash inflows divided by the present value of the net initial investment. The present value of the future net cash inflows is $326,556. Hence, the profitability index is 1.089 ($326,556 ÷ $300,000).
Answer (B) is incorrect because 1.106 does not consider the income taxes on the salvage value. The asset was fully depreciated, so any sales receipts would be taxable income. Answer (C) is incorrect because 1.315 ignores all cash flows for income taxes. Answer (D) is incorrect because 1.063 does not consider the salvage value.

15. Refer to the information on the preceding page(s). The payback period for this investment is

A. 2.84 years.

B. 1.76 years.

C. 2.08 years.

D. 3.00 years.

Answer (C) is correct. *(Publisher, adapted)*
REQUIRED: The payback period.
DISCUSSION: The payback period is the time required to recover the original investment. The annual net after-tax cash inflows for Year 1 through Year 3 are $138,000, $150,000, and $150,000, respectively, as determined by the following: In Year 1, the after-tax cash inflow is $170,000 minus taxes of $32,000 {[$170,000 – ($300,000 × 30%) depreciation] × 40%}, or $138,000. In Year 2, the after-tax cash inflow is $170,000 minus taxes of $20,000 {[$170,000 – ($300,000 × 40%) depreciation] × 40%}, or $150,000. In Year 3, the after-tax cash inflow (excluding salvage value) is again $138,000. Also in Year 3, the after-tax cash inflow from the salvage value is $12,000 [$20,000 × (1.0 – .40)]. Accordingly, the total for Year 3 is $150,000 ($138,000 + $12,000). After 2 years, $288,000 ($138,000 + $150,000) will have been recovered. Consequently, the first $12,000 received in Year 3 will recoup the initial investment. Because $12,000 represents .08 of Year 3 net after-tax cash inflows ($12,000 ÷ $150,000), the payback period is 2.09 years.
Answer (A) is incorrect because 2.84 years does not consider depreciation. Answer (B) is incorrect because 1.76 years does not consider taxes. Answer (D) is incorrect because 3.00 years is the time required to depreciate the asset fully, not the payback period.

16. Refer to the information on the preceding page(s). Assume that the salvage value at the end of the investment's useful life is zero. What is the new payback period?

A. 2.84 years.

B. 1.76 years.

C. 2.08 years.

D. 2.09 years.

Answer (D) is correct. *(Publisher, adapted)*
REQUIRED: The payback period assuming zero salvage value.
DISCUSSION: The payback period is the time required to recover the original investment. As determined below, the annual net after-tax cash inflows for Years 1 through 3 are $138,000, $150,000, and $138,000 (excluding salvage value), respectively. In Year 1, the after-tax cash inflow is $170,000 minus taxes of $32,000 {[$170,000 – ($300,000 × 30%) depreciation] × 40%}, or $138,000. In Year 2, the after-tax cash inflow is $170,000 minus taxes of $20,000 {[$170,000 – $300,000 × 40%) depreciation] × 40%}, or $150,000. In Year 3, the after-tax cash inflow (excluding salvage value) is again $138,000. Also in Year 3, the after-tax cash inflow from the salvage value is $12,000 [$20,000 × (1.0 – .40)]. Accordingly, the total for Year 3 is $150,000 ($138,000 + $12,000). After 2 years, $288,000 ($138,000 + $150,000) will have been recovered. Consequently, the first $12,000 received in Year 3 will recoup the initial investment. Because $12,000 represents .09 (rounded) of Year 3 net after-tax cash inflows ($12,000 ÷ $138,000), the payback period is 2.09 years.
Answer (A) is incorrect because 2.84 years includes salvage value and does not consider depreciation. Answer (B) is incorrect because 1.76 years includes salvage value and does not consider taxes. Answer (C) is incorrect because 2.08 years includes salvage value.

Questions 17 and 18 are based on the following information. McLean, Inc. is considering the purchase of a new machine that will cost $160,000. The machine has an estimated useful life of 3 years. Assume that 30% of the depreciable base will be depreciated in the first year, 40% in the second year, and 30% in the third year. The new machine will have a $10,000 resale value at the end of its estimated useful life. The machine is expected to save the company $85,000 per year in operating expenses. McLean uses a 40% estimated income tax rate and a 16% hurdle rate to evaluate capital projects.

Discount rates for a 16% rate are as follows:

	Present Value of $1	Present Value of an Ordinary Annuity of $1
Year 1	.862	.862
Year 2	.743	1.605
Year 3	.641	2.246

17. What is the net present value of this project?

A. $3,278

B. $5,842

C. $(568)

D. $30,910

Answer (B) is correct. *(CMA, adapted)*
REQUIRED: The NPV of the new machine.
DISCUSSION: The NPV is the excess of the present values of the estimated net cash inflows over the net cost of the investment ($160,000). The future cash inflows consist of $85,000 per year savings minus income taxes. Given salvage value of $10,000, the depreciable base is $150,000 ($160,000 cost − $10,000). The first and third years' depreciation deduction is $45,000 ($150,000 × 30%), leaving $40,000 ($85,000 − $45,000) of taxable income. Thus, first- and third-year tax expense is $16,000 ($40,000 × 40%). Accordingly, the net cash inflow in both the first and third years is $69,000 ($85,000 − $16,000). The $60,000 ($150,000 × 40%) depreciation deduction in the second year results in $25,000 ($85,000 − $60,000) of taxable income. Second-year tax expense is therefore $10,000 ($25,000 × 40%), and the second-year net cash inflow is $75,000 ($85,000 − $10,000). The net cash inflow from sale of the machine is $10,000. No tax is paid on this amount because the remaining book value is also $10,000. The present value of these net cash inflows is determined using the appropriate PV of $1 factors for a hurdle rate of 16%. Hence, the net present value is $5,842 ($165,842 PV − $160,000 cost).

$69,000 × .862	=	$ 59,478
$75,000 × .743	=	55,725
$69,000 × .641	=	44,229
$10,000 × .641	=	6,410
PV of net cash inflows		$165,842

Answer (A) is incorrect because $3,278 assumes that taxes must be paid on the salvage value. Answer (C) is incorrect because $(568) omits salvage value from the calculation. Answer (D) is incorrect because $30,910 equals the present value of a 3-year annuity of $85,000 discounted at 16%, minus $160,000.

18. The payback period for this investment would be

A. 1.88 years.

B. 3.00 years.

C. 2.23 years.

D. 1.62 years.

Answer (C) is correct. *(CMA, adapted)*
REQUIRED: The payback period for an investment.
DISCUSSION: The payback period is the number of years required for the cumulative undiscounted net cash inflows to equal the original investment. The future net cash inflows consist of $69,000 in Year 1 and 3, $75,000 in Year 2, and $10,000 upon resale. After 2 years, the cumulative undiscounted net cash inflow equals $144,000. Thus, $16,000 ($160,000 − $144,000) is to be recovered in the Year 3, and payback should be complete in approximately 2.23 years [2 years + ($16,000 ÷ $69,000 net cash inflow in third year)].

Answer (A) is incorrect because 1.88 assumes an $85,000 annual net cash inflow. Answer (B) is incorrect because 3.00 is the estimated useful life of the machine. Answer (D) is incorrect because 1.62 results from adding income tax expense to the cost savings each year.

Questions 19 through 23 are based on the following information. A proposed investment is not expected to have any salvage value at the end of its 5-year life. Because of realistic depreciation practices, the net carrying amount and the salvage value are equal at the end of each year. For present value purposes, cash flows are assumed to occur at the end of each year. The company uses a 12% after-tax target rate of return.

Year	Purchase Cost and Carrying Amount	Annual Net After-Tax Cash Flows	Annual Net Income
0	$500,000	$ 0	$ 0
1	336,000	240,000	70,000
2	200,000	216,000	78,000
3	100,000	192,000	86,000
4	36,000	168,000	94,000
5	0	144,000	102,000

Discount Factors for a 12% Rate of Return

Year	Present Value of $1 at the End of Each Period	Present Value of an Annuity of $1 at the End of Each Period
1	.89	.89
2	.80	1.69
3	.71	2.40
4	.64	3.04
5	.57	3.61
6	.51	4.12

19. The accounting rate of return based on the average investment is

A. 84.9%

B. 34.4%

C. 40.8%

D. 12%

Answer (B) is correct. *(Publisher, adapted)*
REQUIRED: The accounting rate of return.
DISCUSSION: The accounting rate of return (the unadjusted rate of return or rate of return on the carrying amount) equals the increase in accounting net income divided by either the initial or the average investment. It ignores the time value of money. The average income over 5 years is $86,000 [($70,000 + $78,000 + $86,000 + $94,000 + $102,000) ÷ 5]. Dividing the $86,000 average net income by the $250,000 average investment ($500,000 cost ÷ 2) produces an accounting rate of return of 34.4%.

Answer (A) is incorrect because 84.9% equals the NPV divided by the average investment. Answer (C) is incorrect because 40.8% equals Year 5 net income divided by the average investment. Answer (D) is incorrect because 12% equals the after-tax target rate of return.

20. The net present value is

A. $304,060

B. $212,320

C. $(70,000)

D. $712,320

Answer (B) is correct. *(Publisher, adapted)*
REQUIRED: The net present value (NPV).
DISCUSSION: The NPV method discounts the expected cash flows from a project using the required rate of return. A project is acceptable if its NPV is positive. Based on the interest factors for the present value of $1 at 12% and the annual after-tax cash flows, the NPV of the project over its 5-year life is

$240,000 × .89 =	$ 213,600
216,000 × .80 =	172,800
192,000 × .71 =	136,320
168,000 × .64 =	107,520
144,000 × .57 =	82,080
Total present value	$ 712,320
Purchase cost	(500,000)
NPV	$ 212,320

Answer (A) is incorrect because $304,060 is the present value of the net income amounts. Answer (C) is incorrect because $(70,000) is the excess of the net initial investment over the sum of the undiscounted net income amounts. Answer (D) is incorrect because $712,320 is the present value of the cash inflows.

21. Refer to the information on the preceding page(s). The traditional payback period is

A. Over 5 years.

B. 2.23 years.

C. 1.65 years.

D. 2.83 years.

Answer (B) is correct. *(Publisher, adapted)*
REQUIRED: The traditional payback period.
DISCUSSION: The payback period is the number of years required to complete the return of the original investment. The cash flows are not time adjusted. When the annual cash flows are not uniform, a cumulative computation is necessary. Thus, the total payback after 2 years is $456,000 ($240,000 + $216,000), and another $44,000 ($500,000 – $456,000) must be recovered in the third year. The third year fraction is found by assuming that cash flows occur evenly throughout the period. Dividing $44,000 by the $192,000 of third year inflows yields a ratio of .23. Hence, the payback period is 2.23 years.
Answer (A) is incorrect because the payback period would exceed 5 years if the calculation were based on net income instead of cash flows. Answer (C) is incorrect because 1.65 years is based on the sum of cash flows and net income. Answer (D) is incorrect because it is based on discounted cash flows--not actual cash flows.

22. Refer to the information on the preceding page(s). The profitability index is

A. .61

B. .42

C. .86

D. 1.425

Answer (D) is correct. *(Publisher, adapted)*
REQUIRED: The profitability index.
DISCUSSION: The profitability index is the present value of the estimated net cash inflows over the investment's life divided by the present value of the net initial investment. If the profitability index is greater than 1.0, the investment project should be accepted. The present value of the cash inflows is $712,320, which is calculated as follows:
Based on the interest factors for the present value of $1 at 12% and the annual after-tax cash flows, the NPV of the project over its 5-year life is

$240,000 × .89 =	$ 213,600
216,000 × .80 =	172,800
192,000 × .71 =	136,320
168,000 × .64 =	107,520
144,000 × .57 =	82,080
Total present value of cash inflows	$ 712,320

Thus, the profitability index is 1.425 ($712,320 ÷ $500,000 net initial investment).
Answer (A) is incorrect because .61 is the present value of the net income amounts divided by the net initial investment. Answer (B) is incorrect because .42 is the NPV divided by the net initial investment. Answer (C) is incorrect because .86 is the sum of the undiscounted net income amounts divided by the net initial investment.

23. Refer to the information on the preceding page(s). Which statement about the internal rate of return of the investment is true?

A. The IRR is exactly 12%.

B. The IRR is over 12%.

C. The IRR is under 12%.

D. No information about the IRR can be determined.

Answer (B) is correct. *(Publisher, adapted)*
REQUIRED: The internal rate of return (IRR).
DISCUSSION: The NPV method discounts the expected cash flows from a project using the required rate of return. A project is acceptable if its NPV is positive. Based on the interest factors for the present value of $1 at 12% and the annual after-tax cash flows, the NPV of the project over its 5-year life is

$240,000 × .89 =	$ 213,600
216,000 × .80 =	172,800
192,000 × .71 =	136,320
168,000 × .64 =	107,520
144,000 × .57 =	82,080
Total present value	$ 712,320
Purchase cost	(500,000)
NPV	$ 212,320

Given that the NPV is positive, the investment project should be accepted assuming no capital rationing. Furthermore, the IRR (the discount rate that reduces the NPV to $0) must be greater than the 12% hurdle rate that produced a positive NPV. The higher the discount rate, the lower the NPV.
Answer (A) is incorrect because the IRR would be 12% if the NPV were $0. Answer (C) is incorrect because the IRR would be under 12% if the NPV were negative. Answer (D) is incorrect because whether the IRR is equal to, less than, or greater than the after-tax target rate of return can be determined from the amount of the NPV.

Questions 24 through 27 are based on the following information. Yipann Corporation is reviewing an investment proposal. The initial cost, as well as other related data for each year, are presented in the schedule below. All cash flows are assumed to take place at the end of the year. The salvage value of the investment at the end of each year is equal to its net book value, and there will be no salvage value at the end of the investment's life.

Investment Proposal

Year	Initial Cost and Book Value	Annual Net After-Tax Cash Flows	Annual Net Income
0	$105,000	$ 0	$ 0
1	70,000	50,000	15,000
2	42,000	45,000	17,000
3	21,000	40,000	19,000
4	7,000	35,000	21,000
5	0	30,000	23,000

Yipann uses a 24% after-tax target rate of return for new investment proposals. The discount figures for a 24% rate of return are given.

Year	Present Value of $1.00 Received at the End of Period	Present Value of an Annuity of $1.00 Received at the End of Each Period
1	.81	.81
2	.65	1.46
3	.52	1.98
4	.42	2.40
5	.34	2.74
6	.28	3.02
7	.22	3.24

24. The average annual cash inflow at which Yipann would be indifferent to the investment (rounded to the nearest dollar) is

A. $21,000

B. $40,000

C. $38,321

D. $46,667

Answer (C) is correct. *(CMA, adapted)*

REQUIRED: The average annual cash inflow at which the investor will be indifferent to the investment.

DISCUSSION: This problem requires the use of the net present value (NPV) method of investment analysis. The objective is to determine what average annual net cash inflow will equal the initial cost when discounted at a rate of 24%. Given that the investment has an expected life of 5 years, the appropriate time value of money factor is that for the present value of an ordinary annuity for 5 years at 24%. In this case, the annual net cash inflow is unknown, but the product of the factor (2.74) and the inflow is $105,000. Thus, dividing $105,000 by 2.74 results in an average annual net cash inflow of $38,321. In other words, if annual inflows are $38,321 per year, the present value is $105,000. This present value is equal to the initial cost, and the net present value is zero. At a net present value of zero, the investor is indifferent as to whether to undertake the investment.

Answer (A) is incorrect because $21,000 is the initial cost divided by the life of the asset. Answer (B) is incorrect because $40,000 is the average of the net after-tax cash flows. Answer (D) is incorrect because $46,667 is the initial cost divided by the payback period.

25. The accounting rate of return for the investment proposal over its life using the initial value of the investment is

A. 36.2%

B. 18.1%

C. 28.1%

D. 38.1%

Answer (B) is correct. *(CMA, adapted)*

REQUIRED: The accounting rate of return using the initial value of the investment.

DISCUSSION: The accounting rate of return (or unadjusted rate of return) is computed by dividing the annual increase in accounting net income by the required investment. The average net income over the life of the investment is $19,000 [($15,000 + $17,000 + $19,000 + $21,000 + $23,000) ÷ 5 years]. Consequently, the accounting rate of return is 18.1% ($19,000 ÷ $105,000).

Answer (A) is incorrect because the accounting rate of return (or unadjusted rate of return) is computed by dividing the annual increase in accounting net income by the required investment. Answer (C) is incorrect because the accounting rate of return (or unadjusted rate of return) is computed by dividing the annual increase in accounting net income by the required investment. The average net income over the life of the investment is $19,000 [($15,000 + $17,000 + $19,000 + $21,000 + $23,000) ÷ 5 years]. Answer (D) is incorrect because 38.1% is calculated by dividing the average net after-tax cash flows by the required investment.

26. The net present value of the investment proposal is

A. $4,600

B. $10,450

C. $(55,280)

D. $115,450

Answer (B) is correct. *(CMA, adapted)*

REQUIRED: The net present value of the investment proposal.

DISCUSSION: The net present value is computed by deducting the initial cost of the investment from the present value of the future net cash flows. The present value of each of the future net cash flows is determined by multiplying it by the appropriate factor for the present value of an amount as shown below. The net present value is $10,450 ($115,450 – $105,000).

$50,000 × .81 =	$ 40,500
45,000 × .65 =	29,250
40,000 × .52 =	20,800
35,000 × .42 =	14,700
30,000 × .34 =	10,200
Total	$115,450

Answer (A) is incorrect because the net present value is computed by deducting the initial cost of the investment from the present value of the future net cash flows. Answer (C) is incorrect because $(55,280) is calculated by discounting the annual net income rather than the future net cash flows. Answer (D) is incorrect because $115,450 is the present value of the future net cash flows.

27. Refer to the information on the preceding page(s). The traditional payback period for the investment proposal is

A. .875 years.

B. 1.833 years.

C. 2.250 years.

D. Over 5 years.

Answer (C) is correct.   *(CMA, adapted)*

REQUIRED: The payback period for the proposal.

DISCUSSION: The payback period is the time required to recover the initial investment. The net cash inflows used to determine the payback period are not discounted. The initial cost was $105,000, and inflows during the first 2 years were $95,000 ($50,000 + $45,000). Thus, the first $10,000 ($105,000 – $95,000) of the third year's net cash inflows will complete the recovery of the initial investment. This amount is one-fourth of the third year's inflows. Hence, the payback period is 2.25 years.

Answer (A) is incorrect because .875 is calculated by adding the book value and cash flows to figure the recovery of the initial investment. Answer (B) is incorrect because 1.833 is calculated using the book values instead of the cash flows to figure the recovery of the initial investment. Answer (D) is incorrect because over 5 years is calculated using net income instead of cash flows to figure the recovery of the initial investment.

Use Gleim's *CMA Test Prep* for interactive testing with **over 2,000 additional multiple-choice questions!**

STUDY UNIT TWENTY
RISK ANALYSIS AND REAL OPTIONS

(5 pages of outline)

This study unit is the **last of four** on **investment decisions**. The relative weight assigned to this major topic in Part 3 of the exam is **20%** at **skill level C** (all six skill types required). The four study units are

Study Unit 17: The Capital Budgeting Process
Study Unit 18: Discounted Cash Flow and Payback
Study Unit 19: Ranking Investment Projects
Study Unit 20: Risk Analysis and Real Options

After studying the outline and answering the multiple-choice questions, you will have the skills necessary to address the following topics listed in the IMA's Learning Outcome Statements:

Part 3 – Section E.5. Risk analysis in capital investment
The candidate should be able to:

   a.   identify alternative approaches to dealing with risk in capital budgeting
   b.   demonstrate an understanding of sensitivity analysis and certainty equivalents
   c.   identify qualitative considerations in making capital investment decisions
   d.   explain why a rate specifically adjusted for risk should be used when project cash flows are more or less risky than is normal for a firm
   e.   distinguish among sensitivity analysis, scenario analysis, and Monte Carlo simulation as risk analysis techniques
   f.   describe how the CAPM can be used in the capital budgeting process

Part 3 – Section E.6. Real options in capital investments
The candidate should be able to:

   a.   demonstrate an understanding of the concept of real options in the capital budgeting process
   b.   identify the four common real options, e.g., the option to (1) make follow-on investments if the immediate investment project succeeds, (2) abandon a project, (3) wait and learn before investing, or (4) vary a firm's output or its production methods
   c.   identify these real options as either put or call options
   d.   demonstrate an understanding of the variables and factors that affect the value of options

20.1 RISK ANALYSIS IN CAPITAL INVESTMENT

1. **Risk analysis** attempts to measure the likelihood of the variability of future returns from the proposed investment. Risk cannot be ignored entirely, but mathematical approaches can be impossible because of a lack of critical information. The following approaches are frequently used to assess risk:

    a. **Informal method.** NPVs are calculated at the firm's desired rate of return, and the possible projects are individually reviewed. If the NPVs are relatively close for two mutually exclusive projects, the apparently less risky project is chosen.

    b. **Risk-adjusted discount rates.** This technique adjusts the rate of return upward as the investment becomes riskier. By increasing the discount rate from 10% to 15%, for example, the expected flow from the investment must be relatively larger or the increased discount rate will generate a negative NPV, and the proposed acquisition/ investment would be rejected. Although difficult to apply in extreme cases, this technique has much intuitive value.

    c. **Certainty equivalent adjustments.** This technique is directly drawn from the concept of utility theory. It forces the decision maker to specify at what point the firm is indifferent to the choice between a certain sum of money and the expected value of a risky sum. The technique is not frequently used because decision makers are not familiar with the concept.

    d. **Sensitivity analysis.** Forecasts of many calculated NPVs under various assumptions are compared to see how sensitive NPV is to changing conditions. Changing or relaxing the assumptions about a certain variable or group of variables may drastically alter the NPV. Thus, the asset may appear to be much riskier than was originally predicted. In summary, sensitivity analysis is simply an iterative process of recalculated returns based on changing assumptions.

    e. **Simulation analysis.** This method represents a refinement of standard profitability theory. The computer is used to generate many examples of results based upon various assumptions. Project simulation is frequently expensive. Unless a project is exceptionally large and expensive, full-scale simulation is usually not worthwhile.

    f. **The capital asset pricing model.** This method is derived from the use of portfolio theory. It assumes that all assets are held in a portfolio. Each asset has variability in its returns. Some of this variability is caused by movements in the market as a whole, and some is specific to each firm. In a portfolio, each security's specific variability is eliminated through diversification, and the only relevant risk is the market component. The more sensitive an asset's rate of return is to changes in the market's rate of return, the riskier the asset.

2. Stop and review! You have completed the outline for this subunit. Study multiple-choice questions 1 through 9 beginning on page 459.

20.2 REAL OPTIONS IN CAPITAL INVESTMENTS

1. **Real (managerial or strategic) options** reduce the risk of an investment project. A real option is the flexibility to affect the amounts and risk of an investment project's cash flows, to determine its duration, or to postpone its implementation. A real option is ordinarily part of a major (strategic) project and involves real, not financial, assets.

    a. The **value** of a real option is the difference between the project's net present value (NPV) without the option and its NPV with the option. Similarly, the worth of the project (true NPV) equals its NPV without the option plus the value of the option.

        1) Moreover, the greater the **availability** of real options and the **uncertainty** related to their exercise, the greater the worth of the project. The reason is that increased uncertainty (greater variability of potential cash flows) enhances the likelihood that an option will be exercised and therefore increases its value.

      2) Real options are not measurable with the same accuracy as **financial options** because the formulas applicable to the latter may not be appropriate for the former. Thus, other methods, e.g., **decision tree analysis** with recognition of probabilities and outcomes and simulations, are used in conjunction with discounted cash flow methods.

         a) An approach that exploits the availability of derivatives and other securities that are sensitive to specific risks is the **replicating portfolio**. This method involves identifying securities trading in efficient public markets with cash flows that are the same as those of the real option. Accordingly, these securities must have cash flows and fair values that respond to the **same risks** as the real option. Given the known prices of the securities, the firm may calculate the value of the portfolio and, presumably, the real option with the same cash flows.

            i) An advantage is that this method does not require estimating a discount rate for a discounted cash flow analysis.

            ii) A disadvantage is the need to estimate the effects on cash flows of multiple sources of risk.

         b) Also, see the option valuation models in Study Unit 8.

   b. Management accountants should be able to determine what real options are embedded in a project, to measure their value, and to offer advice about structuring a project to include such options. The following are among the types of real options:

      1) **Abandonment** of a project entails selling its assets or employing them in an alternative project. Thus, the abandonment value of a project may be approximated. Abandonment should occur when, as a result of an ongoing evaluation process, the entity determines that the abandonment value of a new or existing project exceeds the NPV of the project's future cash flows.

         a) The abandonment option enhances a project's worth by allowing the entity to profit from favorable conditions while allowing it to reduce its risk when conditions are unfavorable. Thus, a project should be designed so that it has **multiple decision points** and **total commitment** of resources to project completion is deferred.

      2) The option of making a **follow-up investment** (expansion) may be the factor that renders a project feasible. NPV for the initial project may be negative because its scale is inefficient. For example, a new factory may lack the capacity to be profitable even if it can sell all of its output. However, if demand is expected to increase, a subsequent investment to expand capacity to an efficient scale may be profitable.

      3) The follow-up investment option is based on the assumption that the expansion would not have been possible without the first-stage investment. Otherwise, the entity might have chosen the option to **wait and learn**, that is, to postpone the project (also called a timing option). Postponement permits the entity to undertake the project with greater information and preparation, but it forgoes earlier cash flows and the possible advantage of being first into the market.

        4)   Other real options include the following:

            a)   The **flexibility option** to vary inputs, for example, by switching fuels

            b)   The **capacity option** to vary output, for example, to respond to economic conditions by raising or lowering output or by temporarily shutting down

            c)   The option to enter a **new geographical market**, for example, in a market where NPV is apparently negative but the follow-up investment option is promising

            d)   The **new product option**, for example, the opportunity to sell a complementary or a next-generation product even though the initial product is unprofitable

        5)   Real options may be viewed as **call options** or **put options**. For example, an abandonment option is in essence a put option, and a wait-and-learn option is in essence a call option.

    c.   **Qualitative considerations.** Although real options may often not be readily quantifiable, adding them to a project is always a consideration because doing so is frequently inexpensive and the potential risk reduction is great.

        1)   The option is usually more valuable the later it is exercised, the more variable the underlying risk, or the higher the level of interest rates.

  2.   Stop and review! You have completed the outline for this subunit. Study multiple-choice questions 10 through 12 beginning on page 462.

20.3 CORE CONCEPTS

Risk Analysis in Capital Investment

- **Risk analysis** attempts to measure the likelihood of the variability of future returns from the proposed investment. Several approaches can be used to **assess risk**.

- Under the **informal method**, NPVs are calculated at the firm's desired rate of return, and the possible projects are individually reviewed.

- With **risk-adjusted discount rates**, the rate of return is adjusted upward as the investment becomes riskier.

- The **certainty equivalent adjustments** technique forces the decision maker to specify at what point the firm is indifferent to the choice between a certain sum of money and the expected value of a risky sum.

- Under **sensitivity analysis**, forecasts of many calculated NPVs under various assumptions are compared to see how sensitive NPV is to changing conditions. Changing or relaxing the assumptions about a certain variable or group of variables may drastically alter the NPV.

- **Simulation analysis** represents a refinement of standard profitability theory. The computer is used to generate many examples of results based upon various assumptions. Project simulation is frequently expensive.

- The **capital asset pricing model** is derived from the use of portfolio theory. It assumes that the return on each asset in a portfolio has variability. In a portfolio, each security's specific variability is eliminated through diversification, and the only relevant risk is the market component.

Real Options in Capital Investments

- **Real (managerial or strategic) options** reduce the risk of an investment project. A real option is the flexibility to affect the amounts and risk of an investment project's cash flows, to determine its duration, or to postpone its implementation.

- The **value of a real option** is the difference between the project's NPV without the option and its NPV with the option.

- Real options are **not measurable with the same accuracy** as financial options because the formulas applicable to the latter may not be appropriate for the former.

- Management accountants should be able to **determine what real options are embedded** in a project, to measure their value, and to offer advice about structuring a project to include such options.

- The following are among the types of real options: abandonment; the option of making a follow-up investment; the option to wait and learn; the flexibility option to vary inputs; the capacity option to vary output; the option to enter a new geographical market, and the new product option.

QUESTIONS

20.1 Risk Analysis in Capital Investment

1. For capital budgeting purposes, management would select a high hurdle rate of return for certain projects because management

A. Wants to use equity funding exclusively.

B. Believes too many proposals are being rejected.

C. Believes bank loans are riskier than capital investments.

D. Wants to factor risk into its consideration of projects.

Answer (D) is correct. *(CMA, adapted)*
REQUIRED: The reason for selecting a high hurdle rate for certain projects.
DISCUSSION: Risk analysis attempts to measure the likelihood of the variability of future returns from the proposed investment. Risk can be incorporated into capital budgeting decisions in a number of ways, one of which is to use a hurdle rate (desired rate of return) higher than the firm's cost of capital, that is, a risk-adjusted discount rate. This technique adjusts the interest rate used for discounting upward as an investment becomes riskier. The expected flow from the investment must be relatively larger or the increased discount rate will generate a negative net present value, and the proposed acquisition will be rejected.
Answer (A) is incorrect because the nature of the funding may not be a sufficient reason to use a risk-adjusted rate. The type of funding is just one factor affecting the risk of a project. Answer (B) is incorrect because a higher hurdle will result in rejection of more projects. Answer (C) is incorrect because a risk-adjusted high hurdle rate is used for capital investments with greater risk.

2. A company uses portfolio theory to develop its investment portfolio. If the company wishes to obtain optimal risk reduction through the portfolio effect, it should make its next investment in an investment that

A. Correlates negatively to the current portfolio holdings.

B. Is uncorrelated to the current portfolio holdings.

C. Is highly correlated to the current portfolio holdings.

D. Is perfectly correlated to the current portfolio holdings.

Answer (A) is correct. *(CIA, adapted)*
REQUIRED: The relation of the next investment to the existing portfolio that results in optimal risk reduction.
DISCUSSION: A common general definition is that risk is an investment with an unknown outcome but a known probability distribution of returns (a known mean and standard deviation). An increase in the standard deviation (variability) of returns is synonymous with an increase in the riskiness of a project. Risk is also increased when the project's returns are positively (directly) correlated with other investments in the company's portfolio; that is, risk increases when returns on all projects rise or fall together. Consequently, the overall risk is decreased when projects have low variability and are negatively correlated (the diversification effect).
Answer (B) is incorrect because uncorrelated investments are more risky than negatively correlated investments. Answer (C) is incorrect because correlated investments are very risky. Answer (D) is incorrect because correlated investments are very risky.

3. Mega, Inc., a large conglomerate with operating divisions in many industries, uses risk-adjusted discount rates in evaluating capital investment decisions. Consider the following statements concerning Mega's use of risk-adjusted discount rates.

I.   Mega may accept some investments with internal rates of return less than Mega's overall average cost of capital.

II.   Discount rates vary depending on the type of investment.

III. Mega may reject some investments with internal rates of return greater than the cost of capital.

IV.   Discount rates may vary depending on the division.

Which of the above statements are correct?

A. I and III only.

B. II and IV only.

C. II, III, and IV only.

D. I, II, III, and IV.

Answer (D) is correct. *(CMA, adapted)*
REQUIRED: The true statement about use of risk-adjusted discount rates.
DISCUSSION: Risk analysis attempts to measure the likelihood of the variability of future returns from the proposed investment. Risk can be incorporated into capital budgeting decisions in a number of ways, one of which is to use a hurdle rate higher than the firm's cost of capital, that is, a risk-adjusted discount rate. This technique adjusts the interest rate used for discounting upward as an investment becomes riskier. The expected flow from the investment must be relatively larger, or the increased discount rate will generate a negative net present value, and the proposed acquisition will be rejected. Accordingly, the IRR (the rate at which the NPV is zero) for a rejected investment may exceed the cost of capital when the risk-adjusted rate is higher than the IRR. Conversely, the IRR for an accepted investment may be less than the cost of capital when the risk-adjusted rate is less than the IRR. In this case, the investment presumably has very little risk. Furthermore, risk-adjusted rates may also reflect the differing degrees of risk, not only among investments, but by the same investments undertaken by different organizational subunits.
    Answer (A) is incorrect because discount rates may vary with the project or with the subunit of the organization. Answer (B) is incorrect because the company may accept some projects with IRRs less than the cost of capital or reject some project with IRRs greater than the cost of capital. Answer (C) is incorrect because the company may accept some projects with IRRs less than the cost of capital or reject some project with IRRs greater than the cost of capital.

4. Sensitivity analysis, if used with capital projects,

A. Is used extensively when cash flows are known with certainty.

B. Measures the change in the discounted cash flows when using the discounted payback method rather than the net present value method.

C. Is a "what-if" technique that asks how a given outcome will change if the original estimates of the capital budgeting model are changed.

D. Is a technique used to rank capital expenditure requests.

Answer (C) is correct. *(CMA, adapted)*
REQUIRED: The true statement about sensitivity analysis.
DISCUSSION: After a problem has been formulated into any mathematical model, it may be subjected to sensitivity analysis, which is a trial-and-error method used to determine the sensitivity of the estimates used. For example, forecasts of many calculated NPVs under various assumptions may be compared to determine how sensitive the NPV is to changing conditions. Changing the assumptions about a certain variable or group of variables may drastically alter the NPV, suggesting that the risk of the investment may be excessive.
    Answer (A) is incorrect because sensitivity analysis is useful when cash flows or other assumptions are uncertain. Answer (B) is incorrect because sensitivity analysis can be used with any of the capital budgeting methods. Answer (D) is incorrect because sensitivity analysis is not a ranking technique; it calculates results under varying assumptions.

5. An analysis of a company's planned equity financing using the Capital Asset Pricing Model (or Security Market Line) incorporates only the

A. Expected market earnings, the current U.S. treasury bond yield, and the beta coefficient.

B. Expected market earnings and the price-earnings ratio.

C. Current U.S. treasury bond yield, the price-earnings ratio, and the beta coefficient.

D. Current U.S. treasury bond yield and the dividend payout ratio.

Answer (A) is correct. *(CMA, adapted)*
REQUIRED: The components of the capital asset pricing model.
DISCUSSION: The capital asset pricing model adds the risk-free rate to the product of the market risk premium and the beta coefficient. The market risk premium is the amount above the risk-free rate (approximated by the U.S. treasury bond yield) that must be paid to induce investment in the market. The beta coefficient of an individual stock is the correlation between the price volatility of the stock market as a whole and the price volatility of the individual stock.
    Answer (B) is incorrect because the price-earnings ratio is not a component of the model. Answer (C) is incorrect because the price-earnings ratio is not a component of the model. Answer (D) is incorrect because the dividend payout ratio is not a component of the model.

6. The proper discount rate to use in calculating certainty equivalent net present value is the

A. Risk-adjusted discount rate.

B. Cost of capital.

C. Risk-free rate.

D. Cost of equity capital.

Answer (C) is correct. *(CMA, adapted)*
REQUIRED: The proper discount rate to use in calculating certainty equivalent net present value.
DISCUSSION: Rational investors choose projects that yield the best return given some level of risk. If an investor desires no risk, that is, an absolutely certain rate of return, the risk-free rate is used in calculating net present value. The risk-free rate is the return on a risk-free investment such as government bonds. Certainty equivalent adjustments involve a technique directly drawn from utility theory. It forces the decision maker to specify at what point the firm is indifferent to the choice between a sum of money that is certain and the expected value of a risky sum.
Answer (A) is incorrect because a risk-adjusted discount rate does not represent an absolutely certain rate of return. A discount rate is adjusted upward as the investment becomes riskier. Answer (B) is incorrect because the cost of capital has nothing to do with certainty equivalence. Answer (D) is incorrect because the cost of equity capital does not equate to a certainty equivalent rate.

7. When the risks of the individual components of a project's cash flows are different, an acceptable procedure to evaluate these cash flows is to

A. Divide each cash flow by the payback period.

B. Compute the net present value of each cash flow using the firm's cost of capital.

C. Compare the internal rate of return from each cash flow to its risk.

D. Discount each cash flow using a discount rate that reflects the degree of risk.

Answer (D) is correct. *(CMA, adapted)*
REQUIRED: The acceptable procedure for evaluating cash flows when the risks of individual components of the project's cash flows are different.
DISCUSSION: Risk-adjusted discount rates can be used to evaluate capital investment options. If risks differ among various elements of the cash flows, then different discount rates can be used for different flows.
Answer (A) is incorrect because the payback period ignores both the varying risk and the time value of money. Answer (B) is incorrect because using the cost of capital as the discount rate does not make any adjustment for the risk differentials among the various cash flows. Answer (C) is incorrect because risk has to be incorporated into the company's hurdle rate to use the internal rate of return method with risk differentials.

8. A manager wants to know the effect of a possible change in cash flows on the net present value of a project. The technique used for this purpose is

A. Sensitivity analysis.

B. Risk analysis.

C. Cost behavior analysis.

D. Return on investment analysis.

Answer (A) is correct. *(CMA, adapted)*
REQUIRED: The technique for measuring the effect of a change in cash flows on NPV.
DISCUSSION: Sensitivity analysis is a technique to evaluate a model in terms of the effect of changing the values of the parameters. It answers "what if" questions. In capital budgeting models, sensitivity analysis is the examination of alternative outcomes under different assumptions.
Answer (B) is incorrect because probability (risk) analysis is used to examine the array of possible outcomes given alternative parameters. Answer (C) is incorrect because cost behavior (variance) analysis concerns historical costs, not predictions of future cash inflows and outflows. Answer (D) is incorrect because ROI analysis is appropriate for determining the profitability of a company, segment, etc.

9. A widely used approach that is used to recognize uncertainty about individual economic variables while obtaining an immediate financial estimate of the consequences of possible prediction errors is

A. Expected value analysis.

B. Learning curve analysis.

C. Sensitivity analysis.

D. Regression analysis.

Answer (C) is correct. *(CMA, adapted)*
REQUIRED: The method used to recognize uncertainty about economic variables while obtaining an immediate financial estimate of prediction errors.
DISCUSSION: Sensitivity analysis recognizes uncertainty about estimates by making several calculations using varying estimates. For instance, several forecasts of net present value (NPV) might be calculated under various assumptions to determine the sensitivity of the NPV to changing conditions or prediction errors. Changing or relaxing the assumptions about a certain variable or group of variables may drastically alter the NPV, resulting in a much riskier asset than was originally forecast.
Answer (A) is incorrect because expected value analysis provides a rational means for selecting the best alternative for decisions involving risk by multiplying the probability of each outcome by its payoff, and summing the products. It represents the long-term average payoff for repeated trials. Answer (B) is incorrect because learning curves reflect the increased rate at which people perform tasks as they gain experience. Answer (D) is incorrect because regression analysis is used to find an equation for the linear relationships among variables.

20.2 Real Options in Capital Investments

Questions 10 and 11 are based on the following information.

A company is evaluating the possible introduction of a new version of an existing product that will have a 2-year life cycle. At the end of 2 years, this version will be obsolete, with no additional cash flows or salvage value. The initial and sole outlay for the modified product is $6 million, and the company's desired rate of return is 10%. Following are the potential cash flows (assumed to occur at the end of each year) and their probabilities if the product is marketed:

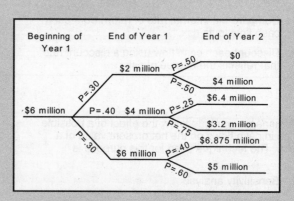

The following interest factors for the present value of $1 at 10% are relevant:

| Period 1 | .909 |
| 2 | .826 |

10. The project's net present value is

A. $878,050

B. $3,242,050

C. $3,636,000

D. $6,000,000

Answer (A) is correct. *(Publisher, adapted)*
REQUIRED: The NPV.
DISCUSSION: The expected value of the cash flows at the end of Year 1 is $4 million [(.3 × $2 million) + (.4 × $4 million) + (.3 × $6 million)], and the present value of this amount is $3,636,000 (.909 × $4 million). The expected value of the cash flows at the end of Year 2 is $3,925,000 [(.3 × .5 × $0) + (.3 × .5 × $4 million) + (.4 × .25 × $6.4 million) + (.4 × .75 × $3.2 million) + (.3 × .4 × $6.875 million) + (.3 × .6 × $5 million)], and the present value of this amount is $3,242,050 (.826 × $3,925,000). Hence, the NPV is $878,050 [($3,636,000 + $3,242,050) − $6 million initial outlay].
Answer (B) is incorrect because $3,242,050 equals the expected present value of the Year 2 cash flows. Answer (C) is incorrect because $3,636,000 equals the expected present value of the Year 1 cash flows. Answer (D) is incorrect because $6,000,000 equals the initial outlay.

11. Assume the company has the real option to abandon the project at the end of Year 1. If the salvage value at that time is $3 million and the desired rate of return remains at 10%, what is the project's net present value?

A. $878,050

B. $1,200,550

C. $2,746,450

D. $4,454,100

Answer (B) is correct. *(Publisher, adapted)*
REQUIRED: The NPV with an abandonment option.
DISCUSSION: If the cash flows at the end of Year 1 equal $2 million, the expected value of the Year 2 cash flows is only $2 million [(.5 × $0) + (.5 × $4 million)]. If the cash flows at the end of year 1 equal $4 million or $6 million, the expected value of the Year 2 cash flows equals $4 million [(.25 × $6.4 million) + (.75 × $3.2 million)] or $5.75 million [(.4 × $6.875 million) + (.6 × $5 million)], respectively. After discounting these expected values to the end of Year 1, the present values are $1,818,000 (.909 × $2 million) given a $2 million Year 1 cash flow, $3,636,000 (.909 × $4 million) given a $4 million Year 1 cash flow, and $5,226,750 (.909 × $5.75 million) given a $6 million Year 1 cash flow. Accordingly, the real option of abandonment is preferable if the Year 1 cash flow is $2 million. The $3 million salvage value exceeds the expected value of the Year 2 cash flows discounted to the end of Year 1 in this case only. If the real option of abandonment is exercised only when Year 1 cash flows equal $2 million, the expected value of the cash flows at the end of Year 1 is $4.9 million {[.3 × ($2 million + $3 million salvage)] + (.4 × $4 million) + (.3 × $6 million)}, and the present value of this amount is $4,454,100 (.909 × $4.9 million). The expected value of the cash flows at the end of Year 2 if the real option is exercised only when Year 1 cash flows equal $2 million is $3,325,000 (.3 × 1.0 × $0) + (.4 × .25 × $6.4 million) + (.4 × .75 × $3.2 million) + (.3 × .4 × $6.875 million) + (.3 × .6 × $5 million), and the present value of this amount is $2,746,450 (.826 × $3,325,000). Consequently, the NPV with an abandonment option is $1,200,550 ($4,454,100 + $2,746,450 − $6 million initial outlay). This amount is substantially greater than the NPV with no abandonment option.
Answer (A) is incorrect because $878,050 equals the NPV with no real option of abandonment. Answer (C) is incorrect because $2,746,450 equals the expected present value of the Year 2 cash flows. Answer (D) is incorrect because $4,454,100 equals the expected present value of the Year 1 cash flows.

12. Which of the following is not an example of a real option in a capital budgeting decision?

A. Abandonment.

B. Follow-up investment.

C. Option to wait and learn.

D. Risk-adjusted discount rates.

Answer (D) is correct. *(Publisher, adapted)*
REQUIRED: The item that is not an example of a real option in a capital budgeting decision.
DISCUSSION: Real options include such factors as the ability to abandon the project early, the opportunity for follow-up investments or ability to create new products, the ability to base additional cash outflows on a wait-and-learn opportunity, or the option to change capacity during the project. Risk-adjusted discount rates are not real options but are a form of sensitivity analysis.
Answer (A) is incorrect because abandonment is an example of a real option. Answer (B) is incorrect because follow-up investment is an example of a real option. Answer (C) is incorrect because the option to wait and learn is an example of a real option.

Use Gleim's *CMA Test Prep* for interactive testing with **over 2,000 additional multiple-choice questions!**

APPENDIX A
IMA MEMBERSHIP AND EXAMINATION FORMS

You must apply and become an IMA member in order to participate in the IMA Certification programs. The cost is $195 per year for Regular or International membership. Recent graduates (associates) have discounted fees of $65 their first year out of school and $130 their second year out of school. Full-time faculty dues (in the U.S., Canada, and Mexico) are $98 and dues for full-time students are $39 per year (must carry at least 6 equivalent hours per semester and reside in the U.S., Canada, or Mexico).

The IMA offers three member interest groups at $75 per year: the Controllers Council, the Cost Management Group, and the Small-Business Council. Everyone except students and associates must pay a $15 IMA registration fee.

The following two pages can be photocopied and used to apply for IMA membership, or call the IMA at (800) 638-4427, ext. 510, and ask for a CMA "kit." You may also email the IMA at info@imanet.org to request an information kit or apply online on the IMA's website at www.imanet.org.

Completion of the registration form on the two pages following the IMA membership application is required in order to take any of the examination parts.

NOTE: The ICMA application has been replaced by the IMA Certification Program. You can apply for admission into the Certification Program by checking the appropriate box on either the IMA Membership Application or the Exam Registration Form. The fee is $200 ($75 for students).

466

INSTITUTE OF
MANAGEMENT
ACCOUNTANTS®

| + + + MEMBERSHIP APPLICATION + + + |

☐ **New Application**   **PERSONAL INFORMATION** *(please print)*

☐ **Renewal**   ☐ Mr. ☐ Ms. ☐ Mrs. ☐ Miss ☐ Dr.   Last/Family Name/Surname: _____

☐ **Certification**   First/Given Name: _____   Middle Initial: _____   Suffix: _____
  (IMA membership required)

  Date of Birth (month/day/year): ____/____/____

Please indicate your contact preference:

☐ **BUSINESS MAILING ADDRESS:**
(See reverse side to enter SIC, job title, and responsibility codes)

Title: _____

Company Name: _____

Street/P.O. Box: _____

_____

City: _____

State/Province: _____

Zip Code/Postal Code: _____

Country: _____

Business Phone: *(Include Country/Area/City Codes)* _____

E-mail Address: _____

☐ **HOME MAILING ADDRESS:**

Street/P.O. Box: _____

_____

City: _____

State/Province: _____

Zip Code/Postal Code: _____

Country: _____

Phone: *(Include Country/Area/City Codes)* _____

Fax: _____

EDUCATION HISTORY

| | Name of Institution | Degree | Major | Date Received/Expected |

Undergraduate: _____

Graduate: _____

Professional Designations Earned: ☐ U.S. CPA ☐ CFA ☐ CIA ☐ Other: _____

CHAPTER AFFILIATION
See a list of Regular/Student Chapter options by visiting our website www.imanet.org, or call (800) 638-4427.

Chapter Name: _____   Chapter Number: _____   ☐ Member-At-Large (Check here if no chapter affiliation is desired)
    ☐ International Member-At-Large

A. MEMBERSHIP INFORMATION *(All payments must be in U.S. Dollars)*

☐ **Regular Membership** $195.00
  (You must reside in the U.S., Canada, or Mexico)

☐ **International Membership** $195.00
  (Available to professionals residing outside the U.S., Canada, or Mexico)

☐ **Student Membership** .... $ 39.00
  (You must be taking 6 or more hours per semester and reside in the U.S., Canada, or Mexico)
  Expected Graduation Date (Year) _____

☐ **Associate Membership**
  (You must apply within 2 years of completing full-time studies and reside in the U.S., Canada, or Mexico)
  Select One: ☐ 1st year after graduation .... $ 65.00
      ☐ 2nd year after graduation $130.00

☐ **Academic Membership** .... $ 98.00
  (You must be a full-time faculty member and reside in the U.S., Canada, or Mexico)

B. OPTIONAL SERVICES
(IMA membership required. All payments must be in U.S. Dollars)

☐ **Member Interest Groups** .... $ 75.00 each
  ☐ Controllers Council ☐ Cost Management Group ☐ Small Business Council

☐ **CPE Offerings** *(Prices valid through 12/31/08)*
  ☐ IMA Ethics Series: Success Without Compromise (4 CPE) .... $ 75.00*
  ☐ IMA Ethics Series: Fraud in Financial Reporting (2 CPE) .... $ 59.00*
  ☐ IMA Knowledge Exchange   (Unlimited CPE) $274.00**
  ☐ IMA Advantage   (Unlimited CPE) $274.00**
  ☐ IMA Knowledge Exchange/Advantage Combo $409.00**
  ☐ IMA CPEdge (24+ CPE) $187.00**
    *Valid for 60 days from date of purchase.   **Valid for 365 days.*

☐ **Certification** ☐ CMA
  ☐ Certification Entrance Fee *(One-time payment)* $200.00
  ☐ Certification Entrance Fee for students in the U.S., Canada,
    and Mexico *(One-time payment)* $75.00
  ☐ **Exam Waiver Fee** *(See www.imanet.org for more information)* $190.00

INSTITUTE OF MANAGEMENT ACCOUNTANTS, INC.

· 10 Paragon Drive, Montvale, NJ 07645-1760 · (800) 638-4427 or (201) 573-9000 · fax (201) 474-1600 · ima@imanet.org · www.imanet.org ·

C. REGISTRATION FEES

☐ **Membership Registration Fee** $15.00
(All new members except Students and Associates)

☐ **Reinstatement Fee** $15.00
(If your membership has lapsed for 90 days, a $15.00 reinstatement fee applies)

┌───┐
│ **TOTAL DUE (add sections A, B, and C)** . . . . $ _____ │
└───┘

APPLICANT STATEMENT

☐ Check here if you have ever been convicted of a felony. Please enclose a confidential letter with a brief explanation of circumstances to the attention of President & CEO.

I affirm that the statements on this application are correct, and I agree to abide by the Statement of Ethical Professional Practice.

Signature: _____ Date: _____

IMA occasionally makes available its members' addresses (excluding telephone and e-mail) to vendors who provide products and services to the management accounting and finance community. If you prefer not to be included in these lists, please check this box. ☐

PREFERRED METHOD OF PAYMENT
(All payments must be in U.S. Dollars)

☐ **Wire Payments** . . . .
All wire transfers must be made with bank fees prepaid. Please notify IMA by e-mail *(dhuckins@imanet.org)* that you are paying by wire transfer. Include your name, amount sent, and wire transfer receipt number.

☐ **Check Payments**
My check for $ _____ , payable to IMA, is enclosed.
No checks drawn on foreign banks will be accepted unless they are payable through U.S. correspondent banks and in U.S. dollars.

☐ **Credit Card Payments**
Charge my credit card: ☐ AMEX ☐ Discover ☐ MasterCard ☐ VISA

Card Number: _____ Exp.: _____

Cardholder Name: _____

Signature: _____

CMA CERTIFICATION PROGRAM

IMA membership required. If you are applying to the certification program for the first time, please check the appropriate box and enclose the Certification Entrance Fee ($200.00) required of new certification applicants only. (Students in the U.S., Canada, and Mexico must pay the reduced fee of $75.00)

☐ Applying as a Student *(U.S., Canada, and Mexico only)* — Upon graduation, arrange for an official copy of your transcript to be sent.

☐ Applying as Faculty *(U.S., Canada, and Mexico only)* — Please provide a letter on school stationery affirming full-time teaching status.

Please complete the Additional Educational Information below:

ADDITIONAL EDUCATIONAL INFORMATION

Check the appropriate box and make arrangements for supporting documents to be forwarded to the IMA certification department. Only one form of credentials is required.

☐ **Later** — By selecting this option, many applicants choose to provide their educational credentials after completing the exams.

If you would like to have your credentials reviewed prior to taking the exams to ensure that they are acceptable, please select one of the options below. Please note that the educational requirement must be fulfilled prior to certification.

☐ **College Graduate** — Submit official transcript (translated into English) showing university degree conferred and official university seal, or arrange to have proof of degree sent directly from university.

☐ **GMAT or GRE Scores** — Provide copy of scores.

☐ **U.S. CPA Exam, U.S. CFA Exam, or other acceptable certification or license** — Arrange to have proof sent directly from your certifying organization. Acceptable designations are listed at www.imanet.org.

Strategic Finance Magazine

Subscription rates per year:
Members: . . . . $ 48 (Included in dues, nondeductible)
Student Members: . . . . $ 25 (Included in dues, nondeductible)

Management Accounting Quarterly

Subscription rates per year:
Members: . . . . $ 10 (Included in dues, nondeductible)

SIC CODE – STANDARD INDUSTRY CLASSIFICATIONS
(Please Circle One)

01 Education
02 Healthcare
03 Media and Entertainment
16 Construction, Mining, Agriculture
21 Manufacturing
41 Transportation, Communication, Utilities
51 Wholesale/Retail Trades
61 Finance
63 Insurance
81 Business Services
82 Real Estate
86 High Tech
90 Nonprofit
93 Government
96 Pharmaceuticals & Biotechnology
99 Other _____

JOB TITLE CODE
(Please Circle One)

05 Executive Officer
11 Corporate Officer
15 Vice President
31 Controller
33 Chief Financial Officer
35 Director/Manager
41 Supervisor
47 Accountant
51 Analyst
55 Programmer
57 Administrative
59 Consultant
65 Academic
99 Other _____

RESPONSIBILITY CODE
(Please Circle One)

01 General Management
05 Corporate Management
10 Public Accounting
15 General Accounting
20 Personnel Accounting
25 Cost Accounting
30 Government Accounting
33 Environmental Accounting
35 Finance
40 Risk Management
45 Budget and Planning
50 Taxation
55 Internal Auditing
60 Education
65 Information Systems
70 Student
75 Retired
80 Other _____

MEMBER PROFILE

1. Do you have international responsibilities?
☐ Yes ☐ No

2. Does your company have international locations?
☐ Yes ☐ No

3. Who will pay your IMA dues?
☐ Me ☐ My Company

4. What are you looking for most from your IMA Membership?
☐ Career assistance ☐ Professional networking
☐ Certification ☐ Industry news
☐ Education ☐ Leadership training
☐ CPE ☐ Research
☐ Other (please specify) _____

5. Are you a member of any other association?
☐ AAA ☐ AFP ☐ AICPA ☐ ASWA
☐ CFA Institute (AIMR) ☐ FEI ☐ IIA
☐ Other (please specify) _____

6. Is your organization:
☐ Public sector ☐ Nonprofit
☐ Private sector ☐ Government

8. How did you learn about IMA?
☐ Chapter meeting ☐ Marketing piece
☐ IMA educational program ☐ Company recommended
☐ IMA website ☐ Industry associate
☐ Industry publication ☐ Professor
☐ Other _____
☐ Other website _____

9. How many employees are in your company or organization?
☐ Under 50 ☐ 51-100 ☐ 101-200 ☐ 201-500
☐ 501-1,000 ☐ 1,001-10,000 ☐ Over 10,000

10. What is your company's current annual revenue?
☐ Under $1 million ☐ $500 million - $1 billion
☐ $1 - $10 million ☐ $1 billion - $5 billion
☐ $10 - $100 million ☐ $5 billion - $10 billion
☐ $100 - $500 million ☐ Over $10 billion

Please send your completed application and payment (made out to IMA) to:

INSTITUTE OF MANAGEMENT ACCOUNTANTS, INC.

Rev. 0308

· 10 Paragon Drive, Montvale, NJ 07645-1760 · (800) 638-4427 or (201) 573-9000 · fax (201) 474-1600 · ima@imanet.org · www.imanet.org ·

468

Institute of Certified Management Accountants
10 Paragon Drive • Montvale, New Jersey 07645-1759
(201) 573-9000 • (800) 638-4427 • FAX: (201) 474-1600

CMA EXAMINATION REGISTRATION FORM

PERSONAL INFORMATION　　　　　　　　　　　　　　　　　　　　*TYPE OR PRINT CLEARLY*

☐ **Please check box if you are applying to the ICMA program, complete side two and pay the $200 entrance fee.**
　No exam will be authorized without remitting the entrance fee. If the exam is not completed in four years, fee will expire.

☐ Mr. ☐ Ms. ☐ Miss ☐ Mrs. ☐ Dr.　　　　　　　　☐ IMA Member # _____

_____

Last Name/Family Name　　　　　　　　First Name/Surname　　　　Middle Initial　　　Suffix
☐ **Please check box if this is a new address.**　　　　Please Specify　☐ **Home**　　☐ **Business**

_____

Mailing Address/Street/P.O. Box

_____

City　　　　　　　　　　　　　　　　State/Province/Country　　　　　　　Zip Code/Postal Code

_____

Daytime Telephone (include area code or country/city code)

_____

E-mail　　　　　　　　　　　　　　Fax Number: (Include Area/Country/City Codes)

NOTES:

(1) Examination Fees and Certification Entrance Fees are **NOT REFUNDABLE.**

(2) You are required to take all the parts you register for within the same 120 day authorization period. (For Part 4 your authorization period is the month for which you are registered.)

(3) Parts 1, 2, and 3 must be passed before registering for Part 4.

(4) Part 4 is given the second month of every quarter. (Feb., May, Aug., and Nov.) at Prometric Testing Centers.

PLACE A CHECK MARK IN THE BOX(ES) BELOW FOR THE PART(S) YOU WISH TO TAKE AT THIS TIME

| ☐ **Entrance Fee** | ☐ **PART 1**
Business
Analysis | ☐ **PART 2**
Management
Accounting
& Reporting | ☐ **PART 3**
Strategic
Management | ☐ **PART 4**
Business
Applications
(Please select a testing window.
See Notes 3 & 4 Above) | ☐ **February**
☐ **May**
☐ **August**
☐ **November** |

TOTAL PARTS _____

$200 Regular Member Entrance Fee if applicable (<u>MUST BE PAID PRIOR TO TAKING FIRST EXAM</u>), expires in 4 years. .... $ _____

$ 75 Student Member Entrance Fee if applicable (U.S., Mexican and Canadian college students) (<u>MUST BE PAID PRIOR TO TAKING FIRST EXAM</u>), expires in 4 years. .... $ _____

$190 Examination Registration Fee per part .... $ _____

Less: Student/Faculty Discount (50% students, 100% faculty) (U.S., Mexican and Canadian college students/faculty only) .... $ _____

Faculty Retakes at 50% of cost .... $ _____

$190 Part I Waiver Fee if applicable (Arrange to have proof sent directly from the certifying organization) .... $ _____

AMOUNT DUE .... $ _____

PLEASE COMPLETE BOTH SIDES　　　　　**NOTE: PAYMENT IN FULL MUST ACCOMPANY REGISTRATION FORM - FEES SUBJECT TO CHANGE**

7/08

CERTIFICATION PROGRAM APPLICATION

If you are applying for admission to the certification program, please complete the following.

☐ **Applying as a Student** (U.S., Mexico and Canada) – Upon graduation, arrange for an official copy of your transcript to be sent.

☐ **Applying as Faculty** (U.S., Mexico and Canada) – Please provide a letter on school stationery affirming full-time teaching status.

ADDITIONAL EDUCATIONAL INFORMATION

Check one of the following and make arrangements for supporting documents to be forwarded to the IMA certification department.

☐ **Later** - By selecting this option, applicants choose to provide their educational credentials after completing the exams. If you would like to have your credentials reviewed prior to taking the exams to ensure that they are acceptable, please select one of the options below. Please note that the educational requirement must be fulfilled prior to certification.

☐ **College Graduate** - Submit official transcript showing university degree conferred and official university seal or arrange to have proof of degree sent directly from university.

NOTE: Please pay the entrance fee before submitting your educational credentials.

Name on transcript (if different from front of registration form)

☐ **GMAT or GRE Scores** - Provide copy of scores.

☐ **Professional Certification** – Arrange to have proof of certification sent directly from the certifying organization. See listing of acceptable certifications at http://www.imanet.org/certification_started_education_professional.asp

CONFIDENTIALITY STATEMENT & PAYMENT INFORMATION

I hereby attest that I will not divulge the content of this examination, nor will I remove any examination materials, notes, or other unauthorized materials from the examination room. I understand that failure to comply with this attestation may result in invalidation of my grades and disqualification from future examinations. For those already certified by the Institute of Certified Management Accountants, failure to comply with the statement will be considered a violation of IMA's Statement of Ethical Professional Practice and could result in revocation of the certification.

I affirm that the statements on this registration are correct and agree to abide by IMA's Statement of Ethical Professional Practice.

Signature of Applicant: _____ Date: _____

PREFERRED METHOD OF PAYMENT (All payments must be in U.S. Dollars)

☐ **Wire Payments**

All wire transfers must ne made with banks fees prepaid. Please notify IMA by e-mail (dhuckins@imanet.org) that you are paying by wire transfer. Include your name, amount sent, and wire transfer receipt number.

☐ **Check Payments**

My check for $ _____, payable to ICMA, is enclosed. No checks drawn from foreign banks will be accepted unless they are payable through U.S. correspondent banks and in U.S. dollars.

☐ **Credit Card Payments**

Charge my credit card: ☐ VISA   ☐ MasterCard   ☐ American Express   ☐ Discover

Credit Card Number: __ __ __ __ – __ __ __ __ – __ __ __ __ – __ __ __ __   Expiration Date: ____/____
                                                                                            MM/YY

Card Holder Name: _____

Signature of Card Holder: _____

IMA occasionally makes available its members' addresses (excluding telephone and e-mail) to vendors who provide products and services to the management accounting and finance community. If you prefer not to be included in these lists, please check this box. ☐

PLEASE COMPLETE BOTH SIDES   **NOTE: PAYMENT IN FULL MUST ACCOMPANY REGISTRATION FORM - FEES SUBJECT TO CHANGE**

7/08

INSTITUTE OF MANAGEMENT ACCOUNTANTS
Advancing the Profession™

10 Paragon Drive • Montvale, New Jersey 07645-1760 • www.imanet.org
(201) 573-9000 • (800) 638-4427 • Fax (201) 474-1600

CERTIFIED MANAGEMENT ACCOUNTANT
Professionals Driving Business Performance™

APPENDIX B
ICMA CONTENT SPECIFICATION OUTLINES

The following pages consist of a reprint of the ICMA's Content Specification Outlines (CSOs) for Part 3, effective July 1, 2004. Please use these CSOs as reference material only. The ICMA's CSOs have been carefully analyzed and have been incorporated into 20 study units to provide systematic and rational coverage of exam topics.

We are confident that we provide comprehensive coverage of the subject matter tested on the revised CMA exam. If, after taking the exam, you feel that certain topics, concepts, etc., tested were not covered or were inadequately covered, please call, fax, or email us. We do not want information about CMA questions, only information/feedback about our *CMA Review* system's coverage.

Content Specification Outlines for the
Certified Management Accountant (CMA)
Examinations

The content specification outlines presented below represent the body of knowledge that will be covered on the CMA examinations. The outlines may be changed in the future when new subject matter becomes part of the common body of knowledge.

Candidates for the CMA designation are required to take Parts 1, 2, 3, and 4. Part 4, Business Applications, may only be taken after successful completion of Parts 1, 2, and 3.

Candidates are responsible for being informed on the most recent developments in the areas covered in the outlines. This includes understanding of public pronouncements issued by accounting organizations as well as being up-to-date on recent developments reported in current accounting, financial and business periodicals.

The content specification outlines serve several purposes. The outlines are intended to:

- Establish the foundation from which each examination will be developed.
- Provide a basis for consistent coverage on each examination.
- Communicate to interested parties more detail as to the content of each examination part.
- Assist candidates in their preparation for each examination.
- Provide information to those who offer courses designed to aid candidates in preparing for the examinations.

Important additional information about the content specification outlines and the examinations is listed below.

1.   The coverage percentage given for each major topic within each examination part represents the relative weight given to that topic in an examination part. The number of questions presented in each major topic area approximates this percentage.

2.   Each examination will sample from the subject areas contained within each major topic area to meet the relative weight specifications. No relative weights have been assigned to the subject areas within each major topic. No inference should be made from the order in which the subject areas are listed or from the number of subject areas as to the relative weight or importance of any of the subjects.

3.   Each major topic within each examination part has been assigned a coverage level designating the depth and breadth of topic coverage, ranging from an introductory knowledge of a subject area (Level A) to a thorough understanding of and ability to apply the essentials of a subject area (Level C). Detailed explanations of the coverage levels and the skills expected of candidates are presented below.

4.   The topics for Parts 1, 2, and 3 have been selected to minimize the overlapping of subject areas among the examination parts. The topics within an examination part and the subject areas within topics may be combined in individual questions. Questions within Parts 1, 2, and 3 will only cover subject areas outlined in the respective content specifications. The exception is Part 4, Business Applications, which may include any of the subject areas tested in Parts 1, 2, and 3.

5.   With regard to Federal income taxation issues, candidates will be expected to understand the impact of income taxes when reporting and analyzing financial results. In addition, the tax code provisions that impact decisions (e.g., depreciation, interest, etc.) will be tested.

6. Candidates for the CMA designation are expected to have a minimum level of business knowledge that transcends all examination parts. This minimum level would include knowledge of basic financial statements, time value of money concepts, and elementary statistics.

7. Parts 1, 2, and 3 are 100% objective and consist of carefully constructed multiple-choice questions that test all levels of cognitive skills. Parts 1 and 3 are three-hour exams and contain 110 questions each. Part 2 is a four-hour exam and has 140 questions. A small number of the questions on each exam are being validated for future use and will not count in the final score.

8. Part 4, Business Applications, consists of several essay questions and problems that are delivered in a computer-based format. Both written and quantitative responses will be required. Candidates will be expected to present written answers that are responsive to the question asked, presented in a logical manner, and demonstrate an appropriate understanding of the subject matter. It should be noted that candidates are expected to have working knowledge in the use of word processing and electronic spreadsheets.

9. Ethical issues and considerations will be tested on Part 4, Business Applications. At least one question in this part will be devoted to an ethical situation presented in a business-oriented context. Candidates will be expected to evaluate the issues involved and make recommendations for the resolution of the situation.

In order to more clearly define the topical knowledge required by a candidate, varying levels of coverage for the treatment of major topics of the content specification outlines have been identified and defined. The cognitive skills that a successful candidate should possess and that should be tested on the examinations can be defined as follows:

Knowledge:	Ability to remember previously learned material such as specific facts, criteria, techniques, principles, and procedures (i.e., identify, define, list).
Comprehension:	Ability to grasp and interpret the meaning of material (i.e., classify, explain, distinguish between).
Application:	Ability to use learned material in new and concrete situations (i.e., demonstrate, predict, solve, modify, relate).
Analysis:	Ability to break down material into its component parts so that its organizational structure can be understood; ability to recognize causal relationships, discriminate between behaviors, and identify elements that are relevant to the validation of a judgment (i.e., differentiate, estimate, order).
Synthesis:	Ability to put parts together to form a new whole or proposed set of operations; ability to relate ideas and formulate hypotheses (i.e., combine, formulate, revise).
Evaluation:	Ability to judge the value of material for a given purpose on the basis of consistency, logical accuracy, and comparison to standards; ability to appraise judgments involved in the selection of a course of action (i.e., criticize, justify, conclude).

The three levels of coverage can be defined as follows:

Level A:	Requiring the skill levels of knowledge and comprehension.
Level B:	Requiring the skill levels of knowledge, comprehension, application, and analysis.
Level C:	Requiring all six skill levels, knowledge, comprehension, application, analysis, synthesis, and evaluation.

The levels of coverage as they apply to each of the major topics of the Content Specification Outlines are shown on the following pages with each topic listing. The levels represent the manner in which topic areas are to be treated and represent ceilings, i.e., a topic area designated as Level C may contain requirements at the "A," "B," or "C" level, but a topic designated as Level B will not contain requirements at the "C" level.

Part 3 – Strategic Management

A. **Strategic Planning (15% - Level B)**

1. ***Strategic and tactical planning***

   a. Analysis of external factors affecting strategy
   b. Analysis of internal factors affecting strategy
   c. Long-term mission and goals
   d. Alignment of tactics with long-term strategic goals
   e. Characteristics of successful strategic/tactical planning
   f. Contingency planning

2. ***Manufacturing paradigms***

   a. Just-in time manufacturing
   b. Material requirements planning (MRP)
   c. Theory of constraints and throughput costing
   d. Capacity management and analysis
   e. Other production management theories

3. ***Business process performance***

   a. Value chain analysis
   b. Value-added concepts
   c. Process analysis
   d. Benchmarking
   e. Activity-based management
   f. Continuous improvement (kaizen) concepts
   g. Best practice analysis

B. **Strategic Marketing (15% - Level A)**

1. ***Strategic role within the firm***

   a. Link between strategic planning and the marketing process
   b. SWOT analysis
   c. Designing the business portfolio

2. ***Managing marketing information***

   a. Developing marketing information
   b. Analyzing marketing information

3. ***Market segmentation, targeting, and positioning***

   a. Market segmentation
   b. Market targeting
   c. Selecting a positioning strategy

4. ***Managing products and services***

   a. Product attributes and branding
   b. Product line and product mix decisions
   c. Product development
   d. Product life-cycle
   e. Marketing strategies for service firms

5. **Pricing strategy**

   a. Internal and external factors
   b. Pricing approaches
   c. New product pricing strategies
   d. Product-mix pricing strategies

6. **Promotional mix and distribution strategy**

   a. Advertising, sales promotion, and public relations
   b. Personal selling and direct marketing
   c. Setting the overall marketing communications mix
   d. Distribution channels

C. **Corporate Finance (25% - Level B)**

1. **Risk and return**

   a. Calculating return
   b. Types of risk
   c. Relationship between risk and return
   d. Risk and return in a portfolio context
   e. Diversification
   f. Capital asset pricing model (CAPM)

2. **Financial instruments**

   a. Bonds
   b. Common stock
   c. Preferred stock
   d. Derivatives
   e. Other long-term financial instruments

3. **Cost of capital**

   a. Weighted average cost of capital
   b. Cost of individual capital components
   c. Calculating the cost of capital
   d. Marginal cost of capital
   e. Use of cost of capital in capital investment decisions

4. **Managing current assets**

   a. Working capital terminology
   b. Cash management
   c. Marketable securities management
   d. Accounts receivable management
   e. Inventory management

5. **Financing current assets**

   a. Types of short-term credit
   b. Minimizing the cost of short-term credit

D. **Decision Analysis (25% - Level C)**

1. **Decision process**

   a. Steps in the decision process
   b. Evaluation of decision results

2. **Relevant data concepts**

   a. Future oriented revenues and costs
   b. Sunk costs
   c. Opportunity costs

3. **Cost/volume/profit analysis**

    a. Breakeven analysis
    b. Profit performance and alternative operating levels
    c. Analysis of multiple products

4. **Marginal analysis**

    a. Special orders and pricing
    b. Make versus buy
    c. Sell or process further
    d. Add or drop a segment

5. **Cost-based pricing**

    a. Comparing to market-based prices
    b. Setting prices
    c. Target costing

E. **Investment Decisions (20% - Level C)**

1. **Capital budgeting process**

    a. Definition
    b. Stages of capital budgeting
    c. Incremental cash flows
    d. Income tax considerations

2. **Discounted cash flow analysis**

    a. Net present value
    b. Internal rate of return
    c. Comparison of NPV and IRR

3. **Payback and discounted payback**

    a. Uses of payback method
    b. Limitations of payback method
    c. Discounted payback

4. **Ranking investment projects**

    a. Capital rationing
    b. Mutually exclusive projects
    c. Ranking methods

5. **Risk analysis in capital investment**

    a. Sensitivity analysis
    b. Certainty equivalents
    c. Other approaches to dealing with risk

6. **Real options in capital investments**

    a. Definition and types of real options
    b. Valuation of real options

APPENDIX C
ICMA SUGGESTED READING LIST

The ICMA suggested reading list that follows is reproduced to give you an overview of the scope of Part 3. You will not have the time to study these texts. Our *CMA Review* system is complete and thorough and is designed to maximize your study time. For all four parts, candidates are expected to stay up-to-date by reading articles from journals, newspapers, and professional publications.

Part 3 – Strategic Management

Strategic Planning
Hill, Charles W. L., Jones, Gareth R., *Strategic Management, An Integrated Approach*, Houghton Mifflin, Boston, MA, 2002.

Thomas L. Wheelen and J. David Hunger, *Strategic Management and Business Policy*, 10th edition, Prentice Hall Inc., Upper Saddle River, NJ, 2006.

Blocher, Edward, J., Chen, Kung, H., and Lin, Thomas W., *Cost Management: A Strategic Emphasis*, 3rd edition, Irwin/McGraw Hill, New York, NY, 2004.

Horngren, Charles T., Foster, George, and Datar, Srikant M., *Cost Accounting: A Managerial Emphasis*, 12th edition, Prentice-Hall Inc., Upper Saddle River, NJ, 2006.

Strategic Marketing
Armstrong, Gary, Kotler, Philip, *Marketing, an Introduction*, 6th edition, Prentice Hall Inc., Upper Saddle River, NJ, 2003.

Kotler, Philip, *Marketing Management*, 12th edition, Prentice Hall Inc., Upper Saddle River, NJ, 2006.

Corporate Finance
Brealey, Richard A., and Myers, Stewart C., and Allen, Franklin, *Principles of Corporate Finance*, 8th edition, McGraw-Hill Inc., New York, NY, 2006.

Van Horne, James C., and Wachowicz, John M., Jr., *Fundamentals of Financial Management*, 12th edition, Prentice-Hall Inc., Upper Saddle River, NJ, 2005.

Decision Analysis
Blocher, Edward, J., Chen, Kung, H., and Lin, Thomas W., *Cost Management: A Strategic Emphasis*, 3rd edition, Irwin/McGraw Hill, New York, NY, 2004.

Horngren, Charles T., Foster, George M., and Datar, Srikant M., *Cost Accounting: A Managerial Emphasis*, 12th edition, Prentice-Hall Inc., Upper Saddle River, NJ, 2007.

Investment Decisions
Blocher, Edward, J., Chen, Kung, H., and Lin, Thomas W., *Cost Management: A Strategic Emphasis*, 3rd edition, Irwin/McGraw Hill, New York, NY, 2004.

Horngren, Charles T., Foster, George M., and Datar, Srikant, *Cost Accounting: A Managerial Emphasis*, 12th edition, Prentice-Hall Inc., Upper Saddle River, NJ, 2006.

Brealey, Richard A., and Myers, Stewart C., Allen, Franklin, *Principles of Corporate Finance*, 8th edition, McGraw-Hill Inc., New York, NY, 2006.

Van Horne, James C., and Wachowicz, John M., Jr., *Fundamentals of Financial Management*, 12th edition, Prentice-Hall Inc., Upper Saddle River, NJ, 2005.

478

APPENDIX D
TYPES AND LEVELS OF EXAM QUESTIONS

The following is an excerpt reprinted from the ICMA's Resource Guide for the Revised CMA exam, July 2004.

TYPES OF EXAM QUESTIONS

All items within the CMA parts 1, 2, and 3 are of the 4-option multiple-choice type, with one and only one correct answer for each question. There are, however, a number of variations on this type of item used in the CMA exams. In the examples below, the term "stem" refers to all the information that precedes the answer options or alternatives.

Closed Stem Item

This item type is characterized by a stem that is a complete sentence which concludes with a question mark. The options may be complete or incomplete sentences.

Example:

Which one of the following would have the effect of increasing the working capital of a firm?

a. Cash payment of payroll taxes payable.
b. Cash collection of accounts receivable.
c. The purchase of a new plant, financed by a 20-year mortgage.
d. Refinancing a short-term note with a 2-year note.

Key = d

Sentence Completion Item

This type of item is characterized by a stem that is an incomplete sentence. The options represent conclusions to that sentence.

Example:

If a product's elasticity coefficient is 2.0, this means the demand is

a. perfectly elastic.
b. elastic.
c. inelastic.
d. perfectly inelastic.

Key = b

Except Format

This type of item is employed when you are required to select the option that does not "fit." In this case, three of the options will fit or be defined by the stem, and one option (the correct option) will not fit. A variation on this type of question is to use the word **not** instead of **except** in the stem, in the form of "Which one of the following is **not**...".

Example:

All of the following are considered tangible assets **except**

a.   real estate.
b.   copyrights.
c.   prepaid taxes.
d.   accounts receivable.

Key = b

Most/Least/Best Format

This type of item requires you to select an option which is either better or worse than the others. In all cases, the correct answer represents the collective judgment of a group of experts within the field.

Example #1:

Which one of the following **best** describes a production budget?

a.   It is based on required direct labor hours.
b.   It includes required material purchases.
c.   It is based on desired ending inventory and sales forecasts.
d.   It is an aggregate of the monetary details of the operating budget.

Key = c

Example #2:

Which one of the following is **least** likely to help an organization overcome communication problems between the Accounting Department and other departments?

a.   Job rotation.
b.   Cross-functional teams.
c.   Written policies and procedures.
d.   Performance appraisals.

Key = d

All items within the CMA part 4 are written-response questions, which will be delivered via computer at Prometric Testing Centers in the same manner as the other exam parts. For essay questions that require a purely written answer, you will have a box in which to type your response. For problems that require quantitative responses, a form resembling a spreadsheet will be available along with a free-form area to present your calculations.

QUESTION LEVELS

In addition to the variety of item formats previously described, the CMA exams present test items at varying cognitive levels. These levels range from questions that require a recall of material to questions that require a sophisticated understanding such that you must apply your knowledge to a novel situation, or judge the value of information as it may apply to a particular scenario. A description of each of these levels, along with sample questions, appear below. The cognitive level required for each major topic area of the CMA exams is shown in the Topic/Resource outline.

Level A

This cognitive level represents the "lowest" or most basic level, and includes items that require the recall of facts and the recognition of principles. This level includes the categories of knowledge and comprehension.

Knowledge: This is the lowest level of learning. Items in this category are those that require the recall of ideas, material, or phenomena related to the topic of interest. In these questions, you will be asked to define, identify, and select information.

Example:

A market situation where a small number of sellers comprise an entire industry is known as

a.   a natural monopoly.
b.   monopolistic competition.
c.   an oligopoly.
d.   pure competition.

Key = c

To correctly respond to the item above, you must recall the textbook definition of an oligopoly.

Comprehension: Items in this category require you to grasp the meaning of the material presented in some novel way. A question testing for comprehension describes some principle or fact in words different from those used in textbooks, and often uses a situation as a way to present the idea. In order to answer the item correctly, you must recognize the principle demonstrated in the problem; memory alone will not be sufficient for identifying the correct answer.

Example:

Social legislation, such as the Occupational Safety and Health Act (OSHA) and the Environmental Protection Act (EPA), is frequently criticized for being inefficient because the agencies

a.   use flexible rather than rigid standards.
b.   rely heavily on the free market to allocate resources.
c.   rarely consider the marginal benefits relative to the marginal costs.
d.   enforce their policies too leniently.

Key = c

In order to answer this item correctly, you must know something about the issues or principles in connection with OSHA and the EPA. Other questions dealing with this level of testing are those that ask you to identify an option which best explains, illustrates, or provides an example of the concept in question.

Level B

This cognitive level includes items that test for the application of material to novel situations and the ability to analyze or break down information into its component parts. Items that require application or analysis are included in this level.

Application: Items in this category measure understanding of ideas or content to a point where you can apply that understanding to an entirely new situation. The objective of these items is to test whether you can use the knowledge in an appropriate manner in a real-life situation.

Example:

The balance sheet for Miller Industries shows the following.

Cash	$ 8,000,000
Accounts Receivable	13,500,000
Inventory	7,800,000
Prepaid Expenses	245,000
Property, Plant, & Equipment	4,700,000

Based on this information, what are the Total Current Assets for this firm?

a. $21,500,000
b. $29,300,000
c. $29,545,000
d. $34,245,000

Key = c

Rather than rely on memory or comprehension alone, the situation presented in this item requires you to draw on your knowledge of the calculation of Total Current Assets and apply that knowledge to the particular data presented in the problem. Other items dealing with this level of testing might ask you to identify a specific situation requiring a certain course of action, or the most appropriate procedure or steps to apply to a particular problem.

Analysis: Analysis involves the ability to break down material into its component parts so that its organizational structure can be understood. It involves the ability to recognize parts, as well as the relationships between those parts, and to recognize the principles involved. Items in this category ask you to differentiate, discriminate, distinguish, infer, and determine the relevancy of data.

Example:

A firm is considering the implementation of a lock-box collection system at a cost of $80,000 per year. Annual sales are $90 million, and the lock-box system will reduce collection time by 3 days. The firm currently is in debt for $3,000,000. If the firm can invest the funds designated for the lock-box at 8%, should it use the lock-box system? Assume a 360-day year.

a. Yes, it will produce a savings of $140,000 per year.
b. Yes, it will produce a savings of $60,000 per year.
c. No, it will produce a loss of $20,000 per year.
d. No, it will produce a loss of $60,000 per year.

Key = c

In this item, you are presented with a novel situation, and asked to identify the data that are relevant to the problem at hand, which in this case involves the determination of the savings or loss of implementing a lock-box type of collection system. You are required to apply principles to determine savings or loss, and then to make an analysis of the outcomes of the alternative courses of action.

Level C

This cognitive level is considered the "highest" or most challenging level, and includes items that require you to evaluate information.

Evaluation: Items in this category are those that require the ability to judge the value of material for a given purpose, based on definite criteria. These questions include those that ask you to appraise, conclude, support, compare, contrast, interpret, and summarize information.

Example:

A home services organization has been using the straight-line depreciation method for calculating the depreciation expenses of its equipment. Based on recently acquired information, the firm's assistant controller has altered the estimated useful lives of the equipment. The corresponding changes in depreciation result in a change from a small profit for the year to a loss. The assistant controller is asked by the controller to reduce by half the total depreciation expense for the current year. Believing he is faced with an ethical conflict, the assistant controller reports the problem to the Board of Directors. In accordance with **Statement on Management Accounting Number 1C (Revised)**, "*IMA Statement of Ethical Professional Practice*," which one of the following is the correct evaluation of the assistant controller's action?

a.   The assistant controller's action was appropriate as an immediate step.

b.   The assistant controller's action would have been appropriate only if other alternatives had first been tried.

c.   The assistant controller's action was not appropriate under any circumstances.

d.   Not enough information has been given to evaluate the assistant controller's action.

Key = b

The situation presented in this item requires you to evaluate the course of action that the assistant controller has taken. Option b is the correct option. While the assistant controller's action is appropriate, the situation may be resolved by less drastic means first. You are asked to make a judgment on the appropriateness of the actions to the situation described, and answer the question on the basis of this information.

INDEX

492

494

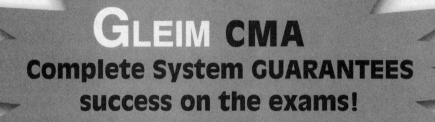
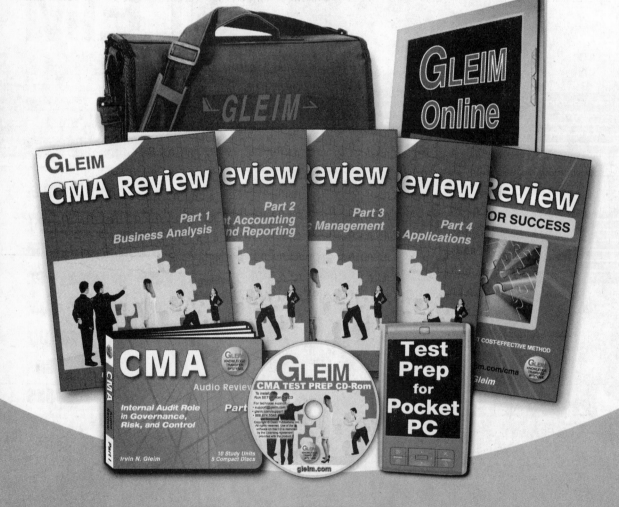

COMPLETE GLEIM CPA SYSTEM

All 4 sections, including Gleim Online, books*, *Test Prep CD-Rom*,
Test Prep for Pocket PC, Audio CDs, plus bonus book bag.

Also available by exam section @ $274.95 (does not include book bag).

*Fifth book: *CPA Review: A System for Success*

☐ $989.95

$_____

COMPLETE GLEIM CMA SYSTEM

Includes: Gleim Online, books*, *Test Prep CD-Rom*,
Test Prep for Pocket PC, Audio CDs, plus bonus book bag.

Also available by exam part @ $213.95 (does not include book bag).

*Fifth book: *CMA Review: A System for Success*

☐ $739.95

$_____

COMPLETE GLEIM CIA SYSTEM

Includes: Gleim Online, books*, *Test Prep CD-Rom*,
Test Prep for Pocket PC, Audio CDs, plus bonus book bag.

Also available by exam part @ $224.95 (does not include book bag).

*Fifth book: *CIA Review: A System for Success*

☐ $824.95

$_____

GLEIM EA REVIEW SYSTEM

Includes: Gleim Online, books, *Test Prep CD-Rom*,
Test Prep for Pocket PC, Audio CDs, plus bonus book bag.

Also available by exam part @ $224.95 (does not include book bag).

☐ $629.95

$_____

"THE GLEIM SERIES" EXAM QUESTIONS AND EXPLANATIONS

Includes: 5 books and *Test Prep CD-Rom*.

Also available by part @ $29.95.

☐ $112.25

$_____

GLEIM ONLINE CPE

Try a FREE 4 hour course at gleim.com/cpe
- Easy-to-Complete
- Informative
- Effective

Contact
GLEIM PUBLICATIONS
for further assistance:

gleim.com
800.874.5346
sales@gleim.com

SUBTOTAL $_____
Complete your
order on the
next page

GLEIM PUBLICATIONS, INC.

P. O. Box 12848   Gainesville, FL 32604

TOLL FREE:	800.874.5346
LOCAL:	352.375.0772
FAX:	352.375.6940
INTERNET:	gleim.com
E-MAIL:	sales@gleim.com

Customer service is available (Eastern Time):
8:00 a.m. - 7:00 p.m., Mon. - Fri.
9:00 a.m. - 2:00 p.m., Saturday
Please have your credit card ready,
or save time by ordering online!

SUBTOTAL (from previous page) $_____
Add applicable sales tax for shipments within Florida. _____
Shipping (nonrefundable) 25.00

TOTAL $_____

Fax or write for prices/instructions on shipments outside the 48 contiguous states, or simply order online.

NAME (please print) _____

ADDRESS _____ Apt. _____
(street address required for UPS)

CITY _____ STATE _____ ZIP _____

____ MC/VISA/DISC ____ Check/M.O.   Daytime Telephone (____)_____

Credit Card No. _____ - _____ - _____ - _____

Exp. ____/____ Signature _____
     Month / Year

E-mail address _____

1. We process and ship orders daily, within one business day over 98.8% of the time. Call by 3:00 pm for same day service.
2. Please PHOTOCOPY this order form for others.
3. No CODs. Orders from individuals must be prepaid.
4. Gleim Publications, Inc. guarantees the immediate refund of all resalable texts and unopened software and audios if returned within 30 days. Applies only to items purchased direct from Gleim Publications, Inc. Our shipping charge is nonrefundable.
5. Components of specially priced package deals are nonrefundable.

Prices subject to change without notice.
06/08

For updates and other important information, visit our website.

gleim.com

GLEIM
KNOWLEDGE
TRANSFER
SYSTEMS

Please forward your suggestions, corrections, and comments concerning typographical errors, etc., to **Irvin N. Gleim • c/o Gleim Publications, Inc. • P.O. Box 12848 • University Station • Gainesville, Florida • 32604.** Please include your name and address so we can properly thank you for your interest.

1. _____

2. _____

3. _____

4. _____

5. _____

6. _____

7. _____

8. _____

9. _____

10. _____

11. _____

12. _____

13. _____

14. _____

15. _____

16. _____

17. _____

18. _____

Remember, for superior service: <u>Mail</u>, <u>email</u>, or <u>fax</u> questions about our materials.
<u>Telephone</u> questions about orders, prices, shipments, or payments.

Name: _____

Address: _____

City/State/Zip: _____

Telephone: Home: _____ Work: _____ Fax: _____

Email: _____